Client-Centered and Experie
A Paradigm in 1

CW01395314

Robert Hutterer
Gerhard Pawlowsky
Peter F. Schmid
Reinhold Stipsits
(Eds.)

Client-Centered and Experiential Psychotherapy

A Paradigm in Motion

PETER LANG

Frankfurt am Main · Berlin · Bern · New York · Paris · Wien

Die Deutsche Bibliothek - CIP-Einheitsaufnahme

Client centered and experiential psychotherapy : a paradigm in
motion / Robert Hutterer ... (ed.). - Frankfurt am Main ; Berlin ;
Bern ; New York ; Paris ; Wien : Lang, 1996
    ISBN 3-631-48137-3

NE: Hutterer, Robert [Hrsg.]

The publication has been supported
by Bundesministerium für Wissenschaft
und Forschung in Wien.

ISBN 3-631-48137-3
US-ISBN 0-8204-2985-6

© Peter Lang GmbH
Europäischer Verlag der Wissenschaften
Frankfurt am Main 1996
All rights reserved.

Printed in Germany 1 2 3 4   6 7

Preface

The Third International Conference on Client Centered and Experiential Psychotherapy (ICCCEP) took place in autumn 1994 in Gmunden, Austria, under the patronage of the Austrian Vice–Chancellor and Federal Minister of Science, Dr. Erhard Busek. Altogether the conference was an intellectually and socially stimulating event. For one week more than 250 participants from literally all continents met at Kongreßhaus Gmunden, a state–of–the–art convention center surrounded by centuries old Austrian tradition, the blue water of Traunsee and snow–capped mountains of the Salzkammergut. The conference assembled participants of 25 countries and the program included more than 100 lectures, presentations, workshops and panel discussions. Far from being unanimous we hope the results of the conference will be interesting to more therapists and practicioners in the field than those actively attending the conference.

Now we are glad to present the present volume, which is an outgrowth of this conference. It contains 48 articles covering theory, research and practical applications including clinical practice. Unfortunately—due to restrictions by the publisher—we were not able to cover all the papers presented at the conference in this volume. So many outstanding manuscripts are not included and it was a difficult task to make editorial decisions taking into account the publisher's restrictions. So, this book offers a representative selection of papers presented at the conference.

The title of the book—"*Client–Centered and Experiential Psychotherapy. A Paradigm in Motion*"—makes reference to an impression which was intensified from conference to conference: *the increasing diversity of client–centered theory and practice.* Client–centered psychotherapy has alway been seen and presented by Carl Rogers and others as "in process" refering to the ongoing process of revising theory and rethinking practice on the base of growing experiences and research. Since in the first two decades of the history of client–centered therapy the persons responsible for all these activities were a clearly defined and relatively joined group of practicioners and researchers able to communicate and exchange their ideas on a common ground of experiences, values language and cultural background, the term "in process" was a very appropriate one. However —paradoxically—the "success" of client–centered therapy in terms of attracting people from all over the world, from different countries with different languages, different cultures and professionals from various fields of applications have naturally weakened the commmon ground. So the present diversities in theory and practice, tensions and frictions between them, cultural influences, diversities in professional, legal and organizational preconditions and even diversities in clinical experiences make *the future developments of client–centered psychotherapy more unpredictable than ever.* This is not the place to discuss implications and solutions. But it may be more realistic to characterize our approach to psychotherapy as "in motion" than "in process".

In particular the foreword is another opportunity to express a sign of appreciation to all those who contributed to the organization of the conference. A special appreciation goes to the commitee whose members were joined in a deliberately difficult adventure, to prepare, organize and accompany the conference in general. Our appreciation and gratefulness go to *Lore Korbei, Sigrid Spudich–Sperl, Johanna Uljas–Lutz, Elisabeth Zinschitz and Peter Frenzel.*

Also we wish to thank the *Österreichische Gesellschaft für wissenschaftliche, klientenzentrierte Psychotherapie und personorientierte Gesprächsführung (ÖGwG)* and the *Arbeitsgemeinschaft für Personenzentrierte Psychotherapie und Gesprächsführung (APG)* for sponsoring the conference as well as the *Ministry of Science* for financially contributing to the conference book.

Since this volume is an outcome of a common investment we have to thank all the authors and wish them a broad reception and recognition. We hope that the professional community will appreciate the intellectual efforts represented in this book.

On behalf of the editors,

Robert Hutterer

Vienna, June 1995

CONTENTS

DEVELOPING THE PARADIGM: THEORETICAL PERSPECTIVES AND BROADER VIEWS

RESEARCH AND EVALUATION

THERAPEUTIC RELATIONSHIP, CORE CONDITIONS AND TECHNIQUE

7

SEVERE DISTURBANCES

GROUP PSYCHOTHERAPY AND FAMILY THERAPY

Developing the Paradigm:
Theoretical Perspectives and Broader Views

On the Way to a Client–Centred Psychopatholgy

EVA–MARIA BIERMANN–RATJEN

PSYCHIATRISCHE UNIVERSITÄTSKLINIK HAMBURG, GERMANY

ABSTRACT

Processes in which changes in the process of psychotherapy occur are characterized as processes in which experience is emotionally evaluated in the context of a relationship. The process of selfdevelopment is defined as a process of integrating emotional self–experience into a self–concept. The process of selfdevelopment–stagnation or defence is interpreted as the result of a split in the actualizing tendency: selfactualization tendencies run counter self–defending tendencies which means the processes in which the emotions aroused by existentially threatening experience are not accurately and completely symbolized as self–experience.

Outside circumstances have done a lot to encourage me to define more exactly what I think about psychopathology. During the last couple of years client–centred therapists in Germany have had the opportunity to discover the value of a formal request in forcing them to formulate their positions – just like Carl Rogers did, 35 years ago.

German client–centred therapists had already spent a great deal of time thinking and writing and arguing and publishing books and papers on the development of the person and its disorders, when we were faced with a new situation. The "Kassenärztliche Bundesvereinigung (KBV)" formally requested a statement on how we define and approach psychopathology.

On the one hand of course this seemed a good chance, as Carl Rogers put it 35 years ago, "to join with others who were endeavouring to formulate their own theories and to use, so far as possible, a common outline – this seemed to be both an obligation and an opportunity" to explain client–centred thinking on psychopathology.

On the other hand in 1959 Carl Rogers was not very enthusiastic about being "asked to cast our theoretical thinking in the terminology of the independent–intervening–dependent variables, so far as this is feasible". The terms seemed to him "to smack too much of the laboratory".

We too had mixed feelings. We are expected to produce an aetiological differential theory on mental illnesses – not just disorders – which can be cured by the client–centred method, or rather methods, or best of all differential methods of doing psychotherapy – and it must be feasible to work out a theory like this.

Trying to outline psychopathology from the client–centred point of view I started out from Carl Rogers' conviction, which I share: "Every theory deserves the greatest respect in the area from which it is drawn from the facts and a decreasing degree of respect as it makes predictions in areas more and more remote from its origin" (p. 191). The core of Carl Rogers' theory, "the earliest portion, most closely related to observed facts, most heavily supported by evidence, is the theory of psychotherapy and personality change which was constructed to give order to the phenomena of therapy as we experienced it" (p. 192).

"This theory is of the if–then variety. If certain conditions exist ... then a process ... will occur which includes certain characteristic elements. If this process ... occurs, then certain personality and behavioral changes ... will occur" (p. 212).

"For therapy to occur it is necessary that these conditions exist:

1. That two persons are in *contact.*

2. That the ... client is in a state of *incongruence*, being *vulnerable,* or *anxious.*

3. That the ... therapist is *congruent* in this *relationship.*

4. That the therapist is *experiencing unconditional positive regard* toward the client.

5. That the therapist is *experiencing an empathic* understanding of the client's

    internal frame of reference.

6. That the client *perceives,* at least to a minimal degree ... the *unconditional positive regard* of the therapist for him, and the *empathic* understanding of the therapist "(p. 213).

The common characteristic elements of these conditions are: They are descriptions of processes in which *experience is evaluated.* This evaluating process takes place in the context of a *relationship.* And these *evaluating processes are felt*: The client *feels*, at least to a minimal degree, his incongruence and the unconditional positive regard and empathic understanding of the therapist. And the therapist *feels* his unconditional positive regard toward and empathic understanding of the client's internal frame of reference.

Now, if this process ... occurs, then certain personality and behavioral changes ... will occur" (p. 212).

Rogers described these personal and behavioral changes in his process–continuum:

When therapy starts, the client is anxious about his feelings, behaves as if they were objects in the outside world. The felt sense of the experience is of no real importance. The individual does not symbolize most of his experience. The experience is interpreted in the framework of rigid constructs, which have been developing in the past. So the evaluating processes of the organism as a whole and the process of evaluating the experience in awareness are incongruent. The client does not like do talk about his personal experience, and he is afraid of being close to other persons. He does not consider his problems as being his personal problems and does not want to undergo personal change.

At the end of therapy the client feels open towards his experience, the fluid process of experiencing. He symbolizes his experience and feels the sense of his experiencing. So he is more congruent, there is less anxiety. The experience is no longer interpreted within the framework of rigid constructs drawn from the past. The cognitive functions are free to recognize the meaning of the experience here and now. Selfexploration is possible and there is less anxiety in personal relations. The individual discovers his problems as his personal problems and is no longer unwilling to undergo personal change.

Carl Rogers always described these changes which he observed in therapy processes as changes in the way experience is evaluated: Fear of experience turns into openness towards experience. Experience which was evaluated to be fended off and remained subconscious and unsymbolized turns into conscious, understood, meaningful experience. Incongruence, which means vulnerability and anxiety, turns into congruence: the organismic evaluation of the experience as either beneficial or dangerous for the maintenance and further growth of the organism as a whole is increasingly in line with the value an experience is given as being beneficial and not dangerous for maintaining and enhancing the self–concept and as satisfying the need for positive self–regard. In this way fear of introspection turns into an ability for selfexploration, anxiousness about close relations turns into the ability to communicate about the self in close relations.

To say it again: This is the description of a change in the *process of evaluating experience*. Experience is evaluated as being more or less dangerous for the concept of the self, as being more or less *anxiety–arousing*. Felt incongruence is anxiety.

And it is the description of the changing relationship between a person and his experience. We put it into the formula: The congruent person's relationship to his experience is like the relationship the client–centred therapist offers: empathic understanding and unconditional positive regard.

Now: when these changes take place within the psychotherapeutic process, then the effect of psychotherapy is further development of the self. More and more self–experience is integrated into the self–concept so that less and less experience is evaluated as possibly threatening its consistent gestalt.

I am sure, that the conditions for the development of the self–concept in early childhood to occur are similar to the conditions for the development of the self–concept to occur in therapy.

For a process of self–development in early childhood to occur it is necessary that the following conditions exist:

1. That the baby is in *contact* with a significant other.

2. That the baby is preoccupied with *evaluating experience* which might possibly arouse *anxiety*.

3. That the *significant other person* is *congruent in the relationship* to the baby, does not experience anything inconsistent with her self–concept while in contact with the baby when it is preoccupied with evaluating his experience.

4. That the significant other is *experiencing unconditional positive regard* toward the baby's processes of evaluating his experience.

5. That the significant other is *experiencing an empathic understanding* of the baby's experiencing within his *internal frame of reference*. This "means to sense the hurt or the pleasure of (the baby) as he senses it, and to perceive the causes thereof as (the baby) perceives them, but wihout ever losing the recognition that it is as if I were hurt or pleased, etc.

If this "as if" quality is lost, then the state is one of identification and not of empathic understanding" (p. 210 f).

6. That the baby gradually *perceives* both the unconditional positive regard of the significant other person for him and the empathic understanding so that in the baby's *awareness* there is gradually a *belief or prognosis* that the unconditionally positively regarding and empathically understanding object would when reacting to other experiences of the baby also exhibit positive regard and empathic understanding (see p. 199).

In this concept the process of evaluating the baby's processes of evaluating his experience is defined as: unconditional positive regard for empathically understood experience.

So if we assume, there is a selfactualizing tendency, the need to represent or integrate a part of the experience as self–experience into a concept of the self,

we may equally assume there is a *need for positive regard.*

Positive regard is the precondition for selfdevelopment to occur.

This need for positive regard is the only need that has to be conceptualized within the frame of client–centred theories. It is the need to be empathically understood in processes in which experience is evaluated, and to be oneself given unconditional positive regard throughout this process.

At this point of the discussion new questions arise:

1. In what way does the baby experience his need for positive regard?

2. In what way does empathic understanding work?

3. And in what way does the baby perceive the empathic understanding and positive regard of the significant other person?

Rogers gave us the following definition:

> The state of empathy, or being empathic, is to perceive the internal frame of reference of another with accuracy, and with the emotional components and meanings which pertain thereto, as if one were the other person, but without ever losing the "as if" condition. Thus it means to sense the hurt or the pleasure of another as he senses it, and to perceive the causes thereof as he perceives them... (p. 210 f).

In these sentences we again encounter descriptions of evaluating processes: If you feel hurt or if you are pleased with an experience, then you are evaluating this experience within your own personal internal frame of reference.

And if you sense the hurt or the pleasure of another person then you sense his process of evaluating his experience in his personal internal frame of reference.

I want to emphasize the following sentence:

The process of evaluating experience from the very beginning of life takes place in the *emotions*, it is an emotional process.

What is an emotional experience?

Most researchers into emotions agree that an adult's consciously experienced emotion consists of at least six different components:

1. changes in the internal physiological and probably hormone status,

2. somehow correlated with changes in expression facial mimic for instance, gestures or vocalisation,

3. readiness to react on the motor level, for instance running away in fear,

4. the individual becoming aware of these three changes,

5. the individual's interpretation of this awareness,

6. the interpretation of the whole behaviour sequence by observers.

The so–called signal components of the emotions (vocalizing, mimic, gestures) exist at birth or develop very soon after – the human face has 46 different pairs of muscles for showing emotions – and are recognizable to others. The motor and cognitive components of the emotions only develop later. There are inborn programs for having and expressing the basic emotions: pleasure, interest, amazement, hurt, revulsion, rage, fear and shame, all of which are evident straight after birth or during the first months of life and are clearly identifiable (Deneke, p. 154). This means that others can empathize with the baby and experience an unconditional positive regard toward the baby's processes of evaluating his experience, can satisfy the baby's need for positive regard from the very beginning of life (see Krause, 1983).

Sullivan has described these links as follows:

> At an indeterminately early age the tensions which appear in the infant connected with his relationship to the physicochemical environment tend to be relatively localized and marked with the *prototype of what later we call emotional experience* (p. 42). The living cannot live when separated from what may be described as their *necessary environment* (p. 31). Human life ... requires interchange with an environment which includes culture (p. 32). Culture is an abstraction of pertaining to people, man requires *interpersonal relationships*, or interchange with others (p. 32).

There is a general need for tenderness which is

> ingrained from the very beginning of things as an interpersonal need (p. 40). The observed activity of the infant arising from the tension of needs induces tension in the mothering one, which tension is experienced as tenderness and an impulsion to activities toward the relief of the infant's needs (p. 39). The manifest activity by the mothering one toward the relief of the infant's need will presently be experienced by the infant as the undergoing of tender behaviour, and these needs, the relaxation of which require cooperation of another, thereon take on the character of a general need for tenderness (p. 40).

In Sullivan's Interpersonal Theory of Psychiatry we do not find a definition of the significant other in a state of incongruence or being unable to empathize with and to give unconditional positive regard to the infants experiencing. Nevertheless one of the central concepts of Sullivan's theory is the mothering one in a state of anxiety.

> Anxiety is a tension in opposition to the tensions of needs and to actions appropriate to their relief. It is in opposition to the tension of tenderness in the mothering one (p. 44). The tension of anxiety, when present in the mothering one induces anxiety in the infant (p. 41).... the interpersonal situation is destroyed, it breaks up (p. 95) ...the relaxation of the tension of anxiety, the re-equilibration of being in this specific respect, is the experience not of satisfaction, but of interpersonal security (p. 42). The need for interpersonal security might be said to be the need to be rid of anxiety (p. 43).

This concept comes close to the client–centred concept of the incongruent significant other. Felt incongruency in client–centred theory is felt anxiety. And the need for interpersonal security might be said to be the need for positive regard.

Let me summarize my thoughts about selfdevelopment up to this point:

Within the client–centred framework there is one and only one single principle of development which is seen as axiomatic: a basic *actualizing– tendency*. "This is the inherent tendency of the organism (as a whole) to develop all its capacities in ways which serve to maintain or enhance the organism ." (Rogers 1959, p. 196)

The actualizing tendency "expresses itself also in the actualization of that portion of the experience ... which is symbolized in the self" (p. 196). We may call this part of the actualizing tendency the *self–actualizing–tendency* (Rogers, p.196). It is the tendency to symbolize experience (to become aware of it), to experience one`s own experience, to develop experience into self–experience and to integrate this self–experience into a *concept of the self.*

"The term *experience* is used to include all that is going on within the envelope of the organism at any given moment which is potentially available to *awareness*" (p. 197). It is always only a part of the whole organism's experience which is symbolized. Experiences which support and enhance the organism are distinguished from those which threaten or restrict it.

The process in which experience is evaluated is an emotional one.

The process whereby experience reaches consciousness is the process of symbolization (to become aware of, to symbolize, to realize are all synonyms) (Rogers p. 198)

In the *process of symbolization* (see Gendlin 1970) *physical sensations, visual imaginations, feelings, thoughts* and *words* occur which are connected to one another, giving each other expression and above all meaning. The successful end of a symbolizing process, the *"felt sense"* is accompanied by a marked drop in tension in the sense "That's right, that's where I am at the moment". If the felt sense cannot be fully developed, there is no sense of relaxation.

Experience can turn into self–experience, e.g. the conscious experience of seeing a flower can turn into the personal experience "*I* see a flower". Such personal experiences accumulate to form a structure which is the *self–concept* (the self, picture of self, self–structure) – on certain necessary conditions.

Self–experience and the concept of the self develop in interactions with the environment – experiencing oneself in these interactions – especially in *relating to significant others*, into an object which is available to awareness though not necessarily in awareness (Rogers, p. 200).

In the framework of the client–centred approach it is assumed that there is one need which takes priority above all others: the *need for positive regard*. Satisfying this is a precondition for development. Failing to satisfy it in babies can result in them dying.

Need for positive regard means wanting to experience being empathically understood and unconditionally positively regarded by a congruent significant other person.

The process of empathic understanding is also a symbolizing process. While sensing what another person is experiencing an individual identifies what the other is going through by referring to his own physical sensations, images, thoughts, feelings and words.This *empathic symbolizing process* may be more or less complete: A mother may for instance grasp what her child is experiencing physically but develop quite different images or feelings in this process than the child would if it already could do the same. In this case she is not experiencing unconditional positive regard toward all of the child`s experiencing. The effect of such incomplete empathizing of the significant other is that the child cannot completely "see" himself in his experience and therefore cannot integrate a complete self–experience into its self–concept.

Now that the self–concept has gained an outline, here is the next step: as well as we need positive regard we need *positive self–regard*. There have been developing *conditions of worth*. This means: New experiences are not just evaluated as either maintaining and enhancing or threatening the organism as a whole. They are also monitored as either confirming or questioning the self–concept and as possibly not satisfying the need for positve self–regard. The individual wants to accept and understand himself with all his experiencing and feel that it belongs to him. This too is an emotionally tinged experience.

Rogers has described these links as follows:

The actualising tendency is also revealed in the attempt to maintain that part of the experience which is symbolized and represented in the self. This means the organism as a whole evaluates experiences as to whether they are useful for confirming the self–concept.

This evaluating process can result in a split in the actualising tendency for efforts to develop the self can collide with efforts to maintain the self–concept: An experience may be helpful in enhancing the organism as a whole. Remember that the selfactualizing tendency is part of the actualizing tendency and the self–concept can only develop by integrating experience as self–experience. But equally the experience may endanger the self–concept and fail to satisfy the person`s need for positive self–regard. These experiences which contradict the self–concept and would not foster positive self–regard if they were to reach awareness as self–experiences are kept at bay. They are for instance banished from consciousness by that part of the actualizing tendency which I propose to call the tendency towards self–preservation or the *self–defending–tendency*.

Defence mechanisms, i.e. all operations which prevent an experience reaching *awareness as self–experience*, are an expression of the self–defending tendency. If experiences which do not support the self–concept and the positive self–regard are not completely banished from consciousness – that is one form of defence – they are symbolized in such a way that they are not identified, understood or accepted as self experience. If the defence is unsuccessfull or only partially so, as well as feeling uneasy and anxious the individual simply cannot understand or accept some of his self–experience. It seems unintelligible or unbelievable, not me and/or undermining his self–respect.

When the organismic process of evaluating experience as either maintaining and enhancing the organism as a whole or not

runs counter the process of evaluating experience as maintaining the self–concept and enhancing positive self–regard – a state is reached which we call *incongruence*.

Being incongruent means there is a split in the evaluating processes of the actualizing tendency: The self–defending tendency runs counter the selfactualizing tendency.

So far I have tried to point out that if we ask what sort of experience under which conditions develops into healthy or disturbed experience, the answer is:

it is emotional experience, which is evaluated emotionally by the experiencing individual himself and evaluated emotionally by significant others as well as by the selfsystem later on as being either beneficial or not for the self–concept and the feeling of positive self–regard.

The precondition for healthy development is that emotional experience is perceived by the individual as being empathically understood and as being emotionally experienced as unconditionally worthy of positive regard by significant others right at the beginning of selfdevelopment, and as enhancing the feeling of positive self–regard later on.

The preconditions for an unhealthy development is that emotional experience is perceived by the individual as being only partially understood and/or as being only conditionally emotionally evaluated by significant others as worthy of positive regard at the beginning of selfdevelopment and as threatening the self–organization and the feeling of positive self–regard later on.

Within the client–centred theoretical framework ideas about defence and selfdevelopment stagnation are closely linked to ideas about conditions of worth.

It may well be for instance that a child's emotional experiences are not empathically understood and positively regarded just for what they are, but rather interpreted or valued by a significant other in a way that they confirm this person's self–regard and fit in with the welcome or unwelcome feelings associated with this: A mother may proudly register: "My son feels like a boy!" This boy has in this situation no chance of integrating the self–experience: "I feel I am a boy" into his self–concept. He is not identified empathically and with unconditional regard as he himself. As the result of this he identifies with what he is supposed to be. In the language of client–centred thinking conditions of worth which do not stem from his own organismic evaluating process have been introjected into his self–concept, giving birth to an ideal self.

Rogers has defined the ideal self as the self–concept which the individual would most like to possess, upon which he places the highest value for himself (p. 200). The term may sound attractive, but in fact developing such an ideal self is no help, for every "I ought, I must" gets in the way of "I am" and therefore hinders genuine growth.

Rogers (p. 209) reports that Standal has introduced the term conditions of worth to replace the term "introjected values" to describe the fact that a self–experience may be sought or avoided simply because the individual considers it more or less "worthy of self–regard", has "assimilated into his own self–regard complex" the conditional positive regard of significant other.

Sullivan has called "the system involved in the maintenance of felt interpersonal security" (p. 108), which is reflected to us in the respect others offer us, the selfsystem and has defined it as an anti–anxiety system. He defined it as purely the product of interpersonal experience with a "mother" who conveys she is anxious, and as intended as a way of dealing with the anxiety the anxious "mother" inflicts on her child.

Sullivan assumes that this selfsystem is extraordinarily resistant to change by experience, just as we assume that the self–defending tendency organizes resistance against the symbolization of experience which challenge the structure of the self–concept and self–regard.

From my point of view tracing the similarities between the client–centred explanation of how defence functions and Sullivan's Interpersonal Theory of Psychiatry would be a greater help in developing a client–centred psychopathology than tracing the similarities between client–centred and classical Freudian thinking about defence mechanisms.

I have attempted this by using the *neuroses as a model* and looking into how they come about.

I have already pointed out that the changes which we observe in psychotherapeutic processes are changes in the way emotional experience is evaluated. Incongruent experiencing turn into more and more congruent experiencing. Less and less emotional experience is evaluated emotionally as threatening the concept of the self and self–regard.

Now I want to talk about what the acute state of incongruence, when you feel the threat to your self–concept, feels like.

The prototype of experiencing incongruence, the situation where the threat to the self–concept is most acutely felt as well as the absence of positive regard and positive self–regard, which are the preconditions for the integration of experience into the self–concept, is the acute stress reaction. It occurs in reaction to unusually upsetting events which seriously threaten our own safety or physical wellbeing or that of someone close to us: catastrophes, accidents, war, crime, rape, but also unusual sudden changes in our social position or social network, for instance a series of deaths in the family (see ICD–10, WHO 1991).

Within a few moments the individual typically develops a kind of anaesthesia, limiting consciousness and narrowing his range of attention; he is also unable to cope with stimuli and becomes disorientated. This condition can be succeeded by a further withdrawal from the outside world into a dissoziative stupor, but equally it may be followed by restlessness and hyperactivity, attempts to escape and actual flight. Usually there are vegetative signs of panic such as tachycardia, sweating and flushing.

After the initial stage of anaesthesia, new symptoms appear like depression, fear, anger, despair, hyperactivity and withdrawal. None of the symptoms lasts long.

The acute reaction usually starts to abate after a few hours if the stressful event is over. There may be partial or complete amnesia about the episode. If the strain continues or cannot be reversed, the symptoms usually gradually subside 12 to 24 hours after the disaster and are almost imperceptible after three days.

Traumatic situations are those in which the organism as a whole is faced with an existential threat and/or there is no form of "positive regard" or "positive self-regard".

Such events arouse anxiety in combination with the prototype of defence against experience, reduced awareness: the experience is not permitted to reach consciousness, and is blotted out. The emotional reaction, anxiety, is symbolised only on the physical level, in bodily reactions and motor programmes. When the numbing effect wears off more emotional reactions associated with the traumatic experience start to surface, those linked to the motor programmes well known to ethologists: running away, attacking, feigning and playing dead. These emotional states are appeals to fellow beings and are understood as such, i.e. they awaken or stop certain impulses to react.

The posttraumatic stress disorder, also known as the traumatic neurosis, is the result of a traumatic experience and occurs after a latency period of weeks or months; it can lead to a lasting change of personality. It can be regarded as the prototype for the *course* of our efforts to either integrate experience into our self-concept or persist in clinging to selfdefence which shows up in symptoms of selfdevelopment stagnation.

In a posttraumatic neurosis the traumatic experience repeatedly crops up in awareness, flashes across the inner eye in daydreams or in dreams. At the same time the person suffering from the posttraumatic stress disorder feels numb and emotionally paralysed, has no interest in others, is passive, anhedonic and avoids situations and activities which might remind him of the trauma. His vegetative system is often permanently on the alert, making him hypervigilant, and his mood can be anything from gloomy to suicidal. There are singular dramatic outbursts of fear, panic or aggression, brought about by sudden reminders or a repeat of the trauma or the original reaction to it.

In the posttraumatic stress disorder the traumatic experience is treated like an enemy; in other words we can see what happens when someone has to fend off experience and is unable to integrate it as his own experience into his self-concept:

Repeated efforts are made to symbolise the traumatic experience but the symbolization remains restricted to the physical or imagery level, for even more effort is made to avoid once again being confronted with the feelings associated with the traumatic experience.

The danger is however that defence generalizes and may block out experience altogether:

• What began as a restricted anaesthesia can turn into emotional withdrawal or bluntness. Emotional experience is ignored.

- What began as an impulse to run away from danger can develop into excessive vigilance, so that the person is ready to flee from any kind of new experience.

- In the individual who has sensed that his own life and feelings are regarded as completely worthless to the powers threatening him a tendency to play dead may turn into a desire to be really dead.

- Reacting aggressively may turn into a strategy applied under all circumstances.

We assume that in the course of the growth of self in early childhood such acute reactions result not only from situations which are life–threatening – and the child of course cannot protect itself. They result too from a lack of empathic understanding and positive regard for the child, or from situations in which the psychic organisation's capacity to cope with experience is overstrained for instance by a repetition of an experience which could not be integrated as self–experience into the self–concept the first time. So the repetition of the experience includes a threat to the self–concept and/or the positive self–regard. The child reacts to this threatening experience by anaesthesia, emotionally withdrawing, doubting its own value, and/or with readiness to attack or escape.

For the child's further development as a person it is especially important that these stress reactions as such – in German, as in English, one can word this neatly by saying someone is outside himself – are understood for what they are and not interpreted and valued as something else.

It is however very likely that the significant others will react to these emotional experiences of the child according to their own emotions and therefore be blind and deaf to the child's feelings – actually they are symptoms, indicating incongruence – or at least respond in a very conditional way.

We assume that later on the adult will regard these reactive symptoms as belonging to him or as alien and not part of him depending on the degree of empathic understanding and unconditional positive regard these affective experiences received from others.

It is characteristic of neurotic experience that some or all of these symptoms of acute incongruence cannot be symbolized as self–experiences or this is only feasible in certain defensive ways. When neurotic persons suffer from limited consciousness, fear, depression or hostility they are not aware that they are reacting to an experience which threatens them and their idea of themselves. They cannot perceive that their acute stress reactions are an expression of the way they evaluate their experience emotionally: as endangering their self–respect or self–concept.

In fact however the acute stress reaction is a completely intelligible and logical message conveying how the whole organism reacts to finding itself physically or psychically in mortal danger: it makes sense. The reaction awakens an impulse to flee; it protects consciousness against the traumatic experience; it mobilizes aggressive impulses, i.e. defending oneself, and in depression it adopts submissive behaviour which is intended as self–defence.

Traditionally neurotic disorders have been classified as anxiety neurosis, dissociative disorders, obsessional neurosis, depressions – in line with the stress reactions frozen into neurotic behaviour patterns:

- incomprehensible fear

- limited consciousness of one's own experience

- obsessions

- depression

The impulses behind these unintelligible emotional states have been discovered and named:

- the phobic patient's urge to flee
- the hysterical patient's need to pretend
- the obsessional patient's hidden rage
- the depressive patient's self–abandonment

It is also possible – as Hans Swildens (1993) has shown in incomparable manner – to analyze these symptoms of incongruence from an phenomenological angle:

- a fearful patient runs away from experience and avoids maturing further
- a hysterical patient's insistence on being positively regarded without regarding his real experience himself is the equivalent of refusing to live his own life
- the obsessive patient's concern with keeping everything under control hampers his own growth
- the depressive's urge to abandon all responsibility for himself prevents him from living

For me it is striking how often patients describe their parents in such a way that I can well imagine that they did not understand their children's emotional reactions, especially their stress reactions, and tended instead to respond with corresponding own emotions:

Anxious patients describe their parents as nervous, especially as far as the children's own abilities are concerned, as unhelpfully uncaring or overprotective.

Hysterical patients report highly dramatic battles with their parents, or that they were so clinging and involved with their children that they failed to give regard to their feelings.

The obsessives were kept in firm check by overstrict and domineering parents.

And the depressives were either emotionally abandoned by depressive or guilt–ridden parents or actually physically abandoned.

So in the language of framework neurotics suffer from a vulnerable self–concept and self–respect brought about by experiences in early childhood when they had to contend with a lack of empathy, positive regard or congruence from a significant other, with the result that they could not integrate these experiences as self–experiences.

Let me say it again:

The empathic process is also a symbolization process in which one person develops own physical sensations, ideas, thoughts, feelings and words in which the others person's experience is identified. This attempt to understand can fail; a mother for instance may grasp what her child is feeling physically but may react with own feelings and interpretations, which are quite different from the child's. The effect of this incomplete empathizing process in the significant other person is that the child cannot be more aware of his experience than it is understood and as a result cannot integrate parts of its experience as self–experience into its self–concept.

If such misunderstood or partially understood experiences repeated themselves they could not be symbolized properly, and the inability to integrate them induced a state of alarm and uneasiness. This state of mind too may be more or less completely grasped by significant others and thus more or less completely integrated into the self–concept: "That is how I feel and think and fantasise if I am not understood, not unconditionally accepted, if I upset someone with my emotions and induce him to react emotionally and not at all unconditionally positively regarding."

When in later life a neurotic person experiences something which endangers his self and his self–respect, he will find himself suffering from this state of alarm and uneasiness again. Because in addition the symptoms or some aspects of the initial state of alarm have not been completely understood and/or unconditionally positively regarded, the neurotic person equally cannot symbolize them or can do so only partially.

So to develop a neurosis one has to repeat an experience, which cannot be integrated as a self–experience. The neurotic *disposition* develops usually not as a result of a single traumatic event but as the outcome of years of living with significant others who are not able to accept the child for its own sake but only if it meets with certain expectations, for instance being male, or can only conditionally accept it, for instance because it is as intelligent as they expected their child to be.

The significant others for persons who later become neurotic in addition to only accepting their child conditionally were unable to understand or accept their child's emotional alarm reactions and reacted in an emotional way, because for instance they themselves sensed that their self–concept and self–respect were under attack.

A neurotic disorder *decompensates* when the experiences which could not be integrated are repeated, reactivating the defence, the stress reaction. These, or at least some of them cannot fade away again because the neurotic patient cannot symbolize them accurately and completely and so become aware of them as his own experiences. And so the neurotic patient remains burdened with one or other of the stress "symptoms" which are partially symbolized emotional stress reactions.

As therapists treating neurotics we should therefore first of all focus on the client's symptoms, which are a sign of a state of alarm, of defence, and grasp their significance so that we can help the client to symbolize them and to accept and understand them. Only then can we proceed to join the client in exploring which experiences are repeats of earlier experiences which he has so far been unable to integrate into his self–concept.

Client–centred therapy with a neurotic client must always be process–oriented, as Hans Swilders has recommended: first comes the symptom phase, where the symptoms have to be understood as a sign that the client has got stuck in the process of becoming himself, and only after that can one start off with the client–centred therapy proper.

In an article entitled "Why are borderline patients mostly female? On the role of trauma in the development of borderline disorders" Christa Rohde–Dachser conjectures that borderline disorders may be the result of traumatic experiences and characterized by specific kinds of emotional alarm reactions.

8 out of 10 patients with the diagnosis "borderline", which is used to label certain nontypical clinical symptoms which do not fit into the usual list of mental diseases and are ranked somewhere between neurosis, character defect, and psychosis (p. 1) are female, and in no other group of patients are there so many reports of sexual abuse, mostly by the father (see Westen et al. 1990, p.15) as in this group.

Certain characteristics of the borderline personality disorder can be understood right into the smallest detail as reactions which according to research into posttraumatic behaviour are attributable to coping with traumata. This applies particularly for the borderline–patient's tendency to inflict wounds on themselves, to attempt or commit suicide, and to enter into unstable relationships (p. 12).

As a rule the (abused) patients do not connect their current symptoms with being abused as children. Long–term observations of trauma victims have revealed that in the course of time fragments of the trauma are transformed and relived in a completely disguised fashion, for instance as bodily sensations, as states of mind, in visualized scenes, in acting out and in dissociated fragments of personality. Research into posttraumatic stress furthermore has unanimously shown that there is an especially high correlation between trauma and dissociation (see Spiegel et al. 1988, p. 11).

The criteria for the diagnosis borderline personality disorder largely consist of typically female coping patterns.

To these belong amongst others a willingness often encountered in borderline personality disorder to enter into intense, clinging, unstable relationships which seem bound to prove disappointing and therefore usually do. The same applies to their autoaggressive ways of dealing with aggressive impulses; according to the cohort study by Schepank (1987) "alloplastic acting out is apparently a more male solution to inner and outer dilemmas, whereas women tend more to make use of autoplastic coping strategies directed against themselves" (Schepank 1987, p. 131). Seen in this light male patients with a borderline diagnosis would be mostly those who were prevented from reacting in a male (alloplastic) manner (in fact one often comes across the kind of self–inflicted injury typical of borderline patients in men in prison) (p. 5).

So using our terms borderline patients suffer from:

1. the after–effects of traumatic experiences of which they have still not been able to become aware. Repeated attempts to symbolize these remain on the level of "physical sensations", "states of mind", "inner pictures" and "acting–out" or are apparent in "dissociated fragments of personality". Borderline patients can suffer from psychotic episodes.

2. the outcome of not having had their emotional reactions linked to these traumatic experiences, their responses and feelings in an emergency properly understood. At best they could only fall back on "female" ways of expressing these emotions, being depressive, seeking shelter, ignoring danger or pretending not to notice it; they were not permitted "male" belligerency or active self–defence.

If they nowadays are faced with a disappointing experience, for instance, and cannot banish their "male" angry alarm reactions quite out of awareness, but are forced to feel them, this anger will seem quite alien and ego–dystonic, or a dire threat to their whole person and relationships.

So it is obviously essential when working with borderline patients to keep "oriented on the process" in Swildens's sense too: If during the symptom phase these patients are not understood as evaluating emotionally their emergency reaction called aggression to be an unintelligible and acutely dangerous threat to their self–concept and self–esteem and probably to other persons, then one cannot move onto the next stage and start working through recent and perhaps later on old "traumatic" experiences.

REFERENCES

Biermann–Ratjen, E.–M. u. Eckert, J. (1982). *Du sollst merken – wie willst Du sonst verstehen.* Plädoyer für das tiefenpsychologische Modell der Entwicklung der Person in der

Gesprächspsychotherapie. In: E. Biehl, E. Jaeggi, W.R. Minsel, R. v. Quekelberghe & D. Tscheulin (Hrsg.), Neue Konzepte der klinischen Psychologie und Psychotherapie (S. 36–40). Tübingen und Köln: DGVT u. GwG.

Biermann–Ratjen, E.–M. (1988). *Was bedeutet gesprächspsychotherapeutisches Arbeiten mit Patienten mit einer Borderline–Störung?* In Gesellschaft für wissenschaftliche Gesprächspsychotherapie (Hrsg.), Orientierung an der Person, Bd. 1, (S. 58–61). Köln: GwG.

Biermann–Ratjen, E.–M. (1989). *Zur Notwendigkeit einer klientenzentrierten Entwicklungspsychologie für die Zukunft (Weiterentwicklung) der klienten–zentrierten Psychotherapie.* In R. Sachse & J. Howe (Hrsg.), Zur Zukunft der klientenzentrierten Psychotherapie (S. 102–125). Heidelberg: Asanger.

Biermann–Ratjen, E.–M. (1990). *Identifizierung. Ein Beitrag zu einem klientenzen–trierten Modell der Entwicklung der gesunden und der kranken Persönlichkeit.* GwG Zeitschrift, 78, S. 31–35.

Deneke, F.–W. (1992). *Die Strukturierung der subjektiven Wirklichkeit.* In B. Andresen, F.–M. Stark & J. Gross (Hrsg.), Mensch, Psychiatrie, Umwelt. Bonn: Psychiatrie–Verlag.

Gendlin, E.T. (1970). *A theory of personality change.* In J. T. Hart & T. M. Tomlinson (Eds.), New directions in Client–Centered Psychotherapy (129–173).Boston: Houghton Mifflin.

Krause, R. (1983). *Zur Onto– und Phylogenese des Affektsystems und ihrer Beziehungen zu psychischen Störungen.* Psyche, 37, 1016–1043.

Rohde–Dachser, Ch. (1994). *Warum sind Borderlinepatienten meist weiblich?* Über die Rolle des Traumas in der Entwicklung der Borderline Persönlichkeitsstörung. Unveröffentl. Manuskript.

Rogers, C.R. (1959). *A Theory of Therapy, Personality and Interpersonal Relationships, as developed in the Client–Centered Framework.* In S. Koch (Ed.), Psychology: A Study of a Sciene. Volume 3. Formulations of the Person and the Social Context (184–256). New York, Boston, London: McGraw–Hill.

Sullivan, H.S. (1953). *The Interpersonal Theory of Psychiatry*, New York, London: W. W. Norton & Company

Weltgesundheitsorganisation (1991). *Internationale Klassifikation psychischer Störungen.* ICD–10 Kapitel V (F). Klinisch–diagnostische Leitlinien. Herausgegeben von H. Dilling, W. Mombour & M.H. Schmidt. Bern, Göttingen, Toronto: Hans Huber.

The Integrative Statement of Carl R. Rogers

JEROLD D. BOZARTH
UNIVERSITY OF GEORGIA

ABSTRACT

This article asserts that Carl Rogers' (1957) statement concerning the necessary and sufficient conditions of therapeutic personality change is an integrative statement for psychotherapy and helping relationships that is separate from his statement (Rogers, 1959) concerning the conditions as part of client–centered therapy. The failure to consider his statement as integrative has resulted in misunderstandings and misdirection of investigation. The misunderstanding of the integrative statement is that the experience of empathic understanding and unconditional positive regard for another is sculptured in a particular form rather than existing as an attitudinal embodiment in the experiencing of one person for another. As a result, the directions of investigation have focused on behavioral forms of communication rather than upon the experiences of the therapist and the client. It is speculated that therapists must achieve their own congruence including the use of their own "technique system" in order to maximize their capacity for experiencing empathic understanding and unconditional positive regard for the client. In short, techniques and theoretical formulations are for the therapist rather than particular clients and this, essentially, allows therapists freedom to enter the person to person relationship with their clients in the best possible way.

Carl R. Rogers (1957) formulated a revolutionary hypothesis when he proposed that there are certain necessary and sufficient conditions for therapeutic personality change. This statement was NOT about Client–Centered Therapy as often assumed. Rather, it is a statement that is meant to integrate therapies and helping relationships through assumptions of common therapeutic variables. Our thesis in this paper is that Rogers' integrative hypothesis has not been thoroughly investigated nor even adequately understood. It is further suggested that the direction of investigation of this hypothesis has resulted in probable limitations to the understanding and manifestations of the hypothesis.

THE STATEMENTS

Rogers' most significant theoretical statements were published near the same time. He (1957) first postulated an integrative statement related to his theoretical investigations. His (1959) second statement was directly related to client–centered theory.

Rogers' (1957) integrative statement has been widely referred to in the literature and is specifically stated by Rogers as follows:

1. Two persons are in psychological contact.

2. The first, whom we shall term the client, is in a state of incongruence, being vulnerable or anxious.

3. The second person, whom we shall term the therapist, is congruent or integrated in the relationship.

4. The therapist experiences unconditional positive regard for the client.

5. The therapist experiences an empathic understanding of the client's internal frame of reference and endeavors to communicate this experience to the client.

6. The communication to the client of the therapist's empathic understanding and unconditional positive regard is to a minimal degree achieved. (p. 96)

Rogers wrote the1957 statement while still working on his rigorous theoretical delineation of, "A theory of therapy, personality, and interpersonal relations as developed in the client–centered framework" which was then published in 1959. There are subtle differences in Rogers' hypothesis as stated in 1957 and his theoretical statement in 1959. The primary differences between his formal statement concerning the necessary and sufficient conditions for therapeutic personality change in 1957 and 1959 is that in the 1959 statement, he *no longer states that the therapist must strive to communicate* his or her experiencing of empathic understanding and unconditional positive regard to the client. The client, however, must perceive the therapist as experiencing these two conditions to, at least, a minimal degree. He also *no longer* designates the pre–condition as being *psychological* contact in 1959. It is difficult to determine whether or not these subtle differences have any meaning; however, it seems unlikely that Rogers would be cavalier with statements that were incorporated in what he considered the most rigorous expositions of his belief and of his theory. It might mean that for Client–Centered therapists the core attitudes are implicitly integrated and therefore present. As a result, Rogers would just expect that they would be perceived by most clients. Whereas therapists operating out of other theoretical frames of reference in which the core conditions are not implicit, explicit delineation of communicating these conditions then became necessary. Whatever, there are some minor differences in the statements of the core conditions. The major difference is, however, more momentous.

THE MAJOR DIFFERENCE

The major difference between Rogers' 1957 and 1959 statements has vast implications. This difference is that in 1959 the hypothesis is presented as a core and integral part of client–centered theory but, in 1957, it is considered as essential in all theories of therapy and, indeed, of all helping relationships. In 1959, these conditions which Rogers considered to be so important are embedded within the context of the foundation block of the theory, the actualizing tendency. As well, the 1959 statement included the importance of the self–concept, non–directivity and the "technical" forms (e.g. reflection, restatement rule, empathic understanding responses) for implementation of the theory. This is not necessarily so in1957 where Rogers is quite clear that he is *not* referring to conditions that are essential for only client–centered therapy. His statement refers to "..conditions which apply to *any* situation in which constructive personality change occurs, whether we are thinking of classical psychoanalysis, or any of its modern offshoots, or Adlerian psychotherapy, or any other" (p. 230). Rogers (1957) hypothesized the following: "that effective psychotherapy of any sort produces similar changes in personality and behavior, and that a single set of preconditions is necessary." (p. 231)

The 1957 statement is truly meant as an integrative medium for all psychotherapies and, even for integration of helping relationships into every day life. As Rogers stated: "It is not stated that psychotherapy is a special kind of relationship, different in kind from all others which occur in everyday life" (p. 231). He explains further:

> Thus the therapeutic relationship is seen as a heightening of the constructive qualities which often exist in part in other relationships, and an extension through time of qualities which in other relationships tend at best to be momentary. (p. 231)

Rogers even refers to the hypothesis being relevant to programs that are aimed at constructive personality change and mentions programs of leadership, educational programs, and "Community agencies aim(ed) at personality and behavioral change in delinquents and criminals" (p.233). He suggests that if the hypotheses are supported, "..then the results, both for the planning of such programs and for our knowledge of human dynamics, would be significant" (p.233). Thus, Rogers' integrative statement is referring to conditions which exist as qualities for therapists in all therapies and for helpers in all situations which exist for the development of personality change. The relevancy of this hypothesis and manifestations of the integrative statement of the conditions in different contexts other than therapy are evident today as illustrated by the authors' experiences in facilitation of a nuclear industry in management reorganization based on an embodiment of the conditions within the values of the organization, and coordinating and facilitating state and community agencies toward a model of collaboration and empowerment through the integration of the conditions into the collaborative relationship among the participants.

MISUNDERSTANDING

Although Rogers is quite clear about his hypothesis being offered for all therapies and other realms of helping, the literature seldom differentiates the integrative concept from his conceptualization of the role of the attitudinal qualities as central concepts in Client–Centered Therapy. The upshot is that the therapist conditions posed as necessary and sufficient for all helping relationships and therapies has been confounded with the conditions as central attitudes in client–centered therapy. Moreover, they have been understood as somewhat separate actions different from other therapist activities rather than viewed as an integral experiencing of the therapist towards a client regardless of the channels of communication.

Nevertheless, the therapist conditions have either come to be considered as synonymous with client–centered therapy or as therapist dimensions separate from the therapist's being. We are, then, left with a misunderstanding which may have important implications having to do with such questions as:

Do the manifestations of the conditions vary according to the situational and theoretical factors which are present at a given time?

Do the perceptions of the conditions exist at a different level than the behavioral referents which occur?

Are the conditions more potent change forces when they exist in the context of the theory of client–centered therapy?

Questions such as these may inform the directions of future research.

MISDIRECTION

Study of the conditions from other theoretical frameworks have resulted in a confounding of the conditions as originally stated in Rogers' 1957 statement. The direction of investigation wascharacterized by a decided focus on communication and delineated forms of behavior that are closely associated with assumptions in client–centered therapy. This is further complicated by the operational definitions necessary for measuring the conditions. What the therapist is doing or not doing is assessed with varying degrees of specificity rather than examination of the person of the therapist experiencing attitudinal qualities towards the client. An example of a couple of the questions used in rating scales depict this directional bias. From one checklist (Cormier & Cormier,1991) for facilitative conditions, the following questions are asked:

For Empathy:

>"Did the counselor reflect *implicit*, or hidden, client messages?"
>
>"Did the counselor refer to the client's feelings?"
>
>"Did the counselor pace (match) the client's nonverbal behavior?"

For Genuineness:

>"Did the counselor match the client's predicates and phrases?"
>
>"Was the counselor appropriately spontaneous (for example, also tactful)?"
>
>"Did the counselor self–disclose, or share similar feelings and experiences?"

For Positive Regard:

>"Did the counselor demonstrate behaviors related to commitment and willingness to see the client (for example, starting on time, responding with intensity)?"
>
>"Did the counselor convey warmth to the client with supporting nonverbal behaviors (soft voice tone, smiling, eye contact, touch) and verbal responses (enhancing statements and/or immediacy)?" (p. 37–38)

As a result of specificity of behavior, the attitudinal conditions were relegated to specificity techniques instead of the experiencing of the therapist with another person. It is clear that the therapist behaviors are perceived as a certain form that conveys the therapist's experience of the client. The difference in meaning between particular behaviors and attitudinal conditions is a very pertinent consideration in attempting to understand the misdirection and misunderstanding of the conditions.

Some sense of the misdirection from an investigative and from the integrative intent can be realized when Rogers' statements are further examined. When he responds to the theoretical usefulness of his hypothesis, Rogers explicitly cites a variety of techniques that he viewed as having "essentially" no value to therapy; such as, interpretation of personality dynamics, free association, analysis of dreams, analysis of transference, hypnosis, interpretation of lifestyle, and suggestion. However, Rogers (1957) adds:

>Each of these techniques may, however, become a channel for communicating the essential conditions which have been formulated. An interpretation may be given in a way which communicates the unconditional positive regard of the therapist. A stream of free association may be listened to in a way which communicates an empathy which the therapist is experiencing. In the handling of the transference an effective therapist often communicates his own wholeness and congruence in the relationship. Similarly for the other techniques. But just as these techniques *may* communicate the elements which are essential for therapy, so any one of them may communicate attitudes and experiences sharply contradictory to the hypothesized conditions of therapy. (p. 234)

An implication of Rogers' integrative statement and of his comments is reflected in his comment that "..the techniques of the various therapies are relatively unimportant except to the extent that they serve as channels for fulfilling one of the conditions" (p.233). Rogers' statement is really quite astounding. He suggests that a person may do a technique that is conceptually antithetical, for example, to the concept of empathic understanding (e.g. interpretation) while still *experiencing* and *communicating* empathic understanding and/or unconditional positive regard.

The misunderstanding of the integrative statement which has occurred is that the experience of empathic understanding and unconditional positive regard for another is sculptured in a particular form rather than existing as an attitudinal embodiment in the experiencing of one person for another. It is a personal and person–to–person level of a certain type of experiencing with another person. The misdirection emerges from this misunderstanding in that thinking and research have been designed from the perspective of these conditions as particular forms. Rogers' liberal and inclusive theoretical definitions have given way to pseudoscientific and exclusive definitions. Although some forms, such as the restatement rule (Teich, 1992) and empathic understanding responses (Brodley, 1994), may be less interfering and more pure channels to allow for client perceptions of therapist experiencing, *they are not necessarily called for in the integrative model.*

A PARADOX

A paradox exists if the thesis that the personal embodiment of the conditions transcend behavior and method is correct. That is, a therapist, or any individual working with an aim toward constructive personality change, focusing on an external referent may be in some other way communicating empathic understanding of the internal referent of the person with whom they are working. In addition, the external referent may somehow even be a channel for the internal referent. How can this be so? One explanation is that the experiencing of unconditional positive regard and empathic understanding with another is a highly personal experience that exists in another way or that, in some way, the therapist's experience of congruence is communicated through, to what amounts to, the incongruent channel. Two examples of this paradox, one in a counseling course and the other in an organization, may give us a basis for exploring this phenomenon:

Counseling Course

One person role played the scenario of a female client who had been seen by one of the authors. The woman came to therapy discussing how her four year old son was disrupting her family. Four students talked with her for just fifteen minutes each on a rotational basis. The students who were not the active therapist at a given time observed the session until it was their time to be the therapist. The students were asked to operate from the Egan (1994) model which we define as fundamentally problem oriented and therapist driven. As such, all but one of the therapists focused on the problem of the child's disruption of the family. Questions raised included the following examples: Has he been evaluated for a physical problem? Have you tried rewarding him for good behaviors? Does your husband help? What does he (husband) think about it? Have you tried to communicate to your husband? In addition to the questions, the therapists attempted to summarize the client's communications. The client's comments were essentially presented in the following sequence:

> My four year old is disrupting the family (This was a continuous communication interlocked with all of her other comments).

> My husband works late on construction and isn't there to help.

> My husband doesn't really care. He doesn't understand the

> problem. He thinks boys will be boys and it's natural.

> My husband doesn't give me any support.

> I'm just there dealing with it all alone.

The only person I ever talk with is a friend who comes over sometimes. He tries to talk with my boy.

The therapists focused on the boy's behavior, sometimes wondering how the client's husband could help her more and even suggesting that her husband come with her for counseling in order to increase their communication with each other. One therapist communicated that this might help her husband to better understand the situation. The last therapist primarily summarized his understanding of her in an attempt to embody more of Rogers' integrative model. This model is viewed as more condition–centered and person–driven. With the continuous summarizing of the therapist's understanding of the client's meaning, the client added to her sequence:

I'm just all alone. No one supports me.

My boy is angry at everyone... at me ...

He's even mad at people he doesn't know very well.

He's even mad at my friend who comes over.

I'm just alone in all of this.

At this point, we stopped to discuss our experiences and observations. These included:

1. The client's intent was to resist telling the therapists that she was having an affair.

2. The therapists experienced something else other than the boy's behavior as going on but continued to focus on the problem as presented. In doing so, they missed hearing several of the client's comments; for example, that she had a male friend visit her. One therapist expressed a sense that she felt everyone was "flipping her off." This was not, however, discussed in the session.

3. The role play session went in a direction remarkably similar to the direction of the actual client. The actual client quit discussing the boy's behavior (never to be mentioned again) during the second session and discussed her affair. She then quit discussing the affair (never to be mentioned again) and talked about her feelings of being alone, discontent etc.:. This was the direction the role play was going during the ten minute integration model.

4. The client felt that she might have eventually discussed the affair with any of the therapists. She felt that their questions kept her active and she felt that she "knew that they knew" that there was something more than the boy's behavior.

The paradox of the phenomenon is somewhat illustrated in this instance. The student therapists focused on the problem and held a predominantly external assessment. Yet, they also had a sense of the client's perceptual view and seemed to be gaining an understanding of her internal frame of reference. The client felt as though she would have talked about her affair and feelings of aloneness if they had continued the session. This may be an example of the resiliency of individuals as clients but the point is that the client "knew" at some level that the therapists "knew", at least, vaguely that there was something else and that they were acceptant of her.

Facilitation of a reorganization model in a nuclear industry

Working in the capacity of facilitators, the authors worked with a nuclear industry whose intention was to change the structure of the organization and the relationship among the work force. This involved a paradigm shift from a formerly autocratic, controlled method of management of the organization to a more empowering organizational management model.

The empowerment model of management included adoption and integration of expressed core values of trust, consistency, openness and acceptance, and a willingness to pursue and allow others to pursue their highest potential in a supportive environment. A critical element of the empowerment model is the presence of a facilitative, secure environment in which the individuals can risk pursuance of a more effective and economical method of performance delivery. Some of the identifiable criteria for selection under the new empowerment managerial structure included individuals who were highly developed in communication and interpersonal skills, hard working, highly aware of stress factors, supportive, team players, skill appropriate, strong believers in the empowering process, secure, open–minded, flexible, radical and persistence.

The facilitators' responsibility was to enhance closer working relationships by providing a facilitative climate for the change process to occur. The context for this environment was team–building workshops. As the facilitators endeavored to embody the conditions as expressed by Rogers and work through the principles of the integrative statement, tension arose within the group pertaining to their expectations of directiveness in accomplishing creation and experiencing of the prescribed environment and subsequent methodical integration of the core values. These expectations were influenced from the earlier and consistent experiencing of management from a formerly authoritative paradigm. Consistency in experiencing the attitudes and not prescribing behavioral techniques to the methodology of the workshops, resulted in a paradoxical directive behavioral action. One of the facilitators, after checking with one of the participants about his stated desire to receive personal feedback from each of the participants, forcefully placed a chair in the middle of the group. The participant then chose to sit in the chair and from that point received individual feedback from his peers who joined him in the middle of the group. Additionally, the facilitator offered his internal experiencing of each participant, individually, in the same context. Subsequent informal remarks from the participants included a wide range of impressions. Some of these are as follows:

> I really liked the technique you used in order to get us to talk.

> I will never forget you for helping me move. When I finished talking with everybody, I didn't think I could move from that chair. But then when you came and sat by me and shared with me your experience of me, I felt accepted and you gave me the time I needed to enable me to move from that spot.

> I'm glad that you heard me, understood me, and helped me to seek out what I had wanted yet were unsure of how to accomplish it.

The paradox in this situation is that the facilitator acted from his own experiencing in an effort to clear himself toward a deeper level of embodiment and integration of the conditions. The "behavior" or "perceived technique" became a channel for him to become more fully absorbent of the participants and his own personal experiencing. It was an unsystematic idiosyncratic occurrence. However, it was experienced differently by the participants and serves as an illustration of the paradox of the phenomenon of Rogers' integrative statement. Several of the participants experienced the conditions through their perception of a behavioral technique.

RESEARCH

The salient points of our examination of varied experiences in the context of viewing Rogers' statement as integrative parallels findings in the research literature (Bohart, 1994). First, clients most often find what they need in whatever the therapist offers. That is, client factors, or extratherapeutic variables, account for forty per cent of the variance in psychotherapy outcome efficacy (Lambert, Shapiro, & Bergin, 1986). As person–centered therapists, we believe that they may seek and find whatever the therapist is experiencing by way of empathic understanding and unconditional positive regard (seeking their own nurture as part of the actualizing tendency). Second, common factors account for thirty per cent of the variance of outcome therapy efficacy (Lambert et. al., 1986), of which the most frequently researched is the therapeutic relationship (Lambert, 1992). Third, fifteen per cent of outcome variance is attributed to techniques or variables unique to specific theoretical orientations (Lambert, 1992). Consequently, Duncan and Moynihan (1994) state the following:

> the outcome literature challenges the inherent and invariant validity of a specific orientation, given that specific technique seems largely insignificant when compared with common factors and extratherapeutic variables. (p. 294)

We view this from a perspective that the therapist has to find his/her own best way to communicate his/her experiences of the client. Tom Malone (1981) provides a tidy summary of this point in his correspondence with Carl Whitaker when he points out that thousand of therapist of all orientations and training consider themselves to be "experiential psychotherapists." Malone (1981) states:

> They use a myriad of psychotherapeutic systems and techniques. They use their experience of their persons in psychotherapy and apparently are convinced that technique and system approach is significantly subordinate to their use of their personal experience to catalyze the patient's growth. (xxvii–xxviii)

He continues:

> The key concept is congruence. The congruence between the therapist's technique–system and his/her person allows the maximal personal participation in the relationship to the patient. This differs for different therapists. (xxviii)

It is this personal participation in the relationship in which we suggest that the empathic and caring experience is actually conveyed via or even in spite of a respite of techniques and therapist activities. If this is so, it is plausible that for therapists to maximize their experiencing of empathic understanding and unconditional positive regard with a client they must achieve first and foremost their own congruence. This congruence going beyond their own experiencing with their behaviors may include their own "technique system" maximizing their capacity for the experiencing of the core conditions. This may be why Rogers expressed congruency of the therapist as the most important of the conditions.

SUMMARY

It is asserted that Carl Rogers' (1957) statement concerning the necessary and sufficient conditions of therapeutic personality change is an integrative statement for psychotherapy and helping relationships that is separate from his statements concerning the conditions in client–centered therapy. The failure to consider his statement as integrative has resulted in misunderstandings and misdirection of investigation. The directions of investigation have focused on form of communication rather than upon the experiences of the therapist and the client. It is speculated that therapists, particularly those working from other orientations other than client–centered therapy, must achieve their own congruence including the use of their own "technique system" in order to maximize their capacity for experiencing empathic understanding and unconditional positive regard for the client.

REFERENCES

Bozarth, J.D. (1992). *A theoretical re–conceptualization of the necessary and sufficient conditions. Paper presented at the Fifth International Forum on the Person–Centered Approach, Terschelling, Holland.*

Brodley, B.T. (1987). *A client–centered psychotherapy practice.* Paper presented at the Third International Forum of the Person–Centered Approach, La Jolla, California.

Cormier, W. H. & Cormier. (1991). *Interviewing strategies for helpers.* Belmont, CA.: Brooks/Cole Publishing Co.

Duncan, B. L. & Moynihan, D. W. (1994). *Applying outcome research: Intentional utilization of the client's frame of reference.* Psychotherapy, 31 (2), 294–301.

Egan, G. (1994). *(The skilled helper: A problem–management approach to helping Fifth edition).* Pacific Grove, CA.: Brooks/Cole Publishing Co.

Lambert, M. (1992). *Psychotherapy outcome research.* In J. C. Norcross and M. R. Goldfried (Eds.), Handbook of psychotherapy integration (pp. 94–129). New York: Basic.

Lambert, M. J., Shapiro, D. A., & Bergin, A.E. (1986). *The effectiveness of psychotherapy.* In S. L. Garfield and A. E. Bergin (Eds.) Handbook of psychotherapy and behavior change (3rd ed., pp. 157–212). New York: John Wiley.

Rogers, C. R. (1957). *The necessary and sufficient conditions of therapeutic personality change.* Journal of Consulting Psychology, 21, 95–103.

Rogers, C. R. (1959). *A theory of therapy, personality, and interpersonal relationships, as developed in the client–centered framework.* In S. Koch (Ed.), A study of a science. Study 1. Conceptual and systematic. Vol. 3 Formulations of the person and the social context (pp. 184–256). New York: McGraw Hill.

Teich, N. (1992). *Rogerian perspectives: Collaborative rhetoric for oral and written communication.* Norwood, N. J.: Ablex Publishing Corporation.

Whitaker, C. A. & Malone, T. P (1981). *The roots of psychotherapy.* New York: Brunner/Mazel.

Change Processes in Experiential Therapy

LESLIE S. GREENBERG, JEANNE C. WATSON, RHONDA GOLDMAN
UNIVERSITY OF WINDSOR , YORK UNIVERSITY

ABSTRACT

Early client–centered and experiential theorists emphasised the importance of two factors in the change process: the therapeutic relationship and the role of clients' experiencing (Gendlin, 1982; Rogers, 1965). A later generation of experiential theorists increased our understanding of the change process by identifying additional client and therapist tasks, characterised by more active interventions, to faciliatate enduring client change (Greenberg, Rice, & Elliott, 1993).

The aim in this paper is to present some preliminary findings with respect to the efficacy of adding more active interventions to a purely relational treatment for a depressed population and to examine more fully the role of experiencing in the change process. First, the theory of process–experiential therapy will be discussed briefly, followed by an overview of the results from a process and outcome study of client–centered and experiential approaches in the treatment of depression conducted at York University. Finally the differential change processes which have been observed in the two treatments will be presented and exemplified.

GUIDING PRINCIPLES OF A PROCESS–EXPERIENTIAL APPROACH

The Process Experiential Approach (Greenberg, Rice & Elliott, 1993) relies on therapists providing genuine,prizing, empathic relationships and being highly attuned and responsive to their clients moment by moment feelings and experiences. One of the primary functions of the relationship conditions is to create a safe working environment within which therapists can facilitate clients' experiential processing to assist them to realize their goals in therapy.

Within a safe working environment (Elliott, Clark, Kemeny, Wexler, Mack & Brinkerhoff, 1990; Greenberg, et al, 1993; Lietaer, 1990; Rennie, 1992; Watson & Greenberg, 1994) process–experiential therapists use active interventions in a process diagnostic and process directive fashion. Process diagnosis occurs as therapists listen for markers of particular types of affective problems with which their clients are currently struggling, such as splits between two parts of the self, or particular behavioural or affective reactions of theirs, that they view as problematic. After the emergence of a marker, therapists may become more process directive and suggest specific in–session tasks to facilitate resolution of the affective problems that clients have articulated (Greenberg et al. 1993).

Five major sets of markers and tasks have been identified and delineated. These are: two–chair dialogues for the resolution of splits . empty chair dialogues for unfinished business systematic evocative unfolding for problematic reactions . focusing at markers of an unclear felt sense . empathic affirmation at markers of vulnerability The combination of relationship and task–oriented interventions adopted in this approach combines the benefits of both more active and more responsive therapeutic stances. In adopting this flexible dual style, balance and judgement are the guiding characteristics. Therapists need to constantly assess the best combination for their clients at specific times, judging whether more active stimulation or more responsive attunement would be most helpful, all the while keeping the overall balance of autonomy in favor of client–directed exploration. The optimal situation in the process–experiential approach is a synergistic interaction in which client and therapist work together, with neither one leading or simply following the other. Instead, the interaction is characterised by an easy sense of mutual collaboration and co–exploration.

Clients are viewed as experts on their own experience and therapy is a discovery oriented process. Thus, while the therapist may be informed about how and when to facilitate particular kinds of exploration of experience they are not the expert on the content of clients' experiences. Therapists' interventions are always offered in a non–imposing, non–authoritative manner, as suggestions or offers to facilitate clients in their goals rather than as instructions or statements of truth. At times of disjunction or disagreement therapists defer to clients' as the experts on their own experiences. Therapists therefore make suggestions to clients to help guide their experiential processing in different ways at different times in order to promote the type of cognitive and emotional processing that is likely to be most productive at various points in the session and to lead ultimately to the resolution of clients' specific affective problems.

DIFFERENTIAL CHANGE PROCESSES

Client–centred and experiential therapists have focused on the therapeutic relationship and clients' experiencing as factors in the change process. Rogers (1959) and Gendlin (1962; 1974) defined experiencing as the basic felt referent of awareness that can progress from elusive to clear. Rogers (1959) posited that in the process of successful therapy people would become more open to their feelings and that this constitutes constructive personality change. Experiencing was thought to be the way in which movement from rigidity to fluidity was manifested in therapy interactions. A number of early studies showed that there was a clear relationship between deeper experiencing and positive outcome in psychotherapy, but they were unable to demonstrate a relationship between changes in level of experiencing over the course of therapy and final outcome (Tomlinson, 1967; Tomlinson & Hart, 1962; Van der veen, 1967; Rogers, Gendlin, Kiesler & Truax, 1967). Kiesler (1971) found that more successful cases had deeper levels of experiencing than less successful cases at all points in therapy but that more successful cases could not be differentiated from less successful ones by shape or slope of experiencing. Thus Rogers' (1959) initial hypothesis that successful therapy was characterized by a steady increase in experiencing over the course of therapy, or a gradual move from fixed functioning to open processing was not supported in the early studies. More recently, other processes in addition to the relationship factors and client experiencing have been thought to facilitate clients' resolution of affective problems in therapy. In a recent study of clients' subjective experiences of exploring problematic reactions three activities: symbolic representation, emotional arousal, and reflexive self–examination, were identified as important aspects of the change process (Watson, 1993; Watson & Rennie, 1994).

Symbolic Representation

Symbolic representation refers to the verbal representation of experience in psychotherapy. The definition of experience employed here includes both a sense of being which is affected from without, feelings and emotions, as well as observations and perceptions of self and world, that provide knowledge of the latter.

The symbolic representation of experience in therapy has a number of important functions, including the clarification of difficult or problematic aspects of experience. In the process of speaking out loud to another person, troublesome issues become more concrete and have to be acknowledged. In representing their experience clients formulate problems and areas of concern which focus their attention on a line of inquiry during the session which facilitates exploration of the problematic issues.

The questions clients pose about their experiences act like compasses in terms of both the paths which need to be explored as well as their ultimate destination and resolution. Process–experiential therapists facilitate clients' representations of problematic aspects of their experience by listening attentively to the questions they pose. Experiential therapists attend to specific client statements or markers that indicate which problems are particularly salient and current for their clients, and actively help them to articulate and symbolically represent these in therapy.

Emotion and emotional arousal

An important assumption in experiential therapy is that clients need to access their inner, emotional experience in order to resolve affective problems (Greenberg & Safran, 1987; 1989; Greenberg & Korman, 1993). Like symbolic representation and reflexivity, emotions are a fundamental human capacity, which serve an adaptive, problem solving function. Emotions inform us of the impact of our environment, trigger reaction tendencies in response to environmental impacts and provide a means of communicating with others. Emotions are evoked in experiential therapy in order to help people make sense of what they feel and to promote emotional reorganization by synthesising previously unavailable internal resources. Clients' access to their emotions and increased emotional processing in therapy is seen as leading to enduring change.

Client–centered and experiential therapists have emphasised the symbolization of feeling and a bodily felt sense as productive processes in therapy. Techniques like reflection of feelings and focusing were devised to facilitate clients access to their inner experience and to promote its representation in therapy. More recently process–experiential therapy has provided additional ways to facilitate clients' access to their emotions and inner experiencing in the session and to help them to represent it symbolically, for example by requesting them to vividly, and concretely evoke events, or to imagine a significant other.

Clients' descriptions of their external world and the events in their life are usually regarded as indicative of poor process by experiential therapists, who tend to favour more internalised accounts that reveal clients' inner phenomenological experience of those events. In contrast Rice (1984; 1986) proposed that clients and therapists work together to provide vivid descriptions of the scenes in which problematic reactions occur using concrete, specific and imagistic language.

The use of vivid language facilitates clients recall of events as well as the reexperiencing of their inner subjective state during the event which they can then represent symbolically in words to come to a fuller understanding of its impact. There is in this process a dynamic interaction between clients recollections, descriptions, and emotional responses to events.

Clients' representations and perceptions of their environments highlight the double edged nature of experience as defined earlier.

Three important conditions contribute to the usefulness of clients' descriptions of their environment in the therapeutic context. First, clients' descriptions of their external environment is more productive, if it is in the service of exploring an experiential question.

Second, clients' recollections can be enhanced if the participants use evocative, concrete and vivid language to describe the situation. Third, therapists faciliate clients' symbolic representation of their subjective experience of events by asking them about their impact and their feelings in response to them.

Another way of helping clients to access their inner experiencing is in two chair work (Greenberg, et al, 1993). One of the primary functions of accessing the critic is not only to make the criticisms known, but also to help clients get in touch with their inner experience in response to those criticisms as an aid to fighting back and challenging them from within. Similarly in empty chair work the act of recalling a significant other promotes clients' access to their feelings and subjective sense of the other so that this can be represented during the session. One of the primary functions of clients' symbolically representing experience by either vividly describing a specific situation, accessing the critic or imagining a significant other, is to promote their emotional arousal during the session. Once clients have become emotionally aroused they are more easily able to label their feelings so that they can know them better.

By identifying different emotional states, clients understand how they feel about situations and events and acquire insight into their own behaviour and the impact of their environment on themselves. They thereby acquire a clearer understanding of their needs, desires, and goals so as to formulate ways of acting in future.

Reflexive self examination

Once experience has been symbolized, clients can reflexively question, examine and evaluate it. An important function of symbolically representing experience is that clients acquire a certain distance from it, which facilitates its examination and evaluation in ways not fully possible while it remained covert and subjective. Reflexivity is a defining feature of human consciousness, that psychotherapy researchers have tended to ignore as an explanatory variable in the change process. Client–centered and experiential theory, with its emphasis on feelings and organismic experience, has tended to downplay the role of values and evaluation in adaptive human functioning and the change process.

Action and experience result from an interaction and dynamic synthesis between clients' needs, desires, values, goals and environmental constraints as they seek to reconcile these potentially competing interests. In order to fully represent human potentialities for change and growth, it is important to remember that people are not only capable of discerning the impact of their experience and its significance for themselves, but they can choose to act in ways that may be contrary to certain needs, desires or values. However, if they are to act in ways that fully enhance their functioning, it is necessary for them to have information from all available sources, so that they are free to determine the best course of action or the one that is most congruent with the majority of their needs, values, desires and goals at specific points in time. An important dimension of experiential therapy is that the choices people make between competing courses of action are evaluated not only rationally but in terms of clients emotional responses to the alternatives (Greenberg, et al, 1993; Rogers, et al, 1967).

When engaged in reflexive self–examination clients reflect on their experience in a number of ways. First, they monitor the accuracy of their symbolic representations against memories of events. Second, as Gendlin (1974; 1982) has observed clients have recourse to an internal barometer or a bodily felt sense that something fits. They may experience a sense of relief when the right label for a feeling or inner subjective sense is found. Third, as they question their experience and observe patterns of behaviour across different situations, they may seek to determine the validity of these observations by checking across different situations to determine if these patterns recur or what their origins are. As they examine their behaviour clients also evaluate their behaviour in terms of their values, goals, needs and desires and begin to formulate alternative ways of being which may be more congruent with all of these. The tasks of experiential therapy facilitate a number of important client processes. First, by listening for and attending to clients' markers of affective problems, experiential therapists assist clients with the identification of their own specific experiential problems. Second, they promote clients' identification and articulation of the impact of, and their responses to their experiences. Third, experiential therapists help clients to access their inner desires, needs, and goals with reference to the problematic aspects of their experience, and fourth, they facilitate clients in formulating plans for future action.

CLIENT–CENTERED AND PROCESS–EXPERIENTIAL TREATMENTS OF DEPRESSION

Comparative outcome study.

A study was undertaken at York University sponsored by the National Institute of Mental Health to determine the efficacy of client–centered and experiential therapy in the treatment of depression and to ascertain whether the addition of more active interventions enhanced a purely relational client–centered approach. Another aim of the study was to increase understanding of the differential change processes in the treatment of depression in both client–centered and experiential therapy.

Thirty–four clients suffering from major depression were randomly assigned to either a client–centered treatment or a process–experiential treatment involving the client–centered relational conditions plus marker guided active interventions. A more comprehensive review of this study may be found in Greenberg and Watson (in press). Differences between groups at the termination of therapy were examined on the Beck Depression Inventory (Beck, Ward, Mendelson, Wok & Erbaugh, 1961), The Rosenberg Self–Esteem Questionnaire (Bachman & O'Malley, 1977), The Inventory of Interpersonal Problems (Horowitz, 1988), The global symptom index of the SCL–90–R (Derogatis, 1977), and the Target Complaints Box Scale (Battle, Imber, Hoehn–Saric, Stove, Nash & Frank, 1966). There was no significant difference between the client–centered and the process–experiential group in the alleviation of depressive symptoms on the Beck Depression Inventory. Moreover the pre–post treatment effect sizes (2.6) for both groups were equivalent to those demonstrated for other major psychotherapeutic approaches in the treatment of depression (Greenberg, Elliott & Lietaer, 1994). These findings lend strong support to the effectiveness and viability of both client–centered and process–experiential approaches in the treatment of depression. However, there were significant differences between the two groups on some of the outcome measures with clients in the process–experiential therapy showing significantly greater improvement on the Rosenberg Self Esteem Questionnaire (p < .02), the Inventory of Interpersonal Problems (p < .000) and the general symptom index of the SCL–90–R (p < .01). Furthermore, clients in the process–experiential treatment had a quicker response to treatment showing greater remission of their depressive symptoms by session 8 than the clients in the client–centered group. The results from this study indicate that while depression in both groups remitted over the course of treatment, process–experiential therapy is more effective in producing changes in clients' self–esteem, inter– personal functioning and general level of symptom distress. These findings support the idea that the addition of the active interventions to the purely client–centered treatments facilitates greater changes within clients.

Process Study

A further aim of the study was to examine more closely the role of experiencing in facilitating change. Given our observations that clients engage more productively in therapy once they have symbolically represented a specific affective problem and begun to explore it in depth by accessing the relevant material about themselves and the world in order to achieve resolution, it was decided to examine clients level of experiencing in relation to segments of therapy that were thematically relevant to their core problems.

Researchers recognized the importance of examining client process in context (Kiesler, 1971). The research question was informed by a view that resolution of specific problems through affective exploration and affective problem–resolution leads to change. Client process was therefore extracted from sessions in which they were working on their core problem and rated on the experiencing scale (Klein, Mathieu, Gendlin, & Kiesler, 1969) and then related to final outcome. The experiencing scale (Klein, et al, 1969) identifies 7 "stages" that define the progression of clients involvement in therapy. Clients descriptions of their experiences are rated as either impersonal and superficial; externalized with limited references to feelings; inwardly focused on inner referents and internal feelings; posing experiential questions; or finally as synthesizing newly realized feelings and experiences to produce personally meaningful structures and resolve issues. Clients' themes, defined as the three most important issues that they worked on in therapy, were identified by therapists and clients' reports at the termination of therapy. Subsequently an independent rater identified the three sessions from the last half of therapy during which clients spoke most on theme. A total of three, twenty minute, theme–related segments were selected for each client. A fuller explication of the method is provided by Goldman (in press).

Relationship Between Process and Outcome

In a preliminary examination, four poor and four good outcome cases from the depression study were investigated. In these cases, clients' modal and peak levels of experiencing on core themes and changes in experiencing from early to late in therapy were related to outcome. For the more successful group, there was a significant main effect for peak ratings on the experiencing scale ($p < .01$), indicating that for this group, peak ratings increased from the beginning of therapy ($X = 3.00$) to the end of therapy ($X = 5.5$). In the less successful group, there were no significant differences between modal ratings and peak ratings of clients experiencing from the beginning to the end of therapy. Thus it seems that in the small number of successful cases clients' level of experiencing increased over the course of therapy when they were actively engaged in exploring their core problem.

In a larger sample of 27 clients from client– centered and process–experiential therapy, it was found that mean level of experiencing in the last half of therapy was related to outcome and that in particular, a higher frequency of responses rated at level 6 on the experiencing scale, was strongly associated with changes in clients depressive symptoms ($r = .62$), and an increase in their self–esteem ($r = .56$), demonstrating that higher levels of experiencing on core themes, especially levels that identified the resolution of problems, correlated with outcome.

Early Therapy Process

An interesting finding was that there was a significant difference between the most successful ($X = 3.00$) and least successful groups ($X = 2.00$) in the modal ratings of clients' level of experiencing at the beginning of therapy ($p < .O$). Thus it seems that more succesful clients began therapy at a higher level of experiencing. In contrast to less successful clients, who provide accounts of their external experience, more successful clients begin therapy presenting both accounts of their experiences in the external world and their subjective reactions and feelings to those events.

A closer examination of early therapy dialogues revealed that a distinguishing feature of the more successful cases was a clearer conceptualization by clients of their problems. The more successful clients showed an initial clarity in conceptualizing their problems which helped them to define a focus of inquiry during the session. In addition to clearly posing a question, more successful clients also showed a sense of personal responsibility in relation to their problems and seemed motivated and committed to working on their difficulties.

For example, one client who showed an increase in experiencing over the course of therapy and general improvement on all the outcome measures stated her problem in these terms at the beginning of treatment:

C: Yeah its more of um, I understand it but then, you know, the anger and the resentment is still there, so I guess that's still part of um, I–I hold it, I don't know why (T: uh huh), but I do.

T: So its like its there and its not going away.

C: No... it recurs (T: uh huh), kind of, if something happens, um, I step back into the–merry go round again.

In the less successful cases, while clients recognized that they had difficulties, there was not the same sense of ownership in relation to their problems or sense of agency. For example this is how one such client spoke about his problems:

C: Yeah, that is not a bad analogy and I ... maybe I am starting to struggle less lately and that is probably why I am sitting here talking to you, cause I don't like the way it is going and I am obviously not capable of handling it, and I am hoping that somebody else can give me some insight, you know whatever.

T: That somehow you can feel that there is something that you can handle, that you can become more active, you can become active about all of this.

C: well, I don't know. like I really have my doubts about... for lack of a better word, talk therapy.

I have an open...mind with regard to it, I'm like, I'm here, so that is the bottom line.

These examples illustrate the difference between level two and level three on the experiencing scale, with level two reflecting a more superficial, impersonal involvment, and level three containing more personal, direct references to the self. In the first example the client is talking about events but is also providing a description of their impact on her. In contrast the client in the second example is speaking about his problems as if they were disconnected from himself. He does not represent clearly the events in his environment nor does he clearly reveal their impact on him.

Discussion of Process Findings

These preliminary findings support the idea that depth of experiencing is predictive of change on particular outcome measures. Moreover client responses rated at level 6 on the experiencing scale are predictive of positive outcome especially with respect to the remission of clients depressive symptoms and increases in their overall level of self–esteem.

Observations of clients in this and other studies suggests that clients' do not necessarily move from a general state of being closed to a more open state of experiencing, as suggested by the constructive personality change hypothesis. Rather what is important is the resolution of specific affective problems and themes in which clients symbolically represent specific aspects of their experience, moving between accounts of their perceptions to their subjective reactions and phenomenological sense of being in the world in relation to a specific experiential problem. This enables them to refelexively examine and evaluate their experience to formulate resolutions of the particular affective problems which are the focus of therapy. The resolutions might consist of revised views of themselves, others, environmental contingencies, needs, desires, values or goals, or any combination of these. Clients do not necessarily become more open and fluid to all aspects of their experience at all times as a function of being in therapy as Rogers (1959) first suggested. Rather, they acquire a way of problem solving that they can access and implement as necessary.

In addition to facilitating clients in session processes, the active interventiions may also implicitly promote clients learning new ways of solving interpersonal problems. For example, in resolving intrapsychic splits, clients actively represent both sides of a conflict first stating differences, then their feelings in response to these differences and finally they negotiate a way to resolve the difficulty. In examining problematic reactions clients acquire greater understanding of their reactions and the links between their behaviour and their environment which enhances their ability to control their reactions in an interpersonal context.

By engaging in these activities clients gain in a number of ways. First, clients' self esteem is enhanced and they learn to be more assertive as they actively challenge their internal critic. Second, clients consolidate their enhanced self esteem by stating and affirming their positive qualities and by asserting their desires and needs. Third, clients learn to experience and express both positive and negative feelings in the presence of another person. All these beahviours help clients to feel more confident in their interactions with others and better about themselves in general as they feel more resourceful in the interpersonal domain.

Some of these changes can be exemplified by a client, who entered therapy feeling very depressed and trapped in her marriage. She was disappointed in her husband, a compulsive gambler, who continually indebted the family. She presented herself as submissive in the relationship and charaterised her husband as emotionally and verbally abusive. On her inventory of interpersonal problems prior to beginning therapy she had endorsed items indicating that she had difficulty being assertive, was overly submissive, and assumed too much responsibility for the welfare and happiness of others.

During therapy she engaged in a number of two chair events which she resolved successfully. During these times she became clearer about her own feelings in response to her husbands behaviour, her desires and needs within the relationship more generally and was able to separate herself from him to make room for her own needs and to protect herself more in her interactions with him.

Her inventory of interpersonal problems post treatment reflected these changes. She reported that she was no longer as submissive, felt more friendly and sociable, and felt more able to express her desires needs, and feeling to others.

The common change factors

Having discussed the distinguishing features of experiential therapy, it is appropriate to look at some of the factors which facilitated change across both treatments. First, the quality of the therapeutic alliance (Bordin, 1979; Horvath & Greenberg, 1989; Watson & Greenberg, 1994; Rennie, 1990) distinguished successful from unsuccessful cases in both the client–centered and process–experiential groups. In cases with poor outcome therapists were unable to obtain clients' collaboration on the tasks and goals of therapy. Two clients in the client–centered treatment expressed frustration at the lack of direction and structure in therapy. One said:

"I could do this with my friends" while another requested more direction. In the process–experiential treatments two clients with the poorest outcome did not engage in experiential tasks until late in therapy. One of these complained that the more active interventions were too artificial, while the other felt his therapists directions were inaccurate. From these observations it seems clear that therapists and clients need to establish a sufficiently strong therapeutic bond and agreement on the goals and tasks of therapy for treatment to be successful irrespective of modality. Once the alliance was firmly established there seemed to be three different types of treatment foci that helped clients to resolve their depression in the two treatments. The first resulted from the provision of a safe environment in which clients primary task was to find their own voice and become more self accepting.

This focus emerged most clearly in the client–centered therapies with therapists primary task being to confirm and validate clients' experiences to enable them to become stronger and value themselves more. The second type of treatment focus was characterised by intensive exploration. This was promoted by therapists in both treatments with the primary goal being to help clients explore the leading edge of their experience. In this way clients became aware of hidden aspects of their experience which allowed them to reformulate specific issues. The third treatment focus, which occurred primarily in the process–experiential therapies, was characterised by clients exploration of the leading edges of their experience and by their experiencing and expressing deep emotion in the session. These processes resulted in clients altering their views of themselves and devising different ways of being in a variety of different contexts.

From these observations it is clear that the therapeutic relationship remains an important factor in the change process in therapy. However, while necessary, it is not as effective in promoting optimal process and change for all clients at all times. Other factors that contribute to change include high arousal and emotional expression along with the exploration of the outer edges of clients experiencing. These are promoted by the addition of the active interventions and enabled depressed clients to attain high levels of experiencing with respect to key issuess, resolve interpersonal difficulties and improve their general functioning. It will be important to determine in future whether the activation of these processes in the therapeutic encounter provides clients with improved capacities to resolve future difficulties and maintain optimal long term functioning.

REFERENCES

Bachman, J., & O'Malley,P. (1977). *Self–esteem in young men: A longitudinal analysis of the impact of educational and occupational attainment.* Journal of Social and Personality Psychology, 35, 365–380.

Battle, C., Imber, S.D., Hoehn–Saric, R., Stove, A., Nash, E., and Frank, J. (1966). *Target complaints as criteria of improvement.* American Journal of Psychotherapy, 20, 184–192. Beck, A., Ward, C., Mendelson, M., Wok, J. & Erbaugh, J. (1961). An inventory for measuring depression. Archives of general psychiatry, 4, 561–571.

Bordin, E.S. (1979). *The generalizability of the psychoanalytic concept of the working alliance.* Psychotherapy: Theory, research & Practice, 16, 252–260.

Derogatis, L.R. (1977). *SCL–90–R Administration, scoring and procedures manual–II.*

Elliott, R., Clark, C., Kemany, V., Wexler, M., Mack, C. & Brinkerhoff, J. (1990). *The impact of experiential therapy on depression: The first ten cases.* In A. Lietaer, G. J. Rombauts & R. Van Balen (Eds.). Client–centred therapy and experiential psychotherapy in the nineties. Belgium: Leuwen University Press.

Gendlin, E. (1982). *Focusing.* New York: Bantam Books.

Gendlin, E. T. (1974). *Client–centered and experiential psychotherapy.* In D. Wexler & L. N. Rice (Eds.), Innovations in Client–Centered Therapy. New York: Wiley, pp. 211–246.

Gendlin, E. T., (1962). *Experiencing and the Creation of Meaning.* New York: Free Press of

Glencoe. Goldman, R. (in press). *The relationship between depth of experiencing and final outcome in process– experiential therapy with depressed clients.* Unpublished doctoral dissertation, York University, North York, Canada. Greenberg, L.S. & Korman, L. (1993). Assimilating emotion into psychotherapy integration. Journal of Psychotherapy Integration, 3, 249–267.

Greenberg, L., Rice, L., & Elliott, R. (1993). *Process– experiential therapy: Facilitating emotional change.* New York: Guilford Press.

Greenberg, L.S., & Safran, J. (1989). *Emotion in psychotherapy.* American Psychologist, 44, 19–30.

Greenberg, L.S., & Safran, J. (1987). *Emotion in psychotherapy.* New York: The Guilford Press.

Horvath, A. & Greenberg, L.S. (1989). *Development and validation of the working alliance inventory.* Journal of Counselling Psychology, 24, 240–259.

Horowitz, L.M., Rosenberg, S.E., Baar, B.A., Ureno, G. & Villasenor, V.S. (1988). *Inventory of Interpersonal Problems: Psychometric properties & clinical applications.* Journal of Consulting and Clinical Psychology, 56, 885–892.

Kiesler, D.J. (1971). *Patient experiencing level and successful outcome in individual psychotherapy of schizophrenics and psychoneurotics.* Journal of Consulting and Clinical Psychology, 37, 370–385.

Klein, M.H., Mathiew–Coughlan, P.L. & Kiesler, D.J. (1986). *The experiencing scales.* In L.S. Greenberg & W.M. Pinsof (Eds.). The psychotherapeutic process: A research handbook. New York: Guilford Press.

Klein, M. H., Mathieu, P. L., Kiesler, D. J., & Gendlin, E. T. (1969). *The Experiencing Scale: A Research and Training Manual.* Madison: University of Wisconsin, Bureau of Audio Visual Research.

Lietaer, G. (1990). *The client–centred approach after the Wisconsin project: A personal view on its evolution.* In G. Lietaer, J. Rombauts & R. Van Balen (Eds.). Client–centred and experiential therapy in the nineties. Belgium: Leuwen University Press.

Rice, L.N. (1980). *Therapist manual for unfolding problematic reactions.* Unpublished manuscript, York University, North York, Ontario, Canada.

Rennie, D.L. (1992). *Qualitative analysis of the client's experience of psychotherapy: The unfolding of reflexivity.* In S. Toukmanian and D. Rennie (Eds.). Psychotherapy process research: Paradigmatic and narrative approaches. Newbury Park, CA: Sage.

Rogers, C.R. (1965). *Client–centred therapy: Its current practice, implications and theory.* Boston: Houghton, Mifflin Co.

Rogers, C.R. (1959). *A theory of therapy, personality, and interpersonal relationships, as developed by the client–centered framework.* In S. Koch (Ed.), Psychology: A Study of Science: Volume 3 Formulations of the Person and the Social Context. New York: McGraw–Hill, pp. 184–256.

Rogers, C.R., Gendlin, E.T., Kiesler, D.J., & Truax, C.B. (1967). *The Therapeutic Relationship and Its Impact: A Study of Psychotherapy with Schizophrenics.* Madison: University of Wisconsin Press.

Tomlinson, T. M. (1967). *The process of psychotherapy as related to outcome.* In C.R. Rogers, E.T. Gendlin, D.J. Kiesler, & C.B. Truax (Eds.), The Therapeutic Relationship and Its Impact: A Study of Psychotherapy With Schizophrenics. Madison: University of Wisconsin.

Tomlinson, T. M.& Hart, J. T. (1962). *A validation of the process scale.* Journal of Consulting Psychology, 26, 74–78.

Van der Veen, F. (1965). *Effects of the therapist and the patient on each other's therapeutic behavior.* Journal of Consu ting Psychology, 29, 19–26.

Van der Veen, F. (1967). *The effects of the therapist and the patient on each other.* In C.R. Rogers, E.T. Gendlin, D.J. Kiesler & C.B. Truax (Eds.), The Therapeutic Relationship and its Impact: A Study of Psychotherapy With Schizophrenics, Madison, University of Wisconsin.

Watson, J.C., (1992). *The process of change when exploring problematic reactions: An inquiry into self.* Unpublished doctoral dissertation, York University, North York, Ontario, Canada.

Watson, J.C. & Greenberg, L.S. (1994). *The alliance in experiential therapy: Enacting the relationship conditions.* In A. Horwath & L.S. Greenberg (Eds.). The working alliance: Theory, research and practice. New York: John Wiley & Sons, Inc. Watson, J.C. & Rennie, D. L. (in press). A qualitative analysis of clients' subjective experience of significant moments during the exploration of problematic reactions. Journal of Counselling Psychology.

Anger and Congruence Reconsidered from the Perspective of an Interdependent Orientation to the Self

T. LEN HOLDSTOCK

AMSTERDAM

ABSTRACT

Anger is a frequently experienced and expressed, yet little understood emotion which poses a special challenge for the Person–Centered concept of congruence. Congruence entails the matching of experience, awareness, and communication. In order to express our anger congruently, according to this definition, we need to be in touch with the precise nature of that experience. But what is this experience and how do we come to label it as such? It is now being realised that the experience and expression of anger is greatly dependent on the manner in which the self–concept is conceived. In cultures with an interdependent orientation to the self, anger is regarded as an ego–focussed emotion which impedes harmony in interpersonal relationships. Despite an independent orientation to the self, harmony in interpersonal relationships is certainly also of importance in Western cultures, and especially in the Person–Centered approach. It would seem advisable, therefore, to reconsider the focus on ego–focussed emotions, such as anger, and conditions facilitating the experience and expression of such emotions in Western cultures. Within the context of the Person–Centered approach, it is especially an ego–focussed orientation to congruence, and the independent orientation to the self, that need consideration.

The initial stimulus for this paper is to be found in my discomfort with the way anger is generally regarded in clinical psychology and handled in the Person–Centered (PC) approach specifically. In the context of the PC approach and theory, anger seems to be of special relevance with respect to the concept of congruence. Since Rogers (1961) defined congruence as "an accurate matching of experiencing and awareness...further extended to cover a matching of experience, awareness, and communication" (p.308), we need to be aware of the exact nature of our experience of anger in order to guide the subsequent expression of that experience as appropriately as possible. In a sense, dealing congruently with our anger requires the same precision in defining the nature of our experience as is required of any scientific definition. Since congruence is interrelated with empathy and positive regard, the two other attitudes considered to be necessary for effective psychotherapy, anger, or any emotion for that matter, is not only of relevance to congruence, but has implications for PC theory in general.

Surprisingly, or perhaps not so surprisingly, a relative dearth of information exists in both the scientific and clinical literature regarding the nature of anger. The statement by Likierman (1987) that anger, "being a familiar everyday feeling of an obvious kind, has received minimal attention in analytic thinking" (p. 143) reflects, not only analytic thinking, but the thinking in psychology and psychotherapy generally. According to Averill (1983) "discussions of anger in the psychological literature are most conspicious by their absence" (p. 1147). Moreover, the work that has been done, focussed mostly on laboratory studies of anger. Detailed "surveys of the everyday experience of anger can be counted on the fingers of one hand" (Averill, 1982, p.150). According to Smedslund (1993) the "ordinary language concept of anger is fuzzy" (p.

9). Everyone seems to know what anger means, yet "it is difficult to formulate the necessary and sufficient criteria involved" (p. 6). Smedslund stresses that it is important to distinguish "between the *phenomenon* of anger, the *ordinary language term* anger and a *scientific term* anger" (p. 9).

The lack of information with regard to anger is even more surprising if one considers the importance of this emotion in human behaviour and relationships. The purpose of this paper is to draw attention to anger and the way it has, or has not been handled, in the PC or Client-Centered (CC) approach. Greenberg and Safran (1989) recently stated that the cognitive revolution has had the legitimization of studying affective processes as an interesting side-effect. These two authors are amongst the theorists who explore "the functional role of emotion in the human information processing system" (p. 20). In the context of the PC approach an understanding of the nature of anger can perhaps be understood best in terms of a framework which incorporates the whole person. In such a holistic perspective anger is constituted by the meaning attributed by the individual to antecedent conditions experienced as stressful, and to the accompanying physiological changes, which the person may, to a greater or lesser extent, be aware of.

Defining anger in such general terms leaves a great many questions unanswered, however. For instance, is anger biologically determined or cognitively constructed? If anger is cognitively construed, what is the nature of the conditions preceding the experience of anger? Is the cognitive construal of anger social in nature, as is assumed by Averill (1983)? Does anger serve a purpose and if so, what is it? Does it defend the individual against the perceived threats involved at either of the two extremes of closeness or separation, as suggested by Munschauer (1987)? Is anger used to maintain control or at least the illusion of a sense of control and mastery (Barlow, 1991)? Does the experience of anger come about when the power struggle for recognition is thwarted (Benjamin, 1980)?

What distinguishes anger from such experiences as anxiety, annoyance, irritability, frustration, aggression, and rage? Where does it fit on a hierarchical scale of `negative' or `aggressive' emotions, as proposed by Stone (1991) and Kernberg (1991)? The relation of anger to other emotional experiences is important in determining whether it is a primary or secondary emotion. Apart from aspects related to the experiencing of anger, it is also important to know what the consequences are of the expression of anger on other people, and on the self. Furthermore we know little about issues related to the duration and time course of anger. The same is true with respect to the question of gender and cultural differences in the experiences and expression of anger. For instance, indications are that considerable differences exist between cultures and subcultures in the experience and expression of anger (Markus & Kitayama, 1991; Mesquita & Frijda, 1992; Russell, 1991).

ANGER AND CONGRUENCE

In the context of the many unanswered questions about and importance of anger, the lack of attention this emotion has received amongst PC theorists and practitioners, is all the more glaring. It is likely that this lack of attention has given rise to an approach to anger which is everything but optimal. The undifferentiated understanding of anger seems to find an all too readily available outlet through the concept of congruence, which also seems to be in need of more urgent attention. In essence, the increasing ease with which anger is expressed in PC circles highlights the problematic nature of the relationship of congruence with empathy and positive regard, the two other `necessary and sufficient' conditions. We seem to have become so totally focussed on being true to what we perceive as our inner experiences and on expressing ourselves, that we seem to have lost sight of the recipient of our expressiveness and the effect it has on that person.

In his own professional behaviour Rogers managed to maintain a balance between the expressive aspect of congruence and the world of the other person. During the latter part of his career he became freer to express his feelings towards clients, especially when the feelings were of a positive nature. Think of the instances when he told Gloria that she would make a very nice daughter and that he felt close to her during the interview. Instances of expressing `negative' emotional experiences of his experiences during his many recorded interviews, are hard to find. Offhand, I can recall one instance from the encounter group film, *Because That's My Way,* that may, somewhat tentatively at that, be classified in this category. This is when he told `George' that he refused to be a revolutionary in the way `George' wanted him to be.

In my own contact with him over a period of 27 years, I can recall two instances of feedback which reflected a measure of irritation. In contrast, there were many instances of positive expressions. I am sure that everyone who has been in contact with Rogers, has had the same experience, even though Rogers was sparse in expressing himself. He has even been criticized in this regard, and with respect to his failure to express anger (see Gendlin, 1988). However, the possibility exists that his ability to indwell into the world of the other prevented the experience and expression of anger. Rather paradoxically though, his theory of self and the concept of congruence provide the space for the expression of ego–centered emotions.

As indicated elsewhere and in the other paper at this conference, a discrepancy exists between the theory of the self and the theory underlying the actual practice of PC therapy (Holdstock, 1990; 1991; 1992; 1993; 1994). This discrepancy pertains primarily to the orientations to the self as an independent or as an interdependent unit of the social system. The concept of self underlying the theory of self is that of an independent entity, while it is the concept of self as an interdependent entity that seems to underlie PC therapy. However, within the theory of therapy a differentiation needs to be made between the three conditions considered to be necessary and sufficient for succesful therapeutic outcome. Empathy and positive regard are in keeping with an interdependent view of the self. Congruence, on the other hand, is that aspect of the theory of therapy which seems to be most in keeping with the theory of the self as an independent unit of the social system.

While Rogers, in his therapeutic behaviour, implicitly corrected for the discrepancy between the independent and interdependent focusses in his theories, adherents of the PC approach seem to be less able to do so. The impression gained in PC forums and workshops during the past few years, would seem to indicate a sharper focus on the self as an independent entity and a consequent shift towards congruence as the most basic of the necessary and sufficient conditions. While such a shift is understandable in the context of the present zeitgeist prevailing in the mainstream culture subserving PC therapy, the emphasis on the self as an independent unit of the social system is not in keeping with the other–centeredness required in empathy and positive regard.

CULTURAL VARIATIONS IN THE EXPERIENCE AND EXPRESSION OF ANGER

That the self–focus, apparent in the experience and expression of anger, and the sanction of that self–focus by the PC concept of congruence reflect the ethnocentric orientation of Western culture, is becoming increasingly more apparent. Cultures vary in the experiece and manifestation of anger. In terms of the prevailing cognitive approach an emotional experience is embedded in the social situation as construed by the person. The way the social situation is construed, in its turn, depends, to a very large extent upon the way the self is construed. Thus, whenever an emotional activity or reaction implicates the self, the outcome of this activity will be dependent on the nature of the self–system, and the way the self–system is construed varies markedly between cultures (see Holdstock, 1993 for references).

The distinction which Markus and Kitayama (1991) make between ego–focussed and other–focussed emotions is of great value in trying to come to a better understanding of the discrepancy evident in PC theory. According to these two authors anger belongs to the class of emotions which "have the individual's internal attributes (his or her own needs, goals, desires, or abilities) as the primary referent...the expression of one's internal attributes is the culturally sanctioned task of the independent self" (p. 235). Frustration and pride are other examples of ego–focussed emotions. In contrast to the ego–focussed emotions are those emotions which have another person, rather than one's internal attributes, as the primary referent. Examples of such emotions are sympathy, shame, and feelings of interpersonal communion.

Whereas other–focussed emotions "result from being sensitive to the other, taking the perspective of the other, and attempting to promote interdependence" (Markus & Kitayama, p. 235), ego–focussed emotions serve to maintain the self as an independent and autonomous entity. In fact, "the expression of one's internal attributes is the culturally sanctioned task of the independent self" (p. 235). In order for those with independent "selves to operate effectively, they will have to be `experts' in the expression and experience of these emotions...Experiencing and expressing these emotions further highlights these self–defining, internal attributes and leads to additional attempts to assert them in public and confirm them in private" (p. 235). "Not to attend to one's inner feelings is often viewed as being inauthentic or even as denying the `real' self" (p. 236). However, "The public display of one's own internal attributes can be at odds with the maintenance of interdependent, cooperative social interaction, and when unchecked can result in interpersonal confrontation, conflict, and possibly even overt aggression" (p. 235).

"In contrast, among those with more interdependent selves, one's inner feelings may be less important in determining one's consequent actions...For those with interdependent selves, it is the interpersonal context that assumes priority over the inner attributes, such as private feelings. The latter may need to be controlled or de–emphasized so as to effectively fit into the interpersonal context" (p. 236). An other–orientation is likely to be experienced negatively by, and have a negative impact on those with independent selves.

"For those with interdependent selves (composed primarily of relationships with others instead of inner attributes), it may be very important not to have intense experiences of ego–focused emotions, and this may be particularly true of negative emotions like anger. Anger may seriously threaten an interdependent self and thus may be highly dysfunctional" (Markus & Kitayama, 1991, p. 236). As a result very little anger is elicited in some interdependent cultures. According to Markus and Kitayama it is not that these cultures have learned to inhibit or suppress their `real' anger, but that they have learned the importance of attending to and considering others, of being gentle in all situations, and to avoid disruption of the harmony of the social situation. The Ukta Eskimos, who "are said not to feel anger, not to express anger, and not even to talk about anger...use a word that means `childish' to label angry behavior when it is observed in foreigners" (p. 236).

In those interdependent cultures where the overt expression of anger is frowned upon as a disturbance of the social harmony, it is especially in close relationships where the expression of anger is to be avoided. "When anger arises, it happens outside of the existing interdependence, as in confrontation with out–groups...In contrast, Americans and Western Europeans report experiencing anger primarily in the presence of closely related others" (Markus & Kitayama, 1991, p. 237).

Thus, the basic question seems to be whether the expression of anger has the same negative impact on persons who function within an independent framework as it has on those with interdependent selves. Even though the degree of the impact is likely to be less, I think it is safe to assume that the impact will still be negative. Although Western cultures with their orientation towards the independent self try to become totally self–sufficient, the success of Rogers' theory of therapy, which in my opinion, is best exemplified by the attitudes he portrayed in his own therapeutic behaviour, demonstrates the opposite. Try as we may to deny our relatedness to each other, being related remains the single most basic aspect of our humanness.

An additional reason for being circumspect in the expression of our anger relates to the fact that we know so little about the precise nature of the experience. It would seem that those of us who operate within the PC mold have a special responsibility, both with regard to getting in touch with the exact nature of our experience and with the subsequent expression of that experience. In an attempt to come to a better understanding of anger, I have embarked upon a number of studies, using the Self–Confrontation Method (SCM) of Hermans (1991). The SCM offers an excellent means of indwelling into the world of the other by eliciting `valuations' from the individual pertaining to that which is of importance to him or her with respect to the topic of interest. At the same time the method allows for the quantification and nomothetic processing of the data. Each valuation is rated on a 6–point scale with respect to 16 affective terms, comprising orientations towards self and other, as well as negative and positive orientations. Content analyses of the valuations can be done, as well as correlating the various valuations with each other. In any case, the purpose is not to describe the method, but to invite those of you who may be interested, to join in an investigation of anger from the perspective of different cultures. By indwelling into our experiences of anger, we may, hopefully, be able to obtain a somewhat better understanding of the important emotion.

REFERENCES

Averill, J.R. (1982). *Anger and aggression: An essay on emotion.* New York: Springer–Verlag.

Averill, J.R. (1983). *Studies on anger and aggression. Implications for theories of emotion.* American Psychologist, 38, 1145–1160.

Barlow, D.H. (1991*). Disorders of emotion.* Psychological Inquiry, 2, 58–71.

Benjamin, J. (1980). *The bonds of love: Rational violence and erotic domination.* Feminist Studies, 6, 144–174.

Gendlin, E.T. (1988). *Carl Rogers (1902–1987).* American Psychologist, 43, 127–128.

Greenberg, L.S., & Safran, J.D. (1989). *Emotion in psychotherapy.* American Psychologist, 44, 10–29.

Hermans, H.J.M. (1991). *The person as co–investigator in self–research: valuation theory.* European Journal of Personality, 5, 217–234.

Holdstock, T.L. (1990). *Can Client–Centered therapy transcend its monocultural roots*? In G. Lietaer, J. Rombouts, & R. van Balen (Eds), Client–Centered and experiential psychotherapy in the nineties (pp. 109–121). Leuven: Leuven University Press.

Holdstock, T.L. (1991). *Het individuocentrisme in de klinische psychologie: Quo vadis?* In J.A.M. Winnubst, P. Schnabel, J van den Bout, & M.J.M. van Son (Eds), De matamorfose van de klinische psychologie (pp. 199–207). Assen: Van Gorcum.

Holdstock, T.L. (1992). *Incongruence beween the Person–Centered theories of self and of therapy.* Paper presented at the Fifth Forum for the Person–Centered Approach, Isle of Terschelling, The Netherlands.

Holdstock, T.L. (1993). *Can we afford not to revision the Person–Centered concept of self?* In B. Brazier (Ed), Beyond Carl Rogers (pp. 229–252). London: Constable.

Holdstock, T.L. (1994, September). *Implications of cultural concepts of the self for mental health, mental illness and psychotherapy.* Paper presented at The XVI International Congress of Psychotherapy, Seoul, Korea.

Kernberg, O.F. (1991). *Sexual excitement and rage: Building blocks of the drives.* Sigmund Freud House–Bulletin, 15, 3–38.

Likierman, M. (1987). *The function of anger in human conflict.* International Review of Psycho–Analysis, 14, 143–161.

Markus, H.R., & Kitayama, S. (1991). *Culture and the self: Implications for cognition, emotion, and motivation.* Psychological Review, 98, 224–253.

Mesquita, B., & Frijda, N.H. (1992). *Cultural variations in emotions: A review.* Psychological Bulletin, 112, 179–204.

Munschauer, C.A. (1987). *The patient chase: A bridge between the theories of Kernberg and Kohut.* Psychoanalytic Inquiry, 7, 99–120.

Rogers, C.R. (1961). *On becoming a person.* Boston: Houghton Mifflin.

Russell, J.A. (1991). *Culture and the categorization of emotions.* Psychological Bulletin, 110, 426–450.

Smedslund, J. (1993). *How shall the concept of anger be defined?* Theory and Psychology, 3, 5–33.

Stone, M.H. (1991). *Aggression, rage, and the `destructive instinct,' reconsidered from a psychobiological point of view.* Journal of the American Academy of Psychoanalysis, 19, 507–529.

The Self as a Systemic Process of Interactions of "Inner Persons"

SYLVIA KEIL
WIEN

ABSTRACT

On the basis of Rogers' concept of the self, the self is regarded as an autopoetic system which. as a result of its ability to refer to itself, is continually evolving. One's relationship to oneself is subject to the same systematic correlations as the relationship between separate persons. Accordingly, regularities such as those identified in communication theory also apply to inner relationships. The self is understood as an ensemble of "inner persons", similar to the family. In this view, incongruence is seen as the result of a dysfunctional inner relationship. A person is congruent when the various parts of his or her personality act together in an advantageous way and are capable of reacting openly newly awakening aspects of the personality. The empathy of the therapist must therefore be directed toward the specific interrelationship of the "inner persons", i.e. toward typical basic patterns and their significance for the whole person's contact with the outside world. In conclusion, a brief discussion of the therapeutic implications of this viewpoint is presented.

SELF AS A SYSTEMIC PROCESS OF INTERACTIONS OF "INNER PERSONS"

Introduction

I would like to make use of this conference to present to you my opinion concerning the processes governing the self. I have made the discovery that communication processes similar to those known from family situations take place in a person, within the self. On account of that I have attempted to view the processes within the self in the same way as interpersonal relations with the help of concepts adopted from communication– and system–theory. One goal of client centered psychotherapy is irrefutably that therapy should bring about a change in the relationship to oneself – so what I tried to do was to look upon and also to treat these inner relations in the same concrete manner I was accustomed to from my work with families. Among other things, family–therapy is aimed at finding ways how family members should deal with each other in order for all to be satisfied. When I began to study my clients' inner relations from this view point I came across some surprising results that made it considerably easier for me to show them empathy and acceptance. I hope that my ideas might be of some use for your own psychotherapeutic work.

The Self in Rogers' work

Originally Rogers ignored the term "self" because it seemed too vague and therefore scientifically irrelevant. Only after clients used the expression themselves and because therapeutic success could be traced back to the clients change in attitude towards himself did Rogers introduce "self" as a central construct in his theory. In his theory of personality self is directly linked to the term "organism". Organism here is not the physical body but a psychological factor: the human ability to make experiences and to evaluate these as hindrance or improvement to his development. The organism is essentially motivated by the actualizing tendency, i.e. not only to strive to sustain the (physical) organism but furthermore the tendency to differentiate and expand in terms of growth as well as the development away from heteronomy towards autonomy.

As a result of the actualizing tendency the organism creates the self by means of interactional exchange with other people. The individual's experiences, i.e. his existence and actions, are partially registered by consciousness.

The function of self

The development of consciousness makes possible a leap in evolution whereby the actualizing tendency towards *expansion* plays a significant role. Only a fully developed self enables us to exist in what Sir K. Popper terms "world 3" (Popper & Eccles, 1982). Human intellect developed parallel to the development of language thereby creating "world 3" which includes all that is man–made, invented or thought. On account of the fact that human thinking can directly influence world 1 and 2 it creates realities. In this manner diverse means of transport have enabled us all to attend this conference here in this constellation. Similarly the development of the client–centered approach has brought about noticeable changes in my and probably also in your psychological as well as material "worlds". This all just goes to show that self is never "selfless" but that it is compelled to *inter*fere with the surrounding world and so make itself noticeable. In phenomenological terms that means: human consciousness is intentionally oriented towards the world. Gordon Allport postulates that psychology cannot evade the concept of self if it aims to explain the coherence, homogeneity and application to purpose of human behaviour (quoted in: Pervin, 1993, p. 30 f.).

A further facet of the functions of self must be accounted for: in principle we can say that every organism has the fundamental drive to satisfy the needs it becomes aware of in itself. Even when looking at such a basic need as that for food, one need only reflect on the enormous number of cookbooks already published to become aware of the numerous ways of satisfying this need. The organism can recognise *which* needs one has. *How* these experiences are symbolised, resulting in the strategies applied to satisfy these needs, is *culturally dependant, must therefore be learnt and are as such subject to the influence of the self.*

Thus self has the further important function to mediate between the organism and the environment (cf. Sommer, 1994, p. 31). I would like to put it this way: the organism can be said to care for its self according to the same mechanisms and in the same way as parents care for their children.

The Self as a Self – Reflexive Phenomenon

The term self was initially introduced to psychology by William James. He was occupied with the study of a certain "doubling–effect" of self (Ludwig–Körner, 1992, p. 21 f.). That is what he calls the fact that self always unites two separate aspects; these are the "I" and the "Me". Note that he speaks of differentiable aspects and not of separate things, because "I" and "Me" are experienced as one person even during differentiation.

Self can comprise several "Me"s. To me it seems particularly significant that the different "Me"s can only recognised by consciousness through the contact with the "I". The process of experiencing can only take place within the framework of this self – reflexive consciousness i.e. I am aware of myself as "I", that in turn is aware of itself, etc. "I" eludes to all scrutiny because it (in itself) becomes an object i.e. "Me" through the self scrutiny. I see this as follows: "I" has a similar function as a light beam in a dark world, in that it illuminates objects, making these visible. The light source, however, cannot be seen. Nevertheless one can observe *what* and *how* the light ray illuminates something. That in turn lets us deduce some qualities of the light source.

In a sense the source "illuminates' itself, which respectively requires the creation of a new "I". On account of "I" being self–reflexive it creates itself. In other words, we are dealing with an autopoetic process. Concerning "I" we thus conclude: "I" is in relation. Even: "I" is relation (Wiltschko, 1994). This means no less than that by taking reference to ourselves a piece of our self is created, e.g. during the therapeutic process.

Carl Rogers also confronts us with a certain "doubling–effect" of self. With the 'coming about' of self the individual develops a need' for positive regard. A particular behaviour will let the individual experience positive self regard if it has received positive regard from others often enough (for the same behaviour). This makes the individual independent of 'concrete' interactions with others. As a result the individual develops a need for positive self regard – thereby "he becomes in a sense his own significant social other." (Rogers, 1959, 224) *Again*: "I" & "Me".

That by the way is the theoretic background why we client–centered therapists should not focus empathy so much on the client's emotion but rather on the value he 'appoints' to the specific feeling. (I have found this viewpoint particularly well discussed in the publications of Biermann–Ratjen, Eckert, and Schwartz, (1979) as well as in those by Binder, U. & Binder, J. (1991)) In this manner we empathise not only with the experience recounted by the but also with the way the client experiences the experience (i.e. how he feels about it!) Not only a client's fear of something is of importance; more important is whether he wishes to suppress or ignore his fear or to see it as a warning signal.

THE SELF REFLEXIVE NATURE OF SELF AS A COMMUNICATION PROCESS BETWEEN "INNER PERSONS"

One can visualise the above processes as inner dialogues: one perceives an emotion to which the other takes a stand. This basic statement can be spun endlessly: the one in turn will assume a position regarding the position of the other, etc. On account of this I believe that self is an interactive process. Though difficult to account for precisely because of the speed of thought at which the process takes place, we can at least observe the following sequence: perception – evaluation – reaction – perception – ....etc. (cf. the description of communicationcycles in: Bandler et al., 1978). We react not only to our environment but just as well to ourselves, we perceive ourselves, evaluate our perceptions and in turn react to the evaluation. More so than for external relations it holds true for inner interactions that one cannot not communicate. Thus inner communication takes on a cyclic / recursive structure and that on its own is reason enough to speak of a process of systemic interaction.

A very clear literary example for this recursive / cyclic structure can be found in "The Little Prince" by Antoine de Saint Exupéry :

> The next planet was inhabited by a tippler. This was a very short visit, but it plunged the little prince into deep dejection.
>
> "What are you doing there?" he said to the tippler, whom he found settled down in silence before a collection of empty bottles and also a collection of full bottles.
>
> "I am drinking," replied the tippler, with a lugubrious air.
>
> "Why are you drinking?" demanded the little prince.
>
> "So that I may forget," replied the tippler
>
> "Forget what ?" inquired the little prince, who already was sorry for him.
>
> "Forget that I am ashamed," the tippler confessed, hanging his head.

"Ashamed of what? insisted the little prince, who wanted to help him.

"Ashamed of drinking!" The tippler brought his speech to an end, and shut himself up in an impregnable silence.

And the little prince went away, puzzled.

"The grown – ups are certainly very, very odd," he said to himself, as he continued on his journey. (The Little Prince, Chapter XII)

The literary compression makes this example extremely concise and can taken to show a number of relevant problems concerning inner communication that I have encountered in my clients and for myself too. – One possible method to avoid plunging into deep dejection like the little prince is to visualise such inner conflict as the conflict between physically different persons.

Thus: person 1 drinks to forget that person 2 is ashamed of him. Person 2 is ashamed because person 1 gets drunk. – This inner relation is not dissimilar to the relation between a nagging wife and her alcoholic husband. New interpretations may be achieved by projecting the same relation on father and son. The more the father is ashamed of his son, the more the son will drink and vice–versa. To be able to work with inner communication therapeutically, it is extremely important to visualise the inner parts as complete persons i.e. with emotions, reason, own wishes and the ability to set actions, – in a way similar to that in which the minds eye can complete a partially destroyed photograph. Only when one assumes this position does it become obvious e.g. that the inner father is merely ashamed instead of keeping his son from drinking. On the other hand the son just gets drunk to show his dissatisfaction instead of confronting the inner father to demand that he actually ought be proud of him. Herein lies the incredible advantage of the inner persons, that they have the power to change what others do or are doing.

I imagine "as if"[1] (ann. 1) it were so and realise that with the help of this presumption my possibilities to become sensitive for the client's inner world increase incredibly. – For example: how can one explain that the inner father does not intervene? Could it be that he feels inferior to the other person or is he maybe secretly quite happy to be better than the alcoholic? Inner relations also differ from "outer" relationships in the directness of access and the security that inner persons cannot just run away from each other; they can merely change themselves and their manner.

The application of the laws of communication to inner relations

Watzlawick, Beavin, and Jackson (1969) formulated the following general laws concerning communication, which I believe can also be applied to intrapersonal relations.

1. It is impossible not to communicate.

2. All forms of communication comprise a content – and a relational component whereby the content is subordinate to the relational component.

When one person is ashamed he will influence the drinker and vice–versa. The drinker might interpret that as, "I don't like you." while the other might "hear", "You're a loser." It is obvious that one takes to drink not only because one received too little love or attention from one's parents but also out of anger at one's own attitude towards oneself which oddly enough is brought about – unintentionally – by one's inclination to drink. This phenomenon can be referred to as intrapersonal circular causality. It is in fact this relational aspect of inner communication that is frequently neglected or at least not accounted for in terms of mutuality. – In our example the atmosphere of the intrapersonal relationships is characterised by mutual rejection.

That also implies that if one is at peace with oneself this aspect of the relationship can be the source of a good deal of energy in seemingly hopeless situations.

3. All communication is structured differently by separate partners in a manner perceived as stages in series of events. – So, what came first, the chicken or the egg, getting drunk or being ashamed of oneself? Coming back to the above example, it is very well possible that the feeling of shame came first. That leads to a new idea however: did the tippler already feel shame before beginning to drink? If yes, then why and for what reason? That is what makes systemic reflexion absolutely necessary in this approach.

4) Human communication can take place in digital (verbal) and analogue (non–verbal) form. Modified for the application to inner communication it can either occur in form of thoughts, inner voices (digital) or in form of emotions felt, actions set or symptoms (analogue).

5) Communication–processes can either be symmetric or complementary. That does not pose any problems as long as symmetrical and complementary processes alternate in a sensible context–sensitive manner. When one has a psychic/psychological problem one is always confronted with escalating symmetrical or escalating complementary inner relationships. In our example the inner relation is symmetrically escalating. We are faced with complementary escalation if e.g. the one "person" complains while the other feels compassion; the more the one sympathises with the other, the more the other will find to moan about. – A vicious–circle commonly known as self–pity. Theoretically this condition follows simple rules: in symmetrical relations the partners negate each others positions , in a complementary relation the partners approve of each others points of view. To end an escalation it is necessary to change complementarity to symmetry and vice–versa. In reality that is easier said than done. Keeping all this in mind it becomes simple to explain the great success of traditional client–centered methods: empathy and unconditional positive regard as practised by Rogers and which in German is termed VEE (Verbalisierung emotionaler Erlebnisinhalte = verbalising of the emotional components of experiences). By endeavouring not to value but to understand or rather to meet with unconditional positive regard we can achieve a (non–affirmative, non–negating) neutral position concerning the contents–level of inner communication while remaining complementary on the relational level.

SELF AS A GESTALT LIKE CONFIGURATION OF MUTUALLY RELATED "INNER PERSONS"

Having shown that the relation to oneself also obeys the laws of communication, I will now turn to a further point: correlation/interaction between inner and outer relations. Each inner person can (at the same time) also interact with the (real person's) environment. In his major theoretical publication Rogers (1959) describes the self as follows:

> Consideration of this phenomenon made it clear that we were not dealing with an entity of slow accretion, of step by step learning, of thousands of unidirectional conditionings. These might all be involved, but the product was clearly a gestalt, a configuration in which the alteration of one minor aspect could completely alter the whole pattern. One was forcibly reminded of the favourite textbook illustration of a gestalt, the double picture of the old hag and the young woman. Looked at with one mind set, the picture is clearly that of an ugly old woman. The slightest change, and the whole becomes a portrait of an attractive girl. So with our clients. The self –concept was clearly configurational in nature.(Rogers, 1959, p. 201 f.)

I believe that this configuration is brought about and maintained by the inner communication process continuously taking place. A similar illusion is presented by the relatively stable picture of a candle–flame although it is brought about by the erratic motion of gas particles during combustion. As long as the inner persons get along with each other all is well; however, even the mere perception that dusk is falling can cause the inner relation of a patient suffering from problems in getting to sleep to become dysfunctional. – Then the configuration would change very suddenly. On the other hand critical outer situations can be responsible for the fact that inner conflicts abate and perfect co–operation by the patient is made possible. Therein lies the reason why one might feel better in bad times than in good times.

I am convinced that the predominant everyday atmosphere concerning our inner relations determines our mental condition or sense of well–being. Clients are likely to suffer even more since they are not capable of verbalising the conditions governing the inner relations. They are as familiar with their inner relations as with the air that they breath and they know no alternative. Instead of influencing their inner relations they make up or cause problems that justify their inner conflicts, although easy to see through: for example an absolutely unnecessary marital row. Naturally, diversion of conflict works in the opposite direction too: instead of seeking the necessary confrontation with an outer partner, a conflict is created in the inner relation. In the same manner as we distinguish between different family or group atmospheres, we can also speak of an inner atmosphere.

By acquiring a therapeutic relation one has the possibility to start a relation with each and every inner person, enabling us to influence the structure of the relational network – the inner atmosphere – directly.

The Development of Incongruence According to Rogers

In the beginning, Rogers concentrated on analytical and behavioristic concepts until practical experience convinced him of the necessity to create suitable outer conditions enabling the client to attain a certain inner harmony. For this reason Rogers introduced the terms congruence and incongruence. Rogers describes the phenomenon thus: incongruence is principally caused when organismic experiences are symbolised incorrectly, since the evaluation by the self of the experience as perceived contradicts the organismic experience. "The self–structure is characterised by a "condition of worth" when a self–experience or a set of related self– experiences is either avoided or sought solely because the individual discriminates it as being less or more worthy of self–regard." (Rogers, 1959, p.209) *"An experience may be perceived as if it were organismically satisfying, when in fact this is not true."* (loc. cit., p. 210) Because such a condition of worth disturbs the valuing process, it hinders the individual's ability to behave and act free and effectively. Incongruence develops on account of the need for self–regard. The individual perceives an experience selectively, depending on the condition of worth developed. The result of incongruence of self and experience is the same incongruence in the individual's behaviour: some behaviour is compatible with the self–concept and is symbolised correctly, other behaviour maintains, enhances and actualises those aspects of the organism that do not correspond with the self–structure. Rogers illustrated the relation of organism and self very generally with the following well–known diagram (Rogers, 1951, p.526 f.).

congruent
symbolised

not
symbolised

incongruent
symbolised

organism   self

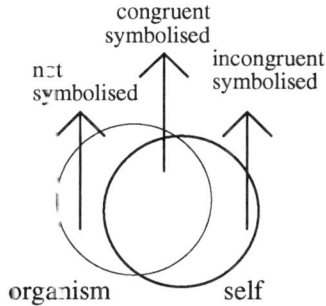

Misunderstanding of Rogers' Concept of Incongruence

Contrary to Rogers who developed his theory as a *result* of his practical therapeutic experience, I applied his theory from the beginning of my therapeutic career. Although Rogers warns us to regard the above diagram critically and in observation of its limits, since all diagrams of complex matter tend to simplify too much, I was induced to a misconception. I began to classify clients' statements and behaviour as congruent or incongruent and tried to deduce the development the client would have to undergo. e.g. A client complaining about a guilt– complex because of too little time and attention for his spouse because he would rather do something for himself. I would have regarded the feeling of guilt as incongruent, "to do something for himself" could have been taken as an expression of the organismic (= good) desire. That would lead me to deduce it would be congruent if he would accept his need to do something for himself and take the risk of coming into conflict with his spouse. That poses an unallowed simplification of a complex procedure. Precise examination would bring to light that the part "wanting to do something for himself" is probably trying to hide his fear of emotional nearness and is therefore not quite so "organismically-good" after all. In this way I learnt that in the individual's problem areas, conflicts never arise between wholly congruent and completely incongruent parts but that each aspect is partly congruent and partly incongruent. That lead me to develop my own explanation regarding the origin of incongruence which in general coincides with Rogers' but places different stress on certain details.

The Self as a Communicator

When one conceives the self as communication it becomes the organism's answer to its environment. Since this point of view makes it also necessary to accept behaviour as a form of communication, I give the self the credit for all behaviour and experiences of the "inner persons". The inner persons do not have to be conscious of such behaviour and experiences. I would act as if for example something does not exist, be it out of anger or as a means of protection. The organism would then be the recipient, the self would be the sender of the communicated message.

Encoding and Decoding

This way of viewing the situation confronts us with the question of encoding and decoding. When you ask someone why he wants to commit suicide, he might reply, "I want some long–deserved rest". The requirement for "some rest" would be encoded as "committing suicide". Hence encoding is at the same time also a strategy to satisfy one's needs.

Decoding also poses problems. How does a child notice that it receives sufficient regard? It is sadly not enough that I as mother offer unconditional positive regard. What children need to feel that they are positively regarded is the expression of parental love in the form of a multi-facetted network of parental care and chores. Lending a loving ear, sewing a fancy–dress co-stume, working intensively in one's own interest too, talking to and explaining things to the child, getting angry, being sad, being happy, giving one' best, refusing an effort, even turning away and "ignoring" the child, etc. – these are all ways of behaving that can at the right mo-ment be experienced by the child as positive attention but possibly also as negative attention. As far as the child is concerned, parents should always offer precisely what it needs at the mo-ment to develop ideally. If one refuses to give the child that, it will experience that as negative attention. That makes it possible that a child can experience something as positive attention even though the mother does feel as though that is the case and vice–versa.

THE DEVELOPMENT OF "INNER PERSONS" AS A REACTION TO THE OUTER ENVIRONMENT

Because it is impossible for parents to meet all these requirements, let alone at the right mo-ment, a challenging tension results in which the individual develops his personality. – Its very own answer to its very specific environment. This is at the same time an adaptation towards and an active attempt to change one's environment or else to care whether optimised conditi-ons exist. Even if that does not succeed, one has contributed to one's personality and retains one's claim on the best possible terms of existence. One stays true to oneself if one can at least be convinced, "I actually deserve the right to those conditions." This is a very powerful motive expressed by one's specific personality. This calls to mind some clients who do not want to give up certain problems because their parents might then believe that they were good parents. Then the disturbance is no less than the attempt to force their parents to admit their mistakes even if the client is not at all convinced of the success of his strategy.

The individual is exposed to numerous environmental influences; it cannot react only to its mother but also to all that has influenced her, it has to react to the mother's position in the family too and also to the predominant global atmosphere. In practical terms, the child is actually born into the scene of a drama with an uncertain ending and to live means to play one's part; one must find roles that allow one to play a part and enables one to actively influence the turn of events according to one's own needs and desires. The reply to one's environment is given by slipping into a particular role (= person in the original sense; PERSONA is Latin for mask). Since the environment is a very complex structure, one role is not sufficient for all si-tuations, so one develops many and adapts found roles to suit one's needs. Therefore the net-work of inner relations is built up between persons created in response to one's environment and persons developed in reaction to persons already developed; again in reference to the "doubling–effect" of self. In detail every inner person is a configuration in itself with both con-gruent and incongruent aspects. The sum of all relations between all inner persons and all inner persons with the environment is equal to the complete configuration of the self. That allows for infinite combinations and relations. A few such "sub–configurations" can be very stable and reliable and as a result are responsible for continuity and stability and the typical personality-structure. Flexibility, on the other hand, is reached by means of:

1) change in the interrelations between the stable persons according to changing demands of the environment,

2) new persons being created at any time and

3) part involved only irregularly or for a short while.

INCONGRUENCE BETWEEN INNER PERSONS AND BETWEEN INNER PERSONS AND THE ORGANISM

The specific constellation of inner relations is responsible for the outward interactions of the person as a whole. That is to be understood in the sense of compelling mutual causality. It takes two different constellations depending on whether one can hardly manage to get up in the morning or to "rise and shine" full of energy to begin a new day. It's as if the inner actors would get together and decide which characters will play which part in dependence of the perceived outer stage.

Congruence is the result if the decision is unanimous. A common answer to the problems posed by the environment is found by the sum of experiences made by the organism. I have tried to demonstrate this graphically. The combined effort corresponds to the full ellipse; stable inner persons are shown as full circles. potential new aspect as dotted circles. The superimposed circles symbolise that each "person" can combine congruent and incongruent aspects in itself.

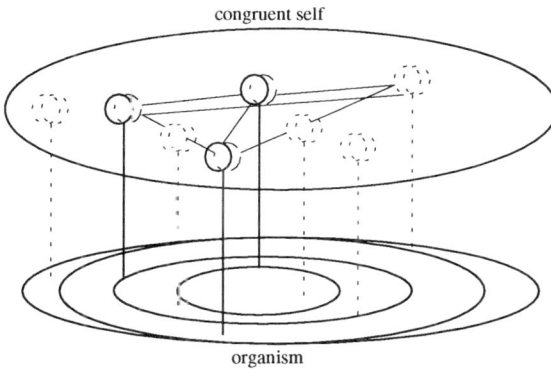

congruent self

organism

We all know about peer pressure in groups of "outer" persons. Transferring this power to our "inner family" makes it seem possible that we might succumb to the inner dynamics and lose control of ourselves. This is a similar situation to that of the sorcerer's apprentice in Goethe's "Zauberlehrling" who cannot get rid of the spirits he has called upon; – We are then faced with incongruence. The inner persons are interacting dysfunctionally; they are carrying out an inner conflict that costs more than the organism can gain from it.

A short illustration based on one of my clients:

Imagine an inner relation showing the following characteristics:

The first person suffers under the impression that all her friends and colleagues are of better upbringing, they have more money and intellect. She is so hopeless that she is too exhausted to achieve anything; we shall call her the "Pitiful".

The second person is "Good" to "Pitiful", but she is absolutely helpless, really feeling sorry for pitiful.

So far, so good. But no.3 is disgusted by all this because she cannot stand needy, helpless people. This "Bad" person does not want anything to do with Good and Pitiful, so she draws back and remains silent in the background.

If emotional cocktail persists for a few days my client would seem deeply depressed to an outside observer.

I have attempted to illustrate the above situation graphically.

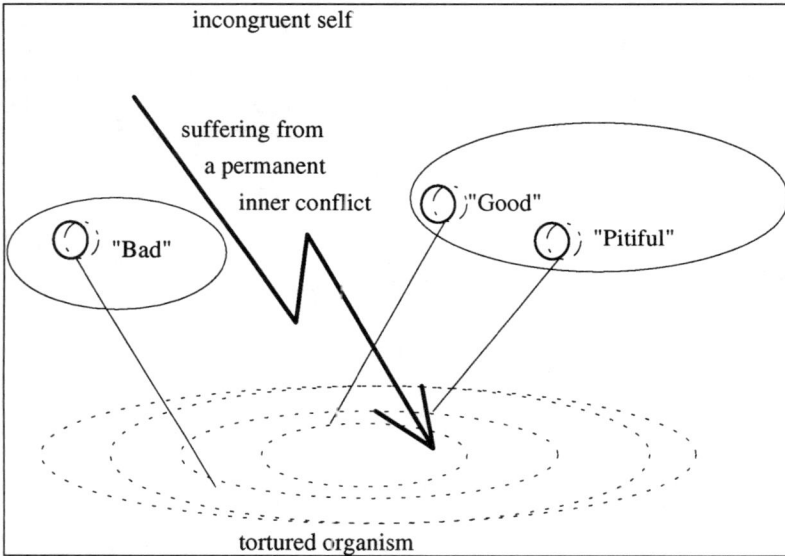

The example implies that, seen from the opposite angle, if for some reason one might want to be depressive, one must create a comparable inner relation. It isn't enough just to decide: I am depressive now!

Such a constellation costs very much energy to maintain. Every single thought of these inner persons must reach the organism as an unpleasant experience. The erroneous symbolising of these unpleasant organismic experiences causes the inner atmosphere to escalate – everything gets worse. Good will hopelessly try bringing Pitiful to her friends or to a psychiatrist. In the meantime, Bad will act as if she didn't even exist. In the systemic approach we must also regard the implications of these synchronous processes. That is the whole self crying out to its environment, "I have already done so much for all of you , do something to help me for a change!" Pitiful has plenty of friends that are willing to help. But they can only relieve the symptoms for a short while, not bring about any change in the situation. Why not? – Because Bad would only increase her rejection, if Pitiful now continues to moan about what a pain in the neck she really is and if she carries on that way she soon won't have any friends left.

Just how do these persons get into a single person?

Pitiful is the product of the contact with the mother who was always there for her daughter when she could not cope with something. So being pitiful is a strategy adopted to achieve something.

Good develops as a copy of the mother, whose understanding nature is regarded as a positive quality in correlation with the common ideal that one should help those in need. She is also the motivation for the client to become a religion teacher in order to propagate this noble ideal.

Bad is the result of the unpleasant experiences that come hand–in–hand with poor social background. She decides "never to be underprivileged and pitiful again"; she aquires an intellectual profession so that one should actually call her "socially successful".

Each of the personality aspects develops as a logical reaction to particular experiences made during childhood. If these three persons become active in the adult individual, they cannot communicate in a congruent manner since their strategies are divergent. Whenever the person as a whole has a desire she does not feel, "I want this" but she "suffers"; that in turn is something no. 3 cannot cope with. It means she still has not achieved enough after she was motivated "never to be pitiful again". Since we develop new needs and desires all the time, the third person will never succeed in satisfying the first. Like Sisyphus she is condemned to continuous work but never to reach her goal. When this "person" finally puts down her work for lack of hope, we arrive at the above situation and the inner chaos is perfect. Even though the second person is very understanding, she is just as helpless. "Pitiful" never gets to hear from any of the other two that she isn't poor but just wants something she can't have right away. On the other hand no. 3 would never permit no. 1 to accept help from "outside". Hence Pitiful is justified in her behaviour to attain at least some attention from outside. This inner relational chaos gives rise to another person: "the patient"

In confrontation with its complex environment the individual develops inner persons that can realise suitable strategies to cope with the confronting situations. Incongruence results when these strategies are

1) not well enough adapted to cope with the adult environment,

2) not compatible so that they cannot enhance one another but prevent each other from functioning effectively and

3) such that their use costs more energy than it will bring the organism.

Implications for Therapeutic Practice

To conclude I shall sum up the practical therapeutic implications of this hypothesis.

We all know what it sounds and feels like when a client is in contact with his inner self. During the process of self–exploration he is in a high experiencing level. Using my model one can formulate that he is in an advantageous confrontation with himself. That leaves little work for us except to be wary not to disturb the process.

A) The effectivity of the above method is clear in therapeutic processes when the client is still stuck in structure–bound experience. The method effectively prevents me from subconsciously being pushy and helps me to understand how the client prevents himself from aquiring helpful contact to his self. It is necessary to keep the following points in mind:

1) I am each of my parts as well as the whole. i.e. no part is more important, healthier, saner or more congruent than any other. Often parts of the self create tremendous pressure on the intra-personal level of relations by demanding to be happy or loved, etc. They behave like spoilt

brats without realising that they are only making life difficult for themselves. We are required to centre our empathy on all parts contributing to the conflict on the nature of the relations between them and on the resulting person.

2) It is more important to find ways for all parts concerned to co–exist positively than it is to find ideal solutions regarding the "outer world". They should be fond of each other; in the same way as we cannot expect everything to work perfectly in a real family, but only that its members begin to appreciate each other. – That is also the therapist's goal in therapy.

3) With a little practise one develops a feeling for which "person" one is talking to and can learn to take part in the inner communication. A few typical problems that this poses are:

a) Some clients speak as though they have no inner dialogues. Is it because they don't want the others to say anything; don't the others want to take part in the "conversation" i.e. that no answer is an answer too?

b) Some clients will make it difficult to tell the different personality–aspects apart. This is a very confusing condition even for the client; it may be that the inner persons will not take on clear positions.

c) Some clients might discuss endlessly with themselves and it seems as though they do not want to come to a decision. Often they are not trying to objectively differentiate but to tell if it is "good" or "bad" what they are feeling. In that way the client is avoiding to become independent from outer evaluation.

d) Sometimes inner persons will become the victims of their own strategies. If someone has learnt to draw back in unpleasant situations, that can cause utter chaos in the inner dialogue: if the "persons" reject the other inner person they simply draw back from themselves too. The client does not experience that he is in conflict with the inner others but will probably complain about an inner vacuum.

B) Encoding and decoding pose the greatest problem in the therapeutic situation. Rogers defines the 6th requirement for the therapeutic process: for a therapeutic process to occur, the client must "perceive, at least to a minimal degree. conditions 4 and 5, the unconditional positive regard of the therapist for him. and the empathic understanding." (Rogers, 1959, p. 213) I guess, the more a therapist is capable of communicating his unconditional positive regard and empathy, the more effective the therapy will be. It is not enough just to be empathic, only the therapist can learn how best to communicate his empathy and unconditional positive regard so that his client also experiences it as such. Sometimes a very unorthodox approach might work. For example,. if a client says, " I feel taken seriously when you are angry at me." that would be a possibility. Since only congruent behaviour can be the starting point of an effective therapeutic strategy, the therapist is faced with some tedious learning; a process that I call "therapist's self–healing in the face of his client". The second consequence from a systemic point of view would be to act as an "expert on processes" – a kind of family–therapist for the "inner family".

C) In an advanced stage of therapy i.e. when the problems concerning the inner relations are known and the sense of these patterns is understood, one can consciously practise the inner confrontation. That requires the development away from therapy towards autonomy. Every inner person should answer the following questions in connection with the conflict:

– What is the outer situation from my point of view?

– What do I feel for the other "inner persons"? (The relational level is often neglected)

– How should the other "inner person" be, how should he behave towards me? (One can more readily change the others inside!)

– What is it that I want as an individual "inner person"? (Some inner people are like overprotective mothers that don't think of themselves and so cause an unclear situation)

– What do I want for the person as a whole?

It is important that these questions lead to a constructive inner discussion aimed at finding a solution acceptable to all concerned.

I can also imagine this method to find application in crisis–intervention and diagnosis. For intervention in crises as an aid to serving as a "helping–I" and in diagnosis to enable the examination of the structure of the inner relations in case of such outer symptoms as addiction, suicidal tendency, phobias and psychoses.

On the one hand the systemic approach greatly simplifies the therapeutic process and on the other hand it helps to explain why it is sometimes so difficult to help. – It is an appeal to our "true me"s to be more humble within us, for we are many (cf. Casey & Wilson, 1992).

I would now like to conclude with a quotation taken from a lecture by Max Reinhardt which Carl Rogers attended as a student in New York City in 1928, which appeared in the book "Towards Creativity" by Peter F. Schmid and Werner Wascher (1994).

"We all carry in us the potentialities for all passions, for all destinies, for all forms of life. "Nothing human is strange to us!" If it were not so, we would not be able to understand others, whether in life or art. But the hereditary transmissions, education, individual experiences fertilise and develop only a few of the thousands of seeds in us. The others gradually wither and die" (loc. cit. p. 8).

REFERENCES

Bandler, R., Grinder, J., Satir, V. (1978). *Mit Familien reden.* Gesprächsmuster und therapeutische Veränderung. München: Pfeiffer

Biermann–Ratjen, E.–M., Eckert, J., Schwartz, H.J. (1979). *Gesprächspsychotherapie. Verändern durch Verstehen.* Stuttgart: Kohlhammer

Binder, U. & Binder, J. (1991). *Studien zu einer störungsspezifischen Psychotherapie. Schizophrene Ordnung – Psychosomatisches Erleben –Depressives Leiden.* Eschborn bei Frankfurt / M.: Klotz

Casey, J.F. & Wilson, L. (1992). *"Ich bin viele".* Eine ungewöhnliche Heilungsgeschichte. Reinbek bei Hamburg: Rowohlt

Ludwig–Körner, Ch. (1992) *Der Selbstbegriff in Psychologie und Psychotherapie.* Eine wissenschaftshistorische Untersuchung. Wiesbaden: Deutscher Universitätsverlag

Pervin, L.A. (1993). *Persönlichkeitstheorien.* München: Reinhardt. (3., neubearb. Aufl.)

Popper, K.R. & Eccles, J.C. (1982). *Das Ich und sein Gehirn.* München: Piper

Rogers, C.R. (1951). *Client–Centered Therapy.* Its current practice, implications and theory. Boston: Houghton Mifflin. Dt.: *Die klientbezogene Gesprächspsychotherapie.* München: Kindler, 1972

Rogers, C.R. (1959). *A theory of therapy, personalitiy, and interpersonal relationship, as developed in the client–centered framework.* In: Koch, S. (Ed.): Psychology: A study of science. New York: McGraw–Hill. Dt.: Eine Theorie der Psychotherapie, der Persön-

66

lichkeit und der zwischenmenschlichen Beziehungen. Entwickelt im Rahmen des klientenzentrierten Ansatzes. Köln: GwG, 1987

Saint-Exupéry, A. de (o. J.). *Le Petit Prince.* Paderborn: Schöningh. (Französ. Schulausgabe)

Schmid, P.F. & Wascher, W. (1994). *Towards Creativity.* Ein personzentriertes Lese- und Bilderbuch. Linz: Edition Sandkorn

Sommer, K.F. (1994). *Das eigene und das enteignete Selbst. Gedanken zum Verhältnis von Machen und Lassen in der klientenzentrierten Psychotherapie.* In: Keil, W.W. et al. (Ed.): Selbst-Verständnis. Beiträge zur Theorie der Klientenzentrierten Psychotherapie Bergheim bei Salzburg: Mackinger

Watzlawick, P. (1991). *"Willst du erkennen, lerne zu handeln."* In: Zeig, J.K. (Ed.): *Psychotherapie.* Entwicklungslinien und Geschichte. Tübingen: DGVT

Watzlawick, P., Beavin, J.H., Jackson, D.D. (1969). *Menschliche Kommunikation. Formen, Störungen, Paradoxien.* Bern: Huber

Wiltschko, J. (1994). *Haben Sie schon einmal ein "Selbst" gesehen? Zur Phänomenologie des Ichs.* In: Keil, W.W. et al. (Ed.): Selbst-Verständnis. Beiträge zur Theorie der klientenzentrierten Psychotherapie. Bergheim bei Salzburg: Mackinger.

---

[1] I am referring here to the famous "Pascal's bet". Watzlawick (1991, p. 178 f.) cites this as an example in his discussion of the construction of reality through actions. In § 223 of his *Pensées,* Pascal posed the question whether a non-believer can attain faith by himself and maintains that faith could result from actions, if the non-believer acts as if he believed.

Partial views

DOUG LAND
LA JOLLA

A METAPHOR FROM NORSE MYTHOLOGY: IT WAS SAID THAT IN THE OLD DAYS

Thor would circle around middle earth each year in order to fight back the enemies of order. But Thor was getting older and the circle occupied by men and gods was growing smaller. So the wisdom god, Woden, went out and lay in wait for the king of the trolls. He ambushed him, got him in a hammerlock, and demanded to know from him how the forces of order might eventually gain the victory over the encroaching chaos. "Give me your left eye," said the king of the trolls, "and I will tell you." Without any hesitation, Woden gave up his left eye."Allright, now tell me," he said. "Well," the troll king said, "the secret is, you must watch with both eyes."(Gardner, 1978)

The few things I have time to talk about tonight I call "partial views" first because that's all I've got. When I was younger everything seemed whole and clear to me, but time has brought a more realistic acceptance of my limited vision. These are not new ideas, but they are ongoing concerns of mine as I observe the Person Centered scene. I will throw in a few partial definitions of terms as we go along to keep us on the same track.

The dictionary definition of *partial* for instance, is: first, pertaining to, constituting, or involving only a part. So I know I can only offer a fragment of the big picture, which no one point of view could encompass anyway. The second and third definitions of *partial* also fit. They are: (2) favoring one side; prejudiced; biased; and, (3) having a special liking for, being partial to. Mine are partial views also because I am partial to them. They are the prejudices and biases which have grown out of my own experience. I accept them as working assumptions, even though they are incomplete and subjective, and could change. If I am seen as a Person–Centered person, then I suppose these ideas might be a partial expression of person–centeredness.

But is there a real Person–Centered Approach? Or are there as many different Person–Centered Approaches as there are self–centered approachers? Do we need "a" real approach? "Do we need "a" reality?" someone has asked (Rogers, 1978).

The term, "Person Centered" does seem to have many meanings these days, from conservative "purist" formulations to concepts resembling a kind of inkblot, adaptable to whatever current interest or technique one wishes to project onto it. And who am I to claim the true and final definition?

I know that much of the time I would just like to *be* person centered. I think that could be described rather simply, and it would not require a systematic philosophy to defend it. Such a modest, simple definition might be this:

The Person Centered Approach is a way of being which manifests persistent interest in, and trust and encouragement of persons, in their quest for positive growth and human fulfillment.

From its earliest days, this approach has been proud of its lack of orthodoxy or rigidity, representing itself as an open process of discovery and constant reformulation. Initially it was only trying to identify the elements of any effective therapy, regardless of its methods or philosophical roots. Then, gradually, with ever–widening general applications, client centered therapy became the PCA, and seemed to have something to say about almost everything.

It sounded sometimes like a new school of thought tending toward an ideology. Its leading proponent said he never intended to inaugurate a "school" of psychotherapy, and never claimed to have the last word about it. He encouraged others to follow their own experiences and directions, to develop their own theories and applications and take responsibility for them. He listened, supported, cared, shared his opinion, but hardly ever imposed it. He avoided taking either credit or blame for the ideas and insights of colleagues and students and encouraged them to go beyond him. He often quoted the saying: "If you meet the Buddha on the road, kill the Buddha," so some of his disciples, who mostly don't believe in transference, made him into a father figure anyway and used his words the way preachers use holy writ, accommodating them to give authority to their own ideas. But, as far as I can see, any appeal to the canon of his writing to support "correct" or "authorized" Person Centered thinking is a contradiction of the spirit of what he actually taught and stood or. He spoke for himself and expected others to do the same.

Carl also always welcomed any critical questioning of the PCA and in this regard at least I tried to please him.

I have always become uncomfortable when I observe any dynamic and vital ethos defining itself in formulaic thinking or as a panacea, or when it tends to sound doctrinaire, producing faithful disciples or authoritarian teachers who claim to have the "true" version.

I am especially put off by what seem to me to be false dichotomies or forced choices. A friend of mine made up a bit of doggerel that I like:

"I abhor either/or.

On both/and I'll take my stand."

For instance, I will not choose either objective or subjective reality. Of course accepting and understanding our own and others' separate subjective realities is necessary and basic to therapy and to good relationships generally. But our personal realities are our various relative attempts to make sense of our place in the larger given reality.

These internal realities are made up of the metaphors and images and stories and myths and worldviews which reach toward and point us to that ultimate reality which is beyond us. The human abilities to abstract and imagine are great gifts, gifts which can catch a sense of the universal in the particulars of here and now, but they can also become dead ends when they are disconnected from the very whole of which they are only a part. Even if we cannot fully see or explain the mystery of that larger reality, we do need to acknowledge it and face up to it or we reduce the Person Centered Approach to mere solipsism.

Solipsism is the theory that the self is the only thing that really exists and that reality is therefore merely subjective. This is over against *objectivism*, the doctrine that reality is external to the mind and distinct from our subjective existence.

But there are more things in heaven and earth than are dreamed of in a Person Centered philosophy, or included in any single or culturally approved world view.

Certainly any pressure to surrender to some group–authorized view of reality is always wrong, and should be resisted. And the individual realities we live with must be acknowledged and accepted, but the hopeful result of such acceptance and respect is to open us up to the possibility of reconciliation with the larger meaning of reality.

You have undoubtedly heard it said: We don't know who discovered water, but we're pretty sure it wasn't a fish. Objective reality is the sea of given conditions we need in order to be able to create our own subjective realities. It is the context within which we live and move and have our being. Yes, Carl we do need "a" reality! A more interesting question might be "does reality need us?"

The philosophical definition of *reality* is: the absolute or ultimate, as contrasted with mere phenomena, or what is only apparent.

Therefore reality would seem by definition to be that which exists beyond our merely subjective and phenomenological realities.Even so, in my view reality is both subjective and objective.

I have emphasized my partiality to this view because I believe that it is the avoidance of that given objective reality which accounts for the consistent disorientation and waywardness of humanity. Subjective realities which do not come to honest terms with objective reality are disconnected abstractions which produce the pathologies which threaten to destroy a large hunk of both hard and soft realities.

Again, caring empathy for separate personal realities, along with appreciation for the pluralism of local narrative, cultural integrity, relative truth, ethnic differences, etc., is a necessary component of communication and survival in the modern global village. But any of these can also be our ways to avoid seeing ourselves and each other realistically and thereby perpetuate the more horrendous effects of a fragmented and alienated human condition.

Which brings me to another partial thought. I have come to feel that reports of humanity's essential goodness are premature. Any openminded observation of human behavior must validate innate destructiveness as at least an equal possibility.

Here is a joke: A man in a restaurant calls the waiter over and complains:

"Waiter, there is a needle in my soup."
"A needle?" the waiter says, "Impossible. Let me see."
"There. See? A needle," says the customer.
The waiter says, surprised,
"Oh, Yes, you are right. I'm so sorry sir. It's merely a typographical error. It should be a noodle."

In the minds of many modern observers, one of the greatest achievements of humanistic psychology, especially the Person–Centered Approach, was to declare the commonly observed age–old human tendency toward evil just a typographical error. People of good will had justifiably become fed up with the abuses and damage done by doctrinaire proponents of shame and guilt throughout history, and tired as well of the shrill, nagging insistence of Christians on total human depravity and original sin, and the world was more than ready for a long–overdue backlash. Then one day a school of prophets descended from a mountain somewhere to the west of here with an inspired body of well–researched clinical evidence which demonstrated that in controlled situations where three necessary and sufficient conditions were observed, (you know them), persons consistently made integrating positive and constructive choices and moved in self–actualizing directions. This seemed to confirm what other thinkers had already suspected and said, and at this point hosts of sanguine and hopeful people–watchers began to sense a millennial possibility.

To refresh your minds, this has been called the phenomenological approach.

A popular definition of *phenomenon* makes it any unusual occurrence; an inexplicable fact; a marvel. And this gift of scientific proof of the essential spark of goodness in humanity did seem something of a miracle in the light of the human record.

More soberly, though, in philosophy and psychology, a *phenomenon* is anything that can be apprehended by the senses, an appearance, or an object as it seems to us on the basis of our perception of it. *Phenomenology*, then, is the scientific investigation and description of phenomena. It is to be contrasted with *ontology*, which is a philosophical theory concerning the nature of reality, an attempt to state the universal characteristics of existence. The word ontology is taken from the Greek, *ontos*, meaning *being*. Ontology is the discipline having to do with the study of being itself.

So, on the basis of so great a cloud of phenomenological witnesses doing controlled research on persons under desirable conditions, the previous verdict of inherent evil in the human animal was, presto chango (zimzalabim), reversed. Naturally, this was a huge boost for the self–esteem industry and has since produced a whole library of books celebrating human wonderfulness and how to help yourself to get the most out of it.

The good–news prophets of phenomenology were careful to point out that they were only citing their own research and experience, their own clinical perceptions of first–hand phenomena, and God forbid that they should make or recommend metaphysical judgments. The fact that this phenomenological report had been subtly translated for some into a new ontological doctrine of the essential goodness of human nature, was barely noticed and certainly not resisted. If their phenomena were selective it was easily justified because they were not focusing on pathology but were only seeking to discover the conditions which make therapy and positive growth more likely, which they did. But many of us bought the abstraction and the generalization anyway, because we wanted it to be true, and because feeling good about ourselves after oppressive centuries of stern moralistic guilt–wallowing was a welcome change.

Of course, phenomenologically speaking, the general quality of human behavior in the world has not changed much at all – certainly not for the better (excepting those of us here in this room, of course).

It seems to me that any approach to psychology which seeks to make extrapolations and applications beyond psychotherapy, which the PCA does, must surely deal with and try to account for and speak to the general human condition outside of psychotherapy. Otherwise we end up offering answers to questions that are not being asked and trying to apply solutions that don't fit the real problems. It reminds me of the student who told her professor, "I just love your lectures. They are like cold water to a drowning person."

For well–intentioned humanists to dismiss the more pessimistic psychological, philosophical, religious and sociological assessments of human nature is to deny a huge and convincing body of additional phenomena. This evidence seems clearly to demonstrate an ineluctable and continuous tendency toward destructiveness operating throughout history down to the present day, in and through the willful agency of the human person.

I definitely don't feel like returning to notions of fear and loathing and sin and guilt, but in my view rosy assumptions of humanity's innate goodness or even the presence of an inevitable positive principle of self–actualization cannot be inferred from general observation beyond controlled clinical conditions. Selective observations of the human person in action might provide plenty of reason to be alternately both encouraged and discouraged but the larger question of what we are and what we may yet be, our being and becoming, is still a matter of moment by moment choice.

Rollo May provides a definition of *being*:

> ... being is the potentiality by which the acorn becomes the oak or each of us becomes what he (or she) truly is.... The significant tense for human beings is thus the future – that is to say, the critical question is what I am pointing toward, what I will be in the immediate future. Being is the tendency in all of us to become what we may be. Actualization is not automatic under any conditions. It is self–chosen cooperation with being and becoming. (although) The right conditions can clarify and inspire and encourage. (May, 1983)

We still have only partial views of the nature and destiny of humankind. We do know that the human being has been persistently bent toward wonder and meaning and realization, and carries within her and him a deep longing for completion, a kind of restless nostalgia for the filling out of our partial vision. This is surely a source of hope for our participation in a larger realm of being, but that hope for human actualization or fully functioning personhood cannot be taken as a guaranteed destiny when we also look at the reality of the human condition and how catastrophically humankind has responded to it so far. William James wrote:

> There is no doubt that healthy–mindedness is inadequate as a philosophical doctrine, because the evil facts which it positively refuses to account for are a genuine portion of reality; and they may after all be the best key to life's significance, and possibly the only openers of our eyes to the deepest levels of truth. (James 1958, p.187)

In a series of remarkable books, Ernest Becker has synthesized contemporary thought concerning evil and heroism and the human condition. The basic human situation is presented convincingly, with supportive data from an wide array of authoritative sources. Becker describes our dilemma:

> Man has a symbolic identity that brings him sharply out of nature. He is a symbolic self, a creature with a name, a life history. He is a creator with a mind that soars out to speculate about atoms and infinity, who can place himself at a point in space and contemplate bemusedly his own planet. This immense expansion, this dexterity, this ethereality, this self–consciousness gives to man literally the status of a small god in nature,...Yet, at the same time,..., man is a worm and food for worms. This is the paradox: he is out of nature and hopelessly in it; he is dual, up in the stars and yet housed in a heart–pumping, breath – gasping body that once belonged to a fish and still carries the gill–marks to prove it. His body is a material fleshly casing that is alien to him in many ways–the strangest and most repugnant way being that it aches and bleeds and will decay and die. Man is literally split in two; he has an awareness of his own splendid uniqueness in that he sticks out of nature with a towering majesty, and yet goes back into the ground a few feet in order blindly and dumbly to rot and disappear forever. It is a terrifying dilemma to have to live with. (Becker 1973, p. 26)

If it seems that we are not directly or consciously in touch with that terror it is because we are so ingenious in devising ways to pretend it away. We deny, ignore, avoid, postpone, sublimate, repress, or otherwise try to transcend the concrete reality of being creatures who are neither beast nor angel, but both/and.

To avoid facing that paradoxical reality, we hide from ourselves in affectations which both distract and reassure us, affectations like patriotism, religion, ideology, visions of ethnic superiority, social status, professional position, titles, etc., anything which seems to offer escape from the threat of personal oblivion and the anxiety of life lived under that threat. It is in the name of such pretexts, these subjective realities expanded to cultural abstractions, that we seem able to justify every human excess and perpetuate our alienation from each other and the real world around us.

Soren Kierkegaard understood the human condition as well as anyone and modern psychology has not really added much new to his conclusions. But he did not offer an easy and comfortable assurance of self–actualization through psychotherapy or break–through peak experience. His was rather a challenge to every individual person to face the strenuous and threatening reality of his or her particular life. Kierkegaard recognized the angst of the human paradox: „If man were either a beast or an angel," he wrote, „he would not be able to experience dread. But since he is a synthesis, he can be in dread... in fact man himself produces dread."(Kierkegaard 1957, p. 139)

He also saw the potential despair of living with that dread, and he called that despair „the sickness unto death." He then declared that the way to master this despair is not to retreat into abstract promises of deliverance, religious or secular, and not through anesthetizing cultural conformities or the easy answers of psychological platitudes. The challenge is to accept the painful paradox of human nature as a fact, and take a leap of faith into the reality of the human condition with radical purity of heart. "Further than this," Kierkegaard wrote, "psychology cannot go." (Kierkegaard, 1957)

But what is "Purity of heart?" You know it of course. "Purity of heart is to will one thing:" he said, "to will to be that self which one truly is." These are familiar words now, but whether Carl Rogers was saying them it in 1957 or Soren Kierkegaard in 1847, to accept, to decide, to choose, to fully intend to be that self which you truly are is by no means the easy product of a self–help cliche. It requires courage to thus open oneself to new possibility and choice, to face anxiety of possible non–being head on in the hope of broader perceptions and experiences, to risk unexpected revelations and the elasticity of freedom. This is certainly not a choice which can be determined by any conditions which we can contrive.

As far as I am concerned, this call for the courage to be is the core of any Person Centered Approach, and makes the vision of Carl Rogers and the work of Person Centered psychotherapy all the more relevant and important. I have never thought of the PCA as an unbiased, scientifically proven way of sharing a few basic conditions in order to make positive personal growth somehow automatic. To me it has always been an active personal commitment to use any and all means available to offer aid and comfort, encouragement, healing, empowerment and inspiration to persons who are trying to discover and live out their own experience of becoming the persons they most deeply are in a world which is both overtly and subtly hostile and repressive to this quest, and makes it difficult and costly to follow it. I think of the Person Centered Approach is an all out crusade a quiet revolution, perhaps too quiet most of the time, against those ubiquitous conditions in the world which lead us so seductively toward depersonalization.

Person Centered psychotherapy is one aspect of this approach which can help persons to discover and face the given realities of their own lives, and encourage and strengthen them in the choice to brave their own unique and personal destinies.

The human person is not a problem to be solved through clever psychology, or a dysfunctional system in need of technical reprogramming. When we stand before a person we face a profound mystery where the difference between what is before me and what is me becomes blurred and the distinction between the subjective and objective breaks down. I think the Person Centered therapist's approach to persons is notable in its willingness to enter into and participate in this mystery, to accompany others in their exploration and effort to come to terms with any reality that bears on their lives.

Inevitably I see this as a spiritual quest. By that I don't mean searching about in otherworldly realms, but rather an urgent stretching toward unconditional reality as it approaches us here in the particurality and partiality of our conditional everyday circumstances.

"To understand unconditional spirit as an abstract concept is not so difficult," writes Lionel Trilling, "but there is no knowledge rarer than the understanding of spirit as it exists in the inescapable conditions which the actual and the trivial make for it." (Trilling, 1957)

I have decided that there is only one necessary and sufficient attitude or predisposition or condition which I can intentionally and rather consistently bring to therapy. Everything else unfolds naturally or is discovered or experienced or invented along the way. [The only efficient *cause* of therapy, of course, is the client's own ability and choice to change for the better, although clients and therapists clearly need each other.] That one attitude which I can intentionally bring and which I know the client surely needs from me is a sustained and generous interest.

I have sometimes noted that so-called people-experts can become fascinated by their subject matter and their knowledge about research in psychology and developmental theories and techniques of therapy, and all the while show very little personal interest in the actual folks they address and claim they are trying to help. Indeed, they often seem to find people a distraction or even a nuisance.

I believe merely being sincerely interested in those persons themselves would do more good than all the clever theories and formulas about them.

I offer a partial definition of interest, along with some related definitions.

Interest is a feeling of curiosity or attentiveness. It is also the ability to inspire or elicit curiosity or attentiveness. To have an interest in something or somebody is to be involved or invested or concerned, that is, sharing an interest. *Curiosity* as a feeling is the eager desire for knowledge, especially of the novel or unusual. Another meaning of curiosity is an interest in the private affairs of others. *Attentiveness* is giving or showing attention, being observant; thoughfulness. *Attention* is the concentrated direction of the mental powers; close or earnest attending. *To attend* is to be present, to minister to, to accompany, to listen to. Originally *to attend* meant to await; to expect.

This deceptively simple attitude of sincere and persistent interest is the essential launching of a therapeutic relationship with a client, and if I sustain and follow that interest with curiosity and attentiveness, it leads naturally, without any special effort on my part, to all the other effects of a helping relationship, those that we have called necessary and sufficient conditions and others which in context are often surprising but equally important and facilitative. The self-generating twists and turns of therapeutic movement seem to become possible and even likely just because I have chosen to be present and genuinely interested without leaping on ahead or lagging back as a companion on the other person's journey toward reality.

In closing, let me share one more feeling to which I am partial.

I admit to having become a rather naive and sentimental therapist. I blame my clients for this. I also thank them.

There is actually a more representative word to embody that effective attitude which I have called a sustained and generous interest. It is a word which captures the full range of creative possibilities and resources of the therapeutic relationship. In spite of its frequently being misused or itself made into an abstraction, it is still the most necessary and sufficient attitude of all in our common quest for the meaning of being human together.

In Sophocles' play, *Oedipus in Colonus* we are shown the old and completely blind Oedipus, who has been forced through a long lifetime of heroic suffering and tragedy to come to terms with the harsh and fateful realities of life and death. And yet in facing his own death he has been given a special power to impart grace to those he meets. When Oedipus finally succumbs to death, his end is, in Sophocles' words: "wonderful if mortal's ever was." And at the last, when a messenger returns to the people to relate the wonderful manner of Oedipus' death, he tells them of the old man's final words to his daughter, and I leave those words with you this evening (Sophocles, 1958):

"...and yet one word frees

us of all the weight and pain of life:

that word is love."

REFERENCES

Becker, E. *Angel in Armor: A Post–Freudian Perspective on the Nature of Man,* New York, Braziller 1969.

Becker, E. *The Birth and Death of Meaning,* New York: The Free Press 1971.

Becker, E. *The Denial of Death,* New York: The Free Press 1973.

Becker, E. *Escape From Evil,* New York: The Free Press 1975.

Gardner, J. *On Moral Fiction,* New York: Basic Books 1978.

Henderson, V. and Kirschenbaum, H. (Eds.) *Carl Rogers Reader,* Boston: Houghton Mifflin 1989

Henderson, V. and Kirschenbaum, H. (Eds.) *Carl Rogers: Dialogues,* Boston: Houghton Mifflin 1989

James, W. *The Varieties of Religious Experience,* New York: Mentor 1958.

Kierkegaard, S. *The Concept of Dread,* Princeton: University Press 1957

Kierkegaard, S. *Fear and Trembling & the Sickness Unto Death,* New York: Doubleday 1954

May R. *The Discovery of Being,* New York: Norton 1983.

Rogers, C. R., *On Becoming a Person,* Boston: Houghton Mifflin 1961

Sophocles, *The Oedipus Plays of Sophocles,* New York: New American Library 1958

Trilling, L. *"Anna Karenina" in The Opposing Self,* New York: Hartcourt Brace 1955

The Infant, the Person and the Psychotherapy

GERHARD PAWLOWSKY

VIENNA

ABSTRACT

What I would like to show in this paper is that the effects of person–centered psychotherapy lie mostly in the extraverbal domain of the client's experiences, although it is a verbal therapy. And only that way it can be successful. If this theory can be proven, a number of phenomena, that have theoretically so far been difficult to explain, become understandable. The results of the infant research that has been done during the 1980's, will play an important role here, because they make it possible to describe the extraverbal domain of human experience more thoroughly. Following up the outlined thoughts I came across many parallels to the philosophical approach of Michael Polanyi that he had developed during the 1950's and 60's. Most of his ideas are verified by the scientific research done by infant experts – a fact that remained unknown up until today.

INFANT RESEARCH

Let me present my approach to you in detail. The infant research done during the 80's has come up with stunning results. It showed that the infant is much more autonomous, much more independant than had been assumed, that it is even a person in its own right who is not at all symbiotically connected with its mother. At least as important is the fact, that the infant has an often entirely different personality and way of experiencing the world during its first year, that is before the acquisition of speech, than after it has acquired the ability of verbal expression.

What does all this have to do with the person–centered approach and with Rogerian psychotherapy? It's a legitimate question to ask yourself, although the connection is a tight one. We see the person undergoing therapy as a human being in the process of changing, we experience, encourage and talk about the potential of change – often without knowing exactly where we started or where we're going. Evolving from here is the question to the development of that person, the client, in the present, but also – if the client wishes to know – in the past. He often digs down deeper in his past, especially when he feels understood.[1] The client seems to sense that the presence is tied to the past. And that something he has not been able to utter in his past might be easier to be said in the understanding presence of the therapist. [2] In some respects this – that is the return to the past and the sense of the connection to the present – shows the structure of experiencing which will turn out as the structure of tacit knowledge or (in terms of infant research) the structure of pre–verbal experience. It can be superimposed by new experiences without leaving memories of the past. This phenomenon is comparable to a computer–text that often is written over, the last version is stored, previous versions are not preserved.

In more theoretical terms: the development of a client during successful therapy obviously has structural parallels to the development of infants and children – the developmental process seems to be of the same kind.[3]

I'll continue my description of therapy: When the client feels understood – I remind you, we are thinking in a growth oriented therapy direction and not in a direction related to deficits and their compensation or to bringing to awareness – he will spontaneously come to talk of those circumstances that were bad conditions of growth to him. Remembering those he experiences restriction, depression, pain and sorrow. At the same time in the here and now of the therapy there is a chance to find relief, to work things out, to begin anew. Rogers' theory of healing[4] by encounter, by contact in the present and the presence of therapy is still valid. How does this work then? We find ourselves in the middle of theories of healing in psychotherapy.

Digression 1: Theories of healing

It is the relief, the catharsis, the expression and thereby elimination of unarticulated, not yet symbolized feelings, which lead to cure and renewed development. This psychoanalytically oriented drive–model of the change of personality, that's connected to the idea of removing repression by bringing to consciousness was the beginning of non–directive psychotherapy (Rogers 1942) which stressed catharsis and the acquisition of insight. But this model of healing was methodically and theoretically not satisfying: methodically it lead to forcing insight by explanations of the therapist (Rogers 1942/1972, 41), theoretically it was too simple, too naive. Therapy must be more than enabling the client to live his emotions – a deeper understanding of the deficit or the conflict must be achieved.

By introducing empathy as a central variable instead of insight, the idea of healing changed from one of catharsis to that of reintegration of those parts the client experienced as incongruent before. The conflict between the preservation of the client's self–concept and the actualizing tendency in the understanding of the client–centered approach had to be resolved by working it out, by renunciation and partial integration (Rogers 1951). The model of healing by working out, however, is still problem oriented and concerned with finding solutions rather than focusing on the personal development of the client.

After 1961 the term „person–centered" is more forward oriented, stressing genuineness, congruence. The fresh start, the re–entering into the process of development – under the ideal circumstances therapy provides – are most important in Rogers' last concept of healing. The problem itself stays in the background, whereas the development of the person's potential and his personality is stressed. The process of becoming a person is focused on by the therapist. The presence of the therapist and the relationship to the client are the healing factors in this approach.

Let me go back to infant research. The following are the characteristics of an infant in his first year: awareness of the whole, which becomes more differentiated all the time (see endnote IV), a procedural memory without single iamges, a way of experiencing that can be described in terms of rhythm and contour and – later – in terms of attunement of affects with the mother – all in all a reality related perception and the adaption to the interpersonal reality. Stern says:

> Deficit is the wrong concept, however, for these reality based events. From a normative and prospective vantage, the infant experiences only interpersonal realities, not deficits (which cannot be experienced until much later in life) and not conflict resolving distortions. It is the actual shape of interpersonal reality, specified by the interpersonal invariants that really exist, that helps determine the developmental course. Coping operations occur as reality–based adaptions. (Stern 1985, 255)

After the first year those abilities are superimposed by a development, which we know much more about, by inner images, by a concrete pictorial memory, and finally by verbal learning.

From there norms and ideals evolve, but also lacks and deficits are experienced when the present experience is compared to the ideal.

It is interesting to see that the different approaches in psychotherapy have hardly acknowledged these discoveries and where they have, they were not very happy with them. The classical, Freud–oriented psychoanalysis has always given great credit to the verbal encounter in coping with the neurosis, therefore it feels threatened by the results of infant research because they reverse the traditional beliefs of psychoanalytic developmental psychology. The most important development of psychoanalysis since Freud, which is Kohut's self– psychology, has at least started moving towards integrating the nonverbal, the extraverbal experiences by greatly emphasizing the concepts of empathy and understanding, both included in Kohut's first theory about the development of the self.[5] Person–centered psychotherapy has hardly gone in the direction of such a world of experiences, since it disapproves of thinking about one's childhood and of a person–centered developmental psychology resulting from that. Biermann–Ratjen is the only exception here, but her theory was not yet connected to modern infant research. The theory of the infant researchers that's important for our connection to psychotherapy research is that the ways of experiencing and the abilities the infant acquires during his first year remain part of the person during his whole life, although they are superimposed by the sense of a verbal self. This in turn proves my theory that person–centered psychotherapy above all aims at changes in the nonverbal, originally preverbal experiences.

I will now try to sketch the parallels between the results of infant research about the structure of the preverbal experiences during the first year and the theory of the philosopher Michael Polanyi.

THE PHILOSOPHY OF TACIT KNOWING

Polanyi presupposes that each of us knows more than he is able to say. (Polanyi 1966/1985, 14) A simple example for that are the human features: we are able to recognize someone although we can't explain how this process of recognition works. This unstateable, but nevertheless present and effective knowledge Polanyi calls „tacit knowing". The first characteristic in this process is a ‚from – to" movement, that is a functional element of structure (and as such a description of a process): while concentrating on expressable knowledge – through presentiment – the unstateable, tacit knowledge is mobilized and, although we are unable to explain how this works (Polanyi 1966/1985, 14) – it's connected to the expressable, explicit knowledge, but at the same time it comprises much more and is often even more important than the explicit knowledge. To put it in the words of anatomy: The distal (bodydistant) term is expressable, the proximal (bodynear) term isn't. In our case that means the single features of a person's face are nameable, whereas the entity of the face and the recognition based on it are not.

Another example shows a first parallel to an infant's experiences: Dornes describes that the infant researchers have found two possible patterns in the interactive behavior of a two– to three–week–old infant, depending on wether the object that comes into the infant's view is human or inanimate. One of the researchers, Brazelton, even claims to be able to tell by the behavior of a filmed four– to six–weeks–old infant whether its interaction partner, who is not visible in the video is live or inanimate. At the same time it has been proven that the infant is able to distinguish his mother from other people. These examples show that the structure of an infant's experience obviously remains unmodified even in our adult world. And – what's more – it has been acquired long before the ability to verbalize things.

Polanyi describes other aspects of tacit knowing as semantic, which means that single features are interpreted into an entity, and as ontological, which describes the aspect of historical understanding. Polanyi's approach to the term of wholeness is this: the entity of explicit and tacit knowledge is made functionally and phenomenologically availabe, it is interpreted semantically, that ist wholly and is understood as a complex entity.

Therefore when we talk we often really only understand each other on an unexpressed, extraverbal level where single features, the distal term, are only understood in connection with the entity, that is the proximal term, the only one that really counts.

However, we are also capable of directing our attention towards the other pole: when that happens, the proximal and the distal term switch places. We know this phenomenon well in the optical domain: If we focus in closely on something with our eyes the things around it get blurred; as soon as we put some distance between us and the object we only realize the single features in their importance for the entity, the ensemble. A test frequently used to show this phenomenon is the Rorschach–test, where there are answers concerning the entity and others concerning the details. Take a poem for instance to exemplify differences in perception: looking at the details and the vers–structure paints one picture before your eyes, simply listening esthetically and emotionally produces an entirely different picture.

Sometimes the taking apart, the explicit naming of details and their re–integration lead to a more profound understanding of the entity, most of the time, however, the explicit integration of details cannot replace the tacit integration. The tacit understanding of the poem – without ever being able to express what exactly this tacit knowledge is – leads to an entirely different inner knowledge. Or, another example: my knowledge of my own body is completely different than the much more detailed knowledge of a physiologist.

I'll focus on psychotherapy for a moment now: the above mentioned theory also describes the phenomenon of the pressure suffering causes: the depression, the uncomfortable feeling, the sorrow and the pain become overdimensionally great, one perception is now directed extremely toward details, whereas the entity, the feeling of inner balance are lost.

Polanyi continues to explain that this understanding is only made possible by indwelling and empathy. He quotes Dilthey, who said around 1900 already, that empathy is the real mode of human knowledge and also of the sciences of man: „To understand the spirit of a person, you have to live through his works again." (Polanyi 1966/1985, 24)[6]

Polanyi goes on to think that the ideal of science, to come up with objective knowledge, is very much questioned considering that tacit thoughts make an indispensable part of any knowledge. (Polanyi 1966/1985, 27)

ABOUT THE STRUCTURE OF EXTRAVERBAL EXPERIENCE

Infant researchers now describe how tacit knowledge is acquired and the kind of structure extraverbal experience and learning have. Here another connection becomes important: The understanding of the entity is only possible by means of indwelling and empathy[7], and this entity is subjective, the tacit knowledge is connected to the explicit knowledge of this person. The currently most popular infant researcher, Daniel Stern, looks for the subjective entity of the child through understanding the infant. He doesn't set out to study the objective but the subjective experiences of the child – his sense of the self. Put another way: he interprets the objective results by means of empathy in the meaning of the results for the infant's sense of self. He distinguishes between different stages in the child's sense of self: the sense of an emergent self, the sense of a core self alone and together with the other, the sense of a subjective self as a step towards intersubjectivity and especially the affect attunement and finally the sense of a verbal self. (Stern, 1985)

These modes of experience build on each other in chronological order, reaching one stage is at the same time the basis for the next, however, the previous stage is not lost. In every mode of experience further experiences can be made. In the mode of experience of the sense of an emergent self it is the experience of process and product, the crossmodal perception, the heights and depths of affects (vitality affects versus categorial affects). Upon these modes of perception and experience the experience of the interpersonal invariants of the core self is based: to have agency or authorship of action, self–coherence, (self–)affectivity, and a history (a memory), for the person himself and together with the other. The next stage, which is the sense of a subjective self needs those acquired abilities to proceed further in a mutual focus of attention, in sharing intentions, in experiencing and sharing affective states. Stern describes the interaction of feelings between mother and child with the term affect attunement. This term stresses the mutual empathic accepting, in which the mother shares the feelings of the child, but often also influences them in an unintentional – tacit – way. Nonverbal symbolization is possible in this stage. A verbal sense of the self with its symbolizations is based upon all of the previous stages.

We can see now that these terms go together well with Polanyi's description of structures: the components of tacit kowledge can – as mentioned earlier – be described as functional, phenomenological, semantic and ontological. The components contain articulation, intellectual passion and conviviality. Only when we consider verbal expression do higher forms of personal knowledge, that is the justification of personal knowledge, become describable. Those forms are the logic of affirmation, the critique of doubt and commitment. (Polanyi, 1958)

One could say that some components of tacit knowledge fit Stern's sense of a subjective self together with the other, both of them have the same structure. Personal knowledge, affirmation, doubt, commitment are only possible with the acquisition of the sense of a verbal self. [8]

APPLICATIONS IN PERSON–CENTERED PSYCHOTHERAPY

If you have listened carefully you will have noticed descriptive elements of the person–centered therapy. I'll try to explain a few of the phenomena of the person–centered psychotherapy with the terminology of the extraverbal experience.

Why person–centered therapy often has late effects

Rogers often described how his clients only noticed the helpful effects of a therapeutic interview a long time after it had taken place (for example in the discussion after a demonstration interview he gave in Salzburg, April, 7th, 1981). They said – put in my own words – that they experienced changes without being able to tell what made them happen. At this point you might say the clients haven't yet worked on themselves long enough and are not clear about the decisive way of experiencing. The phenomenon, however, occurs much too often and continously to be put off so easily.[9] Obviously tacit knowledge has different dynamics of change than does explicit knowledge. It can't be adressed directly in the process of therapy, either.

Rogers' „slightly altered state of consciousness"

In the commentary of his demonstration interview with Ian during the workshop in South Africa in 1984 Rogers describes his experience as a therapist at some times during the interview as a „slightly altered state of consciousness" and later even as „a kind of trance" (Kirschenbaum & Henderson 1989, 148). He obviously managed to focus all of his attention on feeling, on sensing, on tacitly knowing instead of on what was explicitly said. He was able to respond to that, to give resonance to it.[10] I'd like to stress the term resonance because it stands for a slightly passive attitude which is related to the more active form of empathy. Whereas, however, empathy is understood in a more emotional or cognitive way, resonance – in its original meaning – stands for the mostly not explicitly expressable vibrations.

The crying of the therapist in front of the client

I've often experienced a certain phenomenon: whenever I was, as a therapist, caught up in a very moving story of one of my clients I felt tears coming to my eyes a few seconds before the client would start to cry. For a long time I've explained this phenomenon by saying that the client's story brought back similar memories of my own like a bell starts ringing and I believed that I started crying because of the pain my own experiences caused me. In a few cases I could even secretly name those experiences, more often though, I couldn't. That leads me to explain this phenomenon through my tacit knowledge, which is mobilized, whereas the concrete experience connected to it doesn't even have to come clear. Put another way: It doesn't help to remember the concrete experience which would cause my resonance with the moving experience of the client because the tacit knowledge is irreplaceable.[11]

The shortening of the „Gesprächstherapie"

One of the main arguments against client–centered / person–centered psychotherapy is its „exclusively verbal" mode of communication. By overcoming the limitations of „Gesprächstherapie" – which I in fact think is a very inappropriate term because of its historical connection to a client–centered psychotherapy which is defined only by characteristics due to scientific study and observation – ecclectic, „body–oriented" or „other valid ways of interventions" are included. (Tausch 1988) I, on the contrary, believe that talking always comprises explicit and tacit elements and that verbal experience is always linked to extraverbal experience. I have called this phenomenon „acting within speaking". In this sense an especially emphasized body–oriented form of intervention becomes arbitrary because the dimension of body experience through tacit knowledge is always included in the extraverbal sense of the self. I believe furthermore that the best way to tell the client is to resonate with him because explicitly stressing a body–oriented intervention evokes separation rather than integration, it evokes the disintegrating experience of the details rather than the integrating experience of the entity.

Resistance in therapy

With these ideas the phenomenon of resistance in therapy[12] is given a new explanation. The client's resistance often originates from an extraverbal domain, from a feeling[13], but also from a tacit knowledge that is unstateable. The client now „knows" that the therapist is wrong. The way of self–assertion of tacit knowledge can be taken for a means of defense – contrary to those of defense mechanisms acquired lateron. The latter you can address directly because there the images, ideas and phantasies are hidden. To the former you have to react since acting within speaking is important.

Digression 2: a completed theory of healing

Starting from these thoughts I'd like to add another feature, concerning the idea of expressing thoughts and feelings in therapy, to the theory of healing. The importance of doing so, of articulating those thoughts and feelings, for the client seems to be

– that he realizes he's not being judged which gives him relief [14],

– that he tacitly notices through the tentative tries of the therapist to move around in the client's world, that it's okay to be searching and to express uncertainties,

– but most of all the importance seems to be that by articulating uncertainties more of the tacit knowledge, which can never be stated exactly, is expressed.

The idea behind this theory is that articulating presentiments, vague feelings and what is merely implied makes a fresh start easier, it re–initiates the flow of tacit knowledge.

Explicit integration cannot replace tacit integration. Only the client himself is able to accomplish tacit integration – there lies the simple reason for stressing the autonomy of the client in the person–centered psychotherapy. This autonomy is in turn constituent to the person: any person is capable of having tacit experiences.

UNANSWERED QUESTIONS

Of course a few questions remain unanswered:

Does the term „incongruence" need revision?

Does incongruence prevail mostly between explicit and tacit knowledge? In a first approximation I would say, it could often happen that way. An extremely uncomfortable feeling, we know that something is wrong, but we can't tell what it is and what's more we can't tell how we know something is wrong, either.[15]

At the same time tacit knowledge is – if we believe the infant researchers – more flexible, more easily adaptable, and more superimposable than the explicit knowledge of the verbal sense of the self. Incongruence can thus also be caused by explicitly contradictory knowledge, but the tacit components, the procedural attunement will always resonate with it.

How do tacit knowledge and feelings work together?

In any case they're connected with each other right from the start, otherwise the parallels of affect attunement and of the other components of tacit knowledge wouldn't be so clear. However, the exact connection isn't defined; there might be an attunement of tacit knowledge as well. In that case the term „intuition" would fit as well. (Rogers in Kirschenbaum & Henderson 1989, 148) An other important correlation exists between feelings and rational intellect. (see again ann. 13)

How important is exact symbolization?

The idea of exact symbolization is that the more exactly the client is able to express his feelings and the meanings of his feelings the more chance he has in becoming congruent. (Rogers 1959) It is interesting, however, that Rogers didn't pay as much tribute to this idea as it deserves according to its position in the theory. It might be that the term „exact" needs new definition.

The tacit and the unconscious

The tacit and the unconscious are not identical: the extraverbal domain has nothing to do with repression, on the contrary it is open to experiences and willing to learn, but again the connection is unclear. (Rogers in Kirschenbaum & Henderson 1989, 148: „My nonconscious intellect takes over.")

CONCLUSION

This paper speaks about the meaning of the extraverbal experience. There is more and more evidence today, that the extraverbal perception which we are only partly aware of, is a wide field of learning and plays a very important role as a special source of experience. It is of less importance whether the content or the process of this kind of experience comes fully to consciousness or not, it is more important that there remains (or can be recovered again) an ability of learning in this field. As mentioned in the beginning, person–centered psychotherapy (and problably every type of psychotherapy) need to have impact in this field of extraverbal experience at least as well as in the other fields of emotional or even cognitive experience when it tries to be helpful for the client.

Infant research has drawn attention to the preverbal experiences. That might help to take extraverbal experiences more seriously. Tacit knowledge means acting together with the client all the time. There therapy becomes creative and artistic, research done on therapy becomes research about creativity.

REFERENCES

Biermann–Ratjen (1991), *Kann eine aus dem personzentrierten Konzept abgeleitete Entwicklungspsychologie die Empathie des Therapeuten erleichtern?*, in: Personzentriert, Zeitschrift der ÖGwG, 1/991, 17–33

Dornes, Martin (1993), *Der kompetente Säugling. Die präverbale Entwicklung des Menschen*, FiTB 11533, Fischer 1993

Glover, Edward, *The Technique of Psychoanalysis, Baillière, Tindall & Cox, London* 1955

Kirschenbaum, Howard, and Valerie Land Henderson (eds.), *The Carl Rogers´ Reader*, Houghton Mifflin Company, Boston 1989

Kohut, Heinz (1969), *The Psychoanalytic Treatment of Narcissistic Personality Disorders. Outline of a Systematic Approach*, in: The Search of the Self. Selected Writings of Heinz Kohut 1950–1978, Vol. I, 477–511, dt.: Heinz Kohut, Die psychoanalytische Behandlung narzißtischer Persönlichkeitsstörungen, in: Heinz Kohut, Heinz, Die Zukunft der Psychoanalyse, stw 125, Suhrkamp 1975, 173–204

Kohut, Heinz (1975), *Remarks about the Formation of the Self – Letter to a Student Regarding Some Priciples of Psychoanalytic Research*, in: The Search of the Self. Selected Writings of Heinz Kohut 1950–1978, Vol. II, 737–770, dt.: Bemerkungen zur Bildung des Selbst, in: Kohut, Heinz, Die Zukunft der Psychoanalyse, stw 125, Suhrkamp 1975, 252–285

Kohut, Heinz (1977), *The Restoration of the Self*, The International University Press, 1977, dt.: Heinz Kohut, *Die Heilung des Selbst*, Suhrkamp 1979, auch stw 373, Suhrkamp 1981

Kohut, Heinz (1984), *How Does Psychoanalysis Cure?*, The University of Chicago Press, Chicago and London 1984, dt.: Heinz Kohut, *Wie heilt die Psychoanalyse?* Suhrkamp, Frankfurt 1987

Mahler, Margaret, (1968), *On Human Symbiosis and the Vicissitudes of Individuation*, Int. Univ. Press 1968, dt.: Symbiose und Individuation, Klett, Stuttgart 1972

Polanyi, Michael (1958), *Personal Knowledge*. Towards a post–critical Philosophy, The University of Chicago Press, Chicago & London 1958

Polanyi, Michael (1966), *The Tacit Dimension, Doubleday & Co*, Inc., New York 1966, dt.: Michael Polanyi, *Implizites Wissen*, stw 543, Suhrkamp 1985

Rogers, Carl R. (1942), *Counseling and Psychotherapy*, Houghton Mifflin, Boston 1942, dt.: *Die nicht–direktive Beratung*, Geist und Psyche, Kindler, München 1972

Rogers, Carl R. (1951), *Client–Centered Therapy, Houghton Mifflin*, Boston 1951, dt.: Die klient–bezogene Gesprächstherapie, Geist und Psyche 2175, Kindler, München 1973

Rogers, Carl R. (1959), *A Theory of the Therapy, Personality and Interpersonal Relationships, as developed in the Client–Centered Framework*, in: Koch, Sigmund (ed.), Psychology. A Study of Science. Study I: Conceptual and Systematic. Vol. III: Formulations of The Person and The Social Context, McGraw Hill, New York, Toronto, London 1959, dt.: Eine Theorie der Psychotherapie, der Persönlichkeit und der zwischenmenschlichen Beziehungen. Entwickelt im Rahmen des klientenzentrierten Ansatzes, GwG–Verlag, Köln 1987

Rogers, Carl R. (1986a), *Reflection of Feelings and Transference, in: Kirschenbaum, Howard, and Valerie Land Henderson*, The Carl Rogers Reader, Houghton Mifflin, Boston 1989, 127–134

Rogers, Carl R. (1986b), *A Client–centered/Person–centered Approach to Therapy*, in: Kutash, I. and A. Wolf (Eds.), Psychotherapist's Casebook, Jossey–Bass 1986, 197–208, also in: Kirschenbaum, Howard and Valerie Land Henderson, The Carl Rogers Reader, Houghton Mifflin, Boston 1989, 135–152

Stern, Daniel N. (1985), *The Interpersonal World of the Infant*, Basic Books, New York 1985, dt.: Daniel N. Stern, Die Lebenserfahrung des Säuglings, Klett–Cotta 1992

Tausch, Reinhard (1988), *The Supplementation of Client–Centered Communcation Therapy with Other Validated Therapeutic Methods: A Client–Centered Necessity*, Paper, given at the I. ICCCEP, Leuven/Belgique 1988, in: Lietaer, Germain, et al. (eds.), Client–Centered and Experiential Psychotherapy in the Nineties, Leuven Univ. Press, Leuven 1990, 447–455

Wolf , Ernest (1987), *Comments on the therapeutic process in psychoanalysis*, in: Buirski, P. (ed.), Frontiers of dynamic psychotherapy, Brunner/Mazel, New York, 1987, dt.: Wolf, Ernest, Anmerkungen zum therapeutischen Prozeß in der Psychoanalysee, in: Wolf, Ernest, et al. (eds.), Selbstpsychologie. Weiterentwicklungen nach Heinz Kohut, Verlag Internationale Psychoanalyse, München, Wien 1989

---

[1]Understanding a client well usually has two effects: For one thing everytime the client feels understood, his pressure caused by suffering of incongruence that has brought him to therapy diminishes. Secondly, as soon as the pressure has become bearable, it often contributes to a desire of the client to understand him better and even to find out who he is and how he became who he is (this is an important stage in the developmental process of the client, which for the therapist is a relief).

[2] In fact the healing effect comprises two components: On the one hand the articulation of suffering limits it, on the other hand it does become less severe because it doesn't happen again in therapy.

[3] As a comparison examine Biermann-Ratjen's theory: If empathy is so important in a therapy it has to be equally important in the development of a child. (Biermann-Ratjen 1991) Similarly Polanyi says that the processes of realization in the acquisition of knowledge are the same as the ones in discovering and investigating new connections.

[4] Healing in this context stands for re-producing conditions that are necessary to make growth possible and are growth-promoting. Healing is therefore re-entering development. This is a procedural view.

[5] In his theoretical research the psychoanalyst Kohut found the same communication-model independently from the infant researchers. He claimed that the infant has a self(,) right from the very beginning (he called it „virtual self", Kohut 1979, 96), which becomes more and more differentiated. „... not the parts constitute the self, they are merely integrated in it." (Kohut 1975, 262f; see also Kohut 1979, 94ff.) The earlier and very popular psychoanalytic developmental model mentioned parts and part-perceptions, that melt into a perception of the self and of objects during the first year. (Mahler 1968, Glover's „Ego-nuclei" 1955)

[6] Both Rogers and Kohut have to be mentioned in this context. Rogers named empathy as a core variable in the attitudes of the therapist, Kohut puts his idea of empathy that way: for him empathy defines the field of observation. (Kohut 1979, 295) Only the knowledge gained through empathy is important in the human sciences.

[7] Academic psychology describes this as subception. (Polanyi 1985, 17) That, however, neither explains how this perception comes about nor how it is reacted to.

[8] It's to be investigated where the terms describe a tacit sense of the self and where they don't. In articulation there are obvious parallels to pitch, contour, etc. in Stern's categories in the explicit description of affect attunment. This is also true for intellectual passion, individual attention, and conviviality. The same way affirmation is assigned to the second year as tacit completion of verbal expression. (See the „shining in the eyes of the mother", Kohut 1977) Assigning the other terms is not easy, they'd have to be looked at separately.

[9] One of my clients described her experience not after a few sessions but at the end of a 4 year therapy with the words: „I've learned a lot without noticing it."

[10] Kohut's term of the self-object seems to express just this relationship between mother and child, that is to provide resonance for the child. Kohut describes particular dimensions of resonance which are mirroring, affirming, asserting and functioning as an idealizable object. (Kohut 1975, 173-204) Those descriptions, however, which lateron the dimension of being together was added to (Kohut 1984), are less important for our case. We'll focus on the term „resonance".

[11] This consideration is valid also for Psychoanalysis. One of the scholars of Heinz Kohut, Ernest Wolf, says in a paper about the technique of psychoanalytic self-psychology, that all the (psychoanalytic) goals of bringing the unconscious to consciousness or solving unconscious conflicts, and others are secondary after the affirmation and strengthening of the self (Wolf 1987/1989, 109f.). This change and development of the self - in our person-centered context we would say, the recovery and development of a more adequate and integrated selfconcept - is the primary goal of psychotherapeutic treatment.

[12] Rogers was very consistent in his thinking about resistance in psychotherapy. 1942 he said, resistance in psychotherapy is a consequence of an inadequate technique (of the therapist) in handling the expression of problems and feelings of the client (Rogers 1942/1972, 139), 1986 he wrote, „... there are two types of resistance. There is the pain of revealing ... the feelings ...(and) there is also the resistance to therapist, created by the therapist. ..." (Rogers 1986a, in Kirschenbaum & Henderson 1989, 133).

[13] I remember, that my psychoanalyst (who was not in his theory but in his practice strongly person-centered) once said: „The feelings are always prior to the mind." He meant that we are aware of our (in the beginning often diffuse or awkward) feelings, before they come clearer to our mind and we can give a name to them.

[14] Rogers said 1942, that the structure of the situation (of the therapeutic session) first of all is defined by that what does not happen. There are no moral judgements, there is no pressure in a specified direction, ... (Rogers 1942/1973, 87).

[15] For the emerging incongruence and about the formation of the self see Rogers 1951 or 1959: In his theory of the psychotherapy and the personality he states, a part of the perception develops to the self. Incongruence then starts with nonintegrated perceptions, later shifts to nonintegrated feelings.

"Intimacy, Tenderness and Lust"
A Person–Centered Approach to Sexuality

PETER F. SCHMID

HOCHSCHULE ST. GABRIEL / VIENNA

ABSTRACT

Until now sexuality has been paid little attention in person–centered theory. Instead therapists very often derive their thoughts from other theories. By presenting a number of theses, the attempt is made to explain sexuality from a genuinely person–centered viewpoint and to emphasize its particular significance in the context of man's actualizing tendency ("fulfillment") and inclination towards relationships ("devotion, self–transcendence"): as an incarnated encounter, as a body language of the person. In this way the sexual dimension of Carl Rogers' basic attitudes becomes surprisingly clear. A notion of congruent sexuality and its trustworthy, creative dimension is developed. The conditions under which so–called abnormal or perverse sexual behaviour can be considered as incongruence are analysed. In addition, the subject turns the spotlight on man's corporality and the difference between the sexes — subjects which are also widely neglected in person–centered theory.[1]

While in other psychotherapeutic approaches, especially in traditional psychoanalysis, many elaborate theories are applied to sexuality, this is certainly not the case with PCA. On the contrary: sexuality has so far not played a very important part in person–centered theory; in fact, the criticism is often heard that it is being neglected.

In the following I would like to deal with the question of how sexuality can be understood on the basis of person–centered theory and of what the consequences could be for practical use, particularly in psychotherapy. I will do this by formulating theses which, however, I consider to be tentative thoughts and perspectives rather than an all–embracing theory of sexuality. I also hope that they will stimulate a discussion on the subject within our approach.

INTRODUCTORY THOUGHTS ON THE RELATIONSHIP BETWEEN SEXUALITY AND A *PERSON*–CENTERED APPROACH

When PCA talks about sexuality, it means sexuality.

It is extremely difficult to give an exact and comprehensive definition of sexuality. But perhaps that isn't even necessary for our purposes. In PCA sexuality has the same meaning as it usually has in everyday speech, and not, as in Freud's psychoanalysis for example, everything libidinous (cf. Laplanche & Pontalis, 1972, p. 466). When we talk about sexuality from a person–centered point of view, we are neither arguing in favour of fixation on actual genital activity nor extending it almost without limits to cover everything that has to do with lust and desire. Perhaps this is one of the reasons why it is not so easy to talk and to write about sexuality in PCA: the scientific meaning might be exactly the same as our private meaning.

For various reasons Carl Rogers paid very little attention to sexuality.

These reasons include, apart from biographical aspects, in particular the holistic view of the person, which was more important for Rogers than sexual or drive–related aspects, the emphasis on freedom rather than on any dominance of drives as well as the rejection of the psychoanalytic paradigm in general. The explicit discussion of the sexual dimensions desire, passion, surrender, fulfillment is in any case not found in Rogers' work.

The person–centered concept of the person must not be misunderstood as being sexually neutral. Personality in a person–centered sense does not mean ignoring sex, it means the congruent assignement of sexuality and personality.

In emphasizing the holistic approach and the person it can easily happen that the detail, in this case the sexual and sex specific element, is overlooked or denied (Winkler, 1992; Teichmann–Wirth, 1992a). The human being, woman and man, is a person.[2] Speaking of the human being as person one must neither overlook the sexual component of the personality (and there is a particular danger of this in PCA), nor should one underestimate the fact that the person of a human being consists of more than his mere sexuality and role (which PCA has always specifically emphasized).

Especially because of its anthropological basis — approaching the human being as a person — PCA is however certainly ideal to conquer the cliché of traditional sexual roles and diagnosis categories and to put in doubt the traditional sex specific socialisation (expressed by the Anglo–American word "gender"), if it is not reduced to being sexually neutral, thus excluding such questions entirely. The prejudice (which is often justified in person–centered practice) that PCA *as such* ignores the sex specific — particularly the feminist — challenges is not correct, because the reflection of the concrete relationship between the people involved in the person–centered process in their individuality and thus also in their specific sexuality is an essential element of the understanding of the person and the person–centered relationship (cf. Schmid, 1992; 1994).

To develop a person–centered notion of sexuality use of other theories should be avoided: it should truly be generated from personal experience and person–centered anthropology.

The attempts to borrow from the more developed theories of other psychotherapeutic schools as a basis for formulation of a person–centered theory of sexuality, which sometimes can be seen (e. g. Teichmann–Wirth, 1992a), should be rejected as incompatible with this concept. Difficulties which arise while developing a genuinely person–centered theory should rather be taken seriously and considered in this process.

SEXUALITY AS ACTUALIZATION

Sexuality is part of the human nature. On the one hand it can be understood as an expression of the actualizing tendency. Accordingly sexual needs, wishes and activities are actualizations of the sexual potential of a person.

Sexual strivings[3] and the expression of sexuality are the expression of the actualizing tendency.

The sexuality of man is part of the

> inherent tendency of the organism to develop all its capacities in ways which serve to maintain or enhance the organism. It involves not only the tendency to meet [...] "deficiency needs" for air, food, water, and the like, but also more generalized activities (Rogers, 1959a, p. 196)

— even if Rogers himself at this point does not mention sexuality. Because the term "involves development toward the differentiation of organs and of functions, expansion in terms of growth, expansion of effectiveness through the use of tools, expansion and enhancement through reproduction. It is development toward autonomy and away from heteronomy" (ibid.).

The sexuality of a human being is actually particularly an expression of the actualizing tendency insofar as it contains the potential for many different forms of human fulfillment and actualization: the wish for procreation (reproduction), lust and desire as well as their fulfillment (i.e. the build–up and release of tension) and the wish for security and unification and for love.

Therefore we can say: Man's sexuality uniquely consists in a basic way of being, basic needs and basic possibilities of the person. Only this is important enough to justify the special position of sexuality as I will refer to later.

Like human nature in general man's sexuality is primarily to be considered as potentially constructive and trustworthy, not primarily as dangerous or even destructive, and so it should not be treated with reserve or subjected to taboos or (moralizing) reglementations.

The actualizing tendency is a "constructive tendency" (e. g. Rogers, 1979a, p. 101) which is trustworthy (e. g. Rogers, 1961a, p. 194). This trustworthiness and constructiveness of human nature are the pillars of the person–centered anthropology.

In contrast, sexuality very often meets with a great deal of mistrust, which can be observed throughout history, in all cultures and in the various life and maturation stages of an individual. This is shown amongst other things in ignoring, establishing taboos, moralizing, imposing rules and forbidding, and also in mystifying, generalizing, idealizing and overestimating.

A person–centered notion of sexuality thus differs considerably from traditional views of sexuality, and also from many concepts of other psychotherapeutic orientations. Here the different approach of person–centered anthropology with its fundamental trust in the constructive actualization of the human potential under suitable conditions radically becomes visible and tangible.

When a human being really is living — not occupied with "surviving" as is the case in exceptional situations —, any expression of sexuality should be regarded as an expression of his search for growth, creative development and greater fulfillment of personal potential.

> Certain wants of a basic sort must be at least partially met before other needs become urgent. Consequently the tendency of the organism to actualize itself may at one moment lead to the seeking of food or sexual satisfaction and yet unless these needs are over-poweringly great, even these satisfactions will be sought in ways which enhance rather than diminish self–esteem. (Rogers, 1979a, p. 102).

Depending on the self–concept and the given possibilities this search may attain quite different even very restricted or distorted qualities. However congruent sexuality means the maximum openness to experiences. The temporary or complete renunciation of instantaneous satisfaction increases the chances of experiencing something new, increases the desire for something new and increases creativity (cf. the actualizing tendency as personalisation, Schmid, 1994, p. 413–423); to the same extent the tendency to repeat and the reduction of everything to mere satisfaction of needs is decreased.

The sexuality of a human being has always to do with the core of the person: therefore it is crucial for identity and alienation.

Sexuality is thus something central, has something to do with the core of the person, his individuality and his ability and inclination to form relationships: discussing human sexuality is also always discussing the question of how one copes with oneself and with relationships, and therefore finally always concerns the person. Sexuality touches "me myself" more than anything else; sexual rejection is easily experienced as a rejection of the whole person. Thus sexuality is largely concerned with the development of the personality, with personalisation, with becoming whole. Therefore sexuality is one of the keys to the alternative "identity versus alienation", which repeatedly confronts every person.

Genuine sexuality consists in a maximum congruence between the experiencing of sexual strivings and their correct symbolization. Thus, "fulfilled sexuality" means the autonomous and free fulfillment of the potential which is inherent in these strivings.

The term *"fulfillment"* does not only seem more suitable than "satisfaction" (because it is more growth–oriented), it also covers more: fulfillment can also be experienced through the decision not to seek satisfaction. Therefore one could also speak of *"fully functioning sexuality"* by analogy with "fully functioning person" — in the sense of ful*fill*ment: "Thus, to me it is meaningful to say that the substratum of all motivation is the organismic tendency" "toward constructive fulfillment of its inherent possibilities" (Rogers, 1979a, p.102, 99).

Congruent and fulfilled sexuality is an expression of emotional and physical *freedom*, it means in particular freedom from paralyzing or inhibiting fear, it implies a maximum of openness to experience and an absence of inhibitions (cf. Teichmann–Wirth, 1992a). This includes the freedom to pursue satisfaction of lust — or not.

Such a freedom — in the personal sense of the word — must not be confused with being arbitrary, it can certainly be a freely chosen involvement in a relationship (in the sense of loyalty which is also a category of relationship). To achieve congruence, a *decision* about the personal form of sexuality is thus necessary in any case (which always implies an either–or question: finding an identity as a man or a woman, as a heterosexual or a homosexual, etc.); the opposite would be (as is the case in many traditional heterosexual partnerships) "to slip" into a relationship without reflecting and thus into a heteronomous form of sexuality rather than an autonomous one.

The creative, generative dimension of sexuality can be regarded as an expression of the formative tendency.

Rogers (1979a, p. 102–107) himself describes the formative tendency as a "creative tendency" (ibid. 107). Above and beyond its creative forms of expression, sexuality is generative insofar as it creates new life.[4]

Sexual striving for lust, the "concept of lust", as the sexual aspect of the self–concept is determined by the self–actualizing tendency.

If the sexual striving — I would like to call this the *"concept of lust"* by reference to Rogers' term "the concept of self" — is in harmony, i.e. congruent, with the organismic experiences and the actualizing tendency, it serves to enhance the possibilities of the individual and is experienced as satisfying and constructive. If the concept of lust as a part of a distorted concept of self is incongruent with the experiencing organism, it can partially or to a large extent block sexual fulfillment and development. More will be said about this in relation to sexual incongruence.

Sexuality, in particular mature sexuality, is characterized by a movement in a specific direction, i.e. by attraction.

Sexuality can be regarded as the embodiment of emotional experience just as, in reverse, emotional striving can be understood as an expression of physical "attraction". Sexuality is something by which human beings are particularly "moved" (physically and emotionally). According to Rogers (1979a, p. 99) the actualizing tendency generally is a "total directional process". Sexual desire triggers a specific search. Sexuality produces movement. Characteristics of congruent, personal sexuality therefore include: physical as well as emotional movement (in contrast to immobility), activity and excitement (in contrast to rigidity, resignation, rest), warmth (in contrast to cold), creativity (in contrast to repetition and technique), variety (in contrast to uniformity).

Sexual possibilities — sexual potency — merit particular attention amongst man's possibilities as an expression of self–transcendence.

The concept of the actualizing tendency does not only contain "such concepts of motivation as are termed need–reduction, tension–reduction, drive–reducation", but also "the growth motivations which appear to go beyond these terms: the seeking of pleasurable tensions, the tendency to be creative [...]" (Rogers, 1959a, p. 196). The person–centered notion of sexuality therefore (in contrast to some concepts of the orthodoxe psychoanalysis) does not see this primarily from the angle of release of tension but as a stimulation to pleasurable action and thus to the development of constructive tension.

The consequence is that particularly in sexuality — perhaps more strongly than in any other of its expressions — the progressive and creative character of the actualizing tendency can be seen. Here it becomes visible in its self–transcending dimension (from the individual relationship through to procreation). Sexual potency is from this point of view the most powerful potency (power, force, capacity) of a human being, as it radically questions him in his individuality in regard to relationships and it demands self–transcendence.

SEXUALITY AS ENCOUNTER

Now we have reached the second fundamental concept of person–centered anthropology, the concept of encounter: sexuality is also an expression of man's inclination towards relationship.

Sexuality is a category of relationship. Sexual encounter is an overall and not only physical dimension of personal encounter.

Sensuality and "Leiblichkeit" (not only corporality) are intrinsically part of the person–centered notion of a person (cf. Plessner, 1970; Rombold, 1984; Schmid, 1994). Personal encounter[5] basically has also an embodied, sensual dimension. In reverse sexual encounter includes the other dimensions and cannot be reduced to corporality.

Sexuality is basically linked to the personal identity and becomes visible in its essence as a dimension of relationship (relational aspect of becoming a person), not merely as a dimension of the individual (substantial aspect of being a person) (Schmid, 1991).

Personal sexuality is incarnated encounter. Sexuality is a central "interface" between physical and emotional processes.

The development of the personality, becoming a human being, personalisation ("becoming a person") always also means incarnation ("becoming flesh"). This "incarnatory process" ("embodiment", to use an expression of Brian Thorne, 1991b, p. 63) — the process of unification of word and flesh, of the greater mutual penetration of the spiritual and embodied dimensions of the person, of becoming a human being — reaches a climax in the sexual encounter as a physical expression of love and personal encounter. Personalisation is incarnation: personal sexuality is embodied, incarnated encounter. As we say in German: "The relationship becomes flesh and blood".

A positive attitude to the body is therefore an important condition for inner freedom as far as sexuality is concerned, especially as regards the concepts of what is normal. This requires confidence in one's own values and loyalty to one's own inner standards.[6]

Every person is responsable for his own values and standards concerning sexuality.

Especially in regard to sexuality there can be no general standards which would not have to be examined afresh in each personal relationship. If sexuality is an element of personal encounter or is aiming to be so, the persons involved have to be responsible themselves for the way they live it. The same applies to external values; they are also to be rejected particularly in sexuality: this is true for rigid attitudes and behaviour as well as for counterpositions adopted on principle.

Only the unconditional regard which grows out of deep empathy can conquer such introjected values in favour of criteria established by oneself.

Sexual standards often are applied by human beings to use or to misuse power.

Power and sexuality are closely linked — just think of the term "potency". Where sexuality is not meant for encounter, there is a danger of misuse of power, of people dominating people.

External values often are aimed at the exercise of power. "Sexuality is one of the key approaches to man and to the exercise of power." (Schmid, 1989b, p. 107) Dominators have preferred and prefer to use the control of sexuality to impose themselves and to achieve their aims. "Suppressing lust in others seems to be a strong symbol of power = potentia = potency that will not tolerate anything else on the same level." (Strotzka, 1985, p. 157) — Thus power itself can be experienced as being erotic. The dominating moral standards should therefore also always be seen as the moral standards of the dominating people. The argument that people are being protected, in reality often is used to deprive them of their rights.

Frequently people who do not agree inwardly with the prevailing moral standards, but who do not protest against them openly, develop a double moral standard (often unnoticed), which is destructive on a psychological and social level. Free communication however is the most effective means of keeping power in check (Schmid, 1989a; 1989b; 1996).

VARIATIONS OF CONGRUENT AND INCONGRUENT SEXUALITY

As regards sexuality in particular it is true to say: "What is most personal is most general."
(Rogers, 1961a, p. 26)

If access to a very personal aspect tells so much about the actual person, then an experience-oriented approach, which sees the personal relationship as central, interprets exactly this aspect as being decisive for man as such simply as a person. However as decisive elements of the personality can be found in the sexual dimension, we can learn something important about the conditio humana in general from the concrete and personal experience of sexuality.

In reverse we can also say: if sexuality has to do with the very personal dimension, one has to ask the person himself whether something "is sexual" (has a sexual significance) and one cannot generalize or interpret using external criteria.

A concept which includes both sexes allows a more differentiated view of the actualizing tendency.

Gender–specific feeling and understanding must be expressed adequatly in terms of language. We can take as an example the actualizing tendency which also shows that in this way the meaning of this notion is being expanded:

The concept of the actualizing tendency as a "directional", "striving", "forward moving" force (Rogers, 1979a, p. 99f, 101) is characterized by male experience and male language ([self–] realisation); a female concept could on the other hand assume that a human being is in relationships from the very beginning and because of this, development is a differentiating process of giving form to relationships (Gaul, 1993). A similar differentiation must be made with language and concept as regards homosexuality versus heterosexuality: for instance if one speaks of a "tension between the sexes" instead of "sexual tension between people".

If sexuality is the body language of the person, then the various forms and expressions of sexuality can be compared with the dialects of this language.

If one only speaks and understands his dialect, one will also be limited in one's relationships. If one only speaks the standard language, one will lose a lot of the color of the spoken language. If the dialects differ too much from each other, it may happen that people no longer understand each other if they do not speak the standard language or another common language.

The forms and expressions of sexuality are many and varied. There is no one "correct" sexuality. Every human being has in principle the opportunity to choose the variety of sexual behaviour that suits him.

The various forms of sexuality — including many of the so–called perversions — are to be regarded primarily as variations of the actualization and not as incongruence. Thus "abnormal" sexual behaviour — ignoring the necessary question of what is normal — is never *generally* definable.

Many theories are based on the assumption that every human being is born with a particular sexual orientation: just think of the discussion about the genesis of homosexuality. In contrast to this type of "sexual racism", the person–centered position is rather that every human being has the disposition to a variety of sexual possibilities and options. (This represents a parallel to Freud's formulation that man as a small child is "polymorphously perverse".)

If we assume therefore that so–called "normal sexuality" is one of many varieties of sexual behaviour, this means that in principle every person has the freedom (and the responsibility) to realize those possibilities that he wants to live — a freedom that admittedly can be considerably restricted by the specific conditions around him and by the moral external pressure. This also means however that it can be enriching to actualize more of one's sexual potencies — and to live them in such a way and in those relationships in which the person chooses to do so according to his values. This includes the decision to choose hetero–, bi–, or homosexual behaviour or the decision in favour of so–called perverse sexual behaviour or the decision in favour of sexual restraint.[7]

So–called "abnormal sexual feeling and behaviour" is only to be seen as incongruence if the person concerned is not able to correctly symbolize his experiences.

"Abnormal" sexual behaviour, sexual "perversions" are to be seen as incongruence if they do not serve the actualizing tendency of the person or if they are not integrated into the self of the person. Then we have a conflict between the self–actualizing tendency and the actualizing tendency, an incongruency between self (the concept of lust) and experience (in which case there is often a "splitting off" of the impulses produced by the actualizing tendency so that they seem strange to the person himself) and the person concerned generally suffers. Social standards are usually the trigger for this. Only accepting the impulses, i.e. the organismic actualizing tendency, its power (potency, force) and a confidence in its constructive tendency, and not fighting them or trying to push them aside can thus lead to greater congruence.

CONDITIONS FOR FULFILLED SEXUALITY

The conditions for "fulfilled sexuality" are, like the conditions for the development of congruent sexuality, identical with the basic attitudes which Rogers describes as necessary for person–centered relationships.

Here the aspect of development is particularly important: as in other areas of life man must first discover his own wishes, needs and possibilities specially in sexuality to then be able to unfold them in a creative way. The person–centered basic attitudes are essential for a constructive way of dealing with one's own sexuality. As the unconditional positive regard, empathy and genuineness (as attitudes which are experienced from someone else as well as attitudes towards oneself) are all the more important if a topic is very personal and very profound, this also obviously applies for the area of sexuality: differentiated perception, in fact becoming aware of experiences in general, is extremely important and in the sexual area often achievable only through the corresponding empathy and regard towards oneself. Personally significant people — in therapy the therapist — are facilitators of these attitudes.

Deeply felt and correct empathy in sexual experiencing encourages precise perception and symbolisation and thus a change of the self–concept in this area.

Non–judgmental sharing facilitates the positive regard of the client for the aspects of his own sexual experiencing, which are so often connected with negative judgements or are totally rejected or until then totally denied, as well as for the corresponding aspect of the experience and the self–concept. It is a question of getting to know one's own concept of lust with as few prejudices as possible. The esteem for oneself in central aspects, the fundamental self–respect is thus encouraged. This also applies in particular for the understanding of one's own history and thus for the finding of one's own identity.

The "fearless and lustful" authenticity and the related transparency of the therapist similarly encourages the congruence of the client, yes, it even helps to be in sexual respect what one is in a more fearless and lustful way — more independent from external values determined by others.

In summary this means for therapy: a truly non–sexual, caring attention of the therapist for the client, which values him also in his sexuality and which tries to enter empathically into this, encourages a self–concept which is more realistic, more open to the organismic process of experience and thus is more constructive in general.

Carl Rogers' basic attitudes may also well be understood sexually: as "intimacy", "tenderness" and "lust".

Nobody will deny that the attitudes of sensitive, gentle empathy, loving regard and sincere transparency actually contain a tender, sometimes erotic aspect. In addition however they can be understood in their sexual dimensions:

Empathy creates nearness, *intimacy:* this means a conscious and loving approach towards the other person and a gentle entering of his inner being ("male aspect") or gentle embracing (Gaul, 1993) and acceptance of the other ("female aspect"); a temporary fusion and a temporary unification with the other without complete self–surrender, the also physical resonance with the experiencing of the other which allows the other to feel himself even more.

The unconditional positive regard for the other and the gentle care for him implies an attitude of *tenderness* and a warmth as a nonpossessive attention and an unlimited openness towards the other without any superfluous self–protection; the respectful regard for the other which does not intend to control him, but to win him over; "loving words and caressing hands" — but also strength and firm action — that induce the other one to love himself and produce a delightful, sometimes ecstatic feeling in him.

By authenticity in the sexual area is meant the mentioned correspondence between sexual experience and the self (concept of lust) which manifests itself in the feeling of *sexual lust:* the congruence between the tension of needs on the one hand and activity to increase or eliminate it on the other hand is also experienced as lust in the sexual sense as can be applied for the search for the scientific or verbal ("until something is right") authenticity: if one searches authentically (i.e. "in the right way") and makes progress accordingly, getting closer and closer to what he is looking for until he finally is successful (although he may perhaps find something different from what he originally looked for or in a different way than he expected), one experiences this in a lustful manner just like rising and falling sexual tension.[8]

It can also be said the other way round: intimacy, tenderness and lust, the "sexual variables or basic attitudes", are necessary conditions for fulfilled sexuality.

Carl Rogers' dimension of the "presence" in the sexual sense comes close to the meaning of an orgasm shared by both partners which is experienced as satisfying and self–transcending.

Rogers' statements on experiencing presence in therapy or encounter groups are, from the sexual point of view, particularly revealing:

> When I am at my best [...] as a therapist [...] when I am perhaps in a slightly altered state of consciousness in the relationship, [...] in those moments [of presence] it seems that my inner spirit has reached out and touched the inner spirit of the other. Our relationship transcends itself and has become a part of something larger. (Rogers, 1986h; cf. Schmid, 1991, p. 120).

Brian Thorne (1991a, p. 81: cf. 1987) describes the same experience as *"tenderness"*, which becomes a possibility at the moment "when two human persons meet and are able to give way to the liberating urge to trust without anxiety." Elsewhere he writes:

> It is as if energy is flowing through me and I am simply allowing it free passage. I feel a physical vibrancy and this often has a sexual component and a stirring in the genitals. I feel powerful and yet at the same time almost irrelevant. (Thorne, 1991a, p. 77)

Fulfilled sexuality consists in full devotion in presence, in the undivided and fearless presence.[9]

INCONGRUENT SEXUALITY AS ALIENATION AND ITS THERAPY

One of the conditions for "the estrangement of man from himself, from his experiencing organism" (Rogers, 1961c, p. 157), is sexual repression.

Congruent sexuality has to do with identity and incongruent sexuality with alienation. If "man loses the ability to trust his organismic needs" (Teichmann–Wirth, 1992a, p. 296) the consequence is a discrepancy between experience and symbolisation. Since until today much education is repressive, particularly where it concerns sexuality, the result, particularly in this area that — as already mentioned — is central for man, is alienation with all its negative aspects. The many consequences that arise for developmental psychology and for educational sciences cannot be described in more detail here.

Sexual incongruence results from defence against fear.

The denial or distortion of sexual inclinations and orientations because of "defensive behaviour" (Rogers, 1959a, p. 227) occur out of fear of their threatening appearance: in order not to have to be integrated into the self–concept, these inclinations are denied (i.e. declared as meaningless), dismissed (i.e. rejected as experience) or symbolized in a distorted way (i.e. admitted selectively into the awareness: the content of the experience is changed to fit the self–concept, thus symbolized inadequatly. The self changes the experience in order not to experience it as new and therefore not to have to change itself.) (cf. Rogers, 1959a, p. 227f)

"The fixity and remoteness of experiencing" (Rogers, 1961a, p. 132) may be expressed insofar as a person in his sexual activities is guided more by concepts than by his organismic desire (cf. Teichmann–Wirth, 1992a), but can also show itself quite differently: in fixations on particular people or parts of the body or objects etc. With such forms of incongruence a possible differential diagnostic approach could be found.

A "splitting off" of sexuality from the organismic experiencing in particular takes place when in the emotional (and thus sexual) development sexuality is experienced as threatening.

Sexuality is central in the life of a human being and therefore its splitting off signifies a central and not only marginal incongruence, an incongruence that includes many other aspects and therefore often is no longer perceived explicitly as sexual incongruence.

Therefore therapy is also an incarnated process to subdue sexual alienation.

In the opposite process (for instance in therapy) it is then often first experienced as threatening when "heart and genitals come together" again (cf. Teichmann–Wirth, 1992b). The fear resulting from this threat can (under protected conditions, as for instance in a therapy) also be seen as a chance, because it signalizes that important experiences are pushing towards awareness (cf. Rogers, 1959a). In that case a trustful relationship is even more important to regain self–confidence.

Just as sexual alienation often becomes tangible and experiencable as corporal alienation ("to have a disturbed relationship to one's own body"), the possibility of getting in touch (e. g. through therapy) with one's own body — as an "incarnatory" process, as an "embodiment" — admits a new approach to the understanding of one's own corporality. Therapy as an attentive, empathic and authentic sensual and corporal event is in such a manner also an experiential basis for an attentive, empathic and authentic sexual relationship.

The Person–Centered Approach does not consider suffering in sexuality as a "sexual disorder", but as an expression of the suffering of the person. Thus it has no specific "techniques for dealing with sexual disorders", but trusts in the corrective experiences which the client will have in the person–centered relationship.

The person–centered therapist therefore does not meet so–called sexual disorders by applying rigid concepts, explanations or fixed moral standards, but rather by asking the question: "In which way does this specific human being express his relationship to himself and to others in his personal sexuality?" (Teichmann–Wirth, 1992a, p. 298)

In therapy the therapist therefore is very important as a *person*. His attitude, in particular a large degree of transparency, a nonjudgmental acceptance and empathy which also includes the perception of physiological signals, should provide the client with a feeling of security to think about himself with less fear and to adopt the same attitude towards himself: in this way a corrective experience of sexual feeling can become possible.

A specific setting for specific sexual orientations generally does not seem to be necessary, especially when the therapeutic conditions are fulfilled to a large extent.

By analogy with feminist therapy the question is discussed if for specific sexual orientations specific forms of therapy, therapeutic settings or specific therapists (for example gay therapists for gay clients etc.) are more suitable. The possible primary advantage for the client of being understood by his peer is counteracted by the disadvantage of being understood "only" by a peer. Therefore according to my opinion such a specific setting is not necessary when the therapist succeeds in realising to a large extent the conditions of being genuine and empathic, but in particular the unconditional positive regard, which however may hardly be achieved without sufficient self–experiencing in the clinical sector. To have empathy for sexual inclinations of other persons is more difficult if one has only reflected and accepted such inclinations and experiences in oneself to a small degree (cf. Silbermayr, 1988).

In a very general manner we can say: anyone who really is willing to occupy himself with people who — also in a sexual way — experience differently, will find this to be an enrichment rather than a threat.

On the other hand PCA offers the possibility of specific therapeutic settings where this seems to be temporarily necessary because of sexual discrimination.

People who regard feminist therapy as necessary under the present conditions, find in the Person–Centered Approach the anthropological basis and the objective which can make transparent and eliminate at least in part the discrimination (between sexes) and the situations of domination. The same can be applied regarding the slowly growing new self–concept of men which is developing as a reaction to the feminist challenge. (Schmid, 1992)

and all forms of other sexual discriminations (for instance with homosexuals).

The fitting attitude towards sexuality in therapeutic relationships is characterized on the one hand by a strict abstinence by the therapist from sexual activities in the present relationship with the client, on the other hand by a large openness to sexual subjects in general and the given therapeutic relationship in particular.

In a relationship which contains in principle a situation of dependency and an unbalanced situation of power, as is the case in every therapeutic relationship, sexual activities are contraindicated, as they fundamentally aim at equality and free decision of the partners, which is not affected by any dependency. Apart from that, therapy always concerns only one person (the client), in sexuality both are concerned.

The needs of the therapist (of both sexes) should be reflected meticulously in the therapy; a sexuality which in the moment of encounter is under control would however be a contradiction in terms. To say that active sexual attention from the therapist towards the client, even with the consent of the latter, would for him mean a possibility to liberate himself from inhibitions and would be a new experience, would instrumentalize sexuality or simply disguise the needs of the therapist himself to seduce or be seduced — a "sexuality bare of interest" does not exist (cf. Ellinghaus & Große–Rhode, 1990).

What applies to the therapeutic relationship in particular goes for any other relationship which is in principle characterized by hierarchy or dependency (parents, superiors, every relationship in which one has to assess the other, as for instance is the case with teachers or trainers, etc.).

It is important — also independently of therapy — to find a congruent language for sexuality.

Even if communication concerning sexuality does not always have to succeed verbally, it is important to name, to find words, i.e. to understand what one is doing and by what one is thus moved. This is not only true for therapy; there however it is important to say "what we are talking about", to speak about things "one usually does not speak about".

There hardly exists a language which fulfills the need of an adequate personal communication about sexuality — neither the medical and the psychoanalytical language nor the very often vulgar jargon do so. Nevertheless it is important to speak about sexual things and experiences — not with the aim of speaking about sexuality instead of living it, but of symbolising and exchanging sexual experiences in an adequate manner. Particularly in therapy, of course, it is important not to avoid sexual subjects.

SEXUALITY, EROTICISM, LOVE

Sexuality is an expression of encounter as a "game of love", a "love full of force".

Sexuality is something tremendous, a tremendous force. The objective of sexual development can only be to unfold and facilitate such a sexuality which is facilitative for the personality of the individual and constructive for cohabitation. The essence is to find an authentic way of living interpersonal relationships. There is more involved than "sexual potency", more than "power over and through one's own sexuality": sexuality is to be understood as an expression of *love* and to be facilitated by love. It is a matter of the art of loving, of a love that has *force* (as is also expressed by the term "agape" from the New Testament used by Rogers, e. g. 1962a). Sexual encounter is an expression of this love. It can only happen in freedom and disinterest. By analogy with the concept of encounter we can say: fulfilled human sexuality is an authentic game, a "game of love" (Schmid, 1991, p. 121; 1993).

Fulfilled sexuality is every sexuality that has a truly liberating effect, that respects and values the personality of the partner and one's own personality as a whole, that gives and receives trust, that seeks mutual lust and fulfillment, that is — in one word — an expression of personal love (cf. Schmid, 1989a, p. 76).

Sexuality, being understood as surrender in a relationship, in the end aims at self–transcendency

Sexuality in the first place means "to give" and not "to take". Sexuality therefore means surrender, means exceeding oneself (self–transcendency) and the person (transcendency over the person). Sexuality is crossing borders: "Live processes do not merely tend to preserve life but transcend the momentary status quo of the organism, expanding itself continually and imposing its autonomous determination upon an ever increasing realm of events" Rogers (1959a, p. 196) writes, quoting Angyal (1941), in defining the actualizing tendency.

Sexuality is more than simply supplementing one individual by another. It moreover opens up the single existence revealing new dimensions of life and transcends the individual person towards the family and other forms of living together as well as towards social dimensions. Finally it indicates the fundamental interconnectedness of life in general and therefore is a central approach to the universe.

Someone who, without asking for it, receives something he had been longing for intensely feels deep satisfaction. From this point of view a successful, fulfilled sexuality is always a gift — as is love —, can never be produced although suitable conditions can be created. The person who concentrates only on himself does not find sexual satisfaction; sexuality is the opposite: the always new exciting experience of self–transcendency (to be compared with ecstacy). In the fulfilled moment of the orgasm it means surrendering oneself. It means experiencing that the person is more then he thinks of himself, more than himself, more than his self.

The fitting image is not a closed circle, but a spiral open towards the top...

REFERENCES

Angyal, A. (1941). *Foundations for a science of personality.* New York: Commonwealth Fund.
Ellinghaus, E. & Grosse–Rhode, L. (1990). *Plädoyer für die sexuelle Abstinenz in Therapie und Ausbildung.* GwG–Zeitschrift, 79, 123.
Emmermann, H.–M. (1991). *Credo an Gott und sein Fleisch. Erfahrungen mit himmlischer und irdischer Liebe.* Hamburg: Hoffmann und Campe.
Frenzel, P., Schmid, P. F. & Winkler, M. (1992) (Eds.). *Handbuch der Personzentrierten Psychotherapie.* Köln: Edition Humanistische Psychologie.
Gaul, S. C. (1992). *Der personzentrierte Ansatz von Carl R. Rogers aus philosophisch–feministischer Sicht.* Vienna: Manuscript.
Gaul, S. C. (1993). Personal communication.
Laplanche, J. & Pontalis, J.–B. (1972). *Das Vokabular der Psychoanalyse.* Frankfurt/M.: Suhrkamp.
Plessner, H. (1970). *Philosophische Anthropologie.* Frankfurt/M.: Fischer.
Rogers, C. R. (1957a). *The necessary and sufficient conditions of therapeutic personality change.* Journal of Consulting Psychology, 21(2), 95–103.
Rogers, C. R. (1959a). *A theory of therapy, personality, and interpersonal relationships, as developed in the client–centered framework.* In Koch, S. (Ed.), Psychology. A study of a science. Vol. III. Formulations of the person and the social context (pp. 184–216). New York: McGraw Hill.
Rogers, C. R. (1961a). *On becoming a person. A therapist's view of psychotherapy.* Boston: Houghton Mifflin.
Rogers, C. R. (1961c). *"Ellen West — and loneliness".* In Rogers, C. R., A way of being (pp. 164–180). Boston: Houghton Mifflin.
Rogers, C. R. (1962a). *The interpersonal relationship: The core of guidance.* Harvard Educational Review, 32 (4), 416–429.
Rogers, C. R. (1979a). *The foundations of the person–centered approach.* education 100 (2), 98–107.
Rogers, C. R. (1986h). *A client–centered/person–centered approach to therapy.* In Kutash, I. L. & Wolf, A. (Eds.), Psychotherapist's casebook: Theory and technique in the practice of modern times (pp. 197–208). San Francisco: Jossey–Bass.

98

Rogers, C. R. & Schmid, P. F. (1991). *Person–zentriert. Grundlagen von Theorie und Praxis.* Mainz: Grünewald; [2]1995.

Rombold, G. (1984). *Anthropologie II.* Linz: Manuscript.

Schmid, P. F. (1989a). *Doppelmoral: Umgang mit Macht und Sexualität in der Kirche.* Diakonia, 2, 73–77.

Schmid, P. F. (1989b). *Macht über die Sexualität? Psychologische Anmerkungen zur Emanzipation.* Diakonia, 2, 106–109.

Schmid, P. F. (1989c). *Personale Begegnung: Der personzentrierte Ansatz in Psychotherapie, Beratung, Gruppenarbeit und Seelsorge.* Würzburg: Echter; [2]1995.

Schmid, P. F. (1991). *Souveränität und Engagement: Zu einem personzentrierten Verständnis von "Person".* In Rogers & Schmid, 1991, [2]1995, 15–164, 297–305

Schmid, P. F. (1992). *Der Therapeut: Bescheidenheit ist eine Zier, doch weiter ... Zum Selbstverständnis des Personzentrierten Psychotherapeuten.* In Frenzel, Schmid & Winkler, 1992, 39–69.

Schmid, P. F. (1993). *A new image of man? Toward male emancipation.* In Theology Digest, 3, 317–220

Schmid, P. F. (1994). *Personzentrierte Gruppenpsychotherapie: Ein Handbuch. Band 1. Autonomie und Solidarität.* Köln: Edition Humanistische Psychologie.

Schmid, P. F. (1996). *Personzentrierte Gruppenpsychotherapie in der Praxis. Ein Handbuch. Band 2. Die Kunst der Begegnung.* Paderborn: Junfermann.

Schmid, P. F. & Wascher, W. (1993) (Eds.). *Towards creativity: A person–centered reading & picture–book.* Linz: edition sandkorn.

Silbermayr, E. (1988). *Ganz schwul im Hier und Jetzt: Homosexualität und Psychotherapie.* Personzentriert, 1, 7–14.

Strotzka, H. (1985). *Macht: Ein psychoanalytischer Essay.* Vienna: Zsolnay.

Teichmann–Wirth, B. (1992a). *Sexualität: "Man darf das nicht vor keuschen Ohren nennen, was keusche Ohren nicht entbehren können". Personzentrierte Therapie: Jenseits der Sexualität?* In Frenzel, Schmid & Winkler, 1992, 293–302.

Teichmann–Wirth, B. (1992b). Lecture *"Sexualität im Personzentrierten Ansatz".* Vienna.

Thorne, B. (1987). *Beyond the core conditions.* In Thorne, 1991c, 82-106.

Thorne, B. (1991a). *The quality of tenderness.* In Thorne, 1991c, 73–81.

Thorne, B. (1991b). *Behold the man: A therapist's mediations on the passion of Jesus Christ.* London: Darton, Longman & Todd.

Thorne, B. (1991c). *Person-centred counselling. Therapeutic and spiritual dimensions.* London: Whurr.

Winkler, M. (1992). *Das Geschlecht: Du Tarzan — ich Jane. Geschlechterdifferenz in der therapeutischen Interaktion.* In Frenzel, Schmid & Winkler, 1992, 193–205.

---

[1] "'Initimität, Zärtlichkeit und Lust'. Sexualität aus personzentrierter Sicht"; translation by Elisabeth Zinschitz.

[2] If in the following I do not use expressions which indicate sex, this is partly done for greater clarity, though it is also intended to express that my personal view is being presented. I am aware, particularly in this context, of the fact that women experience things differently than men, heterosexuals differently than homosexuals etc. and I am not claiming to cover all aspects.

[3] The term "strivings" is preferred here to the term "drive" because of its strong connection with psychoanalytical and biological theories.

[4] Creativity and PCA: v. Schmid, 1994; Schmid & Wascher, 1994.

[5] "Personal encounter": v. Schmid, 1989c; 1991; 1994.

[6] The body in PCA: v. Schmid, 1994.

[7] A person's freedom to live certain ways of sexuality of course always has its limit where another person's freedom to choose or to develop his sexuality is not respected.

[8] Admittedly lust is not the only term with which congruence in the sexual sense can be described: also *loyalty* to oneself and to others ("To thine own self be true, thou canst not then be false to any man" Shakespeare, Hamlet) is a dimension of what genuineness and truthfulness mean — even if "loyalty" may be an unusual word in the person–centered context.

[9] Here it can also become clear that sexuality and spirituality are not mutually exclusive particularly from a person–centered point of view (e. g. cf. Emmermann, 1991).

Embarrassment Anxiety: A Literalist Theory

JOHN M. SHLIEN

CAMBRIDGE, MASSACHUSETTS

Most theories of therapy contain a theory of anxiety; sometimes two or more.

It might be as simple as incongruence between self and ideal. Or it might be as exotic and dramatic as the "Oedipal complex". My effort here is to provide a theory of anxiety in keeping with my own "literalist" position, "experiential" in keeping with the title of the conference, and as a contribution to our understanding of the fundamental things in life..

I have already subscribed to the view that all theories are autobiographical, and can vouch for the validity of this theory. It may not apply to everyone.; some because they are so noble, others because they are so ignoble. We might learn from either of those extremes how to avoid or conquer this anxiety. What recommends the theory besides its validity is that it is literal,– not abstract, mythological, literary, or metaphorical. Perhaps that takes much of the fun out of it. But anxiety is not for fun,– it is misery, and those who coat it with the amusement of clever symbolic analysis are probably putting a layer of defense between themselves and the real pain of the experience. The experience of which I have in mind is Embarrassment.

People speak of "anxiety attacks" – described as "massive and terrible". I would simply call anxiety, "That which cripples". As examples of the characteristic theories, here are some of the more famous ones. "Separation anxiety" is my literary favorite, developed by Otto Rank. As you know, it relates to the concept of the "birth trauma", that shock of being rudely ejected from the pleasant homeostasis of the womb. That is a fascinating but inferential theory, abstract and metaphorical. Separation anxiety could have more literal origins; disorientation, loneliness, ambivalence about growth, without reference to birth trauma . These are experiences that can happen at any time, any age, for any observable cause. And these are real, quite real. There really IS, for instance, ambivalence about growth. We talk of growth as glorious development , a motive we only admire and enjoy, but in fact, learning to walk has many bumps and falls, is painful. Luckily, the rewards of independent mobility more than offset the pain. But then, each step in growth has in it the potential consciousness of death,– not generally contemplated with pleasure. So separation has ominous overtones without resort to the struggle to be born. And children who are lost have very good reason to feel anxious without ANY previous referent. Of course, parents who have lost their children are also anxious, sometimes more so than the children. Everyone lost may feel scared, and everyone has been born, but one is scared because one is lost, not because one was born. It was actually for another reason that separation anxiety was linked to "birth trauma". That has more to do with the psycho–genetic outlook of early psychoanalysis. "Find the origin" was the motif. On that scale, *in utero* is hard to beat; Rank won, and thereby disgruntled his mentor, Freud.

For Freud had already proposed "the" basic anxiety, fear of castration. That comes after the child (son) is born and in is in competition with father for mother.. This might be a metaphor for a power struggle within the family,– otherwise, it excludes the female gender. That would be inappropriate, since the majority of early patients were women. But then the formulators of theory were men— some of whom later reasoned that the vagina was a symbolic wound, in the service of penis envy. Fascinating as all this may be, attractive, arcane, I consider such concepts as a form of "packaging". Packaging does work. It does attract, may even convince, whether or not it contains the truth.

Here now is another, more literal theory of anxiety (that which cripples), with no packaging. It is a major anxiety, traumatic in the instant of its experience, at any age, and with long remaining consequences of fear that it might be re–experienced. Anxiety, "massive and terrible", is the result of Embarrassment. More accurately, Fear of embarrassment. Perhaps eventually, fear of that fear.

At first, embarrassment may sound slight, a small thing, temporary. It is no small thing. Not exotic, not glamorous, you will not see it in any diagnostic manual, but not small. Perhaps you will remember more about it when you hear the reported experience of other people.

a) For instance, there is a "phobia" called Fear of Flying. Not a joke to those who suffer from it. They are quite inconvenienced, sometimes disabled by it. Work with such sufferers indicates that it is not so much a fear of sitting in a plane from one point to another. People can grit their teeth, grip the arms of the seat, close the eyes, , etc., and complete the trip. What stops them is fear of Embarrassment at being SEEN trembling, sweating, – being perceived as cowardly, foolish, perhaps being ridiculed, laughed at.

So, in "support groups", they take a section of seats in a plane, sit together, have a bearable, even humorous time, and increasingly overcome the disability. They are not impressed nor are they helped by interpretations of the body of the airplane as a womb, or of flying as a sexual metaphor. But if they can look each other in the eye, look at themselves in a mirror, be relieved of the dreadful embarrassment and ridicule they fear, they can, for the moment and in principle conquer the fear of flying.

b) Fear of embarrassment is a major factor in most reports of being "blackmailed". Why else would victims pay so dearly for matters often of relatively little consequence?

c) In a large newspaper poll, people said they would "rather have a root canal than purchase a car". Why? Because it was such an embarrassment to haggle over the price, especially with someone who knew all the facts and felt no such uneasiness. (Incidentally, since buying a car has long been a special anxiety for Americans, one psychologist who interviewed Carl Rogers thought it would be a telling and testing question to ask him, "What if you were buying a car,– would you be person centered, or, how would you be?" (Rogers' answer;–"Shrewd")

d) More surprising, it is reported in the Book of Records, and quoted by the New Yorker Magazine, that the fear ranked as the most dreadful by Americans is not death, not not fear of mutilation, not fear of divorce. These are three of the four worst fears. The number one rank by far, is,– fear of public speaking.

e) All fears are serious to the sufferer, but here are some which we cannot fail to recognize as very serious indeed. Frequently, women do not report rape or other sexual abuse. For the majority, the reason given is their fear of embarrassment. There is international testimony to this fact.

f) Similarly, incest, physical abuse, alcohol and drug addiction, is often suppressed by families for fear of embarrassment.

g) Expert beggars in the New York subways, when interviewed, said that eye contact was the most effective factor, because only then could they make the fear of embarrassment work for them.

h) Most shocking to me was the confession of a Viet Nam veteran, who said that he was "too embarrassed not to kill"! He had been with other soldiers who destroyed a village. He was afraid that if he did not join in the murder, they would laugh at him,feel scorn for him.. Terrible, is it not, to murder because you fear being embarrassed if you do not follow the crowd? That tendency is common to all sorts of teen age male exploits. It is not just fear of embarrassment, but of ridicule,which is a form of punishment well known.

Teachers use a dunce cap on children, and Mao's Red Guards used the same device to torment their teachers.

i) How bad is this fear? People sometimes say, " I could have died of embarrassment". Some actually do! A restaurant owner has reported two cases in which a patron (female) was choking on food. The Heimlich maneuver was used, and after it had partially succeeded, the woman ran into the restroom, because she had vomited on her dress) and there, behind the locked door, suffocated to death. A second case was reported at a garden party.

j) A man who had claimed to be a good swimmer and sailor took small sailboat out on the sea in a high wind. He could not control the boat,– it capsized, and he was rescued, unconscious, from the water. Why had he not signaled for help from a nearby boat? He told his therapist that he was too embarrassed to admit that he had lied about his ability.

k) A well known literary celebrity was depressed, and about to commit suicide. He remembered some pornographic photos in his safe deposit box Where he also kept his will). When he thought of the embarrassment it would cause, he postponed his suicide, sailed back to New York from Europe to hide the photos, and by the time he arrived there had changed his mind. In this case, fear of embarrassment saved his life. In others, it has caused death.

These are a fraction of the incidents that could be presented. If they are enough to remind you of the experience, you can reflect upon your own observations. Some say that this anxiety is a disease of adolescents. Others say that there is a new generation immune to embarrassment. It is true that many topics and behaviors once shunned are now commonplace. TV talk shows in America and Europe present discussions and displays of every kind of oddity and perversion. Some young people, at an age we think typically most sensitive about appearance, wear spiked purple hair, safety pin through the nose, carry a nipple pacifier to school.pendant around the neck. I think that in place of courage, they use defiance. One young man said to me, "No one can ridicule us more than we do ourselves, – that makes us safe, and scares you."

 Perhaps the Fear of Embarrassment can be outgrown. I do not know. It would be wonderful to see some serious studies of the Phenomenology of Embarrassment.. Part of the difficulty in such study is that the experience begs or demands not to be observed. It wants above all to hide. One of our colleagues, Regina Stamitiades wrote, "To be embarrassed is one thing, – and being seen to be embarrassed is another. The second is worse, or the worst! I truly believe that a person may prefer to die, (but can't) especially when being embarrassed means being ashamed of oneself."

Shame, it seems to me, is closely related, but may be equally powerful in isolation, while embarrassment is more likely to be a public event. Embarrassment is an intensely immediate experience. It is a feeling of being excruciatingly alive and wishing one were not. Of being intensely present, and wanting to be anywhere else. There is no escape. Time stops! One is frozen in place, stiff, paralyzed, exposed with a sense of naked vulnerability, unwanted intimacy, transparency. To the witness(es) the victim says in a silent shriek, "Don't look". To which the witness, feeling either pain or glee, may feel drawn in to the experience. In either case, there is a reverberation of embarrassment. Neither sufferer or witness is in a good condition to analyze or report.

Let me mention now some instances in the history of psychotherapy in which fear of embarrassment has played a role, influencing contemporary ideas and practices . First, you may remember that Freud confidently used hypnosis, until, one day, a maid servant entered the room as a woman patient coming out of a trance threw her arms around his neck Shortly thereafter, he dropped the technique of hypnosis, saying that it was superficial, and that his was "not the role of the cosmetician but of the surgeon." I believe that embarrassment was a factor in his decision.

This was at a time when angry husbands were already voicing jealous suspicions about psychoanalysis and the stolen affections of their wives. And it is worth noting that Freud once said, "There is an incomparable fascination in a woman of high principles who confesses her passion". That seems to me an astonishing confession and self indictment on Freud's part, but true. It was and still is the case that a therapist often meets such ladies, frequently above his own social and moral status, and only in the avenue of his practice. That same fascination, and the embarrassment about it, still exists.

And also, there was the famous case of Breuer and Fr. "Anna O", a young woman he treated in a most caring way, using hypnosis and cathartic methods, sometimes feeding her, sometimes taking her for rides in his carriage. At a critical point, as he was thinking her treatment should end, he received an urgent call from her mother, and found his patient "writhing in the throes of an hysterical psuedo–pregnancy". He quickly fled from the house, in a cold sweat, (leaving his umbrella, Ernest Jones does not fail to mention) and left the city the next day for a trip to Italy with his wife. It was the beginning of his separation from Freud, who was barely able to persuade Breuer to join in the writing of the "Studies in Hysteria" that came from their work together. Is it not clear that embarrassment played a part in these events? Remember the fact that both Freud and Breuer were Jewish physicians needing to guard their hard won reputations in an already somewhat anti–semitic Vienna. Later, when Freud "discovered" transference (invented would be a better word) he wanted to explain to Breuer this meaning of the embarrassing incident, but for Breuer, the relief came too late. He did not continue in the business of psychoanalysis.

And what about Carl Rogers? For one obvious example from his life, again take the matter of technique. At an early point, he developed a method of response called "reflection" (of feeling, more than of content). It was an enormous aid to the practice of client–centered therapy.[1] Made it teachable and learnable. And do not underestimate the importance of technique in this regard .Beginning therapists are certainly looking for methods of practice. They want to know, "what do I do, how do I do it?" Methods precede and implement philosophy as means precede ends. In fact, means are ends, at earlier levels, and sometimes the means are the only expression of the ends the clients ever know. Rogers and others of his colleagues refined and promoted this method in much the same way as the psychoanalysts promoted interpretation. Sometime later, he became unwilling to be identified with the method he said had become "a wooden mockery". Still later, he asserted, "I do not reflect"! This was not entirely true. In the first place, shortly after this published assertion, he did a private study of some of his recent interviews, and found that about 75% qualified as "reflections". In the second place, what he meant by his assertion was that he "checked his understandings" as an alternative to and/or refinement of "reflection". Did embarrassment play a part in his statement, "I do not reflect"? You have probably read, or heard him say, he "winced",—it made him "cringe" to be identified with such a technique. This is an expression of embarrassment, painful embarrassment. What happened? Here is my version.

At Wisconsin, Rogers hoped that the project with "schizophrenics" would be his greatest test and crowning glory. Instead, it became a failure, and a source of personal anguish as well. Why the failure? For one reason, and a very large factor it was, that staff was not prepared to provide client centered therapy that was adequate to test the hypotheses. As Rogers later wrote of "flaws that were nearly fatal" , "...I did not take the time to develop a staff that was unified in philosophy and outlook...". That puts it mildly. They were not trained and not committed. It was a staff torn with personal and political as well as philosophical disagreement, and laced with desperate innovations in practice. I must say here, in the most serious way, that it did damage to client centered therapy, damage from which we have never recovered. Nor do I see the wisdom of allowing that failure be the basis for prescriptions of our techniques! But to return this to the topic of embarrassment: There were on that staff two younger men of talent and ambition, on whom Rogers pinned some of his best hopes; Gendlin and Truax.

What did they make of "reflection"? (You must understand,– they were both bitterly angry at Rogers and at each other). After Wisconsin, one, Gendlin, calls reflection, "the method of saying back'. The other, Truax, employed reflection as part of a "skill training' program, just the kind of technical emphasis that Rogers hoped to avoid. What a disappointment. Trivializing by one friend, technologizing by the other. This, after a lifetime of scorn by enemies who ridiculed his method as "parroting". Even though he knew that the technique itself can be raised to the level of a refined art, as well as lowered to a "wooden mockery", he was tired of defending, tired of being type-cast and thus seemed to abandon a mainstay of his method. In so doing, he contributed to the loss of discipline and definition, and to the "anything goes–as long as it is congruent' condition we have now.

In this, I see a sad disillusionment, and a sort of detachment from the public effort of leading a school of thought. In a letter written January 2, 1987 he said, "I have come to feel that good therapists are few and far between".

That comes from a man who at one time hoped to see widespread applications of this form of counseling and psychotherapy. In the end, he wanted no more to be a model for others, nor to be called upon for approval or endorsement of the ideas of others,– only to do what he wanted, in his own way. Finally, he came to rely on what he called his "presence", a healing, "almost another condition", but not one he could call upon at will, much less model for for imitation by others.

There you have it.

I have tried to suggest another theory of anxiety: experiential, not metaphoric; directly observable, not inferential; literal, dynamic, contemporary, not psycho–genetic; so traumatic that people say they would rather face mutilation or death; – and with lasting effects.

It is also the case that some of our leading theoreticians changed their methods and careers because of personal interactions that caused them embarrassment. They, and we, do not live or work in a sanitary laboratory of ideas, but in an atmosphere of personal interactions. Some of these interactions involve this commonplace but powerful experience we call "embarrassment". It is not such a small thing. It can cripple, kill, and change the history of ideas.

The study of this subject awaits your attention. The data is near by.It is a kind of "psychopathology of everyday life" without the cleverness of the sly jokes, slips of the tongue, and the magic paraphanalia of the "unconscious".

It does not carry any prescription for treatment, but it should advance our understanding of the human condition, or it will have missed its mark.Even in that case, it would at least be a model for the kind of theory I believe the world needs,– literal and true to life.

Embarrassment, the experience and the fear of it, may be a major factor in the lives of your clients. Study of it is difficult, but can be accomplished if we will have the courage, and the "openness to experience", to NOT do what embarrassment asks us to do : –Avert our eyes; Pretend that is does not matter, is not happening. As we are so inclined to do, partly because of this very embarrassment.

---

[i] Surprisingly, there is still some loyalty to the method. P. Pentony writes in an article just published (The Person Centered Journal, v.1, Issue 3, 1994) "The discovery and development of this response was a major technical innovation in psychotherapy. If he had done nothing else, Carl Rogers would deserve to be remembered for this contribution".

Person–Centred Therapy : The Path to Holiness

BRIAN THORNE

UNIVERSITY OF EAST ANGLIA, ENGLAND

ABSTRACT

The writer explores his early experience and then reflects on twenty–five years of professional life as a person–centred therapist. He perceives himself as a 'boundary' person and relates this to the ultimate challenges in the therapeutic enterprise. The risk–taking involved in moving into unknown terrain with a client is likened to a spiritual journey and the writer then struggles to find appropriate language to make sense of the totality of his experience. The search for wholeness and the yearning for holiness are seen as synonymous and, unlike Carl Rogers, the writer explicitly defines person centred therapy as a spiritual discipline with its roots firmly in the Western, Christian tradition and the Trinitarian doctrine of God as relationship.

PERSON–CENTRED THERAPY: THE PATH TO HOLINESS

Some years ago I was invited to contribute to a book entitled *"On Becoming a Psychotherapist"* and I underwent the discipline of subjecting my life to rigorous scrutiny in order to elucidate why and how and when I had become a therapist. It was a task which, because of publishers' deadlines, I had to accomplish very rapidly and, looking back on it, I am faintly amazed by what was unearthed during that time of concentrated self–exploration. In the first place, I realized that almost from the moment of conception I had known the proximity of death. My mother suffered from a heart condition and giving birth to me almost resulted in her own death. I was her only child and when I entered the world I was a sickly, jaundiced and premature creature whose survival was by no means certain. Secondly, I came to see how deeply significant it was that I grew up during the Second World War. I was two and a half when war broke out with Nazi Germany and my childhood was spent with the whine of air–raid sirens constantly in my ears and with the nightly possibility of being exterminated by one of Hitler's bombs. On one occasion my mother and I missed a bus on a summer's afternoon only to learn later that, within ten minutes, the vehicle had been destroyed in a freak air attack. Many of my contemporaries had fathers serving in the Forces and not all of them returned to continue their paternal role. My days at primary school were punctuated by frequent visits to the large, dark air–raid shelters in the playground where I learned to entertain myself and others by telling long, rambling stories about little boys and girls who somehow survived adventures of unimaginable complexity. Thirdly, I remembered the agony and the ecstasy of being naturally empathic. There was no choice in the matter, as I recall it. It was simply the case that I sensed what was going on in other people's minds and hearts and had to live with that knowledge. I still have a vivid memory of a teacher in my infants school who was mercilessly tormented by a class of over sixty children and whose suffering I shared imaginatively without having any power to alleviate it. She put her head in a gas oven one Saturday morning and I have never forgotten her.

These early experiences clearly affected me profoundly and as I reflect upon them I realise that they marked me at the outset as a boundary person. I became accustomed to moving between worlds, to traversing continually the gap between my own inner reality and that of others: most importantly, perhaps, I learned what it meant to be alone and yet not alone. As an only child who was constantly invited into the homes of others I knew the paradox of belonging and yet not belonging. Above all, however, there came the familiarity with the no man's land between life and death – the recognition of the permeability and fragility of existence. When I was eleven my grandfather and my uncle (his son) both died within three weeks of each other and, although I was grief–stricken, I was somehow prepared for the experience and saw it as part of the natural order of things. This, I am sure, was not unconnected to a mystical experience which I had on Good Friday 1946 when I was unexpectedly plunged into a deep apprehension of the Passion and Crucifixion of Christ and was overwhelmed by uncontrollable grief which eventually gave way to a sense of peace and serenity. In short, before my childhood was over, I knew that life and death are not in opposition but belong to a greater unity and that to stand at the boundary between them is to be open to the world of spirit.

In a sense I have never left this particular boundary country throughout my twenty–five years as a therapist. It seems to me that at any moment of the day or night a therapist may find himself or herself wrestling with the other's fear of death or, more devastatingly perhaps, with the allurement of death. Clients so often come to therapists because they are no longer sure that they can face life or that they can cope with death. They experience the utter loneliness of the boundary position and do not know where to turn. The therapist who is familiar with the terrain and who is safe in the knowledge of his or her own nature can be a loyal companion to the client who is stranded between life and death. For me, accompanying, being a companion to, coming alongside, are of the essence of the therapeutic task and yet in order to fulfil such a demanding function the therapist needs to combat fear. The boundary between life and death is no place for the faint–hearted: it demands courage which even the most conscientious companion cannot simulate. I am glad that I grew up in a world where it was commonplace to find courage on that boundary although I remain infinitely sad that a war was apparently needed to bring that about. There must be better ways of equipping us as a species to cope with our mortality and our immortality.

Another of my early memories concerns women – or, more accurately, little girls. At junior school I had a devoted following. In some ways it was rather embarrassing, in others utterly delightful because it consisted entirely of girls. I can remember them now: Marilyn, Sylvia, Mary, Jennifer, Judith and Catherine. They would walk home with me and see me to the back garden gate. I don't remember much of what we talked about but I do recall the sense of being cherished and liked. With the passage of time the following diminished and by the age of nine or ten I was spending all my time with the boys and was totally caught up in cricket and football. For the next fifteen years I lived in an almost completely male environment – public school, army, ancient university and then back to public school as a teacher of languages. For some time I wondered about my sexuality and was much attracted to writers of homosexual orientation. Looking back on it all, I believe now that I experienced what it meant to live on the boundary of the male and the female within my own personality. The study of language and literature greatly aided this particular boundary living for such study demands a willingness to enter into the most profound areas of human experience and to savour language at its most richly expressive – that is to say, language which attempts to do full justice to the whole range of male and female sensitivity and vulnerability. As a therapist I continue to live at this boundary and it is not without its risks. Many men regard male counsellors, for example, with great suspicion. They see them either as doing women's work or as seducers who wish to ensnare women in forced intimacy. Some women, too, avoid male therapists like the plague because they cannot believe in their trustworthiness. And yet to flee from this boundary area is to close oneself to that complexity of feeling, reason, intuition and sensation which so often constitutes the confusing terrain where clients risk losing themselves but also have the opportunity of discovering the nature of their own unique identities. I have come to love the male and the female in myself and increasingly value the boundary territory where the two converse with each other with serenity. Such converse remains vital, I know, if I am to continue to respond particularly to those many women in our society whom our culture threatens to condemn to half a life, to half an identity, to an existence so threaded through with the pernicious strands of patriarchy that there is little chance of fulfilment or of the realisation of the self. Living at the boundary of maleness and femaleness becomes a responsibility for any therapist who sees himself or herself as providing a sanctuary from the ravages of a culture and a society which clings to stereotypes as if they were bulwarks against disintegration.

The therapist regards the society of which he or she is a member with circumspection. In some ways I have, I know, cultivated for myself a boundary position in this respect, too. The ability to belong and yet not to belong has been essential in this strange endeavour. Again, it is not, I believe, a stance which can be simulated. I work for the most part in a university, I remain a member of the established Church, I wear ties and I genuinely enjoy dinner parties and the ritual of formal occasions. And yet at the same time in my heart I know that none of these things are of ultimate importance. If for one moment I was to give my total allegiance to an institution, to the form of things, to structures however hallowed by time and tradition, then I would no longer be free to meet the other where he or she is. What is more I should have given up on the possibility of development for myself. I find this thought particularly frightening because with the passage of the years I know more than a little the attraction of the status quo. Institutions, despite their frustrations and often bureaucratic processes, offer security, a modicum of status and, most importantly, a regular salary. Such advantages are not easily renounced and they can be insidiously blocking. Perhaps in many professions this would not matter overmuch but for the counsellor there is something disquieting about the possibility of being stuck in one's own life when the whole object of a counselling process is to enable the client to move out of a trap or to take the risk of moving forward into unknown terrain. I must confess that these thoughts sometimes perturb me in the night when I am feeling particularly exhausted or when hope seems at a low ebb. How can it be, I ask myself, that a person who is committed to movement, to accompanying individuals on unpredictable journeys has remained in the same institution for nearly twenty years and is still a regular worshipper in the church of his baptism? The boundary position, however, is not necessarily vitiated by institutional membership or, for that matter guaranteed by non–allegiance. It is more about an attitude of mind and the willingness to remain true to that whatever the institutional or societal context. As I think back over the years, or consider the present time for that matter, I am aware that continuing to occupy the boundary place where the individual's uniqueness matters more than the institution's or society's demands is no easy task and often brings with it a heavy cost. I count myself fortunate that I work in a place where individuals still matter, despite the unrelenting government and economic pressures to reduce us all to statistics, but I know only too well that the cost in terms of personal energy and commitment for me as for most university counsellors at this time is often well–nigh intolerable. Remaining in an institution has not, I believe, resulted, for me, in the abandoning of the boundary position but has in many ways accentuated that position and heightened its cost. Indeed, there is a sense in which universities themselves are facing a crisis of identity. It is clear that government and some sections of society do not want them any longer as they have been and are demanding continual reforms and changes which will make them little more than increasingly privatised production lines for the brave new world. If that gloomy prophecy has more than a glimmer of truth about it then it may soon be the case that not only university counsellors but whole institutions will find themselves in the boundary position fighting for their very right to continue their existence as autonomous institutions in a so-called democratic society. Seen in this light it may be that my lengthy period in this same university is more excusable. When an institution itself is in a state of flux and transition it is less easy to fall victim to the psychological complacency and inertia which more easily descend in reasonably settled times.

I suppose much the same could be said about my membership of the Church but here, I believe, the issues are more complex and more profound. I do not sense that I have in any way chosen to move to this boundary zone of institutional allegiance let alone to the apparent margins of orthodox belief. On the contrary I recall nostalgically the time when faith seemed relatively uncomplicated and when I could experience the warmth and security of the liturgy and the gentle embrace of the church community. I have been jolted out of this comfortable ambience by a number of factors which are in many ways a direct outcome of my work as a therapist. It has been a source of pain for me over many years to encounter, either as clients or as acquaintances, many people who have suffered unspeakably at the hands of organised religion. They have been made to feel wicked, guilty and, most terrifying of all, utterly unloveable. Such feelings have often been engendered by the imposition of judgemental and dogmatic beliefs in the name of a loving God who laid down his life that others might live. The damage wrought on individuals by such practices is often incalculable especially when the people involved are already vulnerable and have been much undermined by life's experiences. Sadly the perpetrators of such psychological violence – and representatives of other faiths and philosophies as well as Christianity must be included – rarely recognise the devastation caused by their behaviour and attitudes, but as a counsellor I am only too familiar with the often long-standing pain of those who have suffered at their hands. It is this repeated experience of accompanying the casualties of punitive religion that has forced me to re-assess the interpretation of much Christian doctrine and the impact of certain traditional practices. In some ways this has been a rewarding experience for not infrequently I have discovered beneath the powerful dominance of fall and redemption theology, with its emphasis on original sin, human wickedness and the need for self-negation, another stream of belief which affirms the unremitting and unconditional love of God for humanity and the whole of creation and the potential divinisation of humankind. The God whom I meet in this tradition is the infinitely compassionate mother and father and lover of Julian of Norwich's revelations, the joyful, paradoxical, almost teasing, God of Meister Eckhart, the source and goal of Teilhard de Chardin's evolutionary order, the life-giving, infinitely nurturing God of Matthew Fox's creation theology. This is a neglected orthodoxy which lies below the surface of so much that passes for the Christian message and which turns on its head the guilt-inducing worm theology which engenders a fear of God's condemnation and rejection rather than an awareness of his unshakeable and unchanging love for the noblest beings of his creation which we are.

Neglected orthodoxy as it might be, however, I have discovered that to hold to such ideas is to be forced to another boundary and to be regarded by some as a threat and a danger within the Church community. And yet my experience both in my own life and in the sharing of the struggles which many of my clients endure leaves me with no option. There is something about being a therapist – at least in the tradition which I have chosen – which in the end leaves no possible escape from honesty and no remaining bolt-holt for the sophisticated practice of self-deception. In some ways this is a sure recipe for metaphorical martyrdom because most of us most of the time are not over–keen to look too closely at our underlying assumptions especially when these are an integral part of a belief structure or value system which has informed our living for some time. It is for this reason that both churches and schools of therapy, too, find it hard to tolerate those individuals who dare to trust their own experience and judgement and as a result cast doubt upon the received wisdom whether of a theological or psychological nature. For the individual himself or herself the struggle to be honest – or, to use the jargon of person–centred therapy, the resolve to be congruent – is fraught with danger. Not only is there the well–nigh certainty of adverse judgement from others but, more devastating still, there is the inevitable agony of self doubt, the fear of folie de grandeur, the self–accusation of arrogance. At times I have felt the full force of these internal conflicts, often inflamed by hostile external forces, and the temptation to recant, to step back into line whether theologically or psychologically has been irresistible. I simply could not bear the pain and readily excused my cowardice on the grounds that masochism is a neurosis or, better still, that humility is a virtue.

Interestingly enough the theological struggle has become easier in recent times. Since the publication of my little book *"Behold the Man"* in 1991 I have had the immense consolation of receiving many letters and not a few invitations from those who are also clearly struggling in boundary territory. For me it has been particularly revealing to discover that many such people are members of religious orders. They have already committed their lives to God and often to a way of contemplation and yet it is precisely they who find themselves at odds with much that has characterised church attitudes and practice in the past. In some of my most despairing moments, when I have felt myself to be on the very edge of the "household of faith", I have drawn the greatest comfort from the shared perceptions of contemplative monks and nuns who have written sometimes from a distance of many thousand of miles, because they have found in the pages of *"Behold the Man"* a fellow pilgrim in the boundary country.

Counselling and psychotherapy are essentially about relationships, however much some practitioners would like to believe they are about developing insight, changing behaviour or alleviating mental distress. They can, of course, be about all these things and often are but at the heart of the enterprise is the relationship – or lack of it – between the counsellor and the client. It is here, I believe, that the preparedness to live at the boundary has led me into the most astonishing and, at times, the most frightening terrain. It is also, of course, the area of greatest professional vulnerability and at the same time the place where the most audacious advances can be made in the therapeutic endeavour. For me, every new counselling relationship marks the beginning of an unpredictable adventure. There can be no certainty about where I am to travel with my client or of the nature of the companionship which he or she will require. Mercifully most clients are modest enough in their needs. They want a compassionate, listening and understanding ear, a warmth without sentimentality, a willingness on the part of the counsellor not to simulate, a preparedness to be faithful in the accompaniment and not to abandon. But every so often – and for me in recent years it has become disconcertingly often – there comes the person whose journey, if it is to be embarked upon, requires a companion who is more intrepid and willing to venture into the unknown where there are few reassuring reference points and no clear destination. The suicidal, the abused, those who have never bonded, those aggressed in the womb are but a few of the persons who have challenged me to go with them to the extreme limit of the relationship boundary. En route we may visit many of the other boundary zones which I have already described: we may hover for a while between life and death, the male and the female struggle for synthesis, society is berated or embraced, concepts of God are put on trial – but there comes the time when what ultimately matters is how we can be with each other for it is our relationship which will carry or extinguish the hope. As so often in this extraordinary profession, I wish it were otherwise. I don't want to be *that* significant for another person for I know that I cannot finally give meaning to another's existence. I don't want the burden of carrying hope: I don't want the task of relating at this depth; I don't want to be loved – and hated – so blindly or so passionately; I cannot bear the sense of combined responsibility and powerlessness. Inside, I am protesting: "I am not God. I am not ultimate reality. I cannot love you into life."

I sense that to some therapists from other traditions this may sound like pretentious nonsense or a kind of mystical hysteria. There are times when I envy – mistakenly, I suspect – the safety of psychodynamic mythology and the defensive ramparts of the transference or the clarity of the business–like contractual systems of cognitive–behavioural therapy. I fantasise about a vast repertoire of skills and techniques or an infallible map of the unconscious leading to a guaranteed programme for recovery. I long to possess the internalised manual of the self–confident expert. But my tradition offers me nothing of this order to protect my vulnerability, nothing behind which to conceal my ineptitude. Instead it invites me to accept unconditionally, to enter empathically into the other's world, to be true to myself. It is scarcely surprising that such invitations, if they are accepted with integrity, sometimes lead unpredictably and unexpectedly, to the heart of the I–thou mystery, reverence before which must ultimately determine whether the human race will come into its glory or cease to exist.

What does all that mean when we get down to brass tacks? For me it has meant going to the very edge of trust in some of my therapeutic relationships. It has involved facing the implications of believing that we have it within us to become the people we are uniquely equipped to be if only we can offer each other the conditions for such becoming. Such trusting, difficult at any time, is increasingly hazardous in the present climate of our society. Violence is all around us; the abuse of human–beings both of themselves and of each other has reached epidemic proportions; government policies encourage us to trust no one, to be in permanent competition, to evaluate, appraise and assess everyone and everything, to assume incompetence and corruption everywhere. The core conditions of the person–centred approach have seldom seemed so naive, so counter–cultural, so open to derision and contempt. It is in such a climate that I am challenged to trust my own integrity and that of my client, to believe in the universal yearning for wholeness, to risk failure, to run the danger of being seen as the fool who drowned in the deep waters of intimacy because he was mad enough to trust that he and his companion would somehow reach dry land.

This is the boundary country which reveals starkly that for me these last twenty–five years have been the working out of a way of life and that much of that work has taken place behind a closed door with an engaged notice firmly upon it. There are times when that makes me feel guilty, almost furtive. It has made me doubly conscious, too, of the privilege of having a family and colleagues who have permitted me to engage in such work without apparent distrust and with only occasional jealousy. On the contrary, I have received only support, encouragement and infinite patience. I am not blind, however, to the cost which has been involved for those who are close to me at home and in my work settings. I shall never fully know what my family has suffered by having to share a husband and father with hundreds of unknown others and to endure the knowledge of countless unspoken intimacies; nor shall I ever really know what it is like for my colleagues to work alongside someone who must seem at times to be the worst of all addicts – a workaholic in an apparently virtuous cause. All I do know is that I am eternally grateful and in need of constant forgiveness for taking so much for granted. Behind the closed door I have struggled with my clients for the gift of self–transcendence both for them and for me and that perhaps is to cross the boundary which lies beyond all boundaries. It is also a gift which nobody can win for himself or herself unaided. Self–transcendence is the outcome of a relationship where we are enabled to do better than our best and to be greater than ourselves through the energy of another's love. In a sense, therefore, the gift of self–transcendence can only come when there is a recognition between two people or between a group of persons that we are essentially members one of another and need each other for our completion.

Perhaps the cynic will conclude that I have now finally blown my cover and admitted clearly and in public that I need my clients as much as they need me. In a sense that is true but the subject is so profound that I may perhaps be permitted a brief parenthesis even at so late a stage in this paper. In some ways the need that a therapist has for his or her clients is self–evident. If there were no clients there would be no therapists and no work to be done. What is more, if there were no clients there would be no money for the freelance therapist to earn and no funded services for institutional counsellors to staff. In brief, I need my clients because without them I would have no function and no money. I could, however, ply another trade and thus find a new function and another way of earning a living. The need of which I was speaking above, however, is of a different order. Perhaps the client needs me because he or she is in great pain and cannot bear the pain alone. I do not need him or her in the same way for I know that my distress, even supposing it is sometimes acute, will not be relieved by someone who is, in all probability, out of touch with his or her own inner resourcefulness. If I seek to have my own wounds healed by my client I shall not only be guilty of professional irresponsibility but I am also singularly foolish. And yet I know that at the most profound level there is no way in which I am superior to my client. I share with him or her the human condition and fundamentally am subject to the same agony and to the same yearnings. In this sense, then, there is no power inequality, no difference of status between us. I sometimes feel that it is only the person–centred tradition which fully acknowledges this essential truth and as a result sees the establishment of a felt intimacy and ultimately of a felt mutuality between counsellor and client as the experiential enactment of an existential reality. To put it another way – you and I belong to each other whatever our present feelings about ourselves and each other may be. Once we begin to experience our shared inheritance at the deepest level we no longer need to be afraid of each other's strangeness but can instead relax into each other's presence and be nourished by the mutual exchange. In this sense, then, I need my clients – as indeed I need all those who enter my life – for they are the means through which I become more fully myself by transcending myself. It is thanks to them that I can break out of the prison of my own fears and self preoccupation and join the human family.

As I say these things, I realize that I have reached the point in my professional life where I am compelled to make coherent and inclusive sense of my experience. I can no longer refuse to face the implications of my daily activity. To be a person–centred therapist, I discover, is to run the risk of becoming fully human and never more so it seems, than when, in order to enter into relationship with my client, I have to move into no–man's land. I do so, however, fortified by the belief that there can be no wholeness without the other. To be a person is by definition to be in relationship and the call to wholeness often demands a venturing into terrain where meeting is only possible at or beyond the boundaries of the known. Let me put it another way by drawing on the context which is familiar to every therapist. I am face to face with the mystery of the other who sits in the chair opposite me. She is withdrawn from me and afraid, locked into an inner world of anxiety and confusion and surrounded, for all I know, by unfriendly and uncomprehending forces without. How can I hope to meet her, barricaded in as she is by her many fears and memories and by a pervasive distrust? In the first place, I must believe that if we can meet we shall both be the richer for our meeting. This requires in me a paradoxical mixture of humility and self–affirmation. I need to recognize myself as both a source of richness and as lacking in completeness. At one and the same time I acknowledge that I am wholesome and not yet whole. This may not sound a particularly revolutionary statement but, in practice, I have discovered that it is not a common stance among therapists. All too often there is the basic assumption that the therapist has knowledge and expertise which in some way or other will be dispensed to the client or patient. There is seldom the genuine expectation that the therapist will be made more whole by the encounter and will therefore be changed by it.

Secondly, if I am to meet the frightened and mysterious other I must be able to dispel her fear of me and face my fear of her. Again, I do not find it common for therapists to speak openly of their fear of their clients. We read much of the client learning to trust the therapist, but far less of the therapist learning to trust the client. Thirdly, I must be prepared to wait in hope and such hope will not be possible for me if I do not willingly embrace a process in the expectation of a future to be welcomed.

This, then, is my attempt to describe my professional life as I experience it at those times when it pushes me to my limits. And yet I am forced to acknowledge that such a description would sit awkwardly in the pages of a conventional text–book on counselling psychology or the psychotherapeutic relationship. It would, I sense, be embarrassingly inappropriate. It is this very inappropriateness, however, that needs to be explored if I am to continue my work with integrity. Interestingly it is a challenge which Carl Rogers himself failed to meet in the last months of his own life. During that time he was engaged with Ruth Sanford on a re–statement of the person–centred approach to therapy which was subsequently published posthumously in a major psychiatric text–book. What I find interesting – and, I must confess, disappointing – is that there is no mention in this reformulation of the very issues with which Rogers had been most passionately and often uncomfortably involved in the final period of his life. Since the death of his wife, Helen, he had with characteristic courage and openness faced the mystery of death, entered wholeheartedly into the agonizing conflicts of the world and, most significantly, discovered new dimensions of relating in therapy to which, almost shame–facedly in view of his earlier position as the psychological scientist, he attributed such adjectives as `mystical', `transpersonal' and `transcendental'. Little or none of this later experience finds its way into the post–humous article for the psychiatric manual and it is difficult to avoid the conclusion that either Rogers himself drew back from including such material or the editors persuaded him and his co–author to avoid risking their reputations in the eyes of the psychological and medical establishment.

I have no such reputation to lose and yet, I, too, find it difficult to state clearly and unequivocally what I can no longer with integrity deny. In brief, the practice of person–centred therapy has become for me a profoundly mystical path where the client's pain and search for healing are likely to involve me in an encounter with the divine in myself, and in my client and in the relationship between us. What is more this human–divine encounter, which so often takes place in boundary territory or in no–man's land, is deeply incarnational. It is not the communication between disembodied spirits but the gradual meeting of hearts, minds and bodies in a relationship where fear gives way to love.

Now that it is said, I am glad for if I am fully honest I have known ever since I read "Client–Centred Therapy" in 1967 that I was being introduced to a most arduous discipline where what was at stake was my capacity to believe and to accept that my humanness has within it the seeds of my divinity. It is this truth which is glimpsed both by me and by my client when we dare to let ourselves meet in the strength of our undefended vulnerability. It is then that our mutual yearning for wholeness is revealed as the call to holiness and to the owning of our divine inheritance.

I have called it an arduous discipline because I have found it to be so. It therefore surprises me when I come across practitioners from other therapeutic orientations who are dismissive of the person–centred approach and seem to perceive it as an easy option which lacks the rigour and the complexity of their particular brand of therapy. Clearly they do no know what I know. They have not experienced the demands of a relationship which asks of the therapist a preparedness and a capacity to enter into the deep mystery of another's world with trusting acceptance of that other and a willingness to be seen and known for what one truly is without the protective armour of rôle, status or professional persona. This is no work for beginners nor for those who are unwilling or unable to accept the personal discipline which must always accompany those who stand on the threshold of the holy of holies.

Perhaps I need to be even more explicit. I am suggesting that person–centred therapists, whether they know it or not or whether they like it or not, are involved in the practice of a discipline which has all the marks of a spiritual vocation. What is more – and here comes the rub for some I suspect – the nature of the spiritual path which is being pursued is quintessentially Western, Christian and incarnational. It rests upon a belief in the transformation of uniquely differentiated persons through the experience both of offering and being offered a relationship characterised by acceptance where there was rejection, understanding where there was indifference, mutuality where there was abuse of power. It is a spiritual path which needs no liturgy beyond itself, no monastery for its perfecting, no temple beyond the human bodies of the persons who celebrate their communion. It demands not self negation but the self–forgetfulness which comes from self–love engendered though relationship. Its deeply Christian roots are perhaps most exemplified by its mirroring of the Trinitarian concept of God, the most inspired of all Christian doctrines which sees God himself or herself as a relationship. The person of God the Father according to this doctrine, has no separate being apart from the person of the Son and the Spirit who continually dances between them: wholeness is possible only in and through relationship and the wholeness thus experienced is greater than the sum of the two persons in their separateness. That, to my mind, is the most profound description of the therapeutic relationship in the person–centred tradition and enables me to grasp why it is that there are moments in my work as a therapist when I feel outside time and space and cannot conceive that heaven itself could be more desirable. I have no inclination to analyze those moments but they are characterised for both my client and me by a sense of radical unconditional, unearned acceptance and by an empowerment within which makes us capable, however transitory, of loving the whole created order. In short, we have ourselves been swept up into the divine relationship. To the doubtless irritation of many of my professional colleagues in the person–centred world I cannot resist adding that Christianity long ago coined words to describe this experience : my client and I, to employ this strangely distant language, are justified by grace and permeated by sanctification. For a moment, however fleeting, we are whole and holy, fully human and therefore the incarnation of the divine. If this is even remotely true of what happens for others in the twentieth–century secular activity called person–centred counselling or psychotherapy, then perhaps I am justified in seeing my own life's journey as in some way representative of a more wide–spread spiritual evolution, hidden and unnamed, which draws nourishment from the discoveries of an American psychologist who rejected God and church in order to have the freedom to become more fully himself while creating the conditions for others to risk more in their own becoming. God will, I know, forgive me for naming the glo-

116

rious relationship which constitutes his (or her) being. The desire to name is in me and not, I am sure, in God and having done so I am content. For the moment, at least, I have made sense of my experience and if in doing so I have used language which bewilders and offends then that, I suppose, is the price which congruence sometimes exacts.

REFERENCES

Dryden, W. and Spurling, L. (eds.) (1989). *On Becoming a Psychotherapis.* London: Tavistock/Routledge.
Rogers, C. R. (1951). *Client–Centered Therapy*, Boston: Houghton Mifflin,
Rogers, C. R. and Sanford, R. (1989). *Client–centered psychotherapy.* In H.I. Kaplan and B.J. Sadock (eds.), Comprehensive Textbook of Psychiatry V. Baltimore: Williams and Wilkins.
Thorne, B. J. (1991)..*Behold the Man.* London: Darton, Longman and Todd.

Theory of Personality Change :
A Comparison of Rogers, Gendlin and Greenberg.

RICHARD VAN BALEN

KATHOLIEKE UNIVERSITEIT LEUVEN, BELGIUM

ABSTRACT

In this paper I will try to formulate similarities and differences in the view on personality change between Rogers, Gendlin and Greenberg.

1. As to Rogers I will start with a statement about his "classical" client-centered theory, followed by his new ideas on the fully functioning person as formulated in "a Process conception...".

2. As to Gendlin I will start with some aspects of his "Theory of Personality Change" and then I will try to formulate some essential elements, as I see them, of Gendlin's more recent ideas, thereby indicating in which way they seem to be a refinement of the original formulations of Rogers.

3. In a third part I will compare the recent work of Greenberg with these latest ideas of Gendlin.

4. I will conclude my paper with a few words about the impact of these newer formulations on the concrete practice of the client-centered therapy.

ROGERS' VIEW

The basic assumption

Rogers' basic assumption about human functioning is, in my opinion, that man has at his disposal, from childhood on, an internal organization, originating in an innate actualizing tendency. Rogers himself calls it in 1959 the only assumption in his system.

This notion of actualizing tendency has been a frequent source of misunderstanding because several remarks about it have suggested it to be a vitalistic drive which would only require a sufficiently favourable environment to complete, in a natural - and as it were in an automatic - way, the genetic blueprint, as is the case in plants and animals.

It would lead us too far afield to describe here in detail the controversy around the proper understanding of the actualizing tendency. I refer again to Rogers' 1959 theoretical dissertation in which he describes the "release" of the pent-up actualizing tendency as the capacity - and hence the willingness - to "reorganize his self-concept in such a way as to make it more congruent with the totality of his "experience" (Rogers, 1959, p. 221).

The typically human form of this actualizing tendency would then, I believe, refer not only to an internal organization - the organismic way of functioning, common to man and other living creatures - but also and especially to the potential of transcending the genetic and environmental determination and to overcome in a corrective fashion the own historical influences. Or, as Rogers worded it already in 1946, the capacity "to discover a new sense or meaning in the influences which he undergoes and in his early experiences, and to change consciously his behavior in the light of this new meaning" (Rogers, 1946). The specifically human form of the actualizing tendency is thus not aiming at the realization of a genetic blueprint but rather at going beyond the determining influence of past experiences. Rogers did however retain explicitly the inalienable connection between the potentiality on the one-hand and the effective exercice of this capacity on the other, provided this natural capacity had not been curtailed in its development. This connection earned him several times the reproach of naive optimism. In line with the above, he described psychic healing as freeing the actualizing tendency and, as a self-evident consequence thereof, as allowing undistorted surfacing of previously denied or distorted content.

A new view in "A process conception of psychotherapy"

In the fifties, Rogers started a study - Gendlin too was involved - in which the accent was shifted from the content, the "what" of the change, to the "how" of the change. He started concentrating on the question: how precisely does the process of change occur within the client? And he arrived at a number of remarkable conclusions.

To his great surprise, his most outstanding conclusion was that he felt he would have to revise what had, until then, been considered as the essence of personality change. It was no longer tenable, he said, to describe mental health as a form of stability at a sufficiently high level of integration. The evolution from disturbed to optimal functioning could indeed still be described as a step-by-step approach to a higher level time and again, but not as an evolution from fixity through change to a new fixity. On the contrary, the essence of constructive change seemed to be in the transition from stability to changingness, from rigid structure to flow, from stasis to process (Rogers, 1958, p. 131).

Within this evolution, Rogers distinguished a few typical moments of change, different from one another.

First, there was sometimes a clear-cut, sudden and surprising breakthrough of (new) emotional meaning, which then fully revealed itself to the client upon further exploration (see Gendlin's later notion of 'shift').

Second, there was a less spectacular emergence of new insights. Rogers described it as slowly and gradually coming into contact with feelings which "seep through" or "bubble up through". (Think of Gendlin's "experiential steps").

In both these cases, it concerned an almost accidental penetration of, or a being surprised by, new feeling accents which emerge from the act of speaking itself. To use a later terminology, it consisted of a better conceptualization of the experiential process.

Alongside this almost unexpected infiltration while speaking, an "inner urge for more precise formulation" manifested itself. In other words, the discovery of new aspects brought with it an increased attention to the precise meaning and verbal expression of a given experience. Or, to put it differently: the emergence of new elements - from below - would reinforce ipso facto - from above - the concern about, and attention to, precise conceptualization of the experiential process.

It was also thought that this positive evolution could, in a successful therapy of long enough duration, develop further till it reached the highest, optimal levels of functioning in which (to use Rogers' words) "experiencing has lost almost completely its structurebound aspects" (Rogers, 1958, p. 152) and "a feeling flows to its full result" (Rogers, 1958, p. 145).

Or, to put it differently still, the gradual decrease of defensiveness and the undistorted admittance of previously denied feelings would ultimately lead to a point where the self no longer functioned as an object with a specific content and volume, to which feelings were admitted or from which they were banned (a self-concept thus), but only as an experiencing subject. The self and the experiencing would now coincide; the self at that moment, thus Rogers, is this feeling (Rogers, 1958, p. 147). Successful therapy would thus, in the end, lead to functioning in a process-manner: a continuous up-and-down movement between deeper feeling levels and the final verbalization (See Rogers, 1958, p. 149).

Remarkable in the description of this process was also the emphasis on its bodily components, as Gendlin did later on. Rogers did not only speak of the noticeable physiological relaxation which seemed to accompany such a process (Rogers, 1958, p. 148), but described also the felt sense of - the emotional insight into - a situation primarily as a bodily event. This event was then made more explicit by adequate verbalization but was, even before the verbalization, carrier of a (preconceptual) meaning. This meaning would perhaps not be understood all at once but remained simmering in the body, allowing the person to return to it until he was sure to have understood its precise meaning. "It is, perhaps, that they constitute a clear-cut physiological event, a substratum of the conscious life, which the client can return to for investigatory purposes" (Rogers, 1958, p 150).

Summarizing these characteristics, we see how a bodily event - a bodily way of being present in a situation, carrier of a preconceptual meaning - is directly accessible to the experiencing person, who puts these experiences into words without being hindered by an existing self-concept. All this happens in such a flowing process-movement that words seem to emerge from feelings. The more careful the attention to the bodily experience, the more adequate the wording.

Does all this ever sound like Gendlin ! Yet it comes from Rogers, six years before the publication of Gendlin's "Theory of Personality Change", but at the time when Gendlin was putting the last touch to his dissertation on "creation of meaning".

GENDLIN'S VIEW

Gendlin's "Theory of Personality Change".

In spite of the similarity described above, Gendlin will nevertheless distance himself to some extent from Rogers in his theoretical views. Even though it is clear to me that both protagonists of the client-centered orientation were in agreement about the characteristics of the process of change and about the new health model, Gendlin was obviously unable to agree with Rogers' belief that perception of a safe environment and the ensuing decrease in defensiveness would constitute the basis of the process of change.

Gendlin's reasons for pointing out the shortcomings of Rogers' model are both empirical and theoretical. I will not discuss here Gendlin's concrete arguments (for which I refer to Gendlin, 1964 and Van Balen, 1991) but will limit myself to pointing out that, at least in certain cases, Gendlin considers the awareness of a secure climate to follow, and originate in a previous personality change. We will thus have to discover another mechanism, thus Gendlin, which causes resistance to turn into change. And he finds it in the basic notion of interaction and interaction-completion.

In line with his existentialist and phenomenological sources of inspiration - and these are much more obvious than Rogers - Gendlin will stress the interactional character of all naturally occuring forms of life and thus also of human life. He thus views interaction as the primary form of life and the absence of important interactions as disturbing the spontaneous process character of this organismic or bodily way of being-in-the-world. Based on this interactional view, Gendlin will come to consider the two generally accepted essential conditions of personality change - "emotional insight" and "therapeutic relationship" - as forms of bringing about process-enhancing interactions. The factual completion of decisive interactions for both these aspects would then not depend on permissiveness originating in consciousness but only on the adequacy - adequate for the moment and the situation - of the interaction offered. Thus, Rogers' basic attitudes would, according to Gendlin, be important, not because they are perceived as such by the client but because, and to the extent that, they orient the therapist towards offering an adequate interaction.

Becoming conscious of new aspects would then only be an offshoot of such previous process-enhancing interactions. Conscious acknowledgment of that information would not, as Gendlin thought Rogers had meant, be the decisive step but only a marginal phenomenon. Becoming conscious was for Gendlin only a by-product of the essential changeprocess which thus becomes the foundation of increased consciousness.

This last statement does not appear unimportant to me, especially because, in my understanding, it shows that, even in 1964, Gendlin still believed - just like Rogers - that continuation of a still progressing therapy would finally and unavoidably lead to the optimal self-process, to an ever-increasing degree of "experiencing as a referent".

Gendlin's subsequent evolution

In the period following the publication of Gendlin's "Theory of personality change" however, discouraging research findings began to appear which did not confirm the hypothesis of a step-by-step increase and more particularly of a gradually growing spontaneous attunement to the own experiencing process (Gendlin, 1969, p. 13).

Rogers did not consider these findings as a good enough reason to review his assumptions. The more present the basic conditions, he kept believing, the greater the possible evolution for the person.

Not the degree but the direction of the change, however modest, seemed to remain his criterion. Indeed, too many other factors played a role in the degree of the possible change. Establishing a norm of minimum change required would again be opening a door to some sort of expert advice which he had always opposed, namely the opinion of the expert who would judge where someone fell short and would then apply himself to that problem. Once again, "the problem would become the focus, not the person".

Gendlin, on the other hand, considered these findings to warrant a reconsideration of their previous all too optimistic views. On the one hand, a positive outcome was highly improbable if the initial experiential level did not reach a certain minimum. On the other hand, while a sufficiently high initial level did correlate with positive outcome, it correlated only very modestly with a movement score on the experiencing scale. Such arguments led Gendlin to conclude that failure of the expected increase in independent spontaneous reference to experience to occur (the focusing attitude as he described it in 1964; the so-called "experiencing as a referent") had to indicate a specific inability which did not, as had so far been thought, decrease with continuation of therapy.

The belief that succesful therapy - the removal of the complaint thus - automatically would lead to a more experiential way of living, was now definitely shaken.

The consequence of this change-over showed initially most clearly in clinical practice. The focusing process, introduced, I believe, in 1964 to describe concretely the notion of emotional insight, in order to illustrate, at a descriptive level, "how it worked when it worked", now received a totally different status. If the focusing ability had to be sufficiently high from the start in order to achieve therapeutic success - and if, besides, it did not increase automatically with continuation of therapy - then the challenge was to look for ways to teach it when it was too low. Hence the step towards focusing-instructions and the beginning of a shift in accent which provoked numerous discussions and tensions within the client-centered camp.

I will mention here only summarily, in some eight points, the theoretical consequences of this change-over as I believe I can deduce them from Gendlin's later works (See Gendlin, 1973, 1991a, 1991b, 1992).

1. Gendlin continues to believe in an original organismic functioning, in a body-subject as total process, with an embryonic self from the start. He distances himself from a conception of man which postulates a medley of incoordinated, separate part-functions which will only gradually be transformed into a coherent whole, under influence of the environment.

2. His earlier opinion about "process unity" has become more differenciated. Gendlin speaks now of a layered structure of this bodily way of being-in-the-world. He distinguishes four levels: (a) the physiological body, (b) the interactions with the physical environment (behaviour in the sense of moving etc.), (c) the interaction with others (interpersonal relationships) and (d) the ability to symbolize and, as part thereof, the reflection on one's own experiencing process (Gendlin 1973). (Compare this with the four levels in Existentialism: Welt, Umwelt, Mitwelt and Eigenwelt).

Important here is that each higher level of functioning adds a bonus to the functioning of the previous ones. This means that the human body is influenced in its functioning by all four levels which makes the body a "verbal" body, for instance - and that the most influential dimension in the total functioning is the fourth one (or, to place it within the evolution from plant to animal and to human being, the most recently acquired one).

This also means that, when the process unfolds in an optimal way, these four dimensions function together as a whole and that symbolization, wether in word or in behaviour, is the fruit of a complex but harmonic total process.

3. Each level of interaction viewed separately is a function of the completion of a sufficient variety of interactions at that level. An impoverishment at each of the interaction levels may result from either a scarse offer of adequate interaction (see for example the caged animal) or from the not, or not complete, unfolding of the own interaction-responses. In this last case, the blocked passage has to be cleared first by completing the obstructed responses. Thus, the tears never wept have to be wept first, or the pent-up rage first expressed, before an evolution at that level can take place. What has to be broken through, first of all, is the paralyzing effect of a powerless and defenseless suffering of traumatic experiences. This is one form of completion, thus Gendlin. The one which has to happen at one of the first three levels.

4. The second form of completion, the form which has to straighten primarily the one-sided and distorting canalization of the course of interaction (think for instance of rigid habits, of preferences, of prejudices), is the completion at the fourth level: attention thus to the functioning of the three lower levels starting from the highest level.

Indeed, reflection on one's own experiencing process, letting a real 'felt sense' emerge, alters immediately the process course at the three other levels. And it is this 'further living', as

Gendlin calls it, which allows man to intervene in his history, to realize himself as a co-actor, instead of remaining the product of heredity and history; it is also the way of coming to an authentic way of life.

But even this fourth level can carry the scars of a previously disturbed interaction experience. In that case, process-enhancing completions have to happen first, precisely at that fourth level. Concretely this 'structure-bound functioning' of the fourth level means that conscious symbolizing activity has been channelled towards end-products (words, signs, emotions etc.), away from the concrete experiencing process, due to the absence of completing interactions. One has forgotten - or never really learned - to pay explicit attention to that underlying experiencing process. (One may wonder, for example, to what extent differences in traditional education between boys and girls result in a more 'structure-bound' functioning at this fourth level in the typical male).

Indeed, reflecting becomes then immediately 'thinking about' instead of 'thinking and living from (within)'. One continues to look for a solution in what one knows, thus Gendlin, instead of trying to gain access to the not yet known, to what is the "more" in it, as Gendlin words it. And the key to this access consists precisely of putting into operation the reflection on the own experiencing process, the 'experiencing as a referent', the letting oneself be shaped by a real 'felt sense'.

5. Primacy of the fourth level. A disturbance at the fourth level will be more drastic than a lower level one. Indeed, interaction coming from this fourth level is not only itself a form of quality improvement, of 'further living' as Gendlin says, or of integration of the experienced in the symbolic order, but has - as only one - a direct and process quality enhancing influence on the remaining three levels.

This makes it clear, once again, that the essence is not the admittance of feelings but the quality of the process which is expressed in the symbolization. Or, to quote Gendlin: "It is not a question of just any kind of feeling 'good'. Some people may feel 'good' when they kill someone. To give in to an urge often feels 'good' (Gendlin, 1973, p. 327). Important is that the fourth level should take an active and integrating part in the emergence of the 'felt sense'. The difference with earlier views is here immediately clear. For Rogers, the accent used to be on unhindered admittance of experiential data: he seemed to see a wrong conscious conceptualization only as caused by a ban on such unhindered passage, the organismic process as such staying intact.

The opposite is the case for Gendlin: the so-called 'admission' of feelings that happens in therapy, rather seems to imply a (necessary) form of 'further living'; a completion process without which transcending the strict product-character - the so-called rigid structures - remains impossible.

6. Only by crowning an experience by means of symbolization coming from the fourth level does one make this experiential knowledge ultimately one's own. Adequate symbolization is the basis of healthy ego-building, thus Gendlin.

Completion of pent-up processes at the first three levels can only be fruitful when occurring withing the context of such adequate and ultimately completing fourth-level attention, because then only will these interactions be raised to a higher level and grow, in this symbolized form, into ego-acquisitions.

7. A real and lasting personality change being function of an efficient reference to the experiencing process, the active and explicit stimulation of this reference may be, in certain cases, decisive for the succes of the therapy.

8. The fourth level is also the specifically human one, which forms the bridge between the original innate organization and culture. At that level, meaning is not only created out of experience but experience is also created out of the meaning reached. As in all interactions, this is a two-way street. A smoothly functioning fourth level of bodily interaction is a constant source of reciprocal action between knowledge and experience, which are thus continuously tested out against one another and adjusted.

This form of interaction allows not only knowledge-processing but also a kind of bodily digestion of this knowledge, which then, when later experienced and symbolized again, has acquired a personal touch and is thus no longer identical to the one that was reached previously.

This last thesis has far-reaching consequences for the concept of man. Gendlin uses this thesis to refute the structuralists and Lacan by positing that there is more than only the form reached by culture. In spite of being strongly susceptible to the influence of cultural regulation, it is typical for human nature, thus Gendlin, not to be totally in its power; the original internal organization makes man capable of interacting with this regulation in such a way as to influence culture as well as to be influenced by it. And he believes this way of functioning to be the most authentic one.

This thesis refutes, besides, the statement that stressing the existence of an original, innate, natural form of organization means, ipso facto, adopting a vitalistic point of view - Rogers was often reproached with this - or accepting that man is born with a blueprint of what he ought to be if he were to be truly himself. What is proper to human nature as described by Gendlin - and less ambiguously than by Rogers sometimes - has obviously nothing to do with a form-essence. No question here of a pre-programmed future such as the so-called realization of one's own specific nature or of one's true self. Natural predisposition in the sense of specific human nature does not refer to an innate whole of natural abilities, proper to a particular person, but precisely to the fourth innate dimension; the dimension which enables man to form symbols, but also the dimension which, when not directed unilaterally towards the world of symbols, functions as a reflection on the own experience. A dimension which, as part of a total functioning (of a bodily being-in-the-world) creates meaning. In other words, a dimension which, on the one hand, should not be allowed to become uprooted, but, on the other hand, because of being deeply rooted, constitutes a meeting place of culture and internal innate organization. The dimension which, as said previously, allows man to process cultural influence in a personal way, of being himself thus, something which should neither be thought of as separate from culture nor be reduced to a product of that culture either.

ABOUT GREENBERG'S VIEW

A third star in the client-centered sky was, and is, in my opinion, Laura Rice. She was repeatedly described as the most important representative of the 'information-processing approach' within our orientation. In the last few years, however, it is mainly L. Greenberg, I think, who takes over and further elaborates her thoughts. This is why I would like to draw, however briefly, Greenberg's views into this dissertation. I am convinced that they deserve more ample discussion than is possible in this chapter, but I will mention a few points.

Let me point out first of all that I believe that the outline I just gave of Gendlin's later evolution, could largely apply to Greenberg's as far as content goes. Not, however, in the wording. This last is no accident. Indeed, one of Greenberg's main goals is to reformulate the theory of classical experiential therapy - rather Rogers' and Perls' versions than Gendlin's - so as to link up its terminology more closely with that of the cognition/emotion theorists and allow its content to be completed by their insights. In doing so, he hopes not only to further the dialogue with academic psychologists but also to make Rogers' valuable body of knowledge more accessible to a considerable group, still prejudiced against client-centered therapy.

A first criticism of Rogers' theory, common to Greenberg and Gendlin, is about the role of the self-concept.

A second common point is that of the so-called double track. As we have seen, Gendlin started in 1969 to emphasize the therapist's double task. He underlined not only the importance of the 'experiential interaction' - the efficient implementation of the relational attitudes - but also the necessity of guarding - and actively stimulating, if necessary - a proper focusing attitude in the client. Along that line, Laura Rice, and in her footsteps L. Greenberg, started to make a distinction between the 'relation-oriented aspects' on the one hand and the 'task-oriented aspects', on the other.

A third agreement, related to the previous one, is Gendlin's and Greenberg's emphasis on the importance of a judicious synthesis between purely subjective experience on the one hand and the so-called objective truth, on the other; or to put it differently, between nature and culture. The difference between Gendlin (and, in fact, Rogers as well, I believe) and Greenberg seems to me that Gendlin considers this synthesis to be part of process-functioning, of the optimal functioning of the 'actualizing tendency' thus, while Greenberg limits the action of what he mostly calls 'growth tendency' to 'development and adaptation', or what Buber used to call merely 'individualization'. (as contrasted to 'humanization'). Contrary to Rogers and Gendlin, Greenberg then posits a second capacity, separate and different from the 'growth tendency', the 'capacity for choice', to account for the 'humanization' deemed necessary by Buber (Greenberg a.o., 1993, p. 72). Wholistic thinking seems to me more pronounced in Rogers and Gendlin than in Greenberg. Where Greenberg tends to think in terms of evolution and emphasizes the building blocks which, when joined together in an ingenious way, make a solid building, Rogers and Gendlin take the building itself as point of reference and value the parts only to the extent that they have lost their separate existence. We find an example of this difference of approach e.g. in the use and appreciation of the term emotion. Greenberg describes emotions in positive terms as leading to 'goal-directed behavior important to survival' (Safran & Greenberg 1991, p. 6). Gendlin on the contrary sees emotion as the desintegration of a more complex 'feeling'; as the consequence of a narrowing of context, and as leading to a premature, one-sided and process-disturbing reaction.

A last agreement wich I want to point out - but, as said, I confine myself here to a first and limited comparison - is how Greenberg considers the dysfunctional secondary emotions as a consequence of the inadequate acknowledgment of the original primary emotions which he calls 'fundamentally adaptive'. This is in line with Gendlin's view that negative functioning is the reverse side of a readiness for positive interaction which, once completed, will counteract the negative behaviour (Gendlin, 1968).

This brief comparison of three important contributions to clientcentered theory of change makes no pretence to reach firm conclusions. Should it help to promote more interest in - and a more vividly discussion of - the :n my opinion often all too neglected theoretical reflection on our client-centered body of knowledge, then the goal of my contribution would have been fully reached.

REFERENCES

Gendlin, E.T. (1964). *A theory of personality change.* In J.T. Hart & T.H. Tomlinson (Eds.). (1970), New directions in client-centered therapy (pp. 129-173). Boston: Houghton Mifflin.

Gendlin, E.T. (1968). *The experiential response.* In E. Hammer (Ed.), The use of interpretation in treatment (pp. 208-227). New York: Grune and Stratton.

Gendlin, E.T. (1969). *Focusing.* Psychotherapy: Theory, research and practice, 6, 4-15.

Gendlin, E.T. (1973). *Experiential Psychotherapy.* In R. Corsini (Ed.), Current Psychotherapies (pp. 317-352). Itaca: Peacock.

Gendlin, E.T. (1991a). *Thinking beyond patterns: body, language and situation.* In B. den Ouden & M. Moen (Eds.), The presence of feeling in thought (pp. 27-189). New York: Peter Lang.

Gendlin, E.T. (1991b). *On emotion in therapy.* In J.D. Safran & L.S. Greenberg (Eds.), Emotion, Psychotherapy and change (pp. 255-279). New York: Guilford.

Gendlin, E.T. (1992). *The primacy of the body, not the primacy of perception.* In Man of World, pp. 341-353. Kluwer Academic Publishers, The Netherlands.

Greenberg, L.S., & Safran, J.D. (1989). *Emotion in Psychotherapy.* American Psychologist, 44(1), 19-29.

Greenberg, L.S., Rice, L.N., & Elliott, R. (1993). *Facilitating emotional change.* New York: The Guilford Press.

Rogers, C.R. (1946). *Significant aspects of client-centered therapy.* American Psychologist, 1, 415-422.

Rogers, C.R. (1958). *A process conception of psychotherapy.* In C.R. Rogers (1961), On becoming a person (pp. 125-159). Boston: Houghton Mifflin.

Rogers, C.R. (1959). *A theory of therapy, personality, and interpersonal relationships as developed in the client-centered framework.* In S. Koch (Ed.), Psychology: a study of science. Vol. 3 (pp. 184-256). New York: McGraw-Hill.

Safran, J.D., & Greenberg, L.S. (Eds.) (1991). *Emotion, Psychotherapy, change.* New York: The Guilford Press.

Van Balen, R. (1991). *Theorie van de persoonlijkheidsverandering.* In H. Swildens, O. de Haas, G. Lietaer & R. Van Balen (Red.), Leerboek gesprekstherapie. De clientgerichte benadering (pp. 139-167). Amersfoort/Leuven: Acco.

Van Balen, R. (1992). *Klientenzentrierte Therapie und Experientielle therapie: zwei verschiedene Therapien?* Wien: Paper presented at Symposion "20 Jahre ÖGwG".

How Does Empathy Cure?:
A Theoretical Consideration of Empathy, Processing and Personal Narrative

MARGARET S. WARNER

CHICAGO COUNSELING CENTER

ABSTRACT

Neither client–centered nor self–psychology theorists have offered a clear, comprehensive explanation of how the communication of empathy should produce positive effects on the process of clients. This paper offers a synthesis of the process theories of Gendler, Rice and Wexler to explain the functioning of empathy. It suggests that the communication of empathy creates an experience of recognition as words or images match the individual's immediate lived experience. Expressions of empathy that create this kind of experience of recognition encourage the individual to hold the experience in attention and to lessen judgments directed at him or herself for having the experience. As a result feelings, images, and thoughts emerge which have not been incorporated in the person's current life narrative. The individual is likely to experience catharsis in relation to newly received thoughts and emotions and to revise his or her conceptual schemas to incorporate new understanding. The process theories of Gendlin, Rice and Wexler each capture particular ways that new material commonly emerges and is synthesized by clients.

The quality of empathy is central to therapeutic practice in both the client–centered and self psychology traditions.[1] And, while findings are not consistent, a broad array of research studies find that therapist empathy is a significant predictor of successful therapy outcome.[2]

Yet the precise way that empathy, in and of itself, generates positive change has tended to remain vague within both traditions. Some client–centered theorists believe that therapists' individual ways of manifesting empathy and clients' ways of undergoing change are varied enough that any attempts to generalize are likely to limit a spontaneous, naturally occurring process.[3] Several client–centered theorists –Eugene Gendlin, Laura North Rice, and David Wexler–have proposed models of optimal client processes which often emerge under empathic conditions.[4] Yet, these models have not been integrated with each other. Furthermore, each of these theorists has advocated different ways of stimulating such optimal client processes when they do not occur spontaneously. As a result, it is often unclear how and to what degree they believe that empathy in and of itself is a powerful instigator of such change processes.

While eloquently advocating empathy with narcissistically disturbed clients, Heinz Kohut remained curiously doubtful that empathy in and of itself generates positive effects. In his chapter on empathy in *How Does Analysis Cure?*, he proposes exclusive reliance on empathic responding for substantial periods of time with narcissistic clients.[5] Yet, he suggests that the positive force for change comes from those moments when the therapist fails in his or her attempts at empathy, creating empathic breaks which result in new structuralization.[6] Or, he notes that positive effects of empathy result from the "optimal frustration" clients feel when the therapist understands but does not actually meet the client's infantile needs.[7] As a "value–

neutral tool of observation" the therapist's empathy allows him or her to form interpretive hypotheses. While not having an impact in themselves, such empathically informed hypotheses do form the background for personal interactions which Kohut does see as highly significant and curative.

In his last essay, Kohut notes that:

> ...empathy is never by itself supportive or therapeutic. It is, however, a necessary precondition to being supportive or therapeutic. In other words, even if a mother's empathy is correct and accurate, even if her aims are affectionate, it is not her empathy that satisfies her child's selfobject needs. Her actions, her responses to the child do this.[8]

When Kohut does acknowledge direct benefits of empathy he does so with the greatest reluctance. In the same last essay he notes that he thinks empathic interactions do have *some* positive effects. He seems to see this as a highly controversial position to take within the psychoanalytic movement, since he expresses the fear that he will have aroused the "suspicion of abandoning scientific sobriety and entering the land of mysticism or of sentimentality" in presenting this view.[9] He does not elaborate further on the nature of that positive bond and the ways that it might be involved in client change. Thus, while both the client–centered and self psychology traditions have offered substantial insights into the functioning of empathy within psychotherapy, I do not believe that either tradition has offered a fully articulated account of how empathic interaction in and of itself creates positive effects. In addition, the proponents of both traditions often remain quite isolated from each others work. Real differences of theory, language, and tradition often stop theorists from seeing ways that elements of the two traditions could complement each other in significant ways.

In this paper I will offer an integrated view of how empathic interaction[10] has a direct effect on client change. In creating this overall model, I am heavily indebted to the work of various client–centered and self psychology theorists. Yet, since I am combining elements from a number of independently developed systems, the theorists themselves might or might not agree with the particular synthesis that I am proposing.

I propose that:

1. The communication of empathy in and of itself tends to foster positive, self–directed processing of experience.

2. While there is considerable individual variation, this self–directed processing takes common forms which can be described and are deeply grounded in human nature. Empathic responding creates a particular kind of experiential recognition that tends to bring up new facets of experience, allowing clients' life narratives to be reformulated.

3. Caretaker empathy is a crucial selfobject function which operates as a precursor to mature abilities to hold and process experience.

4. Empathic relating within therapy tends to re–activate thwarted selfobject functions and challenge early decisions about one's own and others way of relating to one's experience.

5. Clients who have suffered early empathic failure are likely to have a fragile style of processing experience. As a result they have difficulty holding experiences in attention at workable levels of intensity or taking in the perspectives of others without feeling that their own experience has been annihilated.

Let us begin by considering the definition of empathy.

EMPATHY DEFINED IN CLIENT–CENTERED AND PSYCHODYNAMIC TRADITIONS

The concept of empathy has had a complex definitional history within psychology. In its everyday meaning, empathy is taken to be an:

> intellectual identification with or vicarious experiencing of the feelings, thoughts, or attitudes of another person.[11]

Metaphorically, empathy is often described as an experience by which one is able to "walk in the other person's shoes" or to see a situation "through the other person's eyes." Empathy is usually seen as involving both cognitive perspective–taking and emotional resonance in some sort of interaction with each other.[12] Understanding another person's world view enables one to feel what particular experiences must be like for that person; feeling with the person enables one to learn about the person's world view. Yet, as many observers point out, the emotional resonance involved in empathy is not so intense or undifferentiated that the person loses track of the distinction between his or her own experience and that of the other person. Up to this point, most scholars agree on the use of the term.

However, an interesting divergence emerges in the use of the word empathy among clinical psychologists. If empathy involves deeply understanding the inner world of another person, does this involve the phenomenological world of the person–the world as the person would construe it him or herself? Or, does it involve a psychologically interpretive view of the person's inner world–the world as the person *would* view it if fully aware of his or her experience or motives as construed by expert observers?[13] This is a crucial distinction which leads to considerable confusion in the literature, since some authors assume the first meaning, some the second, and some alternate between the two without clarification.

Since writers in the psychoanalytic tradition see the therapist's primary role as one of uncovering, conveying and helping analysands assimilate material emerging outside of awareness, they tend toward the second meaning of the word empathy. Empathy, then, is a way that the analyst can become aware of material that the client is not aware of him or herself. Freud initiated this usage with his comment that empathic connectedness can allow analysts to experience association and primary process material within themselves that analysands have blocked from their own awareness.[14] This awareness can be used to construct interpretations and evaluate analytic strategies. Roy Schafer summarizes this position, suggesting that by general analytic consensus, empathy includes:

1. constructing a mental model of the analysand

2. being alert to signal affects and shared fantasies in response to analysands' associations

3. being prepared to use these responses reflectively as cues to the emotional aspects and significance of the analysand's activity in the analysis.[15]

Clearly, the primary process material which emerges in the consciousness of the analyst via this sort of interaction might initially be surprising or foreign to the analysand if conveyed to him or her. Given this usage of the word empathy, the analyst would not need to assume that the interaction was less "empathic" as a result of such discrepancies.

Carl Rogers, on the other hand, is quite clear that he is using the word empathy to refer to the client's own phenomenologically based experience. He notes that:

...the state of empathy or being empathic is to perceive the internal frame of reference of another with accuracy and with the emotional components and meanings which pertain thereto as if one were the person, but without ever losing the "as if" condition. Thus, it means to sense the hurt or the pleasure of another as he senses it and to perceive the causes thereof as he perceives them, but without ever losing the recognition that it is as if I were hurt or pleased and so forth.[16]

This understanding of the word is apparent from Rogers' style of empathic responding, in which he conveys his understanding of the client's meaning to check whether it fits with the client's own understanding. If his expressed understanding diverges from that of the client, he does see this as a failure of empathy on his part.[17]

Kohut seems to use the word empathy in both of these ways at different times without noting the distinction. In his communication with narcissistic clients in early phases of therapy he is clearly trying to put words to the analysand's situation in such a way that the analysand feels understood in his or her own terms. He is deliberately not trying to interpret or convey new information of any kind to the analysand – however true or useful such information might be – since he assumes that such communications would be experienced as narcissistically wounding and retraumatizing for the client.[18]

On the other hand, Kohut uses empathy as "an information–gathering activity" that allows him to formulate an "experience near" model of the client's inner dynamics.[19] Here he sees empathy as a theoretically informed way of understanding the selfobject needs which the client is not aware of within him or herself. In his theoretical explanations, then, he follows the traditional analytic usage, ignoring the fact that his actual practice often follows the first usage of the word.

In the traditional analytic usage of the word empathy, I believe that it is correct to say that empathy has virtually no directly curative effect, but only serves as a background for other potentially useful interventions. However, I do believe that phenomenologically based empathy of the sort described by Rogers (and often practiced by Kohut and others) has substantial change–inducing potential at both an immediate problem–solving level and at longer–term characterological levels. This change–inducing potential operates in therapies that rely almost exclusively on empathic responding as well as in those therapies that are empathically grounded but include some amount of feedback and interpretation in the therapy process.

EMPATHY AND EXPERIENTIAL RECOGNITION

A common–sense question arises: How could the communication of empathy generate change when by definition nothing has been added to the client or analysand's experience in the process? The answer that I would give is implicit in a great deal of empathic practice and theory, but seldom stated fully. The communication of empathy tends to facilitate change because it generates a particular sense of experiential recognition within the other person–both the sense of being recognized in one's experience of the moment by another human being and the sense of recognizing ones own experience in the moment. This experience of recognition is of value in itself as a form of human connection and it also tends to shift one's relation to implicit, bodily felt, non–conscious aspects of experience, opening these to awareness and change.[20] Let me first examine the nature of this experience of recognition in some depth and then consider its impact on relationships with others and with one's own experience.

The phenomenological sense of recognition that I am referring to here is a simple and virtually universal human experience. Yet the capacities involved in generating such an experience are complex, and deeply grounded in early childhood experience. I am speaking of the sense of recognition that one has when one feels that another has grasped–in words or in some other way–the essence of one's situation as it is currently experienced, in the absence of a sense of threat or judgement about that experience.[21] This kind of recognition is often accompanied with a sense of slight release or relief at being seen. At an everyday level, a person might feel this sense of recognition when someone notices that he or she has been waiting in line for service or if someone says "You look like you are tired of all of this" when this is in fact true. Most people experience a fuller version of this experience of recognition at certain rare and valued moments in life. Often in a personal crisis, while many people try to say helpful things, a close friend is able to say something that captures one's experience so deeply that one could say, "Yes, that's exactly how I feel" or "This person understands exactly what I mean."

In this experience of recognition, a person momentarily lessens his or her sense of existential aloneness in the world. That which the person is experiencing has some matching, some comprehensibility to another human being. Or, even within one's experience, the fact of finding words that fit one's experience and make sense of it can give one the confidence that there is a matching between one's experience and some account of that experience that is comprehensible.

What kind of processing goes into that friend's knowing what is central to one's experience in the moment? Certainly there is no explicit formula that could tell a person how to create that experience of interpersonal understanding. The friend may well be responding to things one had said in the moment or nonverbal cues. But, he or she would also be responding out of a whole lifetime of general understandings, perhaps a history of knowing this person in particular, various culturally grounded understandings, and the like.

Eugene Gendlin's theory of experiencing offers some clues as to how this experiential sense of recognition might occur. In his 1984 article "Theory of Personality Change", he notes that:

> ...we employ explicit symbols only for very small portions of what we think. We have most of it in the form of felt meanings.[22]

He notes that explicitly symbolized aspects of our experience exist in relationship with a "direct referent" or "felt meaning."

> ...we can notice that only in direct sensing do we have the meanings of what we say and think. For without our "feel" of the meaning, verbal symbols are only noises (or sound images of noises).
>
> For, example, someone listens to you speak, and then says: "Pardon me, but I don't grasp what you mean." If you would like to restate what you meant in different words, you will notice that you must inwardly attend to your direct referent, your felt meaning...

In discussing such felt referents Gendlin is not referring to experiences that are unconscious, but rather to states of consciousness that may or may not be made the focus of attention at any given moment.

> When felt meanings occur in interaction with verbal symbols and we feel what the symbols mean, we term such meanings "explicit" or "explicitly known." On the other hand, quite often we have just such felt meanings without a verbal symbolization. Instead we have an event, a perception, or some word such as "this" which represents nothing, but only points. When this is the case, we can term the meaning "implicit" or "implicitly felt, but not explicitly known."[23]

He notes that such implicit and explicit meanings are different in nature.

> We may feel that some verbal statement says exactly what we mean; nevertheless, to feel the meaning is not the same kind of thing as verbal symbols. As we have shown, a felt meaning can contain very many meanings and can be further and further elaborated. Thus, the felt meaning is not the same in kind as the precise symbolized explicit meaning. The reason the difference in kind is so important is because if we ignore it we assume that explicit meanings are (or were already) in the implicit felt meaning.[24]

The experience of recognition, then, would tend to occur when another person's account of one's experience resonates with one's own implicit sense of that experience, generating an immediate subjective feeling of rightness.

Of course, there is no such thing as one's "real" experience, only an actively constructed account of one's life situation, grounded within one's social and cultural milieu. I could give any number of accounts of my experience at a given moment; I might give quite a different set of accounts if I reflected on my experience a week or a year later. An outsider can sensibly challenge me as to whether my account of my experience makes sense. Indeed, Gendlin notes that:

> ...even when a meaning is explicit (when we say "exactly what we mean") the felt meaning we have always contains a great deal more implicit meaning than we have made explicit.[25]

Yet not all accounts of one's experience, offer this experience of matching with one's explicitly or implicitly felt meaning–this sense of experiential recognition. And no account of one's experience–however valuable in other ways–is fully satisfying until it does correspond with one's subjective sense of oneself in this way.

To understand the function of empathy, it is crucial to see that this sense of experiential recognition of one's own meaning is different from the experience of receiving new and perhaps useful information from outside one's frame of reference. For example, a person might be angry at someone he or she is close to. A good friend might say, "You think that you are angry, but I think that you are really scared of being hurt and you don't want to admit it." This comment might (or might not) be experienced as right and useful by the person receiving it. But, to take it in, a person needs to let go of his or her current way of experiencing her situation, take in a new idea or perspective and relate that in some way to his or her own experiencing.

Empathic understanding which leads to a subjective sense of being recognized in one's experience does not require a person to leave the immediacy of his or her experience in the same way. As a result, I believe that these two sequences are quite different in the kinds of subsequent experience that they generate and that they are quite differently received by different sorts of clients.

How, then, would this experience of recognition generate positive change processes? Again, the answer is implicit in a great deal of empathic theory and practice, but seldom fully stated. In having one's experience recognized and received by another person, one becomes able to recognize and receive one's own experience, both in a broad sense and in one's particular ability to receive one's own moment to moment experiencing. A shift in the way one receives one's moment to moment experiencing opens a number of natural processes by which one integrates and differentiates the meaning of one's experience. This openness to an ongoing experiencing allows a continuing revision of one's life narrative and the "scripts" by which experiences are organized and interpreted, making possible more mature, differentiated ways of living in relationship with others. Let us look at each of these elements separately.

THE DEVELOPMENT AND INTERNALIZATION OF THE CAPACITY TO HOLD EXPERIENCE IN ATTENTION

Rogers notes the way in which the therapist's empathy toward all aspects of the client's experiencing tends to be internalized by the client as a way of relating to his or her own experience.

> ...Being listened to by someone who understands makes it possible for persons to listen more accurately to themselves, with greater empathy toward their own visceral experiencing, their own vaguely felt meanings.[26]

Notably, the process of internalization which Rogers describes in therapy parallels a crucial aspect of optimal child development. Children relate meaningfully to their own experience only after they have first lived in a "good enough" parent–child diad in which their experiences are responded to and named by another. This partnership leading to an internalization of empathic responding could be seen as one aspect of the holding–soothing and mirroring selfobject functions described by Kohut. Or, it could be seen as an independent selfobject function.

Initially, an infant's experience can be seen as entirely constituted by Gendlin's directly felt, implicit meanings, since the infant has no ability to symbolize in words.

> ...the "implicit" or "felt" datum of experiencing is a sensing of bodily life. As such it may have countless organized aspects, but this does not mean that they are conceptually formed...we complete and form them when we explicate.[27]

Still, the infant engaged in such implicit experiencing relates and undergoes change within relationship.

> ...it is often the case that there is an ongoing experiencing process without verbal symbols. In fact, most situations and behaviors involve feeling in interaction with nonverbal events.[28]

Thus, it can be said that:

> Interpersonal events occur before there is a self. Others respond to us before we come to respond to ourselves. If these responses were not in interaction with feeling–if there were nothing but other peoples responses as such–the self could become nothing but the learned responses of others.[29]

Certainly, in this initial "implicit" relating, an infant is active in initiating and responding to interactions with adults. Daniel Stern eloquently describes the nonverbal "affect attunement" central to early phases of infancy which cultivate a sense of efficacy in relating to another.[30] And, caretakers overall ability to eliminate trauma and to create a benign ratio between positive and negative experiences undoubtedly contributes to an infant's overall association of his or her experiences with "goodness" or "badness."[31]

Early on most parents begin to engage in a particular sort of empathic interaction in which they begin to name infant's experiences and to offer hypothesized reasons for these experiences–perhaps saying that the baby is "tired" when she cries or that she thinks "spinach is disgusting" when she spits it out. Essentially, parents are offering verbal symbols that *could* carry the infant's implicitly felt experience forward into explicit meaning if the infant had words. At some point children come to recognize a matching or mismatching between words and their own felt experience.

I remember seeing such a moment of dawning recognition in my three–year–old nephew. His mother had left the room to pay attention to his younger brother and he had begun throwing his toys. I said "You feel angry." He looked at me with a sense of surprise and discovery and tried on the words "I feel angry." He threw his toys a few more times, saying the words with greater conviction each time. Then he went into the kitchen to tell his mother triumphantly about his new discovery, that he felt "angry."

Of course, there is great variation in the quality of parental empathy in this early naming of infant experience and the clarity of reasons offered for such experiences. Some parents are relatively inattentive or have difficulty leaving their own perspectives. Hence, experiences may go unnamed or be systematically misnamed. Particular sorts of experiences such as unhappiness or anger may be threatening in some families and may be routinely labeled as something else. Or, children of a very volatile or insecure parent may learn to label their experience in the way they find most calming or least threatening to that parent.[32] As result of such empathic failure, children may never develop a capacity to hold experience in attention to check the felt rightness of its meaning. In the process they are likely to rely on more external or socially conventional cues as a criterion for labeling experiences. Their personal senses of experiential recognition, or the lack of it, may be unattended to or actively avoided and disparaged.[33] Such experiences that have never been received empathically in childhood are likely to feel unreal or, in some mysterious way bad or poisonous to the person as an adult.

Therapists who offer empathic understanding, then, can be seen as offering a particular aspect of optimal parental interaction. By expressing their best understanding of the client's experience in the moment, therapists are valuing that version of the client's experience that generates a sense of immediated experiential recognition within the client. The intrinsic satisfaction of this sense of experiential recognition is strong enough that clients are likely to internalize the therapists' stance toward their experience–attending to and valuing the version of their own experience that offers an internal sense of rightness or recognition.

By activating the deeply human wish to have one's experience recognized and received by another, such empathic interaction is likely to bring up clients' reactions and beliefs related to any lack of such empathic recognition in earlier nurturing relationships. As a result it tends to reopen early relationship decisions about intimacy and self worth–with all of the attendant deep wishes, fears and vulnerabilities that go with such early developmental issues.

EMPATHY AND PROCESSING

Several process theorists have suggested that when people hold their experiences in an empathic attention, they tend to spontaneously reorganize their under– standing of these experiences. This reorganization occurs because new, previously unattended associations to the experience come into awareness. Gendlin notes that:

> ...having been heard, checking further inwardly, something new and further will arise there for the person. Having that also responded to, will let further steps arise.[34]

In a more information–processing model, David Wexler observes that:

> ...this range of evoked information...provides the client with a substrate for further processing, and it is from the information evoked by his meaning structures that the

client can bring new information into his field by attending to it and organizing its meaning for subsequent processing.[35]

This process happens to some degree when a people attend to and feel understood in aspects of experience that are already articulated and integrated into their sense of self. Yet, several theorists suggest that this process of spontaneously generating and integrating new experience happens particularly strongly when people attend to aspects of their experience that are not yet clear. Gendlin, Rice, and Wexler describe the way that this happens in quite different, but mutually compatible terms.

Gendlin notes that change tends to occur when:

...whatever is said and done (is) checked against the concretely felt experiencing of the person. There are no words or sentences, speculations and inferences which are themselves correct. Rather do they make touch with the person's directly felt concrete body sense of what is being worked on–or do they fail to make touch with it? If they do touch it, this might be because there is some directly felt power to the words; they result in the person feeling a sharpened sense of what is being worked on, or there might be a release and a new step emerging.[36]

Laura Rice suggests that spontaneous reprocessing of experiencing occurs when clients attend to the immediacy of their images of a life situation rather than limiting attention to their previously articulated "schema" about the situation.

...the client's memory of the experience is fuller than his construction of it. As a client talks about an experience, his account will be a mixture of levels including both his construction of the experience and also some material much closer to the original experience that is not encompassed by the construction.[37]

When a therapist is able to evoke the vividness of such original experiences,

...it is as if the client goes back into the situation with a more or less deliberate suspension of his usual automatic construction. He is able to respond freshly to the full complexity of both internal and external aspects of the situation. Parts of the reaction that have become isolated can become integrated with the rest. Aspects that have been felt with less than their full intensity can be fully experienced.[38]

In a similar vein, David Wexler notes that when a person identifies a particular experience, this is likely to bring a broad range of related aspects of the experience into awareness.[39] For example,

...a client who in describing his state of depression says "I feel very much alone." This may evoke in highly condensed and crude form a whole range of information, which for illustrative purposes might include the following: fleeting thoughts of a lack of someone who cares for him, fragmentary memories such as the image of himself lying on his bed staring at the ceiling on a Saturday night, seeing cold faces on the street car staring indifferently ahead.[40]

He notes that:

...this information...is evoked only momentarily and is held in its crude, unprocessed form in memory for subsequent processing of its meaning.[41]

If the person holds aspects of experience that are not easily subsumed in is or her pre–existing understanding of the situation in attention, new facets of meaning can be differentiated.[42] The client may then organize these facets with a new superordinate structure that captures their common meaning. Such integrating meaning structures:

> ...should not be thought of as a mere summation of the subordinate structures. Rather it is an actively synthesized construction generated from information evoked by these structures. This synthesis not only organizes the differentiated structures with respect to each other, but in so doing they take on new meaning because they are now embodied in and subsumed by a new structure.[43]

EMPATHY AND THE ATTRACTION TO EXPERIENCING THAT IS IMMEDIATE AND UNCLEAR

Since schema are interconnected to each other within the mind, the processing of issues of immediate concern is likely to bring relevant related experiences into client awareness. Laura North Rice notes that:

> Anything that is felt by the client as problematic or "loaded" is inevitably a member of a problem class, although neither the client nor the therapist has any idea where it will lead.[44]

Rice and Saperia note that the immediacy or vividness of such problematic situations can lead clients intuitively to search for what is salient in such situations.

> Saliency was not a matter of cognitive judgement, but more an affective recognition...The therapist would say something like "There was just something that got to you, something about his face or the way he said it–? I don't know–?" Sometimes the client would know instantly. At other times it would start the client on a self–directed search for saliency...And, once they became aware of the salient aspect, it became a powerful evocator of their own subjective construal of crucial aspects of the situation.[45]

In particular, Rice and Sapiera note that processing unfinished aspects of current experience tends to evoke related earlier memories. a phenomenon they call "time–sliding."

> ...two of the three clients, while exploring new facets of their own feelings, had a sudden, very live memory of an earlier situation in which they had experienced that same feeling. It was clearly not an intellectual search, but a spontaneous, vivid memory.[46]

These three process theorists agree that attention to less articulated and integrated aspects of experience tends to stimulate a valuable, self–directed processing of experience leading to new understandings. But why, if at all, should empathic understanding lead clients to attend to such less–articulated aspects of experience? Wexler and Rice address this issue in passing. Wexler notes that:

> We may think of two very basic but somewhat opposing tendencies which underlie this attempt (to elaborate and reorder information): a need for organization and order in processing information and structuring the field, and a need for new experience and change in the field.[47]

John Butler and Laura North Rice make a similar point in "Adience, Self–Actualization and Drive Theory":

...the client is thus, as it were, working on the edges of self–created anxiety. He is adiently motivated to create new experience, new cognitive structures, and avoidantly motivated by the anxiety associated with any impulse to seek new experience. It is the constant prizing permissiveness and understanding of the therapist, serving to create a safe interpersonal climate that tips the scales in favor of adient motivation.[48]

How, then, do clients experience the kind of stimulus hunger which, according to Wexler, Butler and Rice, serves to counterbalance the threat inherent in such unarticulated experience? The following sequence seems plausible. Experiences that are symbolized, articulated and integrated into one's sense of self offer a reassuring sense of order and predictability–even if they are negative. (For example, "I'll probably die an alcoholic like my father.") Yet, such well–articulated experiences tend to be felt as having less immediacy and aliveness than experiences that have not yet been fully articulated. When empathic responding offers the reassurance that one's experience is comprehensible to another, this tends to lessen one's fear of the unknown. Under these circumstances, the sense aliveness present in less integrated, articulated aspects of experience increases its intrinsic attractiveness. And, the deep human tendency to want to have a sense of coherence, to resolve discrepancies in one's experience, becomes more compelling.

For example, a client might explain that she loves her mother and is looking forward to going home. At the same time, she might feel a heavy, sinking feeling in her stomach or an awareness of tears in her eyes, or have the passing thought that her mother should be put into a home. Attention to these experiences that are less integrated into her usual sense of herself opens the possibility of contradicting everything she thinks that she feels about her mother and this visit. And she has no way of knowing how these experiences may disrupt her world if she allows herself to follow them where they lead. Yet, there is some vitality, some juiciness to these aspects of her experience that is missing when she talks about what she believes she already knows about her relationship with her mother.

For the same reasons that attending to these experiences makes someone vulnerable, expressing them to another person involves vulnerability. If one is not able to control where such experiences are likely to go within oneself, one is even less able to control how another person would understand or react to them. Thus in a relationship a person can feel drawn to the relative safety of only expressing fully articulated aspects of one's experience. But the very risk and aliveness of sharing less articulated experiences tends to make the experience of being understood in these moments feel more personal and more meaningful.

This suggests a very interesting relationship between empathy, the depth of the client's personal sense of experiential recognition, and optimal processing of experience. The same subset of experiences that tend to resonate most deeply, that create the deepest feeling of being understood in the client also have a particularly strong tendency to stimulate a spontaneous, self–directed processing of experience in the client. Empathic understanding in and of itself, then, has a powerful effect in stimulating optimal processing.

Wexler notes that optimal processing experiences tend to be intrinsically reinforcing to the client.

> The client is then likely to engage in this mode more frequently. By engaging in an optimal mode of experiencing, basically the client learns that he can be his own source for creating new experience and change via his own cognitive functioning...By using organizing rules in flexible combination with one another to generate novel and vivid

organizing structures, the client will also be adding to his existent repertoire of ways for organizing and construing information.[49]

SELECTIVE RESPONDING AND EMPATHY

Some critics of empathic responding have suggested that therapists are simply selectively reinforcing the kinds of contents that the therapist wishes the client to pursue. Empathic listening is selective, but in quite a different way. The listener tries to formulate and communicate that sense of understanding that will resonate most deeply with the client. In so doing, the therapist hopes that the client will have that sense of experiential recognition that comes with feeling fully understood, but does not aim to influence or alter the client's experience in other ways. The kinds of therapist response that generate such an experience of recognition are varied and never fully predictable. One time a client may feel most understood when a therapist says his or her exact words at a particularly poignant moment. At other times a therapist may construe a crucial meaning that the client is trying to convey but has not put into words at all, and the client may feel more understood than he or she would have if the therapist restated what she had actually said. Jerald Bozarth has noted that at certain moments a therapist joke or spontaneous gesture may convey understanding more strongly than any more conventional expression of empathy.[50]

A number of theorists, including Rice, Wexler and Gendlin, have suggested that therapeutic responding needs to be selective at certain points to stimulate optimal processing of experience as articulated in their respective process models.[51] Certainly, therapists can use any of these processing theories to introduce or selectively reinforce particular aspects of experience with the intention of introducing or intensifying processing experiences in the client. While such interventions leave the interpretation of content up to the client, they run the risk of introducing the same issues of resistance and conditions of worth related to client process as any other more directive, interpretative responses. Therapists, then, have the added task of assessing client reactions to process suggestions and deciding whether the client would like to follow the therapist's suggestions or continue on some other client–initiated track. Process–directive empathic therapists typically are quite careful of the client's wishes in this regard, abandoning any suggestions that are not immediately well–received by the client. Whatever clinical strategy a therapist adopts, I think that it is important to remain conceptually clear that the kind of selectivity that goes into empathic responding is quite different from the kind of selectivity that goes into process–directive comments in both its intentions and its impact on the therapist's relationship with clients.

EMPATHIC RESPONDING TO CLIENT MATERIAL THAT IS IMMEDIATE AND UNCLEAR

Empathic responding to less articulated and integrated aspects of experience offers a particular challenge to the therapist. Since such experiences are in the process of coming into awareness and being formulated, therapists can easily read in their own more fully articulated meanings and "fill in the blanks" for the client. In so doing, the therapist can easily stop the client's process of attending to the immediacy and aliveness of such experiences and of finding the personal meaning that resonates with the experience for the client.

Process theorists have offered a number of hints as to how therapists can stay in contact with the immediacy of experiencing without stopping the client's process. Gendlin[52] has suggested that therapists can use open–ended words like "something" or "that" which point to the felt referent without specifying its content. He has also suggested that the therapist stay very close to the client's exact words when the client seems to be touching immediately felt experiences which are in the process of being articulated. Under these circumstances, the clients' exact words offer the client a "handle" which allows them to hold a sense of connection to their felt sense of the experience.[53]

Laura North Rice suggests that staying with the vividness and immediacy of particular life scenes recounted by the client rather than summarizing and abstracting allows clients to re-experience and reformulate such experiences. Conative language used by the client is particularly likely to suggest various associated impressions and possibilities beyond the explicit meaning.

> Language based on sensory imagery (auditory, kinesthetic, etc.) as well as visual is especially connotative in its impact. Metaphorical language seems particularly suited to the task of accurately evoking an experience while leaving open all sorts of possibilities that are not yet clear. Metaphors can be both concrete and open.[54]

David Wexler notes that therapists:

> ...should listen carefully for and select those facets of information that seem to refer to central aspects of the client's functioning and that either seem to have an unfinished flavor for the client or which seem to present processing difficulties for him.[55]

He suggests that:

> ...often a quaver of the voice, a quiver of the mouth, or a postural shift can serve as a far more reliable signal to the therapist that the client is moving into significant territory than the particular words he says.[56]

He observes that therapists should be both concise and vivid in capturing the exact point of the client's overall themes and of the specific facts that emerge from such themes.[57]

Wexler notes that therapists frequently fail to capture the exact specificity of the clients central point when they are telling a story or making comments about their lives, making more generic comments about client feelings such as "You seem really upset." Then when the client does begin to articulate new, less integrated facets of meaning in an attempt to expand or check or clarify whether their original point feels right to them, therapists can easily pass over these, discouraging the client's natural tendency to generate and integrate new facets of meaning.[58] Gendlin makes a similar point when he notes that client-centered practitioners have:

> ...developed a great sense for exact specificity. A round, vague approximation is not yet really listening...this recognition enables us to stay with the person's felt datum and with whatever the person actually says, until we get it.[59]

PROCESSING AND THE REVISION OF LIFE NARRATIVES

Human beings have the ongoing capacity to reconstrue the meaning of their lives and the strategies with which they choose to organize experience. The sort of processing that we have been exploring in this paper offers one of the main ways that this ongoing reformulation of life meanings takes place.

One can, of course, adopt a life narrative wholesale from the culture of others' preconceived ideas about one's self. Yet, such preformed narratives will be dry and detached–creating a false self experience–if they have not been integrated with one's organismically felt responses to life. Processing allows a dialectic between the intricacy of lived experience and they ways that lived experience might be construed within one's culture and life circumstances.[60]

This creation of a personally grounded life story is neither totally determined nor totally open to choice. There is always more than one sensible account that one could offer of one's life history. A person has a considerable amount of existential freedom in deciding what to make of his or her life and what strategies to adopt in approaching the future. Yet, not all versions of a person's life story–however outwardly sensible–ring true to the person herself. A rendition of one's life narrative creates a sense of experiential recognition, or the lack of it, much the way that responses to smaller units of meaning do.

HOW DOES EMPATHY CURE?

Virtually all people live within a life narrative that leaves some aspects of their experience poorly explicated. Some experiences that are felt organismically are not named, or are named in ways that do not function well in helping to make sense of one's situation. One's acknowledged reasons for doing things may contradict each other or they may contradict important aspects of reality as seen by other people. And, even if people's articulated understanding of themselves were fully congruent with all of their lived experience, they would still be likely to generate new life goals and aspirations which would need to be integrated with their experiences in life thus far. To the degree that empathic understanding stimulates the processing of experience and the reworking of life narratives, it is likely to be valuable to virtually all people throughout their lives.

However, I believe that empathic understanding plays a particularly crucial role in therapy with clients who have suffered empathic failure in childhood to the point that their ability to hold and process experience has been severely compromised. I believe that such people are likely to experience a "fragile" style of processing as adults.[61] Clients who have a fragile style of processing tend to experience core issues at very high or low levels of intensity. They have difficulty starting or stopping experiences that are personally significant or emotionally connected. And, they are likely to have difficulty taking the point of view of another person while remaining in contact with their own experiences.

Empathic understanding responses are often the only sorts of responses people with a fragile style of processing can receive without feeling traumatized or disconnected from their experience. The ongoing presence of a soothing, empathic person is often essential to the person's ability to stay connected without feeling overwhelmed. In a certain sense, clients in the middle of fragile process are asking if their way of experiencing themselves has a right to exist in the world. Any misnaming of their experience or suggestions that they look at the experience in a different way is experienced as an answer of "no" to the question and is likely to be felt as an annihilation of their right to exist at all.

I believe that such fragile processing accounts for much of the intensity of negative reaction to interpretive comments which Kohut observes in analysands diagnosed as narcissistic. At the same time, it accounts for much of the intensity of dependence and selfobject transference such clients initially experience with therapists who do provide an ongoing climate of empathic understanding.

For clients with fragile styles of processing, an empathic relationship may well create the *only* place in the world that they are able to exist in an existential sense, since it is the only place they are able to hold experiences without being traumatized. Understandably, such clients would feel frantic at the idea of losing the therapist or being away for even moderate periods of time.

Ongoing empathic interaction is directly curative for such clients in that it offers the sort of empathic, selfobject relating that was missing in childhood. Clients with fragile process are initially only able to hold their experience in an ongoing empathic relationship with another—and that with considerable difficulty. The experience of holding their experience in a selfobject partnership with another tends to reengage with the natural developmental sequence by which the capacity to hold and process experience is internalized.

Related capacities—such as the ability to modulate the intensity of experiences and the ability to take in another person's perspective without feeling that one's own has been annihilated—tend to develop spontaneously. This fits with Kohut's observation that after a period of exclusively empathic responding to his analysands they become able to take in experience—near observations without feeling that the empathic bond with the therapist has been ruptured.

REFERENCES

Basch, M. (1986). *Can this be psychoanalysis?* In A. Goldberg (Ed.), *Progress in Self Psychology*, Vol 2 (pp. 59–75). New York: Praeger.

Bozarth, J. D. (1984). *Beyond reflection: Emergent modes of empathy.* In R. F. Levant and J. M. Shlien (Eds.), *Client Centered Therapy and the Person–Centered Approach: New Directions in Theory, Research, and Practice* (pp. 59–75). New York: Praeger.

Brodley, B. T. (1990). *Client–centered and experiential: Two different therapies.* In G. Lietaer, J. Rombauts & R. Van Balen (Eds.), *Client–Centered and Experiential Psychotherapy In the Nineties.* Leuven, Belgium: Leuven University Press.

Butler, J. M. & Rice, L. N. (1963). *Adience, self–actualization and drive theory.* In J. M. Wepman & R. W. Heine (Eds.), *Concepts of Personality.* Chicago: Aldine.

Demos, V. (1984). *Empathy and affect: Reflections on infant experience.* In J. Lichtenberg, M. Bornstein, & D. Silver (Eds.), *Empathy II.* Hillsdale, N. J.: The Analytic Press.

Freud, S. (1912). *Recommendations to physicians practicing psychoanalysis.* In *Standard Edition*, (12:111–120). London: Hogarth Press, 1958. (Quoted in L. Agosta (1984), *Empathy and intersubjectivity.* In J. Lichtenberg et al. (Eds.), *Empathy I* (p. 53). Hillsdale, N. J.: The Analytic Press.)

Gendlin, E. T. (1964). *A theory of personality change.* In P. Worchel & D. Byrne (Eds.), *Personality Change* (pp. 100–148). New York: John Wiley & Sons.

Gendlin, E. T. (1968). *The experiential response.* In E. Hammer (Ed.), *Use of Interpretation in Therapy* (pp. 208–227). New York: Grune & Stratton.

Gendlin, E. T. (1974). *Client–centered and experiential psychotherapy.* In D. Wexler & L. N. Rice (Eds.), *Innovations in Client–Centered Therapy* (pp. 211–246). New York: John Wiley & Sons.

Gendlin, E. T. (1990). *The small steps of the therapy process: How they come and how to help them come.* In G. Lietaer, J. Rombauts, & R. Van Balen (Eds.), *Client–Centered and Experiential Psychotherapy in the Nineties.* Leuven, Belgium: Leuven University Press.

Gendlin, E. T. *The client's client: The edge of awareness.* Paper in draft.

Goldstein, A. P. & Michaels. G. Y. (1985). *Empathy: Development, Training, and Consequences.* Hillsdale, N. J.: Lawrence Erlbaum Associates.

Hoffman, M.L. (1989). *Empathy, social cognition and moral action.* In W. M. Kurtines & J. L. Gewirtz (Eds.), *Moral Behavior and Development.* Hillsdale, N. J.: Lawrence Erlbaum. (Quoted in A. Kohn (1990). *The Brighter Side of Human Nature* (p. 115). New York: Basic Books.)

Kohut, H. (1971). *The Analysis of the Self.* New York: International Universities Press.

Kohut, H. (1977). *The Restoration of the Self.* New York: International Universities Press.

Kohut, H. (1982). *Introspection, empathy, and the semicircle of mental health.* Reprinted in J. Lichtenberg et al. (Eds.), *Empathy I* (1984) (pp. 81–100). Hillsdale, N.J.: The Analytic Press. (Originally published in the *International Journal of Psychoanalysis*, 63: 395–408.)

Kohut, H. (1984). *How Does Analysis Cure?* Chicago: University of Chicago Press.

Lee, R. (1988). *Reverse selfobject experience.* American Journal of Psychotherapy, 42:416–424.

Lee, R. & Martin, J. C. (1991). *Psychotherapy After Kohut: A Textbook of Self Psychology.* Hillsdale, N. J.: The Analytic Press. The Random House College Dictionary, Revised Edition (1988). J. Stein, (Ed.). New York: Random House.

Rice, L.N. (1974). *The evocative function of the therapist.* In D. A. Wexler & L. N. Rice (Eds.). Innovations in Client–Centered Therapy (pp. 289–311). New York: John Wiley & Sons.

Rice, L.N. & Greenberg, L. S. (Eds.) (1984). *Patterns of Change.* New York: The Guilford Press.

Rogers, C. R. (1957). *The necessary and sufficient conditions of therapeutic personality change.* Journal of Consult. Psychol., 21, 95–103.

Rogers, C. R. (1959). *A theory of therapy, personality and interpersonal relationships, as developed in the client–centered framework.* In S. Koch (Ed.), *Psychology: A Study of a Science*, Vol. III. *Formulation of the Person and the Social Context*, (pp. 184–256), 5(2), (pp. 2–10).

Rogers, C. R. (1975). *Empathic: An unappreciated way of being.* The Counseling Psychologist, 5(2), (pp. 2–10).

Stern, D. N. (1985). *The Interpersonal World of the Infant.* New York: Basic Books.

---

[1] C. R. Rogers (1957), (1959); H. Kohut (1971), (1977), (1984).

[2] For a summary of this research, see A. P. Goldstein and G. Y. Michaels (1985), pp. 131–142.

[3] See, for example, B. T. Brodley (1990) and J. D. Bozarth (1984).

[4] See Eugene Gendlin (1968) "The Experiential Response", and (1964) "A Theory of Personality Change"; Laura North Rice (1974) "The Evocative Function of the Therapist"; and David Wexler (1974) "A Cognitive Theory of Experiencing, Self–Actualization and Therapeutic Process".

[5] H. Kohut (1984), p. 177.

[6] H. Kohut (1964), pp. 66–67.

[7] H. Kohut (1984), pp. 102–103.

[8] H. Kohut (1982), p. 85.

[9] H. Kohut (1982), p. 85.

[10] Throughout this paper I am assuming that effective empathic interaction also meets Carl Rogers other "necessary and sufficient" conditions–that the therapist is genuine and prizing of the client in his or her responses, and that these conditions are perceived by the client to some degree.

[11] The Random House College Dictionary (1988), p. 433.

[12] See, for example, A. Goldstein and G. Y. Michaels (1985), pp. 12–61 for a summary of this literature.

[13] For example, Martin Hoffman (1989) takes this position when he defines empathy as feeling what is appropriate to someone else's situation; that is, what the person would feel if he or she were fully aware of the situation.

[14] S. Freud, (1912).

[15] R. Schafer (1983), p. 36.

[16] C. R. Rogers (1959), pp. 210–211.

[17] M. Basch (1986), p. 25, defines empathy in a similar way when he defines it as a "readiness to experience what it is the patient is experiencing in the patient's terms." (Quoted in R. Lee and J. C. Martin (1991), p. 106.)

[18]See, for example, Kohut's (1984) descriptions of empathic responding, pp. 173–184.

[19]H. Kohut (1982), pp. 84–85.

[20]While I believe that this is the strongest change–inducing effect of empathic understanding, there may be other ways that empathy functions as well. Barbara Brodley (1990) notes that these may be various and idiosyncratic to particular individuals.

[21]This, of course, is complex, since being understood or seen may be experienced in itself as threatening under some circumstances. However, in a noninterpretive, empathic relationship the client has the option of shifting to less self–revealing material should the level of threat feel too high.

[22]E. T. Gendlin (1964), p. 112.

[23]Ibid.

[24]Ibid, p. 113.

[25]Ibid.

[26]C. R. Rogers (1975), p. 159.

[27]E. T. Gendlin (1964), pp. 113–114.

[28]Ibid, p. 130.

[29]Ibid, p. 135.

[30]D. Stern (1985), pp. 100–123.

[31]See, for example, V. Demos (1984), pp. 9–34.

[32]See, for example, R. Lee (1988).

[33]D. Stern (1985) elaborates on this process in his chapter on "The Verbal Self", pp. 162–182.

[34]E. T. Gendlin (1974), p. 221.

[35]D. Wexler (1974), pp. 68–69.

[36]E. T. Gendlin (1974), p. 212.

[37]L. N. Rice (1974), p. 300.

[38]Ibid, p. 299.

[39]D. Wexler (1974), p. 66.

[40]Ibid, pp. 69–70.

[41]Ibid, pp. 70.

[42]Ibid, p. 69.

[43]Ibid, p. 72.

[44]L. N. Rice (1974), p. 294.

[45]L. N. Rice and L. S. Greenberg, (Eds.) (1984), p. 42.

[46]Ibid.

[47]Ibid, p. 66.

[48]John M. Butler and Laura North Rice (1963), "Adience, Self–Actualization, and Drive Theory", p. 102.

[49]D. Wexler (1974), p.78.

[50]J. D. Bozarth (1984).

[51]See D. Wexler (1974), pp. 98–99; L. N. Rice (1974), p. 306; and E. T. Gendlin (1974),. pp. 222–226.

[52]Gendlin includes both empathic and process–directive elements in his writings; both Rice and Wexler have presented their models in a process directive format. In quoting them here I am extracting elements that I think apply within a nondirective, empathic understanding response process.

[53]See Gendlin, "The Client's Client: The Edge of Awareness", pp. 15–16.

[54]L. N. Rice (1974), p. 309.

[55]D. Wexler (1974), p. 99.

[56]Ibid.

[57]Ibid, pp. 100–101.

[58]D. Wexler (1974).

[59]E. T. Gendlin (1974), pp. 214–215.

[60]E. T. Gendlin (1990), pp. 213–214, makes a similar point.

[61]A fuller consideration of this subject can be found in Warner (1991) "Fragile Process."

Focusing Therapy
Some Fragments in which the Whole Can Become Visible

JOHANNES WILTSCHKO

WIEN

ABSTRACT

Presentation of theses on the basic principles, attitudes and methods of focusing therapy, as formulated by Gene Gendlin in recent years and further developed by the Deutsches Ausbildungsinstitut für Focusing und Focusing-Therapie (DAF), especially in the field of verbal therapeutic communication and bodywork including some philosophical and political aspects.

PREFACE

I have planned to present, here at this conference, focusing therapy, focusing therapy as a whole, neatly and systematically. In the DAF[1], *the German Training Institute for Focusing and Focusing Therapy*, we have now been using the expression "focusing therapy" for seven years to indicate the method of our psychotherapeutic work and our way of psychotherapeutic training. We have published several papers on this subject and gave birth to a whole series of books. The term "focusing therapy" is also being used in the meantime by several Northern American colleagues. Next year in Germany the *First International Conference on Focusing Therapy* will take place as part of the *International Focusing Summerschool*. So focusing therapy is in the air. And I am delighted to have the opportunity particularly here, at this meeting of client-centered and experiential colleagues, to explain our understanding of focusing therapy.

At the *International Focusing Conference* this year I have already formulated some essentials about focusing therapy. One of them I should like to start with: Focusing therapy is not just any psychotherapeutic method, for instance the client-centered, *plus* some focusing instructions or focusing exercises. No, *focusing therapy takes place when* - as Neil Friedman (1993, p.1)[2] expressed it - "focusing gives therapy its flavour, its atmosphere, its vibration", or, as I should say, when *the entire therapeutic process is pervaded by what Gendlin developed in his experiential philosophy and in its practical version, the focusing.* This does not mean that focusing therapy is merely based on philosophical concepts. Experiential philosophy itself is an experiential process, experiencing is not excluded by this philosophy, the concepts of Gendlin's philosophy are working *with* experiencing, with the ongoing living process.

Focusing therapy is a form of client-centered therapy, is part of the person-centered approach. Nevertheless it is specific enough to deserve a name of its own. The provisional term *experiential psychotherapy* is too general - which therapist would not like to describe himself as experience-oriented - and it cannot be translated into other languages, at least not into German. Even Gendlin recently dropped this term. My desire now is to present this new client-centered form of psychotherapy and I do hope that it will be welcomed and assimilated into the client-centered family.

But, I have to say right at the beginning: there will be no neat, systematic presentation. For two days I have been trying hard to find a thread that would allow to develop such a system. But psychotherapy, especially focusing therapy, is a *living event*, varied in form, complex, intricate, a hologram. Focusing therapy can be looked at from many different angles, every time one will recognize something else, every time one will loose something else. Focusing therapy is a jungle of which one cannot draw an overall map. To trust maps would mean to get lost, to lose.

But there is even a more specific reason why it is very difficult to write about focusing therapy in a common scientific manner. Focusing is connected with and related to a *phenomenological modell* of change processes. This model is a metamodel of how we can create concepts. What is unusual, special and new about these concepts created by this metamodel is that they are *more* and deal with *more* than merely concepts. *In* and *with* this metamodel we think *with* and *about* that which is *more* than verbal, logical forms. This „more" refers to that which we are presently experiencing: the feeling of the living body, the sensing of the momentary situation, the existing within relationships. This „more" is what we call the *felt sense* or the *intricacy* (and this is always an „excess" in regard to logical or linguistic forms). The concepts of this model not only depict the process of experiencing, relationship and change, they *work with* experiencing, relationship and change. Thus these concepts can only be defined *by* and *with* this experiential aspect. Therefore, Gendlin calls them „odd concepts". Odd concepts always are connected with the felt sese.

This is the reason why it is almost impossible to write about focusing in the usual way. I do know this, but in the first two days unfortunately I tried it all the same. It didn't lead to any proper result. Finally I remembered something I already wrote some years ago in the preface of my book „From Language to the Body" (1992)[3]:

> Many people are expecting that there will finally be something like a focusing therapy manual. Even though now and again I also dream of a comprehensive and systematic book ... - God prevent me from ever writing such a thing! It is not just true that - as is always being said - the theory of focusing is still undefined and the practice not complete; no, the essential, new, original aspects in particular of focusing demand philosophy and poetry and not rigid syntactic structures and stringent regulations of behavior.

> Words, terms, concepts are not only signs, defined by a dictionary, bearing logical proportions to each other, words always also have a soft underbelly - as Gendlin once called the implicit aspect of concepts. This "soft underbelly" of explicit forms wants to be experienced, to be felt: this sensing, this dwelling with the soft underbelly, with the felt sense, gives birth to our sentences - also to our sentences about focusing - and it gives birth to our actions - also to our actions as focusing therapists. The truth of our words, the adequacy of our actions we experience through our body: is the "soft underbelly" moving, does it open itself, will a new step follow? Perhaps we also have an "aha-experience" "in our head", an insight, greater clarity, more reality.

> We are creating anew explicit words, explicit actions in every situation, in every interaction - here and now. Focusing is interested specifically in this generating process, this coming into being of new sentences and new actions. It is not primarily interested in the sentences themselves, the actions themselves. Therefore there cannot be a manual with a collection of sentences, of techniques and exercises to focusing and focusing therapy.

When this finally again became clear to me I created a distance of half a meter between me and my computer and asked myself: "Johannes, what do you actually really want to say in this very moment about focusing?" With that a first sentence arose: *"I believe that the correct next step in my life will occur if I turn to myself".* And from this sentence the following just came by itself. All these sentences together received the title "Credo". As credos usually stand at the end, I shall not read it to you yet, but first present some fragments of the hologram "focusing therapy" in which perhaps the whole becomes distinguishable. They came after the credo at least was already there. This first fragment has the heading:

THE STUPID LOOK THAT IN REALITY IS SOFT AND WITHOUT INTENTION

On one of our last focusing seminars for beginners we had a book called "The Magic Eye". Many of you may know it. A participant looked at it when we had a break and afterwards she was overjoyed: "Now I finally understand what focusing is!" From this event I should like to make a little story, a story about the apparently magical aspect of the focusing process.

If you pay attention to one of these „3D" pictures, first you will only see a chaotic swarming of spots, patterns, colours. What is this meant to be? It does not seem very promising. One would prefer to put it away again instantly and to turn to more important and concrete issues. However, a friendly person joins you and encourages you to take a little more time to pay attention to this diffuse picture. He tells you:

"Look at this picture - you don't have to figure anything out."

"Open your eyes, let them become wide - and wait."

"Relax your body - and while you let the image have its effect on you folow your breathing."

"Allow yourself to let the picture blur, stay alert - and don't expect anything."

You breathe and look. Your face starts to relax and you hear yourself saying inwardly: „I hope nobody enters the room and sees me, I must look like a fool, sitting and staring at the picture with this stupid look on my face." Stupid look ... *attentive without intention* the friendly person next to you will call this. Indeed - the picture starts to blur, you discern even less then before - and suddenly it obtains a third dimension, a depth. It turns into space. You feel how surprise is arising within you and how the meaningless image suddenly becomes interesting. It emanates something fascinating as it has started to change somehow "by itself". It has gained depth which first was not discernible. You think: "Ah, now I know how it functions! I *must not* make an effort, I *must* relax " "I must not ...I must ..." starts to draw a loop in your mind, once, twice, three times ... - and the picture soon becomes shallow, boring and meaningless again. You hear the friendly person quietly say: "... look at the picture ... you don't have to find anything ... stay with it ... breathe ... wait ..." Suddenly the depth is there again, the space, and in this space a figure turns into a shape, a new shape, something concrete. You hear how you breathe with relief, you feel how your body relaxes and a childlike wonder, a joy is arising in you. You notice how you can look around in this picture which has become a three-dimensional space, just as if you are walking around in it. You discover more and more figures, different levels. This walking around gives pleasure. - Suddenly the door opens, a friend comes in and asks: "What are you doing there?" In that very moment all the shapes, all the levels, the space are gone - and again you only see this shallow picture, bare of meaning. You are irritated by the interruption and you are a little bit disappointed that this submerging in the picture is over, but you know that you have seen something special, that in this chaotic swarming there is a meaning and a sense and you think: next time I shall look again into this picture, but then I shall first shut the door to have *free space* and time to let this remarkable *process* happen.

This story shows many of the experiencing steps that usually happen when you turn your attention to the *felt sense*, that is when you, to express it badly, "do" focusing. What is a felt sense? I guess most of you know it. A felt sense can come in the middle of your body, if, for example, you ask yourself now in this very moment: „How am I feeling just now while listening to Johannes ... ?" A felt sense is a bodily mood and this mood is always *about* something - in this case it is about the situation „sitting in this room and listening to the lecture". In focusing therapy we are always looking for the felt sense which is about the topic the client is dealing with. We do not want to talk about a problem. We want to let come a bodily felt sense about the momentary issue (problem, question, concept, ...).

Someone who has never experienced focusing can get an impression of what a focusing experience is quite quickly by excercising with the "magic eye": how first one always sits as if in front of a grey wall that does not promiss anything (that is when you are asking your body: „What is the *felt sense* of ... (a specific issue you want to work on)?"), and how one stares at it with a stupid look on one's face, first without hope that anything will happen (that is the *attitude of inner mindfullness without any intention*).

The fact that focusing always begins with this experience which promises nothing, with this „you cannot *do* anything", is probably why always a genuine decision (or a supportive invitation from the person or therapist accompanying a focusing session) is required to start practizing focusing. This first phase is often like being in no man's land, like dwelling at an impossible point, a tiny act of dying, during which you let go of all your intentions, your urges, your desire to act and to be successful. This letting go is not a moral requirement, it is an inner necessity. There's no way around it.

Furthermore, the story shows how one needs patience and confidence (that is the *dwelling* with the felt sense); how a friendly *companion* can help you with that; how the grey wall suddenly changes into a *space* and an *inner world* comes into being in which one can walk around and perceive how the felt sense suddenly "opens up" and a surprising *new step* forward is taken; how this step changes the bodily experience (that is the *felt shift*). This new step forward is always *qualitatively* new, it changes the situation, it changes the problem not only on the cognitive level of insight, but it also changes the direct, concrete, always bodily feeling and experiencing, it changes the whole spirit, the whole mood, *die Befindlichkeit,* of the person towards being more alive, more present, more free.

The story also teaches us how important an undisturbed, *free space* is where one can be what one is; and how easily one can prevent those steps from happening, for instance through pressure ("people would laugh at me if I couldn't do it" or, as in this example: "Ah, I must not ... I must ..."). These are the *structure bound processes* which play a leading part in every psychotherapy.

Focusing - and that is what I should like to say with this little story - is more than just perceive something inwardly. As client-centered therapists, we focusing therapists also want the client to refer to himself - instead of looking at the therapist and expecting a solution from him. Why do we want the client to pay attention to himself? The reason is that we as client-centered therapists are convinced that the client *in principle* knows himself a thousand times better than any other human being ever could. Even as a psychological expert with all my diagnostic instruments and with my clinical eye I should look like a fool if I should have to say who this client is (we only pretend to know for the National Health Service and the assurance companies). As focusing therapists however we are not only convinced of this because self-perception always is immeasurably richer than what we can observe from outside. Our conviction results from the fact that the organism - in focusing-terminology we prefer to say "body", because the organismic experience always is a body-experience -, that the body "knows" more than I consciously have available as knowledge. Why does the body "know" more? I will answer this question in a very brief way in my „Credo" later on.

Our entire client-centered so-called "technique" aims at encouraging the client towards self-exploration and supporting this self-exploration. Self-exploration is commonly understood as a process during which the client gathers inner data, where he finds new information *in himself*, where he gets to know more about himself and during which he communicates what he experiences. One often thinks that increasing self-perception and the increasing of the courage to express these inner perceptions to others adds to self-congruence - and this after all is a kind of goal of therapy. But many client-centered therapists then ask *why* a *quantitative* increase of information about oneself should lead to a *qualitative* change.

This question is answered by practice and concepts of focusing therapy. In the focusing experience it becomes evident that self-exploration is not a linear but a complex, qualitatively changing process, often first perceived as a mysterious one, a living process of bodily change. In the focusing process the tendency for self-actualization is experienced immediately and bodily. It no longer stays merely a matter of belief. There is a very basic well ordered way in which changing steps occur, a way that is not linear, a way that continues in non-logical steps. Gendlin calls this order inherent to changing moves *order of carrying forward*. I will deal with it in the „Credo", too.

To experience this process, this order of carrying forward, again and again, to describe it, to form concepts out of it, to develop methods out of it for accompanying the process, to study the difficulties and details of this changing process with different persons (different clients, different "disorders") and finally also to create the best experiential environment for learning focusing, all that is a reason for an independent "culture" within the client-centered world - and this culture is called "focusing therapy".

Focusing allows us to watch the order of carrying forward "while it is working". And what do we see there? I will try to show you what - for example - I have seen and felt recently during a partnership focusing session[4]. This following fragment ist called:

THE RED WALL AND THE TINY BUBBLE

My topic - here expressed in somewhat abstract terms - was: How can I feel connected with someone and nevertheless feel free? The *felt sense about this topic* was: I'm not getting anywhere with this, I'm stuck. I would like nothing better than to leave this emotional dead-end, to back up and get out of it. Nevertheless, my focusing companion invited me to *dwell* right there at that dead-end and *to wait*. All of a sudden this compact, opaque dead-end feeling began *to open up* and an image came to me: I saw what looked like a huge red wall, blood red and alive. Opposite the wall, I saw a tiny bubble, that was me. The bubble had the feeling that the huge red wall wanted to take it in, swallow it up. The red wall was life-threatening. Mustering all its strength, all its little vital forces, the bubble was bracing itself against being drawn in by the powerful wake of the red wall. It had no energy for anything else. No energy for its own life, to live from within itself and for itself, just energy to fight against this threat to its life. It couldn't let up in this tremendous effort. And there it came again, the *bodily feeling* of not being able to go any further, not having any alternative to not being free. But it somehow felt different, it was more transparent, more understandable, more meaningful. Nonetheless, there was no help, no solution in sight. No one else was there. Remaining there, waiting, watching the inner image, sensing the bodily feeling that went with it ... and then an *unexpected statement* welled up, a *surprising* insight: It - whoever it was - said: „You are just a little bubble, but you're alive. And no one, not even the huge red wall can take your life from you. Because your being alive is more and greater than you, little bubble, it is greater than whatever it is that is threatening you, greater than the red wall. Your being alive is indestructible. You are alive, you are here. That is all."

That is more or less the text that was "folded inside" the bodily feeling of great relief, of taking a deep breath, of inner understanding. Those are the *steps* of the order of carrying forward: a bodily felt sense of having reached a dead-end, of being stuck, an unpromising gray wall opens and takes on depth, becomes - in this example - an inner image with colors, shapes and volume. This bodily feeling suddenly gives way to a new one, a *non-logical next step*, an initial answer to the unsolved question on how freedom and connectedness can be lived. This step takes place *within the body*, it is evident in a bodily felt way. It does not come through the - admittedly tempting - act of interpreting the symbols in the image. It comes when we allow the order of carrying forward to take the next step by creating a space where we are present, where we remain, where we focus, focus on what is really there, which means bodily there.

Do all client-centered therapists know what I have described here from their own experience? Are all client-centered therapists experienced in supporting and guiding such processes of their clients? My experience of 15 years as a supervisor of client-centered therapists tells me: no, most of them don't. For this reason it is important to give a name to this experiencing, this being acquainted with, this being able to, this knowing, to save it, to train it, to describe it, to spread it, to develop forms of social support (for example conferences and a journal), in short to establish focusing therapy as an autonomous field. Perhaps the following examples of techniques typical for focusing therapy will show that it makes sense to do this and that it makes the client-centered family become richer. I should like to present three different methodical fragments of focusing therapy: (1) dis-identification, (2) the joker questions, and (3) an example from focusing bodywork and the model of experiencing and acting modalities.

FIRST EXAMPLE: DIS-IDENTIFICATION

First I should like to describe a technique of verbal focusing therapy. I call it in German "partialisieren". It seems to be something simple and small - as actually are all focusing therapy methods -, but it can help us in studying some important principles. It is very much connected with a main principle of focusing therapy: freeing the „ego", regaining the „I". This is why I present it here, it is not because this technique is the best tool and always successful.

The client from the last example says: "I don't know anymore what to do." Normally a client-centered therapist would verbalize it like this: "You don't know anymore what to do." Or: "It seems as if you are stuck." Or perhaps: "You feel helpless." The focusing therapist says back: "There is something within you that doesn't know anymore what to do."

We'll divide this sentence in three parts. "There is something" - "within you" - "and this something doesn't know anymore what to do". The structure of this sentence illuminates the entire focusing specific scenario.

Thus there is a *"something"*. With this word we describe a *content*, a content of experience. Furthermore the word "something" indicates that this content is *indefinite yet*. It can carry every possible aspect "enveloped" within it, they are implicit. Third the word "something" expresses that it is a "whole", not just some aspect or part, but a whole something.

This may sound complicated, but you surely must know this: you have a problem, an unsolved question, an conflict of decision and feel: There is something there that is important, it is part of my problem, I feel it clearly, but I don't know yet what it is. It is a quite indefinite something, it carries a significance within, but it is as if it is enveloped, not yet unfolded, not yet explicit. By the dis-identificational form of saying back, the client thus is invited to direct his attention to the "soft underbelly", to the felt sense, to the whole something about "not-knowing-anymore-what-to-do".

"Within you" indicates that besides of this "something" there is also: an *"I"*. It is expressed that this *"I" is bigger than the content*. The "I" *has* a content, it *is not* the content. By this way of formulating the client is invited to become aware: „Ah, I'm *here* and *there* is a something" (and this something doesn't know anymore what to do). Because of this the client gets as far as to *turn to* the content, to *get in touch with* this content, to establish a *relationship* between the „I" and the content. Only now this becomes possible, because first the client identified himself with his content ("*I* don't know anymore what to do.") To get in touch there have to be always two: here these two are "I" and "the content". A distance has grown: between the "I", which is free, and the content there is a bit of fresh air. The "I" feels: I am free, I can breathe - and now I can, if I like, turn to this funny part that doesn't know anymore what to do.

"This something *that doesn't know anymore what to do"* says: there is something there, a whole something of which we do not know anything yet, apart from "that it doesn't know anymore what to do." That has been until now the *explicit* part, the aspect that is already known, already symbolized, already communicable.

Through this special form of saying back it is as if an *inner stage* is being put up on which action and interaction can take place: here is the "I", there is a content, between those two there is little distance, a free space of fresh air, the content has an explicit part ("not knowing anymore what to do") and an implicit part, the felt sense, and this felt sense part is paid attention to by the "I". And that is exactly what we need for the focusing process, for the process of personal change: the client turns to a content of experience, to a something. This something is a whole and surrounded, defined something - an object. It objects to the client, he can object to it, face it, surround it, touch it, feel it and look at it. This something always also has an implicit part, a "soft underbelly", already felt, but still vague, not yet communicable. Every something has an "edge of experiencing", something *intricate*, still unclear. This is the felt sense and towards this felt sense the inner attention of the client should direct its light. It is in the light of this attention that the felt sense begins to open, to change.

When the therapist says back in this dis-identificational way, the next - and most characteristic focusing question can be added: "How does this whole "not-knowing-what-to-do" feel?" Or: "While perceiving this part, what do you feel in your body?" Very often this question is not even necessary, because the client may take this step by himself encouraged by this dis-identification. In this way it could be very easy to support the client to reach a true inner process.

Do you feel the big difference created by these two ways of responding: "You don't know anymore what to do" and "There is something in you that does not know anymore what to do"? Focusing therapy aims at getting in contact with an inner something, to pay attention to the already felt but not yet known aspect of this something, to stay with this vague, intricate something and to wait and see what will happen.

Focusing therapy does not treat the problem, the content itself. The content in itself is rigid, an invariable structure. In focusing therapy we direct our attention towards *the relationship between the "I" and the content*. The relation is changed by focusing. And by the change of this relationship the content is changed. A psychic content is *never independent* of the attitude with which we face this content. Gendlin says: contents are *process aspects*. In this processlike unity of content and relationship lies the basis of an important "mystery" of change. It is a decisive factor for the effectiveness of psychotherapy.

SECOND EXAMPLE: JOKER QUESTIONS

A further example of a verbal technique in focusing therapy are the *joker questions*. I call them that because the therapist can deal them out at almost any moment in the process, in particular when *the therapist* has the feeling that he does not know anymore what to do. Let's hope that this often happens. Each of us knows this phenomenon: I listen to the client, I accompany him in his process and I myself have an inner feeling as if there is some clarity ahead about what is happening, that I feel space for the next step, that there is a perspective (even if I don't know definitely and exactly what will happen in the next moment regarding contents). This "clarity ahead" now and then just vanishes. In that case I as a therapist either have the impression that we reached a crossroads and I "don't know", I cannot feel which direction we should take; or the forward view is completely gone. It is as if I am driving in the car through good weather and suddenly - out of the clear blue sky - it's raining cats and dogs. For some seconds I cannot see through the window - until I switch on the windshield wiper. The windshield wipers - they are the joker questions.

In such a situation of indecisiveness or of not knowing anymore what to do therapists usually strain their brains and think more or less desparately about what they should say or do. In this way they lose contact with their client and with their own experiencing - and the journey together really is stuck. The therapist maybe reproaches himself and not for the first time feels his own incompetence. Or, and that is not better either: he wants to run away from his helplessness, he quickly looks for a good idea in his inner instruction manual or for a good therapeutic tool from his tool box and he imposes his own good idea or his tool on the client. The result is that the inner searching process of the client is interrupted, but at least the therapist can maintain the feeling of being a good therapist. You all know this, don't you? I at least experience both in almost every therapy session.

In focusing therapy if such a situation occurs we just ask the client: "What could be the next step now?" or, if the client has recently started his therapy and is not yet used to this specific form of questions in focusing: "If you ask yourself inwardly 'What could be the next step now?', what answer comes up in your body?"

This sounds like a mean trick, like passing on the responsibility. But it is the opposite. Because (1) the question does not concern the explicit knowledge of the client, but his felt sense, that feeling in which the *whole present situation* is folded up, is implicitely there; (2) it makes clear that the therapist is not a wise guy who always looks at the situation from a superior position; the question implies that the client is the one to feel the best where and how the next step can be; (3) it increases the client's attention to what is there now and it invites him to leave for example his structure bound search for solutions and (4) the question points out that the therapeutic situation is really a partnership.

Further examples for joker questions are: "How could it continue now?", "What would suit you best now?", "What would feel right now?", "What would you need now?", "What would be necessary to continue now?", "What is still missing?", "What makes you stuck?", "Where do you feel life inside of you?".

It is very important to accentuate and to understand that these questions are not solutions designed to hide our embarrassment and to save us from helplessness. In the „Credo" I will formulate a basic thesis of focusing therapy: 'The body implies the next step'. The joker questions are directed towards the body as if to say: "Dear body, how can I go on? Let me know what would be right now." Through this joker questions we seriously let the order of carrying forward take over control.

THIRD EXAMPLE: FOCUSING BODY-WORK AND THE MODALITIES OF EXPERIENCING

Let's dwell for a moment on the feeling mentioned earlier: not knowing anymore what to do. A client tells you: "I would like to create more space for myself, but I don't know how." As he says this, he makes a gesture *with his arms and hands* as if he were trying to shove or push something away.

Instead of the therapist saying back the client's words or perhaps (in what would be a better response) describing the gesture, she reflects this gesture directly, in an analogous manner, as it were: She *shows* it *back* to him, she makes the gesture, too, perhaps adding a guiding question such as: "How does that feel, what do you feel there inside you when you do this (pushing away)?" This is a very simple example of a body-oriented focusing technique.

At this point, we could also invite the client to engage in a little *experiment* and offer him physical resistance by pressing against him when he pushes away while at the same time asking him: "What is happening inside you when you push against me like that." Often we also ask the client to do with his body what he tells us verbally (by adopting a posture that fits to the inner feeling or to express by a gesture what he experiences), in short *to do* something instead of talking. Often apart from accompanying this physical process by words we also do so with our body: we touch the client (for example by holding him, not only with our eyes or our voice, but also directly physically), we accompany the movements of his body with our hands (this can give way to a body-dialogue, entirely in analogy with a verbal dialogue). In focusing therapy everything we are used to do with words can be done also with our body.

When I learned client-centered therapy one of my first questions was: "Why do we (therapist and client) always sit in chairs and why do we only talk?" Hadn't Carl Rogers always spoken about the whole person? And isn't the body an important part of the body? Does a person without a body even exist at all? Is talking the only form of action, the only way how persons can communicate? Is the exchange of words the only possible form of relationship?" I presumed it should be possible in the client-centered situation to pay attention to the body without having to leave the basic client-centered attitude. I did not want to combine client-centered therapy with bioenergetics, but to complete client-centered therapy. In client-centered therapy the body is evidently missing. Soon I began to look for possibilities to include the body in the client-centered work. Focusing gave me the key to that.

In a simple chart[5] I shall show how we make the body - and also other modalities of experiencing than feeling and other modalities of acting than talking - live and act in focusing therapy.

Please imagine the circle as a spheric space. The sphere is the *space of experiencing,* a person's inner world. The central part of this sphere is the *implicit, the soft underbelly, the felt sense.*

The arrows going out from the implicit core depict the four primary *modalities of experiencing* within which the felt sense can unfold: the arrow to the east points toward the modality of experiencing we call *cognition* (which refers to words, sentences, thoughts that occur in our mind), the arrow to the north points toward the modality of *imaginations* (inwardly perceived visual pictures, colors, shapes), the arrow to the west points to the modality of *emotions* (to feelings like rage, grief, joy), and the arrow to the south points to the modality of *physical sensations* (and movement impulses).

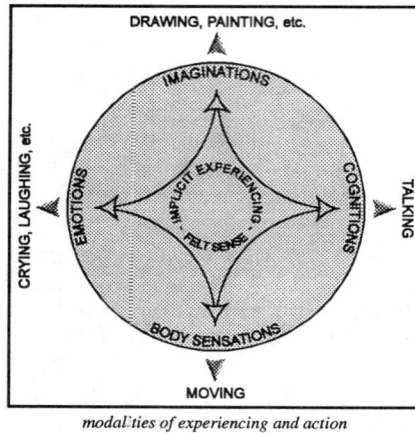

modalities of experiencing and action

Now imagine for a moment that the „I" is sitting with his inner awareness in a little ship and sailing around in the blue sphere of the experiential space. Wherever this little *awareness-ship* stops, it perceives something, a concrete bit of experience. If it happens to be in the northern hemisphere, this bit of experience tends to be more image-oriented; in the southern hemisphere, more physically perceivable. If the little awareness-ship remains more in the center of the sphere, the momentary bit of experience, the given inner datum, is strongly implicit (the soft underbelly is very thick), the character of the experience is holistic but at the same time vague and unclear. If the little ship goes to the edge of the sphere, the bit of experience takes on a more explicit quality, the nature of the experience is clearer, sharper, but the implicit sense of meaning diminishes.

Focusing is like a journey with the little awareness-ship. When it travels from the periphery to the center, we say: I am going to look for the implicit felt sense for an explicit content. When the ship travels from the center to the periphery we say: I am letting come a symbol (a word, an image, feelings, physical sensations) related to the felt sense. When the ship travels from one hemisphere to another (from one modality of experience to another), we call it a *modality change* ("When you see this inner image, is it accompanied by words [or physical sensations, or feelings]?").

Sometimes the awareness-ship lands on the shores of the outside world, the "I" disembarks and does something, it *acts*. The outer world in this graphic model is represented by the square. It is the *space for action* and it, in turn, has different *modalities of action*. They are represented by the dark arrows. Words welling up inside can be voiced, images seen by the inner eye can be painted, feelings that have been experienced can be expressed (e.g. laughing, crying, screaming) and physical sensations can be shown in movements, changes in posture, physical contact, etc.

A lot more could be said about the characteristics of focusing using this simple model. I'd like to stress at least one thing: *sitting, feeling* and *speaking is just one special form,* one of many possible forms, of focusing therapy. By the same token, focusing therapy can also be sitting, imagining, painting; it can be standing, moving, feeling and speaking; it can be lying down, sensing, being held. The model shows how we could develop a focusing imagination or dream work, for example, or a focusing body work.

Finding the right words and expressing them is not the only way a felt sense can be carried forward. This can also be done by allowing oneself to develop inwardly a physical impulse which is expressed by physical action (movement). The process can be accompanied not only by saying back words but also by acting back (e.g. touching). Experiencing seldom is given in words. Expecting the client always to express in words what he feels and senses is like requiring a huge "translation effort", like asking him to digitize analog experiences. This is often not even possible, especially in the case of "early" types of experiences. They don't extend up to the level of word symbols. It is for this very reason that verbal therapy too often excludes many of a person's most significant spheres of experiencing. That's why it can be very enriching to recognize and know how to support and accompany change processes non verbally. These bodily processes function according to the *same* order of carrying forward as the verbal processes. *It is one and the same process, just with a different modality dress.*

The modality model helps us to become oriented within the process while we are accompanying these focusing processes. It can help us make suggestions to the client, suggestions not concerned with *what* he should focus on, but on the *direction* of his focus. The modality model is a good *compass* for navigating the awareness-ship. However, that is all it is good for.

And that is important to remember. Because it can be misleading in conjunction with other aspects of focusing therapy. We *don't* distinguish, for example, between outer and inner, the outer world and the inner world. We certainly *don't* want to distinguish between "spaces" per se, we certainly don't want to relegate the felt sense to a specific location (here, in the center of the sphere). On the contrary, we emphasize that experiencing, the body, is always *situational* and never something only unto itself, existing in an empty geometric space. That's why we also say that the *inner process is at the same time a relational process.* All these aspects are missing in this model. The situation is missing. Also missing, for instance, is the therapist who the client is actually there with, there in a different way than if there were no therapist there, in a different way than if another therapist were there.

Anytime we pin something down, anytime we create a little model, new questions, new errors immediately arise. *That is why it is always false to say anything unequivocal about psychotherapy, to assert that something is true.* And that is also the necessary preface to the following precepts of the focusing therapy credo. This preface is more important than the precepts of the credo themselves.

(MY PRESENT) CREDO OF FOCUSING THERAPY

1. *I* believe the next right step in my life will occur when I turn to *myself,* when I pay attention to my inner experiencing. I do not believe that you know better than I what that next step will be.

2. Who is "I"? „I" is nothing else but „I". "I" cannot be defined by anything else. Beyond the "I" there is no going back. Nevertheless there is more than "I". But this „more" is only accessible by or through the „I". Notice, that the „I" is not the same as the „ego". The „ego" is an object, the „I" is the subject. The "I" is blank. The "I" is free. The "I" is always there - even if it is sometimes or for a long time withdrawn, hidden or lost. It is neither sick nor healthy. It is always intact, inviolable.

3. What does "myself" signify? "Myself" is what I am presently experiencing, everything I perceive within myself at the moment. What I perceive are *contents*. It is good and it does me good to perceive everything, whatever that may be. However, all that is not what I am, all that is what I "have". By becoming aware that I *have* these contents, I feel that the „I" is free. As long as I do not become aware of what is there, I believe all that is what I am. The „I" then is *identified* with contents and thus becomes an „ego". The „ego" is not able to be aware, is not able to face the „adopted" content. Because of the lack of relationsship, of interaction between „ego" and content the content cannot change. The content remains rigid. The manner of experiencing gets *structure bound*. Therefore this *identification* may give rise to many of those states we describe as "ill". This identification confines us, oppresses us, obstructs us, takes our breath away as well as our space.

4. "To turn towards oneself" means open onesself towards the inner world, to be silent and attentive. To listen, to look, to feel inwardly. To listen with friendly ears, to look with soft eyes, to feel with free breath. Inner attention. "To pay attention" means: to be aware without valuing, without explaining, without describing. To become aware without words.

5. Turning towards myself in this way immediately gives rise to a bodily feeling of increased freedom and, in the same time, of increased security. A whole mood of greater lightness comes up, even if the words that usually describe the contents which are in awareness sound unpleasant: loneliness, helplessness, tension, irritation, pain, etc. An inner, bodily felt space is created within in which the „I" is able to walk around, to choose, to look, to feel or to seperate from something, to drop it, to pass it.

6. If the „I" is turning towards a content and directing its attention towards the implicit part of this content, towards the felt sense, the „I" will sense something. This something is obviously already there (it is felt) but it is not complete, not finished yet. It is felt but not known, it is felt but not communicable, it is felt but it does not become an action yet. It is waiting for a carrying forward, it is demanding a next step. This step will cange the something itself.

7. This step forward will come „by itself", I don't have to figure it out. Therefore the step comes as a surprise. It comes because the body, the whole organism „knows" what it needs, „knows" what would be right, „knows" what the next step should be. Why does the body „know" all these things? Our body is not a Newtonian object, no thing in an empty space, but a living process that has always interacted and is always interacting with its environment, in fact it has never actually existed without its environment. There was never first a body that then began to interact with its environment, no, the body was environmental from the very beginning, it *is* its environment. And thus it "knows" about its environment. Our body is an ongoing living process that grows by itself, that takes steps by interactive processes. It is neither a chaotic bundle of drives that one has to impose an order on, nor it is a white sheet on which environment first has to write its story, nor it is an empty box that is only filled by education, by the gathering of knowledge. Because we understand the organism, the body, the creature, the human being as a process that is environmental from the very beginning and that

takes its own steps from this interaction with its environment, we are not working as educationalists, but psychotherapists.

8. All this means: *the body implies its next step.* This is for me, as it were, the first main sentence of Gendlin's philosophy. Gendlin has described this implying, not only within a psychotherapeutic process, but as a philosophical principle of order. He calls it the *order of carrying forward*, in German I call it "Fortsetzungsordnung". This order of carrying forward makes us understand exactly the inner logic of changing processes. *The order of carrying forward defines, governs the changing processes, the therapeutic process.*

9. What is this order of carrying forward? This term says that the way the body discovers the next step that will carry forward the present process of experiencing has a certain order. The next step is not a logical result of what is already there, nevertheless this carrying forward does have a certain order. It is an order which is not yet finished. This order demands a carrying forward. The body is ready for the next step. But it is not easy to find one. Most of the questions or concepts do not lead to an experiential, felt step, do not carry forward the process. In focusing therapy we are looking for those concepts, for those questions, for those words and actions that bring this experiential step forward. Concepts, questions, actions leading to a bodily felt step forward give us the inwardly felt evidence that only these concepts, questions, concepts are right and „true". What was there before the step is changed by the step. Therefore every step changes the whole body - and the whole changed body, the changed felt sense is again ready for a next new step. Thus a changing process occurs. Looking backwards this process seems to be logical. Afterwards we can read an order (a logical one, a dialectical one, ...) into this process. But this later imposed order is not the „natural" order, it is the order made by our construction. The natural order is an order of carrying forward. Each carrying forward step is a new one, not completely determined by what had been happened before the step. In this lecture there is not enough space to say more. I recommend to read Gendlins work. Here I only want to say: *The order of carrying forward governs the process of change, the therapeutic process.*

10. If in focusing therapy we use the word "body" we do not mean the body we can see from the outside, *but the inwardly felt body.* This is an entirely different body from the "medical machine" we look at from the outside.

> Felt inwardly the body is directed towards the world and towards what has not happened yet, but may happen. The body is in the given situation and the situation also is in the body. Feelings are not inner objects, but the life of the body continuing in the environment (Gendlin 1994, p. 8)[6].

This environmental body that has and realizes its own process (that therefore does not have to be pushed and pulled), is - inwardly - directy *accessible* to us. This accessibility allows us to watch the order of carrying forward "while it is working". Provided that I or someone else (for instance my therapist) does not block the access.

11. A focusing therapist will do everything possible to allow a free space in which this crucial process can happen. He is aware not to impede the process, for instance by interjecting intentions, prejudices, theories (for example about what could be right at that moment for the client). Therefore focusing therapists try to be *free of intentions*. They are waiting to be surprised by the next step the body will take. They can only do so if they accept their own helplessness and trust in the order of carrying forward of the living organism. This confidence also means to accept at any moment the possibility of failure. The body is capable, but not

obliged to proceed at any given moment. It may be that the next step won't come now. It is sometimes hard to find the right question, to find the right concept, to find the right symbol that carries forward the process. Insisting means delay, detours are only such in the light of specific intentions.

12. Focusing therapists are nothing more than *companions* in the process of change that is "organized" by the order of carrying forward. It lies within the competence of the therapist, it is the art of psychotherapy, however, to become a companion. But this is not easy. There are two difficulties: firstly, the road to an attentive attitude free of intentions is a long one. Along this road the therapist experiences all the impediments being in the way, he must let go of his own identifications with his contents. And secondly, several attempts are often necessary before the client *allows* the therapist to be his companion. There are many obstacles which impede the client from turning his attention inward. Both roads, that one of the therapist and that one of the client, are the same. The only difference is that the therapist must be the first to set out, he has to start earlier than the client.

13. *Body and environment are one, one living interaction process.* The inner (intrapersonal) process and the relational (interpersonal) process are one process. It is one interaction in which therapist and client take part in the same time. Within the experiencing of each one the whole of both is included. It is always one, one whole process (which could then be divided, on a verbal level, into several aspects). The relationship is thus inseparable from the inner experiencing and vice versa. What happens to the client is thus inseparably connected with the person of the therapist. This means, firstly, that: being therapists we basically "influence" what happens within the client. This makes us responsible. Secondly, it means that whatever the therapist is experiencing, this always has to do with the client. (This changes very basically the traditional concept of „transference".)

14. Therefore the therapist's *self-experiencing is the main source* for understanding the client, the main source for the therapeutic responses, the actions, for the "technique" of the focusing therapist. "To accompany" for the therapist means to pay attention to the client and, *in the same time*, to be attentive to his own concurrent experiencing, to the *resonance* in his own body.

15. *In the therapeutic relationship the whole living ongoing is included.* The relationship is more than the client's momentary content of experience. To respond only to the client's contents reduces and reifies this totality and takes away the strength of the one changing process. The therapist's relationship with himself, the client's relationship with himself, the relationship of the therapist to the client (and vice versa), all these factors are various aspects of the whole. The order of carrying forward dictates that *the way* I ask is the way my body will respond. Contents are not independent of one's relationship to them. The relationship also defines how and what is being experienced. *Therefore in focusing therapy the relationship is primary.*

16. *Experiencing is expressed last of all in words.* It manifests itself in bodily sensations, in feelings, in inner images - and also in words. Speech is not the only means of expression. Expression occurs above all directly through the body: in stopping or changing the body (its breathing, its skin and muscles, its posture, its expressions and gestures). It can also occur in painting, in dancing, in playing. Therefore focusing therapists do not listen primarily to words, but rather to the voice, they also look, they feel and touch.

17. *Focusing therapy cannot be defined by methods.* We cannot describe focusing therapy by listing up specific techniques. *In focusing therapy the client comes first* - and after this we also are creating and using specific methods. Focusing therapy doesn't impose a method on another person. As a focusing therapist I am always looking for: who is this person sitting or lying or standing in front of me? Where in his or her unique experiential situation is this person in this very moment? I always want to be exactly at this point where he or she is, being together with him or her, together in dwelling at this point, awaiting together the bodily implied next step. I, of course, only am able to be there with the client when I am connected *with myself*, with my own experiential process, with my own felt sense, with my own body. Therefore we can say that the focusing therapist always is *at home in his own focusing process*. Focusing therapy is, as one of my students said, a home coming, a coming home to oneself - for both, for the client and for the therapist.

RELATIONSHIP

Actually I wanted to say more about our understanding of *relationship* in focusing therapy, especially about two very central aspects of focusing therapy that are closely tied to this issue: What we call *resonance and response* and what is known *as structure-bound processes*. But since my time is fast running out, I will have to skip them for today. However, I wouldn't think of concluding a lecture on focusing therapy without refering to the fundament of the therapeutic relationship in focusing therapy at least in an anecdotal way. I should like to read what Gene Gendlin said in regard to this on the International Focusing Summerschool in August 1993. He said it in his foreign mother tongue, in German language. Therefore, I will read it in German language, too.[7]

Um für jemanden ein Halt zu sein, oder, wie ich es ausdrücke, um die andere Seite von diesem Rohr, das der Prozeß ist, halten zu können, braucht man nur ein Mensch zu sein. Nichts anderes ist notwendig. Das ist sehr wichtig. Denn auf diese Weise weiß man, daß man das kann. Wenn da irgend etwas anderes nötig wäre, dann wüßten wir nicht, wie das zu tun. Aber es ist nichts anderes nötig. Man braucht nicht gut oder gescheit zu sein oder zu wissen, wie man es machen muß, man muß nur einfach da sein. Und wenn man das einmal weiß, dann ist das sehr entlastend. Du kannst nicht fehl gehen, wenn du nur bereit bist, da zu sein.

Aber auch das Da-Sein klingt so, als wäre es eine spezielle Fähigkeit. Aber das ist es nicht. Man muß einfach nur bereit sein: Ja, ich nehme teil daran, ich bin da. Das ist alles. Wenn wir nur verbunden sind, dann geht es schon und alles andere geschieht von selber.

Das ist immer so. Man sieht's nur nicht so klar. Aber es ist immer so. Wenn man das weiß, dann ist die Hälfte der Arbeit, Therapeut zu sein, schon gemacht. Manchmal denke ich mir, es ist eigentlich der Sessel, der die ganze Arbeit macht. Aber das stimmt natürlich so nicht. Denn der Sessel macht die Arbeit nur, wenn irgend jemand drinsitzt - irgend jemand. Es ist wirklich so. Es ist dieser elektrische oder magnetische Sessel, und um ihn anzutreiben, muß jemand drinsitzen. Der Sessel ohne jemand - das geht nicht.

Und auf diese Weise hat man mich gebeten: „Schau, setz doch hin in diesen Sessel. Wir brauchen nur irgendeinen, der da sitzen wird. Alles andere haben wir schon arrangiert: Der Prozeß ist bereit, alles wird gehen, nur brauchen wir jemanden. Und aus irgendeinem komischen Grund bist du derjenige, der da sitzen soll. Wenn du wirklich nicht willst, also gut, dann werden wir einen andern rufen, irgendeinen anderen."

Unter diesen Umständen kann man das schon machen. Man braucht nur jemand. Man muß nichts machen, nur da sein. Das tiefste Prinzip der Therapie ist so. Es braucht irgendeinen Menschen der da ist, alles andere ist schon bereit.

Und dann, natürlich, soll man den Prozeß, der schon ganz fertig da wartet, auch erlauben. Daß ich also nicht wieder davonlaufe, sondern einfach im Sessel bleibe. Und nicht nur körperlich nicht davonlaufe sondern auch innerlich nicht. Wenn ich z.B. das Gefühl habe, ich muß mich jetzt verstecken, na, also das darf ich nicht. Ich soll schon merken, daß ich mich verstecken will - gut, daß ist schon ganz interessant, später werden wir schauen warum - aber jetzt bleibe ich da. Oder vielleicht, wenn wir Zeit haben, schaue ich sogar jetzt, aber jedenfalls gehe ich nicht weg. Das ist alles.

Mehr als die Hälfte dessen, was für die Therapie gebraucht wird, ist einfach ein Mensch, der da ist und der erlaubt, daß aus dem anderen herauskommt, was eben herauskommt. Wenn du wirklich überzeugt bist, daß das alles ist, was gebraucht wird, dann kannst du auch da sein. Wenn du gescheit sein müßtest und normal oder was immer - das wäre ja unmöglich. Der Usus ist, das anzunehmen, aber wir wissen - hier wenigstens - im Grunde alle, daß das nicht wahr ist.

Denn der Therapeut ist natürlich genauso neurotisch wie der Klient, nicht? Das ist kein Geheimnis. Man kann's geheim halten, das schon. Aber in der Therapie sind wir uns doch alle voraus, nicht? Wir sind viel bessere und stärkere Menschen in der Therapie als sonst. Das muß anerkannt werden. Wenn ich für mich selber arbeite, dann habe ich vielleicht alle möglichen Schwierigkeiten. Aber wenn ich bei meinem Klienten angestellt bin - für ihn kann ich schon, was ich sonst nicht kann. Warum kann ich's? Weil ich es können muß. Denn es ist Berufsethik, daß ich vor meinen Klienten nicht Angst habe. Das heißt natürlich: Ich hab' Angst, aber ich darf darin nicht steckenbleiben. Man muß also mit seiner eigenen Scheuheit und mit seiner eigenen Schwäche und mit seiner eigenen Angst arbeiten. Ich hab' die Pflicht, meine eigenen Schwächen genug zu überwinden, damit ich da sein kann. Ich muß mir Raum verschaffen, wirklich da zu sein, damit jemand da ist. Und der Jemand, der da ist, der hat alle möglichen Schwierigkeiten und Nachteile, aber jeder hat Schwierigkeiten und Nachteile. Und ich bin halt derjenige, der grad da ist. Wenn ich wirklich jemanden besseren weiß, na, dann sollte ich den Klienten dorthin senden. Aber es ist niemand so viel besser. So muß ich also da sein und ich kann nur da sein als derjenige, der ich eben bin. Und der Klient wird dann halt sehen, wer das ist - no, kann ma' nix machen - aber jemand muß da sein. Das ist ein österreichisches Prinzip: Kann ma' nix machen.

END

Anyone who knows Gene Gendlin's theoretical work will have noticed that almost everything I talked about here actually comes from him. Gendlin in the first place is a philosopher and apart from that also a psychotherapist. As a philosopher he's been working for 40 years on something that he modestly calls "a process model". I am fascinated by this philosophy, as it creates a completely new way of thinking. The process model is not simply a new "model", it is a *principally entirely different* model. It is a way of thinking about experiencing, body, language, change, but *with* experiencing, *with* body, *with* change. This way of thinking is so unusual that it seems to be very hard to understand. But I am utterly convinced that no other way of thinking suits so adequately the psychotherapeutic practice and I believe that here a philosophy is being developed that will achieve great significance in the future. For this reason it is extremely worth while to get acquainted with Gendlin's philosophy, to chew and to digest.

Gendlin has said almost everything what we need for psychotherapy. Much he has said as a psychologist, as a psychotherapist and as an empirical researcher. But the most important things he said as a philosopher: not in images, metaphor and stories, but in a stringent form of process logic, in an abstract way. I consider it to be a defiant and important task to let Gendlin's thinking interact with our own experiencing and to express it in an individual language - everyone in his or her own way. This process means to promote the development of focusing therapy. This process of further developing is first of all a personal search and a personal experience of a way, a path ... towards the „simple" being, present as a person. My lecture was meant as an attempt to communicate something of this process to you.

At the very end it is important for me to repeat: The „I" is not a content. The „I" is in principle free from contents. But the „I" frequently is identified with contents. Then the „I" is becoming an „ego". Focusing and focusing therapy are processes which are freeing the „ego" and regain the „I". And this also means that our „I" should not be identified with focusing. If our „I" is identified with focusing, we will become missionars. Focusing then will become an ideology, a religion. And that is the beginning of any kind of fascism. This is the opposite of what focusing means. Let us take care not to go in this direction. Letting go focusing, freeing the „ego" - this is like a daily exercise. It is in fact practizing focusing.

---

[1] The DAF (Deutsches Ausbildungsinstitut für Focusing und Focusing-Therapie) was founded by Johannes Wiltschko in 1988. The DAF emerged from the former IFN-Bureau (International Focusing Network). The IFN-Bureau was established in 1980 by Friedhelm Köhne (Germany), Agnes Wild-Missong (Switzerland) and Johannes Wiltschko (Austria), appointed as focusing-coordinators by Gene Gendlin, as an office for coordination of all focusing activities in these countries. The IFN-Bureau managed the International Focusing Summerschool which is taking place every year since 1981. The Summerschool, now organized and directed by the DAF, is the most traditional and largest focusing event in the world. In the DAF 15 focusing trainers offer training in focusing and in focusing therapy in many different regions of the german speaking countries. The DAF also is publishing the Focusing Bibliothek, a series of books, study papers and videos. The DAF is now directed by Klaus Renn and Johannes Wiltschko. It is located in Würzburg.

[2] Friedman, N., Focusing Therapy. The Focusing Connection, Vol. X, No. 1, Berkeley 1993

[3] Wiltschko, J., Von der Sprache zum Körper. Hinführungen zur Focusing-Therapie II. Focusing Bibliothek, Band 2. DAF, Würzburg 1992

[4] In focusing partnerships first one partner is the client, then the other; both persons accompany themselves in their focusing processes in charging roles. Focusing partnerships of this kind often remain stable for a long period of time and offer a successful model for free self-help.

[5] This model was developped by Johannes Wiltschko and Ernst Juchli in 1982 (Anmerkungen zur Theorie und Praxis von Focusing und Psychotherapie. Materialien zur 2. Internationalen Focusing Sommerschule, IFN, Würzburg 1982).

[6] Gendlin, E.T., Unsere Therapie im Verhältnis zur heutigen Philosophie. Focusing Bibliothek, Studientexte, Heft 2. DAF, Würzburg 1994

[7] "To be a support for someone or, as I express it, to be able to hold up the other side of the pipe which is the process, all that is required is that you be a human being. Nothing else. That is very important. Because it helps you realize you can do it. If something else were required, we wouldn't know how to do it. But nothing is. You don't have to be good or smart or to know how to do it; you just have to be there. And once you know that, you feel very relieved. You can't fail as long as you are willing to be there.
But even "being there" sounds as if it were a special skill. It isn't. You just have to be willing to be there: Yes, I am taking part, I am here. That's all. Once we connect, things start working and everything else takes care of itself.
That's always the case. It's just that people don't always realize it. But it's always the case. Once you know that, half the work of being a therapist is already done. Sometimes I think it's actually my chair that does all the

work. Of course that's not really so. Because the chair only does the work when someone is sitting in it - anyone. That's the actual truth. It's one of those electrical or magnetic chairs and to activate it, someone has to be sitting in it. If the chair is empty, it doesn't work.

It was with this in mind that I was asked: 'Look, why don't you sit down in the chair. All we need is someone to sit there. Everything else is already set: The process is ready, everything will work, but the thing is, we need someone. And for some strange reason you are the one who should sit there. If you don't really want to, ok, we'll call on someone else, anyone else.'

Under circumstances like these, it can be done. "Someone" is all that's needed. You don't have to do anything, just be there. That's the most profound principle of therapy: All that's required is for someone to be there, everything else is already set.

Of course, you also have to permit the process which is there, ready and waiting, to occur. In other words, I can't run away from it, I just have to remain seated in the chair. And it's not just physically that I can't run away from it, but mentally as well. For instance, if I have the feeling I have to hide, well, I must not act on it. I should recognize that I want to hide - hmm, that's very interesting, but let's wait till later to find out why - but for now I will stay here. Or maybe, if we have time, I might even look now, but I will in any case not go away. That's all there is to it.

More than half of what is required in therapy is simply a person who will be there and allow whatever happens to come out of people to come out. If you're really convinced that that's all that is required, you, too, can be there. If you would have to be smart and normal or whatever - that would make it impossible. That is the usual assumption, but we know - at least here - basically all of us know that it's not true.

After all, the therapist is just as neurotic as the client, isn't he? That's no secret. Of course you can cover up that fact, that's true. But in therapy we're all a step ahead of ourselves, aren't we? We are better, stronger people in therapy than we are otherwise. That fact has to be acknowledged. If I'm working just for myself, I might have all kinds of difficulties. But if I'm employed by my client - well, for him, I can do things I otherwise wouldn't be able to do. Why? Because I have to be able to do them. Because it is part of my professional ethics that I not be afraid of my client. Of course in reality I am afraid; I just can't allow myself to become stuck in my fear. In other words, I just have to work with my own shyness, my own weaknesses, my own angst. I'm obliged to rise above my own weaknesses to an extent that enables me to be there. I have to create space for myself to really be there, so someone is there. And the someone who is there is faced with all possible kinds of difficulties and disadvantages, but who isn't faced with difficulties and disadvantages. And I am the someone who happens to be there at this point in time. If I really know someone who is better, I should send the client there. But there isn't anyone who would be all that much better. So, I have to be there and I can only be there as the person that I am. And the client will just have to see who that person is - that's just the way things are - but someone has to be there. That is an Austrian principle: That's just the way things are" (unpublished manuscript, 1993).

The Person–Centered Approach:
Toward an Understanding of ist Implication

JOHN KEITH WOOD

UNIVERSIDADE DE CAMPINAS, BRAZIL

ABSTRACT

The person–centered approach is not a psychology, a psychotherapy, a philosophy, a school, a movement nor many other things frequently imagined. It is merely what its name suggests, an **approach**. It is a psychological posture, a way of being, from which one confronts a situation.

The best known activity it has been applied to is client–centered therapy, which **is** a psychotherapy, has a psychology, a method and a body of research generally supporting its theoretical assertions.

This paper takes into consideration the some sixty years of applications of the person–centered approach which include – as well as psychotherapy – education, encounter groups, and large groups to facilitate transnational understanding, to explore intergroup conflicts, to learn the nature of culture and its process of formation.

Observations from these applications over the last thirty years have revealed inadequacies in the psychology of client–centered therapy. A direction is indicated for the formulation of an appropriate psychology for all the applications of the person–centered approach.

Reflection on this discussion might also inform the practice of psychotherapy as well as suggesting "interdisciplinary" projects which are naturally unified by the paradigm proposed.

AN EXAMPLE OF A PUBLIC MENTAL HEALTH PROJECT INDISTINGUISHABLE FROM AN APPLICATION OF THE PERSON–CENTERED APPROACH[1]

In the late 1960's in the United States many people underwent dramatic life–transitions. Not only young people. Due to political decisions thousands of middle–aged scientists and engineers were unemployed and many were forced to make radical changes in their ways of living. Throughout the nation, some 100,000 scientists were unemployed. This example is about some 250 of this group who lived in San Diego, California.

The crisis began with the government's cancellation of contracts for the construction of a super–sonic aircraft. In one sense, it was a victory for the environment, as this vehicle was expected to cause certain ecological damage. On the other hand, it was a devastating defeat for those who lost their jobs.

Who were these people? The population consisted of technical workers, engineers and scientists, almost all men. A familiar story was the following. A young man joined the armed forces during world war II. He served his country honorably. With the war's end, he took advantage of veteren's benefits and enrolled in a university. After four years he had been awarded a degree in engineering. A couple of more years led to a master's degree. Or perhaps he went on for a doctorate in physics, biology, or an engineering speciality.

On graduating from the university, his services were in great demand. This was the time that the country was rebuilding and expanding. Job offers were abundant, especially in the growing "aerospace industry." He got a good job and began to advance within the organization. He bought a house in the suburbs, a boat, or a trailer for camping excursions, a new car every year. He made investments, provided insurance for his survivors, arranged for his children's teeth to be straightened, put away money for their university education, and, in general, became an important and contented member of his community. Two decades or so later, around age 48, he lost his job.

When I arrived in San Diego (an ex–mathematician and engineer myself), there were some twenty or so engineers and scientists voluntarily organizing a "job bank," to help each other find employment. I joined them. At first, we thought perhaps people could find employment with other manufacturers of aircraft cr aircraft components. All we had to do was to contact the companies, find out what openings they had, and put the right man in the right job.

What we quickly learned was that there were virtually no job openings in the aerospace industry.

So, we began to look into related activities: bio–medical engineering, pollution management, environmental specialties, technical marketing, small business management and so forth. Disappointingly, these industries wanted only young people trained in the technology that they dealt with.

Next, we petitioned politicians such as the mayor and the board of supervisors of the region, the governor. We proposed that every level of community was in need of technical assistance to resolve various problems: control of air pollution, sewage disposal and treatment, crime and security. Why not hire an unemployed engineer? Yes, the problems exist. Yes, we need help. No, we do not have funds to employ your people.

Could the state give a grant for scientific research? Could the county pay for a study of its swamp lands and the ecological threat that housing developments were introducing into the area? Could scientists be hired as teachers in the city school system? We made proposals to every sector of the community: without success.

A "demonstration" was even staged, a quiet march through the downtown streets to advertize our plight. The television journalists loved it, but nothing came from this effort. After a couple of weeks, the journalists were looking for what was new. Unemployed scientists quickly became an old story.

The telephone campaign continued. Engineers and scientists, themselves unemployed, worked on a voluntary basis in a small office the state loaned us. They tried to find jobs for their colleagues who came into the office to register for the meager unemployment insurance. Volunteers telephoned local businesses, factories, and other sources of employment on a regular basis asking for what openings existed and recommending that the enterprise consider our population.

The volunteers also listened to the stories of the recently unemployed who came to the office for help. They told their own stories as well. A common pattern was repeated: At first the unemployed person was not too concerned. He was receiving a few weeks of insurance payments. Also, most received a pretty good payment from funds their previous employer had put aside for their retirement. Thus, they had income for a few months.

At first, they concentrated on looking for a job as good or better than the one they had. They certainly would not consider working for less salary. Without success, they began to apply for lower–level jobs. For example, managers of big engineering departments began applying for jobs as ordinary engineers. Still, with no success and time passing, they began to become worried and applied for jobs well beneath their training and ability. Many related that they had eventually become desperate and had even tried to get work in a gasoline filling station. They were turned down because they were "over–qualified." They were willing to work, but no matter how humble they became, nobody wanted them. This experience was not only humiliating, it left the person depressed and in a desperate state.

While we tried everything we could think of to find work for people and to help them prepare themselves in the best possible way to present themselves in job interviews and while we listened to their stories in the volunteer office, we noticed an inexplicalbe but nevertheless constructive and encouraging phenomenon: Volunteers who came to the office, worked the telephones and talked to people coming in, quickly found employment: if not a formal job, nevertheless, a satisfying new direction for their lives.

Were they to have always found employment in their old line, we could suspect that they were merely privy to inside information about job openings and stepped in to claim the prize, instead of passing it on to one of their colleagues who was waiting for such an opportunity. However, this was not the case. As often as they found similar employment, they resolved their problem creatively: sometimes beginning a completely new career direction.

What was happening? What did this observation mean? Could it be that by merely sitting around the office and drinking coffee, trying to help one's colleagues (and oneself), conversing with each other more honestly than one might converse with acquaintances and casual friends, sharing one's life story, one's aspirations, a person's life transition could be facilitated?

If it were so, we could certainly take advantage of this discovery. To test the hypothesis, a small prototype project was proposed: we would invite unemployed scientists to a group meeting where they would have a chance to do what was taking place within our office spontaneously: That is, learn what they needed to know to look for work effectively, reflect on their common life–situation, share informally their feelings regarding this crisis, explore with others practical solutions to their and other's problems. Although nobody could produce a theory to explain how this might be beneficial, the fact was that in spite of a herculean effort, no other approach had offered the slightest hope of helping, let alone success on a significant scale.

The results of the small group we convened to test this hypothesis, confirmed its potential value. Participants in the group quickly resolved their problems. On the basis of the pilot group's success, the state government gave us a small grant to conduct a longer program that would also be researched to better understand what was going on. Unemployed people were given the opportunity to attend what were called "job clinics." There were some twenty. Each consisted of a group of around 10 unemployed scientists, one or two counselors or supervisors from the state unemployment service (who, through their participation, were also receiving training, in a sense, which they could later use in their work), and two group facilitators (usually a male and a female – only a few facilitators and no participants took part in more than one group). The group met daily for a week which included a two–day intensive experience and afterwards, once a week for three hours in the evening for ten weeks. For the purpose of research, this group was matched with an equal number of similar persons who did not participate in the "job clinics" and did not participate in any government program of counseling or retraining. A third group was constituted from the official reports of people who receive the authorized unemployment counseling from professionals who work for the government agencies.

Six months after a person had completed the "job clinic," he was asked to evaluate his transition. The results were significant. People who participated in the "job clinic" had an *80%* chance of being engaged in a satisfying occupation. Around half of these persons were trying out and were content with an activity they thought they would like which was different from their previous work. Almost one–third were engaged in an endeavor that they had always wanted to do. For example, one fellow became a veterinarian; another, who had invented a   2–cycle gasoline engine as a hobby, was hired by a large motor manufacturer to supervise the design and fabrication of his engine; a metalurgist whose hobby was photography became a crime photographer for the police force; an aircraft stress analyst became a successful film maker, inventing several special effects techniques.

People who "did nothing" had around an *even* chance (57% in San Diego and around 46% nationwide) of realizing these same options. Statistically, these findings are indisputable: the "job clinic" definitely helped people reconstruct their lives in a positive and creative manner. The astonishing finding was that unemployed scientists and engineers who were "helped" by the government specialists had a mere *30%* chance of achieving what the other groups achieved. Thus, it may sometimes be better to "do nothing" then receive certain kinds of "help."

REFLECTIONS ON THIS PROJECT AS RELEVANT TO AN UNDERSTANDING OF THE PERSON–CENTERED APPROACH

Unwittingly, in developing these programs to help unemployed scientists, we had applied an approach indistinguishable from the person–centered approach. What had we done?

First of all, we did not assume that we knew what the problem was. Government officials (without understanding the deeper issues) treated the problem logically: obsolete people need retraining; thus, let's create "re–training programs." Despite enormous expenditures, this approach yielded little.

After testing, to no avail, all the conventional wisdom, we applied no further theories. Without realizing it, we followed the advice of J.W. Von Goethe: "Let the facts themselves speak for their theory. Don't look for anything behind the phenomenon; they themselves are the theory." (Bortoft, 1986) The unemployed person himself spoke for the "theory"and we followed this lead.

It must be emphasized that we were extremely active. We tried everything we (or anyone else) thought of that might resolve the problems of the group or of an individual in the group. Almost every approach we tried was unsuccessful in facilitating the life transitions of a significant number of persons in the unemployed group.

By exhausting every recourse, trying to help the person in crisis formulate his own response to his situation, and observing the subtle realities that were taking place, we finally recognized that there were certain psychological factors that were active in helping people make a successful transition and that these factors could be promoted to be of real help to more people. In this case, we realized the truth in Martin Buber's (1958) insight: "Only when every means has collapsed does the meeting come about." (p.12)

Thus, the successful approach was not at all efficient, but it was *effective*. It was, as I have learned from farming, a bit like nature herself: prefering *potential* to productivity and rewarding *patience*, instead of enterprise.

Therefore, in this case, the person–centered approach might be described, in part, as consisting of:

A *belief* that something can be done and that those who have a problem also have the creativite resources to overcome this problem.

A *respect* for the dignity and autonomy of the person. He or she is the one to decide about his or her life.

A *recognition* of the value of social interaction: one alone is nothing: two is a unity. The majority of persons, both in the "experimental group" and those who "did nothing," said that they found their "new direction in life" through personal relations with others.

A *tolerance* for uncertaintly. We tried things that we understood and they did not work. We did things that we did not understand and they did work.

We turned the best part of ourselves toward the best part of our colleagues in order to accomplish something of lasting value that neither could have done alone.

Attempts at "helping"

At first, because they asked, we tried to teach people how to look for work: how to write a curriculum vita, how to dress for interviews, how to present oneself. Then, when we discovered that there were psychological factors involved, we offered group experiences which were structured in a way to elicit participants to speak about and to reflect on their lives. Later, we discovered that the essential elements were already present in the *meeting*. Our task was to provide the moment and the place and the unencumbered time necessary for deep reflection to take place. This was not as difficult as it may seem because participants intuitively realized this and they themselves provided both the urgency and the creative vitality necessary.

The personal dimension

A promising psychology is beginning to develop around concepts and findings from evolutionary biology, cognitive psychology and brain researches. One small aspect concerns the notion that the brain consists of various "modules," specialized functions having developed to deal with particular necessities of the organism during evolution. Some of the difficulties an individual encounters may be the result of using a "module" or a way of thinking that is not suitable for the problem at hand.

One could notice such a phenomenon among the population of unemployed scientists and engineers. For example, many thought like a twenty–three–year–old first beginning a career: "I must find a good paying job. It must have room for advancement, so that my salary may increase to provide for my growing family: buy a good home, education, and so forth. I may wish to do something else, but I must not think of myself. My family must come first."

However, a forty–eight–year–old man whose children were grown and whose house was paid for and who, for the first time in his life, had the opportunity to do what he *really wanted to do*, and thought like a twenty–three–year–old was surely using the wrong "module."

Often, beginning to think in a more realistic way about what one really wished to do for the rest of his life put him on the road to this new life.

The social dimension

Unemployed persons who shared their feelings, view of life, their hopes and fears with those who were facing similar problems — that is, with those who could understand at a deep level what they were experiencing — seemed to more quickly find the way out of their difficulties.

This was no mere catharsis. In addition to sharing feelings, they offered practical advice to each other. Not gratuitous advice, they offered suggestions which were synchronous with the person's desired direction. For example, an engineer whose lifetime desire was in art, who painted, but never showed his work, was put in touch with the brother–in–law of another group participant who had an art gallery. The contact resulted in the new artist selling several of his paintings and putting his new career on a solid basis.

There is also something to be said for the process of helping each other dream of how they wish to spend their life. This results not only in mutual support and encouragement but also in bringing the dreams more into focus, and somehow bringing them more within reach.

The ambience

The location of the group meetings seemed to influence the initiation of a creative process in group participants. When meetings were conducted in a drab government warehouse where space had been alloted, participants were much more inhibited and much less likely to explore their feelings deeply. When meetings were held in the eucalyptus grove that surrounds the beautiful University of California campus, the process of self–discovery in participants seemed to be facilitated by the place alone.

If a central hypothesis from observations of this project would be stated, it might be something like this: Given the appropriate environmental and psychological conditions, people possess the capacity to reorganize perceptions of themselves and of their reality and to make creative and constructive life–transitions.

With the preceeding example and observations in mind, perhaps we can attempt a preliminary definition of the person–centered approach.

WHAT THE PERSON–CENTERED APPROACH *IS NOT*

First, it is neither a *psychotherapy* nor a *psychology*. It is not a *school*, as in "the behaviorist school." Itself, it is not a *movement*. However, this does not mean that a movement may not attach itself to its name. As William James (1907) has noted about the philosophy pragmatism, "A number of tendencies that have always existed in philosophy have all at once become conscious of themselves collectively, and of their combined mission; and this has occured in many countries, and from so many different points of view, that much unconcerted statement has resulted." (p.5) Likewise, people who have nothing more in common than that they believe in democracy or that they oppose psychoanalysis or whatever, at times gather together at conferences or workshops in the name of the person–centered approach. However, they quickly fall to bickering as it becomes obvious that they are linked by a word and not by a reality.

Although many have noted "existential" positions in its attitudes and others have refered to "phenomenologic" perspectives in its intentions, it is not a *philosophy*. Nor is it any number of other things frequently imagined.

WHAT THE PERSON–CENTERED APPROACH *IS*

It is merely, as the name implies, an **approach**, nothing more; nothing less. It is a psychological posture, if you like, from which thought or action may arise and experience be organized. It is a "way of being." (Rogers, 1980)

In part, it consists of: A *belief* (or perhaps, a *faith*) in a "formative directional tendency" that Rogers (1980, p.133) has described as:

> ... an evolutionary tendency toward greater order, greater complexity, greater interrelatedness. In humankind, this tendency exhibits iself as the individual moves from a single–cell origin to complex organic functioning, to knowing and sensing below the level of consciousness, to a conscious awareness of the organism and the external world, to a transcendent awareness of the harmony and unity of the cosmic system, including humankind.

A *will* to help that includes the conviction that it is possible to help and that to do so is the most important thing in the world at this moment.

An *intention* to be effective in one's objectives. In the case of client–centered therapy, it is the intention to help another human being make constructive personality changes. It does not consist in *showing* that you are trying to help, but in actually helping. It is not trying to do "good therapy," but in doing what favors the best outcome for the client.

Having *compassion* (that would not exclude expressing kindness) for the individual and respect for his or her *autonomy* and *dignity*. In one of Rogers's early attempts to describe his approach as applied to psychotherapy, he proposed that the therapist would have "a capacity for sympathy which will not be overdone, a genuine receptive and interested attitude, or deep understanding which will find it impossible to pass moral judgements or be shocked or horrified." This therapist would have, "a deep–seated respect for the [person's] integrity. ... a willingness to accept [him] as he is on his own level of adjustment, and to give him some freedom to work out his own solutions to his problems." Rogers also thought the therapist should be expected to have "a sound understanding of himself, of his outstanding emotional patterns, and of his own limitations and shortcomings." (Kirschenbaum, 1979, p.96)

A *flexibility* in thought and action. This "way of being" is not bound by concepts or trained behaviors, not even by previous learnings.

An *openness* to new discoveries. Perhaps a "learning posture." One's interest is, "not in truth already known or formulated but in the process by which truth is dimly perceived, tested and approximated." (Rogers, 1974)

An *ability* to intensely concentrate and clearly grasp the linear, piece by piece, appearance of reality as well as perceiving it holistically or all–at–once.

A *tolerance for uncertainty or ambiguity*. From this approach one is able to live without being attached to a particular form or outcome. Like Keats's (1899) Shakespeare, a facilitator possesses a "*negative capability* ... capable of being in uncertainties, mysteries, doubts, without any irritable reaching after fact and reason." (p.277)

Though certainly not the exclusive possession of this approach, a sense of *humor, humility, curiosity* doubtless play a part also.

In less precise language, but perhaps more precise communication, the **approach** consists of turning the best part of oneself toward the best part of the other in order that something of lasting value may be accomplished that neither could have done alone.[2]

THE DIFFERENCE BETWEEN CLIENT–CENTERED THERAPY AND THE PERSON–CENTERED APPROACH

Client–centered therapy and the person–centered approach belong to different **categories**. Client–centered therapy is a *psychotherapy*. The person–centered approach is an *approach:* to psychotherapy, to education, to encounter groups, to large group workshops for transcultural understanding, learning about culture formation, or for the resolution of intergroup conflicts.

Client–centered therapy has a specific and coherent *theory*. (Rogers, 1959) The person–centered approach has no theory.

There is a *method* for conducting client–centered therapy. It is not been so well specified as the theory and varies substantially between therapists. However, Rogers's own technique has been extensively documented (including many films and audio recordings) and can be precisely described. (For recent analyses, see Brodley [1994] and Ellis & Zimring [1994])

On the other hand, the *approach* has no specific method. Methods are developed according to the demands of each application. For example, facilitative behavior in groups is somewhat different, and at times may even be contradictory, to therapist behavior in individual therapy intended to facilitate personality change. Nevertheless, they are derived from the same **approach.** We will return shortly to the subject of method in applying the approach.

For client–centered therapy, a substantial body of *research* has accummulated that has tested hypotheses proposed from studying its theory and practice. Although the research has, in general, been unable to convince the majority of psychologists of the theory's validity, what has been most convincing and has improved psychotherapy on the whole has been client–centered therapy's success in the clinic. The person–centered approach has not been researched as such.

AN APPROACH BY ANY OTHER NAME

The person–centered approach is the same approach that was used to develop client–centered therapy and other activities. Of course, the **approach** has only recently been called "person–centered." In the beginning, it was merely *an* approach. (Rogers, 1939) Then as a distinctive method for practicing psychotherapy was formulated, the approach began to be known by the subsequent developments: the *non–directive approach.* (Rogers, 1942) and then the *client–centered approach.* (Rogers, 1946)

Until the early 1970's, it continued to be called the *client–centered approach.* Then, as applications of the **approach** began to be further developed in fields other than psychotherapy, it became known as the *person–centered approach.* (Rogers, 1977)

The first thirty–year client–centered **approach** period was largely concerned with the development of a system of personality change which concentrated on the individual's subjective world. The following thirty–years of the person–centered **approach** period has been concerned as well with social interactions and has concentrated on learning from doing.

The following schematic may help visualize this history.

```
1935....................  ...................1965 ........................................1995
    ^           ^           ^            ^          ^         ^
                            the approach

        client–centered approach    person–centered approach

    client–centered therapy                    other applications
        I            II          III        IV      V       VI
```

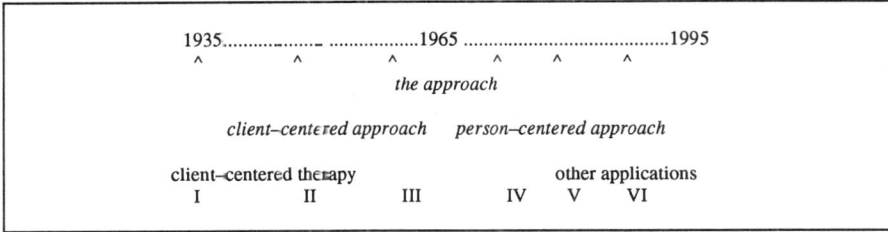

I. **Attitudes of the therapist.** Characterized by Rogers's book, *Counseling and psychotherapy* published in 1942.

II. **Methods of therapy.** Identified by the publication *Client–Centered Therapy* (1951).

III. **Internal process or experience.** Corresponds with the best–seller, *On becoming a person* (1961).

IV. **The facilitation of learning.** *Freedom to learn* (1969).

V. **Interpersonal relationships.** *On encounter groups* (1970).

VI. **Social processes and cultural transformation.** *On personal power* (1977) and *A way of being* (1980).

Although, client–centered *therapy* and the person–centered *approach* are different, Rogers (1987, p.13) made it clear that the **approach** itself, by whatever name, was the same. He insisted:

> To speak of a 'client–centered approach' and a 'person–centered approach' as though they were entities opposed to each other is, in my estimation, a sure road to futile wrangling and chaos. ... I hope I may be allowed to be one whole person, whether I am called upon for help in a relationship deemed to be client–centered or in one that is labeled person–centered. I work in the same way in each.

What did Rogers mean when he said that he worked in the same way in each situation? Did the same empathy exist in his sympathetic and caring gestures toward that poor woman sobbing in the individual therapy interview; as in his cool brashness toward that young "hippy" pointing his finger in the small group, accusing Rogers of betraying "the revolution;" as in his surpressed yawning while that smug university professor was droaning on about Sartre and philosophies of liberty in the large group meeting?

Although his apparent reaction, his manner of expression, his feelings, the circumstances may have been different in each of these situations, I believe that Rogers **approached** them in the very same way. He approached each situation with the same desire to understand, the same good humor, the same humility, the same honesty, the same non–judgemental acceptance of the individual or the group, the same curiosity and openness to learning, the same will to help. He improvised from his knowledge and abilities in each specific case.

The development of effective client–centered therapy has resulted in the formulation of certain *principles*. Some have become part of the theory, some part of the belief system of practitioners, some part of the folklore that inevitably surrounds the activities of a group of people involved in the same endeavor. For the approach, there are no principles as such.

In the case of client–centered therapy, the approach was characteristically expressed through an intense *empathic understanding* within a *genuine* person–to–person relationship, where the therapist *accepted*, without question or judgement, the client's thoughts and feelings.

APPLYING THE APPROACH VS. APPLYING THE PRINCIPLES OF CLIENT–CENTERED THERAPY

Rogers's major descriptions of client–centered therapy (for example, 1946, 1951, 1961, 1980) always included developments in education and groups. In his book, *Client–Centered Therapy*, these subjects were put under the heading of "applications of therapy." However, it is clear from the descriptions of "student–centered teaching" and "group–centered leadership" that these activities are substantially different from client–centered therapy. Nevertheless, the attitudes and orientation (that is, the **approach**) of the educator and the group leader is the same. So, what is more likely being presented are not applications of therapy, but applications of the approach itself.

By the time he described, "A Theory of Therapy, Personality, and Interpersonal Relationships," for Koch's (1959) *Psychology: A Study of Science*, Rogers had already begun to distinguish between applications of therapy and applications of the underlying approach that the therapy was based on. In this case, he called the approach, "the Client–Centered *Framework*."

It is important not to confuse "applying principles of therapy" and "applying the approach they have been based on." In applying the principles of therapy one is doing what one "knows" how to do. In doing so, it may be difficult to avoid therapeutic goals. Thus, in trying to demonstrate the principles of empathic understanding, congruence and non–judgemental acceptance in the classroom, a teacher runs the risk of turning a good opportunity for learning into a bad session of therapy. Education, not psychotherapy is the goal. (If the education is also therapeutic, so much the better. But this should not be the primary motive.)

Applying principles instead of meeting the phenomenon on its own terms may not only be ineffective in achieving one's objectives, it may even be harmful. There is evidence that two large projects based on "models" and principles derived from client–centered therapy may not have been as successful as they could have been. One project was the attempt to modify a private school system. (Coulson, 1989) The other was an attempt to resolve conflict between groups. (Wood, 1994)

An example from encounter groups:

"Attending" each person with "empathic responses," has become for many the customary method of client–centered therapy. This may be effective for some group participants. It may also be ineffective for some persons. It depends on time, place and people. Generally speaking, group participants will not at first tolerate such methods. Of course, for brief periods at the beginning of the group (or in the contrived structure of training or demonstration) it may be permitted. However, even in such cases, prolonged predictable responses from the facilitator, especially those practiced as a facilitative technique, will eventually be challenged by group members. "What about you?" they may demand. "Can you only repeat what we say? How do you feel? What do you think? Who are you?"

Most of all, perhaps, a *pattern* of Rogerian reflective statements or "focusing" advice is annoying. The following example illustrates this point. A participant trained in "communication skills," made what she regarded as a "facilitative response" to each person who spoke in the group. Following what each person said, she repeated the speaker's words, kindly offered some interpretation aimed at demonstrating empathy, and whenever possible, urged the speaker to "focus on his feelings." In spite of her apparent sincerity, the people she tried to "facilitate" promptly ignored her. The gentler speakers would pause until she had exhausted the intervention, then continue. After several such "reflective" interruptions, group participants became visibly annoyed. One irritated speaker ask her to shut up and mind her own business so that he could complete his thoughts.

Later, at the lunch table, she turned to Carl Rogers and said, "This group doesn't seem to appreciate being offered *accurate empathic responses.* Some say they like my effort to reflectively listen, but most of my interventions fall flat." Rogers swallowed a bite of salad and, after a moment's thought, replied diplomatically, "I think the group is challenging us to reach within ourselves for a *deeper empathy.*"

How does one express a deeper empathy? In a way that is sensitive to the present reality. That could even be by reflecting feelings. Or perhaps in silence. Perhaps telling what may seem an irrelevant story. (see Bozarth, 1984) But probably not by thoughtlessly applying the principles of client–centered therapy or any other therapy.

This fact frequently surprises client–centered therapists who cannot believe that, with all their good intentions and conscious effort not to, they are playing a role. Even Rogers himself who adopted the completely innocent posture of "trying to understand every single thing the person was saying," has been called to task for not saying "how you really feel" in a demonstration interview within a large group workshop. The "client" remarking on his impressions of the "therapy" just concluded, related:

I still feel that feeling of sort of a structured – I feel I'm being used. I think you follow your rule book, you know, and I'm sure that if you really let go, you'd sort of look at the heart of these things, you'd open up a bit more and wouldn't be so impassive." (Rogers, 1986; p.25)

Thus, applying the principles of client–centered therapy (in this case "empathic understanding") may not be effective in the group. In addition to confusing empathic understanding, novices in group work may also confuse the therapeutic principles of congruence and non–judgemental acceptance. Attempting to be congruent, they may be brash and impatient. Instead of accepting, they may be passive and inactive.

Naturally, when participants in the group have achieved a person–to–person relation with each other, anyone can be facilitative through "empathic understanding."

Applying the person–centered approach can, and often does, result in a "facilitative environment." This may mean being sensitive to interactions between participants which may be more constructive than those between facilitator and participant. (Yalom, 1985) Even in individual therapy, empathic understanding has been shown to depend more on the client than on the therapist. (Moos & McIntosh, 1970) In the group, perhaps this knowledge may be extended. It may even make sense to facilitate the client's own "capacity for empathic understanding," as it is apparently a better indicator of success than the facilitator's. (Mente & Spittler, 1980)

One of its best–kept secrets is that the person–centered approach seems to function best in situations where conventional methods (including applying the principles of client–centered therapy) have failed.

Applying the person–centered approach

Applying the person–centered approach (as shown in the example opening this article) means confronting a phenomenon (such as psychotherapy, classroom learning, encounter groups or large groups) with that certain "way of being" described earlier and which may also include not only respecting others, but being able to deal with hostility and skepticism. It may mean facing both the unknown and one's own fear and doubt. It may mean fighting for one's own ideas, but giving them up for better ones. It frequently requires an active patience: to allow various perspectives to become apparent before deciding, while, at the same time, not withholding one's vital participation while data is accummulating.

THE PSYCHOLOGY OF CLIENT–CENTERED THERAPY DOES NOT ADEQUATELY EXPLAIN APPLICATIONS OF THE PERSON–CENTERED APPROACH

Although client–centered psychotherapy itself still seems to function effectively, applications of the person–centered approach to education, small groups for encounter and psychotherapy, large group workshops to improve transnational understanding, to facilitate conflict exploration, to learn the nature of culture and its formation have revealed the need to rethink client–centered therapy's psychology. As it stands it does not provide adequate explanations for these phenomena and other current preoccupations.

The victim–of–society myth

The psychology of client–centered therapy revolves around the consciousness of self. In brief, society is seen to be the cause of the individual's problems. It distorts his or her personality. The natural tendency toward self–actualization is then released in a relationship with a client–centered therapist.

Rogers (1981) has insisted that he regarded, "members of the human species ... as *essentially* constructive in their fundamental nature, but damaged by their experience." The idea that cultural influences were to blame for a client's problems was frequently the client's own perception of reality and therefore a perfectly legitimate hypothesis for the initiation of a therapeutic process.

Nevertheless, for group applications there are serious problems with this hypothesis. First, in the group the society is no longer an abstraction. In a manner of speaking, it is the group itself, being created moment–by–moment by participants. Sure, people may be damaged by the group–society, but there are only the participants themselves to blame. Each participant cannot be only a victim. Some must also be victimizers.

The psychology of client–centered therapy proposes that, in a relationship with a therapist, the client may revise his or her concept of self in accord with organismic experience. This revision is based in part on a reflection such as, "Am I living in a way that is deeply satisfying to me, and which truly expresses me?" (Rogers, 1961) There is nothing wrong with this. *Carpe Diem.*

There is no problem, that is, unless *your* "deep satisfaction" prevents any of your colleagues from living in this way also. Martin Buber (1960) expressed the suspicion of many by observing, "I have a lot of examples of man having become very very individual, very distinct of others, very developed in their such–and–suchness without being at all what I would like to call a man."

Indeed, although they may have become more confident individuals, people having completed client–centered therapy could not be shown to have gained more respect and acceptance for

75

others. (Gordon & Cartwright, 1954) However, participants in encounter groups from the person–centered approach apparently could be. (Tausch, 1983)

The task in the group is not merely to reject the rules of "society" and live as one pleases. It is to create a society in which every member may live as much as possible in harmony with his or her organismic experience.

The myth that the individual controls his or her own destiny

Client–centered therapy's psychology includes the belief that people may be counted on to do the right thing and that people are always in charge of their own actions. It is clear that this is not entirely the case. In large group workshops, for example, it is common for participants to behave one way in the group meetings and later, when alone, to regret their actions. Juries and other social bodies sometimes reach decisions that each member voted for but were the individual to have acted, not as a 'representative of the people" but, as a private person, he or she may have decided to the contrary.

This phenomenon also occurs slightly differently, but even more regretfully, on a global scale. Urgent ecological problems have been created by many individuals unwittingly acting in concert. A major difficulty to resolving the problem is that nobody seems to want to give up their inexpensive food (which, in order to produce on a vast scale, wastes substantial soil, a principle patrimony of the planet), their automobile (whose exhaust pollutes the air they must breathe), their refrigerators or bug sprays (whose pressurized gases destroy the ozone, the planet's radiation protection layer), their personal computers (whose fabrication byproducts are among the most toxic). Some are ready to give up these things when everyone else does. The overall effect of this phenomenon is a marvel of cooperation, a well–organized and disciplined endeavor. The problem is that no central control exists. Millions of people conspire to create situations that no single individual admits that he or she wishes and whose solitary withdrawal accounts for practically nothing in changing the system.

Not only are our behaviors coordinated in this obscure way, but also our very biological functioning seems to be tied together in various ways. For example, Lynch (1985), from his researches relating speech with the cardiovascular system, concludes that, "To be human means to live through a body that is both biologically incomplete without other human beings and utterly dependent on others for its emotional – that is, human – development and meaning."(p.276)

Placebo effect is another example of the organism reacting in certain predictable patterns while the governing mind produces all kinds of personal and, at times, fanciful explanations for what is taking place. Patients cured by placebos explain that, "When someone cares about you, you improve." Or, "To improve you must exert effort." Or, "You have within you the power to improve." Or, "Treatment is a reminder that you are trying to change yourself."

What is the placebo effect? Nobody seems to know. Nevertheless, patients improve by digesting chemicals that have been scientifically establised as curative. (Although the drug's effectiveness may be further influenced by color. [Shapiro, 1971]) Patients improve by ingesting completely inert materials. They may also improve when reassured and given a drug that is known to *cause* the very symptoms they suffer. (Wolf, 1950) They improve even when they are *told* that the pills they will be given are "with no medicine, only sugar." (Park & Covi, 1965) When considering this subject one should not forget the reports of *toxic side effects* caused by placebos (Beecher, 1955); and even more astonishing: *addiction* to placebo. (Mintz, 1977)

The myth that individuals are rational and well–intentioned

Individuals may be rational, but they also continue to be tribal. We form into tribes of motorcyclists, football fans, rock music fanatics, professors in academic departments, religious congregations. Each has its own uniform, myths, rites of passage, jargon and so forth. (Morris & Marsh, 1988) Much of the behavior in large group workshops can be seen to be tribal.

And as far as good intentions goes, history is full of examples of well–intentioned people who are quite capable of damaging others. (Milgram, 1974)

The myth that there is only one self

William James (1896) recognized that "the mind seems to embrace a confederation of psychic entities." His observations were passed over for almost a century. However, today there is much talk of interactive "mental organs" or "modules" of mind. Quite a list of supposed modules has already accummulated. It includes one for face recognition, for spatial relations, for tool–use, for fear, for social exchange, for emotion–perception, as well as a "theory of mind" module. (Barkow, Cosmides & Tooby, 1992)

The enormous variety of patterns of thought, varied emotional reactions to the same social situation in large group workshops also suggests a complexity that exceeds the limits of the concept of self proposed by the psychology of client–centered therapy.

Researches of thinking patterns confirms that we may indeed use "modules of mind" to confront certain kinds of experience. However, these studies also suggest that the wrong module may be selected to deal with a problem better suited to another. Furthermore, modules may be "triggered" by certain behaviors of others, even by the phrases they use, and even by certain words. (See Cialdini, 1985, for many examples.) This view also explains why a person may act and feel completely to the contrary when within a group meeting and when solitary; all the time feeling that he or she is a single entity.

Furthermore, there is "divided consciousness," phenomena of the mind that, though largely unrecognized, have enormous influence on behavior. For example, Hefferline, Keenan & Harford (1959) have shown that individuals may be "conditioned" to perform certain tasks without any conscious awareness whatever of anything at all having taken place. Perhaps more astonishing still is the "hidden observer" discovered by Hilgard (1977). There is apparently an entity that may communicate with the outside world without the governing self having any knowledge of its presence, nor its interactions.

In a small volume of lectures, James (1896) has described various "exceptional mental states." Among the subjects he has discussed are dreams, hypnotism, automatism, multiple personality, demonical possession, witchcraft, insanity and genius. James (1890) also admitted that a person "has as many social selves as there are individuals who recognize him and carry an image of him in their minds."

Similar phenomena are readily verified in large group workshops and are not easily, if at all, accounted for in the theory of client–centered therapy.

The myth that historical psychological factors are the only significant influences on consciousness

The various "exceptional mental states," though perhaps difficult for many to accept, are not as astonishing as other subtle, though significant, influences.

For example, an ugly, crowded room can provoke "monotony, fatigue, headache, sleep, discontent, irritability, hostility and avoidance" in inhabitants. (Mintz, 1956) Not only does a beautiful room have opposite effects, Ulrich (1984) has evidence that a view of natural beauty from a hospital room may facilitate recovery from surgery.

The geometry and function of the space may also have an effect on consciousness and even determine behavior. (Barker, 1968)

Obviously, the presence of other people also have an effect on an individual's consciousness. In psychotherapy interviews conducted within a large group, the group itself may have as much influence as the therapist. (Slack, 1985; Rogers 1986)

Seasonal changes in light have been shown to effect the mood of some persons. (Rosenthal, et al, 1984) Colors, music, scents also influence consciousness. Even eating a meal may effect a person's judgement. (Razran, 1938)

Positive ions in certain weather fronts and in polluted air may provoke irritibility, migraine headaches, nausea and respitory congestion. While the inhalation of small negative ions, found near waterfalls, glacial peaks and unpolluted beaches, not only reverses these symptoms but also may provoke inspirational experiences. (Kreuger & Reed, 1976)

Low frequency magnetic fields, such as those surrounding high tension electrical lines and personal computers are suspected of effecting the memory and sense of time of those exposed. (Brodeur, 1989)

Not only mere personal comfort is at stake here. These influences are on the same consciousness that is striving, through psychotherapy for example, to reorganize itself constructively. Thus, they are highly relevant to the practice of psychology. Understanding these effects is especially relevant to studying applications of the person–centered approach because they may have more to do with a participant's experience than the "facilitative" methods used.

TOWARD A PSYCHOLOGY FOR APPLICATIONS OF THE PERSON–CENTERED APPROACH

William James (1890) considered psychology as, "the science of mental life, both of its phenomena and their conditions." In his classic text, he addressed among other things the subjects of stream of thoughts, consciousness of self, attention, concepts, discrimination and comparison, association, perception of time, space and of things, memory, sensation, imagination, perception of reality, reasoning, instinct, emotions, will, and exceptional mental states. Any psychology should contain at least these subjects.

Considering the broad range of questions raised by applications of the person–centered approach, it would be both appropriate to current realities and consistent with the historical trend of Rogers's thinking regarding "organismic experience" to base a psychology for these applications on evolutionary biology.

Perhaps something along the lines of "evolutionary psychology" (Cosmides, Tooby & Barkow, 1992) might be a promising starting point for developing this psychology. Thus, it would assume there is a universal human nature, not as expressed through various cultures but, at the level of evolved psychological mechanisms which are adaptations brought about by hundreds of millions of years of natural selection. Also, it would assume that our present human body and brain – and therefore, mind – adapted to the way of life of Pleistocene hunter–gatherers over some two million years.

The social adaptations also evolved over millions of years of nomadic life but may no longer be suited for the social conditions that began only a few thousand years ago and are now changing at a mind–boggling pace. There has not been enough time for evolution to work its wonders on our minds in this short time. The few thousand years since the outset of agriculture and the beginning of "modern" culture is less than 1% of evolutionary time.

Although our explanations to the contrary may be inventive, we may continue to be governed by certain, for the most part harmless (though at times destructive), adaptations from this substantial history. We can refuse to obey these tribal adaptations only with difficulty. To enter in trance in order to learn from spirits of the dead, to envision directions for a desperate people, or go to war, may be a mere step away from painting the face and throwing oneself into a frenzy for a football match. Firelight dances in the middle of the forrest and sideline theater at the Silverdome stadium may both be the result of the same adaptation. Motorcycle gangs and high society, in choosing their uniforms, may both be motivated by the same impulse. "Movements," religious, popular, or whatever may be seen as attempts to incentivate the group to "centralize," "intensify the will," in order to "move on."

A biological basis for a psychology also would link the mysterious placebo effect (which both biology and psychology have confronted without being able to explain), as well as the various environmental influences on human consciousness: negative ions in the air, the amount of sunlight, low–frequency magnetic fields, planetary orbits. Both the geometry of the local space and the geographic place influence consciousness. This should not be difficult to explain within this theoretical framework proposed.

Finally, individual "psychological mechanisms" also fit conveniently into this orientation. "Material denied to awareness," "defenses," and so forth (Rogers, 1959), may be seen to have developed to deal with the necessities of survival in the hunter–gatherer existence. For example, "denial" may have been very useful for a people who had to cooperate for survival, had to move on quickly and had little opportunity to deal with personal differences or with living in a way that was "truly satisfying." (See Nesse & Lloyd, 1992, for discussion of this aspect.) Under present conditions, it may be unconstructive.

These speculations suggest powerful explanations for why, at the same time we are convincing ourselves to the contrary, there are forces over which we seem to have no control; for why tribal adaptations appropriate for thousands of years ago persist in marginal ways; for why we may be different people, while believing we are but one.

Nevertheless, we should not be overly impressed with these insights. We should take time to test these perspectives, to investigate, to reflect, to learn. A point of view such as this may offer powerful explanations for large blocks of phenomena. However, history suggests that the more powerful a theory is, the more care that must be taken in its use. Remember the epidemics, not only in psychology, sociology and anthropology, but also in art and literature that followed Freud's powerful psychological explanations. Mercifully, most of the more ridiculous have now been retired. Nevertheless, the danger doubtless still exists.[3]

REFERENCES

Barker, R.G. (1968) *Ecological psychology*. Stanford University Press.
Barkow J.H., Cosmides, L. & Tooby, J. (1992) *The adapted mind*. Oxford University Press.
Beecher, H.K. (1955) The powerful placebo. *Journal of the Amercian Medical Associaton, 159* (17) p.1602–1606.

Bortoft, H. (1986) *Goethe's scientific consciousness*. Institute for Cultural Research. Kent: England.

Bozarth, J.D. (1984) Beyond reflection: Emergent modes of empathy. In R.F. Levant & J.M. Shlien (eds.) *Client–centered therapy and the person–centered approach: New directions in theory, research and practice*. N.Y.: Praeger Press.

Brodeur, P. (1989) The hazards of electro–magnetic fields. *The New Yorker*, June 12–26 (three parts).

Brodley, B.T. (1994) Some observations of Carl Rogers' behavior in therapy interviews. *The Person–Centered Journal, 1* (2) p.37–47.

Buber, M. (1958) *I and Thou*. N.Y.: Scribner & Sons.

Buber, M. (1960) Dialogue between Martin Buber and Carl Rogers. *Psychologia, 3*. p.208–221.

Cialdini, R.B. (1985) *Influence*. Glenview, Illinois: Scott, Foresman & Co.

Coulson, W.R. (1989) Founder of "value free" education says he owes parents an apology. *AFA Journal*. April. p.20–21.

Cosmides, L., Tooby, J. & Barkow, J.H. (1992) Evolutionary psychology and conceptual integration. In J.H. Barkow, L. Cosmides & J. Tooby (Eds.) *The adapted mind*. Oxford University Press.

Crick, F. (1994) *The astonishing hypothesis: The scientific search for the soul*. N.Y.: Charles Scribner's Sons.

Ellis, J. & Zimring, F. (1994) Two therapists and a client. *The Person–Centered Review, 1* (2) p.79–92.

Gordon, T. & Cartwright, D. (1954) The effect of psychotherapy upon certain attitudes toward others. In C.R. Rogers & R.F. Dymond (Eds.) *Psychotherapy and personality change*. University of Chicago Press.

Hefferline, R.F., Keenan, B. & Harford, R.A. (1959) Escape and avoidance conditioning in human subjects without their observation of the response. *Science, 130* p.1338–1339.

Hilgard, E. (1977) *Divided consciousness: Multiple controls in human thought and action*. N.Y.: John Wiley & Sons.

James, W. (1890) *The principles of psychology*. N.Y.: Henry Holt.

James, W. (1896) *Exceptional mental states* – The Lowell Lectures. Edited by Eugene Taylor. University of Massachusetts Press.

James, W. (1907) *Pragmatism*. Republished 1978 by Harvard University Press.

Keats, J. (1899) *The complete poetical works of Keats*. Boston: Houghton Mifflin.

Kirschenbaum, H. (1979) *On becoming Carl Rogers*. N.Y.: Delacorte Press.

Kreuger, A.P. & Reed, E.J. (1976) Biological impact of small air ions. *Science, 193*. P.1209–1213.

Lynch, J.J. (1985) *The language of the heart*. N.Y.: Basic Books.

Mente, A. & Spittler, H.D. (1980) *Erlebnisorientierte Gruppen Psychotherapy*. Paderborn: Junfermann.

Mintz, I. (1977) A note on the addictive personality: Addiction to placebos. *American Journal of Psychiatry, 134* (3) March. p.327.

Mintz, N.L. (1956) Effects of esthetic surroundings: II. Prolonged and repeated experiences of a "beautiful" and an "ugly" room. *The Journal of Psychology, 41*. p.459–466.

Milgram, S. (1974) *Obedience to authority*. N.Y.: Harper & Row.

Moos, R.H. & MacIntosh, S. (1970) Multivariate study of the patient–therapist system: A replication and extension. *Journal of Consulting and Clinical Psychology, 35* p.298–307.

Morris, D. & Marsh, P. (1988) *Tribes*. Salt Lake City: Peregrine Smith Books.

Nesse, R.M. & Lloyd, A.T. (1992) The evolution of psychodynamic mechanisms. In J.H. Barkow, L. Cosmides & J. Tooby (eds.) *The adapted Mind*. Oxford University Press.

Park, L.C. & Covi, L. (1965) Nonblind placebo trial. *Archives of General Psychiatry, 12*, April p.336–345.

Razran, G. (1938) Music, art and conditioned response. *Psychological Bulletin, 35*. p.532.

Rogers, C.R. (1939) *The clinical treatment of the problem child*. Boston: Houghton Mifflin.

Rogers, C.R. (1942) *Counseling and psychotherapy: New concepts in practice*. Boston: Houghton Mifflin.

Rogers, C.R. (1946) Significant aspects of client–centered therapy. *The American Psychologist, 1* (10) p.415–422.

Rogers, C.R. (1951) *Client–Centered Therapy*. Boston: Houghton Mifflin.

Rogers, C.R. (1959) A theory of therapy, personality, and interpersonal relationships, as developed in the client–centered framework. In S. Koch (Ed.) *Psychology: A study of a science, 3. Formulations of the person and the social context*. N.Y.: McGraw Hill. p.184–256.

Rogers, C.R. (1961) *On becoming a person*. Boston: Houghton Mifflin.

Rogers, C.R. (1969) *Freedom to learn*. Columbus, Ohio: Charles E. Merrill.

Rogers, C.R. (1970) *On encounter groups*. N.Y.: Harper & Row.

Rogers, C.R. (1974) Remarks on the future of client–centered therapy. In D.A. Wexler & L.N. Rice (eds.) *Innovations in client–centered therapy*. N.Y.: John Wiley & Sons.

Rogers, C.R. (1977) *On personal power*. N.Y.: Delacorte Press.

Rogers, C.R. (1980) *A way of being*. Boston: Houghton Mifflin.

Rogers, C.R. (1981) Notes on Rollo May. *Perspectives, 2* (1) p.16. Humanistic Psychology Institute.

Rogers, C.R. (1986) The dilemma of the South African white. *Person–Centered Review, 1* (1) p.15–35.

Rogers, C.R. (1987) Client–Centered? Person–Centered? *Person–Centered Review, 2* (1) p.11–13.

Rosenthal, N.E., Sack, D.A., Gillin, J.C. et al (1984) Seasonal affective disorder: A description of the syndrome and preliminary findings with light therapy. *Archives of General Psychiatry, 41*. p.72–80.

Shapiro, A.K. (1971) Placebo effects in medicine, psychotherapy, and psychoanalysis. In A.E. Bergin & S.L. Garfield, *Handbook of psychotherapy and behavior change*. N.Y.: John Wiley & Sons. p.439–473.

Slack, S. (1985) Reflections on a workshop with Carl Rogers. *Journal of Humanistic Psychology, 25* (2) p.35–42.

Tausch, R. (1983) Empirical examination of the theory of helpful relationships and processes in person–centered therapies. In J. Helm & A.E. Bergin (eds.) *Therapeutic behavior modifications*. Selected papers from the 12th International Congress of Psychology. Berlin, East Germany.

Ulrich, R.S. (1984) View through a window may influence recovery from surgery. *Science, 224*. p.420–421.

Wolf, S. (1950) Effects of suggestion and conditioning on the action of chemical agents in human subjects: The pharmacology of placebo. *Journal of Clinical Investigation, 29* p.100–109.

Wood, J.K. (1994) The person–centered approach's greatest weakness: Not using its strength. *The Person–Centered Journal, 1* (2) p.69–78.

Yalom, I.D. (1985) *The theory and practice of group psychotherapy.* N.Y.: BasicBooks.

---

[1] This example has been chosen as an illustration of what an application of the person–centered approach may be like because of its clarity and brevity. The very best example of a successful application of the person–centered approach is, of course, client–centered therapy. The history and development of this application is well worth studying also.

[2] Some people seem to like the idea that we might cultivate this *way of being* as a way of life, encountering every kind of day–to–day situation with this attitude and posture. It may be possible, but I doubt it. In any case, it does not need to be a way of life it need only be capable of being applied effectively in various situations that may better life for many others.

[3] The complete understanding of consciousness may never yield to "biological" explanation. Although formative efforts have been made to provide strictly biological explanation, they have yet to be convincing. (See Crick, 1994, for the latest and most uncompromising.)

Research and Evaluation

Therapy and Groups in Context:
A Study of Developmental Episodes in Adulthood

GODFREY T. BARRETT–LENNARD
MURDOCH UNIVERSITY, WESTERN AUSTRALIA

ABSTRACT

Adult life has been viewed as a living out of patterns laid down in childhood, as a progression through regular transitions and stages, and as part of a life–long continuity of learning and growth. The lens advanced here takes progressive change as normative, and highlights the role of intense, unusually vivid or personally eventful episodes in adulthood. While some kinds of life event are broadly shared, each person's life is presumed to be unique in the particular constellation, qualities and meaning of experienced events. Eventful episodes do not occur in isolation; their nature and impact is seen as a matter of context over time—especially the context of previous and subsequent episodes. Thirty persons, broadly in mid–life, answered a low–structure Formative Life Episodes Questionnaire. Thirty–six primary categories of significant life event emerged from these data. Effects of these events were assigned by respondents from a range of possibilities, and about half were specifically identified as causally related to later episodes. The results confirm the promise of the approach and give leads to its further application and potential.

THERAPY AND GROUPS IN CONTEXT:
A STUDY OF DEVELOPMENTAL EPISODES IN ADULTHOOD

This paper focuses on life happenings and episodes viewed in retrospect as highly eventful, or as turning points, in the individual's life journey. Many such eventful episodes are disturbing crises at the time they occur, crises with two–sided potential. One side involves wounding hurt, diminution of life, the seeds of tragedy. The other, more positive, side, includes self–confrontation, new learning and awareness, and growthful adjustment of goals. For the participants in this research, negative effects of events that were disturbing in their occurrence tended not to endure but to spur new consciousness and resolve, and lead on to deeper knowing and more rewarding life quality or meaning.

A way of thinking about developmental change in adult life is first advanced in this report, setting the stage for an empirical study of the nature, interplay and effects of self–identified key life events. Data were gathered by means of a "Formative life episodes questionnaire" from respondents who had at least one potentially formative episode in common—participation *some ten years earlier* in residential workshops that centred on discovery learning through the intensive group medium. Inductive analysis of the episode data generated a three–tier classification of life events. The data are illustrated from several protocols, and the interlocking results portrayed and studied descriptively. Implications for the theoretical model and further research are drawn into relief at the end of the paper.

Intensive groups, particularly open–agenda, sustained experiential learning groups, have interested me for a long time. In the mid–sixties I initiated, and conducted with others, several residential two–week workshops for people in mental health–related fields in Australia. Earlier reports focused on the nature of these eventful groups (for example, Barrett–Lennard, 1974) and their outcomes (Barrett–Lennard, Kwasnik & Wilkinson, 1973/74; Barrett–Lennard, 1974/75). The reported outcome evaluations drew on follow–up data gathered after six months. When the last of these articles was completed I began to think seriously of a long term follow–up study that would tap into possible direct or indirect effects of the workshop experiences, a decade after the event.

STUDYING DEVELOPMENTAL CHANGE LONG TERM: A PERSPECTIVE

The first challenge in connection with such investigation was to work out a way of thinking about the role of discrete life events in experience–based personal change occurring over a broad time span. As I pondered this problem my view of change shifted in focus, in two main respects.[1] First, it seemed clear that change is a tendency and expression of advanced life forms, especially human life where adaptability works as a key to viability both on an individual and species level. Growth and maturation, adaptation and learning, responsive or reactive adjustments to the norms of our communities, and progression through the life cycle, all imply change. Second, it struck me that in an organism of such complexity as the human person, with highly differentiated consciousness and a lifelong memory storage, change that is mediated by experience need not be a gradual, incremental, smooth–flowing process. One would not expect it always to happen little–bit–by–little–bit, as though we were very simply constructed and no synthesising awareness was involved. It is not a novel observation that the grasp of ideas, shifts in perspective, and changes in purpose or direction, often appear to happen discontinuously, almost as a kind of metamorphosis, rather than by an even, gradual motion.[2]

Plausibly, experience–based learning and change can occur on many levels. In some cases, the change is more like the opening of a doorway than immediate or full entry into what is now possible There is movement—in awareness, values, skills, purpose—but not consummation. The shifts trigger new possibilities. The importance of this movement may lie in its effects on significant *future* choices and the person's response to situations that have not yet arisen. Any psychologically eventful experience. any crisis in which the affected person is a contributing agent, most things of consequence that a person does, are likely to have multiple origins and effects. The change may simultaneously be an outcome of prior experiences, a result of immediate circumstance or need, a new life episode with present effects, and an indirect or contributory influence on later steps.

This way of thinking does not support traditional approaches to the study of change or treatment effects, approaches that take constancy of functioning as the norm and which treat change as the exception to be accounted for. Studying a 'treatment' expected to produce developmental change by looking only for immediately visible effects of this treatment, and whether or not these effects are sustained, implies assumptions that are implausible. Such methods can, at best, give a picture that is incomplete and which entirely misses effects that only come into view in interaction with other life events.

In a word, in the perspective now advanced, progressive change is regarded as the norm, and the focus is on the contributing influence of many kinds of life event; events triggered or influenced by previous events, and with bearing on the nature of subsequent ones. Where interest is centred on the consequences of an intended change episode (such as therapy or an experiential learning workshop) the resulting model is not too difficult to approximate in schematic outline. In Figure 1 (below) influential life events and change are pictured as occurring along a time dimension running from left to right. P_{t1}, P_{t2} , etc., in the figure, stand for a "Person at time 1", "Person at time 2", and so forth. FLE stands for "formative life episode" or any very personally eventful experience. Direct or immediate impact on the person of FLE experiences is visually represented by the overlap of episode and person symbols, and the potentiation of further FLEs is suggested by the curved lines connecting them. Some distinct short–duration episodes may have their *main* significance in laying the ground for a later choice or event of great importance in the person's life. An instance of this kind is represented in the figure by FLE_d leading on to FLE_e—both of these events flowing partly from FLE_c.

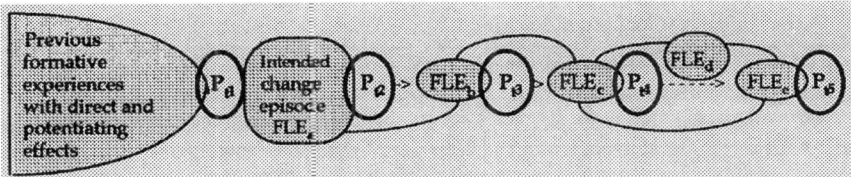

Figure 1: Schematic outline of formative episodes and change, over time

DATA–GATHERING AND SAMPLE

In light of the perspective advanced, and initally motivated by interest in effects of the mentioned workshops, a Formative Life Episodes questionnaire (FLEQ) was devised (see Appendix). As can be seen, the primary questions called on respondents to review a span of years in their (adult) lives and to identify episodes that stand out in perceived importance or impact. I consider the FLEQ to be fairly rough–hewn, not a refined tool. There was no opportunity for trial–run application before the data were gathered from the main sample of respondents. Nonetheless, the instrument elicited a generous measure of pertinent information from those who answered it.

The responding sample was drawn from former participants in three annually held workshops. Everyone for whom we could locate an up–to–date or possible address, 60–65 persons in all, was approached by mail. Results are based on returns from the first 30 persons who provided complete usable responses to the new questionnaire. At the time of this later data–gathering, the responding sample ranged in age from their early thirties to early seventies, with a modal age grouping of 50–54. Thus they tended to be in the middle range of their adult lives. Over half were psychologists, in positions ranging from full time practice, mainly in counselling, to full time teaching and research. Four were social workers, several others focused on marriage and lay counselling, two or three were from sociology or psychiatry, and two recorded themselves simply as "university lecturers".

In the design and the distribution of the questionnaire, effort was made to temporarily disguise its precise origins and context rather than alert participants to any special interest in long range effects of the workshops. Although this effort had limited success, additional questionnaire inquiry and feedback made it seem very unlikely that those who replied were led to exaggerate greatly the impact of the workshops, or of any particular category of life event.[4] More to the point, members of the workshop sample, although diverse in some respects, clearly had interests and values in common. After all, every respondent had earlier chosen to take part in the workshops; and many came long distances or went to other trouble to do so. Their own experience in counselling–related work suggests particular sensitivity to and expectation of change through forms of helping encounter. They may have been more used to thinking, than the majority of people, about personal change through life experiences. On the other side, their views in these spheres would be more considered and less naive than in most groups, and it is difficult to anticipate particular effects on results.

All in all, no presumption is made that the results from this study *would in their specifics* generalise to wider or different kinds of population. And, although further evaluation of the workshops provided a main part of the impetus for the data–gathering, my interest in the work now runs far beyond the issues it began with. It centres on the promise of this kind of approach to studying human development in adult life.

ILLUSTRATION OF THE RAW DATA

The original flavour and quality of the data provided by respondents is best conveyed through excerpts from replies. For example, one man reported as his second–listed episode that the death of his parents some years earlier had been a great shock. He referred to his mother dying following an operation and after complaining to him of specific distress. "The feeling lingers [he wrote] that perhaps some action on my part may have changed the situation. Later, my father took his life. I know I neglected him ..." Of an episode in another sphere he said: "A positive development was my experience, on leave, of comradeship and acceptance.." And, on the personal level again, he speaks of a very special episode of a sharpened sense of kinship with his young son, who said to him on an outing "We are just like brothers, Dad." He speaks also of the impact of separation by her initiative from his wife and children, and finally concludes that in his own case adversity and suffering had been a principal stimulus to growth.

A second participant's first listed episode grew out of an interview for a senior position: "I was told I could not have the position because I was a woman, although I was the only one applying who had qualifications and experience for that particular job". Evidently, similar experiences followed. A further, extended episode was the experience of having a "benign paternalistic senior man" as her immediate supervisor, causing a "string of conflicting reactions in me ranging from sexual fantasies to dreams of killing him." Another item centred on relationship experiences that led her "to realise I would not be able to tolerate a relationship with a man lasting 'forever'." Later, "I was one day consumed with rage against my flatmate [and wanted to destroy her]". And. "I experienced great excitement and generally deep emotional involvement in my work when I finally was given tasks of greater complexity and importance."

For another respondent, an important event was starting a new kind of work, after being "full–time wife and mother", at the point her youngest child began school. This move led in turn to the need to establish new understandings, but with conflict in the process, with her husband. She strongly emphasized the importance of her later workshop experience; in terms of development of deep personal relationships, an evolving new quality of self–examination and, in particular, "more awareness of effect of self on others". Following this was an eventful two-year experience in a therapy group as part of her counselling training. A subsequent, very important decision around possible further university study was singled out, involving "conflict between needs of family and personal needs for fulfilment. Compromise decided on by myself". Later, a promotion of her husband led to "increased pressure on me to fulfil a special sort of role as wife. This I held out against and reached a reasonable compromise".

The same person reported that both her parents suffered long terminal illnesses, involving a "switch in roles—I had to be the one to look after both parents in their frailty and dependency". With the death of her parents, "experiences of grief and loss were easier to bear because of previously–learned ability to live with emotional pain during personal therapy and group experience". Later, she alludes to the relevance of these life experiences in her work with others suffering grief and loss. A special episode, as her children reached maturity, was a conference and travel experience with her husband: both the first extended separation from her children "and first long period of time with my husband for over 20 years". And finally, the consummation of this change, in being a couple again with her husband; and, as well, "A strong sense of identity now as myself, not somebody's wife or mother—although still happy that I am a wife and mother".

These examples are taken, with editing to ensure anonymity, from three of the first four returns, as arbitrarily coded. The completed questionnaires varied in style, specificity and scope; at the extremes, eloquent and moving episodically organized human stories versus relatively terse tabulations of events.

CODING AND ANALYSIS OF THE DATA

Treatment of these data began with the development of a classification system, starting without prior framework and growing out of the data. This was achieved with the aid of student associates, in two main stages. In the first stage, Doug (see footnote), working in close consultation with me, built up a list of 32 ungrouped categories. In the second step, Esther, also working with me but not in contact with Doug, started with his categories and the raw data, and produced a refinement with differentiation of further categories and their grouping into ten clusters.[5] As seen in Table 1, the clustered categories are arranged under three broad headings. The first, Significant Life Happenings, includes common milestones in family life (cluster A), literal life crises including bereavement, serious illness and suicides (cluster B), 'uprooting experiences' such as a temporary or permanent relocation (C), and critical 'career and job change' episodes (D). The second trunk heading, Interpersonal Relationship Episodes, includes a family relations cluster (E), relations with significant others (F), and work–life relationships (G). The third trunk, Self–Initiated Developmental Activities, includes personal development experiences (H), episodes in the educational–vocational development area (I), and a cluster I finally named "Steps in social development and discovery of meaning" (J).

The data for these categories resulted from questions asking the respondent to list life episodes that were particularly eventful and that affected them in some way. Such experiences are variously referred to as 'events', 'episodes', 'particular happenings', etc., in FLEQ questions 1 and 2. Many of the episodes proved to be quite discrete events, producing relatively sudden change in the person's life. Most items in categories under Significant Life Happenings were of this nature. Other episode items were of longer duration, often self chosen developments involving a new activity rather than sudden happenings. Such qualities are found in most categories in the Self Initiated Developmental Activities sphere. Whether resulting from intention or happenstance, and whether over a brief or longer span of time, a reported episode had to be a distinct, externally manifest occurrence or step in the person's life, in order to be coded. The occurrence could be of an emotional nature, for example, an outburst of extreme anger or jealousy toward someone, but mentioned internal shifts, such as experienced new meaning or insight, needed to occur in some visible event context to be counted.

A minority of episodes fell in more than one category in terms of what the respondent emphasised, and thus drew multiple codings. Also, some subjects listed more than one distinct episode of the same kind. Thus, as seen in Table 1, the number of entries in a category often exceeds the number of persons generating those entries. In the course of organising the raw data (including typing and proofing hand–written replies), developing the category system, and rechecking codings as the categories were refined, all of the data came under repeated scrutiny. In an added check on reliability of coding, another rater used the completed category system to independently classify the data from 12 randomly selected returns, with an outcome of 92% agreement with the main classification of these returns (Szeto, 1977, p. 14). The main results (Table 1), and patterns of reply to the additional questionnaire items, form my next focus.

Table 1: Category system and frequencies

Categories (Three tiers: 36 categories in 10 clusters falling in three broad groupings)	Category usage	
	Entries N=358	People N=30
I. Significant Life Happenings		
A. Milestones	(9)	(9)
1. Birth of children/grandchildren	6	6
2. Children leaving home	2	2
3. Retirement	1	1
B. Life crises	(34)	(14)
4. Bereavement	15	8
5. Illness – self or significant other	15	10
6. Suicide (or attempt) – significant other or self	4	4
C. Uprooting experiences	(35)	(18)
7. Relocation of household	8	6
8. Illness – self or significant other	17	14
9. Returning to homeland	6	6
10. Change in financial/material status	4	4
D. Career and job changes	(43)	(21)
11. New appointment, responsibility or promotion	35	20
12. Consideration or rejection of job	4	4
13. Career setback	2	2
14. Resignation or termination of job	2	2
I. Interpersonal Relationship Episodes		
E. Family relationship sphere	(33)	(18)
15. Entry into marriage	13	11
16. Development/adjustment of marital relationship	10	7
17. Intense involvement with whole family	4	4
18. Heightened involvement with child/children	2	2
19. Marital difficulty or breakdown	4	4
F. Significant other relationships (non-family)	(38)	(19)
20. Entry to important or intensive relationship	26	13

RESULTS

The results are presented on a formally descriptive basis. Probability statistics are not convincingly applicable and were not used. I will first look at the leading categories, in terms of frequencies in this sample, with mention also of some general or speculative impressions. A second focus will be on the kinds of effect different categories of event had, as deduced from answers to question 3 (see Appendix). The categories of episode that stood out in terms of evident causal relation to other events (question 4) will be a further focus.

Total entries for the sample numbered 358 classified responses, for a mean of 12 per respondent. Ten of the 36 categories were considered clearly indicated in the answers of *at least one-third* of the respondent sample. The highest-scoring category fell within the Personal Development cluster, and was in fact participation in intensive groups and workshops (category # 29). Such episodes, with primary but not exclusive reference to the particular workshops all sample members had taken part in accounted for almost one entry in eight, and were listed (quite often as more than one distinct episode) by over three-quarters of the respondents. The category "New appointment, responsibility or promotion" (#11 in Table 1) ran a close second, comprising 10% of total entries and involving two-thirds of the respondents. The looser category, "Creative projects undertaken..." (# 33) drew entries from over half of the respondents.

Further categories in the top ten in frequency include some that may particularly characterize mobile professional individuals, as in the present sample. Of this kind are "travel and/or staying abroad" (category # 8); "acquiring a degree or other professional qualification" (# 31); and "impact of a course, book, film, art..." (# 30). In addition, there were categories of more general application: "entering marriage" (# 15), or another important relationship (# 20); episodes of illness of self or a significant other (# 5); and "undertaking a hobby, avocational interest or skill" (# 35). Half of the ten most frequent categories fell in the sphere of Self–Initiated Activities, this whole area accounting for 40% of all episode entries in the present sample. Such emphasis might be usual in groups of similar educational and occupational level but not apply in those of widely differing composition.

Not everyone was comfortable with viewing his/her life as episodic, with periodic high points of impact. An ending question (unnumbered, see Appendix) asked for feedback on this point, namely, whether the respondent's life seemed so even in quality "that it was very difficult for you to discern exceptionally formative episodes or turning points, etc.?" Half of the sample replied with a clear cut "no", often noting that they felt very aware of influential episodes or turning points. Five answered "yes!", they did not see or struggled to discern distinctly formative episodes. Others said "yes" it was difficult to pick out critical (short–duration) incidents, although the idea or sense of turning points was not a problem. A few pointed out other ways in which the answer was both Yes and No.

An overall impression is that the more fully described episodes, of many kinds, gave a distinct sense of something having happened, or been done or entered into, such that past and future were not and *could not be* the same. In some cases, differences in overt choice and attitude stood out and, in others, there were more subtle changes in inner meaning and valuing. New awareness in relationships was quite often implied. *Acutely remembered experiences could, it seemed, work like lookout points in the terrain of inner life, with potential to keep on contributing as the local scene changed.*

Results from FLEQ question 3 relate to this last point. Here, respondents were asked to link particular episodes with particular kinds of short and/or long term effect. The first potential effect was that of impact on the quality of their personal relationships, positive (Q 3.i) and/or negative (Q 3.ii). Intensive encounter–workshop groups (# 29) followed by entering important or intensive new relationships (# 20) and travelling or staying abroad (# 8), stood out in being seen as having greatest positive, short and long term effects on respondents' interpersonal lives. Important new relationships were also seen, with appreciable frequency, as having had short term negative effects, and such effects were noted by one person in reference to experiential learning workshops.

The three categories of episode just mentioned, together with undertaking creative projects (# 33) and advancement to a new position or responsibility (# 11), stood out in terms of perceived importance for *personal* development (Q 3.iv). For the related aspect of positive effects on "your basic sense of worth as a person" (Q 3.v), the picture was quite similar in terms of category selection. Interestingly, events in 30 of the 36 categories were viewed by one or more persons as strongly contributing to self knowledge (Question 3.vi). In the general area of affects on professional abilities, new learning or related new work (Question 3, vii, viii & ix), every FLE category was mentioned at least once by one person.

FLEQ question 4 asked about causal connections among the listed episodes. Perhaps because the question appeared in a small space at the end of the questionnaire, replies to it were mostly brief (and not usable in three cases). Yet, the overall picture has unpredicted, worthwhile substance. Most 'causal' episodes (that is, those seen as triggering or directly influencing other episodes) fell in the Life Happenings and Self–Initiated Activity spheres, rather than the interpersonal relationship grouping, in this sample at least. Specifically, episodes in the human relations workshop/encounter group category were most often identified as causal, for example, by leading to (further) growthful personal–professional experiences, or as prompting further professional training or study leave, or increasing openness to the impact of a course or book, or being the stimulus or launch point for an important relationship. Occasionally, events of more negative valence were evoked: the spouse of one respondent reportedly became ill and depressed over a relationship he developed at a workshop; and another became disenchanted with the conduct of his colleagues back home.

Episodes in the category 'new appointment or responsibility' category (# 11) were also quite often singled out as causal, in reference to varied further professional, educational and personal life steps. "Travelling or staying abroad", "birth of children or grandchildren", "bereavement" and "relocation of household ' were each identified by some respondents as precipitating shifts, for example, in life style or personal outlook and choices. Further episodes noted as causally related to others, included entry to marriage or other intensive relationships, and all of the higher frequency categories in the Self–Initiated Activities area. In many instances, the mentioned 'causal' episodes seemed to trigger a chain reaction or, as Esther Szeto (1977, p. 28) put it, to function as the "activating core to further formative life episodes".

The results tend to confirm that the small group workshops were, over the long haul, a highly valued and influential experience for the persons in this responding sample. However, when comparisons are made of the *relative* frequency with which different classes of episode are cited, it needs to be born in mind that in one respect at least the dice is loaded in favour of some categories over others. Since everyone in this sample had the workshop experience in common there is a "100% potential" for it to be singled out, and this order of frequency (of a single kind of event) may apply to a handful of other episode categories. Plausibly, for example, nearly everyone had received, over the span of a dozen years, a 'new appointment, responsibility or promotion' (#11) and, in this sample, would have 'undertaken some creative new project or programme' (#33). Many would have *either* married (#15) *or* entered into an important or intensive relationship (#20). These are the episode categories (taking the last two not singly but in combination) which in frequency of use approach the frequency of workshop–group mentions.

Life steps reflected in the categories "returning to homeland" (#9), "resignation or termination of job" (#14), "marital difficulty or breakdown" (# 19), "entering counselling or therapy as a client" (#28), and "religious awakening and/or affiliation" (#34) evidently occurred with relatively low frequency, in this sample and over the time span. It seems plausible that they nearly always would have been cited as eventful episodes, when they did occur. High frequency implies that the categories are shared ones, not necessarily that they are more important to individuals within their own selection of significant life events.[6]

SUMMATION

This study has explored new territory in terms of its rationale and method, involves naturalistic investigation not experiment, and has generated results that are plausibly of the same general structure as those that would obtain from other samples using the same procedures. Within this structure, quantitative generality of present results is not claimed. Research with differently composed samples would be expected to yield a different balance of frequency in the life episode categories and groupings.

The idea of episodic development is built into the questionnaire, as a result of the view of change advanced, and is not under formal test in this study. However, direct feedback from respondents indicated that this approach was consistent with the way that at least half of them tended to picture the unfolding of their lives. A minority saw a generally more even, gradual process of change, although not ruling out the idea of turning points or decisive experiences; their problem was in deciphering these. The metaphor of a developmental journey involving a complex causal chain or system is certainly more consistent with the data than the idea of specific effects tied to singular origins. A way of thinking more familiar to ecology than to traditional approaches in behavioural science, is implied.

An empirically–based working chart of the classes of events and episodes that form the significant topography of adult life, and that involve or lead to transitional change, has been produced. Some of the emphasised categories might well have been predicted, but no attempt in fact was made to anticipate them. Viewed after the fact, they appear to fit the lived world that we know from our own experience and other people's lives. New data from differing samples could reveal gaps in the schema or suggest further refinement of some categories. Life events literature, appearing since this study was undertaken, starts with a valuable paper by Sarason, Johnson & Siegel (1978). These authors report the development and application of a Life Experiences Survey (LES) which, in contrast to the approach used here, is a highly structured multiple–choice questionnaire. There is both considerable overlap and visible difference between the events listed in the LES and the categories which emerged from the present study. One general difference is that events encompassed in the Survey tend to be narrower and more discrete as categories than those arising from this research.[7]

In the present work it is very noticeable that activities broadly of a voluntary nature, or steps chosen or agreed to by the respondent, played a much larger part in the critical episodes reported than did events in which the individual had little or no agency. It seems likely, as already suggested, that this balance is related to characteristics of the respondent sample who, for example, would almost certainly rate more highly as 'internalizers' than as 'externalizers' on Rotter's locus of control dimension (Rotter, 1966).

Although a large proportion of the formative episodes reported here were of a crisis nature, very few if any were seen as harmful in the long run; and all were in categories viewed as having had beneficial effects of identified kinds by some one or more persons in the sample. Nearly half of the episode categories were placed in a causative relation to subsequent formative episodes, involving simple A–>B connections and more complex linkages.

The results and yield of this study strongly invite further research on similar lines. I have not myself had good opportunity to gather additional data, but would like to see the same procedure used with a variety of groups. Studies also could target on a particular period of life, shorter or longer time spans might be chosen, and samples could be homogeneous or intentionally diverse in age, occupation, or other circumstance. Initially, use of the present FLE questionnaire method would lend validation and/or refinement to the category system. Later on, the further–tested system of categories could profitably be used as the basis for a highly structured questionnaire, which would be far more practicable for large–scale and comparative research than the open–ended approach called for at the beginning.

There are numerous other potentially interesting variations possible. For example, descriptions of formative episodes could be given for the same person's life by more than one respondent, that is, both from internal and connected–observer frames of reference. Or, couples might be asked to focus specifically on formative events in their lives together. Studies which related

FLEQ data and patterns to independently obtained life–history information, or personality and attitude measures, could lend further meaning to the results generated by each method. A generic feature of all such studies would be that of taking development and change literally as primary principles in the order of life, not merely as departures from stability requiring explanation. This emphasis remains an incomplete and greatly needed 'transition' in the study of the human person.

REFERENCES

Atchley, R. C. (1989). *A continuity theory of normal aging*. The Gerontologist, *29*, 183–190.

Barrett–Lennard, G. T. (1974). *Experiential learning groups*. Psychotherapy: Theory, Research and Practice, 11, 71–75.

Barrett–Lennard, G. T. (1974//75). *Outcomes of residential encounter group workshops: Descriptive analysis of follow–up structured questionnaire data*. Interpersonal Development, 5, 86–93.

Barrett–Lennard, G. T. (1975/76). *Process, effects and structure in intensive groups: A theoretical–descriptive analysis*. In C. L. Cooper (Ed.), Theories of Group Processes (pp. 59–86). London: Wiley (published 1975; corrected soft–cover edition, 1976).

Barrett–Lennard, G. T., Kwasnik, T. P., & Wilkinson, G. R. (1973/74). *Some effects of participation in encounter group workshops: An analysis of written follow–up reports*. Interpersonal Development. 4, 35–41.

Brown, J. D., & McGill, K. L. (1989). *The cost of good fortune: When positive life events produce negative health consequences*. Journal of Personality and Social Psychology, 57, 1103–1110.

Rotter, J. (1966). *Generalized expectancies for internal versus external control of reinforcement*. Psychological Monographs, 80 (1).

Sarason, I. G., Johnson, J. F., & Siegel, J. M. (1978). *Assessing the impact of life changes: Development of the Life Experiences Survey*. Journal of Consulting and Clinical Psychology, 46, 932–946.

Szeto, E. (1977). *Formative life episodes in adult development: An exploratory study. Unpublished master's research essay*. University of Waterloo, Ontario, Canada.

---

[1]My first expression of this refocused view, written about the time the present data–gathering was conceived, appears in Barrett–Lennard, 1975/76, pp. 75–76.

[2]After the basic work for this paper was completed, my attention was drawn to Atchley's (1989) 'continuity theory', which works to integrate the aspects of stability and of change in human functioning. In this theory, stability and change are linked by what is called 'dynamic continuity': "To the extent that change builds upon, and has links to the person's past, change is a part of continuity" It is argued that internal or perceived continuity is adaptive; that it is healthy to see inner or self change as connected and growing out of one's past (Atchley,1989, pp. 183–184).

[3]The questionnaire was sent out by a colleague in another university, who was an early contributor to the workshops but could have been doing research unrelated to them. Respondents were invited to read further information sealed in an enclosed envelope, and from me, after completing the questionnaire but before mailing it back; thus to maximise informed consent. Our modest subterfuge had limited success! A second questionnaire asked respondents whether they had realised while answering the FLEQ that it had a connection with the workshops. The majority 'yes' they thought it had. A further question asked whether this had influenced their replies. Nearly all said "no" or "probably not appreciably"; three who answered 'Yes' implied that their motivation to give a full and/or careful response had been increased by their sense of its source.

[4]I am considerably indebted to both people. Doug Holland worked with me on the initial development of a coding system. Most primary categories were established in this phase. Esther Szeto went on to further differentiate and refine some categories, code the data, analyse responses to the remaining FLEQ items, and

complete a first write–up of the project. In preparing this paper, I closely reviewed the category system, made adjustments in language and sequencing into the form shown in Table 1, and rechecked pertinent codings and counts. (One effect was the merger of two minor categories into others, leaving the present 36.) Although she had no part in the data–gathering, or formulations it was based on, I do wish to acknowledge Esther's significant contribution. We have since quite lost touch, or she might have joined me in authorship of this paper.

[5]In further distinction, most categories emerging from the data of this study may reflect types of event that are typically memorable, and of a kind to have transitional or reference meaning to the individual—perhaps serving as 'lookout points', as earlier suggested. A few of the categories, however (#17 and #21, for example) may involve or flow from types of event which only sometimes have a special potency of impact and meaning.

[6]Subsequent research, using modified versions of the Life Experiences Survey, includes a study by Brown & McGill (1989), who proposed that life events inconsistent with the self concept cause "identity disruption" leading to physical illness. This expected effect was found only in the case of respondents with low self–esteem.

Appendix
FORMATIVE LIFE EPISODES QUESTIONNAIRE

This questionnaire focuses on adult life and is specifically not enquiring about childhood experiences and their influence. We suggest that you read right through it before beginning to reply. Please do not write or sign your name on the questionnaire itself but be sure to fill in and enclose the accompanying identification slip. We will return a Xerox copy of your filled–in form, if you request it.

1.   As you think back over the period since about 1960*, what particular happenings or episodes in the course of your personal life have been exceptionally eventful and significant to you? There is no need to give details, but please identify the essential nature and (as relevant) the time and context of *directly experienced events and episodes that affected you deeply*, for example, in your outlook and values; your personal development or resources; the kind or quality of relationships you have with others; the meaning of your life to you...

Please record your answers after the next question.

2.   As in the case of the previous question, please reflect deeply over the last dozen years or so, this time in the context of your occupational or professional life. What have been key episodes within or relevant to the course and quality of this journey? What experiences of an exceptionally eventful nature *stand out*, for example, in their effects on your work with or on behalf of other people, on your awareness of communicational and other processes between people that deeply affect their living and working together, or on your capacities and/or priorities in your vocation?

[Space for response, and further format suggestion to respondents, is omitted]

3.   Please review the items you have recorded and clearly *number* each one, preferably in the order you have listed them, without repeating any numbers... Now please consider the following questions and indicate by the numbers you have just assigned, which event(s) or episode(s) is/are the best fit in answer to each question.

i)   Which do you feel had the greatest effect on the quality of your interpersonal life,

in the direction of enriching, enhancing and deepening your personal relationships?

_____ in the short run

_____ in the long run

ii)   Which (if you feel any applies) has had a diminishing or negative effect
on the quality of your interpersonal life?

_____ in the short run

_____ _____ in the long run

iii)   Which (if any) has helped you significantly to become more self–reliant?
_____ Answer

iv)   Which of the listed episodes do you perceive as having been particularly

important for your personal unfolding and development?

_____ directly, or in the short run

_____ indirectly, e.g., in opening doorways to further
'growthful' experiences

v)   a) Which has (have had) an enhancing effect on your basic sense of
worth as a person? _____ Answer

b) Which (if any) have had a marked negative effect on your feeling
of your own worth? _____ Answer

vi) Through which episode have you been most strongly (even if painfully) confronted
with some fundamental pattern or quality in yourself, such that you became more
self–knowing in some mportant way? _____ Answer

vii) Which episode seems to have been most critical in its <u>direct and/or indirect</u>   influence on
your resourcefulness in your vocation? If your work involves very clearly different areas of activity,
calling for different answers, please list more than one.

_____ Answer(s)

viii) Which (if any) stand out as a source of basic learning either about the human   person, people
in groups or organizations, or the workings of human society in some wider sense?
_____Answer

ix)   Which ones (if any) led you to do things yourself that recreated, or provided for
others, qualities or opportunities similar to those you had experienced?
_____ Answer

4.   As you review again your answers to the first three items, do you see any order in the
events you describe? Can you see connections between them? For example, do some events
seem to have been causally related to others? Note your clearest observations on this level as
follows: 1—>3; 4—>5—>6; etc.

Did your adult life over the period of review seem to you so even and constant in quality,
in the broad areas considered, that it was very difficult for you to discern exceptionally
formative episodes or turning points, etc.?

_____

_____

_____

Are there any other observations or comments, within or about the general spirit and
scope of the questionnaire, that occur to you to offer us?

_____

_____

_____

Experiencing, Knowing, and Change

ARTHUR C. BOHART AND ASSOCIATES

CALIFORNIA STATE UNIVERSITY

ABSTRACT

A theory of experiencing holds that experiencing is a different way of knowing than cognitive knowing. It is primarily nonverbal, perceptual, holistic, and ecological. It is recognitional, felt, and involves the detection of flowing patterns, or trajectories, over time. Creativity is primarily perceptual and experiential in nature. All forms of psychotherapy facilitate experiential change. Four research projects explored the theory of experiencing. It was found that most subjects recognize the difference between intellectual and experiential knowing. Actors learning a part move from intellectual to experiential knowledge. Creative artists move from an experiential inspiration to a symbolic expression of that inspiration. A study of famous therapists revealed that all did things to make therapy expriential. A study in which empathy responses were "de-experientialized" found that nonexperiential empathy responses disrupted the flow of therapy and such responses were rated by clients as more disruptive and less helpful.

EXPERIENCING, KNOWING, AND CHANGE

Below I discuss four research projects co–developed and worked on by graduate students and myself over the last two years. These are an attempt to explore my theory of experiencing (Bohart, 1993; Bohart & Wugalter, 1991).

Basically I have suggested that experiencing is a different way of knowing than knowing through conceptual thinking. It is primarily nonverbal, perceptual, holistic and gestalt–like, contextual, bodily, and ecological. It is a view based in the work of Eugene Gendlin (1964), George Lakoff (1987), Mark Johnson (1987), and philosophers like Merleau–Ponty.

Basically the hypothesis is that we first and most primarily know ourselves and our worlds through our experiences of them. Experiencing is primarily perceptual and interactive. We are "built" to detect flowing patterns of meaning in our interactions, and we do this perceptually and nonconceptually. We experience our worlds more in an aesthetic manner than in a semantic, conceptual manner (Bohart & Rosenbaum, 1993). Metaphorically we live and know our worlds through our experiences in a manner similar to how we experience works of art, such as symphonic music.

Conceptual knowing, thinking, believing, forming concepts, and the like, all come *from* experiential knowing, and is an attempt to formulate that knowing in words and concepts. This means that we often can sense or 'feel" patterns of meaning which we cannot put into words. Creativity is primarily perceptual and experiential in nature rather than conceptual. In fact, thinking itself is *primarily* perceptual in nature rather than conceptual. In our heads we "rotate" things and "view them from different angles," and a moment of insight is when we quite literally *see* things in a new relationship. It is literally analogus to climbing a hill to get a new perspective on the layout of the land. Seeing things from a new angle, we often see other new relationships which we had missed before.

Therefore, the initial inspiration of creativity is perceptual, felt, or recognitional, rather than conceptual. That is why creative people say that creative ideas "just struck me," or "I just saw it," or the like.

Intuition is basically a sensing or feeling of relationships, nonverbally perceived. We can often have a vague feeling of knowing something or understanding something that we cannot as yet put into words. In this respect many feelings are not emotions, but sensed or felt patterns of meaning. Thus we can "feel" that something is wrong in a relationship before we can cognitively and conceptually identify what it is.

Experiencing is an ecological way of knowing (Gibson, 1979), and is based on the needs of animals to navigate and explore their environments, to detect meaningful patterns of events in those environments, and to cope with them. In order for animals to navigate their environments they need to be able to detect the configurations and trajectories in situations quickly and rapidly. And they do not do this by forming concepts. We *see* meanings, we see configurations and gestalts. We *recognize* people without having to "think" who they are.

The important ecological skill is to detect patterns of meaning flowing over time, that is, to detect the trajectories in situations. Once again, this kind of apprehension is not primarily conceptual. A cheetah chasing an antelope is trying to detect a trajectory, not trying to apply a concept or categorize the event. A human having dinner with a potential romantic partner is trying to sense the "flow" in the relationship (i.e. detect the trajectories). Trajectories are nonverbally sensed or perceived patterns rather than concepts, although concepts may aid in their apprehension.

This view is in contrast to the typical cognitivist view which assumes that all knowing is primarily conceptual in nature. From a cognitivist perspective perception is really conceptual thinking, only at a rapid, underlying nonconscious level. Furthermore, the kind of rapid automatic thinking that underlies perception is seen as relatively rigid and inflexible. Creativity and spontaneity are reserved for conscious, "controlled" processing. In contrast, my view of experiencing holds that it is conscious, controlled processing which is often inflexible and nonspontaneous, and it is nonconceptual experiential knowing which is often the source of creativity and spontaneity.

With regards to therapy, it has long been known that sheer intellectual, conceptual understanding is nontherapeutic. This is because what we want in therapy is an *experiential* shift. We want clients to actually experience themselves and their worlds differently, not merely "think" about them differently. Working to change how we experience the world is a commonality across all different forms of therapy, and all good therapists are experiential in some way or the other.

From this theory several hypotheses follow. First, people should report having experiences ("feelings") that they cannot put into words. They should be aware of sometimes sensing meaningful patterns of interaction in their lives without being able to verbally describe or name them, as one can sense the pattern in a symphony without being able to label or describe it. Second, individuals should be aware of understandings that appear to be "nonconceptual" in the sense that they are more a matter of direct recognition than of "thought." Third, individuals should report occasions when they have had an insight, and it should have the following qualities. It should be not totally describable in words. Further, following the perceptual analogy, seeing things from a new perspective should not only solve the old problem, but open up new vistas as well. In other words, individuals should make new, unexpected discoveries as well.

Fourth, it follows that coming to "really understand" something is to get it at an experiential "gut level." Often individuals start out with intellectual understanding, but we say that they do not really "have it" until they get it at a "gut level." When they get it at a gut level, that is when they should be able to operate from that knowledge in a spontaneous and creative fashion. When it is still "intellectual" they should not. Learning something, such as an actor learning a part, involves the process of using conceptual knowledge to explore until one begins to 'sense" and "feel" the perceptual trajectories involved. Practice in a domain of knowledge does not develop a "habit" so much as it develops a sensitivity to the domain involved—to the pathways involved in the domain. In other words increased practice not only builds motor skills, but leads to increasingly sensed perceptual/experiential knowledge of the domain. This means that one can more and more spontaneously improvise as one comes to know the domain better and better, in direct contrast to the automatized "learning of habits" model.

Fifth, all good therapists should do things to make the learning that occurs in therapy experiential. Sixth, if one reduces the experiential component in a therapy response, that response should lose some of its effectiveness.

Below I describe the projects conducted by myself and my students over the last two years to explore the above hypotheses.

RESEARCH PROJECT ONE

Suzanne Browner, Rachel Muscatine, and Arthur Bohart (1993)

A survey questionnaire was designed to explore the hypothesis that people understand the difference between experiential knowing and intellectual/conceptual knowing. The questionnaire consisted of 33 items which were answered on a five–point scale. The items were designed to explore (a) the idea that people had had the experience of sensing or feeling patterns of meaning that they could not put into words, (b) that they understood or were aware of the distinction between knowing something intellectually and knowing something at the felt or experiential level, and © the idea that gaining an insight or coming to "really understand" something was more of a felt, perceptual/experiential nature than it was of an intellectual, conceptual nature. With regard to ©, it was hypothesized that students reporting on the gaining of some kind of insight or shift after struggling with an issue would report that the the shift involved a sense of direct experiencing or recognizing as much or more than it involved thought, that it would be more like "seeing it from a new angle" than it would be like gaining a new concept, and it would be holistic, it would have the quality of "broadening"— the student would become aware of new and unexpected aspects of the issue,. Finally it would be more than could be put into words.

The questionnaire was administered to 150 introductory psychology students. There were 40 men and 110 women in the sample. There were 41 Caucasian Americans, and 109 subjects of other ethnicities indicating a multicultural sample. There were 61 social science majors, 30 science majors, 40 business majors, and 19 "other" majors. Tests of differences between subjects by gender, ethnicity. and major, revealed the presence of few differences.

Results confirmed our hypotheses. Selected items along with the mean response are given in tables 1 and 2. From table one it can be seen that subjects were aware of having had experiences in which they had experienced meanings that they could not put into words, and that they were aware of the distinction between intellectual and "felt" or experiential knowing. The very small confidence intervals indicate that the means are representative of how the vast majority of subjects answered.

Table One.

Means and Confidence Intervals On Selected Survey Items
Indicating Subjects' Awareness of the Difference
Between Experiential and Intellectual Knowing

Scale: 1 (definitely yes) 2 3 4 5 (definitely no)

1. Have you ever had a sense of understanding something that you could not put into words? X = 1.42; CI = .14

2. Have you ever had a sense of something wrong in a situation or a relationship before you could put it into words? X = 1.74; CI = .18

3. Does the idea of a difference between intellectually understanding something and having a gut level understanding of it make any sense to you?

X = 2.05; CI = .19

10. Has there been a time when you knew something to be true before you were able to intellectually verify to yourself that it was true?

X = 1.62; CI = .15.

X = mean. CI = confidence interval for a value of $p<.02$ (two–tailed).

Table 2 indicates how students rated their experience of having attained a new awareness, a new understanding, or of having "gotten it" after having struggled with some issue.

Table two.

Means and Confidence Intervals on Selected Survey Items
Indicating That Subjects Experience Insights
As Perceptual/Experiential Shifts

Subjects were asked to pick which answer characterized their experience
of their new understanding or awareness.

15.   1. you are directly experiencing the new awareness or understanding

    2. mostly experiencing the new awareness or understanding

    3. both direct experiencing and thinking about it.

    4. mostly thinking about the new awareness or understanding

    5. thinking about the new awareness or understanding.

    X = 2.72 CI = .22.

19.   1. purely intellectual, theoretical, conceptual, and abstract understanding.

    2. mostly intellectual, theoretical, conceptual, and abstract

    3. immediate, direct recognition plus thoughts, concepts, abstractions

    4. mostly direct recognition and some thoughts, concepts, abstractions

    5. immediate, direct recognition along without thought or analysis

X = 3.05 CI = .20.

22.   1. broadening, being able to "see" or "sense" new directions

2. mostly broadening and being able to "sense" new directions

3. some broadening

4. mostly a clearer sense of the one part you were concerned with

5. clearly defined and sharpened understanding of the one thing alone.

X = 2.30, CI = .22.

We had predicted that most subjects would experience a new awareness or understanding as having at least some aspects of direct recognition and perception. However, we expected that they would also experience it as involving thought to some degree. Therefore we expected most subjects to answer somewhere near the middle, but on the side of direct recognition and perception. It can be seen from table two that this was the case. For most subjects the new understanding or awareness involved elements of direct recognition and experiencing, but also elements of thinking. Also, following from the experiencing/perception hypothesis, it was predicted that subjects would find the new insight broadening out into new areas, and this was also confirmed.

In sum, the results confirmed our hypothesis that subjects would generally recognize the difference between intellectual and experiential knowing, and that the gaining of a new understanding or awareness was as much a perceptual as it was a conceptual experience.

RESEARCH PROJECT TWO

Michael Garcia, Aurora Rosales, Suann Hsu, Joan Zirpolo, Kimberly Hagan, Lissa Miller, Suzanne Browner, Rachel Muscatine, and Arthur Bohart (1993)

It was predicted that expert therapists of each of the major persuasions would experientialize the therapy process in one way or the other. A rating scale was designed to assess different ways therapists could make therapy experiential. Eight trained graduate student raters rated videotapes and films of the following expert therapists: Carl Rogers (Client–centered), Leslie Greenberg (Process–experiential), Paul Wachtel (Psychodynamic), Hans Strupp (Psychodynamic), Donald Meichenbaum (Cognitive–behavioral), Aaron Beck (Cognitive–behavioral). A comparison videotape of a television talk show therapist, David Viscott, was also used. Working in a talk–show format, it was predicted that Viscott would be the only therapist who would be rated as being nonexperiential.

It was predicted that while each of the expert therapists would be experiential in one way or the other, they would differ in how they experientialized therapy. A rating scale was developed. The scale had raters rate therapists on a variety of items on a four–point scale, from "yes, very central to this therapist," to "yes, somewhat central," to "yes, but peripheral to this therapist," to "no, this therapist doesn't do this."

It was found that on 22 of the 27 items the reliability was good (.62–.95). Of the other five items it was impossible to calculate a reliability figure on three items because there was virtually unanimous agreement among the raters rating virtually all the therapists the same. Thus there was no variance. The reliability on the other two items was .35 and .51.

Below the results are briefly summarized. The results for the two person–centered/experiential therapists—Carl Rogers and Leslie Greenberg—are specifically highlighted.

We first hypothesized that expert therapists would encourage clients to explore their experience, in contrast to simply thinking about themselves intellectually. This was confirmed as each of the expert therapists was rated as doing something that encouraged clients to explore their experience. All therapists, for instance, encouraged clients to explore their inner experience and their experience of their external circumstances, although there were some differences. For example, Rogers emphasized inner experience over the exploration of external experience. Other therapists, such as Greenberg and Beck, encouraged clients to explore their experience through the use of experiential exercises.

The two person–centered/experiential therapists were rated as follows. Carl Rogers was rated high in facilitating clients exploring their inner experience, and on responding to clients' directly sensed felt meanings. He was rated somewhat high on facilitating clients exploring their external experience. He was not rated as encouraging the use of exercises or as exploring the past.

Leslie Greenberg was rated high in facilitating clients exploring their inner experience, and in exploring their external experience. He was also rated high in using experiential exercises and in responding to clients' directly sensed felt meanings. He was only rated as peripherally encouraging clients to explore their past experience.

Second, we hypothesized that expert therapists who had as a goal the faciltation of gaining understanding or insight, broadly defined, would encourage clients to gain this understanding experientially. That is, they would be interested in clients gaining more than sheer intellectual understanding. They would encourage this by tying abstract cognitive formulations to concrete experiential examples and referents. This would happen, for instance, by only giving interpretations after a good deal of experiential evidence had been amassed so that the client could directly recognize the fittingness of the interpretation.

This hypothesis was also confirmed. Therapists such as Strupp, Wachtel, Beck and Meichenbaum who stressed cognitive understanding or insight, did encourage clients to tie such understanding to experiential referents. This was done by emphasizing the attaining of new understanding only in direct reference to concrete experiences in the client's life.

In general Carl Rogers was not rated high on items in this category, because he did not work to specifically encourage cognitive insight. Greenberg, on the other hand, was rated as moderate in this category. While Greenberg does not emphasize the attaining of cognitive insight, he does encourage tying understanding to experiential referents.

Third, we hypothesized that another way to make therapy experiential would be to encourage the learning of new skills through experience. As might be expected the therapists who were rated as doing this were Beck, Meichenbaum and Greenberg, while Strupp, Rogers, and Wachtel were not seen as doing this to any significant degree. While Greenberg does not explicitly teach skills, as do Beck and Meichenbaum, raters rated him as encouraging the learning of certain skills such as how to test out ideas against experience or how to attend to immediate experience.

Fourth, we hypothesized that the therapy interaction itself would be a source of experiential discovery. Therapists might focus on clients' immediate experience in the session, respond supportively to client emotion, give feedback, share experience with the client, or directly treat the client in new, growth–promoting ways. All of the expert therapists were seen as using the context of therapy as a source of new experiential learning, although they did it in different ways. For instance, Rogers was seen as providing immediate feedback and as self–disclosing, as well as encouraging an open, exploratory atmosphere. Beck was not seen as self–disclosing, but was seen as encouraging an open, exploratory atmosphere.

With regard to the two person–centered/experiential therapists, Rogers was seen as responding to clients' immediate experience of the session, of responding to emotion, and as giving immediate feedback. Further Rogers was seen as supporting an open, exploratory climate, and as encouraging a climate of active participation by the client. Greenberg was seen similarly.

Our fifth hypothesis was that Viscott, operating in an artificial therapy context, a talk–show format, would be rated as more abstract and intellectual than the other expert therapists. In essence we were using the tape of Viscott as a kind of validity check on our scale. While Viscott was rated as doing some experiential things, nevertheless he was rated as generally being nonexperiential. He was seen as giving abstract, conceptual information without significant effort to help the client internalize it experientially. He was seen as focusing on logical exploration and intellectual understanding without much emphasis on developing understanding through experience. In these things he differed from all the other therapists.

Our last hypothesis was that each of the expert therapists would be rated as more like an experiential prototype than an abstract, intellectual prototype, with the exception of Viscott, who would be rated as abstract and intellectual. This was also confirmed. On a nine–point scale, with "1" being most like the experiential prototype, "5" being the midpoint, and "9" being most like the intellectual prototype, the therapists were rated as follows: Rogers, 2.0; Greenberg, 2.0; Meichenbaum, 2.8; Wachtel, 3.4; Beck, 3.6; Strupp, 4.5; Viscott, 6.5.

In sum, our hypothesis that all expert therapists do something to experientialize learning in the therapy process was confirmed.

RESEARCH PROJECT 3

Mark Loesch, Holly Hamilton, Lucy Seferian, Stephanie Rush, and Arthur Bohart (1994)

In contrast to typical cognitivist views, which assume that "controlled" cognitive processing is flexible and creative, while "automatic" processing is stereotyped and inflexible, we hypothesized that it is controlled conscious processing which is often inflexible, while experiential knowing is creative, flexible, and spontaneous. We explored this hypothesis in two ways. First, we studied actors learning a part. We hypothesized that the actors initially try to understand the part intellectually. Gradually, however, the knowledge of the part would move from the intellectual, conceptual level, to the "gut" or experiential level. When the part was grasped at the experiential level, it would be automatic, but it would also be spontaneous. Actors would be more likely to feel they could improvise creatively from the part after they got it at the gut level. They would say that they had a "feel for" the part, and they would feel they had "become" the character (a nonconceptual form of knowing). The whole process of learning the part would be experienced as one of moving from intellectual/conceptual knowing to experiential felt knowing.

Second, we hypothesized that creativity comes from the experiential level. Creativity begins as an "inspiration": a felt, experienced, or directly perceived sense of a new relationship. The creative process is then one of turning that perceived, felt, or experienced sense of a new relationship into words, musical or artistic symbols.

To test these hypotheses we interviewed 10 actors about their experiences in learning a role, and 21 working creative artists. Creative artists included painters, potters, costume designers, composers, screenwriters, and poets. Interviews were based on a set format of questions, patterned after the Rorschach interview. We started with open–ended questions and moved to more specific inquiries. Examples of questions are given in Table 3. The interviews were semi-structured in that interviewers were allowed to modify the questions to some degree to meet the needs of the individual interview. Interviews were then rated by independent raters, with over 90% agreement.

Table Three.
Sample Questions From Interviews with Actors and With Artists.

Actors:

> Please describe the process, from when you first begin to read the part and learn the lines, until when you have the part "down."

> When you had mastered the part, to what degree were you able to operate spontaenously from the part?

> To what degree was your understanding of the part, after you had mastered it, nonconceptual, that is, to what degree did you "just see" what the part was about, without needing to think and analyze?

Artists:

> We are interested in the process of how you came up with the creative idea for you work of art...We'd like you to describe the process, from when you first got the idea or inspiration for the work, through the process of developing it, until its finish.

> To what degree is your creative process describable in words?

> To what degree did you find yourself *discovering* the idea or inspiration, to what degree was it an experience of discovery or realization?

For the actors it was found that on all but 1 of the 11 questions the majority answered in the direction we expected, and results on 8 of these 11 questions were significant at the $p<.05$ level. When raters compared what the actors said to two different prototype models of learning a part, one based on the experiencing notion and the other based on a more cognitivistic view, 8 of the 10 were rated as fitting more with the experiential than with the cognitivistic/intellectual model ($p<.05$). 7 of the 10 subjects spontaneously said that they "got a feel for the part," and 9 of the 10 said either the above or that they "became the character." Signficant at the $p<.02$ level was that when the part was mastered actors were able to operate automatically "without thinking." Yet they also rated themselves as being able to operate spontaneously and creatively from the part.

Our results also supported our hypothesis about creative artists. It was found that for 19 of the 21 subjects ($p<.01$) the beginning inspiration was a feeling, a "just seeing," or an ah–ha. In other words, subjects reported it to be perceptual, recognitional, or felt, rather than conceptual or intellectual. One subject said, for instance, "It occurs on the spot, in an area I like that's pleasing; it makes me feel like painting." In addition, 20 of the 21 subjects said that they had some trouble describing the creative process in words, further evidence for the idea that the process involves experienced, felt, or nonverbal knowing. At the end of the interview we read subjects a description of what we thought the creative process entailed, and asked subjects the extent to which they agreed with the description. 17 of the 17 subjects we asked agreed with our model and said it fit their experience.

In sum, our results supported our hypothesis that felt or experienced knowing is creative and spontaneous, and not automatic and stereotyped as typical cognitivistic theory holds.

RESEARCH PROJECT FOUR

Karen Tallman, Diane Kay, Sylvia Harvey, Ellen Robinson, and Arthur Bohart (1994)

An attempt was made to "de–experientialize" psychotherapy in a therapy analogue study. Using a loosely–based client–centered format, in which therapists tried to respond to clients primarily through empathy responses, therapists attempted to respond in ways that were either "experiential" or "nonexperiential." We defined experiential empathy responses as reponses that not only semantically fit with the client's communication, but also captured the "flavor" or felt or sensed nature of the experience that the client was expressing. In addition, the therapist's body language was also experiential—conveying empathy and understanding through body language.

In contrast, nonexperiential empathy responses were in a general sense semantically congruent with the client's response, but either were at a more abstract, conceptual level than the client's communication, or were at a sufficiently more concrete level so that the sensed or experienced meaning underlying the communication was lost. In addition the therapist tried to adopt a more "informational" nonverbal style. Examples of both experiential and nonexperiential responses are given in Table 4.

Table four:

Experiential and Nonexperiential Empathy Responses

EXAMPLE #1

Client: "My son and I took a long bike ride together. We hardly spoke two

words the whole time, but we didn't need to. It was OK just to be together."

Experiential Response:	*Non–Experiential Response:*
"You felt at peace with each other."	"So you liked being quiet"

EXAMPLE #2

Client: "I was already furious with my boyfriend, then at work, they dumped this Miller project on me!"

Experiential Response:	*Non–Experiential Response:*
"You have *had it* ! Too many	"Now there's this Miller
things ganging up on you at once!"	thing to do."

EXAMPLE #3

Client: "And then my professor told me that it was a 'stupid question'. I feel

　　so humiliated."

Experiential Response:	*Non–Experiential Response:*
"You were really mortified."	"It feels bad when that happens"

The study was a therapy analogue study. The subjects were 21 graduate students in counseling programs. The therapists were four graduate students who were trained to deliver the prescribed responses. Each subject talked about a mild personal problem. Therapists responded with "good" experiential empathy responses for 10 minutes. Then, in the experiential condition, they continued for another 6–8 responses with further experiential empathy responses. In the nonexperiential condition their next 6–8 responses were nonexperiential ones. Interviews were tape recorded. When the session was over an Interpersonal Process Recall (Elliott, 1986) was conducted. The subject listened response–by–response to the last two regular empathy responses given during the initial 10 minutes of the session, and then to the experimental 6–8 responses (either experiential or nonexperiential), and answered a series of questions with regard to each response.

We had two major hypotheses. First we hypothesized that experiential empathy responses, because they would be quickly perceived as "feeling right," would not require clients to "think about" whether they fit or not. Therefore clients would respond quickly and immediately to them. In other words, their latency of response would be very short. In contrast, nonexperiential empathy responses would cause the client to stop and think to see if it fit or not. Therefore the latency of response by the client would be longer. Second, during the Interpersonal Process Recall (IPR), clients would rate experiential responses as less disruptive and more helpful than nonexperiential responses.

RESULTS

The latency of the client's response to the last two "good" empathy responses before we started the experimental responses in each condition was compared to the latency to the subsequent 6–8 experimental responses. In table five it can be seen that in the experiential condition the means were virtually identical. In the nonexperiential condition the latency for the 6–8 "nonexperiential" responses was significantly longer than for the preceding two experiential empathy responses.

The latency of the 6–8 experimental responses in the experiential condition was compared to the latency in the nonexperiential condition. Once again it can be seen from table five that the latency for the nonexperiential condition was signficantly longer than for the experiential condition.

Table 5:

Results of Analogue Study

of Experiential and Non–Experiential Therapy

I.Response Latency (in seconds)

Experiential Condition.

Last Two Experiential	$X = 0.95$
Next 6–8 Experiential	$X = 0.84^a$

Nonexperiential Condition.

Last Two Experiential	$X = 0.68^b$
Next 6–8 Nonexperiential	$X = 5.04^{ab}$

a: $t = 2.86$, $p<.01$ b: $t = 3.79$, $p<.01$

II.Disruption Rated On IPR

Experiential Condition.

    Last Two Experiential   X = 0.43

    Next 6–8 Experiential $X = 0.86^a$

Nonexperiential Condition

    Last Two Experiential $X = 1.38^b$

    Next 6–8 Nonexperiential $X = 4.50^{ab}$

Note: The higher the rating the more the subject thought the therapist's responses were disruptive.

a: $t = 2.98$, $p < .02$; b: $t = 3.66$, $p < .01$

III.Ratings of Growth Experiences On IPR

Experiential Condition

    Last Two Experiential   X = 1.79

    Next 6–8 Experiential $X = 1.62^a$

Nonexperiential Condition

    Last Two Experiential $X = 1.63^b$

    Next 6–8 Nonexperiential $X = 0.98^{ab}$

Note: The higher the number the more the subject rated the response as contributing to one of several "growth experiences."

a: $t = 3.25$, $p < .01$; b: $t = 2.39$, $p < .05$.

From the IPR it was hypothesized that subjects would rate nonexperiential responses as more disruptive than experiential responses. Ratings of the disruptiveness of the last two experiential responses was about equal to the disruptiveness of the next 6–8 experiential empathy responses in the experiential condition. In the nonexperiential condition the 6–8 nonexperiential empathy responses were rated as more disruptive than the preceding two experiential empathy responses. Similarly, the 6–8 nonexperiential responses were rated as significantly more disruptive by subjects than the 6–8 experiential responses.

A composite index of the usefulness of a given therapist response in facilitating a variety of different experiences (gaining insight, getting in touch with a feeling, carrying forward experiencing) was constructed from clients' ratings of therapists' responses during the IPR. It can be seen in Table 5 that experiential empathy responses were rated as leading to more positive experiences than nonexperiential empathy responses.

In sum, experiential empathy responses were more immediately and directly perceived as relevant or fitting the client's experience, and thus responded to more quickly than nonexperiential empathy responses. In addition they were rated by subjects as less disruptive and as leading to more positive experiences.

210

While we have not devised a formal methodology for analyzing this, we were also intrigued by the fact that although on the average nonexperiential responses were not rated as as useful as experiential responses, there were a number of cases where subjects appeared to "work" to take a "bad" nonexperiential response

and turn it to productive use. This supports a new hypothesis of ours (derived from Rogers' views) that in therapy it is really the active client who is the therapist and that therapist responses do not "operate on" clients in any way shape or form to make things "happen." Rather, clients can take even bad therapist responses and use them productively to grow (Bohart & Tallman, 1994). In fact, there were several cases where subjects appeared to make significant progress during the nonexperiential segment of the interview, even though they subsequently rated the nonexperiential responses as unhelpful. This supports our "active client" hypothesis.

CONCLUSION

In sum, our research projects support the hypotheses that experiencing is at least in part a nonconceptual, perceptual, felt way of knowing; that it is creative and spontaneous; that all good therapists work to move clients to experiential, perceptual shifts; and that clients directly experience in a rapid perceptual nonconceptual way good experiential empathy responses as fitting, while nonexperiential responses cause them to "think." Further, experiential responses are experienced as less disruptive and more helpful.

REFERENCES

Bohart, A. (1993). *Experiencing: The basis of psychotherapy.* Journal of Psychotherapy Integration, 3, 51–67.

Bohart, A., & Rosenbaum, R. (1993, August). *Model of the human as aesthetic experiencer.* Paper presented at the American Psychological Association Convention, Toronto, Canada.

Bohart, A., & Tallman, K. (1994). *The active client as integrative therapist; Or, looking for expertise in all the wrong places.* Unpublished manuscript, California State University Dominguez Hills.

Bohart, A., & Wugalter, S. (1991). *Change in experiential knowing as a common dimension in psychotherapy.* Journal of Integrative and Eclectic Psychotherapy, 10, 14–37.

Browner, S., Muscatine, R., & Bohart, A. (1993, April). [Untitled presentation]. *Symposium on "How All Good Therapy is Experiential: Films, Research, and (Nonexperiential) Talk."* Society for the Exploration of Psychotherapy Integration Convention, New York.

Elliott, R. (1986). *Interpersonal process recall (IPR) as a psychotherapy process research method.* In L. S. Greenberg & W. M. Pinsof (Eds.), The psychotherapy process (pp. 503–528). New York: Guilford.

Garcia, M., Rosales, A., Hsu, S., Zirpolo, J., Hagan, K., Miller, L., Browner, S., Muscatine, R., & Bohart, A. (1993, April). [Untitled presentation]. *Symposium on "How All Good Therapy is Experiential: Films, Research, and (Nonexperiential) Talk."* Society for the Exploration of Psychotherapy Integration Convention, New York.

Gendlin, E. T. (1964). A theory of personality change. In P. Worchel & D. Byrne (Eds.), *Personality change.* New York: Wiley.

Gibson, J. J. (1979). *The ecological approach to visual perception.* Boston: Houghton-Mifflin.

Johnson, M. (1987). *The body in the mind.* Chicago: University of Chicago Press.

Lakoff, G. (1987). *Women, fire, and dangerous things.* Chicago: University of Chicago Press.

Loesch, M. E., Hamilton, H. L., Rush, S., Seferian, L., & Bohart, A. (1994, August). *Intellectual versus experiential knowledge: Creative artists and actors learning roles.* Paper presented at the American Psychological Association Convention, Los Angeles.

Tallman, K., Robinson, E., Kay, D., Harvey, S., & Bohart, A. (1994, August). *Experiential and non–experiential Rogerian therapy: An analogue study.* Paper presented at the American Psychological Association Convention, Los Angeles.

Long–Term Development of Borderline Personality Disorder

JOCHEN ECKERT U. MICHAEL WUCHNER

UNIVERSITÄT HAMBURG/GERMANY

ABSTRACT

This report has the purpose to give an empirical answer if borderline patients are destined to suffer for life under their problems.

Findings are presented on the long–term outcome (4 years) and the psychosocial development of 14 patients, which are clinically diagnosed as having borderline personality disorder compared to a group of 16 depressed and 13 schizophrenic patients. Different theoretical conceptualizations (psychoanalytic and client–centered) about the origin of borderline personality are discussed. The autors describe the psychotherapeutic approaches and the goals of client–centered psychotherapy (single and group) for inpatients and outpatients. The findings suggest the efficacy of client– centered group therapy as a treatment for borderline personality disorder.

We studied the question of whether or not patients with a severe personality disorder, particularly those with a borderline personality disorder, are destined to suffer for life under their problems. We examined this question in two ways: For several years, we followed the course and outcome of 14 patients, clinically diagnosed as having borderline personality disorder. At the same time, these patients received client–centered group psychotherapy. There were also two comparison groups of psychiatric in–patients and out–patients with the diagnosis neurotic depression and schizophrenia receiving the same treatment. We examined the question of whether or not client–centered psychotherapy is effective in treating these severe disturbed patients. In the first part we will introduce our findings on long–term development of borderline pathology, examining patients with borderline personality disorder when they were admitted to our research project and after a follow–up time. All patients were admitted to the psychiatric outpatient unit of the University Hospital in Hamburg, Germany, and the psychiatric department of the University Hospital in Luebeck, Germany. The patients were extensively examined and provided with inpatient treatment as well as outpatient psychotherapeutic treatment. In the second part we present the implications of our findings for psychotherapeutic management and client–centered psychotherapy. This part will focus on the modalities of client–centered group psychotherapy.

The first table shows the distribution of the patients and the time between the first clinical examination and the follow–up date.

Table 1:

Diagnostic characteristics and follow–up interval at study intake

	Borderline	Schizophrenia	Depression
Diagnosis	14	13	16
Follow–up (standard deviation)	3,6 years (1 year)	4 years (2,5 years)	4 years (2,3 years)

There were four years between both examinations. There were no significant statistical differences among the 3 groups, although the standard deviation of the schizophrenia and depression group is double that of the borderline group.

The characteristics of age and gender are displayed in the next table 2.

Table 2:

Age and gender characteristics at study intake

	Borderline N=14		Schizophrenia N=13		Depression N=16	
	mean	s	mean	s	mean	s
Age at sudy intake	27.6	6.2	28.5	8.0	30.5	10.1
Gender	male	female	male	female	male	female
N	4	10	6	7	6	10
in %	28.6	71.4	46.2	53.8	37.5	62.5

Patients with borderline personality disorder and schizophrenia were younger at study intake interviews, but this fact is typical for the first psychiatric hospitalization in these groups. Statistical testing yielded no significant differences. The distribution in gender, particularly in the borderline group, is similar to that which is reported in literature: about 70% female and 30% male borderline patients.

The different treatments in our follow–up study are displayed in the next table 3.

Table 3:

Treatment in follow–up interval

	Borderline N=14	Schizophrenia N=13	Depression N=16
Client–centered group psychotherapy	12	5	7
drop–out	2	1	3
no group psychotherapy	–	8	9
Additional treatment in follow– up interval:			
Additional outpatient psychotherapy	43 %	18 %	40 %
Inpatient treatment	29 %	62 %	38 %
Outpatient medical treatment	29 %	62 %	40 %
Psychopharmacotherapy	36 %	77 %	40 %

14 borderline patients were treated in the follow–up interval in an outpatient client–centered group psychotherapy. Two borderline patients dropped out by their own request. Five schizophrenic and seven depressive patients obtained client– centered group psychotherapy together with the borderline patients . Three depressive and one schizophrenic patient dropped out by own request. About 40% of the borderline and depressive patients obtained additional outpatient psychotherapy while only 18% of the schizophrenic patients did. One third of the borderline and the depressive patients were admitted one or several times in inpatient psychiatric treatment in the follow–up interval. Nearly two thirds of the schizophrenic patients were rehospitalized for one or several inpatient stays. About one third of the borderline patients and 40% of the depressive patients obtained outpatient psychiatric treatment, which usually included psychotropic medication. Over 60% of the schizophrenic patients received the same kind of treatment in the follow–up period.

We now want to report the changes in the outcome dimensions in borderline symptoms. The Diagnostic Interview for Borderline was administered to patients at study intake and at the time of the follow–up reinterview. The Diagnostic Interview for Borderlines (DIB) elicits the cardinal characteristics of borderline patients on the basis of a semistructered interview. The following five functional areas are evaluated: Social adaption, impulse/action patterns, affects, psychotic symptoms and interpersonal relations. The Diagnostic Interview for Borderlines and the Axis–II–criteria of the Diagnostic and Statistical Manual (version III) are the instruments, typically used for diagnosing borderline personality disorder. Each section of the Diagnostic Interview for Borderlines is composed of a number of statements to be scored by an interviewer. A patient may obtain a score between 0 and 2 in each section and each of the five sections will have equal weight in determining the overall diagnostic score, which has a range from 0 to 10. As suggested by GUNDERSON, cut–off scores of 7 or above are used to determine the borderline group, with scores under 7 indicating nonborderline status. All our findings were tested by statistical analyses using the two–factor analyses of variance for repeated measures.

Table 4 presents the statements of the impulse/action patterns section.

Table 4:

Impulse/action patterns

–   SELF–MUTILATION – The patient has slashed his/her wrist or otherwise mutilated   him/herself.

–   MANIPULATIVE SUICIDE – The patienthas made a manipulative suicide threat or effort: defined as any suicide attempt or gesture made in circumstances in which someone probably would response from someone. This can include wrist–slashing.

–   DRUG ABUSE – The patient has abused drugs.

–   SEXUAL DEVIANCE – The patient has a pattern of: promiscuity, homosexuality or repititive sexually deviant practices.

–   ANTISOCIAL – The patient has an impulsive pattern not included in statements above. (e.g. runaway, assaults, trouble with the law)

The findings are displayed in figure 1.

Figure 1:

CHANGE IN IMPULSE/ACTION PATTERNS

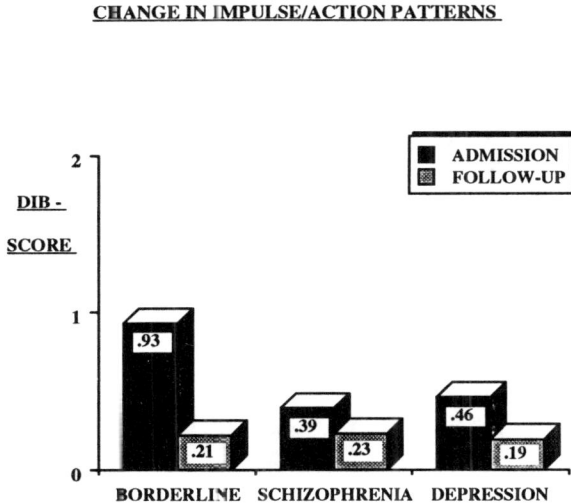

The symptoms of impulse/action patterns, particular those, which are linked with manipulative suicide and self–mutilation showed a drop in the borderline group, which is statistical significant. Depressive and schizophrenic patients showed little change over time. Both comparison group patients had less symptoms in this section at the admission, however, the difference was not statistically significant.

Table 5 presents the statements of the affect section.

Table 5:

Affects

– DEPRESSION – The patient appears depressed or reports recent or chronic symptoms of depression.

– HOSTILITY – The patient is angry, or hot tempered or sarcastic.

– DEMANDING/ENTITLED – The patient is demanding or entitled.

– DYSPHORIA/ANHEDONIA – The patient complains of chronic feelings of dysphoria or anhedonia or emptiness or loneliness.

– FLAT/ELATED * – The patient´s affect is noted to be flat or to be elated.

* This statement is given a negative weight if scored.

The findings are displayed in figure 2.

The affect component of the scale showed a fall from a mean nearly 1.9 to 1.36 in the border-line group. Borderline and depressive patients significantly changed in this component, whereas the schizophrenic patients didn't vary over time. All three diagnostic groups showed significant difference at the time of the initial interview.

Table 6 presents the statements of the psychosis section.

Table 6:

Psychosis

– DEREALIZATION – The patient experiences derealization.

– DEPERSONALIZATION – The patient experiences depersonalization.

– DEPRESSIVE – The patient has drug–free, brief psychotic depressed experiences.

– PARANOID – The patient has drug–free, brief paranoid experiences.

– DRUG–INDUCED – The patient has had psychotic experiences on marijuana or alcohol or persisting psychotic symptoms after psychomimetics (e.g. amphetamines, LSD).

– HALLUCINATIONS/BIZARRE, NIHILISITC, GRANDIOSE DELUSIONS * – The patient has drug–free hallucinations, *or* nihilistic delusions, *or*

grandiose delusions, *or* bizarre delusions.

– MANIA/WIDESPREAD DELUSIONS * – The patient has had manic episodes or pe riods of persistent widespread delusions or hallucinations.

– PAST THERAPY REGRESSIONS – The patient has had transient psychotic experiences which developed in psychotherapy *or* a clear behavioral regression after hospitalization.

* These statements is given a negative weight if scored

The findings are displayed in figure 3.

Figure 2:

CHANGE IN AFFECTS

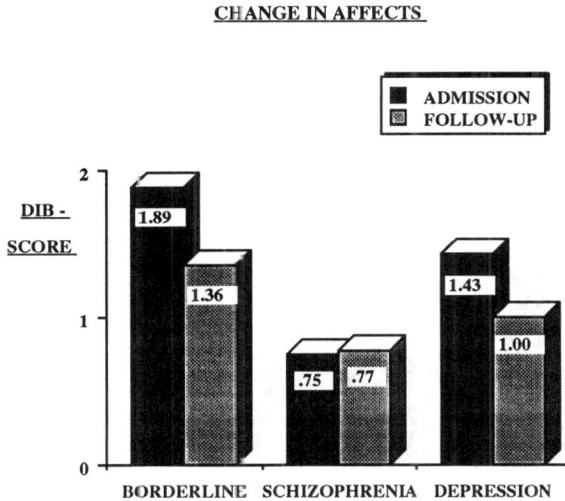

The symptoms of borderline psychosis, like depersonalization and derealization showed an enormous drop from 1.7 to .36 in borderline patients. The drop–off from .8 to .4 in the schizophrenia group is significant as well. The depressive patients show only few symptoms of borderline psychosis before the treatment. The biggest decline in psychotic symptoms was in borderline patients, as revealed by a statistical significant 2 – way interaction between the factors time and diagnostic group. At follow–up, all groups showed an equal amount of symptoms of borderline psychosis.

Table 7 presents the statements of the interpersonal relations section.

Figure 3:

CHANGE IN PSYCHOSIS

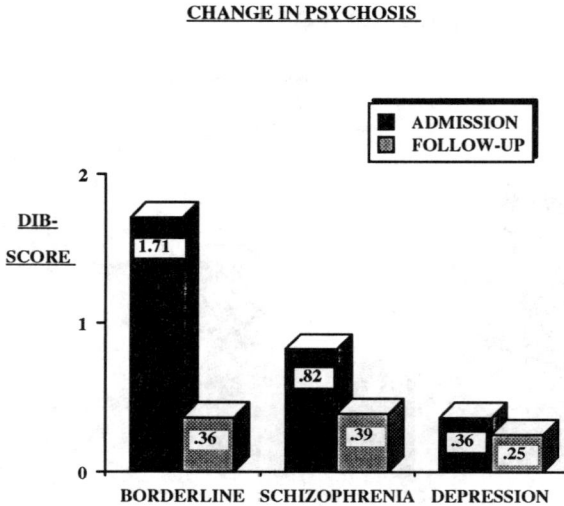

Table 7:

Interpersonal relations

- ALONENESS – Patient is almost always with people *or* patient actively tries to avoid being alone.
- ISOLATION * – Patient is socially isolated, a "loner".
- ANACLITIC – The patient actively seeks a relationship in which he/she takes car of others (e.g. nurse, veterinarian, housekeeper) *or* is in active conflict about giving and receiving care.
- INSTABILITY – The patient forms intense unstable one–to–one relationships.
- DEVALUATION/MANIPULATION – Problems with devaluation, manipulation and hostility recur in the patient's close relationships.

–   DEPENDENCY/MASOCHISM – Problems with dependency and masochism recur in the patient´s close relationships.

–   PAST THERAPY RELATIONS – The patient has involved staff splitting, or formed "special" relationships, or has evoked noteworthy counter–transference problems by a therapist.

* This statements is given a negative weight if scored.

The findings are displayed in figure 4.

There is a significant difference between the borderline patients and the two groups of the schizophrenic and depressive patients in the interpersonal relations section at time of the initial interview. Borderline patients report feel themselves much more disturbed. The symptoms in this section showed a decline in all groups at time of follow–up. The change of the borderline patients in the symptoms of interpersonal behavior is not as large as in the other sections, but it is statistical significant. This result also applies to the schizophrenic and depressive patients.

The last figure 5 displays the overall or global change in the symptoms of borderline personality disorder.

Borderline patients showed an enormous drop from 8.3 to 5.4 at time of follow–up compared to the date of our first examination. This result is statistical significant. The schizophrenic patients and the depressive patients showed less symptoms at admission. The degree of the symptoms in these two comparison groups is nearly equal. The symptoms in the schizophrenic and depressive group are only slightly less at time of follow–up. Although there is a total decline in borderline symptoms in the three groups, we found the drop off in the borderline group dramatic. There is a significant 2–way interaction between the factors time and diagnostic group, indicating a significant in the reduction of borderline symptoms in borderline patients. In conclusion, the following can be stated: Borderline symptoms appear to be influenced in a positive way by client–centered group psychotherapy. Can we say that our empirical results are comparable to other findings in long–term borderline development? A literature review revealed that all studies on course and outcome of borderline personality disorder differ in the length of the follow–up interval. There are four longitudinal studies (Plakun 1985, McGlashan 1986, Stone 1987, Paris 1987) with a follow–up interval of 14 –16 years. The main result is a remission from borderline symptoms, which is linked with a moderate improvement in psychosocial role functioning.

These investigations are lacking in two ways: The diagnosis of borderline personality disorder was assessed in retrospective chart reviews and the follow–up state was examined only by telephone interviews and mail questionaires. There are about 15 follow–up studies (Werble 1970, Gunderson 1975, Pope 1983, Skodol 1983, Barasch 1985, Akiskal 1985, Perry 1985, Tucker 1987, Nurnberg 1989, Modestin 1989, Silk 1990, Links 1990, Armelius 1990, Mehlum 1991, Hoke 1992) with follow–up intervals ranging from a half year to 7 years. Most studies, which can be considered as prospective studies have higher methodological standards. These studies used systematic interviewing procedures including both systematic clinical and structured interviews like the DSM–III or the Diagnostic Interview for Borderlines. The majority of these studies employed a design with at least one comparison group allowing a prospective cohort design.

Figure 4:

CHANGE IN INTERPERSONAL RELATIONS

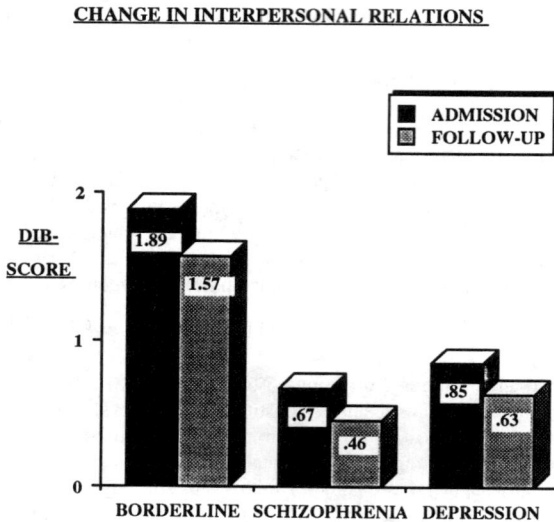

We want to emphasize the difficulties of direct comparisons in the above studies. The authors of the studies used several different measures of change and long-term outcome as well as several different patient treatments. It is important to say, that borderline patients are never without any treatment over years. The different treatments borderline patients receive are included in the following list: Long-term intensive psychoanalytic oriented psychotherapy, long-term supportive psychotherapy, short term hospitalization, residential treatment, psychopharm-cological intervention, crisis intervention and a new approach is cognitive behavioral therapy. How do these results compare to our findings? The outcome of the longitudinal studies can be summarized in the following conclusion: The borderline symptoms remitted at follow–up, but not to the degree that we found in our sample. The psychosocial role functioning of the bor-derline patients is improved, but not in the same way as in the 4 long–term outcome studies. Most of the retrospective studies examined in–patients, who could be considered more dis-turbed, and therefore have a more negative prognosis. These findings are supported by the fact that in retrospective and prospective studies suicide rates of 3–9% were found.

Figure 5:

GLOBAL CHANGE IN BORDERLINE SYMPTOMS

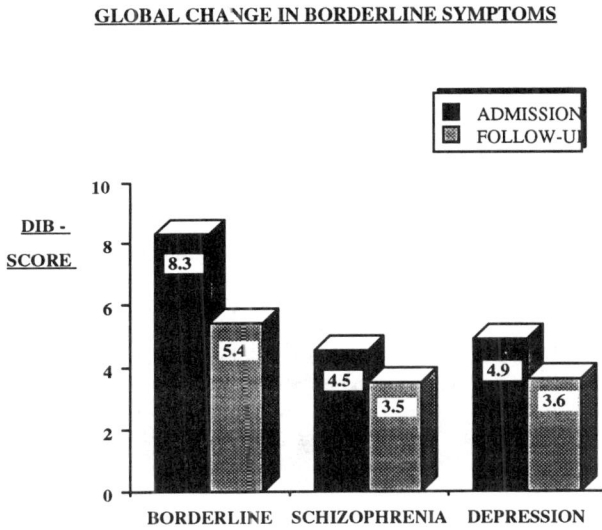

There is evidence indicating that the greatest risk for suicide occurs in the immediate 1 to 2 years after intake hospitalization (Perry 1993). All longitudinal studies on the course and outcome of borderline personality disorder, including our own research work, can be considered as naturalistic studies. No study met all requirements on an ideal methodological design, because of the severity of the disorder and the heterogenity of the individual treatments. To end, I want to ask the question again: Can we say that our empirical results are comparable to other findings in long–term borderline development? If you keep in mind the limited comparison of the different studies on long– term course and outcome of borderline personality disorder our findings, which we presented here, can be considered comparable to other studies. The findings suggest the efficacy of client– centered group therapy as a treatment for borderline personality disorder.

CLIENT–CENTRED PSYCHOTHERAPY WITH PATIENTS WITH A BORDERLINE PERSONALITY DISORDER

The empirical part has sketched the psychopathology of patients with a borderline personality disorder and has also traced how this psychopathology alters in the course of time. It is hard to say which changes are partly or directly due to psychotherapy since our efforts to find a control group with untreated borderline patients failed, and for a very good reason: there aren't any untreated borderline patients.

Before I trace the line of thinking behind our treatment of borderline patients I should like to stress that my ideas on the kind of psychotherapy they need are largely the outcome of how I assume this disorder comes about. As you presumably know, thanks to the American psychiatrist and psychoanalyst Otto F.Kernberg it is now easier for us not just to understand these patients and their disorders, which lie somewhere between neurosis, character defect and psychosis, but also how to treat them. Focussing on ego psychology and object relations from his psychoanalytic perspective, Kernberg has shown that the borderline disorder is a disturbance in ego–development. One of its central features is a characteristic weakness in the defence functions which forces the patient to fall back on primitive forms of defence, particularly splitting and denial. This is accompanied by an internalised pattern of object relations in which the self and the object are grasped exclusively in terms of either/or, black or white; they are either "absolutely good" or "absolutely bad", without any shades of grey between. As a result borderline patients oscillate in their personal relationships between idealising and denigrating themselves and others, and are victims to wild swings of mood. Above all they suffer from two feelings: rage and depression.

Kernberg dates the emergence of this ego disturbance in the second and third years of life, when an excessive and – as he postulates – often inborn high level of aggression hinder the introjects of self and object from losing their sharp division into good and bad and being integrated as a mixture of both. The strict division is maintained to avoid at all costs contaminating the good self and object with the bad self . Borderline patients find their own aggressive impulses so overwhelming and destructive that they assume they can only protect their good, life–saving objects by protecting them from this rage. So the themes of anger, experiencing anger and fending it off are the ones with which we are mostly confronted when treating borderline patients.

In the literature one finds two contrasting ways of explaining how this disorder comes about. The first position, I should like to call it the *drive hypothesis*, is as already hinted shared by Kernberg (1975, 1978). He sees the genetic roots of the borderline structure in an unusually high level of pregenital aggression which cannot be dealt with properly during the appropriate phase. Under its influence there is a "premature oedipus complex" (Kernberg 1975, 1978, p.66ff; Rohde–Dachser, 1989, p.34ff). According to this explanation the rage and the oedipal conflicts are fuelled by unintegrated pregenital aggressive impulses i.e. the borderline patient's rage and object relations are the result of a developmental deficiency.[1]

The other position, which I term the *self hypothesis*, has not been as widely discussed in the literature as the drive theory. It is however the explanation one arrives at if one examines how humans develop, and in particular how they gain a sense of being themselves (Rogers 1959). From this angle being exceedingly angry or highly aggressive is not a sign of certain drives but a natural expression of mental or emotional suffering (Biermann–Ratjen, 1989, 1990, 1993)

A borderline patient finds it impossible to reconcile his profound rage and aggressive feelings with his idea of himself, his self-concept; he cannot accept that these feelings belong to him and are part of his emotional experience. On the contrary the rage or hatred seem like an adversary who threatens his very existence. *Being very angry is for him the same as being wicked,* and this is wickedness understood in the true archaic sense: being wicked means in the patient's view that he has no right to exist, or, even more drastically, he is to be abandoned.

As far as the aggression and defence against it are concerned the two theories differ as follows: the drive hypothesis explains the defence against aggressiveness as the consequence of deep fear of destroying the other, and the self hypothesis explains it as an expression of the fear of being destroyed oneself.

These different positions naturally imply different therapeutic approaches for these patients, and as far as dealing with the aggressiveness is concerned the aims diverge: the drive hypothesis presumes it is helpful to reduce or channel the aggressive impulses which we all have but these patients have in excess so that the destructive feelings can be integrated into the patient's personality . The self hypothesis on the other hand presupposes other goals: first, that the patient gradually becomes aware of the existential fear expressed in the form of rage, and second, that the rage becomes intelligible and acceptable as a (natural) reaction to a existentially threatening (psychic) experience.

In my view one result of the drive hypothesis is that borderline patients have been offered an unnecessarily restricted type of therapy, which seems to be regaining favour (see Aronson 1989). What is usually recommended is supportive, short-term psychotherapy during which the patient should above all be prevented from regressing too far. Just what could happen if there were a transferential reaction in form of a strong regression does indeed sound alarming: we are warned to be beware of transference psychoses, micropsychotic episodes, suicide, murder, loss of employment and hospitalisation (Aronson op.cit.p. 514).

The different views of how borderline disorders come about do not however mean that there is controversy on what generally therapy aims at. So as client-centred psychotherapists we can follow Kernberg who describes the general aims as follows:

The therapy should increase the borderline patient's ability to experience himself and others as coherent, integrated and realistically perceived individuals. At the same time it should reduce the need to fall back on defence mechanisms which weaken the ego-structure by restricting the number of ways of reacting available. So one can expect that the patient develops an enhanced ability to keep his impulses under control, to tolerate anxiety, regulate his affects, sublimate his drives – and while at the same time developing stable and satisfying interpersonal relationships – experience intimacy and love (Kernberg 1989 / 1994).

The differences lie in the therapeutic routes which psychoanalysts and client-centred psychotherapists choose to reach these goals. In what follows I intend to describe the course we have taken. Our report is based on 9 group therapies and a series of individual therapies, most of which took place after group therapy. The group therapies were all time-limited: for inpatients they consisted of about 50 sessions within a three-month period, and for outpatients of about 100 group sessions within a year. The examples given here are therefore taken from both group and individual therapies.

We should like to look into the following points:

1. In what way does the borderline disorder unfold in contact with a psychotherapist?

2. What consequences does this have for the client–centred psychotherapist?

3. What do certain borderline symptoms and behaviours mean?

4. How and when should the therapist convey to the client that he has understood him?

5. Are there certain thematic foci which ought to be dealt with during therapy?

6. How should the therapist organise the therapeutic setting?

In what way does the borderline disorder unfold in contact with a psychotherapist?

1. the "typical" borderline patient:

• idealises and denigrates us

• he avoids real contact, apparently because he is frightened of getting close and of the feeling of helplessness this induces in him.

• he reacts to empathic verbalisations as if they were insinuations or statements about his character.

• he blocks us with his own inner emptiness and emotional void.

• he becomes psychotic

• or suicidal

• or he simply does not turn up for the sessions.

Here is an illustration from a group therapy, showing how the patient tends to idealise or run down those around him: Mr. A. gets the members of the group to focus exclusively on him and his current problem throughout the whole session. For the umpteenth time it seems likely he will lose his job which he got through the employment office; he has only been there a few weeks. He does not manage to get to work on time, and therefore simply stays away, persuading the doctor to give him sick–leave. The group is sympathetic, commiserating with him and trying to discover what stops him being punctual. Mr. A. obviously feels understood and calms down, so that by the end of the session his initial nervousness has vanished. In the next session Mr.A. starts off by scornfully running the whole group down: nothing happens here except a lot of empty chat, the therapist must be mad if he thinks that one cripple can help another. The group is just a bunch of mental wrecks. After the last session he felt terrible. His symptom, a physical sensation that he is shrinking, came back in severity. Again the session is given over to him, though this time it is full of mutual recriminations and insulting retreats. When discussing the session afterwards both therapists remarked on the barely disguised pleasure with which Mr.A presented his complaints and accusations. This course of events, with Mr.A. in one session quite evidently benefitting from the group and the next time pouring derision on its efforts, repeated itself several times.

What consequences does this have for the client–centred psychotherapist?

The client–centred offer of a relationship with the patient is characterised by empathy, congruence and unconditional positive regard. Our example from the group sessions has probably made it clear already: in treating borderline patients the therapist's unconditional positive regard is constantly in peril. So here is a rule to stick to: *as a client–centred psychotherapist treating a borderline patient hang on to your unconditional positive regard as tightly as you can!* It is not just endangered by the patients' direct attacks or idealisations but also because they often seem to ignore you especially in group therapies – or perceive you in a way which has nothing to do with your own personality. A "person–to–person" encounter is impossible: the patient sees in the therapist someone he brings with him. Here is an example of what I mean:

One of my woman patients, who had recently finished an inpatient psychotherapy, rang me and complained that her mother wanted her to work. She was quite desperate, since she could not possibly work. I gave the patient and her mother an appointment and started off by talking to the patient alone. She was very angry and upset, complaining bitterly about her mother and her lack of understanding for her illness. I fetched the mother in and wanted to start telling her that I thought her daughter needed more time before returning to work, but I could not even finish my first sentence before the patient suddenly began to shout at me. How dare I insult her mother like this? If I were a good therapist she would have been able to return to work long ago. Her mother was absolutely right. The patient worked herself in such a rage that she half demolished a chair in my room and sent all the plant pots on the windowsill crashing to the floor.

This example highlights another difference in treating borderline patients compared with neurotic ones. With borderline patients it is often impossible to use one's empathy to understand the patient and convey this to him in a form which he can grasp and make use of. Sometimes empathy can only be used to rescue the therapist's sense of respect and concern for the patient, his unconditional positive regard. In the example just given it is vital to realise the following: for inner reasons my patient found it quite impossible to realise how disappointed she was in her mother as long as she was in her presence. She projected this feeling into me and assumed that I wanted to blame her mother, ie do something wicked which would put her mother in a bad light.

Realising all this was essential before I could sense the specifically borderline anguish which made her behave so violently towards me. In the situation itself I could not have pointed out to the patient what was happening; in her perturbed and confused state she was probably quite incapable of taking in or understanding any such suggestion, or would have thought it was yet another proof of what a bad therapist I was, insinuating that she really was disappointed with her mother.

In our experience there are two stages in the course of therapy where we especially often have to apply the rule: whatever you do hang on to your unconditional positive regard. One is at the beginning of therapy, to get the patient involved and establish a viable relationship, and the other is at the end of treatment, with its partings and farewells. For borderline patients both these phases, allowing yourself to get involved in a close contact and being able to give it up again touch areas so fraught with distress and disappointment that they have to mobilise their defences in a way which is often very hard to bear.

There is one feature of client–centred psychotherapy which is very well attuned to the special problems borderline patients have and makes the contact between therapist and patient easier: its non–directiveness. As a result of what they have already been through these patients are profoundly frightened of being manipulated and misused. One form of misuse they are particularly wary about is that the therapist hopes their symptoms will vanish soon, confirming that he is a "good" therapist. So the client–centred therapist is well advised to aim genuinely at nothing other than really understanding his borderline client. Faced by this kind of fear once I remarked to the patient: "I am not interested in making you better but in helping you to understand yourself better", and the patient was quite obviously very relieved.

What do certain borderline symptoms and behaviours mean?

In contrast to most neurotic symptoms there are several borderline symptoms and ways of behaving which we cannot understand simply by referring back to our own experience. These include for instance symptoms associated with the defence mechanism known as splitting. As therapists we equally do not know about the fears which induce the patients to split, unless we ourselves have a personality structure bordering on the psychotic. This means that the therapist must know with which specific defences they keep off which feared experience.

If a patient recounts impressions, feelings, reactions or symptoms which the therapist cannot understand and leave him confused and uneasy, then as a rule he can conclude that the patient is feeling exactly the same. Even if the patient talks about his symptoms in a quite matter–of–fact tone, the therapist should ask him whether he really understands them.

The therapist should also take the unintelligible parts into account as possible signs of one of the "early" defence mechanisms. For instance if there is a sign of splitting, it is often enough to talk to the patient about it. One can for example point out that he has also other feelings for the person he is so bitterly and ruthlessly criticising, perhaps even gentle and affectionate feelings but he seems to have momentarily forgotten them, even though he talked about them a few hours ago.

In these therapies one often has to remember that the patient's specifically borderline symptoms are likely to become more severe or recur again when he is faced with a situation where others would react with anger or disappointment, or even more likely a mixture of both. Here is an example:

A woman patient who had been in group therapy was picked up by the police right at the end of the subway line and brought to hospital. She still knew her name but could not work out where she was or why. Her plan had been to visit her psychiatrist, but his practice lay in the opposite direction. While talking to her about her state and this episode it turned out that during her last visit to the psychiatrist she had asked him whether she could have an appointment with him once a week instead of only once a fortnight. He had however hardly paid any attention to this request and instead had handed her a list of self–help groups for mentally disturbed persons. When I enquired whether she had been disappointed she replied that she could not remember feeling anything like that. On the contrary, she had blamed herself for bothering her overworked psychiatrist with such a request.

When dealing with the feelings which borderline patients do not permit themselves to have, it is important to realise that the patients should not "learn" to have these feelings, nor should they be encouraged to express anything like them. The first and most important step towards integrating these feelings into the self–concept is that the therapist points out that for some reason otherwise appropriate feelings like disappointment and rage are currently not available to the patient, or presumably are so frightening that the patient feels highly alarmed. The attempt to understand what lies behind this fear is then a further step in the therapeutic process.

Some borderline syptoms are apparently linked to these's patients' fragile concept of self. In this respect they differ most clearly from patients with neurotic disorders. The symptom that borderline patients tend to avoid being alone is presumably one result of this: if they really are alone they are often overwhelmed by a deep sense of insecurity about who they are and whether what they feel really belongs to them. One woman patient reported that she could alleviate this feeling of being unreal by going to the mirror and looking at her own face. Other patients start to ring people up or – this is a more male variation – visit the pub.

Some borderline patients report that when they cannot feel themselves any longer or only have a dreadful sense of being utterly void they start to cut themselves, often with a razor blade, because the self–inflicted pain restores the feeling that they actually exist. (Rohde–Dachser). Hurting themselves, thinking about suicide or actually trying to kill themselves sometimes helps to suppress the unwanted feelings lurking behind the emptiness. A woman inpatient was able to stop hacking at herself with a razorblade when in the course of therapy she realised that she had fallen in love with the sister on the ward.

Generally speaking the following assumptions help one to understand borderline symptoms: most symptoms, but especially the way these patients organise their relationships, have two aims:

1. being able to experience themselves at all.

2. steering clear of any suspicion that they are bad.

How and when should the therapists convey to the client that he has understood him?

Here I should like to remind you of the main task a client–centred psychotherapist has in treating a borderline patient: before he intervenes in any way the therapist should ask himself whether he can do this with unconditional positive regard. If he is certain that he respects his client in this way it is secondary how he conveys to the patient what he has understood about his inner world. He may confront the patient or explain something or point out that the perception of the patient is mistaking something or give a verbalization to an expressed feeling or even interpret a genetic link between the present state of experience and earlier object relations of the patient, and so on.

One very helpful approach for borderline patients because it is often a great relief to them is explaining in a more or less informative manner that feeling disappointed, being very angry or aggressive are very natural reactions to suffering inflicted on them. Many borderline patients are convinced – like Kernberg – that their rage and aggressiveness are an inborn error, that their genes make them wicked people. More specifically I use sentences like these to explain and lighten their burden :" Rage is the oldest autonomic feeling we humans have to defend ourselves. It is a reaction to something bad happening to us, for instance being deprived, not being fed when we need it and so on" or "One painful experience which many children go through is that their parents don't understand them. Many parents – for whatever reason – fail to notice what their children are feeling, or imagine it is something else. But children cannot respond to being misunderstood or ignored by being angry, and so they do not feel hurt but wicked". Or "A little kid can't think: I've got parents who aren't really interested in me. It can only register the experience: "there's something wrong with me, otherwise my parents would love me more".

I cannot provide you with any rules for when to use which kind of intervention. In my experience if a good relationship has been established the patients themselves make sure that the topics which are relevant for them get discussed. This is often presented as a complaint or an accusation; one of my former patients who is also in psychiatric treatment for instance criticised me with the words: "You haven't even asked how many pills I've hoarded up again". The same patient opened the first session after a longish holiday by declaring as she was entering the room: "We're not going to do it like that again!"; the subject of the session was then her disappointment because I had deserted her.

Are there certain thematic foci which ought to be dealt with during therapy?

I have already mentioned the three most important areas to be looked into in an borderline therapy:

1. the special defensive behaviour, especially the patients' tendency to perceive their own and other people's behaviour exclusively as good or bad.

2. the fear of emotions, above all of feelings of disappointment, rage and aggressiveness

3. the psychotic experiences, above all those connected with an instable self-concept.

4. In addition I have found it necessary and in the long term helpful if the patients "learn" in the course of therapy to "look at" their parents i.e. to gain a realistic picture of their real parents.

It is rarely necessary for the therapist to deliberately tackle one of these themes. It is usually enough if he realises how important they are and is prepared to take them up with unconditional positive regard.

When talking about the parents the therapist must protect himself and the patient from giving them the blame for the patient's problems. Even if the parents were in a certain sense responsible, this is not a subject for the patient's therapy. The goal is rather that he gains an allround picture of them, including the sides which caused him suffering, a realistic and complete picture of them as possible.

How should the therapist organise the therapeutic setting?

In many respects I am far less strict about the therapeutic setting with borderline patients than I am with neurotics. Here are three examples:

1. I have nothing against the fact that the patients make use of other therapeutic offers while they are in therapy with me. By this I do not just mean psychiatric care, which is the rule because of the medication the patients require but equally other sorts of psychotherapeutic treatment. My reasons are as follows: the patients should have a chance to widen their range and undergo other experiences to compare with those with me, and possibly prefer them without me rejecting them. This attitude is based on Margaret Mahler's hypothesis, which I have found confirmed again and again, that the difficulties many borderline patients have originate in the individuation/separation phase (Mahler 1975).

2. For similar reasons I try to get in touch with a patient if he has twice missed a session without excusing himself.

3. I always tell neurotic patients in time when I am going on holiday. I tell borderline patients in addition exactly where I am going and what I plan to do there, i.e have a holiday or go to a conference. This is to prevent the patients feeling that I have deserted them and that they might be the reason, because they are so hard to cope with that I have to recover from them in a secret retreat. It also seems to calm borderline patients if they know exactly where their therapist is. Their concept of objects is as unstable as their self-concept. Nevertheless in the many years of working with them I have never been rung up by a patient while on holiday let alone visited by one.

Here finally are some remarks on the setting: Because of these patients' problems with ending therapy we have found it helpful to set firm time limits, especially for the groups. These are furthermore always always closed groups so that all the participants leave at the same time. As far as frequency goes one session per week is not enough; we have found that meeting twice weekly is a good workable arrangement for groups and individual therapies. Treatment is likely to last from between two and six years. This does not mean however that the patients need two sessions a week over the whole period; often after a year they can be seen once a week or even less often. We never exclude the possibility that a patient who has finished treatment, broken it off or gone to another therapist can return to us if he wants to.

CLOSING REMARKS

I should like to close by reminding you of the patient mentioned in the summary to this lecture who anxiously asked whether she was going to be a borderline patient for the rest of her life. Our results so far permit us to reply as follows: if a borderline patient can allow himself to get involved in psychotherapeutic treatment, he has a good chance of being diagnosed as a non–borderliner after three or four years. Whether or not he can then live the life he would like to lead we cannot predict. Our patient was aged twenty–seven when she asked this question; ten years later, at thirty–seven, during a conversation which was not a therapy session she remarked in a resigned tone: I'm afraid I'll be too old to have a child by the time I feel emotionally ready for it.

REFERENCES

Akiskal, H. S., Chen, S. E., Davis, G. C., Puzantian, V. R., Kashgarian, M., & Bolinger, J. M. (1986). *Borderline:An adjective in search of a noun.* Journal of Clinical Psychiatry, 46, 41–47.

Aronson, T. A. (1989). *A critical review of psychotherapeutic treatments of the borderline personality. Historical trends and future directions.* Journal of Nervous and Mental Disease, 177, 511–528.

Barasch, A., Frances, A., Hurt, S:, Clarkin, J., & Cohen, S. (1985). *Stability and distinctness of borderline personality disorder.* American Journal of Psychiatry, 142, 1484–1486.

Biermann–Ratjen, E. M. (1989). *Zur Notwendigkeit einer Entwicklungpsychologie für Gesprächspsychotherapeuten aus dem personenzentrierten Konzept für die Zukunft der klientenzentrierten Psychotherapie.* In Sachse, R. & Howe, J. (Eds.), Zur Zukunft der klientenzentrierten Psychotherapie (pp. 102–125). Heidelberg: Asanger.

Biermann–Ratjen, E. M. (1990).*Identifizierung – Ein Beitrag zu einem Modell der Entwicklung der gesunden und kranken Persönlichkeit.* GwG–Zeitschrift, 78, 31–35.

Biermann–Ratjen, E. M. (1993. *Abschließende Bemerkungen.* In Eckert, J., Höger, D., & Linster, H. (Eds.), Die Entwicklung der Person und ihre Störung (pp. 99–120). Köln: GwG–Verlag.

Gunderson, J. G., Carpenter, W. T., & Strauss, J. S. (1975). *Borderline and schizophrenic patients: A comparative study.* American Journal of Psychiatry, 132, 1257–1264.

Hoke, L. A., Lavori, P. W., & Perry, J. C. (1992). *Mood and global functioning in borderline personality disorder: Individual regression models for longitudinal measurements.* Journal of Psychatric Research, 26, 1–16.

Kernberg, O. F. (1975). *Borderline Conditions and Pathological Narcissism.* New York: Jason Aronson. Dtsch. Borderline–Störungen und pathologischer Narzißmus (1978). Frankfurt:Suhrkamp.

232

Kernberg, O. F., Selzer, M. A., Koenigsberg, H. W., Carr, A. C. & Appelbaum, A. H. (1989). *Psychodynamic psychotherapy of borderline patients.* New York: Basic Books. Dtsch: Psychodynamische Therapie bei Borderline–Patienten (1993). Bern: Huber.

Kullgren, G. & Armelius, B. A. (1990). *The concept of personality organization: A long–term comperative follow–up study with special reference to borderline personality organization.* Journal of Personality Disorders, 1990, 4, 203–212.

Links, P. S., Mitton, J. E., & Steiner, M. (1990). *Predicting outcome for borderline personality disorder.* Comprehensive Psychiatry, 31, 490–498.

McGlashan, T. H. (1986). *The Chestnut Lodge follow–up study III: Long–term outcome of borderline personalities.* Archives of General Psychiatry, 43, 20–30.

Mehlum, L., Friis, S., Iron, S., Johns, S., Karterud, S., Vaglum, P., & Vaglum, S. (1991). *Personality disorders 2 – 5 years after treatment: A prospective follow–up study.* Acta Psychiatrica Scandinavia, 1991, 84, 72–77.

Modestin, J., & Villiger, C. (1989). *Follow–up study on borderline versus nonborderline personality disorders.* Journal of Personality Disorders, 3, 236–244.

Nurnberg, H. G., Raskin, M., Levine, P. E., Pollack, S., Prince, R., & Siegel, O. (1989). *Borderline personality disorder as a negative prognostic factor in anxiety disorders.* Journal of Personality Disorders, 3, 205–216.

Paris, J., Brown, R., & Nowlis, D. (1987). *Long–term follow–up of borderline patients in a general hospital.* Comprehensive Psychiatry, 28, 530–535.

Perry, J. C. (1985). *Depression in borderline personality disorder: Lifetime prevalence at interviews and longitudinal course of symptoms.* American Journal of Psychiatry, 142, 15–21.

Perry, J. C. (1993). *Longitudinal studies of personality disorders.* Journal of Personality Disorders, 1990, 7 (suppl.), 63–85.

Plakun, E. M., Burkhardt, P. E., & Muller, J. P. (1985). *14–year follow–up of borderline and schizotypal personality disorders.* Comprehensive Psychiatry, 26, 448–455.

Pope, H. G., Jonas, J. M., Hudson, J. I., Cohen, B. M., & Gunderson, J. G. (1983). *The validity of DSM–III borderline personality disorder.* Archives of General Psychiatry, 40, 23–30.

Rogers, C. R. (1959). *A theory of therapy, personality and interpersonal relationships as developed in client–centered framework.* In Koch, S. (Ed.), Psychology: A study of science. Vol. III. Formulations of the person and the social context (pp.184–256). New York: McGraw–Hill.

Rohde–Dachser, C. (1989). *Das Borderline–Syndrom.* Bern:Huber.

Rohde–Dachser, C. (1994). *Warum sind Borderline–Patienten meistens weiblich? – Über die Rolle des Traumas in der Borderline–Entwicklung.* Hannover: Unpublished article.

Silk, K. R., Lohr, N. E., Orata, S. N., & Westen, D. (1990). *Borderline inpatients with affective disorder: preliminary follow–up data.* Journal of Personality Disorders, 1990, 4, 213–224.

Skodol, A. E., Buckley, P., & Charles, E. (1983). *Is there a characteristic pattern to the treatment history of clinic outpatients with borderline personality?* Journal of Nervous and Mental Disease, 171, 405–410.

Stone, M. H., Hurt, S. W., & Stone, D. K. (1987). *The PI 500: Long–term follow–up of borderline inpatients meeting DSM–III criteria: I.Global outcome.* Journal of Personality Disorders, 1, 291–298.

235

Tucker, L., Bauer, S. F., Wagner, S., Harlam, D., & Sher, I. (1987*). Long–term hospital treatment of borderline patients: A descriptive outcome study.* American Journal of Psychiatry, 144, 1443–1448.

Werble, B. (1970). *Second Follow–up Study of Borderline Patients.* Archives of General Psychiatry, 23, 3–7.

---

[1] The German psychoanalyst and borderline specialist Christa Rohde–Dachser has recently presented work (Rohde–Dachser, 1994) in which she convincingly argues and shows that the trauma which above all borderline patients had to undergo and to which they could not adequately respond was sexual abuse. Frau Biermann–Ratjen has gone into Mrs. Rohde–Dachser's trauma theory in connection with the genesis of borderline disorders in her paper (Biermann–Ratjen, this volume).

A Process–Experiential Approach to Post–Traumatic Stress Disorder

ROBERT ELLIOTT, PATSY SUTER, JANIE MANFORD, LAILI RADPOUR–MARKERT,
ROBIN SIEGEL–HINSON, CAROL LAYMAN & KEN DAVIS

UNIVERSITY OF TOLEDO

ABSTRACT

In this paper, we describe a process–experiential theory of posttraumatic stress difficulties, emphasizing the role of blocked emotional processing and trauma–related emotion schemes. We then outline the treatment principles, response modes and tasks used in a process–experiential treatment (Greenberg et al., 1993) appropriate for work with victimized clients. Next, we present initial data from a pilot treatment study, summarizing therapist postsession treatment adherence self–ratings. Finally, we offer two illustrative case studies and relate adherence self–ratings and case study data to the treatment model.

From the point of view of Process–Experiential Therapy (Greenberg, Rice & Elliott, 1993), the symptoms of Post–Traumatic Stress Disorder (PTSD) stem primarily from interrupted emotional processing of painful events. As a result, the person experiences a continuing state of internal conflict between aspects of the self which seek to re–experience/resolve the trauma and other aspects of the self which seek to reduce psychological pain by avoiding awareness of the trauma. In addition, the trauma plunges the person into an existential crisis of meaninglessness and personal vulnerability, as cherished beliefs about self, others and the world are threatened and the person finds him– or herself living in a world which is dangerous, others who are malevolent or uncaring, and a self which is powerless, unworthy, and at risk (Janoff–Bulman, 1992).

In this paper, we outline an experiential theory of posttraumatic stress difficulties and a version of process–experiential therapy (Greenberg et al., 1993) which addresses those difficulties. We then illustrate this approach with data from a pilot treatment study, in process.

AN EXPERIENTIAL PERSPECTIVE ON PTSD

A key assumption of humanistic–experiential therapies is that there is a basic human need for growth and mastery. One facet of this growth tendency is the specific need to resolve and master important painful and/or interrupted emotional experiences. More specifically, the process–experiential approach (Greenberg et al., 1993) assumes that emotions are biologically adaptive processes ("deep scripts") which integrate rapid, automatic processing of environmental information with appropriate action tendencies, in the form of action or expression or both. When these emotional processes are interrupted by the either external or internal factors, the person remains in a state of incompletion (referred to by Gestalt therapists as "unfinished emotional business").

In this state, the person continues to experience a conflict between a part of the self which still strives for completion of the emotional expression or mastery of the situation, on the one hand, and another part of the self which, for a variety of reasons, seeks to maintain the interruption. In its simplest form, this conflict is between the need to avoid pain and the need to resolve the painful experience by completing the interrupted action or expression. This conflict generates the characteristic alternation in PTSD between emotional numbing and reexperiencing. The emotional numbing or distancing symptoms represent the continuing self–protective interruption of the painful experience, while the re–experiencing symptoms represent the person's deliberate or automatic efforts to process the experience so that it can be completed.

Re–experiencing the trauma. Thus, from a Process–Experiential point of view, the three main sets of symptoms of PTSD (cf. American Psychiatric Association, 1987), can be explained as follows: First the reexperiencing symptoms, such as intrusive thoughts and images, flashbacks, and nightmares, are not seen as caused by a passive "over–generalization" as a result of traumatic conditioning. Instead, these symptoms are viewed as expressions of an underlying organismic need to finish the unfinished situation. Often, the person is at least partially aware of his or her desire to resolve the painful experiences by re–experiencing them, and attempts at times to deal with them deliberately by reflecting or ruminating on aspects of the trauma. In many instances, however, the need for completion is disowned by the person. When disowned, the need for completion is more likely to express itself in sudden, impulsive or ego–alien forms, such as flashbacks, unwanted images, and recurrent nightmares related to the trauma.

Avoiding pain. At the same time, persons suffering from posttraumatic stress difficulties typically attempt to avoid feelings, ideas, and activities related to the trauma. Often, these attempts are deliberate, as when the person tries to distract him– or herself. However, avoiding painful experiences is a deeply ingrained, frequently–automatic action tendency; automatic avoiding often takes the form of emotional numbing and interpersonal detachment. From a process–experiential perspective, this tendency is seen as a function of the person's biological need to protect the self from pain and to conserve resources.

Hypersensitivity: Experiencing the self as vulnerable. The third set of posttraumatic symptoms involves signs of heightened arousal, including insomnia, irritability, concentration problems, hypervigilance, startle response, physical reactivity, and a sense of foreshortened future. Most centrally, these symptoms suggest a continuing sense of self as vulnerable to further harm from a dangerous world. In schematic terms, the person's "vulnerable self" and "dangerous world" emotion schemes have been strongly activated and the person's experience has come to be dominated by these emotion schemes. These emotion schemes contain the emotion of fear and the action tendencies typically associated with fear, that is, flight (avoiding situations perceived as particularly dangerous), fight (facing the perceived danger with anger or aggression), or hiding or freezing (withdrawing, being "paralyzed," "playing dead").

In addition, these "hyperarousal" symptoms often indicate a continuing state of conflict between the competing needs for re–experiencing/completion and avoidance of pain.

Specific Posttraumatic Emotion schemes. The emotion schemes of vulnerability and danger are so powerful that the person continues to act in these ways even when this danger is not apparent to others, even when the person's actions cause them and others difficulty. However, the person's continuing fear may not be recognized as valid by others, because it is of a pervasive or existential nature. The victimization trauma has shattered a set of cherished beliefs or emotion schemes about the world, others, and self, as described vividly in Wertz (1985) and Fischer and Wertz's (1979) work on criminal victimization and by Janoff–Bulman (1992).

(a) The Dangerous World. First, the person's baseline "safe world" scheme of their physical and social environment as fundamentally benevolent has been replaced with a highly generalized sense of the world as fundamentally unsafe, both dangerous and unpredictable. In such a world, everything is a potential danger and therefore everything is to be feared. However, the biologically adaptive actions associated with fear – freezing, hiding, or fleeing – are no longer effective if the danger is all–pervasive, and so the person is left with emotional avoidance as an alternative strategy, even though this is usually only partially effective.

(b) The Malevolent Other. Second, traumas involving criminal victimization or sexual abuse are fundamentally interpersonal (vs. natural or technological disasters or accidents). Interpersonal violence or violation activates an emotion scheme of a malevolent, detrimental, or predatory other or perpetrator, one who heedlessly and deliberately makes the person their prey. After victimization, this Malevolent Other is seen as potentially present in a wide variety of Others who would formerly have been viewed as innocuous or even helpful.

(c) Unhelpful Others. Third, the person's belief that others can be depended upon to act toward the self in a helpful, concerned or protective way is also shattered. Supposedly helpful others (friends, family, legal authorities) are perceived as unhelpful in multiple ways: To start with, they were unable to prevent the victimization in the first place; then, they were absent or unavailable during the victimization itself; and finally they continue to be seen as ineffectual or uncaring after the victimization. Thus, the victim often experiences others as turning away or abandoning them in their time of greatest need, both during and in the aftermath of the victimization experience.

(d) Vulnerable Self. Fourth, implicit assumptions or emotion schemes of personal power, self–efficacy, invulnerability, or "specialness" ("that will never happen to me") have been shattered by the trauma (cf. Yalom, 1980) Instead, the self comes to be experienced as weak, helpless, vulnerable, and sometimes even deserving of further, future victimizations, perhaps of an escalating nature. The trauma re–activates pre–existing vulnerability schemes left from previous victimizations or traumas, creating a cumulative effect.

The exact nature and combination of the shattered assumptions or cherished beliefs and their replacement by trauma schemes varies with each person and with the precise nature of the victimization experience. Thus, the therapist assumes that the constellation of trauma schemes takes a unique form with each client, and that it is essential for the therapist to understand the client's unique set of experiences and the associated meanings these experiences have for the client. Moreover, recent traumas interact in idiosyncratic ways with traumas from earlier in the person's life.

Comparison to other theories of PTSD. Although the predominant conditioning model of PTSD does a decent job at explaining the avoidance symptoms, the account of reexperiencing symptoms as instances of passive stimulus–generalization appears to be inadequate or at least incomplete. It seems useful to assume instead an active tendency toward completion. Similarly, the behavioral model appears to ignore the existential and phenomenological aspects of PTSD and the way in which the person's whole self and world are altered by their victimization.

OVERCOMING VICTIMIZATION: A GENERAL VIEW OF THE CHANGE PROCESS

According to Fischer and Wertz (1979), three types of change must occur in order for an interpersonal victimization experience to be successfully resolved. These changes thus provide key processes through which the therapist tries to help the client move.

1. Re–empowering the self. The person must actively work to overcome his or her victimization. As part of this process, the self must become re–empowered, so that the person recovers his or her former sense of independence, safety, trust, order, and meaning. This is typically accomplished by the person's efforts to make sense of their experience and to prevent future victimization. In the process–experiential approach, the therapist generally facilitates this by helping the client to explore and express emotions and their associated action tendencies. In terms of empowerment, helping the client to work with his or her anger is especially important, because the adaptive action tendency which accompanies anger is the assertion of one's rights.

2. Offering the presence of a caring other. "Other persons must respond with concern and respect for the victim's full plight, including his or her efforts toward sensemaking" (Fischer & Wertz, 1979, p. 149). Helpful, caring, empathic others provide an alternative, corrective emotional experience to negative images of others as unhelpful or malevolent. This is usually the first task of therapy, and it often takes a number of sessions for a traumatized client to come to believe that the therapist genuinely understands and cares. Indeed, helping the client feel safe enough to reveal their deep sense of vulnerability may be the key change process in an experiential treatment of posttraumatic difficulties.

3. Re–establishing world as partially trustworthy. Finally, the environment must over a period of time show that it is at least partially trustworthy (and therefore that extreme vigilance is no longer needed). As Wertz (1985) points out, the post–victimization world can never be as safe as the pre–victimization world, but some aspects of safety must be reestablished in order for the person to return to a tolerable life. In an experiential therapy, safety or trustworthiness is first established in the therapeutic relationship. However, it is essential for the client to be able to face their environment and to discover that their vigilance can be relaxed, at least under the appropriate circumstances. At the same time, in the process–experiential approach, it is vital the client decide when and where to begin to trust aspects of their world.

According to Fischer and Wertz (1979), all of these changes are essential for recovery from victimization; without all of them, the person is likely to move into a deeper sense of victimization, consisting of "isolation, despair, bitterness, and resignation." In fact, this claim is consistent with the clinical observation that posttraumatic stress symptoms often last for years and do not "spontaneously remit."

AN OVERVIEW OF THE PROCESS–EXPERIENTIAL APPROACH AND ITS APPLICATION TO PTSD

How then do the process–experiential therapists intervene to help clients accomplish these changes? How do therapists help them resolve traumatic victimization experiences and the associated emotion schemes? The general approach of process–experiential therapy has been described in detail elsewhere (Elliott & Greenberg, in press; Greenberg et al., 1993). Briefly, process–experiential therapy is guided by six treatment principles. These treatment principles are implemented at two levels of therapeutic process: the therapist speaking turn and the within–session event or episode. At the speaking turn level, the principles are realized via a set of therapist speech acts or response modes, while at the episode level they are put into practice through a variety of therapeutic tasks (Greenberg et al., 1993).

Treatment principles. Six treatment principles provide the overall guidelines for the treatment. The first three principles involve facilitating a therapeutic relationship, and the last three involve helping the client to engage in work on specific therapeutic tasks (Greenberg et al., 1993):

1.The therapist begins by trying to enter the client's immediate, inner experience, as it emerges and evolves within the session (Empathic Attunement).

2.The therapist then tries to forge a relationship with the client which is characterized by genuine empathy and prizing or caring for the client (Therapeutic Bond).

3.Next, the therapist attempts to facilitate a shared, mutual involvement in the therapy, including the overall goals, immediate tasks and therapeutic activities used to accomplish those goals and tasks (Task Collaboration).

4.Within the context of the therapeutic relationship which has been established, the therapist then gently and noncoercively helps the client to work in the way most likely to help them progress toward resolving their current therapeutic task. This differential task facilitation is guided by a set of explicit stage models of typical task resolution (Experiential Processing).

5.At the same time, wherever appropriate the therapist attempts to foster client growth and self–determination, empathically selecting emergent, self–assertive experience and offering the client choices about the therapeutic process (Growth/Choice).

6.Finally, the therapist tries to help the client to resolve their most important therapeutic tasks, which involves helping the client to persist in difficult tasks or to switch to a more vital task if one emerges (Task Completion/Focus).

Experiential Response Modes. These six treatment principles are realized in two ways: First, at the level of the individual therapist speaking turn, the treatment principles are carried by a set of speech acts, each defined by a characteristic intention. Four of these are essential elements of the process–experiential approach: (a) *Empathic Understanding* responses seek simply to communicate understanding of the client's message, usually in the form of the simple reflections. (b) *Empathic Exploration* responses are most characteristic of process–experiential therapy and the most common experiential response mode (Davis, 1994), including evocative reflections, exploratory questions, and empathic conjectures. These responses simultaneously communicate understanding and help clients move toward the unclear or emerging edges of their experience. (c) *Process Directives* suggest things for the client to try in the session and include suggesting in a nonimposing way that the client try engaging in particular in–session exercises (e.g. two–chair dialogue), attend to a particular immediate experience or carry out a particular in–session action. (d) *Experiential Presence* refers to the therapist's "presence" or manner of being with the client, avoiding interruption and genuinely empathic or prizing vocal quality and nonverbal manner.

A number of other experiential response modes are also used in the process–experiential approach, including experiential teaching, including orienting information (about treatment), process observations, and self–disclosure. In contrast, giving news (interpretation), offering solutions (extra–therapy advisement), providing reassurance from an expert perspective, and disagreeing with the client are all to be avoided, because they violate the treatment principles described above, especially Growth/Self–Determination.

Process–Experiential Tasks. In addition to the experiential response modes, the treatment principles are realized at the level of larger within–session events or episodes, referred to therapeutic tasks. A key aspect of the process–experiential approach is its focus on a discrete set of therapeutic tasks, signalled by client "markers" (signs that the client is ready to work on a particular difficult experience). For each client marker there is a series of steps through which clients typically pass in completing or resolving the task, together with a recommended therapist intervention strategy for facilitating clients' movement through the steps (Greenberg et al., 1993; Rice & Greenberg, 1984).

A total of nine therapeutic tasks have now been at least partially described; as Table 1 indicates, all are relevant in some way to post–traumatic difficulties. However, in working with clients who have been victimized, some of the major therapeutic tasks appear to be (a) *Empathic Exploration* of the victimization (helping the client to narrate or re–experience the traumatic event or trauma–related dreams); (b) *Creation of Meaning* (helping the client to symbolize the cherished belief which was shattered by the victimization experience; Clarke, 1993); (c) *Empathic Prizing* (providing the client with the experience that the therapist cares and accepts them in their most vulnerable moments); (d) *Two Chair Dialogue* (in which the client enacts the internal conflict between the aspects of self which want to either re–experience or avoid the trauma); and (e) *Finishing Unfinished Business* (in which the client imagines a perpetrator or unhelpful other in an empty chair and speaks to him or her in order to complete blocked emotional experience).

Table 1:

Process–Experiential Tasks and Corresponding Post–Traumatic Experience

Intervention/Marker	Relevant Post–Traumatic Experience
Empathic exploration for problem–relevant experiences	Client's need to review or relive the "trauma story" or nightmares
Empathic affirmation for vulnerability (painful self–related experience)	Sense of personal fragility, foreshortened future
Experiential focusing for absent or unclear felt sense	Clearing an internal "safe space", dealing with emotional numbing
Systematic evocative unfolding for self–understanding problems	Puzzling "flashbacks" of trauma
Two–chair dialogue for self–evaluative splits experiences	Self–criticism for victimization; internal conflict: approach v. avoid trauma–related
Two–chair enactments for self–interruption splits	Blocked trauma–related fear, anger
Empty chair work for unfinished emotional business	Lingering bad feelings toward perpetrators or unhelpful others

Meaning creation work for	Cherished beliefs about self,
meaning crises	others or world are shattered by
	trauma
Relationship dialogue for	Distrust, anger at therapist as
alliance difficulties	real or potential unhelpful
	other

Note. Based in part on material from Elliott & Greenberg, in press, and Greenberg et al., 1993.

PILOT STUDY DATA ON PROCESS–EXPERIENTIAL PRINCIPLES AND TASKS

In the rest of this paper, we illustrate the application of the process–experiential therapy to the treatment of post–traumatic stress difficulties, using early data from our current pilot study comparing process–experiential to cognitive–behavioral treatments. We will first report quantitative data on therapists' postsession ratings of the presence of process–experiential treatment principles and therapeutic task elements (interventions and resolution steps). After this, we will describe two clients treated in the study, using a combination of qualitative and quantitative data.

Treatment Principles: Process–Experiential vs. Cognitive–Behavior Therapists. In our pilot study we are comparing the process and outcome of process–experiential (PE) and cognitive–behavior (CB) therapy in short–term (16–session) treatment of post–traumatic stress difficulties. One aspect of this study is the use of therapist self–report as an efficient measure of treatment adherence. After each session, therapists in each treatment condition complete a form which asks, among other things, for ratings of the extent to which they acted on the basis of thirteen treatment principles. Six items correspond to the six treatment process–experiential (PE) treatment principles presented earlier, while seven items represent essential guidelines for the cognitive–behavioral treatment (e.g., "Change dysfunctional belief system through challenging of assumptions and exploring alternative hypotheses"). Table 2 presents very early data from a small sample of sessions (10 cognitive–behavioral, 30 process–experiential).

Table 2:

Comparison of Process–Experiential with Cognitive–Behavioral Treatments for PTSD: Treatment Principles

	Cognitive		Experiential		
	M	SD	M	SD	t
Empathic Affirmation	3.8	.6	4.8	.5	5.6**
Therapeutic Bond	3.5	.7	4.9	.3	6.1**
Task Collaboration	3.6	.5	4.6	.7	4.0**
Experiential Processing	2.6	1.0	4.7	.6	6.4**
Foster Growth/Choice	3.0	.7	2.9	1.3	.2(ns)
Complete Tasks	3.1	.9	4.5	.7	5.4**
Mean PE Principles[a]	3.3	.4	4.7	.4	8.7**
Mean CB Principles	3.2	.5	1.3	.3	11.0**
n sessions	10		30		

ns: not significant; ** $p < .01$

Note. Treatment principles rated by therapists on 5–point presence scales (1 = Clearly absent;

3 = Present but brief; 5 = Present, extended in length).
[a]Minus Foster Growth/Choice.

The data indicate that the process–experiential therapists are giving themselves very high ratings for five of the six treatment principles; Foster Growth/Choice was rated considerably lower, and was the only PE principle not rated higher by PE therapists that by CB therapists. Indeed, the PE therapists rated the five PE principles items very near to the top of the five–point rating scale. In contrast, PE therapists rated the seven CB principles near the bottom of the scale (mean: 1.3). This pattern of responding suggests is open to at least two contrasting interpretations: (a) it may indicate scale problems such an extreme responding set or insensitivity at the top and bottom and of the scale (ceiling and basement effects); or (b) it may suggest that the PE therapists had a very high degree of treatment adherence.

On the other hand, the CB therapists gave mean ratings for most items near the middle of the scale, regardless of whether they were supposed to reflect PE or CB content. The CB therapists thus either did not see themselves as following the CB principles as closely, or they saw the PE principles as encompassed by their approach.

Task Resolution Ratings. In addition to rating treatment principles, each group of therapists completed ratings of tasks specific to their treatment approach. Thus, the PE therapists rated each of the nine treatment tasks in Table 1 on a seven point task resolution scale, an example of which is given in Table 3 (six of these scales were adapted from Greenberg et al., 1993). On these scales, "0" means "no marker"; "1" is given when only the task marker is present; "2" and "3" refer to some degree of client engagement in the task, but without resolution; and "4" through "6" refer to varying degrees of resolution or change on the part of the client. Table 4 gives results for an initial data set of 37 sessions. Task resolution scales are cumulative from scale point 1 up, meaning that each successive scale point implies the previous ones, allowing them to be summarized cumulatively as in Table 4. (That is, ratings 1 through 6 all imply the presence of a marker, as indicated in the first column of data in Table 4, while 2–6 ratings indicate client task engagement and 4–6 ratings refer to varyng degrees of client task resolution or change).

Table 3:

**Example of Task Resolution and Task Intervention Presence Scales:
Empathic Affirmation of Vulnerability**

Task Resolution Scale:

0.   Marker absent.

1.   Mentions strong negative self–related feeling and expresses distress about it.

2.   Describes deeper feelings in response to therapist's empathic affirmation.

3.   Expresses more intense vulnerability.

4.   Seems to touch bottom, expresses dreaded emotion or painful aspect of self in full intensity.

5.   Describes or expresses reduced distress, greater calmness.

6.   Expresses sense of self as whole, acceptable or capable.

Task Intervention: Empathic Affirmation at Vulnerability

Presence Rating Scale:

1.   Clearly absent

2.   Possible present

3.   Present but brief

4.   Present, moderate length

5.   Present, extended in length

Note. Task resolution scale adapted from Greenberg et al., 1993.

Table 4

**Therapist Ratings of Presence of Task Elements
in Process–Experiential Therapy for PTSD**

	Task Resolution Stage			*Therapist Operation*	
	Marker	Engagement	Resolution	Total	Substantial
Intervention	(1–6	(2–6	(4–6)	(3–5)	(4–5)
Exploration/ Experience	.68	.51	.19	.54	.35
Unfolding/ Problematic	.32	.19	.00	.24	.08
Focusing/ Unclear	.46	.32	.16	.38	.27
Affirmation/ Vulnerable	.89	.69	.36	.75	.50
Meaning/ Crisis	.56	.42	.14	.42	.42
Two Chair/ Conflict	.46	.27	.03	.35	.11
Two Chair/ Interruption	.16	.05	.03	.08	.05
Empty Chair/ Unfinished	.49	.19	.05	.27	.16
Relationship/ Difficulty	.14	.03	.03	.14	.05
Out of Mode:					
Give News/ Offer				.18	.00
Solutions/Expert				.08	.00

Reassurance	.27	.05
Disagree/Confront	.03	.00

Note. Proportions of sessions with therapist endorsement of indicated scale points on the Task Resolution and Task Operation Presence scales. n = 36–37 sessions.

Interestingly, the Vulnerability marker was rated as present in almost 90% of sessions, making it by far the most common; it was followed by the Problem–relevant experience (68%) and Meaning crisis markers (56%). Therapists also found that clients were more often able to engage in therapeutic work appropriate to the relevant task for these three tasks ("engagement" column in Table 4, which cumulates both early engagement and later resolution steps). Finally, therapists saw clients as actually resolving the vulnerability task in more than a third of all sessions.

The PE Therapists also rated the degree to which they engaged in the therapist task interventions relevant to each of the nine tasks. They used a 5–point scale (see Table 3), with "3" representing "present but brief" use of the intervention, "4" indicating "moderate" and "5" "extensive" use of the intervention. If brief episodes of task interventions are counted, three–quarters of the sessions involved the Empathic Prizing intervention (which goes with the Vulnerability marker); while half of the sessions contained moderate or extensive Empathic Prizing intervention by the therapist. Over half the sessions were rated as containing at least brief Empathic Exploration interventions; in roughly a third of these, this work was judged to have been at least moderate in length. Meaning creation work was always moderate or extensive when it was conducted (42%).

Finally, PE therapists rated the extent to which they engaged in "out of mode" interventions more typical of nonexperiential therapies. According to the therapists, substantial use of these interventions was almost nonexistent in these data. However, brief expert reassurance occurred in slightly more than a quarter of the sessions, suggesting the possibility that client vulnerability was so common in the sessions that it was difficult for therapists to resist their need to reassure clients.

In summary, these ratings provide a picture of process–experiential therapy with traumatized clients as centered around the three client tasks and corresponding therapist interventions which are relatively close to traditional client–centered work: empathic affirmation for vulnerability, empathic exploration for problem–relevant experiences, and meaning creation work for meaning crises. Chair work was used relatively little, apparently because therapists perceived fewer markers for them, but possibly also because they are more evocative and require "safety conditions" which are more difficult to meet with vulnerable, traumatized clients. In addition, even when therapists went briefly out of mode, they appeared to have been responding to client vulnerability, by offering expert reassurance.

PROCESS–EXPERIENTIAL THERAPY FOR PTSD: TWO CASE EXAMPLES

We will now describe how the process–experiential approach was applied in two case, whom we will refer to at Mark and Melissa.

In our ongoing pilot study pre–session and post–session data are obtained from clients for every session. For example, immediately prior to each session, clients completed an Impact of Event Scale (IES, Horowitz, Wilner & Alvarez, 1979). The IES is a self–report instrument, consisting of 15 statements regarding the client's feelings and responses, during the past seven days, to the presenting victimization experience. Clients responded to a fixed scale, ranging from "Not at all" (0) to "Often" (3), for each of the 15 statements. Based on the client's responses, total impact, avoidance, and intervention scores were computed for each client for each session. Figures 1 and 2 present IES data for the two clients presented in this paper. These show that Mark's scores were quite unstable, and remained relatively high at the end of treatment; in contrast, Melissa showed a striking decline in PTSD symptoms, and was almost symptom–free by the end of treatment.

Immediately following each session, clients also completed a Helpful Aspects of Therapy Form (HAT; Llewelyn, Elliott, Shapiro, Firth & Hardy, 1988). This instrument provides open–ended questions about helpful and/or hindering aspects of the therapy session just completed. In addition, the form asks clients to rate a particularly helpful or hindering event in that session on a 9–point bipolar rating scale, with "1" representing an extremely hindering event and "9" representing an extremely helpful event. HAT data are presented in Tables 5 and 6. Finally, structured interviews were scheduled with all clients at mid–treatment (following session eight) and at post–treatment (following the final session of therapy); the purpose of these interviews was to gather further information about helpful and hindering aspects of therapy and to explore the client's impressions of the course of therapy.

Figure 1

Impact of Event Scale Scores Across Treatment Sessions: Mark

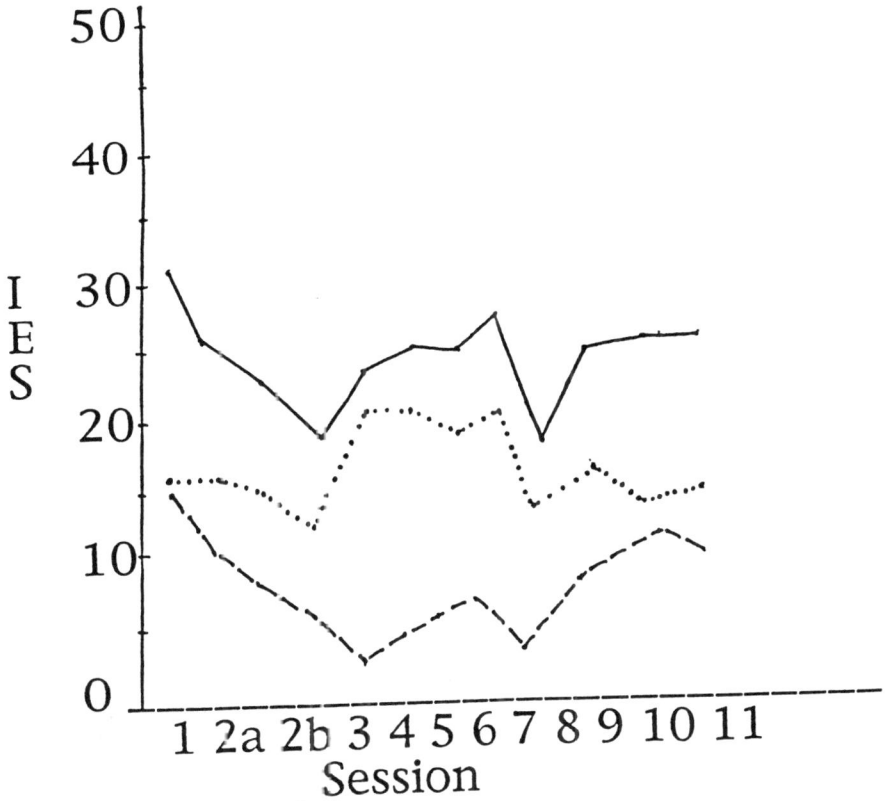

Total Score = ——
Avoidance Score = ---
Intrusion Score = ·········

Figure 2

Impact of Event Scale Scores Across Treatment Sessions: Melissa

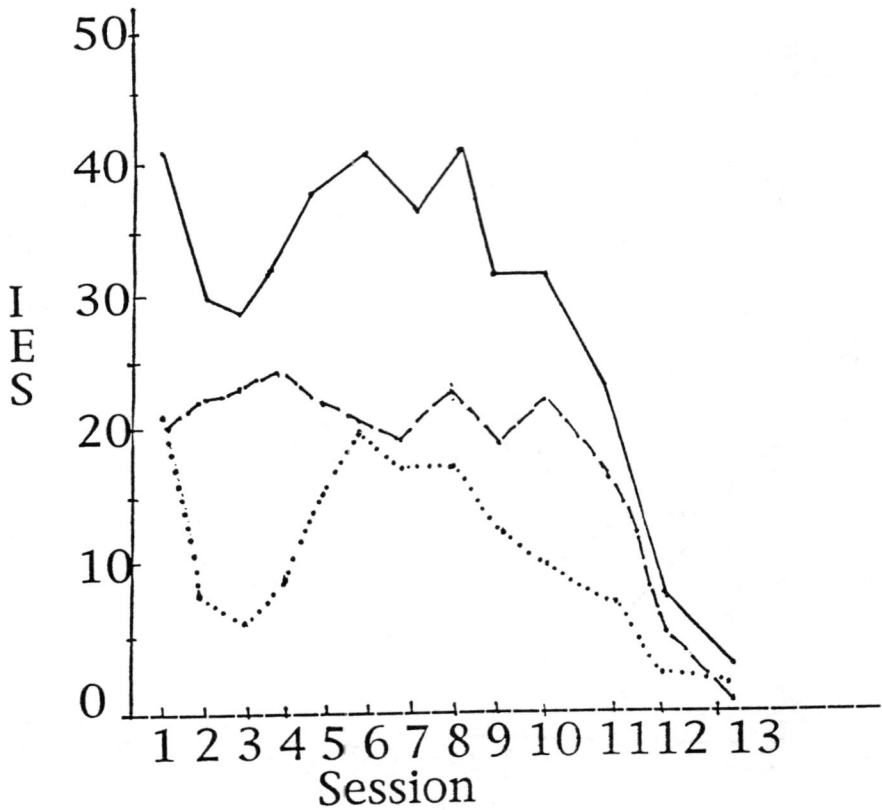

Total Score = ——
Avoidance Score = – – –
Intrusion Score = ·····

Table 5:

Summary of HAT Data for Client Mark

Session	Rating	Helpful/Hindering Event
1	9.0	+Therapist was open and accepting.
		–Presence of videocamera.
2a	9.0	+Discussion of my fears.
2b	6.0	+Concern of therapist.
		–Speaking only English in therapy.
3	8.0	+Therapist attuned to fear.
		Concern with pending trial.
4	9.0	+Therapist doesn't interrupt.
		–Concern with immigrant status.
5	7.0	+Exploration of Hero archetype.
6	9.0	+Admission of negative traits.
		Fear of therapy becoming "standardized".
7	8.0	+Relating past and present experiences.
8	8.0	+Expressing hopefulness for future.
		–Concerns for my family.
9	9.0	+Dialogue with Hero archetype.
10	9.0	+Acceptance by therapist.
		–Concerns for therapist's well-being.
11	8.0	+Feeling hopeful rather than resentful.
		–Continuing concerns with language.

Note. +: Helpful event; –: Hindering event.

Table 6:

Summary of HAT Data for Client Melissa

Session Rating Helpful Event

1	6.5	Getting out of myself.
2	7.0	Discussion of rape.
3	8.0	Reassurance of therapist.
4	7.0	Discussion of rape.
5	8.0	Connections between past and present.
6	No rating.	
7	9.0	Expression of anger.
8	8.0	Crying in session.
9	No rating.	
10	9.0	Talking about what was on my mind.
11	9.0	"I made connections into myself."
12	9.0	Therapist being excited for my progress.
13	9.0	Making it through the program.

Note. Client listed no hindering events.

Although they expressed themselves in somewhat different ways, the two clients presented here moved through similar themes and issues in the course of therapy. Both began treatment with much initial reticence, but eventually identified empathic attunement and the therapeutic bond as key elements in the resolution of their issues. Both dealt in therapy with issues of trust and psychological safety and with the re-acquisition and appropriate exercise of personal power.

Case #1, Mark. Mark, a 29 year old married male manual laborer, had been attacked and beaten by intruders at his place of employment. Mark was born and raised in a third world country and had entered the United States with his wife and daughter after being granted political asylum. Approximately one year prior to seeking therapy, his wife was seduced by the couple's supposed benefactor; when he sought recompense for the seduction, he was attacked and beaten by the supposed benefactor's nephews. At the time of treatment, a court trial on the attack was pending.

The client initially presented with severe difficulty sleeping, problems with concentration, an intense focus on pursuing and obtaining justice, and general moodiness and hypervigilance. The development of a therapeutic bond and task collaboration was complicated by several factors: the pending trial, his recent experience of living under a military dictatorship, and previous negative experiences with therapy.

The therapist was female, in her 50's and had two years of formal psychotherapy experience and training in the process–experiential approach.

Mark was seen for 11 sessions plus an additional brief session labelled in Figure 1 as 2b. The major tasks of sessions 1 through 5 were (a) establishing rapport, (b) empathic affirmation of his vulnerability, and (c) empathic exploration of his traumatic experiences, including the beating and his ongoing anxiety as he planned for his testimony at the trial of his assailants. (The trial was initially scheduled to occur a few days after session 5, but was ultimately delayed for two months, to a time after the completion of therapy.)

The client's postsession HAT data (Table 5) indicate the therapist's empathic attunement and open and accepting manner as the most helpful elements of the therapy. He indicated that this attitude allowed him a place in which to explore his past victimization and to express his fears and reservations in regard to the impending trial. Indeed, at mid–treatment, he noted that he had initially been very concerned that the therapist and other project personnel would be prejudiced against him because he was a foreigner and that he was very pleasantly surprised when this was not the case. Sessions six through ten were pivotal sessions in the therapy; they focussed on Mark's exploration of his Hero archetype, earlier introduced by the client. In this context, he explored his need for a rational sense of his own power in his present and future life. The major tasks of this period were (a) the resolution of conflict splits by means of two–chair work and (b) seeking creation of meaning through exploration of cherished beliefs.

A key element in this period was the ongoing discussion of Wotan as his archetype. He described Wotan as both destroyer and renewer, and through this, was able to begin to resolve his internal split between seeking justice and an opportunituy to move ahead in his life vs. wishing for some sort of revenge against those who had harmed him. As the split began to heal, he began to feel more realistically empowered to manage his own life, care for his family, and move forward into his future. Mark's mid–treatment interview occurred during this time, following session eight; he indicated much pleasure with the course of therapy and described empathic attunement and unconditional acceptance by the therapist as most helpful to him to date.

Session 11 focussed on furthering creation of meaning in his life and termination of therapy necessitated by changes in his life circumstances. He was more focussed on improving living conditions for himself and his family than on pursuing revenge against his benefactor and attackers. Indeed, near the end of the session, Mark indicated that he had found a better job, one which took him away from the scene of his victimization and allowed him to move his family to a safer and more comfortable neighborhood. Unfortunately, this precluded his being able to come for therapy during the hours available. At termination, he indicated that his unfinished business with his assailants and his benefactor had not been completely resolved, but that he did not consider that to be possible until the he knew the outcome of the pending trial of his assailants. Nevertheless, in the full text for the HAT for session 11, he noted

> A feeling of hope for [the] future, putting aside my resentment and [the] violent inherited/acquired side of my personality... I got a feeling of worth, that our [my wife and my] problem and victimization may not have been in vain and that the objective truth speaks for itself...

Post–treatment interview data are not yet available for Mark At the completion of treatment, Mark reported sleeping better, finding more joy in family relationships, and feeling less pressured and stressed than at the outset of therapy. However, his Impact of Event Scale data (Figure 1) show that he remained at clinical levels of traumatic distress.

Case #2, Melissa. Melissa, a 19 year old single female college student, had been raped, in her home, by a former boyfriend. The rape occurred approximately two years prior to her seeking therapy. In addition, Melissa reported having been sexually harassed by neighborhood boys throughout her adolescent years and ongoing stalking by another former boyfriend. While these additional issues were addressed in the course of therapy, they did not seem to interfere with the resolution of her feelings in regard to the rape. At the time of therapy, Melissa was still living in her parents' home, in the room in which the rape had occurred. She initially presented with insomnia, irritability, social withdrawal, hypervigilance, and emotional numbing.

Melissa was seen in therapy for 13 sessions, by the same therapist as in the previous case. She terminated when she felt certain that she had successfully resolved her issues in regard to the rape and was no longer symptomatic for PTSD. As with Mark, there were three readily identifiable phases in the course of therapy. The major tasks of the first four to five sessions with Melissa were (a) developing a therapeutic bond and (b) empathic exploration of her traumatic experiences, including the rape, sexual harassment by neighbor boys during adolescence, and currently being stalked by her former boyfriend. The major challenge in these initial sessions was establishing a "safe place," physically and emotionally, from which to explore and address the reality of having been raped. Melissa's HAT data for these sessions (see Table 6) identify the most helpful factors as having a safe place to retreat to as she began to explore her feelings.

Sessions five through ten focussed on Melissa's recognition and expression of previously numbed feelings. During these sessions she explored her anger and sadness and began to experience her own inner strength and self–efficacy. Primary tasks during this period were (a) ongoing empathic exploration of her victimizations, (b) empathic affirmation of her vulnerability, and (c) initial creation of meaning work.

Sessions six and nine were interesting as transition sessions, with little clear focus and much expression of feelings. For neither of these sessions was Melissa able to provide a numerical HAT rating and for both she noted little memory of content immediately following completion of the session. Sessions seven and ten were particularly focussed sessions. In session seven she explored her sense of strength and vulnerability and in session ten she reported being no longer symptomatic for PTSD, describing her memories of the rape as "simply memories; I have good memories and I have bad memories; the rape memories are bad memories." Melissa's HAT data for this period indicate reconnecting with her past and openly expressing her feelings as being the most helpful elements of therapy. It is interesting to note that in the HAT for session nine, Melissa first used a capital "I" when referring to herself. In all previous HAT's she had employed a small "i" when referring to herself. In her mid–treatment interview Melissa indicated "Not being judged instantly" and "getting out my emotions" as having been most helpful up to that point.

Sessions 11 through 13 focussed primarily on exploring and integrating feeling "normal" into her life and future. The major task of this period was the creation of meaning for her meaning crisis. She reported having aspirations for her future for the first time since the rape, "I have begun to think about getting married and having children; before this I had not expected to live to be more than 30 years old." In all three sessions she expressed great pleasure in the cessation of nightmares and flashbacks along with her becoming more assertive in her everyday life.

Initially she was tentative in accepting these as permanent changes, but by the final session she was describing these changes as real and very acceptable. Melissa's HAT data for this period indicate being supported in her feelings of being real, stronger, and normal as most helpful:

> I feel as though I can deal with life now; it's no longer an overwhelming experience nor a sad place to be. It feels real.

Again, in her post–treatment interview, Melissa identified having a "place to go with my experience" as most helpful in therapy; for Melissa having a safe place appeared to be crucial. Because she showed few markers of splits and worked most efficiently with unfinished business during focussing, little chair work was employed in the course of Melissa's therapy. Indeed, during the only attempt to address her unfinished business with her rapist with empty chair work, she insisted that the empty chair be placed, and remain, as far away from her as the therapy room allowed, literally up against the wall.

At the conclusion of therapy, Melissa was sleeping better and was no longer experiencing nightmares and flash–backs. She reported feeling generally more comfortable around people and taking pleasure in her daily activities. Indeed, she had recently accepted a date with a new male friend and was looking forward to the future. Her IES data (see Figure 2) dropped dramatically over the course of therapy, from 41 to 3.

INTEGRATION AND CONCLUSIONS

The process–experiential perspective on post–traumatic stress difficulties emphasizes two things: First, the symptoms traditionally associated with the PTSD diagnostic category can be explained in terms of interrupted and conflicted emotional processing of painful events. Second, emotion schemes are central to understanding PTSD. In particular, it is vital for the therapist to understand that the client's experience of vulnerability and meaninglessness in the wake of senseless victimization has thrown in question cherished and encompassing beliefs about self, others and the world. This view of post–traumatic difficulties suggests and experiential treatment which emphasizes restoration of a helpful other in the form of the therapist. This conceptualization is supported by questionnaire and case study data from a pilot treatment study currently underway.

Specifically, in terms of the six process–experiential treatment principles, it was the therapeutic bond principle that appears to be most important, at least in the case study data. (Further study is needed to determine the validity of process–experiential therapists' self–ratings of their treatment adherence, as these may reflect either response basis or strict adherence to the treatment model.)

In addition, the data also suggest that even though it is probably not the most common therapist response mode in process–experiential therapy (that distinction goes to empathic exploration responses), the empathic understanding response should not be disregarded. After all, empathic understanding responses are essential to the Empathic Affirmation task intervention which therapists rated as present to at least some degree in 75% of sessions.

Finally, therapist self–report and case study data support the key role of a range of client tasks and therapist interventions in the treatment of clients suffering from post–traumatic stress difficulties. However, interventions consistent with traditional client–centered therapy appeared to be most common in the sample of sessions reported so far on from the ongoing pilot study. These include Empathic Exploration of Difficult Experience, Empathic Affirmation of Vulnerability, and Creation of Meaning for Meaning Crises. Clearly, a more client–centered approach was highly effective in at least one of the case examples presented, while the other case clearly represents not a therapeutic failure but a treatment interrupted by life circumstances. Further study is required to determine whether this therapeutic caution on the part of the therapists is justified or not.

REFERENCES

American Psychiatric Association.(1987). *Diagnostic and Statistical Manual – Third Edition – Revised.* Washington, D.C.

Clarke, K.M. (1993). *Creation of meaning in incest survivors.* Journal of Cognitive Psychotherapy, 7, 195–203.

Davis, K. (1994). *Therapist response modes in process–experiential therapy.* Dissertation in progress, Department of Psychology, University of Toledo.

Fischer, C.T., & Wertz, F.J. (1979). *Empirical phenomenological analyses of being criminally victimized.* In A. Giorgi, R. Knowles, & D.L. Smith (Eds.), Duquesne studies in phenomenological psychology (Vol. 3) (pp. 135–158). Pittsburgh: Duquesne University Press.

Elliott, R., & Greenberg, L.S. (in press). *Experiential Therapy in Practice: The Process–Experiential Approach.* In B. Bongar & L. Beutler, (eds.), Foundations of Psychotherapy: Theory, Research, and Practice. Stanford, CA: Oxford University Press.

Greenberg, L.S., Rice, L.N., & Elliott, R. (1993). *Facilitating emotional change: The moment–by–moment process.* New York: Guilford Press.

Horowitz, M.J., Wilner, N, & Alvarez, W. (1979). *Impact of event scale: A measure of subjective stress.* Psychosomatic Medicine, 41, 209–218.

Janoff–Bulman, R. (1992). *Shattered assumptions.* New York: Free Press.

Llewelyn, S.P., Elliott, R., Shapiro, D.A., Firth, J., & Hardy, G. (1988). *Client perceptions of significant events in prescriptive and exploratory periods of individual therapy.* British Journal of Clinical Psychology, 27, 105–114.

Rice, L.N. & Greenberg, L. (Eds.) (1984). *Patterns of change.* New York: Guilford Press.

Wertz, F.J. (1985). *Methods and findings in the study of a complex life event: being criminally victimized.* In A. Giorgi (Ed.), Phenomenology and psychological research. Pittsburgh: Duquesne University Press.

Yalom, I.D. (1980). *Existential psychotherapy.* New York: Basic.

Using Statistical Experiments with Post–session Client Questionnaires as a Student–centered Approach to Teaching the Effects of Therapist Activities in Psychotherapy

JAMES R. IBERG

ILLINOIS SCHOOL OF PROFESSIONAL PSYCHOLOGY

ABSTRACT

Six students each implemented the same complete factorial experiment, using each distinct factorial combination with a different client in a firs session. Volunteer clients filled out questionnaires after the session. Here we examine ratings of how well cl ents felt understood by the therapist. The three factors tested were 1) two frequencies of understanding response, 2) whether or not the therapist gave general advice, and 3) whether or not the therapist applied the author's "manual for guiding focusing during experiential psychotherapy." Many understanding responses (vs. few) resulted in higher ratings of how well the clients felt understood. The other two factors had no general effects on understanding ratings. There were two students with outcomes at a higher average level than the other four students. Another demonstrated an interaction effect between the frequency of understanding responses and whether or not the focusing manual was used. One student got worse understanding ratings at the higher frequency.

This is another in a series of quality improvement studies done with graduate students in clinical psychology in a course on Client–centered and experiential therapy (Iberg, 1991). The study represents the major vehicle used in the course for providing students with direct feedback from their practice clients regarding the effects of their activities as therapists.

By structuring as a factorial experiment the instructions given to students regarding which activities to use in a given session, we are able to contrast the effects of two or three different kinds of therapist activity on a post session questionnaire of 14 questions derived from the Therapy Session Report (Orlinsky and Howard, 1975), which is filled out by practice clients immediately after the sessions. The two–level factors used have been various ones of interest to novice therapists, such as whether or not questions can be asked, whether or not advice can be given, the frequency of understanding responses (many or few), whether or not the therapist self–discloses, whether or not the session is tape–recorded, etc.

Here I present the results for six students who were part of the Fall, 1993 class, on one of the questions: the clients' ratings of how well they were understood by their therapist. Two sorts of results are examined: first, the results which applied across all students (the more generalizable findings), and second, results which apply uniquely to individual students. These two kinds of outcome increased the personal relevance of the study to the students who participated: they not only saw that one therapist activity had an effect across therapists, but also saw that there were certain activities which had measurable effects specific to the way particular individuals had applied them.

As I continue to use this empirical method of teaching psychotherapy skills, I am pleased with how it takes me out of the position of being the expert therapist who knows how best to do it, and instead puts me in the position of guide and facilitator who organizes, presents, and helps interpret data reflecting the effects of the students' actions on the experiences of their own clients. I am in the position of learning from the experience along with the students regarding "what actions have what effects," making the endeavor more "student centered" than some approaches to teaching.

TWO LEVEL FACTORIAL EXPERIMENTS

The spirit of quality improvement experiments is one of exploring what we can learn from studying a process rather than setting out to refute prior hypotheses (Walton, 1986). Factorial experiments are designed to test the effects of multiple different factors in one experiment, getting as much information as possible out of a given amount of experimental effort, rather than the more inefficient approach of testing only "one thing at a time" (Box, Hunter, & Hunter, 1978). Here we tested three factors, each one at two different levels. For example, one factor was the frequency of empathic response. The two levels we applied were one response every minute ("Few") vs. one response about every half a minute ("Many"). Our results permit us to compare these two levels only, and not others. Should we learn that one level has better outcomes than the other in this study, that would be suggestive for the next study about which levels to include for testing next. Thus, rather than seeking to make claims about absolutely generalizable effects, we have more modest goals: to identify certain levels on the factors tested which seem to have advantages, which will then inform us for further study. Over many such studies, we would like to zero in on advantageous positions in the "verbal behavior space" between client and therapist. These positions would be the settings on various types of therapist activities under therapist discretion to apply or not apply in a given session which produce better outcomes for clients (see Stiles, 1986, for "verbal response modes" akin to the factors we have been testing).

METHOD

Participants

Therapists. Nine graduate students at a professional school of psychology were the therapists for this study. The study was part of a required course on client–centered and experiential psychotherapy. Three of the students did not properly conduct the interviews, so their data were dropped, leaving six students whose results are included here. There were two male students, average age 31, and four female students, average age 30. Four of the students had prior experience in professional mental health settings. The other two students had no prior experience as therapists.

Volunteer clients. Students located volunteers for their clients, 48 during the study (eight for each of the six students included in the analysis). These were to be people who had not had any sessions with the student or any other student in the class before, so they were first sessions. The sample was approximately 67% female, and was generally adult, although there were two children. Many were family, friends and other students, but not students from this class.

Design: A 23 Factorial Experiment to Measure Effects of three therapist activities, each at two levels.

Three therapist activities were chosen for experimental variation from session to session. Two levels of each therapist activity were contrasted: 1) the frequency of empathic response was either "few" (about one per minute) or "many"(about one per 30 seconds), 2) whether or not the student gave any general advice to the client, and 3) whether or not the student gave "focusing guidance" as described and illustrated in the author's "Manual for guiding focusing during experiential therapy" (attached as appendix A). All combinations of these three therapist activities produce the eight treatment combinations delineated in Table 1.

Table 1:

The eight treatment combinations produced by three two–level activity factors

Treatment com–bination number	Therapist activities: Focusing Guidance	Advice	f(Empathy)
1	no guiding	no advice	few
2	guide as needed	no advice	few
3	no guiding	give advice	few
4	guide as needed	give advice	few
5	no guiding	no advice	many
6	guide as needed	no advice	many
7	no guiding	give advice	many
8	guide as needed	give advice	many

For each student, the order of the eight treatment combinations was randomized, and a different client was seen for each treatment combination. Thus, each student saw eight different clients. During the first four weeks of the trimester, students practiced in class responding with these variations of therapist activity. During the study, they received a questionnaire for themselves to fill out as well as the client questionnaires, and at the top of the student's questionnaire, their activity combination instructions appeared in print. They could have this material in front of them to remind them of which combination to use during the session.

The experiment is designed to allow estimation of seven treatment effects: a main effect for each of the three therapist activities, three two–way interactions between therapist activities, and one three way interaction (using seven degrees of freedom).

The design also permits estimation of Student X Treatment effect interaction (using 35 degrees of freedom), as each student performs one entire cycle of the experiment. Thus we can detect if some students obtained treatment effects unique to themselves, in addition to those effects which were common across students.

The remaining five degrees of freedom were used to detect any significant "student" effects, which could occur if one or more students achieved results at significantly higher or lower average levels than the others (mean differences between students).

Measures

Outcomes. An eleven item post–session questionnaire (The "Brief Therapy Session Report," attached as appendix B) was given to clients to complete at the end of each session. It is an attempt to develop a much shorter instrument, for the convenience of the client, derived from Orlinsky and Howard's (1975) Therapy Session Report (the TSR). Items 1,4, and 5 are taken directly from the TSR. The other items were either defined by the author to attempt to capture aspects of a session pertinent to client centered and experiential therapy, or defined as suggested by the factors found by Orlinsky and Howard when they factor analyzed the TSR. Item 2 asks about the extent to which the "doorway" to the client's feelings opened during the session, which is intended to measure the extent to which the client was able to gain access to a body sense (Gendlin, 1981) during the session. Item 3 attempts to measure the degree to which the session was experienced as "non–directive," and was suggested quite directly by two related factors Orlinsky and Howard called "passive dependence" and "independent introspection." Question 6 asks about the degree to which the client came out of the session with new perspectives, which is an attempt to measure the extent of cognitive insight produced in the session. Item 7 asks the client about the degree to which they were able to talk about what was valuable for them to discuss, attempting to assess how much the content of the discussion was "on target" for the client.

Item 9a simply asks if the client feels any better after the session, attempting to measure affective change. Items 10a and 10b attempt to assess the intensity of emotion produced in the session. And finally, item 11 asks about the degree to which the client was able to relate to the feelings and thoughts discussed with an attitude of friendly curiosity. Such an attitude is at the heart of what Gendlin describes as effective "focusing" (Gendlin, 1981, 1969).

For this paper, results are reported for question 4, the degree to which the therapist understood the thoughts and feelings of the client, rated on a five point scale ranging from "understood exactly" to "misunderstood."

Validation of therapist activities. Three questions were appended to the Brief Therapy Session Report to permit us to tell the extent to which the variations in therapist activity executed by the students were perceived in ways we would expect them to be by the clients. Thus, clients were asked

1. Did your listener give you any advice or suggestions about what you could do to improve your situation?
   [ ] Yes
   [ ] No
2. Did your listener make any suggestions about how to relate to your feelings, or how to work on them?
   [ ] No
   [ ] Yes
3. How often did your listener verbalize what he/she understood you to be saying?
   [ ] every step of the way – regularly and often
   [ ] from time to time, after major points

Analytical approach. Stepwise regression was used to identify all significant effects, whether therapist activity effects or their interactions, therapist effects, or therapist by therapist activity interactions. Only significant effects were then included in a simplified multiple regression equation, pooling insignificant effects into error variance. Residuals were examined for normality, autocorrelation, and homogeneity of variance. (In some studies, not including the present one, this diagnostic procedure revealed, for individual students, evidence of improvement or deterioration in performance levels over time).

RESULTS

Validation of therapist activities

In the aggregate, clients did not perceive whether or not focusing guidance was offered, at least not as indicated by the validation question intended to detect this (Table 2).

In the aggregate, clients accurately perceived when advice was given and when it was not (p < .01).

259

Table 2:

Cross–tabulations of Client Impressions and Assigned Levels of Therapist Input Variables

Experimentally assigned level:	Client estimates		Chi–square
	yes	no	
Focusing guidance			
as needed	14	10	
none	14	10	0.086 (n.s.)
	yes	no	
Advice			
given	17	7	
none	5	19	10.154**
	after main points	every step of way	
Frequency of Empathy			
few	11	3	
many	7	17	.8 (n.s.)

p < .05   ** p < .01

In the aggregate, clients discriminated the difference between few and many empathic responses, but not at a statistically significant level (p = .37). Even in sessions designated "few," 54% of clients indicated that there were understanding responses "every step of the way." As a secondary check to see if there was meaningful variation of the frequency of understanding responses, I took a sample of listening from each student at each of the two settings, and counted the responses in a five minute interval. By this measure, there was evidence of variation as required for the experiment, such that the average time between understanding responses in the "few" sample was 65 seconds, and in the "many" sample it was 34 seconds (p < .05). Cross–tabulations between client perceptions of one activity with the assigned values of another therapist activity were also examined (Table 3). There was a significant correlation between the clients' perceptions that suggestions were made about how to relate to their feelings, or how to work on them, and the therapist activity of "advice" (p < .01).

Table 3:

Cross–tabulations of Client Impressions and Assigned Levels of Other Therapist Input Variables

Experimentally assigned level:	Client estimates		Chi–square
	Advice or suggestion? yes, re: what to do in situation	no	
Focusing guidance			
as needed	11	13	
none	11	13	0.084 (n.s.)
Did listener make suggestions?			
	yes, re: how to relate to feelings	no	
Advice			
given	19	7	
none	9	15	6.943**

*

p < .05; ** p < .01

The opposite cross–tabulation, between the therapist's assigned activity of focusing guidance, and the clients' perceptions that they were given advice or suggestions about what to do to improve their situations, showed no correlation whatsoever.

Findings for all therapists as a group

Mean understanding ratings were higher by .45 scale points for the sessions in which more frequent empathic responses were given (Table 4).

Table 4:

Multiple Regression of Understanding Ratings on Five Independent Variables

Variable	Beta	t	p
f(Empathy)	.45	3.318	.0019
Student B level	.375	2.212	.0325
Student C X FocG X f(E)	−.75	2.473	.0175
Student D X f(E)	−.70	2.107	.0411
Student I level	.625	3.687	.0006

Note. Adjusted R^2 = .379; $F(5,42)$ = 6.733; p = .0001

Neither general advice, nor focusing guidance had an effect on understanding ratings in this study.

Findings specific to Individual Therapists

First, the simpler individual effects: two students, B and I, achieved higher mean understanding ratings than the other four students (Table 4). The betas indicate the portion of a scale point by which each was higher than the other four students, so student I was the best performer on this measure in the group. Student B was also superior to the other four.

Students C and D show individual therapist effects in interaction with the treatment variables. Student D had a large negative effect for the frequency of empathy activity variable. Where other students achieved higher understanding ratings when using the higher frequency of understanding response, student D's mean rating was actually lower using the higher frequency (see Figure 1: open circles show the averages as represented by the fitted values of the regression equation).

Student C showed the only significant interaction between two of the therapist activities. For this student, mean understanding ratings were higher when the higher frequency of understanding response was used, but this effect was modified by whether or not focusing guidance was given. When using few understanding responses, ratings were higher when focusing guidance was given. But when using many understanding responses, ratings were higher when focusing guidance was not given.

The pattern of these several different results may be easier to grasp with the help of a graphical display. See Figures 1 and 2, in which observations appear in the order of treatment combination (as in Table 1).

Figure 1:
Observations in Treatment Combination Order within Student Blocks
(indicated by capital letters).

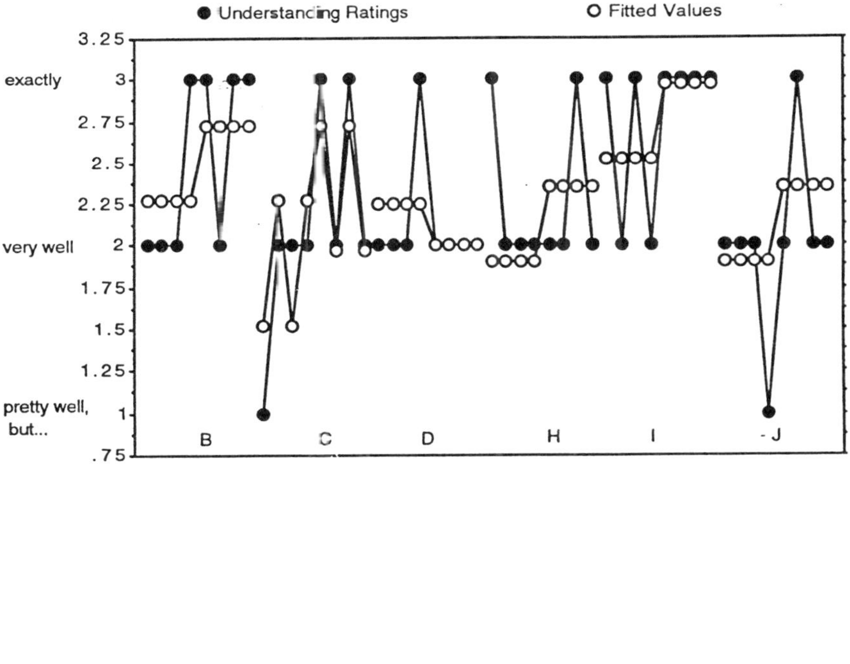

DISCUSSION

Validation of therapist activities

There were some disappointments here. Whether or not the therapist activity of focusing guidance occurred was not validated by the clients' perceptions as measured by the question intended to measure this. From review of audiotapes of some sessions, I know there were some clear examples of focusing guidance as described in the appended manual (appendix A). Perhaps the question was not worded properly for the clients: many of the focusing guiding responses are phrased as questions, so maybe clients did not experience these as "suggestions." The more worrisome possibility is that therapists gave the same level of focusing guidance in all sessions, although that was not my impression from reviewing tapes. It is not the case that focusing guidance was perceived as general advice, since that cross tabulation showed a negligible correlation (Table 3).

It is possible that more training is necessary to achieve enough consistency in the application of the focusing manual so that this activity would be perceptible by clients. The manual is complex, which permitted a wide variation of applications across students. Also, the manual is under continuing development. I now believe the manual is more suited to advanced therapists, than it is to novice therapists. Novice therapists may produce more consistent applications with simpler, more singular focusing interventions, such as "ask where the person feels it in his/her body."

Also, measures of therapist activities other than client perceptions would be desirable. The more subtle therapist activities we may actually be able to test in this fashion may not be perceptible at all by the client. After all, the client should be busy doing something else, rather than paying attention to the therapist's method. Actual tapes of the sessions, which could be rated for the various therapist activities would be ideal, although this would add considerably to the time and expense of doing such studies.

The other problem was with the frequency of empathic response. Although my sample counts indicated adequate distinction between the two settings on this variable, client perceptions didn't correspond as distinctly as we would like. It may be that the wording of the validation question was the problem here, since compared to what people are used to in normal social interaction, even the "few" setting may seem like "every step of the way" to clients.

One additional peculiarity is worth mentioning. The assigned therapist activity of general advice correlated significantly with the client's perceptions of having received suggestions about how to relate to their feelings or how to work on them (which was intended to indicate whether or not focusing guidance was given), as well as with the question intended to validate general advice (Tables 2 & 3). Thus it may be that these therapists gave something more like focusing guidance than general advice when their instructions were to give general advice. My impression from these data is that students were reluctant to give general advice, and lacked confidence about focusing guidance. Their general advice may have been more like focusing guidance than like the other more intrusive forms of advice novice therapists sometimes give.

Therapist activity effects

The only significant treatment effect across all therapists was that more frequent understanding responses resulted in higher understanding ratings by the client. This finding has been found in two other studies of this kind, so it is beginning to stand out as a generalizable finding. I find it somewhat remarkable that purely the frequency of understanding responses would have such an effect: i.e. apart from variation in other forms of quality of understanding, simply more frequent responses achieve better understanding impact. Giving more frequent responses probably requires the therapist to stay in somewhat closer contact, understanding smaller "pieces" of what the client is communicating, and more regularly establishing that what is being communicated is understood. Such sharper, closer following at the level of specific detail is what Gendlin has long recommended to facilitate a focusing process (Gendlin, 1981, 1974).

This effect is not overwhelming in size (less than one half a scale point). Thus it is too small to show up as individual effects for the students in only one cycle of the experiment. But for the six students as a group, it does show up. If you examine Figure 1, you can see that there are clearly more "understood exactly" ratings for the higher frequency sessions (the last four observations for each student therapist). At the "few" setting (the first four observations for each student) the preponderance of observations fall at the "understood very well" level.

Individual therapist effects

Students B and I achieved significantly higher mean understanding ratings from their clients than did the other students. You can see these effects clearly in Figure 2, which shows the fitted values from the regression model. For these two students, their whole set of eight observations fell at an average level higher than the average levels for the other students. Thus, these two students appear to be doing some things well in terms of communicating understanding, and by further study of their listening, we might learn something of use to everyone in the group. This is one of the ways such a study can show the effects of greater experience or aptitude for particular students.

Student C's mean levels were not out of line with the main group, but this student had differential effects depending on the combination of focusing guidance and frequency of empathy. At the lower frequency of understanding, focusing guidance was beneficial, but at the higher level of understanding frequency, also giving focusing guidance was associated with lower understanding ratings. Thus the study suggests that for this student, using the higher frequency of empathy without focusing guidance and the lower frequency of empathy with focusing guidance would result in the best performance in terms of understanding ratings, these combinations putting this student at the same level with student B's superior performance. Using the lower frequency of understanding without focusing guidance resulted in understanding ratings among the very lowest of all those observed in this group, so that combination should be avoided.

Student D was the exception to the general pattern. This student, rather than benefiting from more frequent understanding responses, actually did slightly less well with that frequency than with the lower frequency. Post hoc analysis showed that Student D had the most extreme difference in responses per minute of all the students between many and few responses. The sample of "many" frequency was one per 27 seconds, so perhaps this student was responding too frequently in the "many empathy" sessions. Another student, H, sampled out at this same "many" frequency, and interestingly this student's actual mean understanding ratings for the low and high frequency were identical. It is possible that somewhere below 30 seconds there lies a boundary to the "advantage" zone in terms of frequency of understanding response. Further study is warranted.

Figure 2:

Fitted values in Treatment Combination Order within Student Blocks (indicated by capital letters).

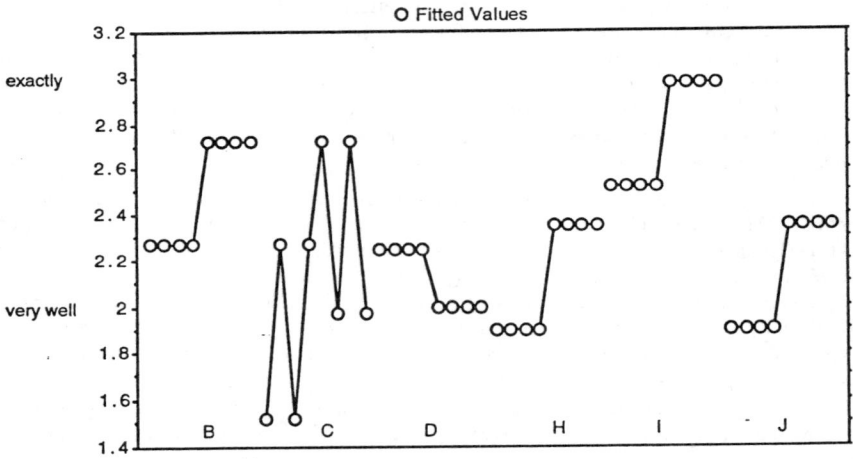

SUMMARY

Once again this approach to teaching client–centered therapy was rewarding and stimulating for me and , I believe, for the students involved. In the class discussion following the presentation of the results, many comments were made by students about the value of doing such a structured form of practice. Several said in different ways that being given instructions to vary these activities led to their varying them in ways they simply would not have done otherwise. Some students discovered more control over their activity than they had realized they have. Participants also discovered that there were corresponding effects on client experience of the session, and not always in ways that they predicted, so I believe the study engendered a bit more humility regarding preconceptions about "what works". And finally, one student said very strongly that she appreciated this "empirical" approach which meant that she learned from her own experience, rather than from the mouth of an expert.

Studies such as this have the advantage that they can be implemented fairly quickly and results can be reported to participants within a one trimester course. The results are based on data that is relevant and meaningful to the participants. The disadvantage of such studies is that little has been done to standardize the behavior of the students to make sure that they are all doing the same thing for each of the therapist activities, which limits the generalizability of the findings. Claims of generalizability require a finding to reappear over more than one study. Designing the study so that each participant performs the whole experiment assures that as long as the individual participant is consistent in his or her performance of the therapist activities, meaningful effects can be detected whether or not they are the same as for other students.

The finding reported here that understanding ratings are higher for responses given about every 30 seconds is one which has occurred in other studies. One of the individual therapist effects reported here suggests that if responses occur even more frequently than that, understanding ratings may begin to drop off. Thus, there may be an "advantage zone" for understanding impact somewhere between one minute and 30 second intervals, and further study should be done to see if the boundaries of this zone can be identified.

One concern voiced by some client–centered therapists is that anything the therapist does other than understanding responses will distract from the empathic impact of the therapist. In this study we find no evidence of such an effect: attempts by these students to guide focusing, and to give general advice had no undesirable effects on understanding ratings. Also, there was no increase in the ratings of how much influence the therapist had over the course of the session (question 3 on the Brief Therapy Session Report) that corresponded to these other therapist activities. These results were for first sessions with volunteers, so results could be different over time, at other points in therapy, or in therapy with regular clients. My conclusion is not that therapist activities other than understanding responses never have undesirable effects – I am sure they sometimes do – but that they don't necessarily always have negative effects for all therapists. Perhaps it would be better to move away from general prohibitions in favor of examining actual results to determine which sets of therapist activities are most effective in which ways for which therapists. Statistical designs such as the one illustrated here have the potential to help us begin to do just that.

REFERENCES

Box, G. E. P., Hunter, W. G., & Hunter, J. S. (1978). *Statistics for Experimenters*. New York: Wiley.

Gendlin, E. T. (1981). *Focusing (2ᵈ. Ed.)*. New York: Bantam.

Gendlin, E. T. (1974). *Client–centered and experiential psychotherapy.* In D. A. Wexler and L. N. Rice (Eds.), *Innovations in client–centered therapy.* New York: Wiley.

Iberg, J. R. (1991). *Applying statistical control theory to bring together clinical supervision and psychotherapy research.* Journal of Consulting and Clinical Psychology , 59, 575–586.

Orlinsky, D. E., & Howard, K. I. (1975). *Varieties of psychotherapeutic experience.* New York: Columbia Teachers College Press.

Stiles, W.B. (1986). *Development of a taxonomy of verbal response modes.* In Greenberg, L. & Pinsof, W. (Eds.) *The Psychotherapeutic Process: a Research Handbook.* New York: Guilford Press.

Walton, M. (1986). *The Deming Management Method.* New York: Perigee Books.

Appendix A: Manual for guiding Focusing during experiential therapy: September, 1993

Keyword descriptions
of client condition   More complete client description with example therapist guiding responses

IF FEELINGS WELL UP
        for client: i.e. If non–verbal cues indicate something feelingful is happening in the client's body (tears, voice cracks, volume drops, rate of speech slows, lips quiver, etc.),

        THEN   Bring attention/awareness to that event as a helpful or useful bodily development.

E.G.   "Now your body seems to be really feeling your sense of this. That will help you move along."
        "There's the felt sense of it. Try to be friendly to that."
        "Something welled up inside you just then, can you describe the quality of that feeling?"

IF Client seems

OFF–BALANCE: i.e. If client seems ambivalent about going into something, or scared of it, or embarrassed,

        THEN   Bring attention to the specific way in which the process doesn't feel comfortable (i.e. does it scare the person, or embarrass them, or what?). Then, if necessary, encourage the person to take a break, or slow down, or otherwise change her/his approach until she/he feels more OK about proceeding.

E.G.   "Take your time with this. We can go at a pace that's comfortable for you."
        "We can take a break if you'd like."
        "Let's check your feelings and see if it's really ok to be working on this right now."

IF Client seems to have

WRONG DISTANCE: i.e. If client seems only intellectual about it, or engulfed by emotion, or talking only about the past, or other people,

        THEN   Assist in making adjustments to a more productive or comfortable distance from feelings. For too much intensity, suggest a short break, or stepping back from it a bit. For too little emotion, ask for or guess about underlying emotion or body sense.

E.G.   Examples from "off balance" work for too little distance.
        For too much, "You have told me a lot about this. Can you stop for a moment and see how all that makes you feel inside, in your body?"
        "I get the impression that you feel pretty strongly about this. Can you tell me the emotional undercurrents you feel about it?"
        "Even though that happened in the past, I suspect you feel something about it now, as you talk to me. Can you tell me what that feeling is?"

IF Client seems to be

NOT CHECKING: i.e. If client seems to be rushing, not taking much care to sense what they are feeling,

        THEN   Ask client to see if words, thoughts, images have corresponding feelings in the body which validate or invalidate the words.

E.G.   "Can you stop for a moment and check with yourself to see if the words we're using really say your feelings right?"
        "See if there's any part of what you've been saying that doesn't quite feel like it fits."

IF Client's words seem

IMPRECISE: i.e. If client seems satisfied with inaccurate, approximate language for what is felt, or speculates deductively about the meaning of what is felt,

        THEN   Ask if he/she can find a quality–descriptive "handle" for the feelings: a word or phrase that says exactly how it feels inside.

E.G.   "Take a moment to try to find a word or phrase that says precisely what you feel in your middle about this."
         "Let's try to be a little more careful about how we describe what you feel. Try to say it just right."
         "Maybe that's what you should feel, or what someone told you to feel, but I'm interested in what you do feel."

IF Client seems to be

thinking
"NOW WHAT?":   i.e. If client seems to be in touch with feelings, but not know what to do with them,

           THEN   Ask the person to find a quality descriptive handle, or suggest an open–ended question for the person to ask him/herself.

E.G.   "You seem to have your feelings right there. Can you find a word or phrase or picture that really captures the essence of what you feel?"
         "What you might try next is to ask those feelings a friendly question, like 'what's the worst of this for me?'"

IF Client seems OVERLY

EVALUATIVE: i.e. If client is focusing, but reacting negatively to what comes from the felt sense,

           THEN   Encourage holding a non–evaluative attitude for a few minutes, being receptive and curious rather than critical. If the person seems unable to do this, reflect the "critical part" of the client which is doing the evaluating until it is accurately described, and then suggest setting that aside for a few minutes while the person describes how he/she feels inside.

E.G.   "See if you can just let your feelings talk for a while without criticizing them or reacting to them."
         "Sometimes our inner critic just won't quit. Can you put that part of you aside for a few minutes?"

IF Client reports body

feelings that are
JUST PHYSICAL: i.e. If client has physical sensations, but maybe not a body sense of the issue,
           THEN   Ask about emotional qualities that come with the sensations, or ask if the client can tell what circumstances produce the sensations.

E.G.   "How do you feel emotionally in connection with those physical sensations?"
         "Do you have a sense what situation makes your body react that way?"

IF Client has CONFLICTING

FEELINGS: i.e. If client definitely has feelings happening, but some feelings seem to oppose others,
           THEN   Ask the client to describe the body quality that comes in response to the conflict or ask how it feels to have this conflict going on.

E.G.   "How do you feel about having those opposing feelings inside of you?"
         "When you think of those conflicting feelings, how do you feel in the middle of your body?"

EVERY ATTEMPT TO GUIDE SHOULD BE FOLLOWED BY AN EMPATHIC RESPONSE TO THE CLIENT'S REACTION.

APPENDIX B: BRIEF THERAPY SESSION REPORT

Feel free to specify between-point marks, or extend the scales. Please add comments, if you like.
1. How do you feel about the session which you have just completed? (circle the one answer which best applies.)

THIS SESSION WAS:
1. Perfect.
2. Excellent.
3. Very good.
4. Pretty good.
5. Fair.
6. Pretty poor.
7. Very poor.

2. To what extent did the "doorway" to your feelings open in this session?
1. Not at all.   I felt closed and guarded.
2. Slightly.   At least once in the session I definitely felt something.
3. Quite a bit.   At a few points, I was in touch with feelings.
4. A lot.   Several times in the session, some feelings opened up.
5. Extensively.   Deep feelings opened up and moved me in unexpected ways.

3. In approximately what proportions did you and the therapist influence the course of the session?
   (i.e. decide what to talk about, change the subject, do the talking, etc.)
1. 20% therapist— 80% me
2. 40% therapist — 60% me
3. 50% therapist — 50% me
4. 60% therapist — 40% me
5. 80% therapist — 20% me

4. How well did your therapist seem to understand what you were feeling and thinking in this session?

MY THERAPIST...
1. Understood exactly how I thought and felt.
2. Understood very well how I thought and felt.
3. Understood pretty well, but there were some things he/she didn't seem to grasp.
4. Didn't understand too well how I thought and felt.
5. Misunderstood how I thought and felt.

5. How helpful do you feel your therapist was to you this session?
1. Completely helpful.
2. Very helpful.
3. Pretty helpful.
4. Somewhat helpful.
5. Slightly helpful.
6. Not at all helpful.

6. How much did the session leave you with changed or new perspectives on the matters you talked about?
1. Extremely much. Things look dramatically different to me now.
2. Very much.   There has been a definite shift in my perspective.
3. Some.   My view is slightly different than before the session.
4. Not much.   My views are pretty much the same.
5. Not at all.   Everything seems just as it was.

7. To what extent do you feel you were able to talk about what was valuable for you to discuss?
1.Completely.   Everything covered felt important/valuable to talk about.
2.Very much.   Most of the session was very valuable to me.
3. Pretty much. Some of the discussion was very good, some so-so.
4. Somewhat.   Some stretches of the session were not so useful to me.
5. Not much.   We didn't talk about much of real importance to me.
6. Not at all. We talked about things of minor or no importance to me.

8. In the context of all the therapeutic conversations you've ever had (with therapists or friends), how does this one compare?
THIS SESSION WAS...
    1. Terrible.   It was worse than any other I have had.
    2. Poor.   It ranks among some of the worst I've had.
    3. Below average.
    4. Average.   This one was comparable to many. Useful, but not great, nor was it lacking in any major way.
    5. Better than average.
    6. Excellent. It was one of the best I've ever had.
    7. Superlative. It was better than any other I have had.

9. Please rate the following two aspects of your feelings.

a. Do you feel any better after this session?

    1. No. I feel worse.
    2. No. I feel just the same.
    3. A little better, but not much.
    4. Yes, there is some relief or improvement in how I feel.
    5. A lot. I feel distinctly better.
    6. A great deal. I really feel better than I did before the session.

b. How were you feeling at the very beginning of the session?

    1. Pretty fine.

    2. O.K.

    3. Not very well.

10. Please rate the following two aspects of the emotional intensity of the session:

a. How intense was the most intense emotion you felt?

    1. extremely intense
    2. very intense
    3. mildly intense
    4. not very intense
    5. not at all intense

b. How much of the time was spent discussing topics of that intensity?

    1. none
    2. very little
    3. some
    4. pretty much
    5. very much
    6. nearly all

11. To what extent were you able to hold an attitude of friendly curiosity toward the emotions, feelings, and thoughts you experienced during the session?

    1. Not at all.   I had a lot of disapproval, dislike, or self-criticism about them.
    2. Barely.   There were only moments of friendly curiosity.
    3. Pretty much. But there were a few times I was unable to have a friendly attitude.
    4. Nearly the whole time.
    5. Completely. I didn't waver from friendly curiosity toward my feelings & thoughts.

For the next three questions, choose the one best answer in each case.

12. Did your listener give you any advice or suggestions about what you could do to improve your situation?

[ ] Yes
[ ] No

13. Did your listener make any suggestions about how to relate to your feelings, or how to work on them?

[ ] No
[ ] Yes

14. How often did your listener verbalize what he/she understood you to be saying?

[ ] every step of the way Ä regularly and often
[ ] from time to time, after major points

An Analysis of Ten Demonstration Interviews by Carl Rogers: Implications for the Training of Client–Centred Counsellors.

T. MERRY

LONDON

ABSTRACT

This paper presents a study of the transcripts of ten of Rogers' "demonstration interviews". Each interview lasted approximately 30 minutes, so a total of approximately five hours of counselling was involved. The method chosen was to examine each of Carl Rogers' responses to his clients, and to attempt to classify each response into one of a number of categories. The total number of responses examined was 640. Responses that consisted of one or two words only, "Okay", "I see", "Hmm", etc. were excluded, though these responses might have been important in that they indicated an attentiveness and awareness on Rogers' part.

Brodley and Brody (1990), in a similar study, categorised the overwhelming proportion (92%) of Rogers' responses as "empathic checking responses", in which Rogers responded "to the client's frame of reference, not the therapist's frame of reference." In this paper, Brodley and Brody remark that, "This type of responsiveness tends to keep the attention and the focus of the interaction within the realm of interests of the client and under the client's control."

The present study was undertaken in an effort to determine the extent to which client–centred counselling, at least as practised by Carl Rogers, showed a consistent pattern of responding to different clients. If such a pattern did emerge, it might be argued that client–centred counselling consists of counsellors acquiring a repertoire of counselling skills (expressed as communication skills, or techniques) which then become mobilised in predictable ways in response to specific client statements. This would tend to contradict the hypothesis advanced by Rogers and others (e.g. Rogers 1957) that effective client–centred counselling depends for its success on the quality of the client/counsellor relationship, rather than on the systematic application of counselling techniques.

The aims of this study, therefore, were firstly to replicate the research of Brodley and Brody (1990), secondly to extend their research with a more differentiated analysis of empathic checking responses (referred to in this paper as "empathic following"), and thirdly to explore fundamental issues for the training of client–centred counsellors.

METHOD

An initial reading of the transcripts suggested that it would be useful to employ the term "empathic following", as one of the categories of Rogers' responses (category 1). Other categories suggested by an initial reading of the transcripts were, 2) "direct questions", 3) "referrals to self", and 4) "offering observations".

The transcripts were then read again, and each of Rogers' counselling responses was placed in the appropriate category. This process showed that empathic following was overwhelmingly the largest category, and it was decided to break this category into five further subdivisions : i) responses using the second person, ("You feel..", "You seem to be saying..." etc.) ii) responses using the first person, where Rogers spoke as if he were the client, iii) formulating the implied question, where Rogers gave voice to the unspoken question in a client's statement, iv) tentative inquiry, in which Rogers included remarks such as, "Is this the way it feels?", or, "Is that what you mean?") v) using metaphors or similes in which Rogers either originated a metaphor, or included one offered initially by the client.

Category 2 is Direct Questions. This category included all responses in which Rogers asked for more information, or asked the client to say more about a particular feeling, idea or experience, e.g. "Can you say more about that?"

Category 3 is Referrals to Self, where Rogers included something from his own past or present experience, thoughts or feelings, e.g. "It occurs to me that...", "I like her", (referring to the client describing the "little child part of me"), "I appreciate being with you."

Category 4 is Offering Observations, in which Rogers commented on something about his client's present way of being, e.g. "You look more peaceful", "You have your standards though", "That was quite a strong statement..."

A second rater separately rated the interviews. Using Pearson's rho test, the observed value of $r = 0.977$ was greater than the critical value of $r = 0.925$ (p < 0 .001, 6 df; 2 tailed test), giving a high inter–rater reliability.

RESULTS AND DISCUSSION

Results, in table form show a) the percentage distribution of categories across all ten transcripts (Table 1), and b) the percentage distribution of each category in each transcript (Table 2).

Category	% occurrence
1.i Second person reflections	62
1.ii First person reflections	10
1.iii Formulates implied question	5
1.iv Tentative inquiry	6
1.v Metaphors/similes	6
2 Asks direct question	2
3 Refers to self	8
4 Offers observation	2

Table 1: Distribution of categories over all ten transcripts (figures rounded up and down).

Category	T1	T2	T3	T4	T5	T6	T7	T8	T9	T10
1.i	51	66	68	58	57	70	68	70	59	56
1.ii	9	12	11	8	11	5	10	12	10	14
1.iii	5	1	3	0	3	15	2	9	3	7
1.iv	9	11	6	10	3	1	8	1	3	6

1.v	5	3	4	4	19	0	5	0	8	6
2	3	1	2	4	0	1	2	0	2	1
3	15	4	6	14	5	8	4	7	10	3
4	3	2	0	2	1	0	1	1	5	6

Table 2: Percentage distribution of each category in each transcript (figures rounded up and down).

1) Empathic Following

Consistent with the Brodley and Brody (1990) study, the present study shows that approximately 89% of all Rogers' responses took the form of empathic following. In other words, 570 of the 640 responses examined were direct responses to the client in which Rogers attempted to communicate his understanding of the client's present state of awareness and experiencing and/or to check the accuracy of his understanding. An analysis of the five subdivisions of this major category is given below.

i) Accurate Empathic Reflection (Second Person)

The term "reflection" is not without its problems. It can imply a rather passive activity in which the therapist is merely repeating clients' words back to them. The term "reflection of feelings" can also be misinterpreted, and as Brodley (1992) points out, client–centred empathy refers to a client's total frame of reference, which includes feelings, but also includes perceptions, ideas and meanings. I am using the term ' accurate empathic reflection" to indicate the active process of listening, checking, exploring, and finally communicating the present level of understanding of the client's experiencing and expression of that experiencing. Accurate empathic reflection using the second person ("You feel...etc) was by far the most common way, (occurring in about 62% of all responses), for Rogers to communicate his understanding. Mainly, he used either exactly the same "feeling words" as the client, or very close approximations that did not add anything to the client's statements of experiencing, or remove anything.

An example is:

Example (1)

Client : ...so I want to be in touch with my feelings, this, uh,...yes... but not in this way, because here I am, and I can't even do what I...uh, like it's... taking up all of me.

Rogers : You want to get in touch with your feelings, but you don't want to drown in them.

Client : Right.

Accurate empathic reflections of this kind were often very brief, such as "You're really quite fearful of what other people might do to you", and "Sounds like you might like to be held, but not gripped", "You're just as frustrated as Hell", to quite complex statements, capturing a range of emotions, " It seems to me you're having a number of feelings right now. You felt frightened; you still realise you are frightened underneath; you're risking; you're feeling comfortable. All kinds of different feelings right here."

That accurate empathic reflection can involve complex feelings, emotions and meanings is illustrated by a further example. "Seems like you can't possibly free yourself from something that is so deep it's right down to the level of every cell in your body. That you're not permitted to be out there."

Very few of Rogers' counselling responses took the form of "advanced" empathic statements that gave expression to a feeling or perception not already expressed in some form by the client. In other words, it was rare for Rogers to include in any response, reference to anything that was not already within the client's experiencing (the number of occasions found in the sample was about one per cent). Whenever he did so, it was always framed in a very tentative manner. Two examples :

Example (2)

Client : Yeah! I feel getting in touch with things again! If I think about these things, I get sort of – reality is so absurd that I, I really have to see that I get in touch with reality again. I will touch things, or at home I grab my cat or something...

Rogers : Somehow have to keep your feet on the ground somehow, or touching something that's real. And I guess that most likely would be... is to touch something that is real in other people too. Client : Yeah, yeah, yeah. Get into touch with people...(etc)

Example (3)

Client : Yeah, very much that. That's entirely it. And now, I am slowly constructing, I feel, an identity that is me — I don't know if I'm constructing something or just dis...uncovering it. I think it's more uncovering than it is constructing.

Rogers : You were discovering a self of your own ... but it sounds as if it's still rather fragile.

ii) Accurate Empathic Reflection (First Person)

The second most common method Rogers had in offering his understanding of his client's experiencing was by speaking in the first person – saying something as if he were the client. About 10% of the total number of responses took this form. Again, they were usually concerned with what the client had expressed in words, they did not attempt to suggest any "deeper" feelings, or to express "hidden" feelings. Rogers often used the same words as the client, or words that were very close in both emotional intensity and meaning. First person reflections were accurate, as shown by client reactions ("Yes, exactly", "That's right", etc.)

Examples are :

Example (4)

Client : [Cries] I can't say anything! ...I really want to, I really want to live, and I think I really, I have a very – I really like living [cries] it's just...

Rogers : It's just a plea: I love life, I want to live. I want to be alive.

Client : [Crying] Yeah. Yeah. [Stammering] I'm so afraid it could be taken away at any minute.

Example (5)

Client : Very much so. What's the extreme end of it, and uh, will it result in a fight? And if it resulted in a fight, would I lose? And then how would I look? Not so much the fight.

Rogers : So it's uh, suppose I lost, then how would I look? How would I look to myself; how would I look to others? A defeated person. Hmmm?

Client : Sort of mocked: (chuckling) he lost; here he is.

iii) Formulating the implied question

A further way Rogers sometimes used (about 5%) to express his present level of understanding was to formulate the question implied in a client's statement. Two examples can be found with the same client :

Example (6)

Client : Yeah. And sometimes in the past when I've had friends who said, "Yeah, we want you to come and visit," and I'm wondering —"Well, what do these people see in me?"

Rogers : Why would they want me to visit?

Example (7)

Client (continuation from above) : Yeah. I've never really done much for them and things, why do they like my company? And now I'm starting to sense that maybe — and also sometimes there have been situations where I accept — maybe intellectually I can accept the fact that maybe they see me as a nice person. But I feel that I've never, we've never been in many situations where I've been able to demonstrate this, or show them, so how do they perceive this?

Rogers : How could they possibly care about me when they haven't seen me do anything? They haven't uh, had much chance. And yet they seem to care for me.

iv) Tentative Inquiry

Whenever he felt some uncertainty, Rogers would check his level of understanding by offering a response in a tentative, exploratory manner, and by underlining his tentativeness with a question or by employing a sensitive questioning manner. About 6% of all responses took this form. For example, "So, you're saying your mother was the model for this organising self. Is that what you're..?", or "A need to hang on so you can kind of make up for the things you feel guilty about –is that part of it?" In fact, when listening to Rogers' tapes it becomes clear that many of his responses were put quite tentatively, especially early in the interview. This is more evident in the tapes through tone of voice and inflection than on the printed page, as would be expected.

v) Metaphors and Similes

Rogers sometimes used metaphor or simile (about 6% of all responses) as part of his communication, but usually only when the metaphor or simile had first been introduced by the client. Whenever such a figure of speech was introduced, however, Rogers always subsequently used it himself. From the ten transcripts, there were only three occasions (two from the same transcript) when Rogers offered a simile himself, and on two of these occasions the simile was rejected as at least partially inaccurate:

Example (8)

Client : So you can see where that puts me. In the...

Rogers : Kind of behind the eight–ball, I guess.

Client : Well, no, I'm farther.. I'm as far as Pluto. That's pretty cold too, but uh...

Rogers : You're way out in cold outer space.

Client : In orbit.

Rogers : In orbit.

Example (9)

Client : Well, my outlook isn't dim, but it's not the shiniest

thing in the world either.

Rogers : Umm. It's about 15 watts.

Client : Maybe 25.

On both these occasions the simile was rejected, not in principle, but because it didn't go quite far enough in capturing the client's experience. The simile was still helpful, though, in that the client subsequently used it to clarify meaning. There was one occasion found in the transcripts where the simile originated from Rogers and was accepted by the client:

Example (10)

Rogers : Maybe the plant is growing and becoming more sturdy and it won't be buffeted about by the wind so easily.

Client : Yeah... And I've got to, I, I, it's a good image because I've got... at the present time I feel... very often I've got to protect that plant against the wind and stuff.

Rogers : Needs a... needs a sort of fence around it to protect it or something.

When a client introduced a metaphor or simile, Rogers always incorporated it in subsequent responses :

Example (11)

Client : Then I'm down. Then I'm like a ship that's just, uh, caught at sea and floundering – I can't get back up.

Rogers : Yeah. I sort of get the feeling you're saying there...

Client : Sink or swim, and I'm not sinking yet.

Rogers : ...these decisions that I feel are mine – – that's my ship, and if I ever let go of that I'd really sink, or I'd be a ship without a rudder, I really wouldn't, I wouldn't have anything.

Example (12)

Client : Not lose control but be controlled, yeah. Being tied up... just the image I have is like an octopus holding me, you know, I just can't get loose... Being taken where I don't want to go... where I'm not ready to go.

Rogers : That's one picture you have of a relationship ... is of

an octopus. Many tentacles that would just hold you down.

2. Direct Questions

This analysis of the transcripts shows that Rogers asked very few direct questions. Thirteen direct questions were found in the ten transcripts examined – about 2% of the total number of responses. Direct questions included, " Can you say more about that fear? What's the feeling of fear?", "Can you say more about the sadness? I'm not quite clear about what it is that feels sad.", "Can you tell him that?", and "Is that what you're fearful of?" Almost all of the direct questions, however, were invitations to say more about a partially expressed feeling, thought or experience, they were not concerned with the "facts" of a client's life. For example, Rogers did not ask questions like, "How many brothers do you have?", or "Do you love your mother?" or "How long have you had these feelings".

Allied to this were the very few (less than 1%) occasions when Rogers would directly ask his client for clarification of something he felt he had not sufficiently understood. For example, "Not quite sure I got that, you mean friendship is a necessary first step, is that what you're saying, or..?", and "I'm not really quite clear, ... is the, um, control and the distancing yourself from people two different issues, or are they the same ... the same issue?" These kinds of responses would contain what Rogers believed his client meant, followed by an explicit " checking out" of its accuracy. His "style" was to say what amounted to, "This is what I've understood about this, but I'm not sure I've got it right." Looked at this way, these kinds of questions also serve to communicate understanding, or at least the genuine attempt to understand.

3. Referrals to Self

Occasionally, (about 8% of total responses), Rogers would offer something to his client that originated from within Rogers' own frame of reference, either in the form of present experiencing or past experiences. Examples of present experiencing include, "I'm, I'm really interested in that experience, when you were away from him, then there was just a little while when it felt safe", "Uh–huh, that's what I was sort of thinking, you've thought your way this far, but then when you do..." and. " It occurs to me you probably wouldn't think of treating your daughter as badly as you treat yourself".

Although the relationship and its qualities are of prime importance in client–centred counselling, there were very few instances found where Rogers made a direct comment about the relationship or his feelings towards the client. Two examples are from the same transcript, "I feel a little baffled by you. And I don't know why", and, "I feel so much more real in my relationship to you than a little while ago."

4. Offering Observations

About 2% of Rogers' responses were formulated as observations about his client's behaviour, presentation or "way of being". For example, "You look more peaceful", "But you know that... your whole face lights up with the idea of a relationship that might open up new and uncharted possibilities, but, wow!, that's also scary", and, "Now I'm seeing a whole different side to you".

Only three times did Rogers offer some experience of his own that was connected with his client's expression, but not directly included in it : "That's one of the most tiring things I know", "I don't know whether it will help you any or not, but I...I don't have any friends my age. I can't stand 'em," and, "The Chinese have a saying – a journey of a thousand miles begins with one step".

GENERAL DISCUSSION AND IMPLICATIONS FOR COUNSELLOR TRAINING

Rogers empathy was built on a purposeful, frequent, restating of a client's communication, capturing it accurately and with the unspoken questions, "Is this what you mean", and "Have I got it right so far?" It was, therefore, clients who deepened the emotional mood of their encounters with Rogers, not Rogers by communicating advanced empathy. This is the very essence of client–centred work; direction and "depth" are matters for clients to decide. Clients explore and communicate more of their inner worlds as a consequence of counsellors' communicating accurate understanding of their clients' present experiencing, as far as clients are able to express it in the immediate moment.

Attempts at referring to unexpressed feelings or emotions, or feelings and emotions that were not within the client's present awareness, were very rare in Rogers' work. There is no sense that Rogers looked for "hidden" feelings, and there were no occasions in any of the transcripts in which Rogers attempted to deepen a client's experiencing directly. Only very rarely did he include in his response reference to a possible feeling (or idea) that had not already been directly or obliquely expressed by his client. (See examples 2 and 3 above). He did not make connections between one experience or set of experiences and similar ones; in other words, he did not "integrate" for the client, though examples of clients integrating experiences for themselves can be found.

Rogers was, in other words, supremely good at staying within his clients' frames of reference. That 89% of all his responses were concerned to express and/or check his understanding of his clients' communication testifies to this. Even though he was not averse to communicating something of his own emotional state, or his own experience, (and both of these, by definition, lie outside the client's frames of reference), actual examples of him doing this are quite rare.

The transcripts do not reveal a systematic application of "skills" or "techniques". There can be no doubt that Rogers was a skilled communicator, and a highly skilled listener, but his communication was simple, economical and idiosyncratic in the sense of personal or individual. One does not get the impression that Rogers' method was to employ a specific linguistic device in response to a specific form of client statement. My impression is, for example, that when Rogers asked a direct question it was because he wanted to know the answer, not because he thought that asking a direct question would be more effective counselling than, say, a reflection.

If Rogers' method was based on the application of skills or techniques, then there should firstly be a variety of skills and techniques observed, and secondly, they would be employed fairly consistently from one counselling interview to the next. This analysis shows a variety of ways in which Rogers communicated with his clients, even though the major method was by offering accurate empathic reflections. The use of "second person reflections" does show some consistency across all ten transcripts and it was the most common form of empathic following. However, the two sub–categories "first person reflections", and "tentative inquiry", for example, present a different picture. If these were simply skills or techniques, it would be reasonable to expect them to occur in roughly the same proportions from one client to the next, especially as all ten interviews were first interviews conducted under similar circumstances. However, first person reflections ranged from 5% of all responses in one case, to 12% or over in three cases. The distribution for tentative inquiry is from 1% of all responses in 2 cases, to between 6% and 11% in 6 cases.

The total number of occurrences of each of these two sub–categories is not large and, therefore, statistical conclusions are of limited value, although first person reflections do account for 10% of all responses. However, it is valid to draw at least the tentative conclusion that there is no consistent application of identifiable skills or techniques in Rogers pattern of communication. The relationships Rogers formed with clients showed a remarkable consistency in that his overwhelming interest was in understanding them coupled with his ability to communicate that understanding. However, the specific way in which Rogers related to each client, as shown by the different ways he chose to communicate his understanding, does vary quite considerably from one client to the next.

The possible exception to this is the largest sub–category (second person accurate empathic reflections). The average percentage occurrence of this form of empathic following was 62%

with a distribution across the ten transcripts of between 51% and 70%, still quite a significant variation. Furthermore, as has already been pointed out, the range of responses included in this sub–category is enormously wide and involves both very simple responses and very complex ones.

This does seem to support the belief that client–centred counselling should not, indeed cannot, be taught as a method in which counselling responses to particular client statements can be learned. In terms of training, it does seem much more appropriate to support trainees' attempts and intentions to understand their clients as far as their clients are presently able to express themselves, and to experiment with their own personal ways of communicating that understanding. It would most probably, for example, be a disaster for someone to adopt speaking in the first person simply because Rogers had shown that for him it was a natural and effective means of expression.

The need that some counsellors have (both beginning counsellors and experienced ones) to be able to sense hidden feelings, or to "hear" feelings that are not yet being expressed appears not to be supported by the data presented here. Empathy, at least as Rogers practised it, consists of the ability to hear feelings, ideas, emotions and meanings that are being expressed. The skill seems to lie in being able to hear those things when they are only tentatively or obliquely communicated, and then to find a way that fits within the counsellor's natural communication patterns of giving them some expression. But it is definitely not the case that Rogers specifically looked for obliquely or tentatively expressed emotions etc. or gave them more (or less) value than directly expressed emotions, etc.

One of the criticisms of discussing client–centred counselling in terms of skills is that it moves the emphasis away from "a way of being" to "a way of doing". The focus is then on "technical responding and leads to the emphases on such conceptualisations as reflecting, client–centred listening, client–centred communication and so on" (Bozarth, 1992). I understand and concur with this criticism, and the analysis given here shows that it is inappropriate to describe client–centred counselling in terms of the systematic application of "technical responding". I agree with Bozarth's (1992) remark that, "It has been my notion that therapist responses may be idiosyncratic to the client, therapist, and the unique relationship". The analysis of the ten transcripts presented here tends to support Bozarth's notion. There is evidence that Rogers responded to different clients in different ways; the underlying intention appears to be a consistent attempt empathically to follow and hence to understand each client afresh.

Brodley (1992) makes the remark that an effect of consistent empathic understanding "is that clients tend to become more consistently and intently focussed on and expressive of the experiential source of what they are talking about". However, it is a subtle but nonetheless crucial point, that the counsellor's intention is not, in client–centred therapy, to produce any particular effect, including a "focussing" effect. Brodley (1992) makes this point very strongly. This study shows that Rogers successfully attempted empathically to understand his clients as deeply as he could, approaching each new person in the same spirit of open communication. Nothing more, and nothing less.

It may be that, for some, the categories chosen to represent Rogers' personal style of communication seem somewhat arbitrary. Perhaps other categories could have been chosen, and some "pieces" of communication could have been put in different categories, or in more than one category. It is most certainly not the intention of this paper to provide a checklist of client–centred ways of communicating with clients. It is also true that the ten interviews used in this paper were all first interviews under "demonstration conditions". It is possible that

Rogers' pattern of communication changed as relationships with individual clients matured. There is some evidence for this observed in Rogers' comment on his interview with Sylvia Slack, "Sylvia is quite correct in her perception of my responses in the second interview. I felt her strength and, hence, was willing to expose more of me and my values in my responses" (Rogers, 1985) . (The Slack interviews were not included in the present work.) However, a reading of the case of "Mrs. Oak", as given in Wedding and Corsini (1989), does not reveal any major variation in Rogers' way of responding from the data presented here. For example, even in the extract from the thirty–ninth interview with Mrs. Oak, Rogers stays within his client's frame of reference and responds empathically to it. There are no examples given in the series of interviews with Mrs. Oak of Rogers responding any differently from his responses summarised in this paper. A typical response from Rogers to Mrs. Oak, taken from the thirty–fifth interview is as follows:

> Rogers: Does this catch it? That as you've gone more deeply into yourself, and as you think about the kind of things that you've discovered and learned and so on, the conviction grows very, very strong that no matter how far you go, the things that you're going to find are not dire and awful. They have a very different character.
>
> Client: Yes, something like that.

If we are prepared to accept Carl Rogers as a model to be influenced and guided by (but not copied or mimicked), then, it seems, we will accept i) an assumption that the actualising tendency is the only motivation of human behaviour, ii) each individual has the capacity for self (and organismic) actualisation, iii) the communication of empathic understanding, personal congruence and non–judgemental respect are necessary and sufficient counsellor activities, and iv) each counselling relationship is a unique product of the interaction between the two people involved, although there are recognisably consistent elements.

These four guiding principles should form the basis of a training in client–centred counselling, but only one of them (iii) is a matter of skill acquisition. Obviously, broader issues to do with counselling psychology, comparisons between competing theories, awareness of the social context of counselling (including issues of race, gender, sexuality, etc.), clinical and professional issues (including supervision of clinical practice) and so on, would be included in any worthwhile counsellor training. In the main, however, this study shows that client–centred counsellor training should emphasise working towards the "psychological maturity" of counsellors so that they are secure enough to enter into relationships that focus almost exclusively on the frames of reference of clients, rather than primarily on the acquisition of skills. In client–centred terms, skills are the means by which counsellors translate their values, attitudes and qualities into observable behaviour. It is essential that the particular means chosen by each counsellor to communicate the "core qualities" is a natural product of each counsellor's personality and preference. In other words, a way of being, rather than a way of doing.

REFERENCES :

Bozarth, J. (1992) *Coterminous intermingling of doing and being in Person–Centred Therapy*, Person–Centred Journal, Vol 1, No.1.

Brodley, B. (1992) *Empathic understanding and feelings in Client–Centred Therapy*, Person–Centred Journal, Vol 1, No.1

Brodley, B., & Brody, A (1990). *Understanding Client–Centred Therapy through interviews conducted by Carl Rogers. Paper presented for the panel Fifty Years of Client–Centred Therapy* : Recent Research, at American Psychological Association annual meeting in Boston, Ma., USA.

Rogers, C.R. (1957) *The necessary and sufficient conditions of psychotherapeutic personality change*. Journal of Consulting Psychology, (21) 95–103

Rogers, C.R. (1985) *Comment on Slack's article. Journal of Humanistic Psychology*, 25 (2), 43–44.

Wedding, D., & Corsiri, R.J. (1989) *Case Studies in Psychotherapy*. F.E. Peackock Publishers Inc.

Single women in their fifties:
Autonomous, agentic, affiliative & happy

SUZANNE M. SPECTOR

CALIFORNIA

ABSTRACT

This study was undertaken to explore the subjective, self–reported experience of single women in their fifties who, by their own definitions, felt good about themselves and their lives. Twenty women who were divorced, separated, widowed, or never–married were interviewed in the United States, Great Britain, Japan, Russia, and Uzbekistan. Unstructured interviews allowed the participants to explore the phenomenon in their own terms. Three major themes emerged from the data: Identity, agency, and connection. Data synthesis suggests a joining of an autonomous, agentic, differentiated self and connection to others in an ever–shifting figure:ground unity. Identity and agency are experienced and expressed in relation to self and in relation to others. The decade between fifty and sixty is experienced as a prime time of self realization.

This study was undertaken to explore the subjective, self–reported experience of single women in their fifties who, by their own definitions, feel good about themselves and their lives. The intersection of three variables was investigated – the decade between age fifty and sixty in the life cycle; the phenomenon of being single heterosexual women – either divorced, separated, widowed or never–married; and the phenomenon of feeling good about themselves and their lives. Interest in these combined phenomena grew out of the author's own experience which contrasted greatly with the old image of the depressed, dried– up, "over–the hill," lonely post–menopausal single woman.

Review of the literature revealed a dearth of information about this decade, lost between interest in midlife crisis and menopause on one hand and gerontology on the other. Because the social movements of the 1960s and 70s profoundly changed the context in which single women live today, past studies of single women are no longer relevant. More recent studies tend to be about older or younger single women, married women, or clinical populations. This is the first cohort to enter their fifties with twenty to thirty years of the Western women's movement in their lived history. Having learned to value and give voice to their own experience, they are not "over the hill." In fact, they feel better about themselves than ever before. The study of these single women has much to contribute to a fuller understanding of women's development that is not limited to married or clinical populations. With millions of baby boomers turning fifty in the next few years, the need for data about positive role models is urgent.

Twenty single women were interviewed in the United States, Great Britain, Japan and the former Soviet Union. Data are presented in Tables 1 – 4. The seventy–five percent who had been married all had children. The majority was educated and leading middle–class professional lives, though, for some, it had taken many years to achieve this status. Although all were heterosexual, Sang's (1991) study of lesbians at mid–life presents similar findings. This was a purposive sample to illuminate the phenomenon of women who felt good about themselves and their lives. The multiplicity of cultures highlighted the diversities and the similarities of women's experience. The focus was not on the cultures, but on the women's perception of themselves and their experiences within their cultures. While multi–cultural, the sample was predominantly ethnic majorities, middle–class, and educated. Participants were located from programs in the Rogerian person–centered approach or from connections with people associated with those activities. Consequently, a particular limitation was that half of the sample had some training in this approach which promotes genuiness, acceptance, and empathic understanding of self and others, qualities which contribute to self and life satisfaction. All participants were interviewed by the author for one and one–half to four hours. An unstructured format allowed the participants' own meanings to emerge within their own contexts (Weiss, 1981). Three major themes emerged: identity, agency, and connection.

IDENTITY: These single women in their fifties, across cultures, feel better about themselves – more whole, competent, secure, and authentic – than they ever did before. Most have integrated many aspects of their personalities and their histories into coherent identities. These identities are also fluid, sustained across and constructed within a multiplicity of relationships. Identities are derived from external connections to family, friends, work, and other activities, as well as from internal connections to self, inner voice, and spirit. As these women matured, they began to rely more on their internal process and less on connections for affirmation of identity.

Many described one or more crises or crossroads in their lives and, particularly, a turning point in their forties, from which emerged a consolidated, positive sense of self. As they describe themselves, the overriding quality is a sense of being or in the process of becoming who they want to be. Alice, an American counselor said:

> Since I became fifty, my sense of who I am and what I know how to do and that I know how to do some things really, really well have come together in a whole new way for me. Knowing and appreciating and feeling comfortable about who I am, I feel settled about myself in a way that I never did before.

Haruko, a Japanese dressmaking teacher, described a turning point in her life about four years ago at age forty–eight. She said,"I felt like a worm coming up from the ground, but unlike the worm, I did not feel able to move freely. Now I am slowly able to start walking on my own."

Without necessarily generating a crisis, midlife, generally, at least triggers a period of assessment. Exploring the unasked questions "who am I?" and "who do I want to be?" leads to a period of integration of various aspects of self into a more whole person. For many, this actualization process involves a recent integration of more "masculine" and/or "feminine" qualities into their being. Maggie, a fifty–two year old English social work administrator, describes this process:

> I've just gone though a great big period of integration that was important. Since entering the crossroads around two years ago, acknowledging myself professionally and trusting that life will bring creative opportunities, I've been on a big inward journey in which I've collected up the male and female bits of myself and brought them together. I feel so alive as a woman and better with myself than I've ever felt and I haven't been in an ongoing relationship with a man for four years now. Because I feel really complete, I can actually face the prospect of celibacy for the rest of my life without feeling, "God, how terrrible," whereas a while ago that would have felt dreadful. I have recognized that what I used to look for in a man to provide are aspects of myself.

The integrated maturity of these women encompasses diverse, sometimes paradoxical elements. Maggie describes "a playful, childlike part" of herself as well as "a deep sadness."

I've always been a positive, optimistic person, but I've also come to see the dark, not as negative but as unseen. Because I can now see the possibility for total destruction and hold it in one hand without denial, I can also have hope for the future and optimism in the other hand. Without denying the negative, I can feel a lot of happy energy and lightness bubbling through me and I'm really enjoying going with that and experiencing the fun, flirtatious parts of myself as well as the intense serious parts. Without going into deep depression, I can feel really sad for the world and sometimes for myself.

For some this integration has meant realizing new aspects of themselves, while for others it has meant re-emergence of qualities from childhood, adolescence, or before their marriages. Sandi, an American therapist, felt like a "bird with one wing" when her husband left her, although she had been a very independent child. When she married at eighteen, she became fused in the "we" of marriage. For her, this decade since her divorce at forty-eight has been a time of not only becoming financially independent, but of remembering, reconnecting, and re-owning her capabilities.

The sense of identity of women in their fifties is usually more multi-dimensional than the self-images they had when they were younger. Jen, an English activist, used to judge herself for "being all over the place and not having just one shape," but then:

I realized with amazement that all these different facets of me were real and that I was solid inside, but the people out there in life were doing their damndest to split me up. I think it's important for women to hold all the different parts of themselves – to know it's all right to dive naked into the pond one night, cuddle your grandchildren the next night and make passionate love the night after that.

NOW SHE APPRECIATES THE "FULLNESS" OF WHO SHE IS

Creativity and spirituality are other aspects of self that single women in their fifties value in their identities. When Mako, a Japanese secretary who never married, was in her late forties, she took up painting so that she would have some expression of herself "to leave in the world instead of children." She has won three awards as an amateur painter and notes, "You might expect dark paintings from someone that had my sad childhood and never experienced the love of a mother, but my paintings are gay and happy because they express the love of Jesus Christ." While her Christian spirit has been at the core of her being since her early twenties, many other women have discovered or reconnected to their spirituality in their fifties.

For many of the women in this study, individual psychotherapy and group psychotherapy, counseling training, support and consciousness raising groups were important vehicles for self-transformation. Unhappy with who they were or how things were, or simply wanting to continue growing, women who wanted to change themselves found others, lay and professional, to help them heal the wounds in their personal and social histories and move on to creating satisfying lives. Ealasaid, a thirty-six year old Scottish widow discovered that she "really was an acceptable person" when she enrolled in a training workshop for counselors in the person-centered approach. Getting some sense of how other people saw her and why they liked her "had a very powerful shaping effect " on her life as she continued developing herself personally and professionally through the workshops and connections with others in this field. This secular belief in and practice of the person-centered approach which began in her thirties led to later development of spirituality. This was true for other women in the study as well, Ealasaid described her life in terms of the triple goddess symbolism of the maiden, the mother and the crone which characterize the stages of woman's life in feminist spirituality:

By tracing my origins of myself as a little girl these last few years, I've been much more able to honor the mother, and connect with the maiden. Now I'm coming into the wonderful mystery of that third stage, wondering what it will hold and bringing it together as a whole with the other two.

To feminist Jungians menopause is viewed as an initiation into a new mode of creativity. When women lose the ability to create babies, they gain the ability to create wisdom from the experience of their lives (Bolen, 1994). To tap this wisdom after years of busy lives, many women, particularly those who raised children, describe their enjoyment of solitude as a time to be quiet and reflective, to listen to their inner voices, feel their feelings, and tap into their spiritual connection to all life. Kathleen, an English woman, enjoying her own house with her own room for the very first time in her life now, remembers reading "solitude described as the richness of spirit and loneliness as the poverty of spirit."

For these single women in their fifties in all the cultures studied, particularly for those who were previously married, identity development has involved a process of individuation, of seeing themselves as individuals, more differentiated and less fused in the relational context. While connections are still important to them, they experience themselves as more separate and whole in their relationships and in other aspects of their lives. About marrying at eighteen, Sandi, the American therapist, said:

I gave up myself and got pregnant right away. The new life growing inside my tummy decided when I slept and when I went to the bathroom and everything that I did from then on. I had no sense of separateness.

For thirty years she totally defined herself as a wife and mother.When her husband left she seriously considered taking an overdose of pills. But now, after a decade on her own, her self-definition is based on who she is as her own person rather in familial roles. Using a tennis metaphor, she says:

The pivotal point of self-definition is like the difference between playing singles or doubles. I really liked doubles, liked the sense of shared partnership. I remember saying to Bob when he left that I could handle all the tragedies, all that went on, as long as I had someone to share it with. I felt terrified at how to do that alone. Interestingly, in tennis I always preferred to play singles because I liked being responsible for the whole court and moving up or back, faster or slower, knowing exactly where I was without having to consider another person.

Several women express an awareness of what is unknown or undone – of pieces of themselves they want to work on, and the growth ahead. Some voice a strong sense of self-responsibility. One asks, "If I'm not as loving or at peace as I want to be, what is in me that I need to clear up; what is blocking that achievement of a way of being?" No longer is responsibility projected onto externals, other than the unavailability of suitable men. Even the absence of a male partner, several women say, is because they are learning to be complete in themselves and not looking to a relationship with a man to give them wholeness. Some fear that they would not be able to maintain their differentiated identity, freedom, and independence if they were coupled. They choose to remain single rather than giving up their freedom. Some muse about an ideal partner with whom they could have intimacy and mutuality while maintaining their autonomous identities.

AGENCY: There is no word in the English language that quite captures the quality of women's experience of acting in the world. The word *agency* is used here in its definition as a "state of being in action or of exerting power." The more common usage of the word pertains to acting on behalf of another which is, of course, most characteristic of women's lives. Bakan (1966) used the word *agency*, manifested in "self–protection, self–assertion and self–expansion" to differentiate the organism as an individual from the *communion* of the organism as a part of a larger context . Somewhere between Bakan's self–centered definition and the common usage of acting on behalf of another, a definition of agency is needed that continues to derive from the Latin root *agere*, to do, and encompasses acting on behalf of both self and other. This agency is affiliative – not so connected as to disregard self, yet not so autonomous as to disregard others.

The picture of typical women's development focused on the care and empowerment of others has been exquisitely drawn by feminist psychologists (Chodorow, 1978; Miller, 1976/86; Jordan et.al., 1991; Gilligan, 1982). All of the women in the study who had married describe their earlier lives in these terms – acting on behalf of others and responding to circumstances and others' needs. In return for nurturing and empowering their husbands and children, the Western women expected to be supported financially and to feel complete as part of a couple. As homemakers, several carried illusions about their husbands' roles, when, in fact, they, not their husbands were the competent ones in the family. The women of the former Soviet Union also fulfilled the nurturing role and they had careers. As a consequence of their financial independence and their identities at work outside their families, it was easier for some of these women to leave their marriages than it was for Western and Japanese women.

Much of these women's agency is responsive rather than initiative. Only a few women spoke of consciously planning, making decisions, and acting to further long–term goals. For all the rest, no matter how creatively they responded to circumstances and how well they did whatever needed to be done, it took many years to become conscious of their own competence and of their "right" to act on their own behalf. Raised on the 'ethic of care' for others (Gilligan, 1982), to act for themselves may have first seemed immoral, or at least unnatural. The phrase "bird with one wing" which defined Sandi's identity when her husband left also defined her feeling about agency. She did not feel capable of surviving on her own. Now she realizes with amazement that she really did a great deal and he was never there in any of the family crises. She has had to rewrite her own story to acknowledge the competence she did not acknowledge during thirty years of marriage.

Being or becoming single was a catalyst that promoted agency for women as they faced taking responsibility for themselves and often their children and/or parents. However, agency usually develops as an evolutionary process that accelerates as it becomes conscious. Joanne recalls a powerful experience when she was still married:

> I wanted to see the United States and not be like my parents with unfulfilled dreams. So I packed my four children into the station wagon, went to AAA for a map, and headed west on a cross country trip without my husband. That was a turning point in my life. I was thirty–nine. Within the first three hours on the road, I felt this absolutely enormous freedom. I felt so proud. I made every decision. Not that I hadn't made the decisions before, I just hadn't realized it.

Since domestic work is not valued, work outside of the home for pay provides a path to agency for most women. Almost all of the women in this study work full time and have worked their entire adult lives or at least since they got divorced. They receive a great deal of satisfaction from their jobs. A few are passionate about their work and a major part of their social lives revolves around work and people from work. Some have been in the same job for many years and others free–lance or change jobs periodically and expect to keep doing that. Work furnishes not only external rewards, but also the satisfaction of expressing a social self through participation in the larger culture beyond the family (Lee, 1987/1959). Most did not consciously choose their work as a job or career initially. Several started out as volunteers and were not even conscious of their need for self-expression. Their work is viewed as both an integral expression of self and a way of helping others. Almost all are employed in facilitating and nurturing the development of others. A few are reluctant to label this "career." Alice said:

> I feel really blessed that my way of being a therapist and a trainer of therapists matches my intention in life of being loving. I don't have to shift my being at all from work to not work. When I was teaching in the college, I didn't become a teacher when I walked into the classroom, it was all who I am.

Strikingly absent in these women's narratives is any sense of conflict between their personal integrity and their ways of being in the world. If, at earlier points in their lives, they felt conflict about acting on behalf of self instead of only supporting and facilitating the growth of others, by their fifties this conflict has been resolved and they feel comfortable with and capable of with making choices for themselves, while maintaining connections with others.

In the context of the women's movement, agency for self became both their right and their responsibility. Several women were very competent in their jobs in their twenties, but did not pay attention to their competence or their satisfaction because they were "on the way to the wedding." Even those who did not marry, expected that they would. Maggie's story illustrates this phenonemon and the evolution of agency. Before she married at thirty she had a full–time job as a social worker and a part–time job three evenings a week as a counselor at a university. Not only didn't she see herself as a professional person, she had the notion that if you were a professional woman, you had to repress your sexuality. Role models of career women with families were rare for this cohort. The models of professional women that existed were of women who sacrificed everything for their careers. When "the crunch came" for Maggie after she married, she realized she was not ready to sacrifice her career either. She kept the part–time counseling job at the university throughout her marriage and feels very fortunate that she was able to have both career and family.

After her divorce, Maggie moved from the counseling service and took a development and training job in social services. She never imagined herself becoming a manager of a service but now she is the manager of the mental health services for a four hundred square mile area. She describes her work style:

> Some people thought I would not be strong enough to cope with the job because I'm more transparent than most people. I don't hide behind a role or cover up my mistakes. I tend to work in a much more organic way than men in similar positions who prefer a lot of structure and getting it right, rather than working with the flow. I'm rigorous enough in looking at standards of service and quality of work and I'm realistic about what can be achieved and without illusions about the institution. But, I also believe in encouraging people and that the best can happen. Because I'm not cynical like many in the social service culture, and employ staff who are creative and have similar attitudes, we create a positive culture and make things possible. I receive positive feedback from my boss and have credibility with colleagues who recognize me as a human being and appreciate how supportive I am and how I recognize the stresses people are under.

THIS IS A VERY FEMALE STYLE OF MANAGEMENT THAT SHE HAS EVOLVED

At this point in their lives, the personal authority with which these women act in the world is grounded in the knowledge and wisdom they have gained from their accumulated life experience. Like many of the women, Maggie has now begun to speak out which she never did before. She does not always have to prepare a speech. Sometimes she will stand up spontaneously and speak publicly about her work or mental health issues because she is confident about what she knows.

While most women express themselves in response to circumstances and needs and some, like Maggie, develop a female style of management, some follow a more traditional masculine path to agency. Naoko is clear about her goals and takes the necessary steps to achieve them. After college, she earned a very good income working part–time as an interpreter in Tokyo where she was exposed to American values. She came from a wealthy family and was particular about the men she dated because she saw her mother as unhappily married. When she was twenty–eight, her mother died and she took over as the dutiful daughter to a "feudalistic" father. After five years, she decided to make a life for herself as an unmarried corporate executive instead of fulfilling traditional Japanese women's roles as either daughter or wife. Assessing her career after she returned to Japan with an American M.B.A., she said:

> I decided to protect myself from being judged 'over the hill' by developing a strategy to improve my marketability. I requested this job in sales so that I would have a unique position for myself as a marketing person who knows sales...The current popular cultural images of the career woman, even in American movies, do not convey the realities of the hard work involved and the extra hard work to overcome male resistance.

Often women have to overcome incredible obstacles to realize their dreams. Haruko tells a story of single–minded purposefulness to become the kind of student–centered teacher she first dreamed of being when she was in junior high school in a tiny mountain village in Japan. Overcoming intense familial resistance to preparing for any role other than dutiful wife, she convinced her parents to allow her to go to dressmaking school which was still within the womanly arts. At age twenty–eight she moved to Tokyo to become a dressmaking teacher. On her own, she learned to cope with urban life and, one course at a time, earned her college degree at age forty–five and her teaching license two years later.

Agency is expressed not only in work, but in lifestyle choices and priorities. Kathleen, a working class English woman who started college and then graduate schools after her children were grown, is not being seduced by her career success and is asking herself when she is going to do all the things she wants to do. She has decided to shift from full–time to part–time employment so that she can do more creative arts activities. To do that, she will "eat jam sandwiches" so that she will have enough for the mortgage and the essentials. She says:

> I feel that time is more important to me than money now. Although my decision will effect my pension, I'm clear that more and more I just need to live in the present; that all I've got is now. I want to explore for myself some things I've never had time for.

Since this study was designed to explore the phenomenon of women who felt good about their lives, it was biased toward zestful women while excluding those more victimized by social, economic, emotional or physical circumstances. Only one women in the study mentioned menopausal difficulty, supporting Greenwood's (1984) medical findings that women who had interesting jobs, steady incomes and a sense of purpose usually report fewer problems with menopause than women who view it as a crisis. Contrary to the medicalization of menopause and recent popularization of a menopause crisis by feminist authors (Sheehy, 1992; Greer, 1992), these single women were, for the most part, actively engaged in their lives and feeling good physically and emotionally without taking hormone replacements.

While agency is usually associated with control over one's life, these women also speak of the paradox of not having control or of choosing not to try to control life. Perhaps, for all of the women who were married and had children, this knowledge of lack of control comes partly from the fact that so much of their earlier lives was tied into the family life cycle. Yet, within the context of lack of control of external events, the women spoke of freedom and self–direction and self–responsibility. The sense of agency seems to revolve around choice. Even those who do not have work as a deep source of satisfaction and sense of purpose, nevertheless, experience agency in their ability to express themselves and to make choices. For most of them agency means that, while life presents the circumstance, what they do with it, what meaning they make of it, and how they act on it is up to them. Reflecting on the spiritual practice that supported her through the loss of her business and subsequent brain tumor surgery, an American woman said:

> Now I feel my wisdom in knowing that everything is important and that nothing is important and I try to maintain that position. When I do, my life is really fun. I make a conscious choice now to view my life from this spiritual perspective, as a life that I chose, instead of telling my story from a "poor me, why me?" victim place that gets a lot of sympathy.

In retrospect, one of the most empowering experiences in many of these women's lives was the decision and action to get out of their marriages, no matter how painful leaving was at the time. For women whose husbands left them, the divorce was even more problematic than for women who ultimately took action to get out of a situation that was not working for them. For women who never married, there was a clear sense of empowerment from the lives they have created for themselves. For all of the women, agency means power – power to choose and to act on their own behalf as well as to nurture and empower others. There is a synergistic relationship between their inner confidence and their potency in the world. Now they are living more fully in the present, listening to their inner voices as the guide for what they want to do, and trusting that the future will take care of itself. Their agency is not usually expressed in opposition to others or without care and responsibility for others. Their autonomy is affiliative.

CONNECTION: This study explores whether the importance of connection in women's development continues to hold in the sixth decade of single women's lives. Caring about others is an intrinsic part of who these women are as human beings.They invested much of themselves in relationships and from connections they have derived much of their sense of being and belonging. Now, in their fifties, many are less directly responsible for the development of others than they were in the past, particularly those who had been married and had raised children. As they went through the process of becoming more autonomous, they were particularly dependent on their connections with friends, lovers, therapists, as well as other sources of emotional support and validation such as growth and training groups. Having derived a sense of identity from significant relationships in the past and other life experiences as well, most of these women feel secure now about who they are. That is not to say that connections are no longer important to them. On the contrary, because they are more differentiated and more authentic and empathic with themselves, they are also able to bring these qualities into their relaltionships. Knowing themselves more fully, they have more of themselves to give in their connections with others. Giving more, they receive more in relationships that are mutual and reciprocal. Consequently, they may experience more intimacy in their relationships than when they were younger. In short, their relationships today may be characterized by less intensity, dependency, or unilaterality, and by more genuineness, mutuality, and intimacy. Refuting Gutmann's (1987) (1992) theory of contrasexual development with men becoming more intimate and women more autonomous as they age, these women are developing their capacities for both intimacy and autonomy.

Continued connection to their families of origin is important to some women, while others feel closer and have more in common with friends than with siblings and other relatives. The only clear pattern that was discernible within or between cultures was that women who never married did not want lives like their mothers. Across cultures, those whose parents are still alive feel an increased sense of responsibility for them, as others felt for widowed parents throughout their lives.

Those who are mothers continue to feel concern for their children, whether their relationships remain parental or have become more mutual now. Perhaps because they are single and have learned to take responsibility for their own lives, it may be easier for them to accept their children's independence and self-direction and their need to take risks and make their own mistakes. Speaking of her daughters, one says,"I think our relationships are so good because I don't live my life through them. I live my own life and encourage them in living theirs." Although they may be very separate from their children geographically, these connections remain very important. One sums up the significance:

> Sometimes I think that my connection to my family is an illusion and that I'm really on my own or ought to be. But when I think about how I would feel if I didn't have my son and daughter, I realize that I would feel diminished, that I wouldn't be the same person.

MOST OF THE NEVER-MARRIED WOMEN ALSO SPOKE OF DEEP CONNECTIONS TO NIECES OR NEPHEWS

Friends, particularly women friends, are crucially important to most single women. Friends provide acceptance, companionship, support, sharing, mutuality, affirmation, and intimacy. These qualities are often experienced in varying degrees through a network of friendships, rather than being contributed and received in one primary relationship. As is the case with familial relationships, friendships do not have to involve regular contact for them to have deep meaning to the participants. Many women feel connected to friends who are geographically distant. These include old friends as well as more recent connections with those with whom they have shared intimate experiences in training groups and travels. Once intimacy has been established, it generally remains, renewed with each contact as if there were no separation. Some single women feel that they give and receive more now than when they were committed to and restricted by a primary relationship.

With more self-understanding and openness to their inner feelings, they no longer need others to the same degree to help them process and understand their experience. Particularly those who raised families may now be turning on themselves some of the energy and attention they formerly directed to the care of others. In learning to take care of themselves, they have become less embedded in relationships. Although processing feelings and experience is a valued activity for many women across cultures, as women get older and more confident in their perceptions of themselves and others, they may choose to do this more as a solitary activity.

Several mention the challenge of balancing work and friendships with their deep need for time of their own now. Maggie describes the shift:

> I used to be very dependent on friends. When I had a problem, I had to get in touch with a friend and talk it all out. The friendship process for me and my friends was based on the need to relate our anxieties and problems. Those friendships have survived and moved to different levels as we've become much more complete and able to handle some of the things alone.

The openness and honesty in their closest friendships is remarkable. Describing a thirty year friendship, Sharon said:

> In some ways, she's like a "life partner." I plan and live my own life – not around her, but we're there for each other. This relationship affirms and support me just as I am. I can share my lowest self and deepest insecurities and still be accepted by her. In fact, we help each other do that. We've cared for each other during physical and emotional life crises and we've shared a lot of personal and spiritual growth experiences over the years. We have no physical or sexual attraction to each other and we do not choose to live together, but we do cherish our connection.

Sometimes women know each other in multiple roles in additon to their friendship. Several mentioned close friends who are also their professional supervisors, and with whom they also work closely as peers, as well as sharing family activities.

While single women may feel whole without a male partner, they nevertheless value male energy in their lives. Sandi explained:

> The male energy feels like my left arm, not my predominant energy, but necessary to balance all that I do. I'm very right–handed, not ambidextrous so I need the male counterpart.While you like following your own drummer, that gets a bit burdensome sometimes. You wish someone had some answers and males often will take that position. They really know and they'll tell you they know. We females leave things so much more ambiguous than they do. Men tend to make it black and white and sometimes that's real refreshing.

Most single women have some men in their social lives – sons or sons–in–law, male friends, connections with men at work, or short term or long term lovers , seen intermittently or regularly. On the whole, friendships with men, other than significant lovers, are not as potent a source of connection as friendships with women and relationships with family. A number of women spoke of connections with male colleagues which fill a variety of needs including guidance, affirmation, mutuality, collaboration, and companionship.

Relationships with lovers may provide deep intimacy, continuity, support, and acceptance while leaving women free to take care of themselves, express themselves, and create their own lives. Some women are not only content with, but may even choose, a sexual relationship that is circumscribed, neither interfering with other aspects of their lives, nor putting undue stress on a relationship that might be lacking in qualities desired in a full–time relationship. Naoko, the executive discusses a sexual relationship with a man whom she has known for fifteen years:

> Initially I was attracted to him because he had studied abroad and became a college pro-fessor at a very young age, but I have outgrown him mentally over the last ten years. The relationship is like staple food, not thrilling but comfortable. I would prefer a more

challenging relationship with someone else, but I'm too busy. I think about having a younger boyfriend to play with but I dont know if that would make me happy or sad.

As women talked about their various sexual connections with men, what their expectations were, and what the experiences meant, it was clear that for some there were valuable learning experiences, while for others, there was a good deal of pain and not much insight. One described a relationship in her late forties :

Literally and figuratively, I was a passenger in someone else's life, on the back of his motorcycle and the cabin of his sailboat. Since then, after I turned fifty, I've clearly chosen to be the creator of my life rather than losing my selfhood in coupledom. I only want mutuality in my relationships with men now and I'm happy to have that on a part-time basis.

Another sometimes feels sad about not being able to live out a complete male–female relationship, but she, too, allows herself to enjoy "incomplete relationships." She says:

At the present time I'm pleasantly physical with a man I see once a month at a meeting. We enjoy each other and touch. It's nourishing without going any further. It's nice to have those kinds of capsule experiences while not meeting men who are actually available for a full relationship.

Although some women still enjoy sexual relationships, or would enjoy them if they were available, most are no longer so dependent on them. They are unwilling to be as accommodating as they once were. One talked about the liberation of no longer needing "little hooks of old relationships to make me feel that I am attractive and desirable as a woman." Some accept or even prefer "incomplete" relationships, while others want only relationships with more spiritual connection and wholeness.

The theme of connection encompasses not only relationships, but participation in other activities such as women's groups therapy and training groups, professional study groups, as well as social, political, religious, creative and physical hobby groups. These connections affirm women's relational selves and fill their affiliative needs, in addition to frequently providing a pathway for agency, competence, and self–esteem. A Soviet woman said the Communist Party had been very attractive to her because she did not have a strong family life. For a Japanese woman, the Christian church substituted for the family she never had with either parents or marriage. Several women mentioned therapy as an important source of connection and support at various times in their lives. For half the women in the study, personal growth groups or person–centered training groups have been an important vehicle for self–exploration, self–acceptance and sometimes exquisite moments of connection with others. Those who are professionally involved now feel an additional level of belonging, support and affirmation as part of an international professional network.

Several women also spoke of their need to sometimes disconnect and be alone for balance. Many spoke of enjoying their own company more and valuing their solitude. Mary, a never married English woman said, "I used to feel something like a maypole, held up by all the connections with people. But now that's the wrong picture because the link goes more inside now, rather than exterior." In solitude, they have become intimate with themselves. In their aloneness, they quiet their minds, hear their inner voices, and, frequently experience profound levels of spiritual connection.

296

CONCLUSION:

The primacy of connection in the theories about the development of women may no longer quite fit the later phases of women's lives or the lives of women for whom autonomy and intimacy are more equally weighted. Learning to take care of themselves, whether by choice or necessity, single women develop identities that are more differentiated and less embedded in relationship than their coupled sisters in the same cohort. The fear of abandonment or loss of significant relationship is no longer an external deterrent to self–development and self–expression. By the time they reach their fifties, they have had sufficient life experience to view themselves and life from an expanded perspective. They can see themselves more as the creators of their own lives in terms of how they cope, what choices they make, and what they learn from experience. They are more conscious of their personal power and responsibility than before, yet they are less reactive and enmeshed in the dramas of life. Paradoxically, they also know that they cannot control the flow of life. Because they are more confident and authentic, they are capable of creating more intimacy in their associations. Most of their relationships with men and women, but primarily with women, are of their own choosing and are characterized by mutuality and reciprocity. Although deeply connected to family, friends, work, affiliation groups, the community and, for many, the universe, they are less dependent on these roles and relationships for their primary sense of integrated identity and personal agency.

Most of the self–in–relation theorists, in doing the necessary and critical job of defining who women are and how they are, have focused on the connection aspect of their being which, as this study demonstrates, is no longer sufficient. Although autonomy has been redefined in feminist theory as the ability to act freely within relationship, it is still considered within the context of connections that either support or constrict self–expression. If not actively present before, the autonomous agent has emerged in the midlife of these single women. Most have found authentic ways to be effective in the world using their affiliative strengths. What these findings illuminate is a female autonomy, defined as being free, independent, and self–governing in a genuine, effective, affiliative way.

Rather than *self–in–connection* (Miller, 1986/76, Jordan et al., 1991) these findings suggest *self and connection* – a bi–phasic construction that joins an autonomous, agentic, differentiated self with connection to others in an ever–shifting figure:ground unity. For these single women in their fifties, identity and agency are experienced and expressed in relation to self and in relation to others. Their autonomy is defined by the ground of connection and their connection by the ground of autonomous self. The decade between fifty and sixty is experienced as a prime time of self–realization for these single women in several countries.

REFERENCES

Bakan, D. (1966). *The duality of human experience*. Chicago: Rand McNally.
Bolen, J. (1994). *Crossing to Avalon*. San Francisco: Harper Collins.
Chodorow, N. (1978). *The reproduction of mothering: Psychoanalysis and the sociology of gender*. Berkeley: University of California Press.
Gilligan, C. (1982). *In a different voice: Psychological theory and women's development*. Cambridge, MA: Harvard University Press.
Greenwood, S. (1984). *Menopause naturally: Preparing for the second half of life*. (Rev. Ed.). Volcano, CA: Volcano Press.
Gutmann, D. (1992). *Beyond nurture: Developmental perspectives on the vital older woman*. In Kerns,V. & Brown, J. K(Eds.), In her prime: New views of middle–aged women. (pp. 221–233). Urbana: University of Illinois Press.

Gutmann, D. L. (1987). *Reclaimed powers: Toward a new psychology of men and women in later life*. New York: Easic.

Greer, G. (1992). *The change: Women, aging and menopause*. New York: Alfred Knopf.

Lee, D. (1987, 1959) *Freedom and culture*. Prospect Heights, Illinois: Waveland Press.

Jordan, J., Kaplan, A, Miller, J.B. Stiver, F. Surrey, J. (1991). *Women's growth in connection*. New York: Guilford.

Miller, J. B. (1986). *Toward a new psychology of women*. (2nd Ed) Boston: Beacon.

Sang, B., Warshow, J., & Smith, A. J. (Eds.). (1991). *Lesbians at midlife: The creative transition*. San Francisco: Spinsters.

Spector, S. (1992). *Realizing their prime: A study of single women in their fifties*. Ann Arbor, MI: UMI Dissertation Services.

Sheehy, G. (1992). *The silent passage*. New York: Random House.

Weiss, H. B. (1981, March). *The contributions of qualitative methods to the feminist research process*. Paper presented to the National Meetings of the Association for Women in Psychology, Boston.

Client–centered Psychotherapy according to the Differential Incongruence Model (DIM)

GERT–WALTER SPEIERER

REGENSBURG

ABSTRACT

The Differential Incongruence–Model (DIM) (Speierer 1994) provides Client–centered Psychotherapy a new and self–reliant theory of disorder on the basis of the incongruence–paradigm, which was introduced by Rogers. Hypotheses of different origins of incongruence, different criteria of incongruence and an incongruence–related classification of disorders allows within the DIM and the framework of Client–centered Psychotherapy to meet the needs of persons with all sorts of psychic disorders according to DSM–III–R and ICD–10 definitions. By the abandonment of the theoretical and therapeutical uniformity–assumptions of the concept of the basic variables and by the redefinition of "Gesprächspsychotherapie" as the treatment of incongruence, the DIM opens the door for a multimodal therapy of the person. The therapy–options can now be offered specifically and variably according to the individual needs of the person and her disorder. The existence and the sources of the individual's experience of incongruence, which are postulated by the model, serve hereby as requirements and guidelines of the indication of client–centered–psychotherapy options also beyond the three basic variables or therapeutic attitudes. The general and specific incongruence–theory of psychic disorders, which was anew developed with the DIM, as well as the therapeutic options, which were derived from it, have been largely confirmed by empirical investigations, primarily of therapy–transcripts. The work was done by using partly existent instruments, partly methods were newly developed. The empirical results in favor of the DIM can continuously be validated or modified by further clinical and empirical research.

Five years ago the first outline of ' a specific illness concept for client–centered psychotherapy (CCT)" was presented in the book "Client–centered and Experiential Psychotherapy in the Nineties" (edited by Litaer, Rombauts & van Balen) (Speierer, 1990a).

It's main theses were:

1. Incongruence is the central construct of the client–centered illness concept.

2. Incongruence is an unpleasant self–endangering experience of which the client is at least partially conscious.

3. The incongruence concept of CCT goes far beyond the psycho–analytic and other conflict–theory concepts of psychopathology.

4. The origins of the incongruence concept can be found in the well–known client–centered social–communicative factors. These factors were postulated in the form of deficits of unconditional positive regard, congruence, and empathy in childhood and later on in life, and in the form of incompatibility between societal and organismic values as a risk–factor of psychic disorder. A non–socially caused bio–neuropsychological inability to reach congruence was introduced as a second source of incongruence. A third source of incongruence was postulated with social and non–social life–changing events.

5. Neurotic disorders, personality disorders and psychotic disorders differ from each other due to differences in the presence or absence of conscious incongruence, and due to differences in the presence or absence of the cognitive, emotional and behavioral disturbances, which are characteristic of psychotic episodes.

6. Specific features of the incongruence dynamic of Dysthymia (formerly neurotic depression), psychological and behavioral factors associated with disorders classified elsewhere (formerly psychosomatic disorders) and of conversion disorders (formerly labeled hysterical neuroses) were proposed and casuistically demonstrated. They can be seen as the contribution of client–centered–therapy to a specific illness concept.

In the meantime the differential incongruence concept was further developed and elaborated into a comprehensive theory of psychic disorders within the client–centered framework: The Differential Incongruence Model (DIM).

The DIM was recently published in a German monograph "Das Differentielle Inkongruenzmodell: Gesprächspsychotherapie als Inkongruenzbehandlung" (Speierer, 1994).

The first part of this paper presents an overview of the Differential Incongruence Model. The second part refers to its impact and consequences for client–centered psychotherapeutic work.

1. THE DIM: AN OVERVIEW

Client–centered–therapy is, according to the redefinition of the DIM, the treatment of incongruence. Its general psychotherapeutic aims include the reduction of experienced incongruence, the improvement of coping with incongruence, the improvement of the ability to self–congruent experiencing, and the enlargement of incongruence tolerance. Within the DIM, the validation and the changing and further development of the existing general and specific hypotheses of incongruence are defined as a task of empirical investigations. Although the existing hypotheses have already been largely empirically confirmed by psychotherapy–transcript analyses of single cases and groups of patients, they may be refuted or changed by the evidence of new empirical data.

A summary of the DIM–relevant categories of transcript analyses, a transcript–analysis–sheet and a life–event–questionnaire are available (until now only in German).

Fig. 1 shows the present state of the DIM. Its hypotheses are arranged in five dimensions:

Fig. 1: Psychic Health and Psychopathology according to the Differential Incongruence Model (DIM): The five dimensions of the model

1. Conditions of Health and Psychopathologic Developments resp. Disorders	1.2 (bio/neuro-psychologic) disposition	1.1 social-communicative experiences	1.3 life events	
2. Psychohygie-nically and Psychopathologi-cally relevant Features of the Person	2.2 dynamic aspect I	The Self (Subject) 2.1 structural aspect II	2.3 dynamic aspect	
3. Psychohygienic and Psycho-pathogenetic Conception of the Model	3.1 congruence-theory	3.2 incongruence-theory and forms of incongruence dispositional i., social-communi-cative i., life-event-conditioned i., non-conflicting i., conflicting i.	3.3 other theories 3.3.1 biologic theories ° 3.3.2 psychologic theories 3.3.3 sociologic theories	
4. Healthy Live Development and Arrangement of Psycho- pathologic Developments	4.1 healthy psycholo-gic live development	4.2 p s y c h o - p a t h o l o g i c d e v e l o p - m e n t s 4.2.1 with partial incongruence resp. with precedence of incongruence 4.2.1.1 compensated disorders	4.2.1.2 decompen-sated disorders	4.2.2 without resp. with secondary or partial contribution of incongruence disorders and/or defects concerning cognit., emot. and behav. functions
5. Arrangement of Psychic Disorders (ICD-10) within the DIM	F0 organic, including symptomatic, mental disorders F1 mental & behav Disorders due to psychoactive substance use schizotypal and delusional disorders F2 schizophrenia, schizotypal and delusional disorders F3 mood (affective) disorders F34. d y s t h y m i a F40 phobic anxiety di F4 neurotic, stress related and somatoform disorders F41 o t h e r a r x i e t y d i s o r d e r s F42 o b s e s s i v e - c o m p u l s i v e d i s o r d e r F43 reaction to severe stress- and adjustment disorders F44 cissociative (conversion) disorders F45 somatoform disorders F48 other neurotic disorders F5 behav.syndr.assoc. physiol.disturbances & physical factors disorders F51 roneorganic sleep disorders F52 sexual dysfunction,not caused by organ.disorder or disease F53 mental and behavioural disorders assoc.with the puerperium F54 psychological and behavioural factors associated with disorders or diseases classified elsewhere F55 abuse substances F59 unspecified behavioural syndroms assoc. With physiological disturbances and physical factors F6 disorders of ad F60.31 emotionally unstable personality disorder (borderline) F7 mental retardation F8 d i s o r d e r s o f p s y c h o l o g i c a l d e v e l o p m e n t F9 behavioural and emotional disorders usually with onset in childhood and adolescence			

The first dimension of the DIM

The first dimension of the DIM covers the conditions of health and of psychopathologic developments or specific psychic disorders. Here, the DIM postulates the interaction between bio–neuropsychologic dispositions, social–communicative experiences and life events as either the main sources of psychic health or the development of psychic disorders with cognitive, emotional, behavioral, social and somatic symptoms. As I already pointed out, the DIM clearly complements the uniformity hypothesis regarding the social–communicative and societal origin of incongruence and the consecutive development of disturbances. This differential etiologic orientation of the DIM is a prerequisite for a differential theory of disorder and therapy.

The second dimension of the DIM

The second dimension of the DIM deals with the psychohygienic and psychopathogenetic relevant features of the self, i.e. the reflecting subject and his dynamic as well as structural aspects.

According to Rogers (1959a), the dynamic aspects (I) include the basic human needs of positive regard, congruence and empathy from other significant persons and the ability of self–

congruent experiencing. The dynamic aspects (I) also include the actualization–tendency, and in addition to Rogers' conceptualizations, the liability for self incongruence, i.e. self–endangering experiencing, incongruence tolerance and coping strategies for incongruence.

The dynamic aspects (II) refer to the conscious and current experiencing stemming from past, present, and future related events. The sources of these aspects are the person's actualization tendency, the personally significant relationships and the previously mentioned life events.

The structural aspects of the self include the current real and ideal self–concept, the organismic values and the conditions of worth according to Rogers (1959a). I extend his thesis and maintain that the structural aspects of the self also refer to the individual's personal constructs and to life–events i.e. personal life–style, life goals, and attitudes about the future.

The dynamic aspects of the self within the DIM do not include the constructs of defense, repression or the unconscious as a constituent of disorders. Therefore, the disorder theory of the DIM can be differentiated from psychoanalytic theory. The DIM postulates conscious experiencing of incongruence and not unconscious processes as source of psychogenic disorders. The deficient or sufficient strategies of coping with incongruence are significant aspects of the DIM disorder theory; however, the concept of defense, which is linked to concepts of the unconscious and of repression, is not essential for the DIM theory.

The third dimension of the DIM

The third dimension of the DIM first defines and phenomenologically differentiates the congruence theory of psychic health.

It includes the concept of the fully functioning person (Rogers 1959a) and its operationalisations with regard to the end stages of the process–scale (Rogers, 1959b; Tomlinson & Hart, 1962, 1970). In terms of the DIM, the healthy psychic development is called congruence dynamic. This dynamic has been broken down into 10 areas of self–references of patients at the end of successful client–centered therapies. The congruence dynamic was empirically validated by therapy–transcript analyses (Speierer, 1986, 1994).

Second, within the third dimension of the DIM, the incongruence theory and 5 forms of incongruence are defined and differentiated.

In general, incongruence is defined as the experiencing of incompatibility of, contradiction between, or of threat of personally relevant parts of experience to the current self–concept. The experience includes dispositional, social–communicative and life–event determined parts. The current self–concept is composed of organismic values, conditions of worth and live–event, life–style and life–perspective constructs. These constructs are summarized as life–experience constructs. The dispositional parts of the self–concept are, more specifically, composed of the individual's organismic "values," i.e. the individual's inherited or constitutional constructs, which allow him to evaluate more or less automatically all sorts of experience as congruent or incongruent and to react accordingly.

So the DIM differentiates dispositional, social–communicative and life–event determined forms of incongruence. Additionally the DIM differentiates two further forms of incongruence.

One is the conflicting incongruence. It results from differences within the individual's self–concept. These differences are between organismic values, the conditions of worth and the life–experience constructs. They constitute internal self–conflicts which have been discussed in the literature (e.g. Perrez, 1976).

The other form of incongruence is new within the DIM; it is the non–conflicting incongruence. This form is based on clinical evidence which has demonstrated that there are numerous patients who do not suffer from a conflicting incongruence. The non–conflicting incongruence experiencing, as it was shown by trans

cript–analyses (Speierer, 1990b), involves no source of contradiction within the self. The patient's self does not cause the suffering. It is the external sources of the suffering which endanger the self in a very holistic way. The individual does not show conflict behaviors as described by empirical conflict research. This non–conflicting incongruence is an important aspect of the DIM. It is also a point in favor of a genuine client–centered disorder theory.

The incongruence theory of psychic disorders includes the phenomenological operationalisations of process–scale's first stages (Rogers, 1959b, Tomlinson & Hart, 1962, 1970). In terms of the DIM the phenomena of incongruence are called incongruence–dynamic. The incongruence dynamic has been defined in 10 empirically validated areas of patients' self–references at the beginning of successful and to some extend non–successful client–centered therapies (Speierer, 1985, 1990c, 1994).

Third, within the third dimension of the DIM, other theories and results have been accepted. They also give plausible explanations for psychic disorders and provide other alternatives for therapeutic change. They can be integrated in client–centered therapy according to the DIM, as long as their hypotheses and results can also be interpreted by incongruence theory.

The fourth dimension of the DIM

The fourth dimension of the DIM deals with the nosological order. The psychopathological developments and disorders are accordingly arranged into three classes.

The first class of the DIM–nosology only includes disturbances with no or a secondary partial contribution of incongruence. Within this class, there are individuals who do not experience incongruence, because the disturbance is self–congruent (ego–synton). An example of this might be a person with a personality disorder, who predominantly suffers from a loss of control; this is mainly a problem for the people around the individual and not for the individual himself (ICD–10 F63). Additionally, there are individuals within the first class who do not experience the symptoms themselves and therefore their personal selves cannot be endangered. A clinical example would be a person with Alz– heimer's disease (ICD–10 F00). Individuals who are mentally retarded (ICD–10 F7) or who suffer from other organic disturbances may also belong to this group.

The second class of the DIM–nosology contains disturbances with a precedent or partial contribution of incongruence which has somehow been compensated for. Persons with compensated disorders show symptoms of incongruence, but they do not experience them as self–endangering, because they have sufficient coping strategies for incongruence and incongruence tolerance. Persons in the latency or compensatory state of incongruence may show compensated, for example phobic reactions (ICD–10 F40.2). These are individuals, who in their own experiencing successfully avoid endangering situations. For example, they do not enter a plane.

In the third nosological class of the DIM are disorders with decompensated precedent or partial experiencing of incongruence. These persons consciously experience internal sources of incon– gruence in addition to experiencing other sources of incongruence. They feel a motivation for psychotherapeutic work. Their actually existing incongruence tolerance and their coping–strategies for incongruence are not sufficient. They suffer from the incongruence because their self–concept is endangered by it. Nevertheless, the reflecting self is intact.

The fifth dimension dimension of the DIM

Within the scope of the DIM, its fifth dimension allows one to arrange the psychic disorders according to the International Classification of Diseases ICD–10 (World Health Organization, 1991).

With the exception of a few cases, most individuals with certain ICD–10 disorders can be located in the first class of the DIM, for example disorders with the classification ICD–10 F0, ICD–10 F6 and ICD–10 F7.

Persons with other disturbances according to the classification of the ICD–10 can, again with the exception of single cases, more often be located in the second or third class of the DIM–nosology, for example persons with the ICD–classifications F34.1, F40 – F44.

Persons with certain ICD–10 disorders can be looked at from a group perspective and, depending on time factors, can be located in all three classes of the DIM, for example persons with the ICD–10 disturbances F2, F3, F42, F8 and F9.

THE DIM'S APPLICATION AND ITS IMPACT
ON CLIENT–CENTERED PSYCHOTHERAPEUTIC WORK

The DIM provides client–centered therapy a new and self–reliant theory of general psychopathology and specific psychic disorders on the basis of the incongruence paradigm.

First, it allows the formulation of the congruence–dynamic as an empirically confirmed client–centered phenomenological concept of psychic health and the endpoint of successful client–centered therapy.

Second, the DIM defines the general incongruence–dynamic. It represents a client–centered phenomenological general concept of psychopathology which has been empirically confirmed. Persons with this "Gestalt" of experiencing can be most successfully treated with the original form of client–centered therapy.

Third, a concept for the investigation of disorder–specific incongruences as the basis of a client–centered differential theory of disorders has been developed with the help of the DIM. This concept is shown in figure 2.

Client Centered Psychotherapy according to the
Differential Incongruence Model (DIM)
Fig. 2: Etiological and Phenomenological Criteria for Incongruence–analysis
(Disorder specific incongruences as the basis for a differential disorder–theory in
client–centered psychotherapy)

Etiological criteria for incongruence:
Disorder specific sources of incongruence (pathogenesis)
o   dispositional aspects
o   social–communicative features
o   life–event determined parts
Phenomenologically relevant areas:
Disorder specific characteristics of the contents of incongruence (symptomatology)
o   the patients'(ideal)self–concept with its
      incongruence–enforcing (pathogenous) parts and
      strategies as well as its incongruence
      reducing (healthy) parts and strategies
o   self incongruent areas and incongruence
      equivalents within the current
      experiences
o   main topics of incongruence

(Copyright G.–W. Speierer, Regensburg 1/1993)

Fourth, client–centered therapy–transcripts and life–event questionnaires of patients with certain ICD–10 defined psychic disorders were quantitatively and qualitatively investigated within this framework. This lead to the formation of disorder–specific incongruence–dynamics. The following elements were included: disorder–specific sources including dispositional aspects, social–communicative features and life–event determined parts; phenomenological relevant areas and parts (in other words the disorder specific characteristics of the contents of incongruence); the patients (ideal) self–concept with its incon– gruence enforcing parts and strategies as well as its incongruence reducing parts and strategies; the self–incongruent areas and incongruence equivalents within the present experiences and the leading theme of incongruence. Up to now, disorder–specific incongruence dynamics have been published for persons with depressive, psychosomatic, delusional, somatoform and conversion disorders, as well as for persons with different forms of anxieties, obsessive–compulsive disorders and dependency of alcohol and drugs (Speierer 1994). Needless to say, all results of the DIM were grounded on empirical research. These results are open for falsification, modification, and/or revision by an enlarged data base.

Fifth the application of the DIM in client–centered therapy leads to several consequences for it's therapeutic practice. They are outlined in Figures 3, 4, 5 and 6.

Client Centered Psychotherapy according to the
Differential Incongruence Model (DIM)
Fig. 3: Consequences for the Practice of Client–centered Psychotherapy (CCT)

1. **Redefinition of CCT as therapy of incongruence**
2. **Differential diagnosis of incongruence:**
    Incongruence analysis
2.1 **Presence or lack of experiencing of incongruence**
2.2 **Etiological orientation: The distinction and weighting**
    of different sources of incongruence
2.2.1 (Disorder-specific) Dispositional sources of incongruence
2.2.2 Life-event determined sources of incongruence
2.2.3 Social-communicative sources of incongruence
2.3 **Phenomenological consideration: The differentiation of the individual**
    incongruence dynamic and contents
2.3.1 The self-(ideal)concept, the pathogenous incongruence-
    enforcing and healthy incongruence-reducing information
    processing strategies of the person (e.g. self-congruentexperiencing,
    incongruence tolerance)
2.3.2 The actual self-incongruent experiences and
    incongruence equivalents
2.3.3 The personally significant content of incongruence
2.4 **The nosological classification of the disorder**
2.4.1 Disorder without, with second order or partialcontribution of
    incongruence
2.4.2 Disorder with compensated incongruence
2.4.3 Disorder with precedent contribution of
    decompensated incongruence

(Copyright G.-W. Speierer, Regensburg 9/1994)

The first application of the DIM for the practice of client– centered therapy is its redefinition as incongruence–therapy.

Instead of defining client–centered therapy from its therapeutic conditions, the DIM favors a redefinition of client–centered–therapy through its therapeutic aims. These aims include: the resolution of incongruence, reducing incongruence, improving the coping with incongruence and enlarging incongruence tolerance.

The second application is the reintegration of diagnosis in client–centered therapy in the form of a differential analysis of incongruence. Its aim is to be able to make use of all client–centered knowledge about psychopathology.

Fig. 3 shows the content and possible results of the incongruence analyses. Its data can be taken from the first five contacts of client–centered therapies, in which the basic attitudes and open–ended incongruence–relevant questions are offered. According to Fig. 3, the analysis confirms the existence of incongruence in the suffering of the person (Fig. 3, 2.1). It includes the distinction and weighting of the three different sources of incongruence (Fig. 3, 2.2) as well as the phenomenological differentiation of the individual's incongruence–dynamic and – contents (Fig. 3, 2.3). Finally, the incongruence analysis leads to the classification of the disorder into the three classes of the DIM–nosology (Fig. 3, 2.4).

The third application consists of practically useful therapeutic options for client–centered therapy of incongruence which have been theoretically grounded (TOI). So, the futile and frustrating endeavors of the patient as well as of the therapist can be minimized by the DIM. Furthermore, the results of the incongruence analysis can, when necessary, open the door for a person's multi–modal therapy. Different therapy options can be offered according to the individual's needs and his disorder. A preliminary list of different communicative therapeutic options which were found in an empirical analysis of behavior of therapists using the DIM, is shown in Fig. 4.

Client–Centered Psychotherapy according
to the Differential Incongruence Model (DIM)
Fig. 4: Therapeutic Options within the DIM (preliminary results)

Basic Variables
unconditional positive regard
congruence
empathy, incl. verbalisation of emotional experiences

Additional Variables

immediacy of patient-therapist relationship
non-offending confrontation
self-disclosure
working with dreams
differentiation,concretisation. relativation, restriction
summarizing
non-specific (psychotherapy) informations
non-specific constructs (i.e. activation of experiencing)
non-specific strategies (i.e. experiencing-activation methods)

client-centered construct-information
(i.e. incongruence-concept, structural and dynamic
parts of self, concept of FFP resp. parts of it,
client-centered theory of disorder etc.)

client-centered strategy-information concern. treatment of
incongruence (pos. (self)regard, (self)empathy &
self)congruence,(differentiation, concretisation, relativation,
restriction

(behaviour-therapy-constructs
behaviour-therapy-strategies
psychoanalytic constructs
psychoanalytic strategies)

Focusing

sources of incongruence (etiology): dispositional, social-
communicative, life-events, and other biograph. Data, relations

between etiological data and onset of present disorder and
phenomena (symptoms/problems) of present state

relationship between actual symptoms, problems and present
experiences/experiencing

current experiences/experiencing: cognitions, emotions,
motives,
actions, personally relev. relationships, body-sensations
self(concept), wishes, ideals, aims (of being)
subjective meanings, evaluations, theory of disorder

incongruence between experience and self-concept
incongruence within the self(concept)
incongruence between different areas of experiences
relationship between patient and therapist
relation between former or present therapy and development of

symptoms, problems, disorder
coping-strategies for incongruence, also (specific) therap.
aids

Guidance
open undirected questions, requests, and incomplete sentences
open directed questions, requests, and incomplete sentences
closed questions
offering topics
active listening
(para)verbal encouragement, reinforcement

(Copyright G.-W. Speierer, Regensburg 9/1994)

Fig. 5 and Fig. 6 show six possible results of the incongruence analysis of persons with
clinically relevant disorders. Its applications for a non–indication or a positive indication of
TOI and some of its therapeutic options are outlined. As the clinical examples show, the DIM
application in client–centered therapy also allows for complex therapeutic plans.

**Client Centered Psychotherapy according to the
Differential Incongruence Model (DIM)
Fig. 5: Consequences for the Client–centered Practice of Psychotherapy:
Differential Therapy of Incongruence (TOI)**

1.   **A person with a psychic disorder who does   not experience incongruence**

      Clinical example: ICD-10 F20.5 Schizophrenic residuum

      Decision of indication: momentarily no TOI

2.   **A person with a psychic disorder experiencing compensated incongruence**

      Clinical example: ICD-10 Z03 Examination by forensic
      reasons

      Decision of indication: momentarily no TOI

3.   **A person with a psychic disorder experiencing decompensated
      incongruence and predominant social-communicative sources of
      incongruence**

      Clinical examples: ICD-10 F34.1 dysthymia, ICD-10 F4
      neurotic-, stress-related and somatoform disorders,
      ICD-10 F54 psychosomatic disorders

      Decision of indication and therapeutic options:
      TOI aimed at reducing incongruence,
      enlarging the ability of self-congruent experiences,
      improving incongruence tolerance and incongruence
      diminishing strategies. CCT basic- and eventually
      additional variables as well as experiencing
      activation methods. The focus of therapeutic work
      in single-, partner-, family- or group-therapy
      may be the self-concept or the experiences
(Copyright G.-W. Speierer, Regensburg 9/1994)

Client Centered Psychotherapy according to the Differential Incongruence Model (DIM)
Fig. 6: Consequences for the Client–centered Practice of Psychotherapy:
Differential Therapy of Incongruence (TOI) continued

4. **A person with a psychic disorder experiencing decompensated incongruence and predominant life-event determined external sources of incongruence**

    Clinical examples: ICD-10 F43 stress-related reactions and disorders of adaptation
    Decision of indication and therapeutic options:
    TOI first in the form of counseling concerning options of psychic, family, social, vocational, medical rehabilitation and changing the situation, aim-oriented reduction of the situative non-personal sources of incongruence

5. **A person with a psychic disorder experincing decompensated incongruence and predominant (disorder specific) dispositional sources of incongruence**

    Clinical examples: ICD-10 F06.4 organic anxiety disorder (e.g. malfunction of the thyroid gland), ICD-10 F23 transient acute psychotic disorders, ICD-10 F3 various forms of acute affective disorders
    Decision of indication and therapeutic options:
    TOI first in form of counseling concerning predominantly medical measures aimed at diminishing the disorder-specific dispositional sources of incongruence

6. **A person with a psychic disorder experiencing decompensated incongruence and dispositional, social-communicative and live-event determined sources of incongruence**

    Clinical example: ICD-10 F42 (Obsessive-compulsive disorder with depressive episodes and repeated aggressive behaviours between family members)
    Decision of indication and therapeutic options:
    TOI aimed at reducing intra-personal incongruence by offering individual therapy with basic variables, construct- and strategy-options; reducing interpersonal incongruence by offering additional family counseling; reducing dispositional incongruence by medically advised antidepressive medication

LITERATURE:

Perrez, M. (1974). *Gesprächspsychotherapie als Therapie inermal motivierter Konflikte*. In P. Jankowski, D. Tscheulin, H.-J. Fiekau & F. Mann (Hrsg.) Klientenzentrierte Psychotherapie heute. Bericht über den 1. Europ. Kongreß für Gesprächspsychotherapie in Würzburg 28.9.–4.10.74. Göttingen: Hogrefe (1976), 82–83.

Rogers, C.R. (1959a). *A theory of therapy, personality, and interpersonal relationships, as developed in the client–centered framework*. In: S. Koch (Ed.). Psychology, a study of a science. Vol. 3, 184–256. New York: Mac Graw Hill. (Dt. Übers.: Schriftenreihe der GwG 1987).

Rogers, C.R. (1959b). *A tentative scale for the measurement of process in psychotherapy*. In: *Research in psychotherapy*. Proceedings of a Conference, Washington 1958. Published by American Psychological Association, Washington.

Speierer, G.-W. (1986). *Selbstentfaltung in der Gesprächspsychotherapie*. Zeitschrift für personenzentrierte Psychologie und Psychotherapie, 5, 2, 165–181.

Speierer, G.-W. (1990a). *Toward a specific illness concept of client–centered therapy*. In: G. Litaer, J. Rombauts, J. & R. van Balen (Eds.) Client–Centered and Experiential Psychotherapy in the Nineties. Leuven: University Press, 337–359.

Speierer, G.-W. (1990b). *Zur Inkongruenzdynamik als spezifischem Indikationskriterium der Gesprächspsychotherapie bei hysterischen Neurosen*. Vortrag auf. AGG Symposion v. 2. 11.–4. 11. 1990 in Essen. In: J. Finke & L. Teusch (Hrsg.) (1991). Gesprächspsycho-therapie bei Neurosen und psychosomatischen Erkrankungen, Heidelberg: Asanger, 59–72.

Speierer, G.-W. (1990c). *Eine klientenzentrierte Krankheitstheorie für die Gesprächspsychotherapie*. In: G. Meyer–Cording & G.-W. Speierer (Hrsg.) Gesundheit und Krankheit, Köln: GwG, 86–114.

Speierer G.-W. (1994). *Das differentielle Inkongruenzmodell (DIM)*. Heidelberg: Asanger–Verlag

Tomlinson, T.M. & Hart, J.T. (1962). *A validation study of the process scale*. Journal of Counseling Psychology, 26, 74–78.

Tomlinson, T.M. & Hart, J.T. (1970). *A validation study of the process scale*. In: J.T. Hart & T.M. Tomlinson (Eds.) New Directions in Client–Centered Therapy, 206–213. Boston: Houghton Mifflin Co.

World Health Organization (WHO) (1991). *Tenth Revision of the International Classification of Diseases*, Chapter H (F): Mental and Behavioural Disorders (including disorders of psychological development). Clinical Descriptions and Diagnostic Guidelines.

An Analysis of Clients' Self-Narratives in Brief Experiential Psychotherapy

SHAKÉ G. TOUKMANIAN AND SANDRA JACKSON

YORK UNIVERSITY

ABSTRACT

This exploratory research was a study of the phenomenon of therapeutic change in a brief perceptually–oriented experiential therapy from the standpoint of changes reflected in clients' constructions of self–narratives. Self–relevant narratives, drawn from all therapy sessions of three good and three poor treatment outcome clients, were evaluated on three measures of client process, the Narrative Process Coding System (Angus & Hardtke, (1990), the Experiencing Scale (Klein et al., 1986) and the Levels of Client Perceptual Processing (Toukmanian, 1986). Data were analyzed descriptively for differential patterns of self–narrative processing across therapy. Results revealed a discriminating pattern for good outcome clients. It was found that, as therapy progressed, their constructions tended to be formulated more often from a reflexive than an external stance. These clients were also found to show a deeper level of experiential involvement in their constructions and to have a higher proportion of narratives formulated through the enactment of more complex mental operations (i.e., analytic, internally differentiating, re–evaluating and integrating) in later than earlier phases of therapy. The analyses yielded no consistent or therapeutically meaningful pattern in the processing of poor outcome clients on any of the measures across therapy. The results are discussed in view of the practice of experiential therapy.

Historically, psychology has been developed within the positivistic tradition of scientific inquiry. In this approach, the quest for "truth" is often judged successful to the extent that scientists are able to sift through information about a particular phenomenon and locate components of some a priorily held notion of external reality (Rorty, 1989). This approach assumes that there is a reality beyond our sense of experience and, in doing so, fails to recognize the impor- tance of subjectivity.

In contrast, the constructivist mode of inquiry is based on the fundamental premise that all knowledge, including scientific knowledge, is constructed by the knower (Fitzgerald, 1992; Howard, 1991). Thus, unlike the positivistic approach, it recognizes the uniqueness of the in- dividual and accordingly, seeks to provide explanations of phenomena that take into account the knower's own subjective experience (Rorty, 1989; Toukmanian & Rennie, 1992).

The impact of constructivist thinking on psychology is apparent in the growing literature on narrative forms of knowing (Fitzgerald, 1992; Polkinghorne, 1988). Recent work in psycho- therapy research also indicates that clients' narratives are increasingly being used for the explo- ration of the processes involved in client change both within and across therapy sessions (Angus & Hardtke, 1994; Chambon, 1991; Nye, 1990; Russel & van der Broek, in press; Rus- sell, 1991). However, as there are varying conceptions of what constitutes "narrative", the usefulness of this method of inquiry for psychotherapy process research is yet to be established.

In this presentation, our objective is (1) to provide an overview of existing perspectives on the relationship between narrative and the psychotherapeutic change process and (2) to present the results of a recent study which explored this process in brief perceptually–oriented experiential therapy from the vantage point of clients' self-narratives.

THE NARRATIVE PERSPECTIVE

Although the term narrative can be used to refer to various forms of communication, generally, it refers to a story and more specifically, to a story as both a process and an end product (Polkinghorne, 1988). In other words, the use of the term narrative implies a construction whereby different components of an experience are put together and organized into a story.

Human beings are narrators of stories. Narratives permeate all aspects of human life. We formulate them to describe and account for our actions as well as those of others. The stories we construct provide the substance of our self–identity. They enable us to perceive where we have been, where we are, and where we are going (Crites, 1986; Polkinghorne, 1988). In short, the narrative form of knowing is a defining characteristic of humanity and one of the few aspects of human nature that is common across cultures and time (Barthes, 1977; Fisher, 1984, 1985).

The Nature of Narrative

There are varying perspectives on the nature of narrative. Some contend that narrative is only a medium, albeit a central one, through which experiences are described and communicated (e.g., Gergen & Gergen, 1984, 1986). Others, however, argue that "truth" does not exist independent of the mind, that people have the ability to construct and describe their experiences of events through language and that it is this ability that gives "reality" its particular form and meaning (e.g., Howard, 1991; Rorty, 1989). From this vantage point, narrative is seen as being more than just a primary mode of communication; it is a fundamental process or an "organizing principle" by which various elements of an experience are contextualized and understood (e.g., Polkinghorne, 1988).

This latter view also implies that narratives perform important functions in the construction of meaning (Barthes, 1977). At an individual level, they provide us with a personal context in which our sense of the past, present and future, i.e., our "self–narrative" or "life–story", develops (e.g., Crites, 1986; Fisher, 1984). Narratives also serve a social function in that it is through our narratives, based on the shared reality of common beliefs and values, that we are able to participate in our social world (Polkinghorne, 1988; White, 1980).

Within the field of psychology, research involving narrative has passed through various phases – from early case studies based on personal stories and biographies, to investigations concerned with the role of language in people's acquisition, organization and communication of knowledge and, more recently, to studies examining the relationship between cognitive processes, experiencing and the construction of meaning via narratives (e.g., Angus & Hardtke, 1994; Bruner, 1990; Polkinghorne, 1988; Russell, van den Broek, Adams, Rosenberger, & Essig, 1991; van den Broek & Thurlow, 1991). By and large, a common theme underlying this body of research is that narratives are central to how people construct meaning about self and about events in their world.

The Narrative Schema

The view of narrative as a cognitive structure has evolved from contemporary schematic information processing formulations of cognitive–affective phenomena. These perspectives are based on the common assumption that the "mind" is an information processing system, that information is stored not as a reproduction but as a constructed abstraction and that the repre-

sentation of knowledge is the function of schemata which develop progressively through people's continuous interactions with the environment (e.g., Anderson, 1981; Neisser, 1976; Rumelhart, 1984).

A typical view of schemata is that they are hierarchically organized and interconnected networks of knowledge structures that people derive from experience for the anticipation, processing and interpretation of new information (e.g., Fiske & Taylor, 1984; Rumelhart, 1984; Toukmanian, 1992; Winfrey & Goldfriend, 1986). It can be seen from this definition that there is a conceptual similarity between narrative, seen as the fundamental process in meaning construction, and schemata as the basic units of cognition through which information is organized and interpreted. The overlap between these concepts is apparent in Sarbin's (1986) "narrative principle" which postulates that human beings think, perceive, imagine and make moral choices according to narrative structures. Such a conceptualization suggests that narrative is an integral part of mental activity; and yet, the connection between narrative forms of knowing and schematic representations has seldom been clearly distinguished in the literature (e.g., Polkinghorne, 1988; Russell et al, 1991).

One way in which researchers have attempted to understand this association is by viewing narrative as a unique category of schematic representation known as the "script" (Abelson, 1981; Bonanno, 1990; Leahy, 1991; Rumelhart, 1984). A script usually refers to a stereotypic or predictable sequence of events. The function of these familiar scenes is to guide expectations and prescribe behaviour (e.g., Abelson, 1981; Bonanno; Leahy, 1991). For example, when we enter a new restaurant for the first time, we anticipate a certain sequence of events (i.e., be given a menu, order food pay bill) and behave accordingly. This is due to an internal "script" of a restaurant which informs and instructs us as to what to expect and how to behave in this particular context. Thus, while "scripts" imply a connection between narrative and knowledge construction, narrative in this form is seen as simply comprising the content of a specific kind of schema. An alternative perspective would be to view mental processes and schematic structures from a narrative framework wherein narrative is seen as supplying the material from which knowledge is constructed.

A recent attempt at integrating cognitive structure and narrative is provided by Russell and van den Broek (1988; in press) who propose that internal representations are held in a narrative format. These authors argue that since events are perceived as a series of episodes organized into coherent stories and since people's internal representations or schemata perform the function of organizing events and interpreting experience, narrative is "a fundamental form of schematic representation". They further argue that (a) human beings tend to link different schematic representations in a manner that results in the construction of experiences into meaningful self "stories" and that (b) it is through the construction of autobiographical stories that one's sense of "self" is developed. Thus, by viewing narratives as schematic structures, Russell and van den Broek's conceptualization represents an attempt at casting narrative into a cognitive framework. Due to the recency of this model, to date there has been very little empirical work on it. As such, its validity and usefulness as a framework for narrative research in general and psychotherapy process research in particular are yet to be established.

Narrative and Psychotherapy

In the current information processing literature on social cognition, the "self" or one's view of oneself is conceived of as a "cognitive prototype" (Rogers, 1981) or as a complex, person specific and attitudinal cognitive structure that develops through experience over time. In other words, it is seen as a social construction and one which plays a central role in determining how people perceive, evaluate, and make judgments about themselves, others and about events in their world (e.g., Fitzgerald, 1992; Markus & Kitayama, 1991).

Thus, if we are to accept the proposition noted earlier that one of the fundamental ways in which knowledge is constructed is through narratives, then it is reasonable to assume that people's narratives would also be importantly implicated in the development of their "self–knowledge" and "self–identity". Furthermore, to the extent that the "self" is a pivotal concept in phenomenologicallyoriented or experiential psychotherapies, the central question with respect to narrative and psychotherapy is: what constitutes therapeutic change from a narrative perspective?

According to Rorty (1989), change is a shift in one's knowledge base. From the vantage point of psychotherapy, this means that change is a shift in the client's "self–knowledge" base. In fact, researchers who have examined therapeutic change from a narrative standpoint (e.g., Schafer, 1980; Spence, 1982) propose that change is the reconstruction of the client's life story. Thus, the therapist's task is not one of helping clients retrieve memories but rather of fostering a more advanced understanding of how they perceive and revise their life story (Bonanno, 1990; Polkinghorne, 1988; Russell et al., 1991). As Chambon (1991) states, the task "is to unglue the client from the story told, multiplying the vantage points and foci, encouraging the construction of a complex narrative and fostering the activity of open–ended interpretation and structuring" (p.4). This, she believes, is accomplished by "making the familiar strange and by impeding automatic, habitual ways of perceiving in order to promote awareness" (p. 4), a view similar to that advanced in Toukmanian's (1990; 1992) perceptual–processing model of experiential therapy.

To date, there are only a few studies which have used the narrative approach to studying client change. A case study by Nye (1990) conducted in the context of psychoanalytic therapy, found that in the early stages of therapy the client provided descriptive, elaborative and factual stories. The middle phase was characterized by a collaborative effort wherein client and therapist examined and reformulated the client's stories. There was also a marked shift in the client's discourse, from telling stories to talking about them, with an increased focus on the present rather than the past and on meaning as opposed to facts. The late phase of therapy resembled the early stage in that there was a return to story telling. However, the stories were qualitatively different reflecting a marked increase in the client's attempts at reformulating the meaning of her narratives.

In a recent study by Angus and Hardtke (1994), the Narrative Process Coding System (NPCS) was used to examine clients' narratives in brief psychodynamic therapy. Results indicated that, during the course of therapy, poor outcome clients had a greater overall percentage of internally and externally constructed narrative sequences whereas good outcome clients had a substantially higher percentage of reflexively constructed narrative sequences.

The exploratory study described below was an attempt to further this line of research and to see whether or not an examination of how clients construct their life stories in therapy would help enhance our understanding of the process of change in brief experiential therapy.

THE STUDY

Our investigation involved the analysis of self–relevant narratives extracted from the verbatim transcriptions of all the therapy sessions of three good and three poor outcome female clients. The six participants were drawn from a pool of 18 clients who had undergone 1–hour long 10 to 12 weekly sessions of treatment in the perceptual–processing method of experiential therapy

(Toukmanian, 1990) and on whom pre- and post–treatment scores were available on the State–Trait Anxiety Inventory (Spielberger, Gorsuch, & Lushene, 1970), the Tennessee Self–Concept Scale (Fitts, 1965), the Social Adjustment Scale – SR (Weissman & Bothwell, 1976) and on the Beck Depression Inventory (Beck, Rush, Shaw, & Emery, 1979). A pre– to post–treatment difference score greater than 0.6 standard deviation of the group's pre–treatment performance on each of these measures was used to identify the good and poor outcome clients.

Assumptions

Our investigation was organized around five propositions drawn from the aforementioned literature. It was assumed that:

1. Psychotherapy provides a natural context in which clients are encouraged to tell their own unique life stories. These stories are autobiographical in the sense that the protagonist is the client, the stories are about the client and are constructed by the client.

2. Narratives are constructions representing the narrator's or client's own sense of reality; they are developed over time and experience; they are elaborated and embellished or alternatively, condensed and reduced based on the client's own perceptions of self in relation to events occurring within as well as outside of him/herself at the time of the experience and subsequent to it.

3. Autobiographical stories cover a variety of content areas which are narrated from any one of three vantage points: (a) from the individual's own (or someone else's) view of what actually happened or is happening with respect to an even external to the person, (b) from the standpoint of the person's own internal subjective reactions to or experience of the event (i.e., what he/she thinks and/or feels about the event) and (c) from the vantage point of the person attempting to reflexively think through, understand and/or find reasons for his/her own actions and reactions to the event (Angus & Hardtke, 1991; 1994). Although clients can and sometimes choose to tell their stories from one vantage point only, more often than not they intertwine all three when communicating their life stories to the therapist.

4. Narratives are constructed and communicated at different levels of personal involvement which are reflected in various linguistic and paralinguistic features of the narrative discourse.

5. Changes in clients' narrative constructions are indicative of shifts in their manner of processing which in turn are foretelling of therapeutic improvement or lack of it.

With these assumptions, the study focused on the exploration of the following three questions: (1) Does the vantage point or stance from which clients construct their self–narratives change over the course of therapy? (2) Are there concomitant changes in the quality or level of clients' involvement in terms of depth of experiencing and the kinds of information processing operations invoked in the production of self–narratives? and (3) Are there different patterns of self–narrative constructions that distinguish clients with "good" and "poor" treatment outcomes?

Procedure

First, following Angus and Hardtke (1991), the transcriptions of all therapy sessions of the six clients were unitized into topic segments. Segments pertaining to the topic "self" were then isolated and rated independently by three expert raters on each of the following three process measures:

The Narrative Processing Coding System (NPCS; Angus & Hardtke, 1991) was used to identify the stance from which clients formulated their self–narratives in terms of one of the measure's three narrative process codes: External (descriptions of events or issues external to the client), Internal (descriptions of subjective experiences) or Reflexive (expressions which reflect attempts at examining, analyzing and interpreting one's own and/or someone else's behaviours, thoughts and feelings).

The Experiencing Scale (Klein, Mathieu, Gendlin, & Kiesler, 1970) was used to evaluate clients' depth of experiential involvement in the construction of their self–relevant stories, i.e., to see whether a given narrative discourse was impersonal, distanced and devoid of personal feelings and awareness or whether it was focused on the client's felt sense of an event(s) and reflected an expanded awareness of the experience.

The Levels of Client Perceptual Processing (LCPP) coding system (Toukmanian, 1986, 1992) was employed to depict the processes underlying the construction of narratives on the level of clients' information processing operations. Each category of this seven category taxonomy taps a qualitatively different pattern of client processing, from shallow to deeper levels, as undifferentiated statement or recognition, elaboration, externally focused differentiation, differentiation with an analytic focus, internally focused differentiation, reevaluation and integration. Coding entails looking at configurations of factors, including (a) whether the client's mode of processing is automated or controlled, (b) the type of mental operation featured most prominently in the process and (c) whether the source of information being dealt with is external or internal to the client.

Results

Figure 1 shows the proportional representation of units coded on the three process measures for the two client groups across therapy. It can be seen that both groups showed a decline in Externally constructed self–narratives from early to late therapy. For the same period, both groups also showed an increase in the proportion of narratives constructed from a Reflexive stance. As well, low levels of experiencing were predominant in both the good and poor outcome groups; and although both groups maintained these low levels, the proportion of higher level Exp–Scale ratings (level 5 or above) for the good outcome group tended to increase slightly in mid and late therapy while for the poor outcome group it remained relatively static. Neither group showed a clear pattern with respect to Level 4 experiencing.

The two groups were strikingly different, however, on the processing dimensions depicted by the LCPP, with the poor outcome group having proportionately more units coded as low (Level I, II and III) processing than the good outcome group. It can also be seen that, as therapy progressed, clients in the good outcome group tended to formulate their self–narratives more often through complex mental operations (LCPP Level V and above) than those in the poor outcome group whose processing remained on relatively simple and undifferentiated levels throughout therapy.

Within these broad parameters there were noticeable individual variations. For example, the processing pattern for Client #1 (Table 1) was characterized by steady and marked gains on all three process measures from early to late therapy. Clients #2 and #3, on the other hand, showed the greatest improvement during the mid phase of therapy. Beyond this phase, both clients' narrative processing across measures was mixed and appeared to be idiosyncratic to each client.

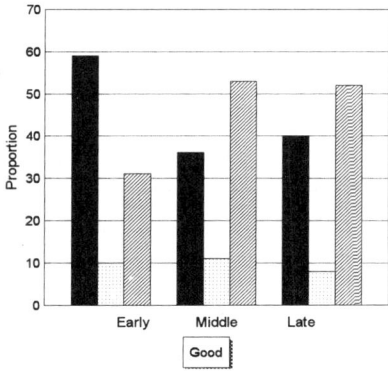

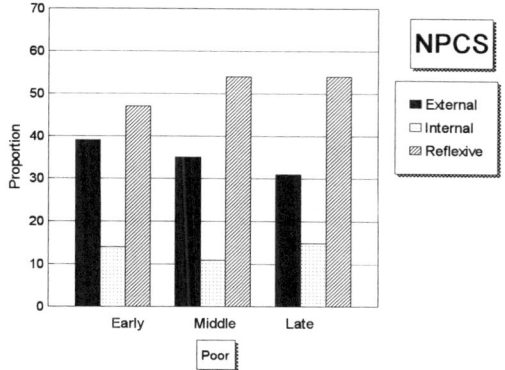

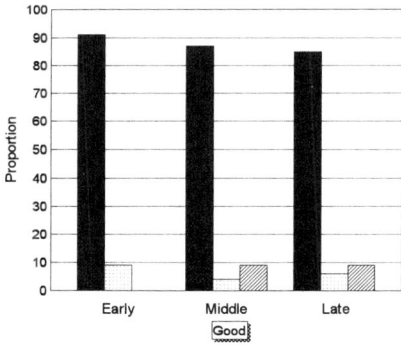

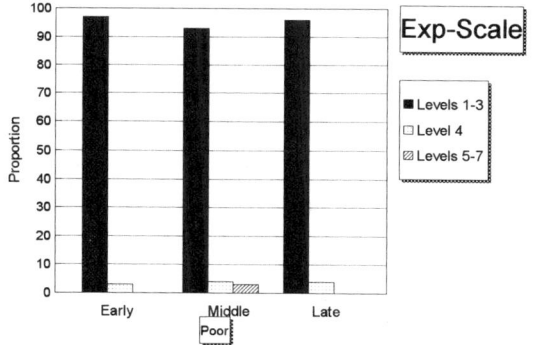

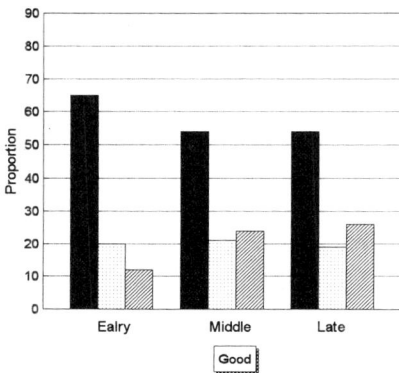

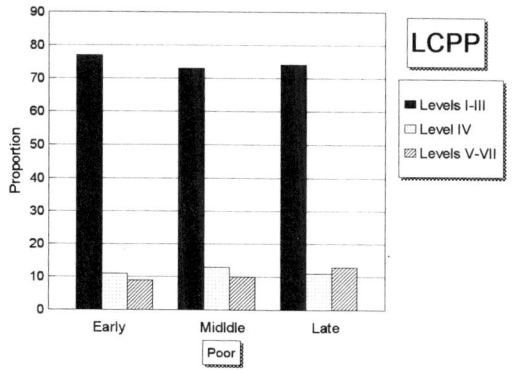

Figure 1: **Proportional Representation of Units Coded on the Three Process Measures**
for both Good and Poor Outcome Groups.

Table 1

**Pattern of Processing Across
Coding Systems for <u>Good</u> Outcome Clients**

	Client #1			Client #2			Client #3		
	E	M	L	E	M	L	E	M	L
<u>NPCS</u>									
Units Rated	(38)	(34)	(31)	(4)	(31)	(36)	(25)	(44)	(50)
External	45%	26%	22%	75%	45%	63%	56%	36%	34%
	(17)	(9)	(7)	(3)	(14)	(23)	(14)	(16)	(17)
Internal	10%	6%	10%	0%	7%	6%	20%	20%	8%
	(4)	(2)	(3)		(2)	(2)	(5)	(9)	(4)
Reflexive	45%	68%	68%	25%	48%	31%	24%	44%	58%
	(17)	(23)	(21)	(1)	(15)	(11)	(6)	(19)	(29)
<u>Exp–Scale</u>									
Mode Units Rated	(98)	(128)	(109)	(13)	(74)	(114)	(65)	(100)	(135)
Levels 1–3	80%	89%	60%	100%	95%	98%	92%	78%	98%
	(78)	(114)	(65)	(13)	(70)	(112)	(60)	(78)	(133)
Level 4	18%	2%	17%	0	4%	0	8%	5%	1%
	(18)	(3)	(19)		(3)		(5)	(5)	(1)
Levels 5–7	2%	9%	23%	0	1%	2%	0	17%	1%
	(2)	(11)	(25)		(1)	(2)		(17)	(1)
<u>LCPP</u>									
Units Rated	(129)	(96)	(116)	(17)	(82)	(120)	(99)	(101)	(148)
Levels I–III	57%	46%	40%	70%	82%	82%	67%	34%	41%
	(74)	(44)	(46)	(12)	(67)	(98)	(66)	(34)	(61)
Level IV	24%	27%	17%	18%	9%	8%	19%	28%	31%
	(31)	(26)	(20)	(3)	(7)	(10)	(19)	(28)	(46)
Levels V–VII	17%	26%	40%	6%	7%	9%	13%	38%	28%
	(22)	(25)	(46)	(1)	(6)	(11)	(13)	(39)	(41)
Other	2%	1%	3%	6%	2%	1%	1%	–	–
	(2)	(1)	(4)	(1)	(2)	(1)	(1)		

Table 2

Pattern of Processing Across
Coding Systems for <u>Poor</u> Outcome Clients

	Client #4			Client #5			Client #6		
	E	M	L	E	M	L	E	M	L
NPCS									
Units Rated	(25)	(47)	(37)	(33)	(66)	(23)	(51)	(80)	(61)
External	28%	32%	24%	49%	30%	26%	39%	44%	43%
	(7)	(15)	(9)	(16)	(20)	(6)	(20)	(36)	(26)
Internal	16%	2%	11%	18%	20%	22%	8%	10%	11%
	(4)	(1)	(4)	(6)	(13)	(5)	(4)	(8)	(7)
Reflexive	56%	66%	65%	33%	50%	52%	53%	46%	46%
	(14)	(31)	(24)	(11)	(33)	(12)	(27)	(37)	(28)
Exp–Scale									
Mode Units Rated	(64)	(136)	(97)	(96)	(192)	(87)	(162)	(240)	(174)
Levels 1–3	100%	93%	99%	90%	90%	93%	100%	96%	96%
	(64)	(127)	(96)	(86)	(173)	(81)	(162)	(231)	(167)
Level 4	0	0	0	8%	9%	7%	0	3%	4%
				(8)	(17)	(6)		(6)	(7)
Levels 5–7	0	7%	1%	2%	1%	0	0	1%	0
		(9)	(1)	(2)	(2)			(3)	
LCPP									
Units Rated	(91)	(169)	(111)	(98)	(195)	(76)	(159)	(244)	(135)
Levels I–III	74%	72%	81%	74%	72%	70%	82%	75%	70%
	(67)	(122)	(90)	(72)	(140)	(53)	(130)	(183)	(95)
Level IV	12%	14%	11%	11%	15%	9%	11%	11%	12%
	(11)	(23)	(12)	(11)	(29)	(7)	(17)	(26)	(16)
Levels V–VII	12%	11%	6%	11%	8%	18%	5%	11%	14%
	(11)	(19)	(7)	(11)	(16)	(14)	(9)	(26)	(19)
Other	2%	3%	2%	4%	5%	3%	2%	3%	4%
	(2)	(5)	(2)	(4)	(10)	(2)	(3)	(9)	(5)

322

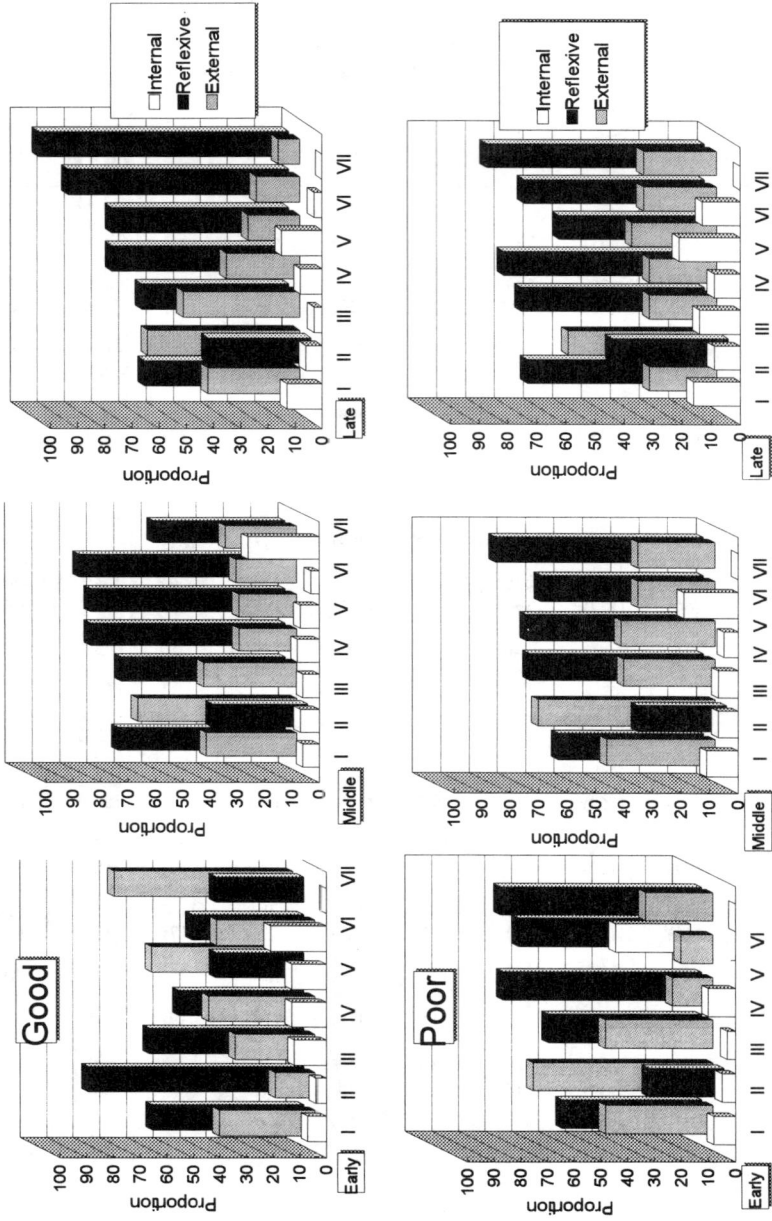

Figure 2: Proportional Representation of Units Coded on the LCPP within Narrative Codes for Good and Poor Outcome Groups

323

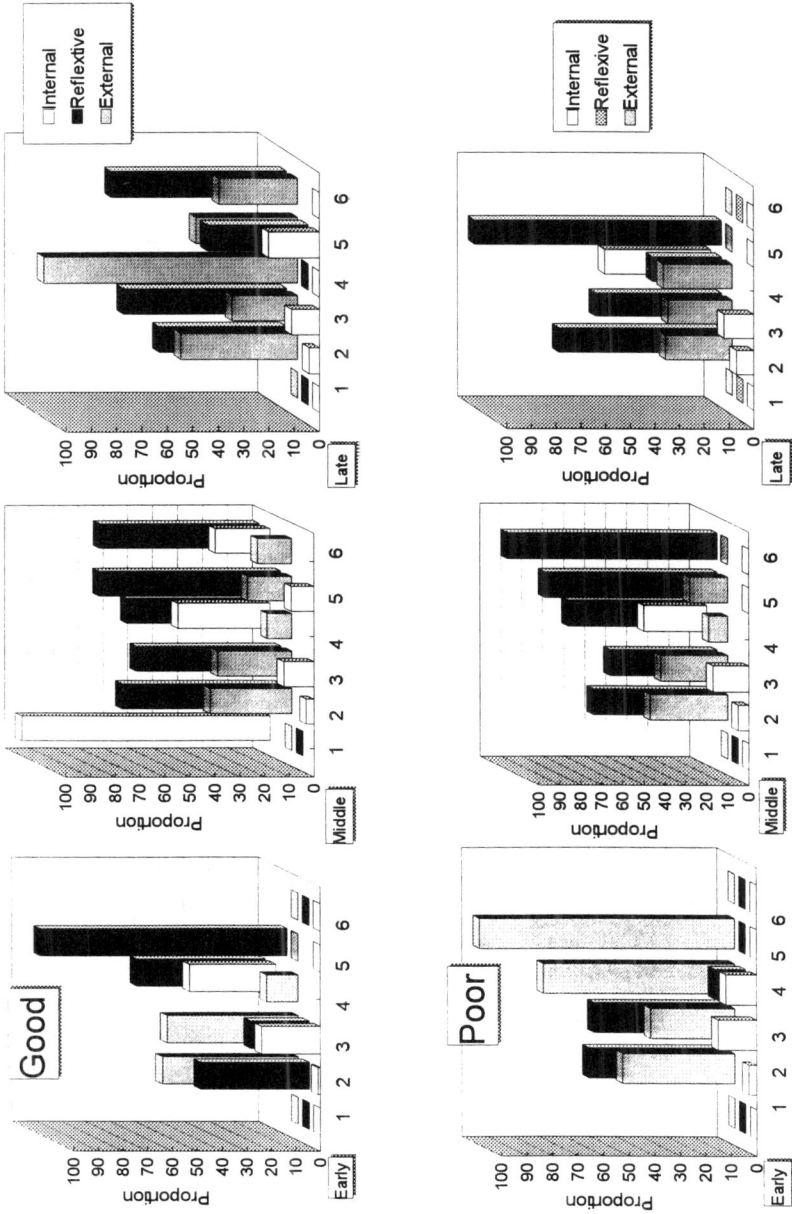

Figure 3: Proprtional Representaion of Units Coded on the Exp-Scale witnin Narrative Codes for Good and Poor Outcome Groups.

In contrast, no particular processing pattern emerged for any of the poor outcome clients both within and across measures. For example, Client #4 (Table 2) began therapy with a relatively high proportion of Reflexively constructed self–narratives which increased and was maintained by mid and late therapy. She also had a moderate proportion of narratives constructed from an External stance which increased by mid therapy and then dropped to a level lower than that in the early phase of treatment. More telling, perhaps, was this client's erratic shifts on both the Exp–Scale and the LCPP which, by and large, showed no therapeutically meaningful changes in processing across therapy. Client #6, on the other hand, showed gradual and meaningful shifts on both of these measures from early to late therapy. These, however, were accompanied by an unexpected increase in the proportion of narratives constructed from an External stance and a decrease in Reflexively constructed narratives.

The proportional representation of units coded for type of processing operations and depth of experiencing entailed within the three narrative codes for each group across therapy is presented in Figs. 2 & 3. It can be seen that the good outcome group had a high proportion of units coded as low levels of processing on the LCPP within Externally constructed narratives, particularly in early therapy. Narratives identified as Reflexive had proportionately more units judged as high levels of processing (Category IV or above), particularly in the mid and late phases of treatment. Units contained in Internally constructed narratives reflected a mix of qualitatively different mental operations of comparable proportions, thus failing to show a clear pattern.

By and large, the processing of the poor outcome group across therapy was characterized by a predominance of Externally and Reflexively constructed narratives containing relatively high proportions of units representing both simple and more complex processing operations. There was, however, some indication that units coded as LCPP Category IV or above were associated more often with Reflexively than Externally formulated narratives. Finally, no meaningful patterns of experiential involvement were found for either group in any of the narrative forms at any point in therapy.

Conclusions

Overall, the results of our study would seem to indicate, albeit tentatively, that good outcome clients reformulate their life stories increasingly more often from a Reflexive stance, engage in more complex processing operations and become personally more involved in their constructions as therapy progresses. Clients with poor outcome, on the other hand, appear to remain relatively stagnant on these dimensions throughout therapy.

This portrayal is consistent with the conception of therapeutic change advanced in cognitive models of narrative processing (e.g., Chambon, 1991; Crites, 1986; Russell et al., 1991; Spence, 1986) which contend that shifts in clients' narratives during therapy are indicative of fundamental changes occurring in their constructions of the "self". Our findings are also consistent with the basic tenets of Toukmanian's (1992) perceptual processing model of therapy wherein therapeutic change is seen to be the function of structural changes occurring in clients' schematic representations over the course of therapy. According to this model, interventions that engage the client in the processing of self– and other–relevant information through qualitatively different mental operations increase the complexity of schematic structures resulting in fundamental changes in the client's perception of experiences and therapeutic improvement. Of particular interest are the results associated with

Reflexively constructed narratives. By and large, our findings suggest a relationship between increases in the proportion of selfnarratives formulated from a Reflexive stance and therapeutic outcome and between this form of narrative and high levels of LCPP processing. An examination of Figures 1 and 2 reveals, however, that although the proportion of poor outcome clients' Reflexive narratives is high and comparable to that of the good outcome group at mid and late therapy, their manner of processing on the LCPP is at comparatively low levels during all phases of therapy. These observations lead us to believe that therapeutic improvement is related more to the kinds of mental operations involved in clients' constructions than to the stance from which they are formulated.

Finally, our failure to find any meaningful pattern with respect to clients' Internally constructed narratives and level of experiencing was disappointing. The generally low frequency of this narrative form and relatively few high level Exp–Scale ratings found across all clients in this study may have obscured any possible pattern from emerging. Alternatively, as the perceptual-processing method of therapy is a cognitively–based therapeutic modality, the findings may have been the function of the focus of this treatment's prescribed therapeutic interventions.

In conclusion, the results of this exploratory study would seem to suggest that therapeutic change, or lack of it, is the function of a combination of some common patterns and individual variations in the manner with which clients process and organize their experiences of events into coherent autobiographical stories. A full scale investigation on self–relevant narratives drawn from a larger sample of clients would be needed to determine the validity of these patterns. We are inclined to believe, however, that the narrative approach provides a useful conceptual framework and a meaningful way of contextualizing clients' discourse for psychotherapy process research.

REFERENCES

Anderson, J.R. (1981). Concepts, propositions, and schemata: What are the cognitive units? Nebraska symposium on motivation. Lincoln, NE: University of Nebraska Press.

Abelson, R.P. (1981). Psychological status of the script concept. American Psychologist, 36, 715–729.

Angus, L., & Hardtke, K. (1991). A rating Manual for the Narrative Sequences Coding System. Unpublished manuscript. [Available from the Department of Psychology, York University, North York, Ontario, M3J 1P3.

Angus, L., & Hardtke, K. (1994). Narrative processes in psychotherapy. Canadian Psychologist .

Beck, A.T., Rush, A.J., Shaw, B.F.. & Emery, G. (1978). Cognitive Therapy of Depression, New York: Guildford Press.

Barthes, R. (1977). Introduction to the structural analysis of narratives. In S. Heath (Ed.), Image–music–text (pp. 79– 124). New York: Hill and Wang.

Bonanno, G.A. (1990). Remembering and Psychotherapy. Psychotherapy, 27, pp. 175–190.

Bruner, J. (1990). Acts of Meaning. Cambridge, MA: Harvard University Press.

Chambon, A. (1991). The dialogical analyses of case materials.

Paper presented at the conference on Qualitative Methods in Social Work Practice, Centre for Social Practice Research, School of Social Welfare, S.U.N.Y., Albany, 1–12.

Crites, S. (1986). Storytime: recollecting the past and projecting the future. In T.R. Sarbin (Ed.). Narrative Psychology The Storied Nature of Human Conduct. (pp. 152173). New York: Praeger.

Fitts, W.H. (1965). Manual: Tennessee Self–Concept Scale. Nashville, Tennessee: Counsellor Recordings and Tests.

Fitzgerald, J.M. (1992). Autobiographical memory and conceptualizations of the self. In M.A. Conway, D.C. Rubin, H. Spinnler & W.A. Wagenaar (Eds). Theoretical Perspectives on Autobiographical Memory. (pp 99–114). Boston: Kluwer Academic Publishers.

Fisher, W.R. (1984). Narration as a human communication paradigm: the case of public moral argument. Communication Monographs, 51, 1–22.

Fisher, W.R. (1985). The narrative paradigm: an elaboration. Communication Monographs, 52, 327–367.

Fiske, S.T., & Taylor, S.E. (1984). Social Cognition, Don Mills: Addison–Wesley Publishing Company.

Gergen, M.M., & Gergen, K.J. (1984). The social construction of narrative accounts. In K.J. Gergen & M.M. Gergen (Eds.). Historical Social Psychology. (pp. 173–189). New Jersey: Lawrence Erlbaum Ass.

Gergen, K.J., & Gergen, M.M. (1986). Narrative form and the construction of psychological science. In T.R. Sarbin (Ed.). Narrative Psychology The Storied Nature of Human Conduct.(pp. 22–44). New York: Praeger.

Howard, G.S. (1991). Culture tales a narrative approach to thinking, cross–cultural psychology, and psychotherapy. American Psychologist, 46, 187–197.

Klein, M. H., Mathieu, P.L., Gendlin, E.T., & Kiesler, D.J. (1970). The Experiencing Scale: A research and training manual. 2 vols. Madison, Wisconsin: Wisconsin Psychiatric Institute. Bureau of Audio–Visual Instruction.

Leahy, R.L. (1991). Scripts in cognitive therapy: the systemic perspective. Journal of Cognitive Psychotherapy: An International Quarterly, 5, 291–304.

Markus, H.R. & Kitayama, S. (1991). Culture and the self: Implications for cognition, emotion, and motivation. Psychological Review, 98, 224–253.

Neisser, U. (1976). Cognition and reality: Priniciples and implications of cognitive psychology. San Fransisco: W.H. Freeman.

Nye, C. (1990). Discourse analysis of narrative process in single case studies. Unpublished manuscript, Smith College, School of Social Work, Northhampton, Mass. (pp.1– 37).

Polkinghorne, D.E. (1988). Narrative Knowing and the Human Sciences. Albany: State University of New York Press.

Rogers, T.B. (1981). A model of the self as an aspect of the human information processing system. In N Cantor & J.F. Kihlstrom (Eds.), Personality, congnition, and social interaction (pp. 193–214). Hillsdale, NJ: Erlbaum.

Rorty, R. (1989). Contingency, irony, and solidarity. New York: Cambridge University Press.

Rumelhart, D.E. (1984). Schemata and the cognitive system. In R.S. Wyer & T.K. Srull Handbook of Social Cognition. (pp. 161–188). New Jersey: Lawrence Erlbaum Associates, Publishers.

Russell, R. & van den Broek, P. (in press). Changing narrative schemas in psychotherapy. Psychotherapy: Theory, Research, Practice and Training.

Russell, R. & van den Broek, P. (1988). A cognitivedevelopmentalaccount of storytelling in child psychotherapy. In S.R. Shirk (Ed.). Cognitive Development and Child Psychotherapy. (pp. 19–48). New York: Plenum Press.

Russell, R., van den Broek, P.S., Adams, S., Rosenberger, K., & Essig, T. (1991). Analysing narratives in psychotherapy: A formal framework and empirical analyses, Unpublished manuscript, New School for Social Research, New York,N.Y., (pp. 1–31).

Sarbin, T.R. (1986). The narrative as a root metaphor for psychology. In T.R. Sarbin (Ed.). Narrative Psychology The Storied Nature of Human Conduct. (pp. 3–21). New York: Praeger.

Schafer, R. (1980). Narration in the psychoanalytic dialogue.In W.J.T. Mitchell (Ed.). On Narrative. (pp. 25–49).Chicago: The University of Chicago Press.

Spence, D.P. (1982). Narrative Truth and Historical Truth. Toronto: George J. McLeod Limited.

Spielberger, C.D., Gorsuch, R.L., & Lushene, R.E. (1970). Manual for the State–Trait Anxiety Inventory. Palo Alto,CA: Consulting Psychologists Press.

Toukmanian, S.G. (1986). A measure of client perceptual processing. In L.S. Greenberg & W.M. Pinsof (Eds.) The Psychotherapeutic Process: A Research Handbook (pp. 107-130). New York: Gulford Press.

Toukmanian, S.G. (1990). A schema–based information processing perspective on client change in experiential therapy InJ. Lietaer, J. Rombauts, & R Van Balen (Eds.), Client–Centered and Experiential Psychotherapy in the Nineties. (pp. 309–326). Leuven, Belgium: Leuven University Press.

Toukmanian, S.G. (1992). Studying the client's perceptual processes and their outcomes in psychotherapy. In S. G.Toukmanian & D. L. Rennie (Eds.) Psychotherapy Processnarrative expressions in psychotherapy. Newbury Park, CA: Sage.

Toukmanian, S.G., & Rennie, D. (1992). Preface. In S. G. Toukmanian& D. L. Rennie (Eds.), Psychotherapy Process Research: Paradigmatic and Narrative Approaches. Newbury Park, CA: Sage.

van den Broek, P., & Thurlow, R. (1991). The role and structure of personal narratives. Journal of Cognitive Psychotherapy: An International Quarterly, 5, 257–274.

Weissman, M.M., & Bothwell, S. (1976). Assessment of social adjustment by patient self–report. Archives of General Psychiatry, 33, 1111–1115.

White, H. (1980). The value of narrativity in the representation of reality. In W.J.T. Mitchell (Ed.), On Narrative (pp. 1–23. Chicago: The University of ChicagoPress.

Winfrey, L.P.L., & Goldfried, M.R. (1986). Information processing and the human change process. In R.E. Ingram (Ed.). Information Processing Approaches to Clinical Psychology.(pp.219–239). Toronto:Academic Press Inc.

Therapeutic Relationship, Core Conditions and Technique

Empathy for a real world

CAROLINE BEECH AND DAVID BRAZIER
NEWCASTLE

ABSTRACT

Empathy is a central concept in the person–centred approach. Brazier (1993) has already suggested that empathy for others is a basic human drive. This paper extends this hypothesis and suggests that empathic engagement, not only with people, but with the world at large, is fundamental to psychological wellbeing. The therapist achieves empathy by setting aside the frame of reference. This paper proposes that the frame of reference is also an obstacle for the client in achieving full engagement with life. It explores ways in which the therapeutic encounter may enhance or hinder the achievement of extended empathy, and its role in helping the client to form a deeper engagement with both inner and outer worlds.

The concept of empathy is central to person–centred theory. Rogers describes the process of empathic connection as follows (1951, p. 29):

> ...It is the counsellor's function to assume, in so far as he is able, the internal frame of reference of the client, to perceive the world as the client sees it, to perceive the client himself as he is seen by himself, to lay aside all perceptions from the external frame of reference while he is doing so, and to communicate something of this empathic understanding by doing so.

Rogers saw the therapist's ability to empathise with the client as a core requirement of the healing process. If the client received sufficient genuine empathic caring, he would grow towards self–actualization.

Rogers suggests that in order to achieve an empathic relationship with the client, the therapist needs to be able to put aside other viewpoints, especially her own, and get into the shoes, or rather the eyes, of the client. She needs to achieve a level of engagement with the client's world and to develop psychological contact through that shared perception. Such a sense of viewing the client's world „as if" from the client's viewpoint is empathy.

In his paper, The Necessary Condition is Love, David Brazier (1993) hypothesised that the development of empathy was in itself a healing process, and as such was a desirable outcome for client as well as therapist. This present paper offers an extension of this hypothesis. It suggests that psychological health depends upon our ability to engage with life. It suggests that the process of such engagement is parallel to the process which Rogers described when he described the empathic engagement which the therapist strives for in the therapeutic encounter.

Empathic engagement depends upon our ability to appreciate people in their own terms, and not through a filter of our own preconceptions and beliefs. Such engagement requires a mental shift as described by Rogers in the passage quoted above. A similar shift can be applied to the world in a more general sense. We can learn to appreciate a work of art in the context of its time and culture. We can appreciate a piece of music in the context of its composition and performance. We can appreciate a natural object in its place in the ecosystem to which it belongs. Each thing or place has its own context; its own way of being. To fully appreciate it, we must get a sense of it within its own framework. We need to develop a kind of empathy for it. We have called this concept *Extended empathy*.

This ability to relate to the world with immediacy, appreciating things in their own terms, and not filtered by our preconceptions, seems to echo Rogers' description of the fully functioning person. In On Becoming a Person, Rogers (1961, pp 151 – 154) describes the final stage of personal growth as one in which the client experiences his feelings with immediacy, and as a constantly changing process. Rogers himself stops short of the notion of extended empathy which we are proposing, yet his statement that „*The self becomes increasingly simply the subjective and reflexive awareness of experiencing. The self is much less frequently a perceived object, and much more frequently something confidently felt in process.*" (Rogers 1961, p153) seems to suggest a putting aside of self as an object of attention and an openness to that which is received by the awareness; ie the external world. The self is experienced not as a separate entity, but in its relation to that which is other.

THE PERCEIVER AND THE PERCEIVED

Rogers's description of empathy is framed in terms of perception. Perception is generally taken to require two components; the perceiver and the perceived. These components are in spatial relationship to each other. The perceiver looks at the perceived. We may think of this as a face–to–object relationship. Developing empathy requires that the counsellor perceives the world as the client perceives it. In other words, it is not the client she perceives per se, but the client's perception that she shares. Client and counsellor both become the perceiver, and the client's world becomes the perceived. Such a relationship between client and counsellor requires a side by side relationship. Even where the client himself becomes the object of perception, Rogers states that the counsellor should perceive him as he perceives himself. In other words, the counsellor is invited to „stand alongside" the part of the client that is perceiving and look at the part that is perceived.

In this model, we have two components, the perceiver and perceived; the subject and the object. We also have two ways of relating: the face to object, and the side by side. Empathic connection seems to relate to the latter. If I see the world through your eyes, we stand together and look in the same direction. We both have our attention on the same field of view, and yet we also have a sense of each other's presence. The shared activity of looking creates a link between us. I am not looking at you, but nevertheless your presence is powerfully there for me. In looking together we create a bond of shared experience. Roger's suggestion that the counsellor should perceive the world and the client through the client's frame of reference is intended not so much to affect the object of perception as the fellow perceiver.

The relationship between the perceiver or co–perceivers and the perceived is described by a visual metaphor. If we extend this metaphor, we may construe a third element in the process. This element is the degree of clarity with which the perception takes place. Do the elements relate to one another in a clear straight forward way, or do other elements create a filter that distorts or muddies the view? Does the perceiver perceive the object clearly, or do other objects obscure the view? Do the co–perceivers achieve sufficient closeness to share the view, or do obstacles prevent them from reaching the side by side position?

If the therapist is to achieve empathy for the client, she needs to work to set aside those obstacles which might obscure her view. Such obstacles might be her preconceptions about the client, her own experiences or beliefs, or an outdated view which she and the client explored together the previous week. If the client is to achieve an empathic relationship with himself and with life, he too needs to recognise and let go of the obstacles to that relationship. In order to do so, he may first need to explore those obstacles, first as objects of his perception, but later, in order to deeply understand their significance, in a more empathic, side by side way. Such a setting aside of the obstacles to clear perception is never complete. There is always some distortion of our ability to see clearly.

We would like to propose here that the distortion which prevents clear vision of the world is none other than the frame of reference described by Rogers. In order to achieve empathy with the client, the therapist must put aside her own frame of reference and see the world as through the client's filtering glasses. For the client to achieve empathy for others and for life, he too must learn to put aside the glasses that cloud and distort his view. He must let go of his frame of reference and begin to see the world in its own terms. Only then can he achieve extended empathy. Thus the frame of reference is itself an obstacle to clear perception, empathy and psychological health.

FILTERED WORLDS

...I had no apprehension about coming. The only consideration that I had was physical, you know, like can I get on the bus that day, and how far will I have to walk? So I had no emotional feelings at all – very neutral about coming. So, coming into the house, I found it very interesting because I am a very visual person. Lots to interest us and look at. It was nice to know that I could sit down and that there was a toilet handy. I've been in a lot of pain today. That was all that was really relevant, physical considerations. I enjoyed the cup of tea. Coming in here was jarred by the seats. I don't like cushions on the floor. They're not practical for me. I think it was the first time I had any emotional reaction that wasn't pleasurable, because I have negative feelings to cushions on the floor. I find it pretentious. (quietly) that's my feelings... But I was relieved to find there was two normal chairs, both comfortable (laughs) and basically I didn't do the thing (part of an exercise the group has just done recalling their arrival in the group) about the conversation. I found it totally unnecessary in the sense that I don't want to clog my brain up with what I talked about half an hour ago, no more than I want to clog my lungs up with trying to rebreathe the breath that I've had to rebreathe half an hour ago. I prefer to go on...

Although, ideally, we might wish to view things „as they are", in fact we all see the world through a filtering lens of our own interests, needs, assumptions and beliefs. Looking at a house, the carpenter may notice the banisters and fence posts, the historian the age and style of the architecture; the child will see the colours in the garden and potential for play in the winding staircase and neglected attics, the mother the dangers of the drop from the second floor landing or poisonous plants in the garden. It is to this filtering lens that Rogers seems to be referring when he speaks of the client's frame of reference.

The passage quoted above is the account given by a participant of his arrival in a research group. It follows a guided fantasy exercise in which the researcher asked group members to recall their arrival at the house where the group was to take place and their interactions with others prior to the group's start, and to become aware of what they had noticed and felt at different stages of this process. Reading the account, we can see that this person's experience of coming into the house and joining the group combines both an „external" reality of places and events and an „internal" reality of ideas, past experiences and interests. This person's account of joining the group is an experience which can only be understood if we take into account the experiencer as well as the experienced. Let us look at this passage in some detail in order to identify some of the elements which may be influencing this experience.

At first sight, we notice that much of this person's attention went to practicalities. As someone who suffered from some degree of physical disability, the first consideration in a new place was the physical comfort or discomfort which that place would provide. Items in the environment were quickly categorised into „good" or „bad" according to their convenience.

If we look further, however, we see other influences on the viewer's perception. Some comments, for example, seem to relate to expectations about the group and the other people present, and particularly about the researcher/facilitator. The focus on the practical aspects of the arrival, can be seen not just as a concern for comfort, but also as an illustration of the assertion that the participant felt *no emotional feelings at all*. This response is clearly prompted by the researcher's invitation to „look at feelings evoked" at certain stages during the fantasy exercise. It does, however, represent selective listening, as the researcher referred to a number of things the participants might observe, of which feelings were only one. It appears that for this person there is an assumption that he is being asked to look at feelings, and that if he is asked to look at feelings, these will necessarily be negative. This assumption may well have arisen from his knowledge that the group was being run by someone whose main occupation was as a therapist, and his view of what therapy might be about. We can hypothesise this chain of thinking from the tone and wording of his response.

Such a hypothesis may in itself be inaccurate, but nevertheless illustrates the possibility that, not only may the client be constructing a series of ideas around a few sentences from the therapist, but also that the therapist may be constructing ideas about the client based upon things the client has said or done. Our minds expand disconnected pieces of information to form pictures of the world. The person–centred approach has been wise to be wary of such constructs, as these can indeed be barriers to empathy. Nevertheless, however hard we try to put aside our own frame of reference, this process will necessarily still be taking place. The process of making sense through extrapolation is basic to human thought. In addition, „hunches" can provide a kind of deep empathic knowing that cannot be arrived at through conscious observation and reasoning. The therapist who is deeply empathic to her client will understand things about the client which have not been openly said. Distinguishing the useful hunches from the less useful constructs is not always easy. Are we seeing clearly, or imposing our own frame of reference? It is often only by being aware of our own assumptions and sharing our own inner processes that we can check out the points at which we become closer to or more distant from the client.

If we return to the passage quoted earlier, we can see that the assumptions which the client is making about the researcher's intentions colour his responses in the group. The tone of this participant's response to the facilitator is not neutral. His comments are challenging. The participant asserts that his experience does not fit into the mould which he assumes the facilitator to be expecting. His comment that the cushions seem pretentious is partly influenced by his disability, but may also be a statement of the difference of values he anticipates between himself and the facilitator. He reports that he stopped participating in the exercise because he *found it unnecessary* and his description of *rebreathing the breath* gives a strong negative image. Such responses seem to arise from his beliefs about what is and what is not useful in a group. It is as if he has a template in his mind of how things should be which he is holding against his experience of events.

Such statements establish the speaker's beliefs and consequently an identity in opposition to the facilitator. The words may also be motivated by his relationship with others in the group, in that they probably also represent a bid for power in the group or an attempt to avoid being overpowered. The contradictory tone of the responses seems to say „I see the world my way, not your way". The speaker makes other statements which seem intended to establish his identity. One example is when he defines himself as „*a very visual sort of person*". His statements about his objection to reviewing past conversations, seem to reflect his beliefs about life, which may be along the lines of „it is unhealthy to dwell on the past", and possibly „life is too short".

As we can see from this illustration, the speaker's description of the world is a complex mixture of what is „there", and his own constructions. These constructions are in themselves complex, influenced by

1. The speaker's needs and interests

2. The speaker's past experience

3. The speaker's beliefs about himself

4. The speaker's beliefs about the world

5. The speaker's relationship with the listener and what he wishes to communicate to her.

When Rogers refers to the client's frame of reference, we may assume that it is to such factors that he is alluding.

At this point, it is necessary to consider the degree to which these processes are conscious for the client. The client is probably aware of his physical needs. He is probably also aware of a degree of irritation. Beyond this, if prompted, he may begin to become aware of some feelings towards the facilitator. He will probably remain unaware, at least for the present, of any power dynamics within the group. Yet all of these can be traced in his responses to life. All seem to contribute to the filter which colours his perception of the world.

Rogers sees a central task of the therapist as being to enter the client's frame of reference. When, however, we look at a piece of interaction such as that quoted above, we see that this task involves a choice on the part of the therapist. Because the communication has many aspects, the therapist necessarily hears selectively. Her experiencing of the client is filtered through her own frame of reference. Even when she is aware of the different layers of meaning, she will not be able to respond to all levels simultaneously. So, the therapist may choose to respond to the „raw experience"; the needs and interests suggested by the selective experiencing; past experiences, whose shadows influence the experiencing of the present; the client's belief system; or the interaction that is taking place within the therapy relationship. Each of these can be separately identified, but will contain elements of the other elements, thus the therapy relationship may contain shadows of past relationships; the expressed needs relating to an event in the client's life may reflect needs felt in the therapy; the beliefs hinted at in statements made may reflect a challenge to the therapist or a prescription for life which might have avoided past hurts.

Thus the client's frame of reference is complex and provides a filter which colours his perception of life. Events of the past or visions of the future influence perception of the present, and prevent a clear vision of the here and now. Experiencing is a combination of „external reality" and the filters which arise from the client's psyche.

THE THERAPY PROCESS

Therapy is concerned with freeing the client's process, increasing his ability to experience life more directly and with more immediacy. In order to achieve this, the client needs to let go of some of the internal structures which colour his perception of the external world. He needs to recognise and put aside the shadows of the past.

Whilst a pure experiencing of life, free from personal bias, is rare, as the client becomes the fully functioning person described by Rogers he is less hampered by prejudices and preconceptions, and more aware of when self–interest and beliefs intrude on his view.

Much of therapy is concerned with identifying those inner structures which prevent a clear experiencing of the present, and finding ways of putting them aside. Past hurts which cloud the present recede into history as healing and forgiveness are achieved. Tyrannical parents cease to wield power over present situations once their humanity is recognised. Life views cease to be as dogmatic once they have been understood and appreciated by another.

Often in therapy, the client becomes aware of the frame of reference which they have been using. When this happens, however, the frame of reference becomes the object of perception, and cannot, at the same time, become the frame of reference from which that object (ie itself) is viewed. The sheer act of recognising one's own frame of reference shifts one to a new vantage point. In fact, we may say, the client moves to a higher, more encompassing point from which a clearer view is possible. To put it another way, the old, narrow frame of reference dissolves. Therapy is not a process of remaining within a frame of reference, but of dissolving it. When Rogers suggests we stay within the client's frame of reference he is suggesting a means for the therapist, not a goal for the client.

ONE FRAME OR MANY?

Rogers refers to the client's frame of reference, but it becomes clear when one is with a client is that what is being described may more accurately be referred to in the plural. We all have a number of filters through which we can view the world. Either we need to see the frame of reference as fluid and multi–faceted, or we need to recognise that the client has not one frame, but many. In either case, we would like to suggest that the frame(s) of reference is one and the same as the filters to which this paper has referred, and that, as such, it clouds, rather than aids clear viewing of the world.

To consider in more detail the multi–faceted nature of the frame of reference, let us take an illustration.

A woman starts to consider the possibility of a new job. At first she greets the idea with excitement. The feelings of anticipation, reminiscent of feelings she experienced as a student some ten years earlier, when preparing for her first job interview, alternate between enthusiasm and anxiety. Will she get the job? How will she feel when her first pay cheque arrives? How good it will be meeting so many new people. She will need some new clothes, and perhaps a car in due course. In her imagination she is both stepping out on her first day in the new post, and reliving those heady days after her final examinations before she started out on her career.

At this moment she remembers that there is a difference between things as they were then, and the way that they are now. She is a mother, with two small children. Taking the job will mean placing her children with a minder during the day. Her mood changes. She is no longer the carefree student. Instead, she remembers her own experiences as a child when her mother went out in the evenings, leaving her with a sitter whom she feared. She feels the panic welling up in her again as she sees the closing door and hears again the car drawing away from the house. Can she leave her own children with a stranger? What if her choice of minder is wrong? Will she know if her children are unhappy? Did her own mother know how she felt about being left?

Then she thinks „Damn it, its always the women who get the blame. These children have a father." She hears in her head the voices of women friends. He should take his turn. Couldn't he get a part time job so he can share the childcare? She feels anger rising in her. Anger at men. Anger at her partner for working long hours and not giving a second thought to her career. Anger at her father for taking more interest in her brother's career prospects than her own.

During this episode, we can see that this woman experiences a number of shifts of viewpoint around her decision to take a job. Each viewpoint is associated with a collection of episodes in her life. First she is identified with her single, student self. From this perspective her way forward seems clear, and although she feels some anxiety, she is basically confident of her abilities and the rightness of her actions. This perspective is not the only one she holds. Her realisation that, as a mother, she has ties which she did not have as a student brings about a shift of mood. She is now able to identify with her position as mother, but also with the possible position of her children. From this position, the whole situation looks quite different. Coloured by her own unhappy memories, she imagines how it might feel for them to be left. Suddenly her way forward looks a lot less clear. Her final shift identifies her with her feminist self. She feels alongside her the women with whom she has discussed her feelings of frustration and her hopes for a more productive life. Their presence in her imagination fires her anger at the men whom she feels have limited her life in the past and the present.

Each position, then, holds within it a number of scenes, feelings and beliefs. Some of these beliefs may contradict each other. As the single person she may feel full of confidence, whilst as the mother she is beset with doubts. As the feminist she is certain that she has a right to self–fulfilment, but as a mother she believes she has a duty to her children to stay with them whilst they need her. We may therefore say that she has at least three frames of reference during this brief episode, each holding its own world view. We may also suppose that there are potentially other frames of reference from which she can view her situation.

Therapy can often involve identifying and exploring different perspectives upon a situation. This process can be one which brings us closer to a complete view of the world. If you take a red filter and look at a specially shot film, you will see a two dimensional representation of a scene. Similarly if you look at the same scene through a green filter, you will see a similar, but slightly different view of the same scene. If you take a pair of specially prepared spectacles with one red lens and one green one, the scene suddenly becomes three dimensional. This cinematic device illustrates the principle which allows us to see the world around us in three dimensions. Because our vision is binocular, we are able to get two fixes on the object of our attention. This places that object in relief against its background. Auditory signals are received in the same way, allowing us to locate a sound to its spatial origin. We are designed to form our picture of the world from two overlapping receptors. Visually, we are limited to two viewpoints, but if we transfer this metaphor to other aspects of our experiencing we may be less limited. The fact that we do have a number of frames of reference, allows us to achieve a multiple viewpoint, and so perceive our world more fully. At the simplest level, finding a new perspective can provide a way out of what seems to be a stuck situation. As she contacts her feminist self, this woman considers the possibility of asking her partner to help with the childcare. More importantly, the more viewpoints we have on life, the richer our experiencing is likely to be. This move towards a multi–frame view of the world seems to echo Rogers' description of the more fluid functioning of the actualised person. It also points to a viewing of life that is closer to, rather than further from an unfiltered view of the world. Paradoxically the more frames of reference we are able to enter, the closer we are to seeing the world in an unfiltered way.

SEEKING THE MULTI-FRAMED VIEWPOINT

If, then, it is psychologically healthy to be able to view life from a number of viewpoints, how is this to be achieved in therapy? Increasing our capacity to see life from different viewpoints can be achieved in a number of ways. Some perspectives or frames of reference are achieved by identifying with a past self or a part of the present self, some by identifying with a role, and some through identifying with the position of a person other than the self. Such shifts of perspective are commonly recognised. We may say „I did that with my teacher's hat on", or „that was my old self talking" or „I said that as if I were my mother". As the counsellor develops in skill and experience, she will learn to empathise with many viewpoints. One may hypothesise that such learning plays an important part in her own growth. She moves from a more restricted world view towards a more complete one. If we see such a process as desirable for the therapist, we may speculate that it is also desirable for the client.

Rogers (1961, p52) states that the therapist needs to be strong in her own separateness not to be „downcast by his depression, frightened by his fear, nor engulfed by his dependency". The client needs the therapist not simply to become a psychological extension of himself, but to remain close but distinct. Although the therapist works to set aside her frame of reference, her success at doing so is, and needs to be, incomplete. This process has parallels to Kohut's optimum frustration model (Kohut 1971).

If we take it that the therapist's role is to help the client to learn to see his world more fully, we may assume that by remaining alongside, but separate, the therapist offers a second viewpoint on the client's world, giving a fuller experience than the client has hitherto been able to achieve. The slight inaccuracies in the therapist's understanding of the client's world view provide the second viewpoint which serves to increase the clarity of its perception. Were the therapist's entry into the client's frame of reference perfect, the therapist's presence as a separate human being would cease to have value. The shared view would be monocular.

In practice, the therapist never becomes so absorbed into the client's frame of reference as to totally share his viewpoint. There will always be small differences of perception, and, far from being failures, these will provide the depth of vision necessary for growth to occur. The therapist's responses offer the client new, subtly different frames of reference from which to view life. The still photograph becomes the three dimensional movie.

BRACKETING

Rogers states that the therapist needs to set aside her own frame of reference in order to empathise with the client. In phenomenological terminology this process is referred to as *bracketing*. The Therapist strives to set aside her preconceptions and enter into the client's world as fully as she is able, viewing it from his perspective. In the phenomenology of Edmund Husserl, the purpose of bracketing is that we should be enabled to perceive „the things themselves", as they are, more clearly.

The process of bracketing involves a deliberate choice to leave one frame of reference aside, and thus to attempt to view the world (of the client) with a naive perception. As such it appears an opposite process to the multi-frame approach suggested in the previous section.

Paradoxes, however often illuminate, rather than destroy arguments. Where apparently opposite statements both appear to contain truth, we may often be able, through them, to glimpse a deeper understanding of the subject. Thus the apparent contradiction between the need to bracket and the need to achieve a multi–dimensional view of the world, provides an example of the usefulness of a two directional approach. Let us look more closely at the processes involved.

If I bracket my preconceptions, I attempt to set aside those views and assumptions that make up my frame of reference. Of course, such a setting aside is always incomplete, as we have already discovered, but, given this, I will achieve a partial bracketing. This will be sufficient for me to become open to a fresh experiencing of the subject. I am likely now to see new aspects which hitherto have been hidden by my assumptions. These will allow me to view my situation from a number of new viewpoints.

So, whilst previously I held a view that was more or less rigid, now I am open to a number of views. Similarly, if I deliberately attempt to adopt a muti–dimensional stand point, I again let go of my rigidity of outlook and am able to see the situation from a number of angles. I recognise that there is not one right view, and that my situation is complex. I become open to receiving new view points. My previous certainties become simply some of many possible viewpoints.

So, whether I attempt to bracket my predominating frame of reference, or whether I deliberately seek out other view points, the effect is to make myself open to a range of possibilities. There is a levelling of viewpoints. My world view becomes more complex and more open to reinterpretation. I no longer hold onto a fixed view of how things are.

A factor in this process, which has already been raised is that of identification. It is often our sense of identity which prevents us from seeing other aspects of a situation. If the woman, whose story is told earlier, depends on her image of herself as a feminist, she will find it very hard to see the choice of work from her children's or partner's perspectives. In order to achieve a more holistic world view, I have needed to loosen my hold on that which I regard as mine. I need to be open to other's view points, not just because I want to take the feelings and needs of others into account, but also because by seeing the world through their eyes, I can enrich my own experiencing of it. I can develop a more fluid experiencing of the world.

THE MITWELT

One particular aspect of the frame of reference is the ever present sequence of scenes and images which we carry with us. We have adopted the term *mitwelt* to describe this phenomenon. The mitwelt is a term used to describe the part of our inner world which we perceive as other than ourselves, but with which we feel identified. Our mitwelt may, for example, be memories of past scenes, our images of our parents or other relatives, our home, possessions, beliefs and aspirations.

As a client describes an event from his life, the therapist may notice that the client is caught up in reliving the event in his mind. As he describes a conversation, he may look towards a particular part of the room, as if seeing the person with whom the conversation took place seated there. Other times he may gaze intently at a distant point whilst describing a scene, as if watching the event being played out on a screen in front of him. The client is here in touch with his mitwelt.

In such cases, the mitwelt is generally experienced as if it were outside the body space of the client. It is projected. (we use the term here to mean any part of the client's inner/internalised world which is perceived by the client as being outside his physical space) Sometimes this projection is onto an empty space. It bears no relationship to the actual physical entities in the room. If it bears any relationship, it is in occupying empty space. The imagined father may be seen sitting on an empty chair. The scene may be placed through the window.

Such projections of the client's mitwelt may easily be distinguished from the external world of the therapy room. In much therapy an exploration of the mitwelt takes a central role. Nevertheless, as with other aspects of the frame of reference, the projected mitwelt is a barrier to clear engagement with the world. In many circumstances the projected mitwelt's presence is not recognised and acknowledged.

If we consider the example given at the start of this paper, the group participant's responses towards the facilitator, we can identify expectations which are not readily understood simply in terms of the actual interaction which has taken place during the group session. We may speculate that the facilitator is perceived through the filter of the participant's projected mitwelt.

Distinguishing the elements in this kind of projection in which the client's response to a place or person contains a mixture of elements from their actual relationship and elements which have been projected from the mitwelt is more difficult than when the projection that is made onto empty space, as when the client imagines a significant person from their past sitting on an empty chair. Recognising that the client's view of the therapist or of another group member is coloured by a projection of their mitwelt requires skill. Disentangling the external from the projection becomes a complex task. The psychodynamic therapist working with such material might make interpretations in terms of transference projections. The person centred therapist is more likely to respond to such a situation by empathising with the client's view of herself, whilst remaining congruent in her sense that she does not fit this view.

The internalised mitwelt, then, is often the filter which prevents us from experiencing the world with immediacy. It can prevent us from seeing others clearly, and can lead us to respond to them in ways that have more to do with our own history than with the other person. It can be a potent factor in preventing us from living fully in the present. We are unlikely to become completely free of the filter which our inner process imposes on our perception of the world, but we can work to recognise and reduce the distortion which it produces. To do this we often need to fully contact the internalised mitwelt and deal with the unfinished business which keeps it in place.

EXTENDED EMPATHY

The concept of empathy is generally applied to human relationships. When we are empathically engaged with another, we are able to experience the world „as if" through their eyes. We are able to share their world view, with the distortions of their frames of reference. Empathy requires intense engagement. It involves experiencing with another. It means appreciating his perspective. Not simply knowing the facts of his life, but having a feeling sense of how it is to be viewing the world and oneself as that person does.

We would like to offer a concept of *extended empathy* which goes beyond the usual definition of empathy to incorporate not just a relationship with another person, but a relationship with the world. Extended empathy can be applied to objects, to phenomena, to ideas. Achieving extended empathy means appreciating things in their own terms. It requires an imaginative entry into their worlds. It means having a felt sense of their essential qualities. If we can achieve extended empathy, we can appreciate the stoneness of a stone, the flowerness of a flower, the dreamness of a dream.

In his paper, „The Necessary Condition is Love" Brazier (1993) proposed that empathy is itself a quality leading to psychological health. His paper highlighted the universal drive towards reaching out to others in a loving and deeply understanding way, and suggested that the need to love preceded and over–rode the need to be loved. Here we would like to suggest that empathic engagement has a far wider application than simply human relationships, and that the development of extended empathy is the route to psychological well being.

Empathy is developed by setting aside one's own frame of reference and adopting the frame of reference of another. Extended empathy is similarly achieved by setting aside our own viewpoint and taking on the „viewpoint" of the object of empathy. In both instances a rigid frame of reference is an obstacle to the achievement of empathic connection.

Extended empathy can be applied to the external world of objects and events, but the concept can also be applied to objects within the inner world. These processes are parallel. Thus, developing his ability for empathic engagement with life allows the client to deepen his sense of his inner world. Both require an attitude of open acceptance.

EXTENDED EMPATHY AND THE MITWELT

As the therapist listens to the client, she will be aware of shifts in the client's perceptual field. At some points the client will be fully engaged with the therapist. They will make eye contact, and speak directly. The therapist will have no doubt that she is being addressed as a fellow adult, and told clearly the details of the client's life. At other times the client may seem more caught up in the story that he is telling. He may perhaps be looking at a distant point, or hardly seem to be focusing his eyes at all. If the therapist responds in a reflective way, he may hardly seem to notice her presence, and if she says something that cuts across his train of thought he may react in a startled way. Sometimes the client's story becomes so vivid that the therapist can almost see the angry relative whom the client is describing as a presence in the room.

The person–centred therapist works to empathically enter the client's world, and to convey her sense of that world through her responses. Empathy requires that the therapist adopt a „side by side" position in relation to the client. That she sees the world that the client sees. Thus the empathic therapist will see not the client, but the client's world. Only on rare occasions, at times when the mitwelt has receded, will the therapist stand alongside the client in reflexive contemplation.

Having stated this, it is nevertheless the case that many therapists, in practice, see their role as being to focus the client's attention on himself. If the client speaks of his mother, the response is often „And I'm wondering how that is for you..". The difference in effect of these two different styles of response becomes apparent if we look at an example.

John, who has been describing vividly a scene in which his father was abusive towards him, tells his therapist „I feel angry with my father".

If John's therapist chooses to focus on John, her response may be „You feel angry". This response is a commonly used empathic reflection, picking up John's stated feeling. Many therapists talk about feelings because they think this will help the client become more in touch with their inner world. If we look at this response again, however, we see that John's attention is probably actually still focused on his father. This being so, the therapist's response to John's anger is based upon her observation of John, and her hearing of his words. It is a face to face response. It does not offer an understanding of how it feels to see the world through John's eyes, but rather of how it is to see John experiencing the world. John is feeling angry, because he has his attention upon his father. If he focuses on his anger, he will step into the „face to face" therapist's viewpoint, and he will probably become less angry.

If, instead, the therapist mentally steps alongside John and sees the world through his eyes, she is more likely to respond „Yes, its like your father is standing here with us." Such a response may be verbally more distant from John's original statement, but it may well offer a closer account of John's actual experience. Both John and his therapist are „looking" in the same direction. Responses of this kind have the effect of making the mitwelt more „real" for both therapist and client. This process, termed *amplification*, is described in Caroline Beech's paper „Looking in, Looking out" (Beech 1993). It tends to help the client to be more in contact with the feelings that his mitwelt evokes.

Reflections which amplify the client's experience of the mitwelt help the client to deepen their engagement with their inner world. By making that world the subject of experience, feelings are evoked in a way that they are not if the feelings themselves become the objects of attention. Thus reflections that centre on the client, and those that centre on the client's mitwelt will have quite different effects upon the course of the therapy.

Feelings arise in relation to an object. If I want to experience joy, I think of an event or object that gives me joy: a new baby, a sunrise, a first snowdrop. If I try to find joy in myself without such an image, I am unlikely to experience the feeling to the same degree. Indeed I may well find that the word evokes an image spontaneously. Similarly, we may ourselves become changed by a perceived object. If I imagine a school teacher who taught me when I was six, I may feel myself to be six once more. If I imagine giving a lecture to an appreciative audience, I may feel more confident.

If we are to let go of those parts cf our inner world that keep us from functioning fully in our present life, we need to recognise and acknowledge their existence and power. More than this, we need to accept and appreciate that inner world and those parts of ourselves that are still caught up in it. If I am to achieve empathy for the external world, I may first have to achieve empathy for my inner world. If I do not, that inner world remains, a rigid aspect of my frame of reference.

EMPATHY FOR THE WORLD

Whilst much therapy is concerned with the client's inner world, the fully functioning person, as described by Rogers, is one who lives is the „real world", and who is in contact with their inner process in as much as it flows through them in response to external events and interactions.

Much of our inner distress arises from a holding onto inner structures. Shadows from the past, rigidly held beliefs, expectations, all colour our perception of the world. In therapy we can work to diminish the effect of such elements, but we can also work to connect more directly with our present experience. Learning to empathise with the external world takes us beyond those things which block our perception. If we learn to connect more fully with our present experience, we can let go of encumbrances.

Working with awareness, then becomes an important aspect of the therapy process, not only in developing awareness of the blocks to engagement, but also in developing engagement itself. The client may need to fully experience his grief in order to let it go, but he may also be able to let go of it by focusing his attention fully in the present. Present focus has tended to be the preserve of eastern approaches to the mind, rather than western psychotherapy. The Buddhist practice of mindfulness centres around a letting go of attachment to all that is not within the present moment. Letting go of attachment to illusion is the practise of full engagement. (Nhat Hanh, 1975)

Some approaches have attempted to bring working with awareness into the personal growth arena (Brooks, 1974), but many of these focus more on engagement with the inner process (for example focusing, Gendlin 1981). Therapies which have as their focus deepening engagement with the world remain a minority.

Yet it has been our experience that through working with awareness in a direct way, clients often achieve a sense of wellbeing and engagement with life that conventional therapy does not provide. Because its nature is experiential and qualitative, such work is hard to document. An account of a session in which awareness and engagement were the focuses is therefore included as an appendix to this paper.

Extended empathy allows us to experience the world in a feeling way; in a way that involves our whole attention. If we can start to feel the stoneness of stones, we will in that moment become absorbed into that stoneness. If we can feel the flowerness of the flower, we will become that flowerness. It is at these moments that we are most fully alive. In becoming most other, we are most self.

APPENDIX 1

The following example gives an account of a group session in which awareness was the primary focus:

I would like to invite you to stand up.

The group stands, forming a circle. Each woman a part of the circle, part of the whole, yet separate. There is a new energy in the group. We have been together for half a day now. We have met each other in different ways, verbal and non verbal. We have just been sitting, sharing our feelings about the morning's activities. It has been good sharing, but our minds have been with the morning and with ideas that the morning has evoked. Suddenly, by standing, we have arrived back in the present.

I see bright eyes, making contact with me. I feel elated. We are here. We are now. Something is happening. I feel anticipation.

Perhaps you would like to look inside yourself. To get a sense of what is going on in your body. To get a sense of how you are feeling about standing here. To share some of what comes up spontaneously.

There is a silence. Each of us turns our attention inwards. Each listens to those small voices and impulses that are so often lost in the hurly–burly of speech.

After a pause we start to share. For one there is wonder in the sense of connection; the circle. Another experiences the central space as special; she is moved by its safeness. Another would prefer not to be in the group at all. Her impulse is to move away, to leave the room even, to break the circle.

In me the excitement flutters under my ribs. my arms feel ready to move. Is it an embrace they seek? Or perhaps a dance? I feel the tiny testing movements in them. They are wanting, longing.

Then why not try following that impulse, see where it leads? Lets each explore where in the room our impulses take us. Lets explore what position they invite us to occupy.

We start to move. One slowly walks around the perimeter of the group. Another takes herself into a corner and curls up on a pile of cushions. Another stands in the sunlight, face up turned. Another moves into what had been the centre of the circle and lies, arms and legs outstretched. Quite quickly there is stillness again.

I move. My feet want to be slow. To touch the ground tenderly. To feel the soft strands of the carpet under my instep and between my toes. My arms want to dance lightly on an unseen breeze. They float before me. Flow and move. Find a resting place against my heart. I reach a stillness. My feet are firmly planted on the earth. My body strongly upright.

As you pause, you might like to take your attention inwards, and notice what is going on for you in this new place. Have things changed? Do you feel differently?

There is a pause, a silence. It is a time for each to explore in her own way. Space for the attention to move around the body or the mind, just as, a few minutes previously, we have moved physically around the space of the group room.

I am strong. So strong. Strong and tall as a tree. My feet are rooted. I can send them down, down into the earth. I can drink my fill from the good soil. My arms can grow tall and free. They are not longing now.

You might like now to start to move your attention outwards. To make contact with your surroundings. To use your senses to explore. What is supporting you? What is in contact with your skin? What contact do your other senses make with their surroundings?

Almost imperceptibly there is a change in the room. More alertness. Bodies that had been slightly slumped become slightly more upright. Attention is outward. Hands, feet, arms, backs move over the surfaces they touch. Feel textures, temperatures. Smoothness and roughness.

I feel the carpet under my bare feet. The pressure under the ball and heel of my foot. The softer caressing fibres of wool where my weight is less intensely focused. I feel the slight give in the pile as I rock very gently to and fro. I play with slight muscle movements, feeling the effects of even the slightest shift of weight from one part of my foot to another, or between my two feet. The intensity of contact is almost unbearable. Moving my attention, I become aware of my hands. My finger ends tingle with anticipation. I reach down now to feel the carpet, as if for the first time. I run my hands lightly over the pile. To my hands, it is softer, lighter. I can push my finger tips into it. Feel them surrounded by its softness. I can move it. Draw patterns in it. Smooth it. I open my eyes, which have been shut, and see the colours. Browns and golds. I see the patterns and the dark and shade.

You might like to experiment with different focuses of attention. Inward attention and outward attention.

There is little outward change in the room. Only the slightest movement. All is peaceful.

I feel the carpet and I feel my body touching it. My feet, caressed by its softness. The muscles of my legs moving as I play with the sensations under my feet. I stand once more. My hands now touch my clothing over my heart. My heart feels brimming over with the softness of my contact with the floor. I feel its steady beating on the palm of my hand and the slight rise and fall of my breath. I feel the warmth of my body, comforting against my hand. I feel the fabric of my T shirt, smooth but firm, slightly creasing between my hands and body.

We have paints and paper here. Perhaps you would like to use them to express something of what you have been experiencing. On the other hand, you may prefer to stay with what you are doing now. In an hour or so, we can maybe come together to talk about what we have been experiencing.

Some women slowly start to move towards the art materials. Others remain where they are. Two women take paper and paints. One starts to cover her paper immediately, with urgent brush strokes and bright primary colours. In a few minutes she has filled her paper and takes a second sheet. The other sits for several minutes with the empty sheet before her before starting to paint, carefully and slowly feeling each brush stroke as she applies it, and stopping frequently to sit and look at the shapes she is producing. An other woman, who has been curled up in a corner of the room takes a pad of paper and returns to her space, where she sits for a moment before starting to write. The words seem to flow in fits and starts and her face looks filled with emotion. Other women take pastels and charcoal and start to draw. Two remain in positions they took up earlier, still wrapped in inner process.

I take some paints. Soft soft colours. The softness of my heart. The softness of the carpet. The curves of hands caressing, touching, letting go. Sweeping strands of paint. Gentle blues and greens. Merging, flowing together. Melting into one another.

Several women seem to finish together. They sit, looking unsure what to do.

You might like to sit with what's going on for you now, or you might like to choose a different medium to work in and see if that takes the process further. As you work, try to allow the materials you are using to speak to you. See what they are able to do.

One sits, the others take new paper. One who has painted begins to write. Haltingly at first, then fast, scribbling and crossing out in her urgency. Another who has drawn with coloured chalks takes a large sheet of paper and starts to daub colour onto it. Others too change their means of expression. One starts to walk around the room again, first slowly, then more quickly and lightly. Her energy seems to infect others. several begin to paint more actively.

Paper. I write. Words, words, chaotic words, hurtling helter skelter onto the page. Faster than I can manage, my fingers tumbling over themselves, trying to express.

We need to be coming together soon. Before we do, you might like to sit with what you have produced, to notice how your body is now, to notice how you respond to this thing that you have created.

There is a settling. The women slowly put paints aside, and sit, pictures and writing spread before them.

I see the energy rising in my painting. Life energy. It is this energy I have been struggling to contain in words, but it feels uncontainable. I look at it and my body wants to move. The upper part wants to flow in the breeze. The tree image returns, and I realise how grounded my lower half feels. Sitting, I make solid contact with the ground. I no longer need to contain. The ground contains me, but my branches flow freely. I look around the room with newborn eyes.

Perhaps we could share now.

The women start to talk. Each shares a little of the process she has been going through. Some have a lot to say, others little. The group begins to reconnect in a new way. We have been on parallel courses, our journeys, like different coloured threads have run together, weaving in and out of one another, but we have also been separate. We have each remained within our personal worlds of images and perceptions, making our individual contacts with the inside and outside processes. As we talk we discover the points at which those processes touched. „I chose that blue, because the blue you were using spoke to me". „I felt your energy as you passed and felt joyful." Sharing, we learn to trust our sense of contact

REFERENCES

Beech C. (1993). *Looking In, Looking Out*. In Brazier, D (Ed) Beyond Carl Rogers, London: Constable.

Brazier D. (1993). *The Necessary Condition is Love*. In Brazier, D (Ed) Beyond Carl Rogers London: Constable.

Brooks C. (1974). *Sensory Awareness, the rediscovery of experiencing*. Santa Barbara Ross–Erikson.

Gendlin E. (1981). *Focusing*. Toronto: Bantam.

Kohut H. (1971). *The Analysis of the Self*. USA: U of Chicago Press.

Nhat Hanh. (1975). *The Miracle of Mindfulness*. London: Rider.

Rogers C. (1951). *Client Centred Therapy*. London: Constable.

Rogers C. (1961). *On Becoming a Person*. London: Constable.

Die Bedeutung des motivationalen Aspektes von Empathie und kognitiver sozialer Perspektivenübernahme in der personzentrierten Psychotherapie.

UTE BINDER

FRANKFURT

ABSTRACT

Es wird versucht Empathie im therapeutischen Prozeß nicht als Basisvariable, sondern als Methode herauszuarbeiten. Ausgehend davon, daß schwere psychische Störungen bereits im vorsprachlichen Bereich durch defizitäres empathisches Beziehungs/Bindungsverhalten primärer Bezugspersonen angelegt sein können, kommt störungsspezifischen empathischen Prozessen zentrale kurative Bedeutung in der klinischen Arbeit zu. Empathie und Empathieentwicklung wird in ihrer Bedeutung und Funktion der kognitiven sozialen Perspektivenübernahme gegenüber gestellt. Diese beiden zentralen Dimensionen sozialer Kompetenz sind motivational und funktional grundsätzlich verschiedenen Bereichen zuzuordnen. Ausgehend von der Priorität von Empathie als veränderungs– und heilungseffizient in der klinischen Arbeit kann die kognitive soziale Perspektivenübernahme als Hilfsmittel zur Erhöhung und Differenzierung von Empathie eingesetzt werden, wenn sie motivational mit dem empathischen Ansatz kongruent ist.

DIE BEDEUTUNG DES MOTIVATIONALEN ASPEKTES VON EMPATHIE UND KOGNITIVER SOZIALER PERSPEKTIVENÜBERNAHME IN DER PERSONZENTRIERTEN PSYCHOTHERAPIE .

Annäherung an eine Begriffsbestimmung

Versucht man den personzentrierten Ansatz von Rogers zu vermitteln, so erweist sich die Darstellung seines Menschenbildes oft als Stolperstein:

Aussagen wie: "Der innerste Kern der menschlichen Natur, die am tiefsten liegenden Schichten seiner Persönlichkeit, die Grundlage seiner tierischen Natur ist von Natur aus positiv, von Grund auf sozial, vorwärtsgerichtet, rational und realistisch" (Rogers, 1961, S. 99) werden entweder mit zustimmender bis sentimentaler Rührung aufgenommen, oder als naiv, undifferenziert und vor allem in krassem Widerspruch zur eigenen Erfahrung und allgemeinem Wissen über menschliches Verhalten in der Geschichte gesehen.

Bei den zahlreichen Beispielen menschlicher Grausamkeit scheint aber so recht keiner an sich selbst oder seine Freunde zu denken, sondern es sind immer die ganz anderen, die ihm einfallen.

Es sieht so aus, als ob zumindest die meisten Menschen bei allen Selbstwertproblemen, Schuldgefühlen und Zweifeln, die sie so plagen, für sich und alle, die ihnen nahe stehen, das positive Menschenbild von Rogers durchaus in Anspruch nehmen. Und zwar ebenso allgemein wie Rogers dies tut, nicht im Sinne von "besser als", sondern eben menschlich, und d.h. im Grunde sinnvoll und in Ordnung.

Wenn sich ein Mensch empathisch verstanden fühlt, dann fühlt er sich, auch wenn die jeweiligen Gefühle durchaus nicht rühmlich sind, meist akzeptiert bis gern gemocht. Er spürt das Motiv des Gegenübers, die Dinge emotional mit seinen Augen zu sehen und damit grundsätzlich prosozial auf seiner Seite zu stehen und so nachzuvollziehen, daß sein Erleben einer verständlichen inneren Ordnung folgt.

Das Motiv der emotionalen Teilhabe ansich ist bereits Verbindung und grundsätzliche Akzeptanzbereitschaft. Besondere Hochachtung, Bewunderung oder spezifisches Interesse schließt es nicht ein. Es bedeutet zunächst ganz frei von speziellen Qualitäten, daß man sich als Artgenossen als wesensverwandt erkannt hat und sich damit "Freund", im Sinne von vertraut, einfühlbar und verbunden ist.

Man kann sich aber auch unter ganz anderen Aspekten als Artgenossen erkennen: z.B. als potentiellen Rivalen oder als Partner, der spezifischen Ansprüchen genügen muß, oder auch als Gegner in einer bestimmten Angelegenheit. Dann gilt es sorgfältig zu prüfen, ob und in welcher Hinsicht man Freund oder Feind ist und wie man welchen Einfluß auf die Beziehung nehmen kann. Hierbei bemüht man sich vorsorglich, Schwächen des anderen zu erkennen und eigene möglichst zu verbergen.

Unter diesem Blickwinkel entsteht ein eher düsteres, ebenso realistisches Menschenbild.

Im ersten Fall ist die Dimension sozialen Verstehens Empathie . Sie setzt eine emotionale Ansprechbarkeit für die bei anderen wahrgenommenen Gefühle voraus und ist als solches eine persönliche, subjektive Erfahrung, die auf Verbindung zielt.

Im zweiten Fall ist die Dimension sozialen Verstehens die kognitive, soziale Perspektivenübernahme. Sie setzt ein kognitives Verstehen der Gefühle und Motive des anderen voraus und ist als solche eine instrumentelle Fertigkeit, die auf eine objektive Einordnung und Bewertung zielt.

Soviel zur Einleitung und vorläufigen Begriffsbestimmung.

EMPATHIE ALS METHODE DER PERSONZENTRIERTEN THERAPIE.

Ich denke, daß es bei der psychotherapeutischen Arbeit ganz wörtlich und unmittelbar um emotionales, empathisches Verstehen geht, und, daß die je spezifischen therapeutischen Handlungskonsequenzen sich aus diesem Verstehen ergeben müssen. Hierbei ist auch die wahrgenommene Absicht, das Bemühen um Verstehen im Sinne einer emotionalen Teilhabe und damit einer auf Verbindung und Nähe ausgerichteten Kontaktaufnahme wesentlich.

Hiermit nehme ich eine Gegenposition zu denjenigen Kollegen ein, die den personzentrierten Ansatz eher im Sinne einer unsystematischen Desensibilisierung verstehen und Empathie und ihre Vermittlung als Basis sehen und als Vehikel benutzen, um einsichtsorientierte Klärungsprozesse in einer bestimmten Zielrichtung, in Gang zu bringen.

Bei aller Wichtigkeit und konstruktiven Prozeßhaftigkeit von Selbstexploration im inneren Bezugsrahmen, scheint doch die Erfahrung des Verstandenwerdens im Sinne einer unmittelbaren emotionalen Teilhabe für psychisches Wohlbefinden und Funktionieren von zentraler Bedeutung zu sein (Vgl. Whitehorn u. Betz, 1975, Bryant, 1990, Christie u. Geis, 1970, negativer Einfluß von Machiavellismus). Die Erfahrung bei der Arbeit mit psychisch schwer Gestörten zeigt, daß der Verlust des emotionalen Bezugs und der Verbindung zu Mitmenschen und Umwelt von viel elementarer Bedeutung ist, als etwa Mängel an realitätsangemessenen Einsichten, Erkenntnissen und Wahrnehmungen.

Nun schließt das eine das andere ja nicht per se aus: Einsichtsorientiertes Klären ist sicher eine sehr gute Methode, um die emotionale Teilhabe mit sinnvollem, wertvollem Zusatznutzen zu transportieren. Hinzu kommt, daß es sich gewissermaßen selbstverständlich anbietet: das gemeinsame Thema ist der Patient mit seinen Problemen, deshalb kommt er, und im Hinblick darauf will er etwas. Und es ist anzunehmen, daß der Patient, wenn er sich zum Thema macht, emotional sehr präsent ist, so daß sich hierbei wohl in den meisten Fällen die günstigsten Voraussetzungen für relevantes empathisches Verstehen in komprimierter Form ergeben. Empathisches Verstehen ist ja keine Sache ansich, die sich im luftleeren Raum vollzieht, sondern muß sich auf etwas zu Verstehendes beziehen und ist dabei auf Signale angewiesen. Tiefe Selbstexploration ist sicher geeignet, dem Therapeuten Signale zu liefern, die ihn zu differenziertem, empathischem Verstehen auf entsprechendem Niveau befähigen; sie ist sicher das, was in den meisten erfolgreichen Therapien meistens geschieht.

Speziell bei der Arbeit mit Schwergestörten habe ich aber oft den Eindruck, daß introspektives Klären einen eher nachgeordneten Stellenwert hat. Es kann sogar destruktiv sein, wenn wir es unbedingt forcieren wollen, weil wir dann schon ein bißchen die Übereinstimmung der Interaktionsebenen und das empathische Verstehen verlassen haben, indem wir – egal wie wohlmeinend – an unseren Maßstäben und Zielvorstellungen orientiert sind.

Unterstützt wird diese Therapieauffassung einmal durch die Tatsache, daß sich die psychische Entwicklung im vorsprachlichen Raum unter Nutzung anderer Kriterien vollziehen muß. Dann, durch die Erfahrung, daß viele psychotherapeutische "Sternminuten" sich im Zusammenhang mit unmittelbarer emotionaler Teilhabe ereignen und, daß es positive Entwicklungen in der Therapie mit Patienten, bei denen störungsbedingt diese Form der Klärungsarbeit wenig möglich ist, gibt.

Rogers sagt über die Therapie mit Mr Vac: "Ich glaube meine fehlerhaften Vermutungen waren unwesentlich im Vergleich zu meiner Bereitschaft seine Gefühle von Wertlosigkeit und Verzweiflung zu teilen, wenn er in der Lage war diese zu äußern". (Rogers, 1967, S. 411)

Die Möglichkeit andere am eigenen inneren Erleben teilhaben zu lassen und das Erleben anderer zu teilen, scheint eine unmittelbare bestätigende Erfahrung an sich zu sein (Stern, 1992, affect–attunement.)

Empathie ist darauf angewiesen, daß die Beteiligten über irgendein wechselseitiges Repertoire im Senden, Empfangen und Entschlüsseln von Signalen verfügen, also eine gemeinsame Sprache nicht nur dem Vermögen nach sprechen können, sondern soviel Interesse an Nähe und Teilhabe am inneren Erleben des anderen haben, daß sie sich nach Kräften und ohne versteckte Hinterabsichten anderer Art darum bemühen, es zu tun und auch zu vermitteln.

Empathie vollzieht sich im Rahmen eines Bezugssystems, das nach den Dimensionen Nähe–Distanz, vertraut–fremd, Freund–Feind, Sicherheit–Angst, Eindeutigkeit–Verworrenheit strukturiert ist (Binder, 1994 a; b).

Empathie setzt keineswegs im Prinzip enge oder tiefe Beziehungen voraus, sondern lediglich eine jeweils bereichsspezifische, situativ ausreichende Klarheit hinsichtlich dieser Dimension und damit eine gewisse Stimmigkeit, einen gegenseitigen Konsens über die wechselseitigen Näheerwartungen, –bedürfnisse, –motive und –toleranzen.

Empathie muß nicht rein altruistisch sein, aber motivational wenigstens tendenziell prosozial auf einen anderen gerichtet, wobei der jeweilige Nutzen für beide Partner gleichwertig und gleichzeitig sein kann oder auch nicht.

Man kann unvollständig, unangemessen, grob, wenig oder in einer gegebenen Situation überhaupt nicht empathisch sein. Man kann auf Täuschungsmanöver hereinfallen. Man kann zu stark identifikatorisch am eigenen Erleben verhaftet sein, oder an dem Bild, das man sich vom anderen gemacht hat und damit den eigentlichen am anderen orientierten Empathieprozeß vorschnell in andere Richtungen treiben. Man kann auch das ursprünglich empathisch Verstandene zu ganz andere Zwecken nutzen. Man kann sich während des Empathieprozesses überfordert, angesteckt oder überschwemmt fühlen und aversiv reagieren, aber dem Ursprung nach ist der empathische Prozeß nicht feindselig.

Dieses zu Beginn prinzipiell auf emotionale Verbindung Gerichtet–Sein von Empathie schließt nicht automatisch Niveau und Qualität ein, und es garantiert auch nicht, daß die aus dem Prozeß resultierenden Reaktionen nicht phantasielos, unbeholfen oder überflüssig ausfallen, aber sehr wohl, daß sie auf der emotionalen Ebene tendenziell nicht destruktiv sind. Hierfür gibt es zahlreiche Beispiele aus der frühkindlichen Empathie, wo die wohlgemeinten Handlungen mangels entsprechender Kompetenz oft völlig mißlingen.

Und nun ein Beispiel von konstruktiver, wechselseitig befriedigender Empathie bei umständehalber ausgesprochen reduziertem Verständnis:

Ich habe drei Wochen allein in einer chinesischen Bauernfamilie verbracht. Meine chinesischen Sprachkenntnisse beschränken sich weitgehend auf das existentiell Notwendige. Ich kann so wenig, daß ich auch kaum falsch verstehen kann, sondern eben nicht. Mit der Zeit begann die Hausfrau mir ihre persönlichen Probleme zu erzählen. Wir bemühten uns beide sehr darum, daß ich möglichst viel auch von den Worten verstand, sodaß ich jeweils auch einen ungefähren Schimmer vom Thema hatte. Ansonsten blieb nichts anderes übrig, als empathisches Verstehen im nonverbalen Bereich. Die Gespräche hatten Prozeßcharakter mit typischem Verlauf. Die Intensität stieg an, erreichte eine gewisse Dramatik mit expressivem Zorn, Angst oder Trauer, die ich jeweils benannte, und ging dann langsam über in zunehmende Entspannung, Ruhe und Nachdenklichkeit, um schließlich in zufriedener Alltagsstimmung mit Alltagsinhalten zum Abschluß zu kommen. Die Bäuerin muß auf emotionaler Ebene etwas davon gehabt haben, weil es keine andere Erklärung dafür gibt, daß eine Frau, die so viel und hart arbeitet, immer mehr Zeit dafür verwendet mit einem Menschen, der ihre Worte so wenig versteht, ihre persönlichen Probleme zu besprechen. Nun war es ja keine Arbeitssituation, sondern mein Urlaub. Was habe ich also davon gehabt? Ich denke, insgesamt ungefähr dasselbe wie sie, wenn auch ganz ohne eigenes Problemthema, das ich geklärt hätte. Es war für mich zwar anstrengend, aber völlig stress– und angstfrei und führte zu einem Zustand ausgeglichener Erlebnisoffenheit und einer zunehmend freundlich offenen, vertrauensvollen Einstellung zu mir und allen anderen Personen in meiner Umgebung.

Das Fazit ist gewiß nicht, daß Nicht–Verstehen günstig ist. Günstig scheinen aber Bedingungen zu sein, die dazu führen, daß weder überverwickelt Gefühlsansteckung und Identifikation möglich sind, noch emotional distanzierende Bewertungen und Beurteilungen, noch auf außerhalb des unmittelbaren Geschehens gerichtete Bedürfnisse und diesbezügliche Strategien und Manipulationsabsichten.

Und doch blieb etwas dabei unbefriedigend: diese ursprüngliche, unmittelbare Empathie konnte sich nicht zu einem tieferen oder spezifischeren Verstehen entwickeln. Wir wurden uns zwar immer vertrauter, blieben aber ganz ohne gegenseitigen weiterführenden Erkenntnisgewinn. Eine Beziehungsgeschichte, die über die konkrete Situation hinausging, hatten wir nicht.

Bei soviel Fremdheit und so wenig Möglichkeit diese über eine sich langsam vortastende, verbale Kommunikation zu minimieren entsteht entweder extreme Angst und Mißtrauen und das zentrale Interesse aneinander ist Einschätzen und Durchschauen oder aber, es entsteht genau entgegengesetzt, großes Vertrauen und eine positive Bindung, die nichts mit der Bewertung der spezifischen Eigenarten und Qualitäten des anderen zu tun hat. Diese Bindung entsteht und wird aufrechterhalten, indem die Beteiligten über empathisches Verstehen und dessen expressive Vermittlung eine emotionale Nähe herstellen, durch die die bedrohlichen Aspekte der Fremdheit ausgeschlossen werden. Hierbei ist dann das zentrale Interessen aneinander nicht, was man sich mit welchem Ziel gegenseitig tun bzw., wie man gegenseitige Qualitäten erforschen und nutzen kann, sondern was man mit einander tun und teilen möchte auf der Basis dessen, was man unmittelbar vorfindet. Hierbei ist das Interesse wechselseitig auf das emotionale Befinden gerichtet; ein Hinterfragen der an irgendeinem normative Wertsystem orientierten Berechtigung eines emotionalen Zustandes findet nicht statt.

Da es sich bei Bindungen der im Chinabeispiel beschriebenen Art um ein Phänomen handelt, das wir üblicherweise inbezug auf kleine Kinder kennen, sind wir gewöhnt, derartiges als kindlich bis primitiv und regressiv zu betrachten und hierhin einen Ausdruck von Abhängigkeit zu sehen. Sicher ist der sprachunfähige Gast in einer fremden Kultur situativ sehr abhängig, aber eine Reduzierung innerpsychischer Autonomie ist nicht gegeben.

Das empathische intensive Auf–einander–bezogen–Sein hat für Erwachsende die selben konstruktiven Qualitäten wie für Kinder auch, und es setzt für Kinder wie für Erwachsene Erlebnisintensität und Energien für Neuerfahrungen und Veränderungen frei. Indem die Dimension Mißtrauen, d.h. bewertende, beurteilende Betrachtungsweisen des Beziehungsgeschehens in den Hintergrund gerückt ist, finden die sozialen Erfahrungen angstfrei und kongruent statt.

Empathisches Verstehen und Verstandenwerden ist eine soziale Kompetenzerfahrung im Bereich der Dimension Vertrauen–Mißtrauen in sich und andere. Die hierin gegebene Möglichkeit der Steuerung sozialer Erfahrungen – man kann das Senden bzw. Unterdrücken von Signalen willentlich beeinflussen – stellt einen Schutz vor Ohnmachtserleben und Verletzungen dar und bedeutet einen Zuwachs von Autonomie ohne Beziehungsverlust.

Entscheiden für Bindung in diesem Sinne sind die strukturellen Qualitäten des Partners. Für die Dauer und Intensität einer Bindung wesentlich sind Verständigungs– und Anlehnungsprozesse, die weniger auf Austausch basieren. Sie werden als dem Selbst zuzuordnende Dimensionen gesehen. Demgegenüber bei Beziehung davon ausgegangen, daß der Partner aufgrund von bestimmten Qualitäten ausgewählt wird, und somit das "Einzigartige" an ihm die notwendige Vorbedingung des Zusammenseins ist, während Bindung, genau umgekehrt, zunächst beliebig, gewissermaßen austauschbar eingegangen wird. Erst eben durch die vollzogene Bindung wird der entsprechende Partner "einzigartig" nicht austauschbar und nicht ersetzbar. (Auckenthaler u. Binder, 1987).

Ich will im Folgenden versuchen Unterschiede zwischen Empathie und kognitiver sozialer Perspektivenübernahme herauszuarbeiten. Ich glaube, daß diese beiden zentralen Dimensionen sozialen Verstehens inbezug auf Bindung und Beziehung im oben beschriebenen Sinne wesentliche andere Funktionen haben.

Die Bindung stiftende Empathie scheint eher fremdbezogen und abgegrenzter vollzogen zu werden als die prüfende, eher beziehungsrelevante Perspektivenübernahme. Empathie richtet sich darauf, wie es dem anderen unabhängig–von–einem selbst in einer Angelegenheit emotional geht. Perspektivenübernahme richtet sich viel stärker darauf, was die Befindlichkeit des anderen für einen selbst im Guten wie im Schlechten bedeutet.

Für die Empathie relevant ist die Gleichheit/Ähnlichkeit der Gefühlausstattung bei gegebener Andersartigkeit der Situation und Person. Für die Perspektivenübernahme relevant ist die Vergleichbarkeit bzw. Relation im situativen motivationalen Bereich und ihre Konsequenzen.

Empathie setzt ein gewisses Ausmaß an Verbundenheit/Vertrautheit mit der emotionalen Ausstattung des anderen voraus. Ausgehend vom kleinsten gemeinsamen Nenner stellt sie eine Verbindung zunächst fest und nicht her, um sie dann aber aufrechtzuerhalten, zu stabilisieren und zu intensivieren.

Kognitive soziale Perspektivenübernahme geht von sozialem Erfahrungswissen aus und zielt auf einen Erkenntnisgewinn im Sinne von Bewertungen und Vorhersagen inbezug auf den anderen.

Es ist mir hierbei wichtig die Empathie in jeder Hinsicht aus einem moralisch bewertenden Kontext herauszulösen: die Vertrauen und Bindung stiftende Empathie ist keineswegs im höheren Sinne moralisch, sondern ausgesprochen parteiisch und solidarisch bis hin zu Ungerechtigkeit und Vetternwirtschaft.

Wird die Annäherungs– und Bindungsmotivation verlassen, so kann sie sich ganz asozial in ihr Gegenteil verwandeln. Gegenüber Angehörigen der Wir–Gruppe entsteht z.B. in einer gegebenen Situation Mitgefühl, gegenüber Angehörigen der Nicht–Wir–Gruppe durchaus Schadenfreude.

Demgegenüber ist durch kognitive soziale Perspektivenübernahme so etwas wie eine objektivere moralische Urteilsbildung möglich, ob und wozu man diese dann benutzt, ist eine andere Sache.

Empathie und kognitive soziale Perspektivenübernahme haben unterschiedliche Funktionen und gründen auf unterschiedlichen Erfahrungsbereichen und diesbezüglichen Bedürfnissen und Erwartungen. Sie pflegen sich real häufig zu überlagern und zu ergänzen. Sie benutzen dieselben Signale. Sie stehen beide im Dienste des Funktionierens in der sozialen Umwelt und sind beide hierzu unabdinglich, aber motivational sind sie tendenziell entgegengesetzt und zwar für den Sender und den Empfänger.

Beide haben etwas mit dem Verstehen und Erfassen der Gefühle, Bedürfnisse und Ziele des anderen in einer gegebenen Situation und den daraus resultierenden eigenen Gefühlen, Erwartungen, Bedürfnissen und Motiven zu tun. Im einen Fall, um sich mit durchaus gegenseitigem Nutzen einander anzunähern und sich emotional zu verstehen und zu binden. Im anderen Fall, um sich voreinander zu schützen, sich abgegrenzt zu durchschauen und Vorhersagen treffen zu können und so das Verhalten primär zum eigenen Nutzen zu steuern.

Empathisches Verstehen vollzieht sich stärker von Moment zu Moment und ist damit zwar nicht erfahrungsunabhängig, aber wird je genuin durchlaufen. Die Wahrnehmung und Dechiffrierung der Signale kann defizitär sein.

Die kognitive soziale Perspektivenübernahme geht aus von Erfahrungen und bildet Hypothesen in die Zukunft. Die entsprechenden Interpretationen und Annahmen können falsch sein.

In beiden Fällen sind Mängel bzw. Fehldeutungen nicht im Bewußtsein repräsentiert.

Um Unterschiede und Überlagerungen deutlich zu machen, kann man sich z.B. folgende Situation vorstellen:

Kommt ein Mensch an einen Badestrand, so pflegt er meist kurz die bereits Schwimmenden zu betrachten; nimmt er nun wahr, daß diese frieren, so kann er das empathisch verstehen und kommunizieren und so einen emotionalen Rapport herstellen.

Er kann aber auch, hiervon ganz unberührt, über Perspektivenübernahme sich ein Urteil bilden, ob er selbst unter den gegebenen Umständen schwimmen möchte oder nicht. Dieser Vorgang ist bindungs– und beziehungsmäßig irrelevant, beinhaltet aber den großen Nutzen, ohne eigenes Risiko aus den Erfahrungen anderer lernen zu können. Dieser Mensch kann aber auch beides tun und z.B. auf einige empathisch verbindend reagieren, auf andere ausgrenzend schadenfroh und gleichzeitig für sich selbst eine Entscheidung treffen.

Überspitzt ausgedrückt: der einseitig empathiezentrierte erfährt etwas über die Empfindungen der Badenden, nicht aber über die Wassertemperatur. Bei dem nur auf Perspektivenübernahme ausgerichteten verhält es sich umgekehrt.

Entwicklung

Um zu einem vertieften Verständnis der beiden wesentlichen Dimensionen sozialen Verstehens zu kommen, möchte ich jetzt kurz etwas zur Entwicklung von Empathie und kognitiver sozialer Perspektivenübernahme sagen.

Bei beiden handelt es sich um arteigene, angeborene Dispositionen, die sich über vielfältige Vorläufer bei gegebener Ich–andere–Differenzierung entwickeln (Bischof-Köhler, 1989). Obgleich zeitlich relativ parallel und funktional für die Regelung sozialer Beziehungen/Bindungen gleichermaßen überlebensnotwendig, unterliegen sie verschiedenen Entwicklungsbedingungen (Bryant, 1990).

Vorläufer von Empathie – wie etwa Gefühlsansteckung – scheinen von Geburt an gegeben zu sein, also zeitlich etwas früher als Vorläufer kognitiver sozialer Perspektivenübernahme. Empathie und ihre Vorformen dürften eher im Dienste der Herstellung und Aufrechterhaltung von Bindung stehen. Perspektivenübernahme ist demgegenüber eher der Umweltkontrolle und realitätsangemessenen Verhaltenssteuerung zuzuordnen. Möglicherweise ist hier die Fremdenangst mit 8 Monaten als ein Vorläufer anzusehen.

Das Beziehungs/Bindungsverhalten der Betreuungsperson stellt hierbei eine ziemlich genaue Entsprechung dar: in frühen Phasen läuft die emotionale Verbindung über motor–mimicry und Wahrnehmung von Bedürfnissignalen, um dann, bezüglich empathischer Reaktionen zu affect-attunement, mit diesem Ausdruck ist die Spiegelung der Emotion in einer anderen Sinnesmodalität gemeint (Stern, 1992), überzugehen. Ebenso tritt bei Zunahme des Aktionsradius des Kindes jetzt auch verstärkt Perspektivenübernahme der Betreuungsperson auf, da nun die Notwendigkeit besteht, Absichten des Kindes vorausschauend zu erkennen und zu steuern.

Empathie und kognitive soziale Perspektivenübernahme sind grundsätzlich bei jedem Menschen als Disposition gegeben, unterliegen aber in Entwicklung, Ausprägung und Gewichtung, also in quantitativer und qualitativer Hinsicht, sowohl inter– als auch intraindividuell einer großen Variabilität (Binder, 1994 a; b). Defizite, unterschiedliche Gewichtungen, individuelle Unterschiede in der Wahrnehmung, Reaktionsbereitschaft und Flexibilität in diesen beiden Dimensionen sozialer Kompetenz sind in ihrer Entwicklung, Differenzierung und Aufrechterhaltung weitgehend unabhängig voneinander (Bryant, 1990). Empathie der Betreuungsperson hat eine zentrale Funktion in der Entwicklung des Selbst, der Ich–andere–Differenzierung, der Identität, der Selbst– und Umweltkontrolle, der Sicherheit und der sozialen Kompetenz und dem Selbstwertgefühl (Hattie, 1992, Krueger, 1989, Stern, 1992). Ein Bewußtsein inbezug auf die eigene Identität – ob dies nun formuliert ist oder nicht – bedeutet auch ein Bewußtsein darüber, zu wem man bindungsmäßig gehört und zu wem nicht. D.h. das Identitätsbewußtsein, das Selbstbild ist entscheidend dafür, ob wahrgenommene Signale in einem sozialen Kontext eher mit den Mitteln der Empathie oder eher mit denen der Perspektivenübernahme verarbeitet und beantwortet werden, oder auch, ob jeweils die Dimension Bindung/Beziehung zugunsten von Sach- und Handlungsinteressen desaktualisiert wird.

Ähnlich wie für die Entwicklung des Selbst auch Erfahrungen kontinuierlicher, zuverlässiger Art und hierauf gründende Erwartungsmuster, die die soziale und auch die unbelebte Realität handhabbar, kontrollierbar und vorhersagbar machen, wesentlich sind, so verhält es sich auch inbezug auf die sozial affektneutrale Beobachtung von Verhalten und Erleben artverwandter Lebewesen, die Modell für zu erwartende eigene wünschenswerte oder zu vermeidende Erlebnisse darstellen und im Dienste der Entwicklung realitätsangemessener Umweltkontrolle stehen.

Auch wenn wir als Rogerianer so sehr viel Wert auf genuine, organismische Erfahrungen und bewertungsfreies, empathisches Verstehen legen, so ist psychisches Funktionieren und die Entwicklung eines ausreichend stabilen Selbst- und Menschenbildes auch auf mehr oder weniger automatisch abrufbare Erfahrungsmuster angewiesen (Binder/Binder, 1994 b).

Auch Pfeiffer (1994) weist darauf hin, daß das Postulat der organismischen Erfahrung von Rogers der Erweiterung bedarf: soziale, kulturelle und informationsgebundene Erfahrungen, die mit den organismischen nicht übereinstimmen, können für psychisches Funktionieren oft auch von entscheidender Bedeutung sein.

Empathie nimmt in der Entwicklung nicht quantitativ zu, sondern durchläuft qualitative Veränderungen in Richtung Differenzierung. Die Differenzierung vollzieht sich erfahrungsbezogen, in dem sie mit der zunehmenden Breite des eigenen emotionalen Spektrums und dessen präziser Wahrnehmung korrespondiert. Nach Harris (1991) können Kinder bei sich und anderen erst etwa mit 10 Jahren zuverlässig widersprüchliche Gefühle wahrnehmen und benennen. D.h. erst etwa zu diesem Zeitpunkt ist Empathie weniger auf Eindeutigkeit der Signale angewiesen.

Weiterhin entfalten sich reifere Formen von Empathie durch zunehmende Abgrenzungsfähigkeit, Desaktualisierungs- und Dezentrierungsfähigkeit und Handlungskompetenzen. Hierdurch wird der Zeitpunkt, an dem empathische Erregung zu belastend wird und in reine Gefühlsansteckung, personal distress Reaktionen und Aversion umkippt, verschoben (Eisenberg, 1986; Hoffman, 1990).

Eine weitere erfahrungsbezogene Errungenschaft inbezug auf empathische Fähigkeiten, in die Aspekte der kognitiven sozialen Perspektivenübernahme mit eingehen, bezieht sich auf die Antizipation von Gefühlen anderer. Eine in der Phantasie durchlaufene antizipatorische Einfühlung ermöglicht entsprechende Verhaltenssteuerungen. So z.B. muß man dann einen anderen Menschen nicht erst verletzt haben, um sein Gekränktsein anhand von Ausdruckssignale wahrzunehmen, sondern man kann es vorwegnehmen und die Verletzung unterlassen, oder aber bei entsprechender Motivationslage bewußt und mit Absicht vornehmen.

In einer Untersuchung von Harris (1991) über die Fähigkeit von Täuschungsmanövern im emotionalen Ausdruck bei verhaltensgestörten und normalen Kindern ergab sich, daß beide Gruppen dem Vermögen nach relativ früh dazu fähig sind, aber daß die verhaltensgestörten signifikant weniger empathisch unecht waren um andere nicht zu verletzen, als vielmehr um sich zu schützen.

Ein empathisch orientiertes, prosozial motiviertes Zurückhalten bis Vortäuschen von Gefühlen beinhaltet keine destruktiven Aspekte von Inkongruenz, da, wenn es transparent wird, die Botschaft "will mir wohl" als kongruent und relevant spürbar wird.

Demgegenüber gründet die kognitive soziale Perspektivenübernahme eher auf einem Erfahrungsschatz im Sinne von abrufbarem Wissen von relativ feststehenden zu erwartenden Verknüpfungen von Situationen und zugehörigen Gefühlen, Motiven und Handlungen (Wilson u. Klaaren, 1992).

Damit erlaubt sie es soziale Einschätzungen und Verhaltenssteuerungen schnell und unaufwendig vorzunehmen, ohne dabei notwendigerweise einen eigenen emotionalen Prozeß durchlaufen zu müssen. So z.B. weiß man einfach, auch ohne sich die Mühe zu machen Ausdruckssignale präzise wahrzunehmen und über Einfühlung zu verstehen, daß, wer im Spiel verliert, sich üblicherweise ärgert, und wer gewinnt, sich freut.

Im Zuge von Lebenserfahrung kann die Fähigkeit zur kognitiven sozialen Perspektivenübernahme im Prinzip an Differenziertheit und Treffsicherheit kontinuierlich zunehmen. Sie kann aber auch in einzelnen Bereichen in festgefahrenen Vor–Urteilen erstarren und genuine Neuerfahrungen blockieren bzw. die adäquate Wahrnehmung von der Erwartung zuwiderlaufenden Ausdruckssignalen und entsprechenden Gefühlen anderer verhindern.

Solche erfahrungsbedingten, abrufbaren Gefühlserwartungsmuster sind inbezug auf das eigene Erleben als Teil des Selbstbildes und inbezug auf die soziale Umwelt als notwendige Orientierungshilfe zu betrachten. Durch sie wird Kontinuität und Sicherheit gewährleistet, schnelles Reagieren ermöglicht und die Fähigkeit zur Desaktualisierung von Widersprüchen, die die Funktionstütigkeit beeinträchtigen können, aufrechterhalten.

Das Erleben und Bewerten anhand von aus der eigenen Erfahrung gewonnenen erstarrten Gefühlserwartungsmustern und erst recht solchen, die über erfahrene Bewertungsbedingungen anderer etabliert wurden, sind ein Prototyp von Inkongruenzen im ursprünglichen Sinne von Rogers, die den Zugang zu genuiner Selbsterfahrung blockieren oder verzerren.

Ganz ohne sie bricht die Vorausschau, Planung und Desaktualisierungsfähigkeit und damit die Lebenstütigkeit zusammen; nur mit ihnen geht die Erlebnis–, Selbsterfahrungs– und Veränderungsfähigkeit, die das Leben im Prozeß halten im Rahmen zwischenmenschlicher Bindungen und Beziehungen verloren.

Wie arteigen und angeboren eine Disposition auch immer ist, ihre Entfaltung und Entwicklung kann defizitär verlaufen und Störungen erfahren.

Und hiermit kommen wir zu den Defiziten und Störungen in Ausprägung und Gewichtung sozialer Kompetenzen.

In der neueren Literatur gibt es zahlreiche Untersuchungen über die Wichtigkeit von Empathie für die Selbstentwicklung.

Hierbei habe ich weniger Ergebnisse gefunden, die die Auswirkungen von Empathie in ihrer ganzen Komplexität beleuchten, als vielmehr solche, die von quantitativen Unterschieden ausgehen.

Um nur zwei Beispiele zu nennen:

Nach Harris (1991) haben autistische Kinder keine relevanten Defizite inbezug auf die Fähigkeit zur kognitiven sozialen Perspektivenübernahme, aber entscheidend hinsichtlich Empathie.

Dasselbe konnte er, wenn auch weniger ausgeprägt, inbezug auf verhaltensgestörte Kinder feststellen.

Nach Feshbach (1990) wiesen Eltern, die ihre Kinder physisch mißbrauchten, erhebliche Defizite bezüglich ihrer empathischen Fähigkeiten im Vergleich mit einer normalen und einer psychisch kranken Elterngruppe auf. Dasselbe traf für die physisch mißbrauchten Kinder zu. Demgegenüber scheinen Defizite in der kognitiven sozialen Perspektivenübernahme weniger eklatante Zusammenhänge zur emotionalen Entwicklung zu haben. Hier scheint eher situativ durch z.B. Migration und Kulturwechsel oder auch überdauernd bei eher isoliertem, weltfremdem Aufgewachsensein oder auch anders bedingten Lernbehinderungen ein geringes oder auch falsches Verstehen sozialer Gegebenheiten als Stressfaktor wirksam zu sein, der dann auch eine emotionale Belastung durch erhöhte Ängste und Unsicherheiten in der sozialen Umgebung zur Folge hat, die durchaus Auslöser für psychische Erkrankungen sein können (Pfeiffer, 1994).

Gehen wir davon aus, daß unsere Patienten in irgendeiner Form defizitären bzw. unangemessenen Gewichtungen inbezug auf Empathie und adäquate Wahrnehmung ihrer Person ausgesetzt waren, so liegt nahe, daß sie ihrerseits Schwierigkeiten haben im Senden, Empfangen und Dechiffrieren von Signalen (Binder, 1994 a).

Die bei geringer Stabilität bzw. Flexibilität des Selbstbildes gegebenen Ängste und Bedürftigkeiten verhindern oft ein realitätsangemessenes Pendeln zwischen den je relevanten Ebenen sozialer Wahrnehmung und Kommunikation.

Hierzu ein Beispiel:

Eine psychotische Patientin, die in ihrer emotionalen Bedürftigkeit und sozialen Unsicherheit und all ihren Identitätsdefiziten stets darauf angewiesen ist, sich in Beziehungen zu definieren und zu positionieren, versucht dies im Sinne von "wer nicht für mich ist, ist gegen mich" zu regeln, was zu einem raschen Wechsel zwischen naiver Leichtgläubigkeit und panikartigem Mißtrauen führt. Sie verliebt sich gern und schnell in ernsthaft und fürsorglich an ihr interessiert wirkende Männer. Hierbei reagiert sie so total auf das Gefühl verstanden, umsorgt und geliebt zu werden, daß sie sich mit dem Betreffenden wie seit Urzeiten vertraut und seelenverwandt fühlt, ohne zu realisieren, daß ihr seine Person gänzlich fremd ist und ihre Wahrnehmung hier ganz diffus bleibt. Als jemand, der irgendetwas von ihr will oder mit ihr beabsichtigt, kommt er gar nicht vor.

Wenn nun im Zuge des Geschehens der auf ihr ruhende Blick der Liebe aktiver wird und eine Phase imponierender, werbender Selbstdarstellung beginnt, kann sie das nicht als solches wahrnehmen und durchschauen, sondern fühlt sich plötzlich klein gemacht, abgewertet und verachtet und reagiert ganz unverständlich hoch aggressiv. Entfällt diese Phase und der Blick der Liebe verändert sich in den der begehrenden Leidenschaft, so kippt ihr Gefühl der Nähe und Vertautheit unmittelbar um in das höchster Bedrohung. Sie dekompensiert und unterstellt dem eben noch innige Geborgenheit ausstrahlenden Liebhaber Mordabsichten und fühlt sich verfolgt.

Die Suche nach empathisch spiegelnden Signalen oder Botschaften, die helfen, Bausteine für ein positives Sebstbild zu finden, ist bei dieser Patientin so drängend, daß sie auf motivationale Veränderungen im Prozeß des Beziehungsgeschehens nicht mehr adäquat reagieren kann. Mit derselben Intensität, mit der sie sich so nah verbunden gefühlt hat, sucht sie jetzt ihr Gegenüber angstvoll als fremde, feindselige Person mit auf sie gerichteten Absichten zu durchschauen.

Indem sie sich und ihr Gegenüber identitätsmäßig diffus verwickelt wahrnimmt, führt der Versuch, sich durch kognitive soziale Perspektivenübernahme zu schützen, hierbei nicht zu der

Möglichkeit einer realitätsgerechten Einschätzung des konkreten Verhaltens einer konkreten Person in einer konkreten Situation, und die emotionale Betroffenheit kann nicht zu Gunsten einer Verhaltenssteuerung desaktualisiert werden.

Die Beziehungsorientierung psychoseerfahrener Patienten geht von der Frage aus, ob das Gegenüber sie ausreichend akzeptiert und achtet, um so zu klären, ob emotionale Nähebedürfnisse möglich oder extrem bedrohlich sind. Diese Frage ist so zentral und existenziell, weil diese Patienten über wenig Kompetenzgefühl hinsichtlich einer möglichen Beeinflussung des Beziehungsgeschehens verfügen, und auch, weil sie im Falle negativer Affekte wenig Abwehrmöglichkeiten haben, so daß ein diesbezüglicher Irrtum für sie entsprechend katastrophal ist.

Paranoid schizoide Beziehungsorientierung geht tendenziell von der Frage aus, was der andere meint und fühlt unter dem Aspekt, was er einem tut und mit einem vorhat und wie sich dieses aus versteckten Hinweisen ermitteln läßt. Diese Patienten brauchen oft mehr Aktivität des Therapeuten als Voraussetzung dafür, die Beziehung klar und eindeutig genug zu erleben, um sie irgendwann so weit ausblenden zu können, daß Selbstbezogenheit ohne Angst vor Kontrollverlust über das Beziehungsgeschehen möglich ist.

Und noch ein Beispiel:

Ein psychotischer Patient, der sehr einsam ist, bekommt hin und wieder Besuch von einem meist mißgelaunten, arbeitslosen Nachbarn, der ihn weniger aus Zuneigung als aus schlichter Langeweile zum Schachspielen besucht.

Die Beziehung ist nicht eng, so daß der Mißgelaunte keinen Anlaß hat, seine Stimmung zu teilen oder zu erklären, er will sie vielmehr möglichst verbergen. Der auf emotionale Verbindung zentrierte, für nonverbale Signale übersensible Patient nimmt sie aber sehr dominant wahr, wobei die Verschleierungsabsicht, die er auch spürt, die Angelegenheit noch verschlimmert. Zuerst reagiert er diffus gefühlsangesteckt und überschwemmt, es geht ihm auf ganz unerklärliche Weise, aber eindeutig im Zusammenhang mit seinem Gast, zunehmend psychisch schlecht. In ihm entwickelt sich ein ihm fremder Groll auf seinen Besucher, den er sich verzweifelt zu erklären sucht, und er unterstellt diesem schließlich die Absicht, ihn durch schlechte Gefühle so zu schwächen, daß er, trotz bekanntermaßen höheren diesbezüglichen Fähigkeiten, im Schach verlieren wird. Dieser Vorgang bleibt nicht ganz ohne Einfluß auf den Mißgestimmten, der sich gemäß kultureller Normen angepaßt und diszipliniert freundlich verhalten hat; er weiß sich seinerseits die massive Ablehnung, die ihm unausgesprochen mimisch entgegenschlägt, nicht zu deuten. Die dadurch gegebene Irritation ist Auftakt für den weiteren destruktiven Verlauf: die Spannung nimmt zu, und der emotional instabilere Patient ist davon so beeinträchtigt, daß er nun wirklich im Schach verliert und sich in seiner paranoiden Unterstellung bestätigt fühlt. In der Folge kommt es zu einer Zunahme psychotischer Symptome, bei denen sich die Wahnthematik um diesen Nachbarn dreht.

Bei Bindung, Zuneigung, Nähe und auch emotionaler Sicherheit, Selbstbewußtsein, autonomer Abgrenzungsfähigkeit und hohem sozialem Kompetenzgefühl nimmt die Empathiebereitschaft zu. Bei Unsicherheit, Fremdheit, Angst, hoher emotionaler Verletzlichkeit, Abgrenzungsmotiven und –schwierigkeiten, aber auch bei Interessenskonflikten, Macht–, Durchsetzungs– und Beeinflussungsstreben, d.h. motivational nicht wertfrei ergebnisoffenen Absichten inbezug auf den anderen, intensiviert sich die kognitive soziale Perspektivenübernahme.

Bei Depressiven ist der aktive, voluntative Bereich häufig wenig entwickelt, und Macht–, Durchsetzungs– und Beeinflussungsstrebungen sind motivational nachgeordnet (Binder/Binder, 1994 b).

Depressive Bindungs/Beziehungsorientierung geht tendenziell von der Frage aus, was der andere braucht, will und fühlt, und wie man ihm was geben muß, um die für sich selbst notwendige Basisharmonie herzustellen. Depressive scheinen im realen sozialen Umgang ausgesprochen empfindlich auf strategische Manipulationen zu reagieren und sie selbst eher wenig einsetzen zu können und zu wollen. Dem gegenüber ist das typische depressive Grübeln gewissermaßen ein Umgang mit sich selbst nach Art gnadenlos kritisch prüfender von Mißtrauen geprägter Perspektivenübernahme. Hierbei wird sezierend detektivisch und ganz unempathisch vorgegangen, um eigene negative Motivationen selbstkritisch aufzuspüren; ehe man riskiert derart von anderen betrachtet und vernichtet zu werden, macht man es lieber selbst.

Ich denke, daß der kritische Umgang mit sich selbst dem Muster folgt, das die Patienten mit relevanten Bezugspersonen erfahren haben; die Tendenz mit anderen empathisch umzugehen entspricht dem Wunsch eben dieses in Beziehungen zu vermeiden.

Fassen wir die schweren Störungen im Bereich sozialer Wahrnehmung noch einmal kurz zusammen:

Kongruenzdefizite, Fragmentierungen im Selbstbild und entsprechend gravierende Unsicherheiten im Senden und Empfangen und Dechiffrieren von relevanten sozialen Signalen führen zu pathogenen Mischungen unterschiedlicher Verstehensdimensionen in der sozialen Wahrnehmung und entsprechend schweren Störungsbildern.

Das quälende Empfinden emotionaler Getrenntheit aktiviert eine extrem verbindungsuchende, gefühlsoffenen Verletzlichkeit, bei der die Empfänglichkeit für emotionale eher nonverbale Signale übersteigert ist und gemäß den Vorformen von Empathie im Sinne von Gefühlsansteckung und –übernahme wirksam wird (Binder, 1994 a).

Aufgrund der Schwierigkeiten hinsichtlich der Einordnung Ich–Andere bzw. Wir–Nicht–Wir und der damit einhergehenden prinzipiellen sozialen Bedrohung wird die Anwendung von kognitiver sozialer Perspektivenübernahme unter dem Aspekt beziehungsrelevante Absichten zu durchschauen, verstärkt.

Hierdurch entsteht die Tendenz alle wahrgenommenen Signale als strategisch beziehungsgerichtete Kommunikation zu mißdeuten. Aufgrund von Bindungsbedürfnissen existentieller Art bleiben die stets als von höchster Beziehungsrelevanz gewerteten Signale als empathische bzw. affektive Erregung mit einer Tendenz zu Gefühlsansteckung, –übernahme und personal distress Reaktionen bestehen, ohne daß die gleichzeitig unternommenen Versuche bewertender Perspektivenübernahme desaktualisiert werden zu können. Der Versuch, sich durch kognitive soziale Perspektivenübernahme zu schützen, führt hierbei nicht zu der Möglichkeit der Einordnung, die die emotionale Betroffenheit relativiert und sich in realitätsangemessene Verhaltenssteuerung umsetzen kann. In der Folge kommt es dann zur Dekompensation mit ihren vielfältigen Erscheinungsbildern.

Und nun zu den therapeutischen Konsequenzen:

Indem der Therapeut vom ersten Moment an eine hohe Empathiebereitschaft für den Patienten aufbringt, gewährt er gewissermaßen rückhaltlos Vorschuß in Sachen Bindung/Beziehung. Dieses emotionale Risiko kann er sich nur leisten, wenn er voraussetzt, daß ihm sein Gegenüber vertraut genug ist, um unbedrohlich zu sein, und, wenn er in sich stabil genug ist, um sich gegen destruktive Gefühlsansteckungen und –übernahmen abgrenzen zu können, und, wenn er seinerseits keine Abhängigkeiten oder andere Arten von Bedürfnissen an den Patienten hat.

Der Therapeut hat auftragsgemäß keinerlei Anlaß, den Patienten inbezug auf dessen Qualitäten für eine wechselseitig lohnende Beziehung zu untersuchen. Demgegenüber hat der Patient sehr begründete Erwartungen an den Therapeuten und eine berechtigt hohe Motivation diesen inbezug auf seine bindungs– und beziehungsrelevanten Qualitäten zu überprüfen.

Wenn der Therapeut vor allem zu Beginn und bei psychisch schwer gestörten Patienten, deren Vulnerabilität inbezug auf negative Affekte so hoch ist, konsequent empathisch orientiert bleibt, ist es ihm möglich ohne Aggressionen zu entwickeln, mit Beziehungsprüfungen wie Provozieren, Agieren etc. gelassen empathisch verstehend umzugehen und nicht reaktiv, verwickelt mit Gegenaggressionen oder Empfindlichkeiten zu reagieren.

Das gegenüber strategischen Manövern des Patienten neutrale empathische Verstehen der dahinter liegenden Erlebnisweisen ist hierbei keineswegs eine defensive oder vermeidende Haltung. Der empathisch bindungsorientierte Therapeut nimmt dies alles durchaus wahr, wobei das Interesse aber gleichbleibend wertfrei auf das Verstehen der Gefühlsbedeutungen ausgerichtet ist und nicht auf strategische Gegenzüge. Hierdurch nehmen meist auch auf seiten des Patienten derartige Verhaltensweisen schnell ab. Dieses radikal unparanoide Beziehungsangebot des Therapeuten ist gewissermaßen das genaue Gegenteil des analytischen Konzeptes, wo Übertragung durch ständige Beziehungshinweise und diesbezügliche Deutungen angeheizt wird.

Ausgehend von einem motivational prosozialen empathisch bindungsorientierten Kontakt führt der Therapieprozeß über Vertrauen, Sicherheit, Angstfreiheit und Unverlierbarkeit nicht in die Abhängigkeit, sondern in eine dialogisch interaktionelle Beziehung (Pfeiffer, 1994). Wenn uns das gelingt, sind dann im Therapieprozeß zunehmend auch beziehungsorientierte Interventionen und Konfrontationen möglich.

Der Zeitpunkt der Verschiebung von Sicherheit/Bindung als zentral zu mehr autonomen Gegenüber von Person zu Person ist störungsspezifisch unterschiedlich. Beide Aspekte sind immer gegeben, aber unterschiedlich gewichtet, je nach dem, ob und inwieweit der Patient in der Lage ist, den Therapeuten fraglos als motivational unverdächtig und ihm positiv zugewandt zu erleben, sodaß Spekulationen über geheime Absichten überflüssig sind.

Es scheint so zu sein, daß Einfühlen konkret in der Situation die einzige Möglichkeit ist, den anderen emotional zu erreichen, ohne ihm schaden zu können. Und, daß Denken, Interpretieren, Wissen, Absichtenverfolgen diesen Prozeß zerstören und ablösen oder auch begleiten und optimieren kann.

Ich glaube nicht, daß Denken über und Sich–einfühlen–in–einen–Anderen im Prinzip Gegensätze sein müssen, sie werden es erst, wenn sie motivational entgegengesetzte Prioritäten setzen, und nicht, wenn es sich um sich ergänzende Modalitäten inbezug auf dasselbe Ziel handelt.

Wesentlich hierbei ist, daß Verstehensansätze, die kognitive soziale Perspektivenübernahme als Grundlage haben, stets den Charakter von Hypothesen bzw. Denkanstößen, die vom Patienten aufgenommen oder verworfen werden können, behalten.

Wenn wir in der Psychotherapie alle unsere Interventionen und Verstehensweisen transparent machen, d.h. die Quelle unseres Verstehers jeweils angeben, können wir auch die kognitive soziale Perspektivenübernahme ohne Schaden anzurichten erweiternd nutzen.

Bei manchen psychisch schwer gestörten Patienten, die dazu neigen, das Verhalten anderer wahnhaft zu interpretieren, ist die gemeinsame Suche nach möglichen anderen Erklärungen über kognitive soziale Perspektivenübernahme oft eine konstruktive Möglichkeit verfestigte Sichtweisen wenigstens wieder zu öffnen und auch, gewissermaßen modellhaft nebenbei, das Pendeln zwischen den beiden Dimensionen sozialen Verstehens anzuregen, ohne daß hierbei die therapeutische Beziehung Irritationen erfährt.

Kognitive soziale Perspektivenübernahme hat zwar auch Prozeßcharakter, kommt aber bezüglich der jeweiligen Situation/Thematik zu einem Abschluß, einem Ziel und endet mit einer Stellungnahme als Grundlage für Planung und Umsetzung von Verhalten.

Empathie ist demgegenüber ein bindungsbegleitender Endlos–Prozeß, der motivational und – zumindest in der Psychotherapie prosozial – an der Teilhabe der Gefühle und ihrer Bedeutung für den anderen und einer entsprechenden Kommunikation orientiert ist. Hier werden die Gefühle des einen gewissermaßen das gemeinsame Dritte in der Interaktion (Pfeiffer, 1994) auf der Basis einer bestehenden sicheren Bindung, die keiner Prüfung und Thematisierung bedarf.

Wenn wir Empathie als die Methode betrachten, werden alle verfügbaren Verstehensmöglichkeiten im Dienste der Herstellung möglichst differenzierter Empathie genutzt. Es werden also störungsspezifisches Wissen, Theorien, Diagnosen etc. zur Optimierung empathischen Verstehens eingesetzt.

Nehmen wir den Begriff personzentrierte, störungsspezifische Empathie als zentrale Dimension unserer Methode ernst, so bedeutet das: unter Berücksichtigung der gleichrangigen respektierenden Einbeziehung der stets gegebenen "gesunden, erwachsenen" Anteile unserer Patienten muß unser Bindungs/Beziehungsangebot je in Abstimmung auf die störungsspezifischen Defizite eine konstruktive Entwicklung im Senden und Empfangen von Empathiesignalen fördern. Auf dieser Basis wird die Bildung eines kongruenten Selbstbildes entsprechend der "gesunden" Entwicklung nachgezeichnet und schrittweise aufgebaut.

Hierbei muß der Therapeut konstruktive Bedingungen anbieten, die jeweils in spezifischer Übereinstimmung mit dem Entwicklungsstand von Empathie und Selbst und den je vorliegenden Gewichtungen in unterschiedlichen Problembereichen des Patienten korrespondieren. Defizite in der Entwicklung von Selbst und Selbstbild, also Diffusität inbezug auf Identität und Kontinuität im Erleben, führt zu einem Mangel an erfahrungsbezogenen Gefühlserwartungen, die ohne jeweils einen genuinen Prozeß durchlaufen zu müssen, einfach abrufbar sind und so Erleben und Verhalten entlastend vorstrukturieren.

Defizite im Zugang zur organismischen Erfahrung aufgrund eines unflexiblen, inkongruenten Selbstbildes bewirken Mangel an veränderungsorientierter genuiner Selbsterfahrung und Stagnation (Swildens, 1991). Von daher bedeutet der personzentrierte Ansatz, ein auf demselben theoretischen, weltanschaulichen und empirischen Hintergrund beruhendes störungsspezifisches manchmal geradezu entgegengesetztes Vorgehen bei unterschiedlichen Patienten inbezug auf Erleben mit zeitlichem Prozeßcharakter.

Den einen müssen wir vorwiegend helfen "eingefrorene" inkongruente Raster wieder genuinen Erleben zu öffnen, den anderen müssen wir vorwiegend helfen überhaupt stabile Raster aufzubauen, die das Erleben zeitlich und gemäß den je relevanten Dimensionen geordnet strukturieren.

Rogers spricht von der Aktualisierungstendenz als konstruktive Entwicklungsrichtung. Gesunde psychische Prozesse sind sowohl auf die intensivierende, realitätsangemessene, innovative Aktualisierungstendenz, als auch auf Desaktualisierungsfähigkeiten angewiesen, damit Erleben im Prozeß bleibt (Binder/Binder 1994a; vgl.: "überschießende Aktualisierung", Speierer, 1994).

Die adäquate Vermittlung von konstruktivem, empathischem Verstehen setzt auch ein Verständnis dafür voraus, wie der Patient was, wann und warum versteht.

Chinesisch lernen ist für uns ungleich schwerer als etwa Englisch oder Französisch, wo neben Fremdem und Neuem auch Vertrautes und Ähnliches gegeben ist. Chinesisch ist keineswegs simultan übersetzbar, sondern erfordert strukturelles Umdenken und Üben ganzer Sätze, bis sich so etwas wie ein Sprachgefühl und ein spontaner Transfer einstellt.

Übertragen wir dieses Bild auf unsere Arbeit:

Je strukturell abweichender unsere Patienten von uns und unseren üblichen Erfahrungen sind, umso mehr Hilfsmittel, Mühe und Aufwand müssen wir aufbringen, um jeweils spezifisch dasselbe Ausmaß an konstruktivem empathischen Verstehen wie im uns vertrauten zwischenmenschlichen Bereich zu entwickeln und adäquat zu vermitteln.

Ein Sprachvermögen hat jeder, aber er kann dadurch noch lange nicht sprechen und verstehen; d.h. wir müssen jeweils die Sprache der Störung lernen.

Empathie kann man fördern, üben und erforschen. Damit empathisches Verstehen überhaupt Empathie ist und sich die darin liegenden Wirkungen in einer zwischenmenschlichen Beziehung entfalten können, müssen wir wirklich jedes mal neu einen empathischen Prozeß mit entsprechenden Emotionen in uns in Gang setzen, durchlaufen, aufeinander abstimmen und vermitteln. Obgleich dieses "neu" sich zwar vor Moment zu Moment vollzieht, ist es aber keineswegs geschichts- oder erfahrungslos.

Der Anspruch die notwendige störungsspezifische Empathie wirklich bei allen Patienten in der notwendigen und ausreichenden Form zu verwirklichen, bleibt eine Illusion, oder erfordert entweder beispiellose Genialität, oder – und dies auch, wenn wir sinnvoller Weise nur an eine Annäherung an dieses Ziel denken – sehr viel Arbeit.

LITERATUR

Auckenthaler, A.; Binder, J. (1987): *Beziehung und Bindung*. Unveröffentliches Manuskript.
Binder, U. (1994a). *Empathieentwicklung und Pathogenese in der klientenzentrierten Psychotherapie*. Eschborn: Klotz
Binder U. (1994b): *Klientenzentrierte Psychotherapie mit Patienten aus dem schizophrenen Formenkreis*. In: Hutterer–Krisch, Wien: *Springer*
Binder, U.; Binder J. (1994a). *Klientenzentrierte Psychotherapie bei schweren psychischen Störungen*. Eschborn: Klotz
Binder, U., Binder, J. (1994b). *Studien zu einer störungsspezifischen Psychotherapie – Schizophrene Ordnung – Psychosomatisches Erleben – Depressives Leiden*. 2. Aufl. Eschborn: Klotz
Bischof–Köhler, D. (1989). *Spiegelbild und Empathie*. Bern: Huber
Bryant, B.K. (1990). *Mental health, temperament, family, and friends: perspectives on children's empathy and perspective taking*. In: Eisenberg et al. New York: Cambridge University Press
Christie, R.; Geis, F.L. (1970). *Studies in Machiavellism*. New York: Academic Press.
Clark, M.S. (1991). *Prosocial Behavior*. Newbury Park: Sage.
Clark, M.S. (1992). *Emotion and Social Behavior*. Newbury Park: Sage.
Eisenberg, N. (1986). *Altruistic Emotion, Cognition and Behavior*. Hillsdale: Erlbaum.

Eisenberg, N.; Strayer, J. Eds. (1990). *Empathy and its development.* New York: Cambridge University Press.

Feshbach, N.D. (1990). *Parental Empathy and Child Adjustment/Maladjustment.* In: Eisenberg et al., New York: Cambridge University Press.

Hattie, J. (1992). *Self–Consept.* Hillsdale: Erlbaum.

Hoffman, M.L. (1990). *The Contribution of Empathy to Justice and Moral Judgement.* In: Eisenberg et al., New York: Cambridge University Press.

Harris, P.L. (1991). *Children and Emotion.* Cambridge: Basil Blackwell.

Hutterer–Krisch, R. Hrsg. (1994). *Psychotherapie bei Menschen mit psychotischen Störungen.* Wien: Springer.

Krueger, D.W. (1989). *Body Self and Psychological Self.* New York: Brunner/Mazel.

Pfeiffer, W.M. (1994). *Personzentrierte Störungslehre aus interaktioneller Sicht.* Vortrag bei der GwG–Fachtagung: Störungs– und Krankheitslehre. Köln: GwG. Im Druck.

Rogers, C.R. (1961). *On becoming a person. A therapist's view of psychotherapy.* Boston: Houghton Mifflin Company. (dt.: Entwicklung der Persönlichkeit. Psychotherapie aus der Sicht eines Therapeuten (1973). Stuttgart: Klett.

Rogers, C.R. (1967). *A Silent Young Man.* In: Rogers et al. Madison: Wisconsin Press.

Rogers, C.R. Ed. (1967). *The Therapeutic Relationship and its Impact.* Madison: Wisconsin Press.

Speierer, G. (1994). *(Das differentielle Inkongruenzmodell DIM).* Heidelberg: Asanger.

Stern, D.N. (1992). *Die Lebenserfahrung des Säuglings.* Stuttgart: Klett.

Swildens, H. (1991). *Prozeßorientierte Gesprächspsychotherapie.* Köln: GwG.

Whitehorn, J.C.; Betz, B. (1975). *Effective Psychotherapy with the Schizophrenic Patient.* New York: Jason Aronson.

Wilson, T.D. and Klaaren, K.J. (1992). *"Expectation whirls me round".* In: Clark. Newbury Park: Sage.

Client–Centered Therapy and Techniques

JEROLD D. BOZARTH

UNIVERSITY OF GEORGIA

ABSTRACT

Can one use techniques and be Client–Centered? The answer, for me, is, "Yes but.." The theory militates against the use of techniques. Techniques are generally problem–centered and therapist driven rather than trust–centered and person driven. They are generally laden in one way or another with the expertise of the therapist. Unless they are emergent in the blending of therapist and client, techniques distract from the attention of the therapist to the world of the client. Emergent techniques occur out of the connection of the therapist's self with the other's self within the therapist's dedication to the world of the client.

The question posed is, Can one use techniques and still be Client–Centered?

Rogers' theoretical position is a view that militates against the use of techniques in counseling and psychotherapy. Techniques are, at best, irrelevant and have no value to the fundamental theory of the client–centered approach. Worse, however, is that techniques may interfere with the client freedom perpetuated by a client–centered stance and can insidiously contaminate the nondirective position of the therapist. Although I believe that techniques may occur in client–centered therapy and be consistent with the theory, such responses are necessarily related to the internal referent of the client and emergent from that internal referent. It is important to keep in mind Rogers' theory since one of the typical discursive traps is "..that of dismissing the fundamental assumption of the approach (that of the actualizing tendency and the self authority of the client) as untenable or questionable and proceeding with criticism of the theory from other frames of reference" (Bozarth, 1993, p. 2). I will begin with a statement of my understanding of the position of those who believe techniques are appropriate in client–centered therapy and react to this position. I will then offer a brief reiteration of the theory, identify Rogers' (1957) view of techniques in his classic integrative article and discuss the only theoretically consistent integration of techniques in the theory.

RATIONALE FOR THE USE OF TECHNIQUES

Art Bohart (personal communication, April 15, 1993) asks a critical question, "Can one systematically try to facilitate experiencing, to work through the problematic reaction points, and to resolve unfinished business, and still be consistent with the person–centered philosophical emphasis on people finding their own solutions" (p.36)? Brodley and Brody (1994) aptly respond to this question in their paper when they remark:

> In our opinion, infusing specific goal oriented treatments and techniques with client–centered values in ways that influence the actual application of the treatments and techniques might well tend to greatly humanize and improve the efficacy of the treatments and the techniques. But they should not be confused with client–centered therapy. (p.2)

To go a bit further, why would one want to use techniques if operating from a client–centered stance? Most techniques are developed from other psychological frameworks holding different basic assumptions. For example, the assumption that clients have unfinished business is alien to the theory. There are no preconceived (nor post–conceived) systematic problem points. The approach is trust–centered rather than problem–centered. Concepts and their concomitant techniques such as unfinished business are not part of and is probably antithetical to the underlying framework of the theory. The belief that certain techniques are considered powerful influencers of behavior is not a valid argument for including them in a contradictory frame of reference.

Other than the non sequitur emanating from other basic assumptions, the only other rationale that I know that argues for the use of techniques is that there is ample research evidence supporting the effectiveness of certain techniques. Brodley and Brody acknowledge that we know of effective specific psychotechnologies such as ".. cognitive and behavioral techniques for alleviating depression, getting through panics, for controlling one's focus of attention and for relaxation" (p.9). However, these techniques are deemed to be effective from frameworks of assumptions of expertise of the therapist and predicated upon the questionable specificity assumption. The position assumes the therapist to have certain information and skills available to the client through which goals can be attained or problems alleviated. In the client–centered position, problem resolution is in the trust of the client's capability and unique directions and not in the therapist's armamentarium of skill and knowledge.

In addition, the research on the question of efficacy of techniques can be questioned prima facie; e.g., generalizability, direct comparison with other treatments, replicability. My skepticism about such data is recorded in a dialogue with Lazarus and Lazarus (Bozarth,1991a) where I point out the very studies which they use to support their assertion for the tenet of specific techniques for effectiveness in treating particular disorders actually raise questions about their own assertion. Furthermore, we seldom know the extent of influence of the common variables of the relationship and of client motivation when techniques are being studied.

In short, do we really know as much about the efficacy of specific techniques as often assumed? We certainly do not have a comparative base that any techniques that we offer is better than the clients emergent directions of self influence. The recent research reviews on outcome efficacy (Bohart, 1994; Lambert, 1992, Lambert, Shapiro & Bergin, 1986; Patterson, 1984; Stubbs & Bozarth, 1994) suggest that application of the research results might better involve an intentional utilization of the client's frame of reference (Duncan & Moynihan, 1994). My personal view is that the potency of the client's frame of reference and self adjusting methods by far exceed other methods *when therapists are able to trust clients' constructive forces and their rights to their own expertise about their own life.*

THE THEORY

Rogers' view of psychological dysfunction is that individuals are thwarted in their natural growth by conditions of worth being introjected from significant others. Psychological growth results from the individual being freed of these introjections. When the individual experiences unconditional positive regard from a significant other, the person begins to develop unconditional positive self regard. As this occurs, the individual becomes increasingly able to deal with problems and life.

If the therapist is congruent in the person–centered relationship, experiences unconditional positive regard and empathic understanding toward the client and if these attitudes are, at least, minimally perceived by the client, then therapeutic personality change will occur (Rogers,

1959). In client–centered therapy, the therapeutic atmosphere created by the therapist fosters the natural process of the actualizing tendency of the client. The greater the extent that the therapist honors the authority of the client as the authority of his/her own life then the greater the probability of constructive personality change and problem resolution. As constructive personality change occurs, the client will also be better able to solve his or her own problems (Rogers, 1977; Rogers & Wallen, 1946). Hence, the amelioration of particular dysfunctions are a result of personality change that involves the experiencing of unconditional positive regard. Interventive techniques are simply extant of the theory. To reiterate, Client–Centered Psychotherapy is founded on the trust of the person and not on problem–centered assumptions.

TECHNIQUES FROM ROGERS' PERSPECTIVE

Rogers' (1957) perspective of techniques is clearly pronounced in his integrative statement. This statement is not about client–centered therapy but has to do with the commonalties which Rogers' viewed across therapies and helping relationships (Bozarth & Stubbs, 1994).

In the integrative statement, Rogers explicitly cites a variety of techniques that he viewed as having "essentially" no value to therapy; such as, interpretation of personality dynamics, free association, analysis of dreams, analysis of transference, hypnosis, interpretation of lifestyle, and suggestion. However, Rogers (1957) adds:

> Each of these techniques may, however, become a channel for communicating the essential conditions which have been formulated. An interpretation may be given in a way which communicates the unconditional positive regard of the therapist. A stream of free association may be listened to in a way which communicates an empathy which the therapist is experiencing. In the handling of the transference an effective therapist often communicates his own wholeness and congruence in the relationship. Similarly for the other techniques. But just as these techniques may communicate the elements which are essential for therapy, so any one of them may communicate attitudes and experiences sharply contradictory to the hypothesized conditions of therapy. (p. 234)

An implication of Rogers' integrative statement and of his comments is reflected in his comment that "..the techniques of the various therapies are relatively unimportant except to the extent that they serve as channels for fulfilling one of the conditions" (p. 233). Rogers could not be clearer. He viewed techniques as valuable only in that they are channels for the core conditions. This view was true for him not only of client–centered therapy but therapy and helping relationships in general.

TECHNIQUES IN CLIENT–CENTERED THERAPY

Techniques must be emergent to be consistent with client–centered theory. Of the techniques which emerge during therapy, there are several contexts which are reasonably prevelent. These contexts are: (1) the client request (2) the setting and (3) the clearing of one's self in order to better absorb the client's world.

Client Request

When the client has a consistent request for the therapist to apply a technique, the therapist needs to be honestly present in the implementation of that desire. In other words, the therapist might indicate the reluctance to give advice or enthusiastically endorse a concentrated behavioral effort to effect particular change I'm reminded of the time that I reluctantly gave advice (without using a specific technique unless it would be called homework) to a couple in marital counseling. During a one time consulting session, the husband was clearly intent on obtaining advice from me. He was a self employed individual who was very goal and activity oriented.

Other therapists had given them advice that he liked (Namely, that they contract for the wife to have sex once a week and he would stop following her around the house when she changed clothes). They had a pattern of talking about their problems from morning through evening. When he asked me for advice at the end of the session, my honest presence was that I understood his wish for suggestions for concrete action. I said to him that I didn't usually give advice and, usually, when I did, it didn't work out very well. However, I expressed my understanding of his need and continued by suggesting that they quit talking to each other about "the problem." Several weeks later, the wife indicated that things had dramatically improved between them. The husband was delighted with the advice. Several years later they worked out an amiable divorce. Both individuals still , after nearly ten years, express their gratitude to me for the session. I think that the same gratitude would be there if I would have advised weekly picnics or if we would have attempted psychodrama.

Setting

Another prevalent context for using techniques seems to me to be requirements of the setting. Techniques are increasingly considered by agencies and institutions, to meet demands of demonstrating the treatment mode and pursuit of specific problem amelioration demanded by insurance guidelines, HMO's and so forth. The client–centered therapist may need to adjust to the system to survive. The setting may have a decided influence on the actual use of techniques in therapy.

Therapist Congruence

The third important rationale for the therapist to use an emergent technique is for the purpose of "clearing" him or herself in order to be better able to accept and understand the client. A brief example of this point occurred in a community group meeting. I kept losing my attention with one of the members when he talked. Over the couple of days, I found that I reacted nearly every time he spoke. My stomach got tight; I got a headache; I had a complete lack of attention to him. I would get up and leave when he talked; discussed my reaction with colleagues and so forth. Finally, I found myself completely annoyed with him as he droned on in a (to me) narcissitic dialogue. I had lost my capacity to just tolerate him let alone understand him. At that point, I got up and stood by the window noticing some mirror tiles that were awaiting construction of the room. Impulsively, I took one of the mirrors to him and asked him to look at himself. I had no thought of possible effect. The only reason for the action was that of clearing myself and making a connection with him. In fact, I thought that he might throw it at me. Instead, he looked at himself for several minutes. At the end of the workshop, he mentioned this as a meaningful technique for him. Others questioned my reason for using the technique (A Freudian one I believe someone said). It was, however, not a deliberated technique with any intention of result. It was simply a way that emerged for me to clear myself and to help me to connect with him. The "technique" did enable me to be somewhat more in concert with him.

For those who adopt the integrative model (and not necessarily the client–centered model), the primary justification for systematically using techniques is the provision of a way for the therapist to be maximize his/her congruency to bring his/her personhood to the client. When discussing orientations and techniques in relation to experiential therapy, Tom Malone (Whitaker & Malone,1981) captures this point:

> The key concept is congruence. The congruence between the therapist's technique–system and his/her person allows the maximal personal participation in the relationship to the patient. This differs for different therapists. (xxviii)

It is ironic that a therapist's techniques that are incongruent with adhering to client authority but which enables therapists to enhance their personal participation withclients might even serve as "conveyors" of the conditions. Evenso, the conditions may be so strong that they override the incongruent techniques.

GUIDELINES FOR THE INCLUSION OF TECHNIQUES

In general, I agree with Art Bohart's (1994) idea that techniques may emerge in the "dance" of the client and therapist. In fact, I believe that one can *do* many things as a therapist as long as one is totally dedicated to the theoretical base of the internal referent of the client and that empathic responding may be multifaceted and idiosyncratic (Bozarth, 1984). Increasingly, I (Bozarth, 1992) believe that one of the most confounding factors in the understanding of the approach is the focus on what the therapist should do in therapy rather than how the therapist should be. The guidelines that I view for using techniques in Client–Centered Therapy are similar to those I have proposed for using tests and assessment. The following quote (Bozarth, 1991b) with substitution of TECHNIQUE for tests and assessment summarizes this position:

Does this theory mean that TECHNIQUES from the person–centered perspective does not exist? Is it plausible to use TECHNIQUE in person–centered therapy and be consistent with the theoretical model? If so, what are the conditions for the use of TECHNIQUES? Responses to these questions revolve around the difference between what the counselor does in counseling and the philosophical dedication to the self–authority of the client. Assuming that the counselor adheres to the person–centered philosophy of honoring the clients perception of the world, what a counselor does in person–centered counseling is quite flexible depending on the idiosyncrasies of the client, counselor, and situation (Bozarth, 1984). Raskin's (1988) conceptualization of the systematic versus unsystematic implementation is significant in this regard. He differentiated *systematic* therapist activities from the *unsystematic* by viewing systematic therapists as having "a preconceived notion of how they wish to change the client and work at it in systematic fashion, in contrast to the person–centered therapist who starts out being open and remains open to an emerging process orchestrated by the client" (p.2). TECHNIQUES and other forms of activity (e.g., dispensation of medicine, behavior modification, homework) are consistent with the theory in that they may occur as unsystematic actions that are decided on by the client from the client's frame of reference in interaction with the therapist. *Any ethical activity or action that is decided upon by the client and emerges from the attention to the internal world of the client is a viable and congruent activity in person–centered therapy.* (p. 45)

SUMMARY

Can one use techniques and be Client–Centered? The answer, for me, is, "Yes but.." The theory militates against the use of techniques. Techniques are generally problem–centered and therapist driven rather than trust–centered and person driven. They are generally laden in one way or another with the expertise of the therapist. Unless they are emergent in the blending of therapist and client, techniques distract from the attention of the therapist to the world of the client. The primary reason for involving techniques in a client–centered frame of reference is to help the therapist clear his/her barriers to absorbing the client's perceptual world. Thus, the remarkable potency of trusting the client's own way, direction and pace can be realized. I personally agree with Rogers when he said, "If I thought that I knew what was best for a client, I would tell him." Likewise, if I thought that I knew that a particular technique was best for a client, I would use it. However, I can't imagine that happening.

368

REFERENCES

Bohart, A. C. (1994). *The person–centered therapies.* In A. S. Gurman & S. B. Messer (Eds.), Modern psychotherapies. New York: Guilford

Bozarth, J. D. (1984). *Beyond reflection: Emergent modes of empathy.* In R. F. Levant & J. M. Shlien (Eds), Client–centered therapy and the person–centered approach: New directions in theory, research, and practice (pp. 59–75), New York: Praeger.

Bozarth, J. D. (1991a). *Rejoinder: Perplexing perceptual ploys.* Journal of Counseling and Development., 69(5), 466–468. Invited article.

Bozarth, J. D. (1991b). *Person–centered assessment.* Journal of Counseling and Develoment, 69, 458–461.

Bozarth, J. D. (1992). *Coterminous intermingling of doing and being in Person–Centered Therapy.* The Person–Centered Journal. 1(1), 33–39.

Bozarth, J. D. (1993, May). *Misunderstandings of the person–centered approach.* Paper presented at the annual conference of the Association for the Development of the Person–Centered Approach, Maryville, TN.

Bozarth, J. D., & Stubbs, J. P. (1994, September). *The integrative statement of Carl R. Rogers.* Paper presented at the International Conference on Client–Centered and Experiential Psychotherapy, Gmunden, Austria.

Brodley, B. T., & Brody, A. (1994, September). *Can one use techniques and still be client–centered?* Paper presented at the International Conference on Client–Centered and Experiential Psychotherapy, Gmunden, Austria.

Duncan, B. L. & Moynihan, D. W. (1994). *Applying outcome research: Intentional utilization of the client's frame of reference.* Psychotherapy 31(2), 294–301.

Lambert, M. J. (1992). *Psychotherapy outcome research.* In J. C. Norcross & M. R.Goldfried (Eds.), Handbook of psychotherapy integration (pp.94–129). New York: Basic.

Lambert, M. J., Shapiro, D. A., & Bergin, A. E. (1986). *The effectiveness of psychotherapy.* In S. L. Garfield and A. E. Bergin (Eds.) Handbook of psychotherapy and behavior change(3rd ed., pp. 157–212). New York: John Wiley.

Patterson, C. H. (1984). *Empathy, warmth, and genuineness in psychotherapy.* A review of reviews. Psychotherapy, 21, 431–438.

Rogers, C. R. (1957). *The necessary and sufficient conditions of therapeutic personality change.* Journal of Consulting Psychology, 21, 95–103.

Rogers, C. R. (1959). *A theory of therapy, personality, and interpersonal relationships as developed in the client–centered framework.* In S. Koch (Ed.), Psychology: A study of science (Vol. 3) Formulation of the person and the social context (pp. 184–256). New York: McGraw Hill.

Rogers, C. R. (1977). *Carl Rogers on personal power: Inner strength and its revolutionary impact.* New York: Delacorte.

Rogers, C. R., & Wallen, J. L. (1946). *Counseling with returned servicemen.* New York: McGraw Hill.

Stubbs, J. P. & Bozarth, J. D. (1994). *The dodo bird revisited: A qualitative study of psychotherapy efficacy research.* Journal of Applied and Preventive Psychology. (Invited article), 3(2), 109–120.

Whitaker, C. A. & Malone, T.P. (1981). *The roots of psychotherapy* (rev. ed.) New York: Brunner/Mazel.

Can One Use Techniques and Still Be Client–Centered?

BARBARA TEMANER BRODLEY

ILLINOIS SCHOOL OF PROFESSIONAL PSYCHOLOGY

ANNE BRODY

CHICAGO COUNSELING AND PSYCHOTHERAPY CENTER

ABSTRACT

Can a therapist who uses techniques still be client–centered? The specific meaning given to this question implies several different answers. Therapists whose client–centered values influence the *application* of goal–oriented treatments and techniques might describe themselves as client–centered behavioral therapists or client–centered relationship trainers, et cetera. However, this should not be confused with the practice of actual client–centered psychotherapy. The question might be rephrased to say, "Does client–centered therapy use techniques?" In this case, the answer is YES. Technique of some sort is intrinsic to all therapy practice. Another meaning of the question might be, "Can specific techniques that have specific goals and effects be applied in the context of true client–centered therapy?" Here, the answer is YES, if they are the result of the client's questions or requests, and NO if they are the result of the therapist's having a diagnostic mindset that determines which goals and techniques are indicated.

CAN ONE USE TECHNIQUES AND STILL BE CLIENT–CENTERED?

Depending upon the specific meanings given to the panel question, there are several different answers. We shall first try to put aside one meaning of the question with a quick, but hopefully clear, answer in order to pursue some meanings of the question that are of greater interest to us.

"Client–centered" can refer to a general framework of theory, a philosophy that attributes high value to the individual person, values an egalitarian and democratic approach to the relations among persons, and also views Rogers' (1957) attitudinal conditions of congruence, unconditional positive regard and empathic understanding as necessary therapist attributes in helping relationships. The term "person–centered" is also used to refer to this general framework.

Some therapists who work from this general framework provide services that involve having specific goals for clients and/or involve specific goal–directed techniques. Examples are teaching relaxation for alleviating pain, teaching behavioral techniques to cope with anxiety or obsession, teaching relationship or parenting skills, psychodrama, gestalt therapy, artistic or expressive procedures, and teaching meditation or focusing techniques. When the general client–centered framework is combined with other therapies or specific goal–directed techniques, the answer to the panel question is a very qualified YES. One can use techniques and still be client–centered — at least sort of.

The meaning of being "client–centered" in this regard is that the therapist is basically not a client–centered therapist but is, for example, a relaxation therapist, a cognitive therapist, a relationship trainer, or a focusing trainer approaching his/her work with client–centered values. Such therapists employ the theory and techniques of their specific therapies in *ways that are as faithful as possible to client–centered values and attitudes*, given the contradictory and limiting features of their basic approach.

Such therapists and trainers might describe themselves as client–centered whatever — client–centered behavioral therapists, client–centered gestalt therapists, client–centered relationship trainers, et cetera. These kinds of applications of the general client–centered theoretical framework to specific treatment goals, using specific goal–directed techniques for the benefit of clients are not, however, client–centered therapy.

In our opinion, infusing specific goal–oriented treatments and techniques with client–centered values in ways that influence the actual application of the treatments and techniques might well tend to greatly humanize and improve the efficacy of the treatments and the techniques. But they should not be confused with client–centered therapy.

A different meaning to the panel question might be phrased: "Are techniques employed in client–centered therapy?" In addressing this question we first wish to clarify the meaning of "technique." A technique is a method or procedure that exists in practical or formal *details*. It involves actions that are usually employed to carry out an artistic work or scientific operation (Webster, 1977, p. 1972). This definition does not obviously fit into our topic of psychotherapy (or at least it raises questions about the nature of therapeutic theories). But basically, putting aside those complexities, a technique is doing something according to some principle or following some steps in order to promote or effect an end or a goal.

Adapting this definition to our topic of psychotherapy, we can say techniques refer to procedures, steps, actions, specific behaviors that implement ideas (that is, our theories) about how to help persons psychologically in order to enhance their well–being and functioning as persons. In terms of this definition, techniques are intrinsic to client–centered therapy. There is no therapy, of any kind, without techniques. And although client–centered therapy is correctly described as a theory of values and attitudes (Rogers, 1951; 1957; 1959; 1986), it cannot be practiced without techniques.

To express this point we quote John Shlien (1993) about client–centered therapy:

> Attitudes are not enough. Techniques are extremely important, because they are what express the attitudes. The theory is not expressed in the grand design, it is expressed in the method. The principles are in the practice. The attitudes are in the technique.

Corroboration of Shlien's statements can be found in Rogers' theory of therapy (1957), which requires that the client perceive the therapist's offering of the therapeutic attitudes for change to occur. This theoretical element mandates that the therapist be present and act towards the client in ways that communicate the therapeutic attitudes, thus giving the client an opportunity to perceive them. The therapist's actions that express the therapeutic attitudes are, in effect, techniques. Thus, the panel question, rephrased as "Does client–centered therapy use techniques?" must be answered YES. Without techniques there would be no therapy because there would be no communication to the client and, consequently, no perception of the therapeutic attitudes by the client.

Another meaning of the panel question can be stated: "Can specific techniques that have specific goals and effects be applied in the context of true client–centered psychotherapy?" This question might mean, more specifically, "Can a client–centered therapist teach relaxation, teach focusing, apply a gestalt or a psychodrama technique, et cetera, in the context of client–centered therapy and still genuinely be doing client–centered therapy?" In order to address this question we need to refer to the conclusion, above, that techniques are necessarily employed in client–centered therapy, and then attempt to answer the question: "Towards what goals are techniques employed in client–centered therapy?"

If it is true, that implementation of the therapeutic attitudes is an application of techniques, then towards what goal or end are these techniques employed in client–centered therapy? Simply put, the answer in Rogers' theory is that the therapeutic attitudes provide a highly favorable interpersonal and intrapsychic environment for the client. This climate promotes the client's own capabilities for self–understanding, problem solving, more effective functioning in the client's interpersonal world and realization of untapped potentialities. Thus the goal of the techniques of client–centered therapy is only the successful provision of the attitudes in ways that communicate to the individual client. If the client perceives the attitudes, the consequent effects on the client are the result of the client's inherent capabilities for growth and healing. The consequences of the client's perception of the attitudes are not the therapist's goals for the client. In fact, the client–centered therapist has no goals for his/her clients other than providing his/her presence and communicating in such a way that the client is able to perceive the therapeutic attitudes.

Rogers was very clear—he had no goals for his clients. He said, "the goal has to be within myself, with the way I am" (Baldwin, 1987, p. 47). He also said that therapy is most effective "when the therapist's goals are limited to the process of therapy and not the outcome" (Baldwin, 1987 p. 47). But even these process goals are not goals for the *client's* process. They are goals for the therapist's inner experience and for the therapist's implementation of inner experience in ways that can accurately communicate to the client.

Rogers elaborated on what he meant about his goals being limited to the process of therapy and not the outcome. He said, 'I want to be as present to this person as possible. I want to really listen to what is going on. I want to be real in this relationship, . . ." (Baldwin, 1987, p. 47). He said he asked himself, "Am I really with this person in this moment?" (Baldwin, 1987, p. 48), and concluded that these are "suitable goals for the therapist" (Baldwin, 1987, p. 48). In other words, the goals of the client–centered therapist are goals for him/herself in the relationship—how he/she feels toward the client and relates to the client. They are goals in respect to the therapist's subjective states and his/her clarity of communication of those states to the client.

In client–centered work the therapist is not occupied with evaluating the client in respect to any expectations about, or goals conceived for, the client. It is not a client–centered concern to be evaluating how well the client's process of self–expression is attuned to his/her experiencing. It is not a client–centered concern to be evaluating how coherently or how deeply or how realistically the client is proceeding in his/her interaction with the therapist. Client–centeredness involves a profoundly non–diagnostic mindset. The therapist is neither reflecting upon the client's clinical diagnosis nor reflecting upon any other scheme for deciding what the therapist should or should not do in relation to the client at that particular time. The mindset of client–centeredness involves the therapist in giving total attention to the client and towards understanding the client's frame of reference and what it is the client is attempting to have understood in the moment.

A client–centered therapist's behavior in relation to the client is affected by the client's behavior and communications, but not in any diagnostic sense. The client–centered therapist is in a relationship with the client, in a dialogue with the client, in order to try to understand the client from the client's frame of reference. In the relationship and in attempting to empathically understand, the therapist is responsive to the client. The therapist needs to be understood by the client in respect to the therapist's intentions to understand, accept and be authentic with the client. Thus, if the client responds to the therapist in ways that communicate that there are misunderstandings, the therapist attempts to adjust his/her behavior so his/her intentions can be accurately perceived by the client.

The therapist wants to accurately understand the client, and to this end makes empathic responses to find out from the client whether or not he/she does accurately understand. And the therapist wants to be accurately understood by the client, at least as far as that is perceptible. The therapist does make adjustments in his/her manner of communication and in his/her expressive behavior on the basis of feedback from the client for the sake of accurate intercommunication and clarity of communication between therapist and client. But even taking into account this adjustive responsiveness on the part of the therapist, it should be evident that client–centered attitudes and their implementation are profoundly non–directive. This fact is crucial in addressing the question of whether one is being client–centered if one is employing techniques that have goals other than the goals the therapist has for him/herself.

Rogers expressed the non–directive character of client–centered therapy in many ways in his writings and in his therapy demonstrations. In the context of his recognition of the political aspect of client–centeredness, Rogers (1977) stated:

> The politics of the client–centered approach is a conscious renunciation and avoidance by the therapist of all control over, or decision making for, the client. It is the facilitation of self–ownership by the client and the strategies by which this can be achieved; the placing of the locus of decision–making and the responsibility for the effects of these decisions. It is politically centered in the client. (p. 14)

The client–centered therapist's techniques when interacting with a self–expressing client are subjective procedures for maintaining total attention to the client, understanding empathically, and correcting experiences of momentary incongruence. The techniques are also behavioral forms that communicate acceptant empathic understanding. In this context of trying to understand, the therapist has no reason to think about specific goals for the client or about techniques to apply in relation to the client. It is not consistent with being an authentic client–centered therapist to apply specific techniques to effect changes in the client's experience, content of focus or process of communication.

Clients usually have specific therapy goals, such as alleviating anxiety or depression, recovering from trauma, getting along better with a partner, deciding what kind of a job to get, as well as having a general goal of improving their overall well–being or of being happier. Client–centered therapists interact with their clients through a process of understanding these specific goals as well as trying to understand any other focus that is occupying the client. The fact of the client's having specific goals does not set the client–centered therapist on a track of trying to figure out how to help the client with those goals in ways other than providing the therapeutic conditions. It is assumed, and it is our experience, that clients' specific goals are reached in a great variety of ways and that the ways are designed or discovered by the clients themselves. Occasionally a client–centered therapist will be called upon by the client to contribute ideas or procedures to help the client towards one of his/her specific goals.

It is consistent with, and actually an implication of, client–centered theory for the therapist to address client's questions and accommodate his/her requests, if doing so is within the therapist's capabilities. Answering questions and honoring client's requests for information, ideas, guidance, or techniques follows from the non–directive attitude (Brodley, 1994) and the client–centered values of respect for and trust in clients. Often, participation in a client's request for help towards reaching specific goals that is other than acceptant empathic understanding involves discussion with the client about treatments or techniques available outside of the client–centered therapy relationship. These treatments or techniques may be available through self–help literature or from therapists, physicians or trainers who are sought as a concomitant or adjunctive form of help by the client.

Sometimes, when requests are made, the client–centered therapist has knowledge and/or expertise in other specific therapies or specific psychotechnologies. For example, we know some cognitive and behavioral techniques for alleviating depression, getting through panics, controlling one's focus of attention and for relaxation. In the context of authentic client–centered therapy, while being responsive and accommodating to the client's direction, some such techniques occasionally may be practiced with a client. When the therapist participates in this manner the procedure is conceptualized as an experiment in the service of the client. It is directed as much as possible by the client. And it is under the client's control throughout the time of the experiment. Its value and benefit is assessed by the client.

Client–centered therapy does not pretend or presume to provide all of the personal and psychological resources a client might need, or believes that he/she may need, in the process of therapeutic personal change. It does show its valuing of clients' autonomy, self–direction and self– responsibility by providing the therapeutic attitudes. It also shows respect for, and trust in, clients by responding to their questions and honoring their requests when it is possible for the therapist to do so. Any specific goal–aimed techniques that the client–centered therapist might provide, however, are not sourced in any kind of diagnostic mindset towards the client.

One cannot employ techniques based on any kind of diagnostic mindset and still be functioning as a client–centered therapist. Thus, in the sense of the panel question expressed, "Can specific techniques, that have specific goals and effects, be applied in the context of true client–centered psychotherapy?" the answer is NO if they are the result of the therapist's having a diagnostic mindset, and YES if they are the result of the client's questions or requests, and if the therapist is able to participate in applying a technique while integrating such participation into his/her maintaining the therapeutic attitudes.

REFERENCES

Baldwin, M. (1987). *Interview with Carl Rogers on theuse of the self in therapy.* In M. Baldwin & V. Satir (Eds.), The use of self (pp. 45 52). New York: The Haworth Press.

Brodley, B. T. (1994, May). *Meanings and implications of the non–directive attitude in client–centered therapy.* Revision of paper presented at the ninth annual meeting of the Association for the Development of the Person Centered Approach. Kendall College, Evanston, Illinois.

Rogers, C. R. (1951). *Client–centered psychotherapy*, Boston: Houghton Mifflin Co. (1957). The necessary and sufficient conditions of therapeutic personality change. Journal of Consulting Psychology, 21, 95 103.

Rogers, C. R. (1959). *A theory of therapy, personality, and interpersonal relationships, as developed in the client–centered framework.* In S. Koch (Ed.), Psychology: A study of a science: Vol. 3. Formulations of the person and the social context (pp. 184 256). New York: McGraw Hill.

Rogers, C. R. (1977). *Carl Rogers on personal power.* New York: Delacorte Press.

Rogers, C. R. (1986). *Client–centered therapy.* In I. L. Kutash & A. Wolf (Eds.), Psychotherapist's casebook: Therapy and technique in practice (pp. 197 208). San Francisco: Jossey Bass.

Shlien, J. (1993, November). *God is in the details* [Videotape]. Lecture presented to Portuguese Society of Client–Centered Therapy and Person–Centered Approach, Lisbon.

Webster, N. (1979). *Webster's new twentieth century dictionary* (2nd ed.). New York: Simon & Shuster.

Mental Health and the Core Conditions

DUNCAN CRAMER

LOUGHBOROUGH UNIVERSITY

ABSTRACT

Person–centred theory holds that mental health primarily results from the core conditions of experienced unconditional acceptance, understanding and genuineness in a relationship. Despite substantial research on this idea, there is still little evidence which clearly shows a causal relationship between these conditions and mental health. Temporal precedence may be explored in longitudinal studies in which the direction and strength of the cross–lagged correlations are compared either directly or in terms of LISREL models with latent variables. Three such studies are described. The first study, on individual psychotherapy, suggested these qualities lead to therapeutic progress as judged by the therapist. The second study, on undergraduates's current closest relationship, implied these qualities resulted in greater self–esteem. The third study, on a representative community sample of adults, indicated mental health (assessed by the General Health Questionnaire) affects the perceived adequacy of close relationships but no such temporal relationship existed for depression.

Rogers' (1959) client– or person–centred theory originally proposed that mental health was solely determined by having a relationship in which a person genuinely felt unconditionally accepted and understood by another. Subsequently, Rogers acknowledged Ellis' (1959) critique that these three core conditions were likely to be highly desirable rather than necessary or sufficient and modified his proposition accordingly (Rogers & Truax, 1967/1976). The relationship between these conditions and mental health is linear such that higher levels of the conditions result in greater mental health. In addition, the conditions are interdependent so that, for example, feeling unconditionally accepted depends on being genuinely understood.

Despite the widespread impact of person–centred theory and its existence for over 30 years, evidence for its central hypothesis that these three conditions enhance mental health is weak and inconclusive (Cramer, 1991). Most of the early research on it was carried out on the professional therapist–client relationship while more recent work has examined it in personal relationships. One reason for the equivocal status of the findings is that almost all of the research has used non– or quasi–experimental designs in which participants have not been randomly assigned to high and low levels of these conditions. Thus, even though higher levels of the core conditions may have been found to be associated with better mental health, the non–experimental character of these studies do not permit the causal nature of this association to be ascertained.

While any such association is consistent with the core conditions facilitating mental health, it is also consistent with three other causal explanations. Firstly, mental health may affect the perception and/or presence of the core conditions insofar that those in better mental health may perceive and/or may have more highly facilitative relationships. Secondly, the causal relationship between the core conditions and mental health may be reciprocal with both variables influencing each other. And thirdly, the association between the two variables may be spurious, resulting from one or more confounding factor. The preferred method for determining causality is to conduct a true experimental design in which individuals are randomly allocated to differing levels of the variable whose effect is being investigated. Although it may be possible to carry out such research on the effect of the core conditions, the greater difficulty of doing so may not justify it until stronger non–experimental evidence for the association of these conditions with mental health has been provided (Cramer, 1990a).

One non–experimental approach for exploring the temporal relationship between two variables is a longitudinal study in which the two variables are both measured at the same time on two or more occasions (e.g. Cramer, 1990a). Two statistical methods for analysing such data are cross–lagged panel correlation analysis and linear structural relationships (LISREL) analysis. The advantage of the first method is that it partly offers a means for determining spuriousness, provided certain conditions are met. Essentially, it compares the correlations between the two different variables across time (i.e. the cross–lagged correlations). If, say, the cross–lagged correlation between the core conditions at time 1 and mental health at time 2 is significantly more positive than that between mental health at time 1 and the core conditions at time 2, then this difference implies that the core conditions are a stronger determinant of mental health than mental health is of the core conditions. If, on the other hand, the cross–lagged correlations are significantly positive but not significantly different, then the association between these two variables may be either spurious or reciprocal.

These interpretations assume that the (synchronous) correlation between the two variables at time 1 is similar to that at time 2, the internal reliablities of the measures are comparable and the test–retest (or auto–) correlations do not differ for the two variables. Two limitations of this method are the data may not satisfy these restrictive conditions and no index is provided of the strength of the cross–lagged correlations which takes account of the associations between the variables. These drawbacks are not shared by the second method which may also be employed to compare the statistical fit of models postulating one–way, two–way and no cross–lagged relationships between the variables. Moreover, the use of latent rather than manifest measures is presumed to give less biased estimates of the variables.

The main aim of this paper is to briefly outline some of the analyses carried out by the author which have generally explored the temporal relationship between the core conditions and mental health in both professional therapeutic and personal relationships with these two statistical techniques. One methodological advantage of studying this issue in individual professional therapeutic or counselling relationships is there is only one relationship which need be described (i.e. that with the therapist or counsellor). This is not the case in group therapy or in personal relationships where it is not clear whether only one relationship should be looked at and if so, which one. A second methodological advantage of examining this hypothesis in psychotherapy and counselling is it is easier to specify the period over which this relationship should be examined and to investigate it from its inception since substantial therapeutic improvement has been shown to take place within the first few sessions (e.g. Howard, Kopta, Krause & Orlinsky, 1986). In personal relationships, on the other hand, it may be difficult to predict which relationships may become important and over what period any change might be expected to have occurred. However, despite these potential drawbacks, it is also important to study this issue in personal relationships which typically characterise and are central to our lives and to which person–centred theory also applies.

PROFESSIONAL THERAPEUTIC RELATIONSHIPS

Two exploratory studies examining the cross–lagged correlation between the core conditions and mental health in the client–therapist relationship have been published so far. The first study examined the temporal relationships between client–rated therapist empathy and acceptance, and both client– and therapist–assessed therapeutic progress after sessions 2 and 6. The 37 clients taking part received weekly individual sessions of long–term psychoanalytic and person–centred therapy carried out by 37 experienced therapists in one of three Dutch psychotherapy institutions (Cramer & Takens, 1992). Six items each assessed therapist empathy (e.g. 'S/he does not always quite understand what my experiences mean to me'), therapist acceptance (e.g. 'I think s/he likes me') and therapeutic progress (e.g. 'I think our interviews are of some use to me'). The therapist acceptance and empathy scales consisted of items loading highly in a factor analysis of a Dutch version of the Barrett–Lennard Relationship Inventory. Therapist acceptance and empathy were only evaluated by the client while therapeutic progress was assessed by both client and therapist.

The cross–lagged relationship between therapist–rated progress and both therapist empathy and acceptance could not be interpreted because either the synchronous or the auto– correlations differed significantly. The necessary conditions for interpreting the cross–lagged relationships between client–rated progress and both therapist empathy and acceptance were met but none of these differences was significant, implying that these relationships were either spurious or reciprocal. The LISREL analyses suggested that the most parsimonious model for the relationship between client–rated progress and therapist acceptance was one which assumed no cross–lagged association between the two variables, while for the relationship between client–rated progress and therapist empathy it was a unidirectional one in which therapist empathy at session 2 was negatively related to client–rated progress at session 6. This latter finding implies that greater initial empathy leads to less subsequent progress, at least when both these variables are assessed by the client. One interpretation of this result is that being understood may satisfy the client's need for such understanding and may reduce their desire for making further progress.

The best–fitting model for the relationship between therapist–rated progress and therapist empathy was a unidirectional one in which therapist empathy at session 2 was positively associated with therapist–rated progress at session 6, while for the relationship between therapist–rated progress and therapist acceptance it was a reciprocal one in which both cross–lagged coefficients were positive. While these two findings are consistent with the person–centred hypothesis that the client's perception of the therapist as empathic and accepting leads to therapeutic improvement, one limitation of this study is that it is not known to what extent the measure of therapeutic progress used is positively related to more standard indices of mental health or therapeutic change.

The second study assessed the relationship between the core conditions and mental health after the first and third session of primarily eclectic individual therapy with 24 clients (Cramer, 1993a). Clients evaluated their therapist's core conditions with the 64–item revised Barrett–Lennard Relationship Inventory and their own mental health on the 12–item Leeds General Anxiety and Depression Scales, the 10–item Rosenberg Self–Esteem Scale and the 10–item Jones' Need for Approval Scale. Because of the small sample size, cross–lagged correlation and LISREL analyses were not carried out. Instead, cross–lagged correlations were computed in which the other variable measured at session 1 was partialled out. Three of the eight partial correlations were significant at the one–tailed level and a fourth was almost significant. Controlling for the core conditions at session 1, greater depression at session 1 was significantly associated with a less positive view of the therapeutic relationship at session 3 while higher anxiety at session 1 was significantly correlated with a more positive perception of the therapeutic relationship at session 3. These two results suggest that initial depression and anxiety determine the subsequent therapeutic relationship or its perception. With the relevant mental health measure at session 1 controlled, a more positive view of the therapeutic relationship at session 1 was significantly associated with greater self–esteem at session 3 and was almost significantly correlated with less need for approval at session 3. These latter two findings, on the other hand, imply that the initial more positive perception of the therapeutic relationship may bring about higher self–esteem and lower need for approval subsequently. Therefore, the results of this study provide mixed support for the person–centred assumption that the core conditions lead to mental health, which appears to depend on the aspect of mental health measured.

CLOSE RELATIONSHIPS

The cross–lagged relationships between self–esteem and the core conditions in one's current closest relationship have been investigated in a small sample of some 60 British students (Cramer, 1988, 1990b, 1994). The closest relationship was specified since close relationships are often seen as including ideal characteristics similar to the core conditions of acceptance, understanding and honesty. Incidentally, in a later study when 262 16–17 year old females were asked which of their closest relationships they had been describing, 74 per cent mentioned the same–sex closest friend, 16 per cent a boyfriend and 9 per cent the opposite–sex closest friend (Cramer, 1993c). Current rather than past relationships were chosen because these were assumed to be more immediately relevant to present self–esteem and also more likely to change with time.

The core conditions were measured with the revised Barrett–Lennard Relationship Inventory which assesses four rather than three core conditions since the core condition of unconditional acceptance has been appropriately subdivided into the two further core conditions of level of acceptance and unconditionality of acceptance. Sixteen items each assess level of acceptance (e.g. 'S/he cares for me'), unconditionality of acceptance (e.g. 'Her/his feeling toward me doesn't depend on how I feel toward her/him'), empathy (e.g. 'S/he nearly always knows exactly what I mean') and genuineness (e.g. 'S/he is comfortable and at ease in our relationship'). An earlier item factor analysis of this inventory for 335 students describing their current closest relationship indicated that four orthogonal factors extracted reflected the items of the four scales, suggesting that these four qualities could be discriminated (Cramer, 1986). Unconditionality of acceptance needs to be interpreted in terms of whether the level of acceptance denotes acceptance or rejection since unconditional rejection may be less facilitative than conditional rejection (Cramer, 1989). Since most people feel accepted by those they describe as being closest to, unconditionality in this context generally refers to unconditional acceptance. For example, the percentage of young people who felt respectively rejected by their romantic partner, same– and opposite–sex friend, and a casual friend was 3, 5, 8 and 31 (Cramer, 1990c). Self–esteem was measured with the Rosenberg Self–Esteem Scale, which has been described as being more an index of self–acceptance than self–esteem. However, the two constructs do not appear to have been differentiated empirically. Examples of items from this scale include 'On the whole, I am satisfied with myself' and 'At times I think I am no good at all'. Both questionnaires were completed on two occasions separated by 15 weeks, during which time it was assumed sufficient change could have been expected to have occurred.

The relationship between self–esteem and each of the core conditions as well as the core conditions combined was examined. The cross–lagged relationships between self–esteem and both unconditionality of acceptance and genuineness could not be interpreted because the autocorrelations differed significantly (Cramer, 1988). The conditions for interpreting the cross–lagged relationships between self–esteem and level of acceptance, empathy and the combined core conditions were satisfied. The cross–lagged correlations were significantly positive but did not differ for the relationships between self–esteem and both level of acceptance and empathy, implying that these relationships were either reciprocal or spurious. The cross–lagged correlation between the combined core conditions at time 1 and self–esteem at time 2 was significantly more positive than that between self–esteem at time 1 and the combined core conditions at time 2, implying that the core conditions have a stronger effect on self–esteem than self–esteem has on the core conditions.

The LISREL analyses suggested that the most parsimonious model for the relationships between self–esteem and the core conditions of levels of acceptance, empathy and genuineness was one which postulated no cross–lagged coefficients, whereas it was a unidirectional one for the relationship between self–esteem and unconditionality of acceptance and the combined core conditions in which later self–esteem was determined by prior unconditionality of acceptance and the combined core conditions (Cramer, 1990b, 1994). Since the combined core conditions obviously include unconditionality of acceptance and as the path coefficient between self–esteem and unconditionality of acceptance was more positive than that between self–esteem and the combined core conditions, the relationship between self–esteem and the combined core conditions is most probably primarily due to the influence of unconditionality of acceptance.

Two recent and as yet unpublished analyses of a longitudinal study by Henderson, Byrne and Duncan–Jones (1981) may throw further light on the association between mental health and the supportiveness of close relationships (Cramer, Henderson & Scott, 1993a, 1993b). Supportiveness was assessed by 12 items which, while not directly measuring the core conditions, may have done so indirectly since these items covered related aspects such as whether respondents considered they could lean on their close relationships, felt close to these people and could share their most private thoughts with them. Supportiveness was evaluated at four times each separated by four months. Mental health was assessed with the 30–item Goldberg General Health Questionnaire on these four occasions and with the 20–item Zung Self–Rating Depression Scale on all but the second occasion. The participants consisted of a representative community sample of 225 adult residents in Canberra.

With respect to the General Health Questionnaire, the conditions for interpreting the cross–lagged correlation between mental health and the adequacy of close relationships were met for the first and second interval (Cramer, Henderson & Scott, 1994a). Although the cross–lagged correlations were significantly negative for both these intervals, they did not differ from one another, suggesting that the relationship between these two variables was either reciprocal or spurious. However, the most parsimonious LISREL model was a unidirectional one in which earlier mental health appeared to determine subsequent satisfaction with close relationships. In terms of the depression measure, the conditions for interpreting the cross–lagged correlations were upheld for the first interval (Cramer, Henderson & Scott, 1994b). Although significantly negative, these correlations did not differ from one another, implying that the relationship between these two variables was either reciprocal or spurious. The most parsimonious LISREL model was one which assumed no cross–lagged relationships. The explanation for the differing results for these two measures of mental health is not clear. One reason may be that since the depression scale assesses a more stable aspect of mental health, the change in depression may have been insufficient for the causal relationship between the two variables to be ascertained. Why the results for this study differed from that of the previous one is also not clear but may have resulted from the use of different measures or samples which may have involved different processes.

SUMMARY AND CONCLUSIONS

Rogers' person–centred approach to mental health postulates that mental health is primarily determined by having a relationship in which the individual genuinely feels unconditionally accepted and understood by another. Despite the inherent plausability of this idea, its widespread influence and the substantial research it has engendered, there is still little evidence which clearly shows that there is a causal relationship between these qualities and mental health. One non–experimental way of exploring temporal precedence is to conduct longitudinal studies in which the direction and strength of the cross–lagged correlations are compared either directly or in terms of LISREL models with latent variables. This paper briefly describes this kind of analysis for three studies. The first of these studies examined this issue in individual psychotherapy where there is only one relationship and where this issue can be more readily studied from the start of the relationship. The results depended on the indices of therapeutic outcome used but suggested that these qualities may lead to therapeutic progress as judged by the therapist, and increased self–esteem as rated by the client. The other two studies investigated this hypothesis in close everyday relationships. The first study on a small sample of undergraduates also implied that these qualities as seen in one's closest current relationship could result in greater self–esteem. The second study, based on a representative community sample of adults, did not assess these qualities directly. The results for the General Health Questionnaire of mental health intimated that mental health affects how adequate close relationships are seen as being while those for a measure of depression implied no temporal relationship between the two variables. The reason for these discrepant findings is not clear but indicate that it cannot always be assumed that supportive close relationships will enhance mental health. If this is more generally found to be the case, then the conditions under which this causal relationship holds needs to be established.

REFERENCES

Cramer, D. (1986). *An item factor analysis of the revised Barrett–Lennard Relationship Inventory.* British Journal of Guidance and Counselling, 14, 314–325.

Cramer, D. (1988). *Self–esteem and facilitative close relationships: A cross–lagged panel correlation analysis.* British Journal of Social Psychology, 27, 115–126.

Cramer, D. (1989). *Self–esteem and the facilitativeness of parents and close friends.* Person–Centered Review, 4, 61–76.

Cramer, D. (1990a). *Towards assessing the therapeutic value of Rogers's core conditions.* Counselling Psychology Quarterly, 3, 57–66.

Cramer, D. (1990b). *Self–esteem and close relationships: A statistical refinement.* British Journal of Social Psychology, 29, 189–191.

Cramer, D. (1990c). *Disclosure of personal problems, self–esteem, and the facilitativeness of friends and lovers.* British Journal of Guidance and Counselling, 18, 186–196.

Cramer, D. (1991). *Personality and psychotherapy: Theory, practice and research.* Milton Keynes: Open University Press.

Cramer, D. (1993a). *Therapeutic relationship and outcome seen by clients in first and third session of individual therapy.* Counselling Psychology Quarterly, 6, 13–15.

Cramer, D. (1993b). *Perceived and desired facilitativeness of one's closest friend, need for approval and self–esteem.* British Journal of Medical Psychology, 66, 97–104.

Cramer, D. (1994). *Self–esteem and Rogers' core conditions in close friends: A latent variable path analysis of panel data.* Counselling Psychology Quarterly, in press.

Cramer, D., Henderson, S., & Scott, R. (1994a). *Mental health and adequacy of social support: A four–wave panel study.* Manuscript submitted for publication.

Cramer, D., Henderson, S., & Scott, R. (1994b). *Depression and adequacy of social support: A three–wave panel study.* Manuscript submitted for publication.

Cramer, D., & Takens, R. J. (1992). *Therapeutic relationship and progress in the first six sessions of individual psychotherapy: A panel study.* Counselling Psychology Quarterly, 5, 25–36.

Ellis, A. (1959). *Requisite conditions for basic personality change.* Journal of Consulting Psychology, 23, 538–540.

Henderson, S., Byrne, D. G., & Duncan–Jones, P. (1981). *Neurosis and the social environment.* Sydney: Academic Press.

Howard, K. I., Kopta, S. M., Krause. M. S., & Orlinsky, D. E. (1986). *The dose–effect relationship in psychotherapy.* American Psychologist, 41, 159–164.

Rogers, C. R. (1959). *A theory of therapy, personality, and interpersonal relationships, as developed in the client–centered framework.* In S. Koch (Ed.), Psychology: A study of a science: Vol. 3 (pp. 184–256). New York: McGraw–Hill.

Rogers, C. R., & Truax, C. B. (1976). *The therapeutic conditions antecedent to change: A theoretical view.* In C. R. Rogers, E. T. Gendlin, D. J. Kiesler & C. B. Truax (Eds.), *The therapeutic relationship and its impact: A study of psychotherapy with schizophrenics* (pp. 97–108). Westport, CT.

Reflections on the self of the therapist

NED L. GAYLIN, PH.D.

UNIVERSITY OF MARYLAND

ABSTRACT

Healers of the soul and spirit (later to become the psyche) existed long before the age of psychology. Before the age of psychological "enlightenment," and the scientific era, these healers (e.g., prophets, priests, shamans) were considered divinely inspired. In other words, they were believed to have "gifts" – talents beyond ordinary men and women. Although these individuals usually apprenticed under masters, they were considered chosen for such training. Despite our present enlightenment, the situation today differs little. Although our metaphors differ, those who are called to the helping professions are most probably impelled to do so by natural talents augmented by positive experiences in dealing with others: they like people, people like them. They are considered by themselves and others to be good listeners and, perhaps most importantly, they genuinely care for others. Many of the attributes of potential psychotherapists are those traits listed by Rogers as the "characteristics of the helping relationship," (Rogers, 1958). These characteristics, by and large, parallel Rogers' "necessary and sufficient conditions" (Rogers, 1957) but go beyond them somewhat by exploring the notion of therapist congruence. Genuineness, transparency—the personhood of the therapist—become focal issues. In our search for understanding the restorative nature of psychotherapy we have followed the medical tradition, focusing on either the "illness" and/or its repository, "the patient." Perhaps it is time to focus on the restorative power of the client–therapist relationship, with particular emphasis on the integrated nature and self of the therist.

THE INHERENT QUALITIES OF THERAPISTS AND THEIR TRAINING

Having been involved in psychotherapy endeavors for over a third of a century, first as a student, then as a therapist, and finally as an educator of therapists, I have grown convinced that God, not teachers nor their models, makes therapists. The best that our education and training programs can do is offer student therapists experience under conditions in which they may safely experiment with who they are in the therapeutic engagement. Our therapy training programs and we, its teachers, are merely the whetstones on which the novice therapist hones his or her instrument—that instrument being the self of the therapist.

Reviewing applicants' records for our family therapy training program, I am always impressed, but not surprised, by what has impelled our students to become therapists. Despite widely differing ages, backgrounds, and routes to our establishment, virtually all of our candidates mention that their friends and relatives have gratefully identified our candidates as good listeners and helpful friends. They in return, acknowledge that they have felt rewarded, gratified, and validated and consequently have developed an aspect of their sense of self, which one might call "helper." The formulation of this helper subself (Gaylin, 1991) usually began relatively early in their lives, often during adolescence, and through maturation continued being reaffirmed by others.

I, therefore, find ironic the anguish–laden puzzlement and frustration that beginning therapists invariably experience when they attempt to apply that "helper" aspect of self in the early stages of work in a professional therapy setting. Somehow, in trying to analyze and enhance apparently innate therapeutic ability, they become awkward, stiff, and often paralyzed. Where once they were intuitively empathic and helpful active listeners with friends, as beginning therapists interacting with their first clients the therapists often feel lost and devoid of the talent that gave rise to their helper subself in the first place. At this point, these novice therapists often become discouraged and lose confidence in that very ability that had worked so well and unquestioningly for them in the past.

This often terrifying sense of impotence—the clumsiness and the corresponding loss of confidence—in large measure derives from the nature of our training programs. We have established a worship of theory and have prematurely attempted to make scientific that which has been, and still is, primarily an art. Our assiduous attention to "pure" theoretical orientations in training (for years eclecticism was considered a dirty word) forces students to lay themselves on Procrustean training beds.

In most therapy training programs, students must dutifully subscribe and adhere to the given psychotherapy model propounded by those programs and their advocates as the one "true" method. By dutifully emulating their trainers, trainees (the term "trainee" as distinct from "student" is purposive here) master the techniques propounded by the model. Trainees are rewarded for conformity and criticized for deviance from it. Training is different from education where students assimilate and integrate new knowledge are accomplished via the encouraged of inquiry and dialogue that includes contrasting points of view.

Our reverence for the "right" theory reflects the general defensiveness of the behavioral sciences, particularly with regard to psychotherapy. In an effort to make psychotherapeutic practice more a behavioral science and less a behavioral art, we press to validate the effectiveness of psychotherapy by constructing theories that are replete with the development of idiosyncratic nomenclature and exotic techniques.

The construction, elaboration, and testing of theory in the behavioral sciences are, indeed, laudable and necessary to the understanding of psychotherapy, its practice and enhancement. However, except for a relatively few basic premises which are integral to all modes of psychotherapy, most theories have proven, at best, incomplete. Furthermore, virtually all of the extant theoretical models have been found flawed when put to the empirical test: We continuously rediscover that psychotherapy, regardless of theoretical orientation, has about a 60% success rate (Lambert and Bergin, 1994). This figure is undoubtedly inflated, for what we have also learned that when prospective clients are put on waiting lists, about half of them report feeling better over time without the benefit of actual psychotherapy services.

Nevertheless, despite these empirical findings, staunch advocates of various theoretical persuasions abound. Such theoretical allegiance undoubtedly arises initially, from personal experiential validation of a chosen theory in the successful practice of psychotherapy and later become entrenched through the continuous investment and commitment of one's professional self to that choice. These choices, usually made during professional training, are perhaps the most important discoveries that therapists make, i.e., which psychotherapeutic methods are right specifically for them: which ones do or do not fit the therapist's natural personal style, which do and do not feel comfortable, which do and do not work. Thus, at least in the best of situations, psychotherapy training is a laboratory for continuous discovery of the self of the therapist. For, rather than technique, or even method, it is this self which is the tool, the elixir of change, in the practice of psychotherapy.

Most training programs conceptually understand and respect the importance of the therapist as tool and, correspondingly, emphasize self understanding on the part of the therapist as a meaningful aspect of training. However, herein lies another hazard of training. Too often, programs believe they are promoting such self understanding by requiring therapy for all of their trainees.

Certainly, it is not a bad idea for therapists to undergo their own self exploration and experience the therapeutic process from the vantage point of the client, but I am not convinced that it is necessary for this experience to occur solely within the context of formal professional psychotherapy. Although I treasured my own experience as client during my training (and believe it has enhanced my empathy as a therapist) I do not believe that all therapists must have therapy themselves in order to be good therapists.

Pernicious dangers lurk in the situation where training programs require that students process self issues in front of other students and their trainers. Even when handled more discretely, self discovery mandated by training institutions is problematic. Forced therapy is a contradiction in terms—more often traumatic than therapeutic, doing more harm than good. The process of self discovery is one which is growth producing only if the individual is, to some degree, in charge of that process.

Furthermore, many experienced therapists believe that in the course of providing therapy we continuously learn about ourselves, even as we learn about our clients. I remember, towards the end of my graduate internship at the Institute for Juvenile Research in Chicago, being supervised by Carl Whitaker. I naively asked him how he knew when therapy was over. Without hesitating, he responded, "when the therapist stops growing in the relationship."

As practitioners, our central focus is, of course, the client. But as theorists and empiricists, a shift from our traditional emphasis on the client to the therapist may be in order to understand better those qualities of the therapist, regardless of therapeutic model, which facilitate therapeutic growth in both client and therapist.

THE THERAPIST IN THE HOUR: PROCESS ELEMENTS OF THE SELF SYSTEM

Psychodynamic (psychoanalytic) psychotherapy, dominated the practice of psychotherapy for the first half of this century and stresses the notion of the therapist as a *tabula rasa*, a blank screen. Thus, clients project certain attitudes feelings onto their therapists which become grist for the therapeutic mill.

In its simplest form, the tabula rasa concept is a good one in so far as the therapist allows the client to initiate the issues which direct the course of therapy; the therapist, presumably, remaining neutral. Because of this supposedly neutral stance, any feelings the client exhibits for the therapist are considered an aspect of the *transference* phenomenon in which the patient transfers feelings for another person (generally a mother or father) onto the therapist. Likewise, the feelings of the therapist for the client are regarded as *counter–transference*.

In reality, of course, like any other human being, the psychoanalytic therapist is hardly a neutral observer, but a participant in the therapeutic process. Freud clearly demonstrated this by involving himself quite heavily in many of his clients' lives. Another flaw in the therapist's presumed objectivity during the analytic therapy hour is that the structural elements of psychodynamic theory undoubtedly color the therapist's perceptions of the client. Nevertheless, for the first half of this century, the pretense of scientific neutrality dominated thought regarding the therapeutic relationship; for many it lingers.

In the middle of this century, Carl Rogers (1957) virtually shocked the psychotherapy community by making the interpersonal relationship between the client and therapist basic and focal to his theory of therapy. This relationship is the first and core element of his "necessary and sufficient conditions for personality change." Carefully couching his premise regarding the nature of the therapist's feelings for the client, he avoids the use of the words "love" and "caring," but certainly allows for their inference by using, instead, terms like "unconditional positive regard," "nonjudgmental stance," and "empathy." Basically Rogers' conditions for change center on the empathic caring of the therapist for the client and, reciprocally, the client's recognition of these feelings as the engine of change behind the psychotherapy process.

Despite Rogers' having established the personhood of the therapist as a central element in his model for change, most of the research that emanated from his theory emphasized aspects of the client rather than those of the therapist. This client emphasis is true for virtually all other psychotherapy models as well. There has been relatively little research on how the personal qualities of therapists (viz. their aspects of self) affect their behavior in the therapy session, and what influence this has on clients. Recently, interest in this area has been growing.

Thirty years after his initial, simple statement regarding the condition of the therapist, in an informal interview with Baldwin (1987), Rogers remarked on his growing awareness of the use of himself—his person—in the therapy hour. Basically, these comments, well towards the end of his life, reflect an earlier notion that Rogers proffered regarding therapist genuineness or authenticity. From the very outset, what is clear in Rogers' thinking about the therapist is that the therapist is fully present as a person in the therapeutic encounter, and that encounter is clearly an interpersonal relationship of two (or more) people engaging each other. The deeply interpersonal nature of the therapist–client relationship is unique to the person–centered philosophy.

Not at all clear, however, are Rogers' meaning of the presence of the therapist, and the ramifications of that presence upon the client. The entire second chapter of *Client–Centered Therapy* (Rogers, 1957) although nominally dedicated to the personal qualities of the therapist, addresses only the therapist's ability to adhere to and maintain the classic necessary and sufficient conditions of nonjudgmental, empathic regard.[1]

What are the qualities, attributes, or characteristics of therapists and the special nature of psychotherapeutic relationships which sets them apart from other interpersonal relationships? First of all, the therapeutic relationship is highly circumscribed and artificially structured. Generally, (a) meeting times are fixed with a mutually agreed upon beginning and ending; (b) therapist–client social contact is limited to the prescribed hours; and (c) therapists are remunerated in some fashion for their time and skill.

Like few other relationships, there is an intensity and one sidedness to the psychotherapeutic relationship. The well–being of the client virtually always takes precedence over the well–being of the therapist. To modify Buber (1937) slightly, the therapy relationship is intensely "Thou–I." The therapist's feelings and emotions are there as backdrop in the service of the client—the focus or "center" is the client. Buber, and later Friedman (1992), employ the word "inclusion" in lieu of Rogers' "empathy." Inclusion by the therapist appears to be a more intense stance than that of empathy and emphasizes the "I–Thou" relationship of Buber. Theologians are less awkward than behavioral scientists in using intimate terms to describe relationships.

The therapist's ability to risk being intimate, to engage, or even to embrace the client, *yet not make demands for reciprocity*, may be another important and little understood features of healing relationships. Thus, "love" according to Fromm (1956), wherein the well–being of the other takes precedent over one's own well being, may, indeed, be the appropriate word. Maybe it is time to examine the caring or loving nature of the therapist as an indigenous aspect of psychotherapy process.

Along with unselfish caring, there is an intensity of focus and concentration that makes the therapist–client relationship unique and, with few exceptions, so unsustainable in normal social intercourse. In the session, the therapist gives over his or her entire concentration to apprehending and helping the client understand his or her experiences and feelings which surround them. These qualities of concentration and focus taken together with the caring nature of the therapist define the special *presence* of the therapist in the psychotherapy hour.[2]

There are qualities to this special presence that complement and articulate with the empathic stance. An attribute that distinguishes truly effective therapists from others is a unique self awareness that could be called self availability. That is, the therapist has a repertoire of experienced selves or subselves each of which becomes awakened in response to the client's recounting of his or her experiences. Thus, as I am listening to a young client relate a hurtful engagement with a parent, I find I begin to subceive or sense in myself a similar childhood encounter which evoked similar feelings within me. The word "sense" refers to the fact that I do not actively search my memory, but rather my focus on the client passively elicits the recall which emerges, along with some re–experiencing. The feelings freshly revived, enable me to relate quite actively to the feelings the client reports experiencing. This kind of special memory, or awareness, breathes dimension into understanding and communicates itself to the client as active experiential understanding—empathy.

Thus, not only is reliance on theory alone unhelpful in facilitating the therapy process, it actually may hinder it. In attending to theory rather than using it as an infrastructure, focus and concentration are drawn away from the client, and the therapist's self availability in service of the client is supplanted by concern for theoretical validation. When working with beginning therapists who are often hungry for theoretical principles and accompanying techniques, I put it to them this way:

> Forget what you have learned and sharpen your listening skills. The client is the theory, and each client is different. Thus, your theory is constantly undergoing change. You are, therefore, to learn the theory from the client in the hour. You are responsible for learning the client's language, not vice–versa.

> Furthermore, I prohibit my students from planning for the next session and enjoin them not to look at their notes or review tapes of previous sessions *on the day of the forthcoming session with a given client.* At first, these dicta tend to be distressing for beginning therapists who have spent much of their time steeping themselves in the theoretical methods and techniques from various models. They are particularly distressing because virtually all of the students' other professors and supervisors (my colleagues) insist upon a strategy and therapeutic plan for at least the next session.

Certainly my students and I debrief on sessions, but never on the day of the client's succeeding session. The major reason for this is a relatively simple one which I discovered during my own training. Therapists, particularly eager beginning therapists, are prone to over–focus on their clients' problems as revealed during a given hour. For the therapist a specific problem too easily becomes a fixed point of reference, often obfuscating the totality of the client's distress. People are far more intricate than just the sum of their problems; even the most distressing problems are a part of a complex life moving in various directions through time.

Listening to or discussing a previous hour tends to fix the issues of that hour in the therapist's mind. Entering a new session with a focus on the concerns of the previous hour can, like a preoccupation with theory, distract the therapist from being fully present for the client at any given moment. Regardless of the amount of time between sessions, the client has had a multitude of experiences outside of the clinical hour. This is true even in classical psychoanalysis where session frequency is often three to five times per week. Many of these new experiences may take precedence for clients over what was bothering them during the previous session (which, indeed, the client may have forgotten or even resolved). With the previous hour fresh in the therapist's mind, the new session begins with the therapist out of sync with the client's needs at that moment. Therefore, it behooves the therapist to let the client set the agenda: It is the therapist's job to follow the client, not visa–versa.

In addition to the requirements that the therapist care and have empathy for the client, Rogers, (1957) in his conditions for psychotherapy change, adds that the therapist must be "congruent" within the therapy relationship. Basically, congruence means that the perception and experience of ourselves are consonant. The ramifications of therapist congruence on the therapy process are vast and far reaching. Therapist congruence implies that the many subselves of the therapist are integrated in some way during the hour. The therapist must be able draw upon these many subselves as a frame of reference in listening, empathizing, and responding to clients as they explore their own subself complex. Thus, for example, in the case of an individual client's exploration of childhood experiences, the congruent therapist may reach back and elicit parallel feelings from that aspect of the therapist's own childhood to explore empathically the client's experience. In family therapy, this particular connotation of congruence is of special importance because the therapist must be in touch with the multiple and often conflicting world views of the various family members in the therapy session. To complicate the therapist's task, these world views are often transtemporal and thus transgenerational.

The concept of therapist congruence also implies another quality, that of genuineness or authenticity. This quality adds to the aforementioned special presence, caring, concentration, and focus of the therapist in the hour. The therapist needs to be available: continuously in touch with his or her feelings and reactions to the client. If these conditions are met—if the therapist is congruent, integrated, fully present, and genuine—the therapist becomes intuitively free to react to the total person of the client. In this manner, the therapist's empathy for the client becomes heightened and shared meaning is enhanced. It is this process that gives clients perspective on their lives and increases their own sense of personhood through feelings of shared meaning with the therapist. This is the process—the availability of the therapist, the caring and focused presence, and the deeply shared meaning within the relationship—that mitigates the existential despair and loneliness that often impel clients to seek therapy in the first place.

PRESENCE

The concentration of the therapist on the client in conjunction with the therapist's empathy for the client make the therapist something of a lens. This lens–like quality enables the client to focus on those internal processes which may have led to the client's incongruence wherein the experience of self and the perception of self are at odds. The client's prior incongruences, confusions, blurring of subselves, and generalized anxieties have blocked the natural growth or actualizing processes. Assisted by the therapist's caring concentration and focus on the client and empathic reflection of the client's feelings and experiences, the client's self awareness is heightened. Specifically, aspects of the client's self that may, heretofore, have been blocked from awareness can thus emerge for examination and eventual self integration.

Most therapists become aware of certain markers during the therapy session, places where the therapist's attention is piqued. One such marker is the client's self judgment which seems to interfere with the client's self exploratory process. Thus, a client may be exploring some incongruent behavior and say something like, "I don't know why I do such crazy things—they make no sense, they just aren't like me, etc." The therapist in his or her non-judgmental stance acts as a model whereby he or she not only is available to the client, but also encourages the client's explorations of self. These explorations most importantly include those "ugly" or otherwise unacceptable aspects of self which tend to act as a kind of black hole, drawing energy away from the actualizing process either through over attention or by attempts to suppress them from awareness.

Especially during those times when the client is in a self-critical (and thus incongruent) mode, descriptive detail becomes a vital tool in aiding the therapist's and, therefore, the client's understanding of the client's incongruence and self blame. Such circumstances are generally situation specific, and clients typically note they cannot remember the details of a given incident. However, if the therapist is empathic and can facilitate experiential recounting (often through the elicitation of some small particular), the details surface with exquisite minutiae and vivid clarity, often to the client's surprise. This unfolding of detail is usually accompanied by the sensation of relief, much like a long mislaid object that is finally recovered.

Herein lie some of the key elements to the experiencing and the reexperiencing of a given event. There is a sense of ordering that is prelude to integration of the experience in a new manner. Working with couples and/or families makes such ordering and re-experiencing clear. The couple often begins a recounting of a heated and usually hurtful disagreement. Typically there will be a difference of opinion attended with confusion and puzzlement as to how the disagreement began. For me this is a marker. At such times I ask the couple to "back up the tape" to a point somewhat before the occurrence of the dispute. Generally what happens is aspects of some barely subceived umbrage are unearthed, the remembered dispute eclipsing (for a variety of reasons) the previous intra and interpersonal incongruence. Such reexperiencing and reintegration are generally followed by a sense of discovery, relief, and lightening, often accompanied by amazement and laughter. Though often more subtle and less evident during individual therapy, the sense of relief in resolving an intrapersonal incongruence is the same. This image of "lightening" is in contradistinction to the notion that psychotherapy is the psychological parallel to open heart surgery.

THE PARAMETERS AND ETHICS OF SELF DISCLOSURE

In attending to the personhood of the therapist in the therapy process, perhaps no one concept causes more anxiety for practitioners, theorists, and even researchers, than that of self disclosure wherein therapists share aspects of themselves with clients. No matter how opaque or neutral one claims to be, there are always aspects of self which are disclosed, even to the casual observer. The question is how much to disclose and when and why. I continuously struggle with how much of myself is appropriate to share with my clients, and why and when I feel impelled to do so.

The obvious danger of self disclosure is that it may lead to abuse of the client. I define abuse of the client as that moment when the therapist's feelings for the client, either positive or negative, take the focus off the client and onto the therapist and, consequently, the activities of the therapist become self rather than client serving. The pursuit of therapist genuineness and transparency should never be construed as a license to use the client.

The most flagrant abuse of the client is his or her as a sexual object. Clients, no matter how needy they be for physical intimacy, are never well served by having their psychotherapist as a sexual partner. Thus, if a therapist is sexually attracted to a client, it behooves the therapist to search inside him or herself to discern the meaning of those feelings. In certain situations this search may warrant outside consultation, the use of a co–therapist, and, if these are not sufficient, directness followed by referral to another therapist.

In dramatic instances of a therapist's sexual attraction to or strong revulsion of a client, the operative word is "response." In maximizing one's self as the tool in therapy, the responsible congruent therapist needs to discern if those feelings incongruent to the therapeutic stance are brought to the session by the therapist or, in some manner, evoked by the client. Generally, in such circumstances, a complex combination of therapist and client interactive factors exists. For a seasoned therapist who is self aware of those situations that kindle strong personal responses, recognition of incongruence, if done with the continuous acknowledgment that the safety of the client is foremost, can often resolve the incongruence of the therapist without the use of disclosure. In these circumstances, such therapist reactions are often a powerful source of interpersonal information which can facilitate the process of therapy.

On the other hand, strong negative feelings such as rage or loathing in response to a given client also require close scrutiny. Clients, no matter how interpersonally provocative and abrasive, are never deserving of verbal abuse by their therapist. It would seem gratuitous to add that physical abuse should be beyond the realm of the therapist's interactive repertoire.

Examples of therapists meeting their personal needs in the process of working with their clients are generally obvious to all therapists except those who are severely incongruent and, thus, by definition, do not fit the conditions of being facilitative of their clients' growth. A therapist's construction that such acts are performed in the service of his or her clients is indicative of the therapist's self–deception and corresponding incongruence.

More difficult to discern are the subtle forms of therapists' self disclosure and their potential impact on clients. At some level, how we comport ourselves, our style (our speech, smile, the manner in which we dress) conveys something about us and is, therefore, at some level, self disclosing. Thus, the notion of the objective therapist, the therapist as a tabula rasa is, at best, somewhat deceptive, but worse, is double binding to our clients and confounding to ourselves in our search to discern the nature of the therapeutic relationship and its impact. Consequently the more the therapist is truly and utterly him or her self, i.e., congruent in the therapy hour, the less confusing and least abusive the therapist is to the client.

Nevertheless, no matter how congruent and integrated therapists may be they will still encounter incongruences. Often less dramatic and more transitory than in the case of sexual attraction and rage, these subtle incongruences may be experienced by therapists either in relationship to a client with whom a therapist normally maintains congruence, or with a given client who presents specific problems which elicit incongruent feelings within the therapist.

I remember attending a workshop given by a very talented colleague, at the 1990 Annual Meeting of the Association for the Development of the Person–Centered Approach (ADPCA).[3] The subject of the workshop was therapist incongruence, and the leader of the workshop reported on a client whom she truly cared about, but with whom she was beginning to have trouble maintaining concentration. She felt increasingly bored as the client told her about certain happenings from his past. The therapist searched for a reason within herself. The client had rarely bored her for such a protracted period before. The therapist genuinely cared for him, yet despite her continuing efforts, she reported being unable to bring her concentration on the client into focus. Finally, she gently and tenderly disclosed her feelings, taking full ownership of them (i.e., not blaming the client for boring her), noting that this condition was unusual in response to the client.

The therapist described how, in response to this self disclosure, the client smiled good-naturedly, admitting that he did not think that what he was telling her about had much relevance to his progress in therapy, but because his previous therapist had thought the issues extremely important, he thought it obligatory to share the incidents with her. In this case it became clear that the therapist's incongruence was a direct reflection of the incongruence of the client. The clearing of the air coupled with profound warmth, gentleness and caring of the therapist allowed for an enhancement of the therapeutic relationship which in turn enabled the therapy to lift off its plateau.

The presumption that a good therapist is a unidimensional unwavering paragon of non-judgmental, unconditionally-regarding empathy is not only inaccurate, it is obfuscating of valuable data regarding the instrument of the therapist. The ability to suspend judgment, care unconditionally and remain intensely focused, all the while conveying an understanding of the client's deepest meanings, is the ideal from which we all deviate to some degree all of the time. With whom, how, when, why, and to what degree we stray from this ideal therapeutic stance can tell us much about the nature of therapists and the therapeutic process. Indeed, such questions form the foundation of my consultations with students. When I see a student foundering in the hour, or struggling with a client, I first ask "Do you like this client?" and, depending upon the answer, then ask "Why?" or "Why not?" The answers to these questions invariably yield important information regarding the therapist, the client, and the nature of each idiosyncratic therapeutic relationship. They shed light on the subtle intricacies of both intra and interpersonal congruences of the relationship. The process of discovery thereby engendered enriches the therapist's understanding of his or her self as a unique and dynamic instrument in the therapy relationship.

THE THERAPEUTIC ENVIRONMENT

The therapeutic environment is a related and, perhaps, even more subtle and rarely discussed extension of the therapist's style and an often unforeseen form of self disclosure. This overlooked and important element of environmental ambience has proven to be a key issue in my own congruence during therapy sessions and, I believe, an equal important one to my clients.

In my early training I was fortunate. The Counseling and Psychotherapy Research Center at the University of Chicago granted its advanced interns their own offices. Indeed, each of the half dozen or so of us was given $50.00 (at that time a worthy sum) to decorate our offices. For most of us, it meant putting a coat of paint on the decrepit oak desks and chairs and, perhaps, buying a rug, desk lamp, or curtains. Our offices became a sort of home for each of us, each quite different and a reflection of our personal styles.

I felt comfortable and secure in my little niche, as did my colleagues. Interestingly, I remember the therapy hours there vividly, in contrast to those of my internship the previous year at the Institute for Juvenile Research (IJR), a state agency in Chicago serving children and their families. At IJR, each therapist (including the senior staff) used common interviewing rooms on the second floor. Each had working offices on the floor above, so the need to conserve space was not an issue. Rather, IJR reflected its psychodynamic values regarding the clinical neutrality of its environment. By contrast, the University "Counseling Center" reflected its emphasis on the person and the personal. I do not think these policies were ever really consciously strategized by the staff of the two institutions but, rather, were a natural extension of their respective models and general orientations.

To this day, I find I do better therapy in my own environment. I lament the fact that our clinic at Maryland cannot afford the luxury of enabling our trainees to design an ambience more reflective of who they are, so that their clients may benefit additionally from having their therapists feel truly at home in their environments. A small issue, perhaps, but one worthy of further exploration.

A small pilot study (Gaylin, Grebe, McCarrick, Millstein, and Werlinich, 1988) adds some credibility to this notion of therapeutic ambience. In this study conducted by a group of private practitioners on the attitudes of clients in private practice, one of the interesting and consistent findings was that clients were very observant of and sensitive to the ambience of the their therapists' offices. As one client noted, "If she [the therapist] can't take care of her plants, what kind of care will she take of me?"

I have noted that the garden which adjoins my office (and is my personal place of solace) attracts much attention from my clients. Not only do they comment about it, they will often come a few minutes early before sessions there: Sometimes, they will linger there afterwards. My garden is clearly an extension of my office, and it is clearly a reflection of me. It communicates something about me to my clients. It pleases me, both in and of itself as well as for the pleasure that it brings to others.

Just as I take joy in sharing the pleasures of my garden, I often will share relatively mundane things about myself with my clients. I have my degrees posted on my walls; it is no secret that I have a family. There are traces of the others who share my life throughout my environment. This is a form of self disclosure that I believe humanizes and balances the therapist–client relationship. In many respects, I enjoy breaking the professional barrier that I believe many of us hide behind. Certainly I have boundaries and I believe my boundaries are clear. My clients respect them, as I respect theirs. The operative word is respect—mutual respect for each other as people.

REFERENCES

Baldwin, M. (1987). *Interview with Carl Rogers on the use of self in therapy.* In Baldwin, M., and Satir, V. (Eds.). The use of self in therapy. New York: Haworth Press, 45–57.

Buber, M. (1937). *I and thou.* Translated by Ronald Gregor Smith. Edinburgh; T. and T. Clark. New York: Charles Scribner's Sons.

Friedman, M. (1992). *Religion and psychology.* New York: Paragon House.

Fromm, E. (1956). *The art of loving.* New York: Harper & Brothers.

Gaylin, N. L., Grebe, S C., McCarrick, A., Millstein, F. & Werlinich, C. A. (1988*). Looking in the mirror:* a pilot study of family therapy research process and outcome in private practice, unpublished study.

Gaylin, N. L. (1991). *Family–centered theory: The client–centered relationship in developmental context.* Paper presented at the Second International Conference on Client–Centered and Experiential Psychotherapy, University of Stirling, Scotland, July 6,

1991.Recommended graduate training program in clinical psychology. Report of the Committee on Training in Clinical Psychology of the American Psychological Association. (1947). American Psychologist,2, 539–558.

Rogers, C. R. (1951). *Client–centered therapy*. Boston: Houghton–Mifflin.

Lambert, M. J., & Bergin, A. E. (1994). *The effectiveness of psychotherapy*. In, Bergin, A. E., & Garfield, S. L., (Eds.), Handbook of psychotherapy and behavior change, Fourth Ed. New York: John Wiley & Sons, pp 143–189.

Rogers, C. R. (1957). *The necessary and sufficient conditions of therapeutic personality change*. Journal of Consulting Psychology, 21, 2, 95–103.

Rogers, C. R. (1958). *The characteristics of a helping relationship*. Personnel and Guidance Journal, 37,1, 6–16.

---

[1]Later, in Chapter Ten, on training therapists, Rogers returns to the idea of the personal qualities of the therapist. Here too, however, he never describes or explores these qualities, but rather concurs with the APA list regarding "Who Should Be Selected for Training," (APA, 1947. pp 434-435). The list of qualities follows:

1. Superior intellectual ability and judgement.
2. Originality, resourcefulness, and versatility.
3. "Fresh and satiable" curiosity; 'self-learner.'
4. "Interest in persons as individuals rather than as material for manipulation--a regard for the integrity of other persons.
5. Insight into own personality characteristics; sense of humor.
6. Sensitivity to the complexities of motivation.
7. Tolerance: "unarrogance."
8. Ability to adopt a "therapeutic" attitude; ability to establish warm and effective relationships with others.
9. Industry; methodical work habits; ability to tolerate pressure.
10. Acceptance of responsibility.
11. Tact and cooperativeness.
12. Integrity, self-control, and stability.
13. Discriminating sense of ethical values.
14. Breadth of cultural background--"educated man."
15. Deep interest in psychology, especially in its clinical aspects.

[2]The above qualities of the psychotherapeutic relationship have few parallels in social intercourse, those few being that of loving parent, and perhaps, loving mate. Such a parallel makes the "transfer of training" (or "transference") phenomenon, far more understandable.

Discrepancy between the Person–centered Theories of Self and of Therapy

T. LEN HOLDSTOCK

AMSTERDAM

ABSTRACT

Developments regarding the self–concept during the past decade are of particular interest with respect to the Person–Centered approach. In contrast to the emphasis on the empowerment of the individual, which is such a hallmark of the Person–Centered approach, the new developments stress the self as an *interdependent,* and not as an *independent* unit of the social system. Interestingly enough, the new developments regarding the self–concept do not seem to be as much in conflict with aspects of Person–Centered therapy as with the Person–Centered theory of the self. While the theory of the self focusses on individual autonomy, the theory of therapy stresses empathy and unconditional positive regard, attitudes which reflect the importance of relatedness. Congruence is the only aspect of the Person–Centered theory of therapy which is really in keeping with the theory of the self. This paper discusses the nature of the discrepancy between the Person–Centered theories of self and of therapy and the implications which this discrepancy has for the future of the approach.

WHY IS IT SO DIFFICULT TO PRACTICE WHAT WE PREACH?

I have, for a long time now, been uneasy about the manner in which the theory underlying the Person–Centered (PC) approach finds expression among those of us who subscribe to its theoretical principles. At first, I thought that the paradox which I perceived between theory and application could be attributed to the failure in shifting from Client–Centered (CC) therapy to the PC approach. It seemed that CC practitioners reserved application of the necessary and sufficient conditions exclusively to the therapeutic situation, and in doing so failed to apply the necessary and sufficient conditions to situations other than that of psychotherapy.

As is known, the shift in emphasis to PC implies the application of the underlying principles in a much broader context than that of psychotherapy (Holdstock & Rogers, 1983). Apart from extension to the educational, organizational, medical, and other professional fields, even to politics, it also implies application of the principles to everyday behaviour. "Rogers formulated the person–centered approach out of the successful practice of psychotherapy but increasingly came to understand that this was a general way of being with others. It was by no means confined to psychotherapy or other special professional–client relationships" (Caspary, 1991, p. 9). In essence, the challenge for the PC person is to practise what he or she preaches in all aspects of his or her behaviour. If we want to alleviate the incidence of mental health problems in the world we have to begin with ourselves. It certainly is not enough to focus only on facilitating those with professed difficulties in living or to restrict the application of PC principles to professional endeavours of a varied nature. It is as essential to have empathy and regard for our family, friends, and colleagues, as for our clients.

Each one of us is certainly aware of numerous instances in which we have failed to practise what we preach within the PC or CC context. Apart from the private instances, many public displays of behaviour not in keeping with the principles of the PC approach occur at conferences, forums, and workshops of a PC or CC nature. At these meetings people regularly report the experience of having their rights violated by those who demand that their own rights be attended to. Attendees at PC and CC gatherings regularly report not being listened to by others who demand that they be listened to.

Let me hasten to say that the inability to put theory into practice in daily life is not restricted to those who function predominantly within a PC or CC framework. A few examples from outside the PC framework will demonstrate the generality of the phenomenon. At the meeting of the *International Transpersonal Association* in Davos, Switzerland, in 1982, a shaman from southern Africa expressed his amazement at how untranspersonal the transpersonal presenters at the conference were. On several occasions, earlier this summer at the conference on the *Evolution of Psychotherapy* in Hamburg, the person next to me remarked how touchy some of the leaders of the various psychotherapeutic orientations were in their response to comments or questions from the audience. A leading exponent of archetypal psychology refused the request for his signature on the conference poster. He considered it 'a waste of his time', yet, he had the patience to search for and hand the person who asked for his signature, an order sheet for his books. Just two weeks before the present conference I experienced something similar at *The 16th International Congress of Psychotherapy* in Seoul, Korea. During a presentation on the nature of *Tao*, a leading Korean psychoanalyst said that *Tao* could best be conceptualised as 'pure' empathy – his frame of reference was Kohut, not Rogers. Yet, scores of Western, as well as Asian participants at the conference, experienced an abysmal lack of empathy in the way he responded to questions and comments from the floor. It was clear that the presenter could talk about, but not model behaviour which he associated with *Tao*. In fact, one of the presentations at this conference raised the very point that I am concerned about here (Kang, 1994). Based on long–term observations of Eastern and Western psychoanalysts, Kang perceived the Westerners to be 'nicer and warmer' in, than outside the psychoanalytic session. He concluded that the warmth of Western psychoanalysts, in contrast to their Eastern colleagues, originated from techniques rather than a genuine relationship with the client.

Contrary to the argument that our inability to practise what we preach is to be sought in the failure of practitioners to generalise from CC therapy to the PC approach, is the contention that it is, in fact, the move towards Person–Centeredness which is responsible for falling short of the ideals set forth by Rogers. I am not sure that I understand this viewpoint. A clearcut distinction seems to be made between the principles underlying professional and everyday behaviour. The contention seems to be that by taking CC therapy out of the consulting room the PC approach has become unprofessional. While this is certainly true in the strictest sense of the term professional, the application of the principles underlying our therapeutic endeavours to other areas need not imply unprofessionalism in the way we conduct ourselves. In fact, what we ought to be striving for is the professionalisation of our everyday life.

The comparison which Hutterer (1993) draws between the English language and PC therapy, provides a possible answer for understanding the viewpoint that the shortcomings of concern here, are to be laid at the door of the PC extension of CC therapy. According to Hutterer it is said that the popularity of the English language is due to the fact that it can so quickly be spoken so poorly. "In a similar way one suspects that client–centred therapy is often taught primarily, and wrongly, because it is believed to be easy to learn. In fact the idea seems to be that everyone can learn it: it just takes some friendly and understanding person. There are probably in no other therapy form so many who think so soon that they have mastered it, even without training" (p. 279).

While the statement by Hutterer (1993) is certainly valid, I doubt that it can fully explain the discrepancy between the theory and the practice of the PC approach. The incongruence between PC theory and practice seems to be more deep–seated. My discomfort relates to an inherent incongruence in the principles underlying the theory and the practice. In searching for a cognitive framework to encompass the discomfort which I experience, recent developments in thinking on the self–concept provide a useful framework with which to approach the paradox.

REVISIONING THE CONCEPT OF SELF

Several aspects of the work on the self–concept during the past decade are of interest with respect to the PC approach. Firstly, the incisive revisioning of the concept of self has far–reaching consequences for the PC approach. Secondly, the large number of divergent disciplines and orientations which contribute to this revisioning lends support to the validity of the revisioned self. The disciplines within which the reorientation to the self as the unit of the social system has occurred, include mainstream psychology, social psychology, social constructionism, clinical psychology, feminist studies, critical theory, deconstructionism, the challenges to liberal individualism, various transcultural disciplines, eg. cultural and psychological anthropology, transcultural psychiatry, cross–cultural and indigenous psychologies, human movement studies, sociology, philosophy, and various developments within the natural sciences (eg. holism, general systems theory, unified field theory, holonomic theory, and nonequilibrium theory) (see Holdstock, 1993 for references).

The reaction is against the prevailing view in the West that it is as an independent, autonomous, and closed entity that the self constitutes the unit of the social system. In fact, it "was around the issue of individualism that psychology constituted itself as a scientific discipline in its own right" (Rose, 1989, p. 119). The emphasis is on "attending to the self, the appreciation of one's difference from others, and the importance of asserting the self" (Markus & Kitayama, 1991, p. 224). There:

> "is a faith in the inherent separateness of distinct persons. The normative imperative ... is to become independent from others and to discover and express one's unique attributes ... behavior is organized and made meaningful primarily by reference to one's own internal repertoire of thoughts, feelings, and action, rather than by reference to the thoughts, feelings, and actions of others' (Markus & Kitayama, 1991, p. 226).

Invariably the approach to the self dominant in psychology and in the Western world in general, has been described as monocultural, monotheistic, monadic, ethnocentric, egocentric, egotistical, egocentric–contractual individualistic, idiocentric, individuocentric, selfish, separate, autonomous, self–contained, bounded, boundaried or limited, closed, linear, self–reliant, independent, a centralized equilibrium structure, abstract, rationalistic, private, bourgeois, saturated, as well as empty, minimal, entrepreneurial, and referential (see Holdstock, 1993 for references).

The alternate model of the self that is being envisioned stresses the self as an interdependent, and not as an independent entity. The self is considered as an agent in relation. Some developments, such as that within the natural sciences and cultural anthropology, even extend the relatedness of the individual to the physical universe and the spiritual realm. The human movement sciences elaborate the activity component without which the self cannot be known, as well as the psychological importance of the body. Hermans and his coworkers (Hermans, Kempen, & van Loon, 1992) consider the self to be a dialogical narrator, "(a) spatially organized and *embodied* and (b) *social*, with the other not outside but in the self–structure, resulting in a multiplicity of dialogically interacting selves" (p. 23).

The revised model of the self challenges the notion of the self as a demarcated entity, set off against the world. Power and control are not considered to rest predominantly with the individual, but within the field of forces within which the individual exists. This revisioned concept of self has invariably been described as sociocentric–organic, bipolar, extended, communal, interdependent, open, ensembled, contextual, collective, embedded, embodied, dialogical, indexical, connected, constitutive, personalised, allocentric, relational, a decentralized non–equilibrium structure, a vital force in participation, oscillating, indexical, polytheistic, pluralistic, and holistic (see Holdstock, 1991).

Since this is not the place to elaborate on each of these concepts, only a brief outline of perspectives pertaining to the way the self is conceptualised in non–Western cultures and in femininst writings, will be presented. Many non–Western cultures (see Holdstock, 1992) have thus far been documented as portraying "the self as constituted by social context rather than by an individuated psychological core" (Miller, 1988, p. 273). Numerous examples exist in the various cultures of the different ways in which the principles of the interdependent self find expression. Among these are the supreme Chinese virtue of *jen*, which implies "the person's capability to interact with fellow human beings in a sincere, polite, and decent fashion" (Markus & Kitayama, 1991, p. 228), and the concept of *simpatico* among Hispanics which "refers to the ability to both respect and share others' feelings" (Markus & Kitayama, 1991, p. 228). Among the Japanese the concept of *sassuru*, which is of the highest priority, means to always consider other people first.

In many non–Western societies being separated from other people implies a personal, cultural sense of hell. The Hindu and African cultures are among such societies. I have written elsewhere of the importance of relatedness in Africa (eg. Holdstock, 1987, Ch. 10). *Umuntu ngumuntu ngabantu*, meaning a person is a person through other persons, embodies the essence of the concept of the person in Africa. It is believed that "I am because we are, and because we are, I am." In contrast to the Cartesian dictum of `I think therefore I am', African people believe that `I belong therefore I am.' Of the many other concepts portraying the importance of relatedness, none is more expressive than *ubuntu* (Nguni) or *botho* (Sotho). Ubuntu conveys the idea of strength based on the qualities of compassion, care, gentleness, respect, and empathy.

The interdependent nature of the African self is also indicated by the belief that each individual is *a vital force in participation* with other vital forces. These vital forces are composed not only of other people but of animals, plants, the ancestors, and even elements of the inanimate world. Many other non–Western cultures also belief in a relatedness with the larger universe and with the past. Since we are part of a system of vital forces we have to have proper respect for the other vital forces even those that are of a lesser order, such as the animal kingdom and the inanimate world.

Several feminist and post–feminist writers have also proposed an alternative to the autonomous and non–relational model of the self. According to them the emphasis on the separation–individuation side of identity reflects the male perspective. The female perspective refers to "`the other voice' with which many women seem to confront the world and in terms of which they frame their understanding. This is the voice of connections and relationships rather than the voice of boundaries and separations" (Sampson, 1988, p.18).

"Women move along in the world through relational connections...The notion of a separate identity or a separate sense of self is not quite the same in women as in men" (Josselson, 1987, p. 169–170). Women grow up with a relational sense of self. Identity means being with. Without others there is no sence of a fulfilled self. The more there is of others the more there is of self, and vice–versa. Identity seems to be a matter of defining the internal experience of the self through attachment to others. Unlike males, who are brought up in a culture stressing self–assertion, mastery, individual distinction, and separateness, women are raised in a culture of communion, stressing contact, union, cooperation, and being together. Skill and success in relatedness become keystones of identity. Women's sense of self is organized around the ability to make and maintain relationships. Josselson (1990) discusses seven dimensions of relationship as foundations and expressions of identity, varying from the most basic needs of holding and attachment to embeddedness (the *we* of *me*), and the offering of tenderness and care.

IMPLICATIONS OF THE INTERDEPENDENT CONCEPT OF SELF FOR PC THEORY

The revisioned model of the self as an interdependent entity seems, on the one hand, to be closely affiliated with the PC approach, and on the other, to be distinctly different from it. Rogers undoubtedly rejected narcissistic individualism (see Caspary, 1991). He wrote that "We seem as a culture to have made a fetish out of complete individual self–sufficiency, of not needing help, of being completely private except in a very few selected relationships" (Rogers, 1979, p. 12). In all his major works Rogers (1951, 1959, 1961), after elucidating the actualising tendency of the organism and the self, acknowledges the inherently social nature of the self. In *Client–Centered Therapy* (1951), he first describes how "The organism actualizes itself in the direction of...increasing self–regulation, autonomy, and away from heteronymous control" (p. 487), and then states: "Finally, self–actualization of the organism appears to be in the direction of socialization, broadly defined" (p. 488). Similarly, in his self–proclaimed magnum opus, "A theory of therapy, personality, and interpersonal relationships, as developed in the Client–Centered framework," Rogers (1959) again sets out by describing the central source of energy in the human organism as the "development towards autonomy and away from heteronomy, or control by external forces" (p. 196), before he acknowledges, later in the chapter, the importance of significant others in the development of a person's sense of self. Thus, it is clear that Rogers realised the importance of others to and for the individual. However, his point of departure always remained the actualisation of the self as an independent unit of the social system. Others are attributed a secondary and not a primary role in the life of the individual.

And although the social outreach of his theory into the political arena during the latter part of Rogers' life does not have a direct bearing on the theory of self, it can perhaps be used to further argue the social dimension of the PC approach. Caspary (1991) states that although the PC "approach began as a strictly personal/psychological/private approach" (p. 8), it evolved, during the latter two decades of Rogers' life, into the political arena. He considers this development to counter the criticism that the PC way of being is inherently individualistic and apolitical. However, even in the social outreach of the theory, empowering the individual remained the focus through which societal change was thought to be brought about (Rogers, 1977). In addition, it has been argued that the inherently individualistic nature of the PC approach and its focus on talking about issues, actually defuses, rather than encourages any real political action (Swartz, 1986), thus maintaining, rather than opposing the status quo of political regimes. O'Hara (1989), though acknowledging Rogers' individualistic or egocentric concept of personhood, nevertheless considers the raising of critical consciousness which occurs in large PC groups, as being of the same nature and political intent as the work of Paulo Freire, whose concept of the self was diametrically opposite that of Rogers.

Brazier (1993), along with others (eg. Caspary, 1991; Ford, 1991), fully acknowledges the inherently social nature of the self in the personality theory of Rogers. Yet, he maintains that instead of regarding self–development as primary and the development of a social conscious-ness as a by–product of self–actualisation, that it is self–development that is a derivative of the altruistic orientation. Brazier argues that the human being is, in contrast to the PC focus on self–orientation, primarily Other directed. He maintains that we are intrinsically organised to focus outside, and not on the self. He reverses the basic assumptions of Rogers. The individual is not primarily in need of receiving the necessary and sufficient conditions, but of providing them. In agreement with Eric Fromm, Brazier maintains that "our basic need is the need to love rather than the need to be loved" (p. 76). Thus, therapy is more growth promoting for the therapist than for the client, unless there is an opportunity for the client to also learn to adopt an altruistic stance.

Gaylin (1993) states that he has "grown increasingly uncomfortable with the person–centred emphasis on `independence' as a key concept in defining psychological well–being" (p. 181). Rather, interdependence defines our species. He argues that PC theory ignores the complexity of the developing person's relationship within the family. Based on his belief in the interdepen-dent nature of the human being, Gaylin prefers to practice PC therapy in the context of the marriage or the family. "Since virtually all therapy deals with issues of interpersonal relations-hips, the inclusion of others should be looked upon not as unusual and odd, but usual and natural" (p. 189).

Geller (1982) attacks the ego–directedness in the self–actualisation theory of Rogers. "Like it or not, Rogers is committed to an atomistic theory of the self, according to which the `true or real self' is asocial in nature and origin. It is what it is independent of and prior to interaction with others" (p. 59). Like Brazier, Geller maintains that the self must originate via social means. Caspary (1991) distinguishes between Rogers' sense of personhood and Harry Boyte's sense of `peoplehood.' In contrast to Rogers, the community orientation of Boyte stresses such traditional ethics as duty, loyalty, and reverence. Contrasted to defining self–actualisation strictly in individual terms, as Rogers did, Boyte considers self–actualisation in terms of community – peoplehood not personhood.

In similar vein to Brazier (1993) and Caspary (1991), Arnett (1989) contrasts the respective contributions of Rogers and Buber to the issue of interpersonal communication. Arnett wrote that "Rogers' emphasis on the psyche, `internal locus of control,' `congruence betweeen self and organism,' and `the innate goodness of the organism,' is incompatible with the fundamental dialogical notion of the `between.' Each of these concepts is based in an internal understanding of communication. The meaning of communication remains *inside* the person, not `between' persons" (p. 44). Like Brazier, Arnett thus argues that the I and Thou of Buber, the dialogic relationship, became for Rogers primarily a means to promote or achieve "self–reliance and autonomy that marks the goal of self–actualisation" (p, 50). Buber, on the other hand, accepts the relationship as an end in itself, with individual growth occurring as a by–product, not the goal of the relationship.

Ford (1991) has provided an elaboration of the nature of the internal dialogue in the theory of Rogers. He highlights the distinction which Rogers made between the *actua-lising tendency* of the organism and the *self–actualising* tendency of the self, which was considered as a subsystem of the actualising tendency. In "1959 the actualizing tendency replaced the self–actualizing tendency as the fundamental and only motivational construct" (p. 104). Rogers employed this distinction between experience and self as the basis for his concept of congruence.

"The important point is that in contrast to 1951, Rogers in 1959 (onward) no longer supported self–actualization as *necessarily* meaning the realization of optimal psychological functioning. In fact, self–actualization being in conflict with actualization is the usual state of affairs" (Ford, 1991, p.105).

Thus, it seems clear that the PC theory of self subscribes, in keeping with the zeitgeist out of which it grew, to an ethnocentric concept of the self as an independent entity. The theory of therapy, on the other hand, although it is based on the theory of self, is not congruent with that theory. The theory of therapy seems to have much more in common with the view of the self as an interdependent entity. To complicate matters even further, not all aspects of the theory of therapy seem to derive from this common base. Two of the `necessary and sufficient conditions' of psychotherapy, empathy and positive regard, are in keeping with an interdependent view of the self. By their very nature, empathy and positive regard, reflect the importance of relatedness. Furthermore, psychotherapy, especially as it is practised in the PC approach, is an interdependent relationship between two or more people. Congruence, on the other hand, primarily reflects an orientation to the self as an independent and not as an interdependent entity. Congruence implies that it is the inner world of the self, rather than of the other, that is of importance. However, to emphasize the independent autonomy and self–focus of the client in psychotherapy, an endeavour which is at heart an interrelated activity, is a contradiction in terms.

I would like to argue that the appeal of the PC approach can be ascribed to the interdependent and related nature of the concept of the self which implicitly underlies the therapeutic relationship, and not, primarily, to the empowerment of the individual person. If one has to talk in terms of empowerment it is empowerment of the individual in relationship, and not as an individuated entity. However, the interdependent nature of the self which underlies therapy has never been acknowledged in the theory. As the variety and great number of disciplines and subdisciplines, stressing the importance of the interdependent self indicate, it is the concept of the interdependent self, and not that of the independent self, which is central and of universal significance.

CONGRUENCE AND THE INTERDEPENDENT CONCEPT OF SELF

While empathy and positive regard reflect the importance implicitly attached to relatedness in the theory of therapy, congruence, the third of the `necessary and sufficient conditions', is as stated, more in keeping with the theory of the self as an independent entity. Rogers defined congruence as the accurate matching of experience and awareness (the experiential component), further extended to cover a matching of experiencing, awareness and communication (the expressive component). Although both aspects of congruence reflect an independent orientation to the self, it is especially the expressive component that is cause for concern within PC theory.

The experiential component of congruence, to be in touch inwardly, seems universally to be considered of importance. It is of as much significance to the healers belonging to the interdependent non–Western cultures, as it is to the PC practitioners functioning within the independent orientation of the West. What Gendlin calls focussing, the San of the Kalahari desert and the indigenous healers of southern Africa call a tapping inside their bodies.

The expressive, or communicative aspect of congruence, on the other hand, can pose severe problems for PC theory and practice. In the other paper presented at the conference, these problems are highlighted with respect to the special situation of anger. It is especially in the context of an independent orientation to the self that problems arise with respect to congruence. In such a context congruence elicits ego–focussed, and not other–focussed emotional experiences and expressions.

In contrast to the ego–focussed nature of congruence in Western cultures, the internal bodily sense and its expression is dealt with in a totally different way in cultures subscribing to an interdependent self. For instance, the indigenous healers of Africa refer to the tapping inside their bodies in order to know what is amiss with their clients. This, I would venture a guess, is also what happens during moments of optimal therapeutic encounter. Here, my bodily sense is placed in service of the other, and not just of myself. It is the point at which empathy and congruence become one.

Within an interdependent orientation, the belief in the fundamental connectedness of human beings to each other determines the overt expression, not only of felt bodily states, but of such inner attributes as abilities, opinions, judgements, emotions, and personality characteristics. Voluntary control of the inner attributes constitutes the core of the cultural ideal of becoming mature. The understanding of one's autonomy and the expression of that autonomy as secondary to, and constrained by, the primary task of interdependence, distinguishes interdependent selves from independent selves for whom autonomy and its expression is often afforded primary significance.

Within an interdependent framework, one's inner feelings and their expression, may be less important in determining one's consequent actions. For those with interdependent selves, it is the interpersonal context that assumes priority over the expression of private feelings. The latter may need to be controlled or de–emphasized so as to allow the individual to fit effectively into the interpersonal context. Especially intense experiences of ego–focussed emotions, such as anger, are to be avoided by those with an interdependent orientation.

Within the framework of the independent self, Thomas Gordon (1974) distinguishes between I– and You– messages. His attempt at concretising the expression of congruence, can also be regarded as an attempt to soften the impact of the ego–focussed expressions of self. While congruent I–messages are certainly more effective than blaming You–messages, it is debatable that ego–based I–messages can, in the long run, be optimally facilitative in establishing a new world order. Perhaps we have reached a stage in our development where the model of the independently competitive individual as the unit of the social system needs to be replaced by that of cooperative interdependence with each other. It seems that the PC approach has, as legacy of the great pioneering work of Rogers, a particular responsibility in this regard.

REFERENCES

Arnett, R.C. (1989). *What is dialogic communication? Friedman's contribution and clarification.* Person–Centered Review, 4, 42–60.

Brazier, D. (1993). *The necessary condition is love: Going beyond self in the Person–Centred approach.* In D. Brazier (Ed), Beyond Carl Rogers. London: Constable.

Caspary, W.R. (1991). *Carl Rogers – Values, persons, and politics: The dialectic of individual and community.* Journal of Humanistic Psychology, 31, 8–31.

Ford, J.G. (1991). *Rogerian self–actualization: A clarification of meaning.* Journal of Humanistic Psychology, 31, 101–111.

Gaylin, N.L. (1993). *Person–Centred family therapy*. In D. Brazier (Ed), Beyond Carl Rogers. London: Constable.

Geller, L. (1982). *The failure of self–actualization theory: A critique of Carl Rogers and Abraham Maslow*. Journal of Humanistic Psychology, 22, 56–73.

Gordon, T. (1974). *T.E.T. Teacher effectiveness training*. New York: Peter H. Wyden.

Hermans, H.J.M., Kempen, H.J.G., & van Loon, R.J.P. (1992). *The dialogical self. Beyond individualism and rationalism*. American Psychologist, 47, 23–33.

Holdstock, T.L. (1987). *Education for a new nation*. Johannesburg: Africa Transpersonal Association.

Holdstock, T.L. (1991). *Can we afford not to revision the Person –Centered concept of self?* Paper presented at the 2nd International Conference on Client–Centered and Experiential Psychotherapy, Stirling, Scotland.

Holdstock, T.L. (1992). *(Clinical) psychology in search of identity*. Amsterdam: The Free University Press.

Holdstock, T.L., & Rogers, C.R. (1983). *Person–Centered personality theory*. In R.J. Corsini & A.J. Marsella (Eds), Personality theories, research, and assessment (pp. 189–227). Itasca, Ill: F.E. Peacock.

Holdstock, T.L. (1993). *Can we afford not to revision the Person–Centred concept of self?* In B. Brazier (Ed., Beyond Carl Rogers. London: Constable.

Hutterer, R. (1993). *Eclecticism: An identity crisis for Person–Centred therapists*. In D. Brazier (Ed.), Beyond Carl Rogers. London: Constable.

Josselson, R. (1987). *Finding herself. Pathways to identity development in women*. London: Jossey–Bass.

Josselson, R. (1990, September). *Identity and relatedness in the life cycle*. Paper presented at the symposium on Identity and Development, Amsterdam.

Kang, J.A. (1994). *Comparison of psychotherapy in the East and West from my personal experience*. In Scientific Programme Committee (Ed), Psychotherapy: East & West (Integration of Psychotherapy) (p.549–556). Seoul: Korean Academy of Psychotherapists.

Markus, H.R., & Kitayama, S. (1991). *Culture and the self: Implications for cognition, emotion, and motivation*. Psychological Review, 98, 224–253.

Miller, J.G. (1988). *Bridging the content–structure dichotomy: Culture and the self*. In M.H. Bond (Ed.), The cross–cultural challenge to social psychology (pp. 266–281). London: Sage.

Rogers, C.R. (1951). *Client–centered therapy*. Boston: Houghton Mifflin.

Rogers, C.R. (1959). *A theory of therapy, personality, and interpersohnal relationships, as developed in the Client–centered framework*. In S. Koch (Ed), Psychology: A study of science (Vol. 3, pp. 184–256).

Rogers, C.R. (1961). *On becoming a person*. Boston: Houghton Mifflin.

Rogers, C.R. (1977). *Carl Rogers on personal power: Inner strength and its revolutionary impact*. New York: Delacorte Press.

Rogers, C.R. (1979). *Groups in two cultures*. Personnel & Guidance Journal, 38, 11–13.

Rose, N. (1989). *Individualizing psychology*. In J. Shotter & K.J. Gergen (Eds.), Texts of identity (pp. 119–132). London: Sage.

Sampson, E.E. (1988). *The debate on individualism: Indigenous psychologies of the individual and their role in personal and societal functioning*. American Psychologist, 43, 15–22.

Swartz, L. (1986). *Carl Rogers in South Africa: The issue of silence*. Psychology in Society, 5, 139–143.

The Core Conditions between Theory and Practice
Critical Remarks to a Successful, but Unpractical Theory

ROBERT HUTTERER

UNIVERSITY OF VIENNA

ABSTRACT

The therapist s task in person-centered therapy is to create person-centered attitudes within him– or herself, and to implement corresponding behavior in the relationship to the client. Furthermore, the therapist is expected to maintain this "way of being" and "doing" even in the face of clients with many different kinds of behavior, varying modes of expression and styles of defending themselves and different forms of vulnerability. Unfortunately the process of developing and maintaining a person-centered way of being or style in therapeutic relationships is poorly discussed in person-centered theory. Traditional client-centered theory of therapy follows an objective, linear and causal pattern (If-then-formulation): The therapist s attitudes and ways of behaviour are components of cause, process and changes in the client (success of therapy), are components of effect. This theory does not take into account ambiguity and complexity, uniqueness and incomparability, as well as uncertainty and conflict, which are unavoidable components of therapeutic practice. The writer argues that traditional client-centered theory of therapy – helpful and successful in conducting empirical research – is a source of dilemmas and constraints, if used as guidance for practice. It causes compulsory self-demands, superstitious behavior and a winner-looser-dynamic, which limits the experience and behavior of the therapist. In the best case traditional client-centered theory of therapy is irrelevant. It is argued that practitioners – successful in developing and maintaining a client-centered way of being in their practice – are guided by "personal principles" of regulating their own attitudes and actions in the therapeutic situation in order to come to a consistent "person-centered style". The bases of therapists' self regulation are tacit processes and implicit knowledge which includes self-reflection, improvisation, experimentation as well as quality control.

INTRODUCTION

Let me present some general considerations first. My argument and the problems I refer to in this article have to do with integrating theory and practice, thinking and acting, attitudes and behavior, bringing together theoretical knowledge and practical knowledge. Also it has to do with professional competence and mastery. I think these problems have not been systematically discussed in client-centered theory.

The integration of thinking and acting might be one of the most pressing and yet least understood problems of our time. In a time of trial-error politics, partial solutions and misplannings in many professional areas, it is competence that is in demand. Competent action requires the perceiving and understanding of relevant factors, relations and elements of a situation, their selective consideration or non-consideration, in order to quickly "forget" them again while acting and thereby making space again for understanding a meanwhile changed situation. This "forgetfulness" or obliviousness was never an impediment for the development of professional competence, it has however always been difficult to understand. Professional competence has some mystery that cats have when they land on their feet every time after a free fall. It is not by chance that we consequently speak of the "secret of success" in all those who are successful, even though they might have unveiled it for the hundreth time. It is this necessity to forget knowledge, the transitoriness of the understanding while acting, that has made the theory-practice-problem into a burdensome problem, frustrating for philosophers, social scientists and psychologists inspite of its fascinating intellectual side.

This problem is no less burdensome for those working as Rogerian therapists, since the integration of thinking and acting, attitudes and behavior is part of the challenge that belongs to the therapeutic element of authenticity.

DIFFERENT WAYS OF THERAPISTS' SELF-REGULATION

The following phenomena I was confronted with during supervision of beginning person-centred psychotherapists direct us to that kind of problem I wish to describe in more general terms: Trainees and young therapists undergoing supervision complain about therapeutic situations in which "nothing happens", they complain about lack of orientation, don't know "what to do", have the feeling of "doing something wrong", and are insecure. Their own response or solutions to these experiences of "being stuck" or "being confused" are almost always claims which derive from the person-centred theory of therapy. They express something like:"Yes, I know, I might not be empathic enough", "I should probably be more accepting", "I should be more authentic, but how shall I do that?" It appears, that in the course of therapeutic sessions the consciousness and thinking of these therapists is largely dominated by these "theoretical justified" self-criticism and doubts in themselves.

On the other hand, more experienced therapists say that they do not think at all if they realise therapeutic conditions or to which degree they express them. The theoretical requirements and preconditions are no explicit subject of reflection during the therapeutic situation.

How can these opposing phenomena be explained or understood? The first example shows that the therapist tries to find orientation for his/her being and doing as therapist from a theoretical statement (empathy, prizing, authenticity of the therapist supports therapeutic changes). The therapist s occupation by theoretical requirements is quite obviously "disturbing" to the attention, the flow of experience and action. The second example shows that the therapist has obviously found a way to apply the theory on a particular client without directly referring to the formulation of this theory. The implementation of the therapeutic conditions have not happened in a rational way and have not been directly taken from the preformulated theory; they have rather happened "on the side" and in a subliminal way.

Both examples represent different relationships between theory and practice: In the first example the therapists turn back to theoretical formulation, they try to direct themselves, influence themselves in correspondence with their theoretical knowledge during the contact with the client. In the mind and consciousness of these therapists there is – again and again – a shift of focus from the client s frame of reference to the therapist s own way of doing therapy.

In the second example the therapists do not directly refer to what theory tells them, but to a different source of knowledge. They obviously follow ways of regulating their attitudes and behavior towards the client, in which official theory has no place and no use. It seems true for these therapists that they have developed a competent way of practicing therapy in spite of or even because theory is faded out or ignored.

My *main argument* arises from these perceptions, which is:

Traditional client-centered theory of therapy, which was helpful and successful in conducting empirical research – is a source of dilemmas and constraints, if used by therapists as direct guidance for their practice. Because of its characteristics, the way it is presented and taught, traditonal client-centered theory of therapy does not determine, but confuse the practice of therapy. It seems therefore appropriate to say that traditional client-centered theory of therapy as unpractical. Successful practitioners – successful in terms of developing and maintaining a client-centered way of being in their practice – do not refer to theory in order to guide their practice. They have developed highly idiosyncratic ways of regulating their own attitudes and actions while involved in and in relation to particular clients in order to come to a consistent "person-centered style". The bases of therapist s self regulation are tacit processes and implicit knowledge which include self-reflection, improvisation, experimentation as well as quality control.

THE CORE CONDITIONS IN TERMS OF TECHNICAL RATIONALITY

My arguments say that traditional client-centered theory of therapy, the way it is presented and taught is not helpful to guide a competent client-centered practice. Let us take a short look at this theory. You soon will recognize that you already know what I mean.

A linear and causal theory

Client-centered theory of therapy, as we know, follows an objective, linear and causal pattern: the therapist s attitudes and behaviour are components of cause, and the changes in the client (success of therapy) are components of effect. Their relationship is characterized by a causal connection: the therapist is the independent factor, the client is the dependent one; the therapist represents the cause, the client the effect. The variability of the cause (i.g degrees of empathy) is in linear connection with the variability of the effect (degrees of self-exploration). This is the classic understanding of theory in the empiric-analytic approach of research.

We can find examples for this formulation that fit into this pattern in relevant literature. In Rogers well-known article "The necessary and sufficient conditions of therapeutic personality change" (1957) he presented the following hypotheses: "If these six conditions .... exist, then constructive personality changes ... will occur in the client. .....If all six conditions are present, then the greater the degree to which conditions 2 to 6 exist, the more marked will be the constructive personality change in the client." (p. 229)

These statements can be found in all kinds of variations. Rogers himself formulated carefully, at times including more of the phenomenological part or, as we can see in the following example, putting more stress on the component of activity:

"If I can provide a certain type of relationship, the other person will discover within him/herself the capacity to use that relationship for growth, and change and personal development will occur." (Rogers 1961, p33). In this quotation Rogers brings the activity of the therapist in contrast to the activity of the client resulting in a formulation which does more justice to this phenomenon, but still remains in a causal context. Rogers was aware of the limitations of a causal theory, but he accepted the disadvantages in order to make his theory accessible to the empirical research.

THERAPEUTIC PRACTICE AS APPLICATION OF THEORY

According to that linear-causal theory there is a view about how this theory should be implemented into practice which follows the principle of technical rationality. The key concept is the concept of "application".

In our example this means: the beginning therapist acquires the characteristic features of empathy, positive regard and congruence as complex attitudes and correponding behaviour patterns. According to the linear-causal theory it follows that the therapist realises his/her way of acting, his/her attitudes independently of the client and his/her way of expressing . The therapist is the independent factor, the one that causes. The theory suggests that the therapist turns on his/her attitudes from the first minute of the session and to the highest degree like spotlights. The therapist illuminates the client regardless of the shadows the client might try to cast. The therapist is expected to maintain this "way of being" and "doing" even in the face of clients with many different kinds of behavior, varying modes of expression and styles of defending themselves and different forms of vulnerability. The supply of energy, the regeneration is a procedure that continues independent of the client. Also occasional short-circuits are within the range of the therapist (spotlight analogy). Furthermore – according to this theory – the therapist's attitudes and qualifications (empathy, etc.) are expected to be so sound that they will not break down even in difficult situations. In case that in unforeseen situations or with specially difficult clients the therapist's style breaks down repeatedly then the therapist must be "repaired" or be "serviced"; the therapist must go back to training (supervision, self-therapy, exercises). But traditonal theory of therapy does not provide on-line-help or on-line-guidance in this case.

INCOMPATIBILITIES AND CRITIQUE

I think the therapeutic situation and therapeutic relationship – as practitioners experience it – is not the way this theory portrays it: there are pressures of action, surprising reactions of the client towards the therapist, uncertainties, value conflicts and unclarities of various kinds. The linear and causal model of theory do not go hand in hand with the conception of mutual exchange. Our theory is not as complex and differentiated that it is able to take into account ambiguity and complexity, uniqueness, as well as uncertainty and conflict, which are unavoidable components of therapeutic practice.

From the traditional theory and the traditional theory-practice-relationship we cannot see how we can achieve the desired therapist's attitudes/behaviour in a therapeutic situation and how these attitudes can be maintained in relation to the client. Special questions arise from understanding the therapeutic conditions as attitudes , from a "lack of technique", from the viewpoint that person-centerdness is a state of being rather than a state of doing and knowing. Therefore the question how it can be maintained is even more complex. Traditional theory offers no real answers. So especially trainees and unexperienced therapists using that theory as guidance for practicing try to model themselves according to the principle of technical rationality.

The consequence is that these therapists limit themselves, they use a kind of self-communication which constricts and confuses them; for instance compulsory self-demands ("I must be empathic", "I must be accepting"). Once these therapists get out of balance they produce different kinds of coping strategies in order to overcome the feelings of not having power over their own attitudes, feelings and behavior. One of that coping strategies is "muddling along"; another one the call for higher efficiency ("I think I should make more efforts and understand them better"), passivity in connection with superstitious behavour of the therapist (motto: "the tendency to self-actualisation will do it", "it will change again, it's only a process"), counterbalancing by using techniques ("one must do something now"), rallying-cries ("I just must stick it out now, another 10 minutes and the session will be over"), panic behaviour (over-activity, hectic calming down of high emotions, agressiveness in case of longer periods of silence, paralysis signs), relapse into an everyday-psychology (giving advices, explanations). These are some examples of coping strategies performed in order to feel a little bit more comfortable in spite of the presence of insecurity, confusion, stuckness, self-constriction. Since the application of client-centered theory of therapy does create insecurity and discomfort, the trainee or unexperienced therapist may be open to adopt techniques from other therapeutic schools (Hutterer, 1993)

The theory does not tolerate errors: little empathy, lack of positive regard are failures of the therapist. The theoretically conceded variability in the therapist's behaviour, the "more" or "less" encourages a winner-loser-dynamic, because it is only the "more" in empathy for instance that is relevant for the practical success of therapy; the "less" (in empathy and accepting), negative feelings, feelings of rejection, misunderstandings are interference factors, they "don't lead anywhere". From the viewpoint of theory they are counter-productive, have no meaning and must be excluded. It is indeed the biggest problem especially of younger therapists how to deal with empathy errors (failures) and negative feelings without insulting or suppressing themselves or their clients.

The main reasons why traditional theory of therapy is unpractical in the sense I described it is that it does not touch the indeterminable zones of practice: ambiguity and complexity, uniqueness.

It suggests to the therapist a way to manage him/herself according to a principle of technical rationality which is not suitable to control one s own complex attitudes and feelings. We cannot change our attitudes by approaching them directly and in a linear way, we cannot push the button and our inner situation as therapist will change immediately. It is as hard to do so as it is hard to come into a good mood intentionally.

Complex attitudes contain many components which can be inhibited or supported by the pressure of a situation. Attitudes are more prone to get out of balance, but also more open to development. Attitudes consist of ways of perceiving which are not fully at the disposal of and cannot be directly controlled by the person involved. They are actualized in situations, they develop in a non-linear way. But the limiting pressure of a situation or relationship can supress them also.

These are some considerations, examples concerning the argument, that our traditional theory of therapy is unpractical: If a therapist does really apply this theory and use it as direct guidance for practising therapy, he or she is lost and will not come to a competent mastery of a client-centered style. So the question arises if there exist competent client-centred therapists at all. Since we only have this unpractical theory we may conclude that there is no competent client-centered therapist. This is definitely not true, although there is some evidence from research that many client-centered therapists do not offer high quality therapy. One writer concluded from this evidence that we should provide to those "average therapists" special means to improve their communication, e.g. teaching them how to give person-centred advice, or how to stop the client when presenting detailed problem descriptions and self-exploration of burdensome feelings.

ACTION THEORY: KNOW HOW AND TACIT SELF-REGULATION

I assume, that we would identify experienced therapists as competent, gradually developing a silent "user theory" which stands next to the "official theory", more or less compatible with the latter, but guiding the therapeutic actions. This "user theory" is not an if-then-theory, it is a how-to-theory: Knowledge about how to be, how to do, how to perceive. The aim of that theory is not to control the client, but to regulate and balance the therapist s own attitudes, feelings and complex actions. They have developed "personal principles" of regulating their own attitudes and actions in the therapeutic situation in order to come to a consistent "person-centered style" in relation to the client s way of expression and adapted to the client s style (of making contact). Strangely enough, if we would ask these therapists what they are doing they would present the official theory (empathizing, staying open and accepting, staying congruent). They do so, because the official theory is a sort of symbol of identificaton, a trademark and certainly still a part of the truth, altough the theory does not determine their practice.

Some characteristics of this user theory or action theory:

1.   This theory speaks about therapist s personal principles of self-regulation that are highly tacit processes. It does not speak about overt behavior and definitely not about principles of controlling the client.

2.   These principles need to be discovered and explored from the inside. We are only able to approach them phenomenologically, with a self-reflective way of investigating in order to make them explicit.

3.   They operate in the background, in the subsidiary awareness, while the therapist s focal awareness is directed to the client s frame of reference. (Polanyi, 1958).

4.   They operate in the sense of self-reflective improvisation or experimentation. That means these principles are not used in a rigid way, it is more an adaptive trying out while having some background awarenesse of doing this and an awarenes of what follows. This improvisation is in relation to the clients unique style of expressing him/herself or the client s vulnerability.

5.   An ongoing, intuitive quality control is included. This is one of the most important things for coming to competence and mastery: to be able to do this intuitive, "enfolded" or "background" quality control. Qualitiy control is not a way of watching oneself self-critically. Self-criticism in this concern would destroy the ability of quality control. It has to do with (counter)balancing, that is possible only if we feel and are in touch with how it is to be in balance. This process is comparable with how to ride a bycicle. We only are able to counterbalance if we feel and know how it is to ride a bicycle in a balanced way. Once we got it then an intuitive qualitiy control could happen. And we need not to control it cognitively. So the therapist – to be able to do this quality control – first does need the experience how it is to do be on the track of the client, in touch, more general how it is to do a high quality therapy.

Examples of principles of therapist s self-regulation

Principle of controlled identification. I would rather say self-reflective identification: Identifying with the client s feelings and ways of perceiving, but being aware of that and not loosing the feeling of being a seperate person.(Rogers, 1942)

The sensible person assumption. That means that the therapist assumes he/she speaks to a sensible person, to keep the perception of the client as a sensible person even the client s behavior and way expressing him/herself forces the therapist to have a different perception. Concerning dealing with unresponsive clients, Gendlin stated: "This assumption has never failed of later confirmation, but in the face of .... unresponsiveness it is an assumption requiring imagination." (Gendlin, 1967, p. 367)

The benevolent witness assumption: the therapist perceives him/herself, the therapeutic interaction and they client s way of expression and feeling from the perspective of a benevolent witness. It is like having a person sitting behind the therapist very closely embracing every moment by expressing a non-evaluative attitude saying: "I see, oh yes this is the way it's going".

Finding the right distance: How the therapist comes to manage closeness in the relationship to the client is also an example of therapist s self-regulation (see Leijssen, this volume).

CONCLUSION

It is argued that traditional client-centered theory of therapy is irrelevant in guiding the therapist s practical actions. Practitioners – successful in developing and maintaining a client-centered way of being in their practice – are guided by "personal principles" of regulating their own attitudes and actions in the therapeutic situation in order to come to a consistent "person-centered style". The bases of therapist s self regulation are tacit processes and implicit knowledge which include self-reflection, improvisation, experimentation as well as quality control.

I am convinced, if these personal principles of therapists' self-regulation were made explicit it would help us to understand in more detail how to achieve more competence and mastery in the practice of client-centered therapy.

A self-reflective approach is needed to explore the therapist s inner communication and inner experiences of the client s being in the therapeutic situation in phenomenological terms. Case examples of therapists inner self-regulation related to their work with different client styles could be of great help for trainees and students seeking competence and mastery.

REFERENCES

Gendlin, Eugene, T. (1967) Therapeutic Procedures in Dealing with Schizophrenics. In: Rogers, C. R. et al. (1967). The Therapetiuc Relationship and its Impact, University of Wisconsin Press, Madison, 369-400.

Hutterer, R. (1993). Eclecticism: an identity crisis of person-centred therapist. In: Brazier, D. (1993). Beyond Carl Rogers. Constable, London, p. 274-284.

Leijssen, M. (1995) Characteristics of a healing inner relationship (this volume).

Polanyi, M. (1958). Personal Knowledge. Towards a Post-Critical Philosophy. University of Chicago Press Chicago.

Rogers, C. R. (1942) Counseling and Psychotherapy. Houghton Mifflin, Boston.

Rogers, C. R. (1957). The Necessary and Sufficient Conditions of Therapeutic Personality Change. In: Kirschenbaum, H & Land Henderson, V. (1989). The Carl Rogers Reader. Houghton Mifflin, Boston. p. 219-235.

Rogers, C.R. (1961). On Becoming a Person. Houghton Mifflin, Boston.

Training Therapy in the Client-centered Approach

Training therapy would seem, at first glance, to be an inappropriate form of training for the client-centered approach. Rogers viewed institutionalized therapy training programs with scepticism and rejected the notion that obligatory therapy should be a part of such a training program. Nevertheless, he was very much in favor of "personal therapy" as part of training. Such a "personal therapy", however, must be regarded as training therapy, since its goals and motivation are primarily didactic and not therapeutic. Proceeding from Rogers' significant tendencies in the training program (the aim to achieve the congruence of one's basic attitudes as well as therapeutic empathy), as well as from Freud's similar definition of training analysis (with its aim of a certain conviction of the unconscious), I regard training therapy as a basic element of a therapy training program. Accordingly, the goal of training therapy in a client-centered training program is to impart fundamental therapeutic qualities as a result of the trainee becoming convinced of the central hypothesis of this approach through his or her own experience. I describe the characteristics of a training therapy by way of the self-experience processes which trainees should generally go through in the course of training. An historical overview of the development of training analysis as the oldest tradition of this kind reveals how important it is to strictly separate training therapy from the rest of the training program and, in particular, not to overburden it with therapeutic expectations, seeing it as a super-therapy. Finally, a discussion of Rogers' concept of significant learning explores training therapy as a paradigmatically person-centered opportunity for learning.

INTRODUCTION

The desire to integrate a training therapy into the training program of a client-centered therapist does not appear to be in keeping with the client-centered approach. As is well known, Carl Rogers was sceptical about or even rejected altogether a formal training program within this approach. He expressed this view very clearly in a conversation with the staff of the GwG in Hamburg: "I have always had an aversion against the kind of training association you have here" (Rogers, 1982, p. 20; transl. by auth.). Furthermore, he stated "I have always felt it to be a paradoxical situation to train someone to be a client-centered therapist" (ibid, p. 18). The main reason why this should be paradoxical is that client-centered therapy is based on a very personal and intuitive relationship, something which, unlike specialized knowledge or methods, cannot be conveyed as part of a training program. Rogers' scepticism also evidenced itself in the fact that, aside from the above-mentioned discussion in Hamburg, he dealt with the topic of training for client-centered therapy in only one of his main works ("Client-Centered Therapy", 1951; German 1972). It is here that Rogers provides an additional reason for his scepticism in this respect, namely the lack of empirical and scientific data with regard to a therapy training program in general. In conclusion he states the following:

> It should be amply evident, from the various points that have been listed, that if we were
> willing to sweep aside all the conventional notions of pre-therapy education and the ve-
> sted interests which are associated with them, and were to start with a fresh considerati-

on of those elements of preparation which experience has shown to have a definite relationship to effectiveness in therapy, we should doubtless emerge with a preparatory curriculum of experience vastly different from that usually required. (Rogers, 1951, p. 440; German 1972, p. 383)

Rogers is also very sceptical about the usual forms of therapy training programs, yet he did not completely develop any alternative to them.

Rogers' rejection of obligatory training therapy can be seen as a logical consequence of his reserve with regard to therapy training programs. "It does not seem consistent with the whole viewpoint of client-centered therapy to require individual therapy of the trainee" (1951, p. 438; German 1972, p. 381). However, here as elsewhere, Rogers does support the purpose of training therapy in substance, as he stresses the considerable significance of the experience of a "personal therapy" for client-centered therapists. In summing up his experiences with training programs, he points out the significant trend of

giv(ing) the student an experience of therapy within himself. This can be done in part through the way in which courses are taught and in part through the way the student is given supervisory help on his cases. The most direct route, of course, is for the student to undergo therapy himself, and a steadily increasing proportion of student counselors have been availing themselves of this opportunity. (1951, p. 433; German 1972, p. 377)

Accordingly, the tradition of so-called "personal therapy" is observed in many client-centered therapy training associations. However, in my view, the specific aims of a "training therapy" exceed those of a "personal therapy". Nevertheless these aims are hardly explicitly supported or discussed within the client-centered therapy movement.

I shall attempt to show that the processes that are essential for client-centered therapy can only be comprehended and learned when the individual has experienced them himself. If this occurs within the context of a personal therapy, then consequently this therapy should no longer be considered personal therapy, but rather, "training therapy". Such a therapy differs from a "normal" therapy in that its goals and motivation are primarily pedagogical rather than therapeutic. This may result in only slight differences in the behavior of those involved, but there will be a considerable difference in the way the entire training therapy is perceived. The most important aspect is that the trainee learns and experiences essential qualities of a therapist, and not that he or she becomes healthier.

At the beginning of my presentation I would like to discuss the aspects that Carl Rogers, on the basis of his experiences, considered to be essential for a client-centered therapy training program and to compare these with the fundamentals of training analysis as it was conceived of by its "inventor", Sigmund Freud, as they seem to me to closely resemble Rogers' aims. This discussion should provide a fundamental perspective from which to gain an understanding of training therapy (point 2). Subsequently I will provide a detailed outline of the goals and characteristics of a training therapy in the client-centered approach (point 3). The brief overview of the historical development of psychoanalytical training analysis as the longest standing tradition of this kind should help us to more closely define the concept of training therapy in our own training programs (point 4). Finally, I shall briefly discuss the concept of training therapy in connection with Rogers' basic principles of teaching and learning in general(point 5).

THE FUNDAMENTAL AIMS OF A CLIENT-CENTERED TRAINING THERAPY

Rogers: Significant Tendencies in a Therapy Training Program

In the above mentioned work on client-centered therapy training programs (the only one of its kind) (1951, p. 432 ff.; German 1972, p. 376 ff.), Rogers sums up his experiences in this area, and delineates four "significant trends" which have manifested themselves. I would like to address two of these trends here, as they, in my opinion, provide substantial grounds for a training therapy in the client-centered approach. First, Rogers describes the trend away from therapeutic techniques and toward the attitudinal orientation of the counselor. The trainees should think about and seek to understand their fundamental relationship to others as well as the attitudinal and philosophical preconditions for this relationship. At first they should not orient themselves toward the client-centered direction, but rather, try to find out how they really act as opposed to how they think they really act. This has to do, therefore, with experiencing one's own congruence and incongruence.

Rogers sees another trend in giving trainees the experience of undergoing a therapy. Although Rogers of course means a "normal" therapy in this case, he does point out that the aim of this personal therapeutic experience does not lie in the trainee freeing himself of conflicts, but rather, in his becoming more sensitive and empathic toward his clients.

Both trends are not about teaching techniques or imparting specialized knowledge or even overcoming one's own problems, but rather, about achieving something like the "professional" (i.e. necessary for a therapist) congruence and empathy that are essential to the client-centered approach. The concept "professional" in this connection should not, of course, imply something inauthentic or superficial, but rather, refers to very personal qualities that are necessary for establishing a therapeutic relationship. Professional experience and behavior have to be personally authentic. This nevertheless suggests that therapeutic congruence and empathy as well as a therapeutic relationship are essentially different from "everyday" congruence and empathy and everyday relationships. It is therefore necessary to look more closely into the question whether this difference is compatible with Rogers' often repeated view that these relationships are the same.

Therapeutic actions require professional qualities

Rogers stressed again and again that all constructive relationships are characterized by the same attributes as a therapeutic relationship. Accordingly, practically everyone would have the ability to become a therapist, and training is superfluous. However, a closer look at Rogers' therapy theory and his theory of interpersonal relationships reveals that there are significant differences between the two types of relationships. In therapy, the dynamics of experience are essentially determined by the empathy of the therapist, whereas in other relationships the congruence and incongruence of those involved are of the greatest significance. Rogers confirmed this in his above mentioned discussion with the staff of GwG by characterizing the difference between therapy and everyday life as follows:

> In therapy, empathy is probably the outstanding characteristic that advances the therapy. In everyday life it is congruence, its authenticity, that usually becomes apparent when there is a problem in a relationship, but on the other hand it seems to me that the qualities that make a good therapy also make a good relationship outside of a therapy (Rogers, 1982, p. 26; transl. by author).

I believe, however, that this diffence is even greater than Rogers acknowledges. I believe that therapeutic empathy has to exceed the empathy of everyday relationships. And since the therapeutic attitudes have to form an internal whole, the same must be true for congruence and unconditional positive regard. Perhaps the difference can most readily be seen in the case of empathy. As Rogers himself suggests, empathy in the therapeutic relationship is somehow greater or more important. In my view, it is greater in the sense that the empathy experienced in the therapeutic relationship does not arise from a "natural" need, but rather, from the "cultivated" intentional impulse to hold back one's own interests and to direct one's complete attention to the inner frame of reference of the other person. Therapeutic experience is therefore both artistic and professional in character, and like any skill it first has to be acquired and practiced. This is normally the case, possible exceptions being geniuses or people with inborn talent. Thus it is in this sense that I would maintain that there is a difference between therapeutic empathy and the therapeutic relationship in general on the one hand, and empathy arising from one's own need and everyday beneficial relationships on the other. If professional qualities are necessary for one to be able to practice therapy, then a professional training program is also necessary.

The basic aims of a client-centered therapy training program

The trends that Rogers perceived in his training experiences (cf. 2.1) can also be regarded as basic aims of a therapy training program. First of all, the training program should enable the trainee to achieve *congruence* in the area of his own attitudes. This should ensure that, on the one hand, the candidates become aware of their own true basic attitudes, and on the other, that they can authentically embody the basic assumptions of the client-centered approach. Furthermore, therapy within the training program should serve to make the trainee more sensitive to clients, to help develop a certain kind of *therapeutic empathy*. By becoming aware of one's own experience, one should acquire a "knowledge" of certain processes and qualities that are essential to psychotherapy.

I would like to explicitly show that these basic goals of a training program can best be conveyed through a training therapy. Training therapy is then the core of a therapy training program. First, however, I would like to go beyond the framework of the client-centered approach and discuss certain ideas from the area of psychoanalysis, as training analysis has formed the core of its training program from the very beginning. In addition, there seems to me to be an astonishing similarity between Rogers' notions of the basic aims of a training program and the goals of training analysis as they are defined by Sigmund Freud (after much experience with it, i.e. towards the end of his career). For this reason, and because the form of a training therapy was, after all, "invented" by Freud, I would also like to consider concepts related to training analysis. Moreover, in my view, Freud's own words can give us a more exact understanding of the basic aims of a training therapy.

Freud: Training analysis for the purpose of giving a firm conviction of the existence of the unconscious

In his work entitled "Analysis Terminable and Interminable" (1937), Freud dedicates one chapter to the problem of training people for that which he terms the "third of those `impossible' professions", psychoanalysis. (Due to their equally insufficient prospects for success, teaching and ruling are the other two "impossible" professions.) After arguing that one becomes ideally suited for this profession after having undergone personal therapy oneself, he writes:

> For practical reasons this analysis can only be short and incomplete. Its main object is to enable his teacher to make a judgement as to whether the candidate can be accepted for further training. *It has accomplished its purpose if it gives the learner a firm convicti-*

on of the existence of the unconscious, if it enables him, when repressed material emerges, to perceive in himself things which would otherwise be incredible to him, and if it shows him a first sample of the technique which has proved to be the only effective one in analytic work. This alone would not suffice for his instruction; but we reckon on the stimuli that he has received in his own analysis not ceasing when it ends and on the processes of remodelling the ego continuing spontaneously in the analysed subject and making use of all subsequent experiences in this newly-acquired sense. (Freud, Standard Edition, 1964, XXIII, p. 248 f.)

Although they are more pointed in form, Freud's views regarding the nature of therapeutic training resemble those of Rogers. According to Freud, candidates for training should first of all acquire something like a basic attitude necessary for their profession. Secondly, this basic attitude can only be acquired through personal experience, that is, by becoming aware of one's own psychic processes. Thirdly, he makes it clear that personal therapy, within which these personal self-experiences are made, should not be understood as a complete therapy, but rather as the beginning of a life-long openness for and interest in one's own self. These are the primary goals of training therapy. It provides a meaningful basis for the acquisition of techniques and specialized knowledge as well as a basis for the first work with clients within the framework of a training program.

It is clear that Freud's understanding of human beings and their psychodynamics as well as of psychotherapy is very different from that of Rogers. However, their views on the essential personal prerequisites for analytical and therapeutic work appear to me to be very similar. Freud's words allow me to make a more pointed statement regarding the basic aims of a training therapy: if Freud regards the goal of training analysis to be the personally experienced, firm conviction of the existence of the unconscious, I would like to formulate in analogy to it the following aim for client-centered therapists: the goal of a training therapy is to convey the personally experienced certain conviction of the central hypothesis of the approach. Rogers regards the central hypothesis to be that the person in himself has vast resources for understanding himself and for constructively changing his way of living and behaving, and that these resources can best be set free and realized within a relationship with certain defined qualities (Rogers, 1980, German 1991). This expresses even more clearly that training therapy is not intended to impart therapeutic congruence and empathy as if they were technical skills, but rather, as inner convictions, an existential attitude.

Training therapy as an appropriate form of learning for the client-centered approach

When it comes to conveying or developing such inner convictions or existential attitudes, what is needed is both an intimate and protected framework and the accompaniment of or the true encounter with someone who embodies this central hypothesis. This applies all the more in the present case since a form of learning of this kind is eminently appropriate for an approach in which self-development, growth and healing are connected to existential encounter in a special way. Seen in this way, it is, to say the least, surprising that personal therapy or training therapy have not been regarded as the core of a client-centered training course and as a paradigm for person-centered learning from the very beginning (cf. Keil, 1986). In my view, Rogers was unfortunately too reluctant in this respect to offer such learning processes himself. He explains this by saying that he does not want to make people do his psychotherapy instead of their own (for example, 1982, p. 21). "The purpose of training is increasingly to train therapists, not a particular brand of therapists. To put it in another way, the present point of view is that no student can or should be trained to become a client-centered therapist." (1951, p. 432; German 1972, p. 377). Of course it is absolutely essential that trainees act therapeutically in congruence with their own basic attitudes. For this reason they should examine, and be examined, as to whether the therapeutic approach in question suits them. If this is the case, then clear learning structures should be made available to them, and they should not have to wait until they have invented their own therapy orientation, as it were. Rogers' refusal to represent such a school of therapy has certainly had the damaging result that hardly any genuinely client-centered forms of learning have been developed. Instead, rather paradoxically, a number of skill-training programs have come about in the U.S. (for example, by Carkhuff, Egan, Gordon, Guerney, Martin, Ivey, among others), and in the German-speaking countries there has been an overemphasis of VEE as the focal point of learning. A genuinely client-centered form of learning has to be based on self-experience while imparting a basic attitude that corresponds to one of the central hypotheses of the approach. This is the fundamental duty of a training program in client-centered therapy and a training therapy can best achieve this.

GOALS AND CHARACTERISTICS OF A TRAINING THERAPY IN THE CLIENT-CENTERED APPROACH

At this point I can outline the aim and the characteristics of a training therapy in the client-centered approach. The aim of this training therapy is to impart, through intensive self-experience, therapeutic qualities, namely congruence in one's own basic attitudes and therapeutic empathy. The therapeutic qualities are not to be understood as technical skills, but rather, as the personally experienced conviction of the essence ("central hypothesis") of the client-centered approach. It is possible to distinguish a number of specific self-experiences or learning processes that are of greater or lesser significance in attaining this goal and by means of which one can describe and determine the process and the results of a client-centered training therapy. I would like to list here only those self-experiences which, on the basis of the theory of client-centered therapy, seem important in this context.

I would like to illustrate these learning processes on three interrelated levels. The personally experienced conviction of the essence of the client-centered approach can develop when:

(1) the candidate becomes aware of certain personal experiential processes (*the experiential level*),

(2) certain convictions come about and are lived by the candidate *(existential level)*,

(3) and a certain therapeutic sensibility and perceptive ability develops *(phenomenological level)*.

(ad 1) Among the experiential processes that the trainee should consciously perceive is the fundamental experience that it is personally significant for one to sincerely venture into oneself. In the words of Gendlin (1970) this means to have experienced how vague feelings become felt sense, and how further clearing is confirmed by a noticeable felt shift.

I would also like to mention the experience of what it feels like to take something seriously that one never liked about oneself or had repressed – or to have it accepted by others. This corresponds to the fundamental process described by Biermann-Ratjen (1989) in which organismic experience can become self-experience merely through empathic understanding. Or once again in the terms of Gendlin (ibid.): experiencing how one can move from structure-bound experience through the personal engagement of others to reconstitute the implicit experiential process.

Finally I would like to refer to an experience that corresponds to the "one more characteristic" which Rogers in a later work (1986, German 1991) adds to the conditions for therapy already mentioned: the experience of being intuitively understood or of one's self-transcendent present being within a personal encounter. On the experiential level, therefore, it is an aim of training therapy that the trainees have experiences of this kind and become conscious of them.

(ad 2) Self-experiences of this kind should result in a certain attitude in dealing with oneself and others. This attitude is characterized by a proven trust in one's own experiencing process or in the process of a relationship, or, put more generally, by the acceptance of the actualizing tendency, the effectiveness of which can be expected from oneself and others. Such an attitude can be perceived concretely in one's reaction to existential situations effecting oneself, such as sickness, age, or social position, in the formation of partnerships and family roles or, more generally, in one's attention to one's own feelings, for example, how much room is given in one's own experience to "primary emotions" such as desire, anger, etc. For this reason training therapy should explore the individual's way of dealing with himself and others.

(ad 3) Finally, a certain sensibility and perceptive ability should result from these self-experiences and basic attitudes. The above mentioned experiences with one's self should lead to the development of an acute sensibility for congruent and incongruent behavior or experience and thus for psychic conditions such as tension or fear or for psychic health or sickness in general.

The exploration of the individual's way of dealing with himself that was also described above should furthermore bring about an increased ability of hermeneutic understanding. By this I mean an intuitive understanding of how the structure of the personality and the self was formed in the personal life history of the individual (particularly in childhood), in his or her encounters with the environment (in particular with the dominant atmosphere in the family) and how it continued to develop. Thus a further aim of training therapy is for the trainee to gain an understanding in paradigmatic form of his own development as a result of his encounter with his personal environment throughout his life. This ability to understand hermeneutically clearly indicates that therapeutic empathy surpasses the empathy of everyday relationships and that specific training and practice is necessary to acquire it.

Training therapy vs. personal therapy

It is important to stress that the above mentioned aims of training therapy do not imply the completeness of such experiences or the attainment of especially good psychic health on the part of the therapist. I will address this point more extensively in the discussion of the danger of regarding training therapy as a kind of "super-therapy". Here I would only like to point out that the primary goals of training therapy are not clinical, but rather pedagogical. It is not a matter of healing one's own diseases, of mastering problems or of recognizing and thus overcoming one's own incongruencies. It is primarily intended to enable the trainee to experience the essence of the client-centered approach himself and to comprehend it fundamentally. Of course the material to be dealt with are one's own problems and training therapy can have significant therapeutic effects. But these are neither the goals of nor an appropriate motive for undertaking a training therapy. Training clients may have this personal motive for themselves during certain phases of the therapy, but in general they must have an overriding motive for the training therapy as a whole that makes significant learning possible. As I have already shown, it is for these reasons that a therapy within a therapy training program can be regarded as a "training therapy" and not as a "personal therapy".

LEARNING EXPERIENCES FROM THE HISTORY OF TRAINING ANALYSIS

Historical development of training analysis

A look at the origins of training analysis, to be found in the work of Sigmund Freud, can lead to a deeper understanding of training therapy. And I believe that the long history of training analysis within psychoanalytic training programs can provide us with a number of important experiences that have been made with this training instrument. For this reason I would like to give a brief overview of the historical development of training analysis, and subsequently to derive several important basic requirements for training therapy. In distinguishing individual phases in the development of training analysis I have primarily adhered to the divisions set forth by Michael Balint (1969, p. 287-298) in a conference paper on this topic in 1953.

First of all it is important to stress that Freud's creation of this form of training represents a significant innovation. The impetus for this innovation surely came from the problem of conveying Freud's discovery, the unconscious. "Freud was soon aware of the difficulty of conveying his discoveries; obviously they could not be presented like other clinical work. There was only one way to verify his claims: through analysis – be it self-analysis or training analysis" (Bernfeld, 1984, p. 441; transl. by author). Moreover, since "no psychoanalyst goes further than his own complexes and internal resistances permit," Freud required in 1910 that "he shall begin his activity with a self-analysis and continually carry it deeper while he is making his observations on his patients" (Standard Edition, 1957,VII p. 145). At that time Freud's first students were preparing for their work through reading and discussions. Lou-Andreas Salomé regarded her six private discussions with Freud as something like a training analysis (cf. Welsch & Wiesner, 1988, p. 328). However, it was soon felt to be necessary to acquire more than just intellectual knowledge. What followed was a short analysis, lasting a few weeks or months. Balint refers to this as the phase of the demonstrative training analysis and illustrates the first training analysis with a quote from a letter by Freud: "Eitington is here, he goes for a walk with me after dinner twice a week and lets me analyze him" (Balint, 1969, p. 287; transl. by author). Bernfeld states in this connection that Freud's teaching was very student-centered. In the course of training analysis, if the students required it, he would also discuss analytic theory, the patients and the theoretical works of his students or the politics of the analytical movement (Bernfeld, 1984, p. 442).

As a result, this demonstrative analysis is attacked (especially by Ferenczi) with the argument that it is unacceptable that training analysis does not go any deeper than a therapeutic analysis. This demand is still generally accepted today, and training analysis is understood as a comprehensive analysis of the individual. "The goal of the training program is that the analyst in training frees himself from unconscious infantile bonds, i.e. he resolves the Oedipal situation and develops a strong, critical ego" (Cremerius, 1987, p. 1068; transl. by author). The pedagogical character of training analysis is foremost. It is not primarily about a therapeutic change, but rather about the fundamental experience "that and how in a special intrapersonal relationship experience is enacted under the influence of unconscious motives" (Thomä, 1991, p. 488; transl. by author). Sensitivity is necessary to be able to grasp and understand processes such as transference and resistance. Balint also states that in the twenties such a training anlysis would last one and a half to two years on paper, but in reality would last from three to four years (1969, p. 289).

At first as a result of the training analysts' dissatisfaction with their own course of training, but later with the growing institutionalization of analytical training and the expansion and refinement of analytical theory, training analysis continued to develop, but not without being criticized on numerous occasions by leading analysts. In terms of content, the originally didactic aims of training therapy change in part to become clearly therapeutic. It is no longer a matter of developing the necessary sensitivity for unconscious processes, but rather, it becomes a complete therapy, what Balint calls a "super-therapy". Training analysis should go beyond the oedipal phase to include the earliest childhood experiences. Depending on analytical direction, the aim becomes working through those psychopathogenetic developments that are regarded as fundamental. Thomä regards this trend somewhat ironically:

> Balint maintains that for the individual to make a new beginning, it is necessary for him to go back to before the traumatization of his basic disorder so that he will be able to lead a more or less harmonious life. In Winnicott's theory, it is the recovery of transitional objects that make a creative life possible. In the school of Melanie Klein, the universal psychopathogenesis is bound to the psychotic core. It should pose no difficulty at all to find in every person some aspects of the narcissistic split that Kohut regards in his psychology of self to be the basis of insecurities and disturbances as well as the corresponding forms of compensation. (Thomä, 1991, p. 489; transl. by author)

In the wake of increasing institutionalization, training analysis usually involves a number of judgements and evaluations within the framework of the training course. Very often the training analyst can determine when the candidate is to be admitted to theoretical training and when he can begin working with patients of his own (and when he can begin to come to control analysis), and when the training analysis can be regarded as completed. The duration of a training analysis has also increased considerably, it can now extend far beyond 1,000 hours. Critics of these developments point out that under these circumstances training analysis can bring about the opposite of self-enlightenment, namely unanalyzable conformity, dependence and the formation of clans (cf. Bernfeld, 1984; Cremerius, 1987; Langer, 1984; Simenauer, 1984; Thomä, 1991).In this connection Carl Rogers states the reasons for his rejection of the founding of a training association for client-centered therapists: "because I have seen the psychoanalytic programs and they became more and more rigid and narrow, and I am not at all interested in that" (Rogers, 1982, p. 20; transl. by author). For the sake of completeness it must be added that there have of course always been opposing opinions with regard to this development. The most significant among them is surely Freud's 1937 statement quoted above in which he speaks out clearly against a therapeutic aim for training analysis. For Freud, training analysis was to result in the firm conviction of the existence of the unconscious. However, the total development of training analysis distinctly shows us the dangers and chances it brings and the effects a certain understanding of training therapy can have.

Conclusions for training therapy

If there is anything we can learn from the history of training analysis in addition to the necessity to remain alert to the dangers of institutional rigidity, then there are, in my opinion, two important things. First of all, training therapy should be clearly separated from all selection and evaluation processes within a training program. This includes the organizational separation of the training course and the training therapy, ensuring that the trainer and the training therapist are two different persons, as well as permitting the trainee to select his own training therapist.

Secondly, training therapy should go deep enough to enable the trainee to make experiential and existential experiences fundamental to the client-centered approach, i.e. it should have a clear didactic goal and should not be overloaded with expectations of a comprehensive therapy and the resulting exorbitant duration of such a therapy. Time and again it seems that training therapy is subject to this super-therapy trend in various schools. This becomes quite clear when the outline of the goals and content of a training therapy take on the form of a long and comprehensive catalogue in which all of the important areas of the personality and a human life are designated to be worked on. For instance, the following experiences were listed in an now outmoded set of guidelines for a gestalt therapy analysis:

> Working through the relationship to the father, mother, siblings and other significant persons of reference, in particular the relationship to the therapist, the attitude to one's own body, sexuality and partner relationship. Further points of emphasis are closeness and distance, pain, fear, disgust, anger, desire, sadness, shame, guilt, responsibility, the question of having children or the relationship to them, work, performance, professional situation, one's own potential and limits, values, love, one's own death, transcendence, etc. (Curriculum, 1976)

Within the framework of my association, Peter Lobner and Johannes Wiltschko (1987, p.56-68) have also tried to describe the contents, aims and processes of training therapy in the form of a detailed list, yet they were careful to point out this list was incomplete and should not be misunderstood as a catalogue of duties. It seems to be difficult to keep training therapy free of the essentially understandable desire to achieve the comprehensive personal and professional competence of the candidates. If this desire is given in to thoughtlessly, the well-intentioned aims all too quickly become illusionary, and the training therapy becomes a delusion therapy (cf. Kuiper, 1987). Psychic health, like congruence, cannot be attained once and for all, and experience can never be made up for through reflection. For this reason it is important to expect only that from training therapy which it is capable of providing: the experienced understanding of the essence of the client-centered approach. I would agree with Rogers when he maintains the following about personal therapy in training:

> The purpose of this therapeutic experience is perceived a little differently than in other orientations. It is not expected that personal therapy will permanently remove all likelihood of conflict in the therapist. Nor is it felt that therapy will permanently rule out the possibility that his own personal needs may interfere with his work as a therapist. He may later need and desire further personal help in relation to some case with which he is dealing. (Rogers, 1951, p. 433; German 1972, p. 377)

Expressed in analytic terms, it is important that the terminable analysis be terminated when the interminable, i.e. self-analysis, has been installed in the analyst (cf. Parin, 1986). Endless analysis with the training analyst can only be an insufficient substitute for self-analysis. (Benedek, 1975, p. 134).

With these additional remarks I hope to have made my understanding of the goals and characteristics of training therapy in the client-centered approach more or less clear. In conclusion I would like to discuss what I regard as the basic issue – whether something like training therapy is fundamentally compatible with the client-centered approach – in connection with Rogers' concept of teaching and learning, which exceeds the area of therapy.

TRAINING THERAPY AND ROGERS' CONCEPT OF TEACHING AND LEARNING

Carl Rogers' reserve with regard to establishing an institutionalized form of training in client-centered therapy did not merely result from his poor impression of the rigid analytic training programs, but rather should be seen in a larger context. In the same way that he took his experiences in counselling seriously and developed the client-centered approach on the basis of them, he tried to take seriously his negative experiences in the academic world of teaching and learning. As is well known, this also led to Rogers personally leaving this area altogether after the Wisconsin project. A representative summary of experiences of this kind can be found in Rogers' "Current Assumptions in Graduate Education: A Passionate Statement" (1969, German 1974). In this work he attempts to formulate the unspoken assumptions that underlie an academic education. Students are regarded as objects to be manipulated and sifted out by means of examinations; examinations continue to be regarded as the best and only criterion for ascertaining professional ability; knowledge should apparently be acquired through the passive accumulation of information; scientific character is not an attribute of ideas, but rather of methods; creative scientists are expected to develop from passive learners, and so on. Basic assumptions of this kind are of course diametrically opposed to an approach which locates the place of evaluation and all resources for the formation of life within the individual. It is therefore only logical that Rogers would reject such views on teaching and learning. In the article "Personal Thoughts on Teaching and Learning" he formulates his theses on the subject. There he writes:

> It seems to me that anything that can be taught to another is relatively inconsequential and has little or no significant influence on behavior... I have come to feel that the only learning which significantly influences behavior is self-discovered, self-appropriated learning ... Such self-discovered learning, truth that has been personally appropriated and assimilated in experience, cannot be directly communicated to another .... As a consequence of the above I realize that I have lost interest in being a teacher ... Such experience would imply that we would do away with teaching. People would get together if they wished to learn. (Rogers, 1969, p. 276 f.; German 1974, p. 153 ff.)

Accordingly, Rogers did not want to be someone who teaches things to others. Despite this, or perhaps because of it, he became one of the most important teachers.

The person-centered approach requires that situations are sought in which self-determined, significant learning is possible and that situations are overcome in which learning is imposed upon the individual in a self-alienating manner. However, this does not mean that all teaching and learning institutions are to be rejected because they are institutions. In my view institutions of teaching and learning are particularly necessary in any complex society, but that they evidence an immanent tendency to alienate and dominate individuals. This tendency is not irreversible, however, and individuals can have an influence upon it. This would be a point of departure where person-centered policies could have an effect (cf. Vogel, 1989). The aims of such policies toward institutions would be to enable the participation and self-realization of individuals. In the case of teaching and learning institutions this would mean making student-centered instruction and significant learning possible.

Significant learning is particularly necessary within the area of client-centered psychotherapy. Of course, this manner of therapeutic practice can only be learned by someone who really wants to learn it and who is truly suited for this approach. Furthermore, this kind of learning has to reach a depth of experience from which one's own existential basic attitudes and self-transcending intuition arise. For client-centered therapy requires a certain way of being with persons and an intuitive presence of being, not simply the application of acquired information or skills. A training program in client-centered therapy should therefore take both aspects into account: both the self-determination and authenticity of learning, and the necessary deepening of this learning. It is especially this aspect that requires that the teacher does not withdraw, but rather that he is effectively present. In his training courses Rogers made the experience that the participants needed this and asked it of him. He reports that the first participants in such a course advised him to stress personal therapy more strongly (1951, p. 447; German 1972, p. 388) and that supervisory processes were of crucial importance both for the work of the participants with one another and for their work with clients (Ibid., p. 468 ff.; German p. 405 ff.). It would therefore be unfortunate to keep trainees from experiencing the deep and intensive learning processes that are possible in a training therapy. Especially in this approach, in which personal encounter is so important, training therapy can serve as a paradigmatic example of Rogers' concept of significant learning.

CONCLUSION

Now that I have discussed the significance of training therapy as part of a therapy training program and have shown its place within the person-centered approach, I would like to conclude with an open problem. Lore Korbei (1988) has called attention to the fact that the term for this kind of therapy in German is Lehrtherapie ("teaching therapy") and not learning therapy (German Lerntherapie). Perhaps this stems from the unreflected adoption of the teacher-centered tradition of psychoanalysis, in which the expression Lehranalyse was coined. Should this be the case, then it should serve as another indication of how important it is to regard existing institutions with a critical eye.

However, if we are to continue to live with the concept of Lehrtherapie ("teaching therapy") , then we should perhaps begin to regard the concepts of Lehrtherapie and learning therapy (Lerntherapie) the way psychoanalysis understands the concepts of terminable and interminable analysis. Seen in this way, a Lehrtherapie would be completed when the trainee has grown into learning therapy. At this point we would be beyond the training phase and would be ready to take on the task at hand: on the basis of what we have already been taught, to continue to learn through and in addition to our activites as a therapist. "Or to put it another way, the degree to which I can create relationships which facilitate the growth of others as separate persons is a measure of the growth I have achieved in myself. In some respects this is a disturbing thought, but it is also a promising or challenging one" (Rogers, 1961, p. 56; German 1973, p. 70).

REFERENCES

Balint, M. (1969). *Die Urformen der Liebe und die Technik der Psychoanalyse.* Frankfurt / M.: Fischer

Biermann-Ratjen, E.-M. (1989) *Zur Notwendigkeit einer Entwicklungspsychologie für Gesprächspsychotherapeuten aus dem personenzentrierten Konzept für die Zukunft der klientenzentrierten Psychotherapie.* In: Sachse, R. & Howe, J.: Zur Zukunft der klientenzentrierten Psychotherapie. Heidelberg: Asanger

Benedek, T. (1975). *Die Lehranalyse in der Vergangenheit, Gegenwart und Zukunft.* In: Scheidt, J.v. (Hg.): Psychoanalyse. Selbstdarstellung einer Wissenschaft. München: Nymphenburger

Bernfeld, S. (1984). *Zur Kritik der psychoanalytischen Ausbildung.* Psyche 38, 5, S. 437 – 459 Curriculum zur Ausbildung von Gestalttherapeuten. Integrative Therapie 2, 2/3, S. 125 – 147

Cremerius, J. (1987). *Für eine psychoanalyse-gerechte Ausbildung.* Psyche 41, 12, S. 1067-1096 Freud, S. (1910). Future Prospects of Psychoanalysis. Standard Edition, VII, London: Hogarth, 1957.

Freud, S. (1937). *Analysis Terminable and Interminable.* Standard Edition, XXIII. London: Hogarth, 1964

Gendlin, E.T. (1970). *A theory of personality change.* In: Hart, J.T. & Tomlinson, T.M.:New Directions in Client-Centered Therapy. Boston: Houghton Mifflin

Keil, W.W. (1988). *Lehrtherapie als Paradigma für die Potenz der klientenzentrierten Therapie*. In: GwG (Hg.): Orientierung an der Person. Bd. 1 Diesseits von Psychotherapie. Bericht vom 7. Symposion der GwG, Okt. 1986. Köln: GwG

Korbei, L. (1988). *Lehr– oder Lerntherapie: Notwendigkeit und Möglichkeiten*. Personzentriert 2/1988, S. 30 – 33.

Kuiper, P.C. (1987). *Ausbildungs– oder Einbildungsanalyse*. In: Brede, K. et al. (Hg.): Befreiung zum Widerstand. Margarete Mitscherlich zum 7o. Geburtstag. Frankfurt / M.: Fischer

Lobner, P.C. & Wiltschko, J. (1987). *Einige Bemerkungen zur Lehrtherapie*. Personzentriert 1/2 1987, S. 56 – 68.

Parin, P. & Parin-Matthèy, G. (1986) *Subjekt im Widerspruch*. Frankfurt / M.: Syndikat

Rogers, C.R. (1951). *Client-Centered Therapy. Its current practice, implications and theory*. Boston: Houghton Mifflin. German: Die klient-bezogene Gesprächstherapie. München: Kindler, 1972

Rogers, C.R. (1961). *On Becoming a Person. A therapist's view of psychotherapy*. Boston: Houghton Mifflin. German: Entwicklung der Persönlichkeit. Stuttgart: Klett, 1973

Rogers, C.R. (1969). *Freedom to Learn. A view of what education might become*. Columbus: Ohio. German: Lernen in Freiheit. München: Kösel, 1974

Rogers, C.R. (1980). *Client-entered psychotherapy*. In: Kaplan, H.I. et al. (Ed.): Comprehensive textbook of psychiatry, III Baltimore: Williams & Wilkins. German: Klientenzentrierte Psychotherapie. In:Rogers, C.R. & Schmid, P.F. (1991): Person-zentriert. Grundlagen von Theorie und Praxis. Mainz: Grünewald

Rogers, C.R. (1982). *Gespräch Carl Rogers mit dem Vorstand der GwG*. GwG – info 48, Okt. 1982, S. 18 – 35

Rogers, C.R. (1986). *A client-centered / person-centered approach to therapy*. In: Kutash, I.L. & Wolf, A. (Ed.): Psychotherapist's Casebook. San Francisco: Jossey Bass. German: Ein klientenzentrierter bzw. personzentrierter Ansatz in der Psychotherapie. In: Rogers. C.R. & Schmid, P.F.: Person-zentriert. Grundlagen von Theorie und Praxis. Mainz: Grünewald, 1991.

Simenauer, E. (1984). *Aktuelle Probleme der Lehranalyse*. Psyche 38, 4, S. 289 – 306

Thomä, H. (1991). *Idee und Wirklichkeit der Lehranalyse*. Psyche, 45, 5, S. 385 – 433 und 6, S. 481 – 505

Vogel, A.-L. (1989). *Das Politische bei Carl R. Rogers*. Frankfurt / M.: Peter Lang

Welsch, U. & Wiesner, M. (1988). *Lou Andreas – Salomé. Vom "Lebensurgrund" zur Psychoanalyse*. München: Internationale Psychoanalyse

Characteristics of a Healing Inner Relationship

MIA LEIJSSEN

KATHOLIEKE UNIVERSITEIT LEUVEN

ABSTRACT

In spite of a good interpersonal therapeutic relationship, some clients do not develop a healing intrapsychic relationship. Eight case studies with "unsuccessful" client and more than 15 years of experience with the integration of the focusing process in ongoing psychotherapy resulted in expanding our view on the necessary conditions for successful therapy. I learned that the therapist can assist the client more actively by showing the client how to be accepting and empathic with the painful, rigid, difficult, critical points of himself...

To develop a healing intrapsychic relationship the client needs help to:

1) find the right distance between himself and his experience, which means to be in touch but not be overwhelmed by his experience;

2) make contact and connect with his body sensations, his emotions, the symbols and his life situation;

3) receive in an understanding way his resistance, his split parts, his interfering voices, his defences; symbolise them and give them a "better place" in his life.

The use of metaphorical language is a powerful means to develop an intrapsychic relationship. Metaphors respect the complexity of what is felt, but at the same time they help to express the implicit and to evoke a new relationship towards the inner felt experience.

In my presentation, I will show how the therapist can facilitate the development of the necessary client attitudes. This will be illustrated by many excerpts from client–centered therapy sessions.

INTRODUCTION

Rogers' main contribution to psychotherapy is in the area of the interpersonal relationship. That he also paid attention to the development of the client's inner relationship, is evident in the following quotation from 'A process conception of psychotherapy' (Rogers 1961).

" The process involves a change in the manner of experiencing. The continuum begins with a fixity in which the individual is very remote from his experiencing and unable to draw upon or symbolize its implicit meaning (p. 156) ... There is much blockage of internal communication between self and experience (p. 133) ... From this remoteness in relation to his experiencing, the individual moves toward the recognition of experiencing as a troubling process going on within him. Experiencing gradually becomes a more accepted inner referent to which he can turn for increasingly accurate meanings (p. 156– 157) ... There are increasingly freer dialogues within the self, an improvement in and reduced blockage of internal communication (p. 142) ... Frequently these dialogues are in the form of listening to oneself, to check cognitive formulations against the direct reference of experiencing (p. 142) ... The self becomes increasingly simply the subjective and reflexive awareness of experiencing (p. 153) ... Internal communication is clear, with feelings and symbols well matched, and fresh terms for new feelings (p. 154)".

In these words, Rogers describes the change which takes place within the experiential process when the client feels received, welcomed and understood as he is. But Rogers continues: "We seem to know too little about the ways in which a person may come to experience himself as 'received'" (p. 135). Rogers does emphasize strongly the importance of the basic attitudes of authenticity, acceptance and empathy; but in spite of the continuous and intensive communication of these attitudes by the therapist, a client may not succeed in developing empathy and acceptance in relation to himself, and thus the healing inner relationship may not develop. In the present paper I would like to show how a therapist can guide a client more actively towards this healing inner relationship, primarily by teaching him to find a receptive attitude towards himself and by showing him how to deal empathically with painful, hurt, blocked, difficult or critical parts of himself. These ideas have taken shape in the course of ten years of searching and exploring of what is helpful at times when clients get stuck in their therapeutic process (e.g. see Leijssen, 1991). Besides, various articles, workshops and dialogues with An Weiser (1991, 1993), Mary Armstrong (1993) and Kathleen McGuire (1993) – all of them colleagues from the 'focusing branch' – have inspired me to such an extent that I want explicitly acknowledge their contribution to my development.

I will highlight successively: 1) the importance of the self's manner of relating with the experience, particularly the right distance which is marked by making contact with experience without merging with it; 2) completing a felt sense by bringing together body sensation, emotion, symbolization and life situation; 3) integrating split– off parts, interfering characters or resistances by receiving them, translating them into symbols and assigning them a new place. In doing so, the importance of using metaphoric language as a powerful aid in facilitating the inner dialogue will be repeatedly stressed. When more than can be put into words, is being experienced, images, at the same time, are able to respect the complexity, while being a concrete help in shaping the complexity and bringing this complexity to expression.

THE RIGHT DISTANCE

With the idea of the interpersonal therapeutic relationship serving as a model for the inner relationship, we will first look at the basic attitude of empathy. The empathically present therapist will be touched by what the client says but will not identify with it; the therapist makes contact with the client without fusing with him. This therapist– client relationship with its 'right distance' is also characteristic of the optimal inner relationship. The healing inner relationship is indeed marked by a 'right distance' between self and experience. This means that the client should be able to get in touch with his experience without merging with it or being overwhelmed by it. Where there is too much or too little distance, the inner relationship is absent. In the event of 'too much distance', the client has no experience with which to get in touch, whereas in the event of 'too little distance' he merges totally with the experience and there is no experience of a self that can relate to the inner feelings. We are not talking here about two diagnostic categories in which to classify people, but about ways of being, which can be present in anybody at certain times. These are process characteristics that allow us to determine the absence of an inner relationship on the basis of an excessively large or small distance between self and experience. We do notice, however, that some clients may be typical in their style, some keeping too much distance whereas others are habitually flooded. Others still swing between one extreme and the other. Most people however can be found somewhere on that continuum and will shift their position according to the more or less threatening nature of the experience. Certain cultures and subcultures also foster certain positions.

Too much distance

In the absence of an inner relationship due to excessive distance, attention is largely directed outwards. In our western culture, with its emphasis on productive efficiency in the outside world, education favours this way of being. The general emphasis is on 'doing', a sure way to substantial achievements in material matters. It is marked by a rational approach which is especially suited to linear– logical issues.

People functioning in this way are not psychotherapy– minded. They prefer to seek their solutions in the outside world, for example by working hard, accumulating material wealth, proper planning of activities, engaging in sports and social contacts. Physical complaints are tackled with medication, insomnia with sleeping tablets and restlessness with alcohol and other substances. In client– centered psychotherapy they are not easy clients. They limit themselves to explaining to the therapist what goes wrong and expect the therapist to come up with a solution; that is what experts are for. Healing has to come 'from outside' just as problems come 'from outside'. These are people who live primarily with their head and expect salvation from a logical analysis of their problems.

I think here of a female client who came to therapy with an addiction to alcohol and sleeping tablets. In the sessions, she 'works' hard at collecting insights which could explain her problems. After two years of therapy, the major improvement is to be seen in her children because she had – to use her own words – learned to 'listen to them'. The interpersonal relationship with the therapist appears thus to have become, to some extent, a model for other interpersonal relationships. In the sessions, however, she never seems to listen to herself. An inner object of reference, the experience of something in herself on which to focus her attention, seems to be lacking. Explanations found in books are her main source of knowledge about herself and the question: "what she feels about that herself", is consistently answered with: "nothing".

Many therapists are in the habit of asking rational clients what they feel about their own explanations or how these explanations effect them. But with clients who are too far away from their experiences, such questions are not very helpful. Often these clients do not know what to do with such well– intentioned questions. This is not just a matter of resistance. It is a rusty pattern, a structure– bound behaviour that had made a lot of sense when it was originally used but for which the client no longer has an alternative. It is the therapist's task to show an alternative, starting with small steps. The step: "how does this feel?" is too big for these people. A major turning point in the therapy of the above– mentioned client came when I suggested we explore together what she can experience inside of herself. Instead of starting the session in *her* habitual way, by her telling long and detailed stories about what had happened the previous week and attempting to find a rational explanation for it, I let her first sit quietly for a while and asked her then to close her eyes and direct her attention inwards by following the rhythm of her breathing, simply becoming conscious of how she breathes in and out without wanting to change anything to it or judging it. The transition from talking to silence, her shifting her attention from outward to inward, from thinking and evaluating to experiencing, is a step which she would never have taken by herself. With a few very simple, but explicit invitations by the therapist, this client is now capable of leaving the horizontal dimension and venturing briefly into the vertical one, even though only in very elementary aspects such as noticing her breathing.

Important is not whether or not the breathing had been observed but the fact an inner way of relating has been initiated in which the client learns to venture into the positions of an observing impartial self which can experience certain events within itself; the client learns to relate to processes or contents in the inner world. Once this awareness of an observable inner world is established, then the content observed can shift from something as simple as breathing to more complex experiences. True, this specific attitude of alert receptivity and sheer attention will at first only be exercised in relation to unthreatening phenomena but it can gradually be extended to a more loaded content.

Other small steps which helped this particular client in directing her attention to her own experiences were among others: letting her gradually evoke situations which mean something to her, such as her relaxed feeling when working in the garden, and then learning to notice that other situations, such as thinking of a conflict with her boss, can push away that relaxed feeling and replace it by another experience. The point is to teach the client step by step how to make contact with something in herself, with an inner referent to which she can then direct her attention.

This is a highly directive intervention but, in my opinion, a highly client– centered one. Instead of allowing the process to stagnate repeatedly in the same manner, the therapist offers help to put it in motion. The therapist does not pull the client through it but shows her a few steps along which she can proceed. The therapist connects with the level where the client happens to be and gives her a hand instead of watching her getting stuck.

In the above– mentioned example, the client remained constantly at an excessive distance from her experience and an inner relationship was unknown to her. The majority of clients however only find themselves occasionally in a position of avoiding contact with their experiential world; and such instances relate mostly to a specific anxiety– provoking content. An example: a male client who works generally well in therapy remains always at a distance from the theme of 'war' and this in spite of the fact that his father has been killed in action and that his mother, a young widow with two children, had suffered a psychological breakdown at the time. The client reports occasionally his inability to experience anything around this topic. During a group therapy session in which music and drawings were also used, he gets in touch with anxiety and abandonment. At that moment, when he starts getting in touch again with this unsafe and chaotic world, the therapist's and the group's steady presence are crucial in helping him 'survive' his traumatic experiences, that is: letting these experiences again become part of the process and finding a new way of relating to them.

It is no accident that I mention the facilitating properties of non– verbal forms of communication under the heading 'too much distance'. Relating with too much distance corresponds to a left– hemisphere dominance which is marked by logical thinking, reasoning, linear causality, influencing and dominating the environment, and with verbal language as its main form of communication. Music, art and poetry, on the other hand, belong to the right side of the brain which corresponds to the emotional, the intuitive, the receptive, the fluid. An excessive respect for left– brain activities sometimes prompts therapists to work exclusively with language. This may perpetuate a way of relating with 'too much distance' in certain clients. Therapists should perhaps examine their own resistance against non– verbal working methods.

We should however keep in mind that relating with 'much distance' may be necessary in various circumstances, particularly those in which survival and control are paramount. Psychotherapy requires however also a capacity for letting go, for allowing oneself to be touched.

Too little distance

The other pole is the pole of allowing, of being touched. In certain clients, this pole may be so dominant that, here as well, a healing inner relationship fails to appear. In this way of being –

again a structure– bound way of experiencing, in which it is possible to get stuck – clients are flooded by their experiences; they merge with everything that touches them. There is no inner relationship because there is no self to relate to certain contents. Whereas clients with too much distance tend to resort to sterile intellectualizations, those with too little distance feel too much. On the whole, client– centered therapists are better at dealing with these. In international meetings it struck me how numerous client– centered therapists readily end up in this position of needing to express overwhelming feelings. Because there is no inner relationship, the need to express oneself to others is great indeed. The quiet stable presence of an empathic listener acts, in that case, as a vessel in which to unburden or leave behind one's load. The therapist's containment function is indeed an important one but for those clients the effects are generally temporary. These are however grateful clients: both client and therapist feel that a lot is happening in the session because a lot of affect is expressed and clients leave the office better than when they came in. Both client and therapist view their relationship as very important. This in itself is something fortunate in which we, client– centered therapists, have become 'specialized'. But it is also our pitfall: relating with the therapist can become and remain more important than the inner relationship. Clients learn to draw strength from the relationship with the other and this can stand in the way of development of an inner relationship. Being without distance, one basically remains stuck; but because there is a lot of accompanying emotion, there seems to be movement; it feels like a 'stirring life'.

An example from therapy practice can illustrate this. The client is a married woman of 45 but gives a girlish impression. Already during the intake interview she presents with much crying and the appeal to me is great. During therapy she lets me know regularly that she benefits greatly from our talks and that she would like to come several times a week. The therapy hour is always too short. She also seeks help from several other helping professionals. She has a preference for father figures. Her own father died when she was 18. Mother has a sickening influence on her; the client cannot stand her but visits her often. Her husband abuses her, but as soon as the man gets ready to leave, she pleads with him to stay. There were a few brief psychiatric admissions following a suicide attempt during the therapist's vacation. After three years of therapy she sees herself as much improved – and in certain respects she is – but she still gets flooded by a multitude of problems coming to her from the environment.

I give the example of a fragment of conversation in which she is guided towards greater distance. The therapist does not follow her in exploring her problems but chooses to help her discover in herself a way of relating in which she does not have to identify with her problems. The client starts the conversation in a very excited manner by talking about a big fight between herself and her husband; she experiences simultaneously an enormous tension in her abdomen. The therapist allows her to blow off steam for a while and asks her then to put at some distance away from her, everything that so excites her and produces so much tension. She calms down, breathes more freely and tears appear. She experiences a feeling of great deprivation and an enormous need for affection and tenderness. These themes have emerged already several times previously. Now the therapist asks the client if she could let this feeling of deprivation know that she has heard it and if she could tell her need for affection and tenderness, in a loving way, that she takes care of it.

The client is offered here a different way of relating than the one she knows from within herself. She is stuck in a structure– bound behaviour of merging with events or with her own needs and the solutions have to come from the outside; people have to react to her needs in a different way. What is new in the approach is that, instead of going on drowning in the problems – and the therapist or others helping her to keep afloat – she learns to get out of the water for a moment, gathers forces on the shore and feels solid ground under her feet. From this position she can then look at the sea instead of drowning in it. In this concrete example, the client discovers in the session: "a warm spot in the region of my heart. It is strange but when I watch from here I can see that all my running after the respect of my husband, my parents and my in– laws is not necessary. Besides, I do not value anything in these people anyway. From this spot here I respect myself and feel quiet". In the weeks following that session, she on her own succeeds occasionally in making the movement of creating distance. Hereby she repeats to herself the invitations which she learned about in that session. For the first time she keeps some peace and inner strength even outside the sessions and she is able to take measures for a divorce in a businesslike manner. It still surprises me as a therapist that the 'simple' invitation to give the problem a place in the therapeutic space, at some distance away from the client, can have such a powerful disidentifying effect. However, the therapist has to guide this process carefully, especially by letting the client check each time whether the place assigned to the problem reflects faithfully how close or how far he or she wants to have it. Also, the degree to which this has to be given concrete form may vary. Some clients may, for example, write down the problem on a piece of paper and actually deposit it at some distance away from themselves. The bodily effect of putting a problem at a distance, is received each time and is sometimes evoked or expressed even more strongly by means of a metaphor such as "unload a heavy backpack and feel what it does to you". A more detailed description of this microprocess can be found in the focusing step 'making space' (Leijssen, 1991).

I suspect that Gendlin introduced "making space" as a first focusing movement just because the clientele attracted to client– centered therapy tends to lean towards too little distance. For these people – and for many client– centered therapists with them – it feels unnatural to let go of problems and, in spite of the fact that a lot is felt, there is no inner relationship; all energy is put into interpersonal relationships at the expense of developing an internal relationship.

Silence

Our study (Stevens, 1990, Wels, 1992) shows that higher levels of experiencing are preceded by silence. This indicates that an inner dialogue can only take place when interpersonal dialogue stops. Thus, with clients who do not spontaneously leave any silence, the therapist can choose to introduce, actively, the silence required for the emergence of an inner dialogue.

In the absence of an internal relationship the client keeps turning to the outside world. This is shown in among others always excessive talking. The therapist can choose to actively break through this structure– bound behaviour, by inviting the client to interrupt the continuous dialogue in the horizontal dimension and to allow some silence.

Process diagnosis

Both ways of being – too much or too little distance – have to do with an excessive orientation outwards which prevents the inner relationship from developing. Both are aspects of a lack of optimal distance and require process– enhancing interventions other than the classical Rogerian ones. An accurate process diagnosis will indicate the way. Personally, I find the use of non-verbal means of communication only meaningful with clients who otherwise remain stuck in a structure– bound behaviour with 'too much distance' whereas I would be hesitant to use these methods with experience– hungry clients who may look for even more experiences and lean towards an all too close way of relating. It is indeed often unnecessary to draw such clients' attention to their bodily experiences as these tend to impose themselves spontaneously.

On the other hand, we do not ask clients with a too distant way of relating to create space. When a client has succeeded only with difficulty in making contact with his feelings, an invitation to 'let go' is totally inappropriate.

The interpersonal relationship

The lack of an inner relationship may be due to an excessive orientation outwards but may also not be the expression of the client's structure– bound way of being. In supervision I often hear therapists complain that their clients do not reach a deeper level of experiencing, whereas, in my view, the first problem lies with the interpersonal relationship. Therapists may, for example, remain too distant and untouched by what the client tells them while at the same time giving process directions which are supposed to help the client make inner contact. The client however may well be unable to do so if the existing interpersonal relationship follows a contrary model. Thus, therapists can, on the basis of their own sensibilities, feel the need to guide the client away from what was in fact the right way of relating for the client; and therapists may do so because they have difficulty with the intensity of the feelings reaching them. Clients can only start concentrating on the inner relationship if the interpersonal one is good, which means that, on the relational level, nothing stands in the way.

This implies that therapists too have to have an inner way of relating which allows them to make contact and be touched without fusing or getting flooded. When a therapist cannot spontaneously be with the client in such a way, then the interpersonal relationship is either too warm or too cold. Both these types of interpersonal relationship constitute an unsafe base for the client and an obstacle in developing an optimal inner relationship.

THE COMPLETE FELT SENSE

Once a client has found the right way of inner relating – fortunately there are clients who find it spontaneously or with minimal guidance – one may proceed to the next step. An inner relationship implies the experience of something meaningful to which one can relate. What develops further in the inner relationship 1) is something that can be experienced in the body, among others such as a tension across the chest, 2) has an emotionally quality, among others such as anger, 3) is related to something in the client's life and 4) can be translated into symbols. I do not name these four components – body sensation, emotion, use of symbols and life situation – at random. In studying fragments of therapy sessions, we have noticed that clients always start with one of the four components and that, regardless of the entry choosen, the felt sense only fully emerges when contact is made with all four components. This model of a complete felt sense is particularly useful at times when clients remain stuck in one or several components and feel that it does not help them any further to keep exploring those. A few illustrations which also show how clients differ in their preferential component can bring this point to life.

Starting with emotions

This example is available on video– tape and has partly been published in transcript (Leijssen 1993). The client, a woman, starts the session by saying that she is *anxious*, even panicky. Next she starts to *sob* and *hyperventilate*. The process diagnosis here is one of a client with "too close" a way of relating. The therapist first helps her to disidentify from her anxiety and asks her to assign a place in space to what makes her so anxious (This takes 37 client– therapist interactions). That the client effectively achieves a distance is shown by the fact that her hyperventilation and sobbing stop and by her saying that she now feels safe. Then the therapist asks her to look again at what threatened her so much, but now from a distance. The client gets an *image* of a "creeping fog". By means of empathic reflections the therapist allows her to further elaborate the fog image. The client describes how this fog can come into her and how it feels as if it were winding itself totally around her spine. At the same time, she feels sucked in by it and can become its center. In this session, three components of the felt sense are already present: emotions, body sensations and images. However rich this inner dialogue may be, it is not yet completely meaningful because an important component is still missing. I mention this because I regularly see therapists who get lost – with their clients – in one of the components. An image, for example, can be so evocative that it is easy to be seduced into dwelling on it. In this session here, the therapist evokes the missing component by asking the client: "Could you feel what in your life feels like what you just described with that image?". The therapist tries to establish a link with a real *situation* which touches the client in a similar way. After some time, the client expresses that she is in danger of being overwhelmed by an existing relationship; she is in danger of loosing 'herself'. "That is threatening", she adds. She starts crying again but now it is not a flood but an acknowledgment of the hurt she has sustained in that relationship. "To loose myself, that is what is painful". These words symbolize what was pressing to be expressed and it obviously relieves her. The experience now carries the proper symbolization, the meaning is complete, the client feels relieved and faces life now in a different way.

Starting with the situation

In this example, a client starts telling me about a *situation* in which he has to address a nasty colleague. He describes with a profusion of details the circumstances and the colleague's attributes, but not what it in fact does to him. The therapist asks: "Could you check what you experience within yourself while you are telling me this?" The client translates it into a symbol: "I am like a rat in a trap". The therapist savours that *image* and includes in her reflections how she sees the client *physically* writhing. The client notices himself that he has a tendency to protect his vital organs "just as he did when he was beaten as a child by a tyrannical teacher who made him suffer a lot". He discovers how an autoritarian man still provokes in him the *fear* of being slaughtered. The situation, the symbolization, the body reactions and the emotions now constitute a complete felt sense which he now words as follows: "Now, that is what bothers me: I start already by setting myself up as the one who will get beaten so that even the most neutral question on his part becomes threatening !". These words provoke an important shift; he even literally sits up straight and looks securely at the therapist.

Starting with body sensations

Some clients have a preference for body sensations: they describe in great detail all sorts of body sensations, as if they were explaining a problem to a physician. When this entry is used, it is important to search for the emotional colour of their sensations. A female client describes, for example, in detail a pain in her arm. In doing so, she uses words such as 'nagging' and 'pulling'. The therapist reflects: "there is something that nags and pulls". This evokes emotions of anger and sadness. The client further discovers that she wants to have everything her way and that life is a big burden like that.

In psychosomatic patients, body sensations are so prominent and so anxiety– provoking that the completion of the felt sense is of crucial importance. Yet it also encounters much resistance. Here the process of achieving the 'right distance' from the pain or symptoms should first receive full attention before the patient can venture deeper into the problem (see Fuhrmann, 1990).

Starting with symbolization

Starting with symbolization is rather exceptional. When it happens, it is often something still lingering from a movie, or a sentence from a book that has stuck. Thus, a client who keeps thinking of the sentence from the bible: "Thou art my Son, my Beloved; on Thee my favour rests". Taking this symbolisation as point of departure, the therapist lets the client make contact with what it does to his body when he repeats it. After a period of silence he becomes aware of being "on the verge of tears". Subsequently he is able to link this to having missed a father figure who gave him the feeling of being loved. Bart Santen (1993) describes the case of a 13 year old girl suffering from multiple personality and how he starts with symbolizations by letting her underline those sentences in Kafka's books which express something of herself. With these passages as points of departure, she makes contact with various feeling qualities within herself.

About the four components which constitute a complete felt sense, I would like to invite those therapists whose client gets stuck in the session, to check wether one of the components could perhaps be missing.

INTERFERING CHARACTERS

When the interpersonal relationship is good and the client is in touch with the problem without being overwhelmed by it, then the process of completing the felt sense can take place according to the above– mentioned process, except that "raiders may sometimes appear on the shore" and may disturb the inner dialogue between self and inner felt sense. These are other forms of structure– bound behaviour which can cause the inner dialogue to get stuck and the healing process to be delayed or even impossible. This is again a moment which requires the therapist to be vigilant and to guide the client actively into finding a new way of relating to this 'disturbance'.

We could compare the inner dialogue to the way a firm, warm, unprejudiced friend kindly listens to what tries to express itself in a hesitant, fresh and often illogical language. The metaphor which appeals to many clients in this respect is that of a dialogue between a loving inner adult and a hurt inner child. The dialogue can be disturbed by other instances operating in the person, such as the one that tries to keep everything under rational control, or the one that does not tolerate vulnerability, or the one that delivers cynical comments all along, or the one that quickly hands down ready– made solutions. This list can be completed with all possible defenses which have been established in the course of a human existence. "It looks like a whole army" said one of my clients. In fact, they are all ways of reacting which can sometimes be helpful but which now thwart the inner dialogue. It is essential that therapists help clients to discover these parts of themselves instead of letting them get stranded yet again in structure– bound behaviour.

To do this, the therapist first and foremost has to keep a receptive empathic attitude, which means here: to admit and give a place both to the part that is being attacked and pushed away and the part that does the attacking. Speaking of resistance, we could say that it has to be treated with respect but should not be allowed to get the upper hand. The client learns to find a way of dealing with resistance instead of coinciding with it (too little distance thus) or denying it (too much distance).

Again, an example may clarify the matter. It concerns the 52nd session of a single 40 years old woman. The fact that she is not married is, among other factors, due to a hypercritical, demanding attitude towards others which has led her to find no partner good enough. In this session she recalls a party where, to her great surprise, she noticed that she is less inclined than in the past to put down everything with cynical remarks. However she discovers in herself suspicion regarding other people's motives when they try to come into contact with her during the party. When we go deeper into this, she suddenly starts to put her own shortcomings sharply to the fore. We have encountered this part of her several times before. Now the therapist asks her whether she can put that part of herself which reacts so strongly to her own little shortcomings, in front of her and see what emerges. After half a minute of silence, in which she changes physically from being cramped to being much more relaxed, she answers: "Then I see before my eyes an English puritanical old spinster who lives next door to the parish priest and passes judgment on the whole village". She laughs and adds: "Let her get lost!". When the therapist reflects it, she corrects: "But I have to be careful with that, because she's been the boss for so long, she had dominated the parish in me for so long; you don't just sack her; part of the village would stage a revolt". The therapist reflects: "As if there would be parts of you that would revolt if you were to send her away". The client continues: "Yes, when I continue with the parish image, I think a number of people are served well by having such a figure around". Therapist: "What can you discover in yourself that would be served by her?". Client: "She protects". The therapist then invites the client to look more carefully at what in herself is helped by the protection of the English puritanical spinster. Client: "It is ... not feeling the pain of being found out about your weakness". After a few moments of silence she adds: "When she's gone ... (more silence) ... then I stand there naked and vulnerable". She starts to weep quietly and says after some time: "I get the impression that I have kept that old spinster going for a long time; she was my only recourse, but I do not want that any more now ... when things hurt, let them hurt". Therapist reflects: "It also seems to feel valuable now to be in touch with that part of you where you are vulnerable". Client: "Yes, I first would like to be able to allow this; this pain is difficult but I do not want any more this sterile invulnerability". This eloquent fragment illustrates the effects of creating distance from an interfering character. It certainly is no accident that this is the 52nd session. The protection which she can now relinquish would, at a previous stage, have been indispensable. After that session, big changes took place in this client's life and later she still mentioned regularly the turning point which this session constituted in her life.

In this context it always strikes me how helpful metaphors can be in symbolizing experiences. Clients easily see a specific figure before their eyes when they are invited to place the interfering part in front of themselves. Sometimes this is a symbolic figure, sometimes a real– life person such as a parent. Recently a female client told me that she becomes extremely restless when she is not working. When asked to put this restlessness in front of her and see what comes next, she was suddenly struck by the image of her mother who never stopped working. In the invitation to put the interference in front of oneself, a disidentification is already implied. It is a very concrete help for clients to disengage themselves and gain a view of the 'interference'. When they choose a symbolic figure, it usually speaks for itself: thus we see a fair number of policemen, watch men, schoolmasters and old aunts ... these are symbols of exactingness and severity, but also of solidity and protection.

When clients succeed in looking the interfering part 'in the face', they mostly realizes that these defenses had an important function at one time in their life, but that they now hinder rather than help. This felt 'in– sight' helps to let go of the defense totally or at least partially. Clients take the wheel again themselves and choose which function they want or do not want to give to this specific part. Thus with a client whose interfering character took the shape of a severe, dutiful and everpresent guard, the client concludes the session with the agreement that the guard could go on vacation every now and then and that he would decide himself when his services as a guard were needed.

This is mostly the moment when humour appears, such as a real liberating laughter which does not ridicule but recognizes with generosity and gratitude what was once important but can now be seen in perspective. In fact, dealing with resistance and interference amounts to helping clients develop a receptive empathic attitude towards everything that presents itself to them and guiding them in finding the right way of relating, which is one of making contact, looking, feeling but not merging or identifying with what emerges. On the basis of this attitude and this way of relating, the healing process can proceed. Becoming 'whole' means then learning to receive the split– off parts of oneself and to reintegrate them in the total personality.

CONCLUSION

Looking back at Rogers' remark that we know very little about how a person arrives at feeling received by the therapist, I would dare to suggest that it is crucial that clients learn to receive what comes forward out of their inner knowledge. This self– empathy which is necessary in order to arrive at healing can be promoted in different ways. We first communicate it to clients through our own authentic basic attitudes of empathy and acceptance regarding all the client's experiences. Secondly we can guide clients more actively towards the development of an attitude of listening to their own inner knowing. In order to facilitate this inner dialogue, the therapist has to pick up on the client's ways of relating – and to focus on these besides the contents. An optimal inner way of relating implies making contact with the problems without merging with them. Metaphors seems particularly apt at putting this complex process into words and to concretize it. Clients can learn to distinguish in themselves several parts which can mutually interact and with which they can learn to deal in ways different from their usual ones. The 'interested adult' in them can devote tender loving care to the 'wounded child' in them and can, besides, explore the function of the 'ever– returning policeman'. Looking for a 'proper place' for everything that emerges is a process of receiving, questioning, naming, revaluing and integrating. Denied, rejected and/or split– off parts of the self are thus reintegrated in the larger whole.

This is the evolution which can come about in therapy. A further movement subsequent to the one usually aimed at in therapy can be experienced, namely the one in which a person feels himself or herself to be part of a larger transcendent whole. The inner experience of this relationship imposes itself upon some as the ultimate healing process.

Well– informed readers will perhaps notice that the process put forward in this paper correspond to well– known steps of the focusing process. Because of the importance of these phenomena I would recommend that we make the knowledge of the focusing process available to other therapists. The fact that similar processes also emerge elsewhere and have been present for centuries in cultures which have, more than our western one, applied themselves to expeditions inwards, says something about the general validity of these processes.

REFERENCES

Armstrong, M. C. (1993). Sexual abuse, dissociation and multiple personality disorder: One experiential therapist's approach to the aftermath of childhood sexual abuse: Dissociation and multiple personality disorder as necessary survival adaptations. The Folio. A journal for fucusing and experiential therapy. 12(2), 35– 44.

Fuhrmann, E. W. (1990). Some aspects of combining focusing with person– centered therapy in working with psychosomatic clients. In G. Litaer, J. Rombauts, & R. van Balen (Eds), Client– centered and experiential psychotherapy in the nineties (pp. 733– 740). Leuven: Leuven University Press.

Leijssen, M. (1991). Focusing in therapie. In J. C. A. G. Swildens, O. de Haas, G. Lietaer, & R. Van Balen (Eds.), Leerboek gesprekstherapie: de clientgerichte benaderin (pp. 195– 221). Amersfoort/Leuven: Acco.

Leijssen, M. (1991). Ruimte maken: een micro– proces in experientiele clientgerichte therapie. Tijdschrift voor Psychotherapie, 17(1), 48– 53.

Leijssen, M. (1993). Creating a workable distance to overwhelming images: Comments on a session transcript. In D. Brazier (Ed.), Beyond Carl Rogers (pp. 129– 147). London: Constable.

McGuire, K. N. (1993). Focusing inner child work whith abused clients. The Folio. A journal for focusing and experiential therapy, 12(2), 17– 34.

Rogers, C. R. (1961). A process conception of psychotherapy. In On becoming a person (pp. 125– 159). Boston: Houghton Mifflin.

Santen, B. (1993). Focusing with a dissociated adolescent: Tracing and treating multiple personality disorder experienced by a 13– year old girl. The Folio. A journal for focusing and experiential therapy, 12(2), 45– 58.

Stevens, I. (1990). Invloed van focusing– leersessies op het zelfexploratieniveau van weinig succesvolle clienten. Niet– gepubliceerde licentiaatsverhandeling, Katholieke Universiteit Leuven.

Weiser, A. (1991). Too close/too distant: Toward a typology of focusing process. Paper presented at the Second International Conference on Client– centered and Experiential Psychotherapy, University of Stirling, Scotland.

Weiser, A. (1993). The Focusing Guide's manual. Focusing Resources. 2625 Alcatraz Av. # 202, Berkeley, CA 94705– 2702; 510– 654– 4819.

Wls, G. (1992). Therapeutinterventies in therapiesessies en leersessies focusing. Nietgepubliceerde licentiaatsverhandeling, Katholieke Universiteit Leuven.

Five kinds of empathy

BERNIE NEVILLE

MELBOURNE, AUSTRALIA

ABSTRACT

In tracing the evolution of human consciousness, Jean Gebser distinguished five mutations, which he labelled the archaic, magical, mythical, mental– rational and integral structures of consciousness.Gebser argued that earlier structures are still present in us in a more or less latent form, while the integral structure is slowly emerging. This paper takes Gebser's structures as a framework for looking at empathy, and finds that Gebser's notion of integral consciousness can illuminate our understanding of the experience of empathy in client–centred and experiential psychotherapy.

The Swiss cultural philosopher, Jean Gebser, after tracing the evolution of human consciousness,concludedithas evolved through five stages or "mutations",each clearly distinguishable from the stage preceding it.[1]

The most primitive state of human consciousness Gebser calls the *archaic* structure of consciousness.It is most primitive both in the sense that it is earliest and in the sense thatit is the least complex.For the first million or so years of human existence, human beings had no sense of themselves as separate from their environment.As far as we can guess, primitive humans were governed by instinct, and their consciousness was exceedingly dim.In this *archaic* consciousness they had no sense of themselves as individuals, no sense of time and space, and lived in a state of ego– less unity with their environment. Their relationship to nature was dominated by impulse and instinct.

With the emergence of *homo erectus* (about 750,000 B.C.)[2], we find signs of human beings acting in a world of differentiated objects, exercising some control over them through the use of simple tools. There was as yet no sense of personal identitynor any ability to distinguish the part from the whole or internal experience from external. They seem to have experienced no sense of identity apart from the clan, and their world was a world of numinous power which could be dealt with only by magic. They had little language;they communicated through the direct experience of physical sensations or images.Their lives were totally enmeshed in the rhythms of nature.Gebser calls this consciousness *magical*.The magical structure, as he determined,"is spaceless and timeless and has an emotional and instinctual consciousness responsive to the demands of nature and the earth" (1983, p.76).

After the last ice age (about 12,000 B.C.) this primal consciousness was displaced by a new kind of consciousness, characterised by the development of imaginative thinking and the development of language.This shift from *magical* to *mythical* consciousness, took human experience from an instinctual/emotional mode to an imaginative/verbal one.Humans ceased to experience themselves as being totally merged with nature. We see the beginnings of individual consciousness, the differentiation of self from other, the separation of internal and external awareness, the expression of human experience of the cosmos in image and story. Through the power of imaginative or "mythical" thinking they were able to develop the sophisticated civilisations and complex societies of the ancient world, and with them the great narratives which expressed their experience of the universe.

About 1000 B.C. a fourth structure of consciousness which Gebser calls *mental* began to emerge in Europe and Asia.Human beings became capable of rational and directed thought, began to identify being with thinking rather than feeling, to be aware of time, space and quantity as we commonly understand them today.The emergence of discursive or abstract thought totally changed the relationship between human beings and their world.They became able to stand outside their world and reflect on it.They even became able to stand outside themselves, finding themselves not merely conscious, but conscious of their own consciousness.They became aware of time as more than duration and natural rhythm. They became fully aware of themselves as individuals, aware of cause and effect, able to act in a directed way on their world, no longer submerged in their environment and social group. They became able to build abstract political structures rather than tribal ones,to develop secular– scientific ways ofperceiving and exploring the world.

With the collapse of the Roman Empire, Europe experienced a regression for some centuries to a magical– mythical consciousness. It was only in the twelfth century that the Celtic and Germanic tribes made the same transition as had been made by the Greeks and Hebrews two thousand years earlier, from mythical to mental consciousness. Gebser makes much of Petrarch's discovery of landscape as the discovery of "objectified space", and of da Vinci's discovery of the laws of perspective.The Renaissance celebrated the discovery of the person. The fully fledged ego entered human history.With the emergence of science, the human ego began more and more to assert itself against nature, against faith,against the darkness of myth and magic.By the seventeenth century, reason reigned supreme.

In his notion of structures of consciousness, Gebser distinguishes between *efficient* and *deficient* structures.Magical consciousness, mythical consciousness and mental consciousness can all have either efficient (positive) or deficient (negative) manifestations.From Gebser's perspective, the *rational* structure of consciousnesswhich has dominated European culture for the past four hundred years is not a higher form of consciousness which has emerged from the mental structure through an inevitable evolutionary progression,but is actually a deficient form of mental consciousness, being cut off from its magical and mythical roots.It is an evolutionary dead end.It has seen the reduction ofthe universe from living organism to a collection of objects, the body from the temple of the soul to a piece of matter.It has seen the privileging of the intellect over other human capacities, the identification of intellect with themale and the relegation of the devalued physical– emotional (magical) and imaginative– intuitive (mythical) to the female.The fantasy of rational egoic control over the human machine andrational scientific control over the planetary one, have proved both futile and destructive.

Gebser's investigation of the evolution of human consciousness came from his sense, in the thirties, that European consciousnesswas undergoing some sort of change, that something new was emerging in the twentieth century.It seems to have started with his studies of Rilke's use of language, finding there a transcendence of dualism,an *aperspectivity* and a notion of qualitative time,which he went on to find also in other European writers, notably Paul Valéry and T.S. Eliot.As a refugee in Paris in the late thirties, he sought in art, literature, music, science,architecture, psychology, the evidence of a new sort of consciousness – against the background of a disintegrating mental–rational world and a regression to magical consciousness.

Three elements stand out in Gebser's analysis of what he calls the *integral*structure of consciousness.The first is time– freedom.Archaic and magical humanity seem to have had no sense of time at all, living in a continuous present.For mythical humanity, time was rhythmical, constantly returning to its beginning.For mental– rational humanity. time became continuous and sequential, and eventually mechanically quantifiable. What identifies an integral sense of time, for Gebser, is the re– owning of pre– rational, magic, timelessness and irrational, mythical, temporicityalongside mental, measured time. This "makes possible the leap into arational time– freedom"(1983, p.289).

The integral structure of consciousness also has a new sense of space. Archaic and magical humanity lacked all spatial consciousness, because it lacked a defined sense of a self as observer. Mythical humanity emerged from this enmeshment in nature, and became aware of an external world, butself– consciousness was still too weak to experience objective space.It is only in the beginnings of mental consciousness that human beings became able to locate events in objective space. Central to this experience was the discovery of perspective, which demands a point from which the world is viewed and an individual to view it.In the emergent, four–dimensional, integral consciousness, it becomes possible to view the world without locating the viewer in a particular position in space.

A third element in Gebser's analysis is the ego.Archaic and magical consciousness were ego-less.Mythical consciousness holds only a dim sense of self as distinct from the clan.Mental–rational consciousness allows the development of separate egoic identity.Integral conscious-ness is, in Gebser's language, "ego–free".

Gebser saw the deficiency in rational consciousness as deriving from its arrogant devaluation and suppression of the earlier structures.He saw in the collapse of this structure in the twentieth century both the danger of slipping back into a deficient magical– mythical structure and the promise of evolution to an integral structure.For the unwillingness of our rational-scientific civilisation to acknowledge the more primitive structures in no way makes them go away.We still think magically and mythically as well as rationally, whether we acknowledge it or not.[3] The past structures are still present in us. We are inclined to equate consciousness with the sense of self we experience at the mental level.Yet we constantly shift between this mental–rational consciousness and the more primitive structures which preceded it.

We still slip back into our archaic unity– consciousness in sleep, or enter it voluntarily or involuntarily through trance, drugs or certain kinds of meditation.We operate at the magical level when we submerge our identity in that of a group, when we experience events or objects as numinous, when we engage in rituals designed to make things happen or make us feel good, when we come closer to a loved one by kissing a photograph or when we share in the power and glory of a football team by wearing its colours.A great deal of healing, both physical and psychological, takes place within a magical structure of consciousness.When we sense in our bodies the pain or joy of a loved one, even in their absence, when we know something "in our bones", when we join in religious ritual, we are acting from our magical consciousness.

We are engaged in mythical thinking when we dream or day– dream, when we watch televisi-on, listen to a story or tell stories about ourselves, receiving or constructing the world in images without any need or attempt to translate them into thoughts.Every metaphor comes from our mythical consciousness.When we give a human name to a car or boat, or talk to an inanimate object as though it can understand us, or get angry with it because it will not do what we want it to, we are thinking mythically.Our mythical thinking enables us to admire and love a work of art even when we would be hard pressed to explain what it is about or why we like it.It is our mythical consciousness which induces us to change our behaviour after hearing a story which has engaged us, and which binds us to a partner or a group of friends through the stories we tell about ourselves.It is through the mythical structure of consciousnessthat we remain enmeshed in the "old stories", the shared narratives by whichour family, clan, tribe or nation defines its identity and its understanding of the world.Such narratives prove to be more potent shapers of behaviour than abstract reasoning.

Some would argue that this is a primitive and inferior form of thinking which has limited value in the modern world.Others would claim that mythical thinking remains a very effective way of dealing with the world, and that it is our capacity for mythical, and even magical, thinking that enables us to find meaning in our lives and gives us a grounding in the concrete world which rational thinking seems bent on destroying.It makes more sense to say that magical and mythical consciousness are neither better nor worse than mental– rational consciousness.They are simply older and different.

Our contemporary consciousness is multi– structured or, to change the metaphor slightly, multi– layered. We may thank Freud and Jung for pointing out to us that even when we are acting "rationally",our magical and mythical consciousness is hard at work.The complexity of human behaviour comes out of the interplay of these several "layers" or "levels" of consciousness in whatever we do.[4]Gebser suggests that the acknowledgement and appreciation of these discrete structures is a step towards their integration with the rational structure in a more "evolved" way of experiencing the world.

I believe there is value in using Gebser's structures of consciousness model as a framework for looking at the many processes and methods of therapy.However, in this paper I intend to focus only on the notion of empathy, and examine whether Gebser's model helps us to illuminate it.

ARCHAIC EMPATHY

In *archaic* consciousness, the therapist and client do not inhabit separate worlds. Human beings can, if they choose, through auto– suggestion or deep relaxation,change their ordinary state of consciousness to a less complex state.Or they can letthemselves be put into trance by hypnosis, or by chanting, music, dancing, or drumming.Or they can meditate.They can stop all mental activity for a time and let themselves slip into a much simpler state of being. If theyjust sit,cease doing anything, remain in a state of passive attention,deal with intrusive thoughts and images by simply *letting them go,*they find they can enter a state of trancein which their sense oftheir individual reflecting ego,their sense of the boundary between their internal and external worlds,become greatly diminished.They can enter a state of *bliss*, not ecstasy or transcendental experience perhaps, but silent, ego– less *bliss*, in which they and the universe are comfortably one. I believe that this simplest form of meditative trance, like the trance induced by repetitive chanting or dancing,is a regressive experience, a return to the archaic structure of consciousness through the shutting down of the other structures.I am also impressed by the evidence that it is desirable and healing to enter this state from time to time. The use of group trance in healing was and is common in pre– scientific cultures.

(Of course, not all meditation is regressive;different forms of consciousness– changing meditation belong to the magical, mythical and integral structures, and we can meditate within the mental structure without changing our mode of consciousness at all.)

We are inclined to think of meditation as a private and personal thing, even when people meditate together.Yet, historically and cross– culturally,meditation, like trance induction, seems most commonly a group activity.

In my experience, the kind of meditation I am talking about is most powerful in its impact when undertaken in a group.Each member of the group lets go the boundary around the self and allows in the experience of the *thisness* of the universe.The group members are in no way focused on each other, but share in the immediacy of what *is*. I think there are grounds for calling this phenomenon, and other group trance phenomena, *archaic empathy*.It may at first sight seem to have little to do with therapy,butGebserargues that he archaic structure of consciousness is the ground of all the others.I suggest that the experience of oneness with the universe is the ground of our empathic experienceof other people.

MAGICAL EMPATHY

In *magical* consciousness, the therapist experiences the client's world *somatically*. Gebser suggests that in this structure consciousness is not so much in the individual human as in *the world*.Magical humanity tried to gain some control over the transcendent power of nature through magic and sorcery, ritual, totem and taboo, experiencing this magical world through a group– ego, sustained by the clan.It is in the magical structure that empathy, considered as an experience of the primal sensing and feeling states of other members of the clan, is first a distinguishable phenomenon.Empathy is, for Gebser, a primitive phenomenon,utterly basic to the human condition.

Magical empathy is found in therapieswhich in which the healer is envisaged as a conduit for a transpersonal, palpable, healing energy (called chi, for instance, or reiki, or the Holy Spirit) rather than as someone whose personal intervention heals the patient, or even as someone who facilitates the patient's self– healing.It is found in traditional healing ceremonies where healer and patient enter a common psychic space through ritual.

Magical empathy is found in the shared consciousness of the group.It may be the shared consciousness of the football crowd, who collectively feel the fatigue, despair and delight of the heroes with whom they identify; the community of knowing and feeling of the religious gathering, involved in a ritual which allows them to relive the creative moment;the *participation mystique* of mother and new– born child;the phenomenon of sympathetic illness or sympathetic pregnancy;the unity of experiencing of two persons who are deeply (or obsessively) in love;the submergence of the individual in group singing or dancing or drumming;or the dissolving of ego– boundaries in the intensive encounter group.In such situations there can be an immediacy of communication,sometimes through body– sense, sometimes through image,which appears independent of space and time.A rational scientistic culture ignores the phenomenon, or labels it "telepathy" and tries to find an explanation for it within the current paradigm.Pre– scientific cultures accept such phenomena as a matter of course, along with other magical phenomena which we label "parapsychological".

In my own experience of intensive group work I have sometimes found myself in a "non-ordinary" state of consciousness, in which I have experienced feelings, even physical tensions or pains, which "belong" to others in the group.I have found myself and others uncannily "intuitive",even precognitive, "knowing" others' internal states without doubt or hesitation. I have found people sharing simultaneous images and sharing dreams.

Many counsellors will admit to experiencing physical sensations, tensions or pains while counselling their clients, sensationswhichseem to "belong" to the client rather than themselves.The counsellor feels a pain in theshoulder, a tightening in the stomach, a cold shiver down the spine,an overwhelming nausea, which does not seem to relate towords the client issaying or thoughts the counsellor is thinking.Or the counsellor has an experience of fear, or despair, or depression, and with it a sense that it is not her own response of fear or despair or depression to something the client has said, but is somehow a direct experience of what is going on in the client.Magical consciousness does not need, indeed does not have, words.

Not all counsellors experience these phenomena, but they are too common to be ignored.In mainstream writing about the therapeutic interactionthe phenomena seem not to exist, or are belittled as "merely projection", evidence of therapists' lack of adequate ego– boundaries.[5]In New Age writing it is more generally viewed as evidence of a higher, or more evolved, consciousness. I want to argue, with Gebser, that the world of magical consciousness knows no ego– boundaries, that we have access to a mode of consciousness which deals with reality in just this way.And in doing so I want to avoid either romanticising or disparaging magical consciousness which, as Gebser asserts, can be either efficient or deficient.

From the viewpoint of our ordinary rational consciousness we are inclined to view such phenomena as the transmission of a sensation or image from one self– contained person to another, in time and across space.We are also inclined to see a cause and effect relationship between the experience of the client and the reflection of it in the therapist. Gebser's notion of a consciousness which experiences an ego– less, time– less, space– less, unitary world "in which each and every thing intertwines and is interchangeable...[and] which operates without a causal nexus" (ibid., p.48). challenges us to look at the phenomenon somewhat differently.If we drop our anthropocentric and egocentric assumptions we can imagine a reality in which both client and therapist are equal participants, in which the shared somatic or imaginative experience of client and therapist are not related as cause and consequence, or transmitted from one to the other, but are literally *co– incidental.*

MYTHICAL EMPATHY

In *mythical* consciousness, the therapist experiences the client's world *imaginatively.* Where the magical structure of consciousness is sensate, pre– rational and pre– verbal, the mythical structure is imaginal, irrational and verbal.It maintains the collective identity of the magicalalong with a fairly dim sense of individuality.Mythical empathy does not give me a direct experience of how you are and feel.Rather, it enables me to imagine how you are and feel.And it enables this because at the mythical level our separate stories are a common story.

Mythical thinking is characterised by image and narrative.Its time is rhythmical or circular time,a continuous reiteration ofthe basic narratives of our relationship to the world.Mythical empathy involves the counsellor entering into the client's story, recognising its universality as well as its uniqueness, being in the storywith the client.

Mythical empathy arises out of a limited (relative to rational consciousness) sense of separate self.The magical structure does not distinguish self from not– self;the mythical structure knows self and not– self as a polarity, a complementarity; the mental structure knows self and not– self as a duality.In our mythical consciousness we are both one and separate. I know your story by knowing my own;I know my story by knowing yours.The more intensely personal your story is, the more universal it is, and the more it is intensely mine.The gap between us is crossed by imagination, not by conceptualisation.

Shamanic healing operates largely within the mythical structure, as the shaman enters the imaginal world shared by healer and client.Imaginal therapies such as Jungian *active imagination* and Assagioli's *psychosynthesis* depend on the ability to engage mythical consciousness.The therapist enters the imaginal world of the client and stays with the client's images, not interpreting, not rationalising,being an affirming presence in the imaginal world, helping the client to *tell the story on.*Likewise, *sand– tray* therapy (often associated with a psychoanalytic orientation), and *psychodrama* (Moreno) depend on a willingness to cross the border into the client's personal story and an ability to recognise in this the universal story.In mythical consciousness the boundary between self and other is permeable.Many therapists utilise the mythical structure when they cease reflecting andand responding, and simply "tune in" to the client and wait for a "vision".

Psychoanalysis labels this crossing of boundaries as either projection or identification, maintaining the assumption that the therapist and patient are two separated, intact entities who are constrained to relationships to one another within an objectively real world. Classical Jungians discuss such phenomena as expressions of a collective or objective psyche.Post–Jungians like James Hillman (1983) take seriously the notion of the *mundus imaginalis*[6], a level of reality located between the material, sensate world and the world of ideas or spirit. This is the world in which therapist and client find themselves enacting together the myth of the Wounded Healer.More spectacularly, it is the world which the shamanic healer enters in order to seek healing for her patient. It is the world of shared stories, shared visions and shared dreams.[7]

For most of us most of the time the mythical world is experienced diluted by reflection, abstraction and pre– conception.To stumble into our mythical consciousness can be a disturbing experience.For this reason, therapists whowork with clients within this structure are likely to invite a crossing into the mythical worldby enacting a ritual of some sort.This is as true for the sand– tray practitionersetting up the tray and its icons and the psychodramatist guiding the protagonist in setting up the scene for enactment as it is for the shaman using his drums, rattles or bells to summon or drive away the spirits.In such therapies the return to ordinary consciousness is likewise ritualised.

The mythical world is far more unitary than the conceptualised world of mental– rational consciousness. It does not manifest the*either/or*of dualistic, rational thinking. Rather, its world is bipolar,*both/and,*taking the rational mind's oppositions (body/mind, conscious/unconscious, self/other, health/pathology, goodness/badness, subject/object, female/male, spirit/matter, one/many, even truth/falsehood) as complementary manifestations of a unitary reality. The mythical world is not a world of "dead matter" like the world of rational, mechanistic science. It is ensouled, alive, replete with divinity (or divinities).The "mythically empathic" therapist is able to move about in this numinous, fascinating and sometimes frightening world with her client.

MENTAL– RATIONAL EMPATHY

The *mental– rational* structure enables the therapist to experience the client's world *conceptually.* In distinguishingthe efficient mental structure of the great classical civilisations and the early renaissance from the deficient mental (rational) structure of the modern age, Gebser notes particularly the discovery of objectified space,the development of the self– contained self, and the development of dualistic thinking.While the early mental structure is closely in touch with its magical and mythical roots, the rational structure is divorced from them. In the logic of a purely rational/materialistic/scientific consciousness,the notion of empathy is a nonsense.In the hubris of positivistic psychology even the existence of consciousness was denied. Carl Rogers defied such absurdities,but in his early theorising about the nature of empathy he was clearly concerned to develop a logical, systematic and abstract way ofexplaining the phenomenon and its implications for therapy.He accepted the assumption that counsellor and client are existing in separate, rational worlds,assumed that one can look only from one direction at a time, that while the therapist knows the client's frame of reference,he does not experience any confusion of identity, or become engulfed in the client's experiencing.The therapist's value to the client depends on the latter's determination to maintain his distinct separateness.Rogers expressed this idea with some emphasis:

> Am I strong enough in my own separateness that I will not be downcast by his depression, downcast by his fear nor engulfed by his dependency?Is my inner self hardy enough to realise that I am not destroyed by his anger,taken over by his need for dependence, nor enslaved by his love, but that I can exist separate from him with feelings and needs of my own? When I can freely feel this strength of being a separate person, then I can let myself go much more in understanding and accepting him (1958, p.15).

Nevertheless, there is some ambiguity here, for Rogers also saw the relationship as something which transcends these separate identities:

> In terms of the therapeutic situation, I think this feeling says to the client, I have a real hunger to know you, to experience your warmth, your expressivity – in whatever form it may take – to drink as deeply as I can from the experience of you in the closest, most naked relationship we can achieve.I do not want to change you to suit me;the real you and the real me are perfectly compatible ingredients of a potential relationship which transcends, but in no way violates, our separate identities(1951, p.164).

Rogers' reflections on this observation sound like an apology for a not adequately "scientific" statement:

> This whole idea seems important to me, not so much from a scientific standpoint, but simply because of its apparent importance in the process which my clients have been undergoing....Whether I'm kidding myself theoretically or not, this feeling of emotional adequacy in a therapeutic relationship seems very essential in creating a free and spontaneous relationship with clients (ibid., p.164f).

We find the same uneasy, ambivalent relationship between practice and "proper scientific thinking" in Kohut, Rogers (1986) himself points to the contradictory nature of Kohut's statements about empathy He cites with approval Kohut's (1978) statement: that "Empathy, the accepting, confirming and approving human echo evoked by the self, is a psychological nutrient without which human life as we know and cherish it, could not be sustained" (p.715).He contrasts this with Kohut's (in Goldberg,1980) reflection that "Empathy is employed only for data– gathering;there is no way it could serve us in our theory– building.In the clinical situation, the analyst employs empathy to collect information about current events in the patient's inner life" (p.483).Kohut's practice may have convinced him of the power of empathy, but he could not entertain the unscientific notion that empathy might, of itself, be healing. This same ambivalence is reflected in Kohut's handling of an incident where as analyst, he was at a loss for something to say to a despairing and suicidal woman client, so he gave her two fingers to hold.Immediately he had to atone for this unwarranted warmth by making an interpretation:"I immediately made a genetic interpretation to myself.It was the toothless gums of a young child, clamping down on an empty nipple" (cited in Rogers, 1986, p.132).

In these extracts from their work Rogers and Kohut seem to me to be struggling, consciously or not, between what Gebser regards as the efficient and deficient mental structures.It is the deficient structure which is represented by their notions of credible science. Rogers is staying in the efficient structure, while acknowledging the incorrectness of his position from the perspective of conventional science.Kohut is drawn by impulse towards the efficient expression, but rejects its apparent irrationality and chooses the more theoretically correct position.Rational empathy aims to understand the inner world of the client, not to experience it.Having a ready– made interpretative system to assist in this understanding tends to turn understanding into diagnosis and reinforce the subject/object duality which is central to rational consciousness.

In *Client– Centred Therapy* (1951), Rogers is consciously and deliberately working within a mental– rational framework.Take his reflections on the proposition:*The best vantage point for understanding behaviour is from the internal frame of reference of the individual himself(p.494).*He argues that human behaviour, no matter how bizarre it may appear to the observer, is always rational and purposive"in response to reality as it is perceived" (ibid).He takes the perfectly rational view that while it would be desirable "to empathically experience all the sensory and visceral sensations of the individual"(ibid), this is impossible.Admitting that a great deal of the client's experience of the phenomenal world is not brought to the conscious level, he argues that on the one hand it is unsatisfactory to try to understand the client'sunconscious experiencing through an external interpretative framework, and on the other that to stay with the client's awareness gives us an incomplete picture.He acknowledges that the counsellor's understanding of the client's phenomenal world will be at least partly derived by inferences from elements of that world which belong to the counsellor and client's common experience.Throughout his discussionthe client's world is clearly the client's and the counsellor's world is clearly the counsellor's.Contents of one can pass to the other only by communication and (less accurately) by observation.

Rational empathy is essentially an act of intellection.The counsellor strives to understandwhat the world of the client is like.It has no necessary connection with feeling, and is certainly not to be mistaken for sympathy.There is no losing of boundaries.What is yours is yours and what is mine is mine, and there must be no confusion.Nevertheless, though"cool", rational therapy might have been consistent with the theoretical constructs out of which Rogers was working at this stage, his experience of what worked drew him to suggest that this was not enough.The therapist must be touched by the experience of the client:

> I think clients are very much aware of the difference between the counsellor who listens and understands, and simply does not react, and the one who understandsand in addition really cares about the meaning to the client of the feelings, reactions and experiences which he is recording (ibid, p.164)

INTEGRAL EMPATHY

Gebser suggests, logically enough, that just as archaic humanity could not feel what the experience of magical consciousness might be, and just as mythical humanity could not imagine what mental consciousness might be like (pre– mental humanity did not have "ideas") rational humanity cannot conceptualise the experience of integral consciousness.Gebser himself claims only to have observed the past and present trajectory of consciousness and on this basis to have guessed at its future direction. I want to suggest that client– centredand experiential psychotherapy is in this trajectory, at least as far as the notion of empathy is concerned.

Both client– centred and experiential psychotherapy belong to the humanistic– existential cluster of therapies which, for all their many differences, have historically defined themselves in opposition to the rational– mechanistic propositions of behaviourism and psychoanalysis.Humanistic– existential therapies have been concerned to challenge the assumptions of high modernism:the dualistic assumption (particularly the mind/body dualism);the mechanistic/deterministic assumption (through a focus on volition and spontaneity); the masculist assumption (through a prizing of the feminine);the assumption of the absolute primacy of intellect (through a focus on experience and feeling);the materialist assumption (through a willingness to acknowledge non– material reality).However, within this cluster of therapies, and even within the smaller cluster of client– centred and experiential psychotherapies, there are different and contradictory voices.In this discussion I will consider only two of them:person– centred empathy as described in the later writings of Carl Rogers, andexperiential empathy as it is described by Alvin Mahrer.[8]

Rogers' mature understanding of the nature of empathy is outlined in one of his later papers.Reiterating his ideas on the nature of the therapeutic relationship he states:

> The third facilitative aspect of the relationship is empathic understanding.This means that the therapist senses accurately the feelings and personal meanings that the client is experiencing and communicates this acceptant understanding to the client.When functioning best, the therapist is so much inside the private world of the other that he or she can clarity not only the meanings of which the client is aware but even those just below the level of awareness.Listening, of this very special, active kind, is one of the most potent forces for change I know(1990, p.136).

While this is not too far removed from Rogers earlier explanations of what he means by empathy, we can note that he is here imaginatively placing himself within the world of the client rather than constructing that world out of communication and observation.He is also less coy about the possibility of being in touch with something of the unconscious world of the client. There is less of a sense of counsellor and client being in their separate, egoic space.

These differences are taken considerably further later in the paper, when he goes beyond what has been confirmed by research and speaks from the edges of his personal experience:

> When I am at my best, as a group facilitator or as a therapist, I discover another characteristic.I find that when I am closest to my inner, intuitive self, when I am somehow in touch with the unknownin me, when perhaps I am in a state of slightly altered consciousness in the relationship, then whatever I do seems to be full of healing.Then simply *my presence* is releasing and helpful.There is nothing I can do to force this experience, but when I can relax and be close to the transcendental core of me, then I may behave in strange and impulsive ways in the relationship, ways which I cannot justify rationally, which have nothing to do with my thought processes.But these strange processes turn out to be *right* in some odd way.At those moments it seems that my inner spirit has reached out and touched the inner spirit of the other.Our relationship transcends itself and becomes a part of something larger.Profound growth and healing and energy are present (ibid., p.137).

Psychologically, theemergence of the aperspectival, arational, integral world demands a disenchantment with narrow rational consciousness and a re– owning of the earlier structures.This allows the emergence of a new structure of consciousness for which we do not as yet have an adequate language. We find in Rogers' statement here, acknowledgement of a phenomenon with magical– mythical elements. Magical– mythical healingoperates through what are for us "non– ordinary" states of consciousness, is independent of linear space and time,does not know the duality of mind/body and self/other,locates core identity not in the individual but in "something larger",and does not know the laws of logic.

Those (inside or outside the client– centred community) who regard rational consciousness as the peak and culmination of evolutionary progress will see this statement of Rogers as an indication that he "lost it" in his old age. They will warn us that this honouring of magic and irrationality is regressive, an unfortunate intrusion of magical– mythical New Age consciousness into a perfectly adequate rational– humanistic system of thought. Indeed, Ken Wilber warns us of the dangers of the "pre/trans fallacy", the tendency of some of us to mistake regressive phenomena for progressive ones, to mistake the pre– egoic for the trans– egoic, the pre– rational for the trans– rational, the pre– personal for the trans– personal, the magical for the mystical. However, he also points to the tendency of others of us to make the opposite mistake.[9] For Wilber, as for Gebser, trans– or post– states are distinguished from pre– states in that they retain the foundation of ego, rationality and control which they transcend.

Rogers is talking in this passage about an experience which he cannot justify rationally. We might be inclined to label it irrational. However, Gebser takes pains to distinguish the irrational from the arational:

> It is of fundamental importance that we clearly distinguish between "irrational" and "arational", for this distinction lies at the very heart of our deliberations.... There is a fundamental distinction between the attempt to go beyond the merely measurable, knowing and respecting it while striving to be free from it, and rejecting and disregarding the measurable by regressing to the immoderate and unfathomable chaos of the ambivalent and even fragmented polyvalence of psychic and natural interrelation (1983, p.147)[10]

Rogers' reflections in this paper are hardly the reflections of some one who has abandoned rationality and slid into an "immoderate and unmeasurable chaos"! Neither has he abandoned his sense of self, but is able to hold the paradox of experiencing self– sense and transpersonal sense simultaneously. In reflecting on his experience he shows an awareness of a paradox, or at least an irony, in finding that a focus on individual experiencing should lead to an experience of oneness. He quotes with approval a participant in one of his workshops:

> I found it to be a profound spiritual experience. I felt the oneness of spirit in the community. We breathed together, we felt together, even spoke for one another. I felt the power of the "life force" that infuses each of us – whatever that is. I felt its presence without the usual barricades of "me– ness" or "you– ness" – it was like a meditative experience when I feel myself as a centre of consciousness. And yet with that extraordinary sense of oneness, the separateness of each person present has never been more clearly preserved (cited in 1990 p. 137)

Rogers notes somewhat apologetically that this account of group empathy "partakes of the mystical".

Later in this same paper Rogers comments on a particular example of an "intuitive response" in a therapeutic interacton he is discussing:

> I have come to value highly these intuitive responses. They occur infrequently...but they are almost always helpful in advancing therapy. In these moments I am in a slightly altered state of consciousness, indwelling in the client's world, completely in tune with that world. My nonconscious intellect takes over. I know much more than my conscious mind is aware of. I do not form my responses consciously, they simply arise in me, from my nonconscious sensing of the world of the other (1990, p.148).

Once again we could argue that an altered state of consciousness, identification with the client and a sense of nonconscious knowing point to magical– mythical structure of consciousness.These are not highly evolved capacities, restricted to the genius, the saint or the shaman, but fairly basic ones which we seem to share with animals.There is certainly no basis for romantically privileging these capacities. However, if we follow Gebser in arguing that the capacity to simultaneously experience these capacities and maintain a reflective awareness of them signals something new in the evolution of human consciousness, we may wish to viewthe whole phenomenon somewhat differently.

The point of this paper is not to argue for the validity of Gebser's model, or even to use Rogers' reflections on empathy to illustrate particular aspects of it. The pointis rather to suggest that Gebser's modelmay be used to illuminate the experience of empathy in the practice of client– centred therapy.I wish to make the same point regarding experiential psychotherapy as described by Alvin Mahrer.

In his critique of the limitations of client– centred therapy, Mahrer (1983, p.143f.) sets out the three assumptions on which he believes the approach is based:

(a)Therapist and patient are assumed to be two fundamentally separate and intact entities.

(b)Their relationship is predominated by the patient's frame of reference. The patient has this frame of reference, and the therapist acknowledges and uses the patient's frame of reference.

(c)Both therapist and patient are assumed to exist within an encompassing world of objective reality upon which the patient's frame of reference is but one perspective.

In Gebser's language, Mahrer sees client– centred therapyoperating within a fairly advanced mental– rational structure.He locates his own experiential therapy within the emerging integral structure.

In the reality in which Mahrer works,"the personhood or identity of the therapist can assimilate into or fuse with the personhood or identity of the patient.""[T]he locus of the therapist can occur internally within the patient."The therapist is "able to share both the internal and external domains of the patient.""When the patient attends to a meaningful focal centre, the therapist can likewise share the same attentionalcentre."In the course of therapy "the locus of relationships radically shifts from that of external, separated therapist and external, separated patient...to either the relationship of patient (and therapist) with the meaningful attentional centre, or to the relationship between patient and deeper personality process (and therapist)."Finally, Mahrer takes it as given that "patient and therapist exist in multiple phenomenal worlds constructed by the patient, the therapist, and both conjointly"(1983, p.145).

Empathy is entirely revisioned in such a context.Instead of maintaining the separation of identities, as the mental– rational expression of client– centred therapy was determined to do,experiential empathy depends on the dissolving of the boundaries between therapist and client:

> Ordinarily, about 80 to 90 per cent of an experiential session is spent with the therapist sharing the patient's attentional centre.During all this time, the therapist is internal to the patient, aligned and fused with the patient...(ibid., p.197).

A precondition to such a unity of experiencing is the minimisation of therapist/patient roles, which Mahrer sees not merely as problematic but as severely inhibiting successful therapy. The experiential therapist's aim is to concretely experience the world of the patient, not to be content with the *as if* of the client– centred therapist.Accordingly, she aims to enter the patient's world from her common personhood, not from within a role relationship.She does not sit facing the patient but beside him;she does not seek to reflect what he is thinking and feeling, but to express what they are thinking and feeling in common;she does not observe him as *the other*, for both she and he have their eyes closed;she does not seek to *relate*to him or even *communicate* with him as self to other but rather she seeks to experience exactly the same world as he does;she does not seek to enter this world by a conceptual or imaginative leap butby sharing the same physical sensations.

Experiential empathy begins with the client becoming aware of the sensations in his own body and describing these to the therapist.The therapist adopts these sensations as her own:

> Something is happening in your body right now.It may be in your throat or chest or head or legs or somewhere.I want to have the same thing in my body.I want to have the same feelings, the same sensations that are going on in your body right now.Describe where the feelings are and what they are like, so that I can have them too, no matter where they are or what they are like.Then we can move ahead (Mahrer, 1983, p.235).

Moving ahead involves the therapist in attending, not to the patient, but to whatever the patient is attending to.The therapist does not guess what the patient is experiencing, butexpresses whatever sensations and images she is experiencing herself.Therapist and patient do not interact with each other but rather they interact as one person with the shifting focus of attention.As the therapist experiences more and more intense sensations, and increasingly precise and vivid images, there is no censoring or selection on the basis of,"This is mine;that is his."

Mahrer's reflections on this practice bear comparison with Rogers' reflections on the practice of empathy.Like Rogers he finds the practice healing in itself.Like Rogers he notices a shift in and out of an altered state of consciousness.Like Rogers he claims to be aware of a deeper potential, a deeper transpersonal reality.Like Rogers he is constantly confirmed in his conviction that beyond the frightening darkness of the client's deeper potential is a positive energy.

Obviously, in evaluating such a practice, we are at risk again of falling into Wilber's pre– trans fallacy, one way or the other. Such a practice clearly involves magical and mythical processes.However, I would argue that it integrates them with mental processes, transcending the constructs of the "merely rational" world rather than resiling from them. The experiential therapist is simultaneously inside and outside the experience,just as the protagonist in psychodrama may be simultaneously a three year old child in hospital and an adult observing his own performance, or the person in hypnotic trance may observe his own trance behaviour.The experience of operating in two or more states of consciousness simultaneously is common enough.Perhaps in our re– owning of the earlier strata of our consciousness this is the best most of us can manage.Fully integrated consciousness may be still emergent!

CONCLUSION

Gebser's exploration of the evolution of consciousness is only a prelude to his main work, which focuses on the nature of the transcendent reality which is manifest in these various structures. What can we say about the *suchness* of the world, the *Itself (Das Sich)*which is revealed in the darkness of the archaic structure, the gloom of the magical, the twilight of the mythical, the brightness of the mental and the transparency of the integral? Gebser challenges the privileging of the scientific world– view as the only legitimate window on that reality.He would have it that what we know of reality through our rational mental– rational consciousness complementswhat we know, obscurely, through archaic, magical and mythical consciousness.It does not falsify it.

Gebser developed his theory in the context of a European culture whichwas in grave danger of regressing to a deficient magical consciousness. He came to hold the view that the destabilisation of rational consciousness could be a sign of the emergence of a new structure.In the nineties it seems that we are again being confronted with same danger and the same promise. I am inclined to see the developments that I have noted in client– centred and experiential psychotherapy as signs of the promise, rather than signals of the danger.

REFERENCES

Achterberg, J. (1985). *Imagery in Healing: Shamanism and Modern Medicine.* Boston: Shambhala.

Corbin, H.(1972)*Mundus Imaginalis, or the imaginary and the imaginal.* Spring

Feuerstein, G. (1987) *Structures of Consciousness:The Genius of Jean GebserLower Lake,* Ca:Integral Publishing.

Gebser, J. (1983). *The Ever– Present Origin.*Ohio University Press.

Goldberg,A.(1980).*Advances in Self– Psychology.*New York:International Universities Press.

Harner, M. (1978). *The Way of the Shaman.* New York:Viking,

Hillman, J. (1983)*Archetypal Psychology: a Brief Account.* Dallas: Spring Publications.

Kohut,H. (1978). *The psychoanalyst and the community of scholars.*In Ornstein, P. (Ed.), *The Search for Self:The CollectedWritings of Heinz Kohut.*New York: International Universities Press.

Lawrence, W.G. (1991). *One from the void and formless infinite: experiencesof social dreaming.Free Association.*

Mahrer, A. (1983) . *Experiential Psychotherapy: Basic practices.* New York:Brunner/Mazel

Rogers,C.R. (1951).*Client– Centred Therapy.*London:Constable.

Rogers, C.R. (1958)*The characteristics of a helping relationship.* Personnel and Guidance Journal. Vol. 37,.

Rogers, C.R. (1986)."Rogers, Kohut and Erickson:*a personal perspective on some similarities and differences.*"Person– Centered Review. 1 (2).

Rogers, C.R. (1990) *A client– centered/person– centered approach to therapy.*In Kirschenbaum, H. & Henderson, V. , The Carl Rogers Reader.London: Constable.

Samuels, A.(1989). *The Plural Psyche.*London: Routledge.

Wilber, K. (1979). *Up from Eden.*New York:Anchor.

Wilber, K. (1980). *The Atman Project.*Wheaton: Quest,.

Wilber, K. (1983), *Eye to Eye,*New York:Anchor.

---

[1]Jean Gebser was born in Posnan (Prussia) in 1905, left Germany in 1929, spent the next ten years in Spain and France, and eventually found a home in Switzerland. His inter-connecting of a broad range of academic disciplines makes it difficult to categorise him as a scholar, but he was happy to accept the label "cultural philosopher".Though he developed his key ideas in the thirties and forties, he was denied substantialrecognition until the sixties, when a professorial chair in Comparative Civilisations was created for him at the University of Salzburg.He died in 1973.

His work is still barely acknowledged in the English-speaking world.His major work, *The Ever-Present Origin* (*Ursprung und Gegenwart*) was first published in German in 1949, but was not translated into English until 1983.His later writings still await translation.

[2]Gebser is very reluctant to ascribe a chronology to the mutations. I have followedFeuerstein's chronology here.See G. Feuerstein, *Structures of Consciousness*, Integral Publishing, 1987.

[3]The development of consciousness in the individual appears to follow a path similar to that of the species.Our intra-uterine experience seems to be characterised by archaic consciousness, the first two years of infancy by magical consciousness (Piaget's sensorimotor stage, Freud's primary process), and our childhood up to about seven years of age by mythical consciousness (Piaget's concrete operations). Ken Wilber applies a Gebserian model of consciousness evolution to personal development in *The Atman Project.*, Quest, 1980.

[4]Gebser prefered to speak of "structures" or "intensities" of consciousness rather than "levels" or "layers" because he wanted to avoid any suggestion of a hierarchy.Likewise, he insisted that hisevolutionary model did not encompass an assumption of "progress" or even "development".

[5]The phenomenon has been reflected on much more within the analytic tradition than elsewhere.Andrew Samuels examines the various waysby which Freudian and Jungian writers explain such phenomena, considering such labels as 'projective identification" (Klein), "syntonic countertransference (Fordham), "reflected countertransference" and "embodied countertransference" (Samuels). .See A. Samuels *The Plural Psyche*, Routledge 1989,In discussing the analyst's physical sensations in the therapeutic encounter, Samuels argues that "the analyst's body is notentirely his or hers alone and what it says to him or her is not a message for him or her alone." ibid p. 164.

[6]Henri Corbin (1972) writes of the *mundus imaginalis*as a "fully objective and real world with equivalents for everything existing in the sensible world without being perceptible to the senses". What the therapist experiences is a "vision" of the client, which comes without a sensory stimulus, without intellection, and often without a deliberate act of imagination.Commenting on this notion, Andrew Samuels argues that "the *mundus imaginalis* functions as a linking factor between patient and analyst and that some of the analyst's counter-transference may be regarded as visions and hence part of this imaginal world" *The Plural Psyche* p.164.

[7]It is commonly observed in working with ongoing "dream groups", that members of a group who meet regularly to analyse/interpret/appreciate each others' dreams,will have an increasing tendency to share common themes and images in their dreams, to an extent not explainable in terms of their conscious communication with each other. Gordon Lawrence's work on "social dreaming" suggests that dreaming is a collective, rather than a purely personal, phenomenon.See W. G. Lawrence, "One from the void and formless infini-te:experiences of social dreaming" in *Free Association*, 1991.

[8]I have taken Mahrer's version of experiential psychotherapy as my illustration in preference to Eugene Gendlin's focusing technique, because of Mahrer's specific challenge to conventional notions of empathy. Gendlin's experiential psychotherapy appears to me to be likewise committed to the integration of archaic, magical, mythical and mental consciousness, as are a number of other humanistic, existential and transpersonal therapies.

[9]See K.Wilber, *Eye to Eye,* Anchor, 1983.Wilber's discussion of the evolution of consciousness is strongly influenced by Gebser's work.See *Up From Eden*, Anchor, 1979.

[10]Gebser points out, as does Feuerstein more recently, many illustrations of the aperspectivity and arationality of twentieth century science.See Feuerstein, op. cit., p.130ff.

The Deep Structure of the Core Conditions:
A Buddhist perspective

CAMPBELL PURTON

STUDENT COUNSELLING SERVICE, UNIVERSITY OF EAST ANGLIA

ABSTRACT

In this paper I explore what seem to me significant parallels between views of the person, and of therapy, in Buddhism and in the work of Carl Rogers.The background parallels involve similar aims, recognition of the essential trustworthiness of human nature, the importance of an internal locus of evaluation, the 'process' view of the self, and the therapeutic process which involves a reduction of 'incongruence' or 'delusion'. Given this background I look in more detail at the nature of the core conditions, relating these to what is seen in Buddhism as the overcoming of the three 'afflictive emotions'. I then explore how both in Buddhism and client-centred therapy the process of therapeutic change can be seen as centred on the 'softening' or dissolution of the self(– concept) insofar as this is experienced as a 'rigid' structure. I conclude with a theoretical reflection on why, given my analysis, there are just *three* core conditions, and a clinical reflection on the implications for which of the core conditions should be given preferential emphasis in different forms of psychological disturbance.

INTRODUCTION

This paper is an attempt to explore the relationship between some central themes of Buddhism andclient– centred therapy. I am conscious of the great gulf in time and culture between Buddhism, an ancientAsian path of liberation, and client– centred therapy, a modern Western school of psychotherapy; yet having been struck by what seem to me to be important parallels (Purton, 1993), I feel impelled to explore them further.

I also want to use the parallel with Buddhism to explore some specific themes in the client–centred approach which seem to me worth exploring, especially what it is about the human situation which makes the core conditions of empathy, respect and genuineness so important. Finally, having developed at least in sketchy form a view of what the core conditions amount to when approached from a Buddhist point of view, I return at the end of the paper to some empirical or clinical consequences of what I have said.

AIMS: CLIENT– CENTRED THERAPY

Clients typically come to therapy because they are confused, depressed, anxious, lacking self–confidence, experiencing difficulties in relationships and so on. In short, they come out of a sense of deep unsatisfactoriness, out of a feeling that all is not well with them as persons.Successful therapy is therapy which helps clients to move to more satisfactory states of being, where clarity replaces confusion, depression lifts, anxiety abates, and respect and understanding both of self and of others improve.

This is the common sense, and phenomenological, picture of the therapeutic progress. However, the client– centred approach also has a *theory,*which attempts to explain the phenomenological changes (Rogers,1959).Very briefly stated, it is that we tend to lose touch with who we really are through the development of a self– concept which does not adequately represent our experience.This happens partly because of the conditions of worth which are imposed by significant others, and partly because of our need for a coherent sense of self.In a word, our self–

concept becomes increasingly *incongruent* with our experience, and this state of incongruence lies at the root of our state of distress or felt unsatisfactoriness.It is incongruence which results in our sense of alienation fromourself; it destroys the possibility of genuine self– respect and self– understanding;and it interferes with our capacity to respect and understand others. In short, from a theoretical point of view, if there is a single aim of therapy it is that of client congruence. The therapist's task is the simple, though difficult, one of helping the client to become what he or she really is.

AIMS: BUDDHISM

In the *Majjhima Nikaya*(i, 130) the Buddha says :"Today and formerly, monks, I teach just two things – suffering and the release from suffering". The word translated as 'suffering' here is *duhkha*,and from the contexts of its use it is clear that *duhkha*doesn't just mean suffering in the sense of pain.It is not exactly the pain, but the 'unsatisfactoriness' of things which Buddhism aims to reduce, just as in therapy we know that on the path to a more satisfactory way of being there may well be as much, or even more, *pain* than before.

The pervasiveness of *duhkha*is the first of the four 'Noble Truths' of Buddhism.The other truths deal with the cause and alleviation of *duhkha,*and what is said is that *duhkha*is esentially rooted in 'craving' and in 'ignorance'.Both these terms need explanation, and I shall say more about them shortly, but I will just remark that although 'craving' is often presented as the cause of *duhkha,*the Buddhist writings emphasise that craving itself is rooted in a deep misperception of the nature of oneself and of the world.It is not a simple matter of suffering arising from our not getting what we want; the deep source of *duhkha,*it is said, lies in our emotional misconception of our self as having a certain fixed nature.We experience ourselves as being essentially such–and– such, and then suffer as a result of the discrepancy between our picture of ourself and what we really are. . I will try to explain this Buddhist approach to the notion of the self more clearly later, but here just want to indicate the sort of parallel that exists with the client– centred approach.It is thatboth Buddhism and the client– centred approach begin with the person (client) in a state of unsatisfactoriness (*duhkha*), and while the superficial cause of this may be certain attachments or fears the deep cause, as identified by the respective *theories,*is that the person misperceives and hence mis– lives what they really are.

BASIC TRUSTWORTHINESS OF HUMAN NATURE

It is central to Rogers' conception of the person that human nature is fundamentally sound, though thissoundness almost inevitably becomes obscured.The corresponding theme in Buddhism is that of the original Buddha– nature. In the *Tathagatagarbha Sutra*the Buddha says:

> "...all the living beings, though they exist among the defilements of hatred, anger, andignorance, have the Buddha's wisdom, Buddha's Eye,Buddha's body sitting firmly in the form of meditation. – Thus, in spite of their being covered by defilements...they are possessed of the Matrix of the Tathagata [Buddha– nature], endowed with virtues, always pure, and hence not different from me." Having thus observed, the Buddha preached the doctrine in order to remove the defilementsand manifest the Buddha– nature within the living beings. (Williams, 1989, p. 97)

This parallel needs little comment.For both Buddhism and Carl Rogers the basic nature of human beings is trustworthy;if there is neurosis or *duhkha*in human life this is because there has been distortion or obscuration of what is at heart good and sound.

INCONGRUENCE AND INTERNAL LOCUS OF EVALUATION

In Rogers' view we lose touch with our experience largely through the pressures of the conditions of worth that are imposed on us. There develops an 'incongruence' between whatwe really are and how we perceive ourself. That which we call our self is not truly our self, but a distorted version thereof, a mask. We come to value things not from our own internal locus of evaluation but from that of others. The mask develops out of the pressure we feel to be what others want us to be, and once established it constitutes our sense of identity. Yet this 'self' which we feel to be ourself is illusory; it is not who we really are. We are in a state of incongruence.

Buddhism emphasises the importance of an internal locus of evaluation in passages such as these: And whosoever, Ananda, either now, or after I am dead, shall be a lamp unto themselves, and a refuge unto themselves, shall betake themselves to no external refuge, but holding fast to the truth as their lamp, and holding fast as their refuge to the truth, shall not look for refuge to anyone besides themselves– it is they, Ananda.... who shall reach the very topmost height – but they must be anxious to learn.(*Mahaparinibbana Sutta*, II, 31– 5, in Foy,978, p. 184)

> Of whatever teachings you can assure yourself in this way: 'These teachings lead to calmness, not to neurotic passion;.... to individuality, not to immersion in the group; ... of such teachings you may affirm with certainty: 'This is the Dharma. This is the ethical life. This is the Master's message.' (Vinaya, II, 10)

CHANGE, FLUX, IMPERMANENCE

Given that we have lost touch with what we really are, it is crucial, if we are to regain our reality, that our nature should be open to change. If the illusory self (or self– concept) is of the nature of a fixed *thing,* then there is no hope for us, but if on the other hand the self is a flux, a process, this process may lead back to our original nature. The latter, optimistic view, is shared by Rogers and Buddhism. The Buddha says in the *Samyutta– nikaya* (35, 43): "All is impermanent. And what is the all that is impermanent? The eye is impermanent, forms are impermanent.....The mind is impermanent, mental objects, consciousnesss, whatever is felt.... is impermanent." And in the *Lalitavistara Sutra*: "The three worlds are impermanent like autumn clouds: the birth and death of living beings is similar to viewing a dance; life is gone like a flash of lightning in the sky, quickly passing like a mountain waterfall."(Batchelor, 1987, p.219)

THE CORE CONDITIONS: TERMINOLOGICAL ISSUES

Thus far the picture presented both in client– centred therapy and in Buddhism is that of the person as basically sound, but suffering from illusory self– perception. The illusory self is open to change, however, and I want to consider now what is involved in such change.

The central theme of the client– centred approach is that therapeutic change consists in a movement from a state of incongruence of self and experience to one of congruence, and that this movement is facilitated by the presence of three attitudes in the therapist, i.e. empathy, respect and genuineness. However, before continuing some remarks are needed about terminology.

(a) Congruence and genuineness

In the definitions section of his major theoretical paper Rogers (1959, p.206) writes

that "when self– experiences are accurately symbolized, and are included in the self– concept in this accurately symbolized form, then the state is one of congruence of self and experience."

A person in a state of congruence is thus genuine or authentic, in the sense that they are themself, that they are not acting out of any *self–* deception. Now congruence in this sense is compatible with various forms of untruthfulness, hypocrisy or play– acting. If someone judges in a particular situation that it is best to lie, or consciously decides to play a particular role, that does not in itself detract from the person's congruence or authenticity, since there need be no incongruence here between self– concept and experience. Conversely, it is quite possible to be open and honest with someone to the best of one's ability and yet be incongruent.

Now from the point of view of therapy, both incongruence and dishonesty in the therapist are detrimental.The client needs to experience *genuine* respect and empathy, so that if they sense that the therapist is either pretending or self– deceived the conditions for therapeutic change are not met.It is combined congruence– and– honesty which is important in the therapist, so that it is useful to have a word which covers this combination. 'Genuineness'or 'transparency' seemssatisfactory terms, since being genuine (or' transparent') seems to rule out both pretence and self– deception.

The aim of client– centred therapy is client congruence (i.e. the client becoming him– or her-self). It is *not* the aim of therapy to facilitate client honesty, for whether or when to be honest is a matter for the moral judgement of the client.

(b) Acceptance

I need also to say something about the relationship between 'respect', 'acceptance'and 'empa-thy'.Person– centred writers often use 'respect' as synonymous with 'acceptance'; however I think that there are significant differences between the two.

Respect involves the acceptance of individuality and difference:when Kahlil Gibran (1964, p. 16) says in connection with marriage "let there be spaces in your togetherness. And let the winds of heaven dance between you" he is touching on just this.However, respect does not necessarily involve any personal closeness or warmth in the usual sense of the word . We may not *like* the other person much or feel we have much in common with them, but this is imma-terial since *we* don't come into the picture.We respect *them* for what *they* are, independently of us.

By contrast, when we feel *close* to someone, when for the moment we share their world, when 'two hearts beat as one', *then* we are accepting our *lack* of individuality; it is as though the boundaries between us have temporarily dissolved.This is also a kind of 'acceptance', but clearly we are heremore in the territory of 'empathy' than of 'respect'.

Although Rogers usually distinguishes rather sharply between the respect and empathy condi-tions he acknowledges the link between them in his paper 'Empathic: an unappreciated way of being' (Rogers, 1980, p. 152):

> A second consequence of empathic understanding is that the recipient feels valued, cared for, accepted as the person that he or she is.It might seem that we have here stepped in-toanother area, and that we are no longer speaking of empathy. But this is not so. It is impossible to accurately sense the perceptual world of another person unless you value thatperson and his or her world – – unless you, in some sense, care.

Empathy thus involves a degree of respect, but equally we might argue that respect cannot be real unless it includes a degree of empathy.I can't really respect *you* unless I have some under-standing of who you are.Respect and empathy can interpenetrate, I suggest, because they are both aspects of acceptance.As I am using the terms, respect involves accepting and valuing people for what they are in themselves, as a reality separate from me, while empathy involves accepting and valuing our commonality, our sharing of a perspective on the world.

THERAPEUTIC CHANGE

With these clarifications let us return to the process of therapy.Rogers (1980, p. 159) writes in this connection:

> The self is now more congruent with the experiencing.Thus the persons have become, in their attitudes towards themselves, more caring and acceptant, more empathic and un-

derstanding, more real and congruent. But these three elements are the very ones that bothexperience and research indicate are the attitudes of an effective therapist.

Looking at the therapeutic process in this way, what the client is doing, with the therapist's facilitation, is overcoming his or her own lack of respect, empathy, and congruence.I stress this way of seeing it so that the process can be compared more easily with what it is that Buddhists are trying to overcome in themselves. namely the three *kleshas*or 'afflictive emotions' known by the tags of 'greed', 'hate' and 'illusion'.In Buddhism it is held that it is these three which in all their varieties and combinations obscure our inherent Buddha– nature.

THE THREE TROUBLES

Buddhism, no less than client– centred therapy, has its problems over terminology and, while the term *kleshas*has been translated in a variety of ways, in what follows I will simply speak of the three 'troubles'.

First, some explanation is needed if we are to grasp what these 'troubles' really amount to. 'Greed' is a common translation of the Sanskrit/Pali *'lobha',*but other renderings can be 'attachment', 'desire', 'clinging', etc.*Lobha*is greedy possessivenes, *having* to possess things or people, a devouring of the world so that I have everything within *me*. *Lobha*cannot tolerate independence or separation, the valuing of something or someone for what they are independently of me.

'Hate' is the common translation of *'dosa',*but it is better translated as 'aversion', since *'dosa'*can cover fear as well as hate.*Dosa*is in a way the opposite of *lobha;*in another way it is very similar.It is the opposite in that while *lobha*insists on 'getting' and 'holding on to', *dosa*insists on 'getting rid of' or expelling from oneself.What they have in common is the insistence, the *having to* get or get rid of.Hence they are often regarded as two aspects of the craving which leads to duhkha.

'Illusion' is the translation of *'moha'* , also translated as 'delusion' or 'ignorance'.It can seem odd, on first acquaintance with Buddhism, that *moha*is regarded as a form of craving, along with *lobha*and *dosa.*.If *moha*is ignorance it is clearly a special form of ignorance, a *motivated* ignorance.*Moha*is the craving not to see clearly, and is thus closely linked with the Western psychological concept of repression.It also has the aspect of 'inertia' or 'stupidity', the clinging to fixed or stereotyped ways of seeing oneself or others.According to Buddhism the central illusion involved in *moha*is that of seeing one's self as a real, independent, 'solid' entity.I will return to that point shortly, but here for purposes of comparison we just need to note that *moha*essentially has to do with illusory self– perception.

I suggest that the parallels between the three 'troubles' and the three core conditions go something like this:

Moha('illusion')seems to be related to incongruence.Incongruence is essentially self– misperception which involves denial or distortion of some aspects of what is really experienced. Incongruence, like *moha,*is motivated. and like *moha*it is to do with illusion in the sphere of self–perception.

The overcoming of *lobha*('greed') is the overcoming of attachment to things, people, ideas, the overcoming of the sense of *having* to have something, to possess, to own.Overcoming *lobha*means coming to accept that other people have their own reality, that they can't (without *duhkha*)be possessed.It means accepting life as it is, situations for what they are, not insisting on changing them into what we must have.It means not being attached rigidly to our own views, accepting that others see things differently. Hence what will counteract *lobha*is respect for people as they are. I suggest that this comes close to what Rogers refers to as'unconditional positive regard', 'prizing' or 'respect.

The overcoming of *'dosa'* is the overcoming of aversion, whether aversion from others or from aspects of oneself. The feel of *dosa* is that of cutting off, cutting out, expelling, getting away from. Overcoming *dosa* means 'bringing together', 'sharing', 'feeling at one with'. It means acceptance of connections and relationships, of the fact that 'No man is an island'. This is different from the sort of acceptance which overcomes *lobha*– it is the acceptance that I am not entirely separate from you, that we can move in and out of each other's worlds. I suggest that it is significantly related to the concept of 'empathy'.

To summarise the comparison I am drawing up, I am linking the Buddhist *moha* ('illusion') with 'incongruence'; Buddhist *lobha* ('greed') with lack of respect, and Buddhist *dosa* ('aversion') with lack of empathy. It is interesting that in both systems of thought there is a tendency to focus on one of the three troubles as being in a sense more fundamental than the other two. In client–centred therapy it is incongruence which is the underlying trouble, while in Buddhism it is illusion.

So if we have to say in a *single* word what troubles people who are appropriately seeking counselling, the answer in both systems is illusion/incongruence. Similarly the goal is enlightenment/congruence. In Buddhism the way to enlightenment is through the elimination of craving in its twin forms of greed and aversion. In client– centred therapy the way to self– actualisation or congruence is through acceptance in its twin forms of respect and empathy. It is of course difficult to get the terminology right. 'Words slip, slide, will not stay in place', but the following scheme is the best I can manage at present:

The 'trouble' (Buddhist terminology)	The 'therapy' (Rogers' terminology)
illusion	incongruence
manifesting in craving which has the	acceptance (in therapist)
twin forms of greed and aversion which result in	respect and empathy (in therapist)
further illusion	congruence (in client)

I am inclined to think that while ultimately enlightenment or self– actualisation has to do with overcoming illusion and becoming congruent, the *path* to this involves acceptance or the overcoming of craving. What the therapist needs to *do* is to respect and empathise with the client. Of course, the more genuine the therapist is the better, and this means that the therapist needs to work at being as self– aware and as honest as he or she can be, but for all its importance therapist genuineness comes into the picture in a different way from the other two conditions. Therapist genuineness comes in through the necessity that the therapist's *respect and empathy* be genuine. This point may be more obvious if we reflect that an encounter with a very genuine person need not be *therapeutically* valuable if their genuineness is expressed in ways which have nothing to do with respect or empathy.

CRAVING, NECESSITY AND THE SELF

What craving amounts to is the sense of necessity, of *having* to do/not do (or be/not be) something. The general notion of necessity is one which has been explored in various ways in Western philosophy, but the particular insight we need here is due to Schopenhauer (1813), i.e. the insight that all necessity is *relative*. That is, while there are indeed things which we must do or be, this necessity is always relative to something else which for the moment goes unquestioned. For instance I must get to the railway station by eight o'clock, but this is so only relative to the fact that I must catch the eight o'clock train. And *that* is relative to the fact that I must get to London by tomorrow morning.

Now there is a problem here about where the chain of necessities ends. It can hardly go on indefinitely, yet if it comes to a stop it seems that we are back with an absolute necessity. So in our example of catching the train, let us look at where the chain of necessity does end.I *must* get to London by tomorrow morning.– What if you don't? – Then I won't be able to meet Annabel for that concert in the evening. – Why *must* you meet Annabel? Well, I said I would meet her, and I must keep my word.– Why must you keep your word? – Because otherwise I would be an untrustworthy person.– Why mustn't you be untrustworthy?– Well, I'm not like that, that's not me – andI'm not answering any more stupid questions!

It is somewhere around here that the chain seems to end: "I can't be untrustworthy"– Why not?– "Because then I wouldn't be me". I stop thequestions where I feel that my self– concept is in question. Surely, I say to myself. I *am* a particular sort of person, and that sort of person doesn't do that sort of thing.That is how we naturally see it, but from a Buddhist point of view this perception is illusory.There is no fixed essential 'self', I don't *have* to be trustworthy because I don't *have* to be any way at all.I may choose to act in a trustworthy way in this situation, I may believe that it is always best to act in a trustworthy way, but I don't *have* to act like that and I don't *have* to have that belief. There is no absolute 'have to'.Lessing (translation: 1972, p.16) put it beautifully in his *Nathan the Wise*. Nathan the Jew is talking to his dervish friend Al– Hafi:"What's this I hear?*Must*?– – A dervish *must*?*Kein mensch muss müsssen* (no one should live by *must*), and certainly not a dervish."

To summarise this section,*duhkha*arises from craving, and craving arises from the illusion that there is a fixed self which I am, a self has to be a certain way.In the Buddha's words (Ñanamoli 1972, p. 132): "When a man perceives impermanence, perception of not– self becomes established in him; and when a man perceives not– self, he arrives at the elimination of the conceit 'I am', and that is nirvana here and now." Removing the sense of a self results in removing the sense that I *have* to be any particular way, I don't even have to be good.And with the release from this necessity comes the sense of freedom:"Just as the Great Ocean has one taste, the taste of salt, so too this Law and Discipline has one taste, the taste of liberation."(Ñanamoli 1972, p.162)

As a parallel to this sense of the fluidity of the self let me quote the following passsage from Rogers (1967, p. 171):

> Clients seem to move toward more openly being a process, a fluidity, a changing. They are not disturbed to find that they are not the same from day to day, that they do not always hold the same feelings toward a given experience or person, that they are not always consistent. They are in flux, and seem more content to continue in this flowing current.The striving forconclusions and end states seems to diminish.

THE SELF AND OTHERS

For Rogers the dissolution of the self– concept returns us to the experiencing self, but this 'self' is not a fixed entity; nor is it isolated from other fixed selves.Rogers (1951, p. 520) remarks that "it is one of the unexpected findings that have grown out of the client– centred approach" that self– acceptance leads to greater acceptance of others. He goes on to suggest a theoretical explanation for this, which is, roughly, that the denial of experiences incompatible with the self– concept leads to defensiveness and distorted ways of seeing other people.Conversely, with the elimination of the self– concept we become more accepting of (respectful towards) our experiences, and feel less need to defend ourself against other people's views of us. "When there is no need to defend, there is no need to attack" (Rogers 1951, p. 521)

It is the reduction of the sense of the 'fixed self' which leads to the improvement in personal relationships, and this theme is echoed in Buddhist teachings on the relation between 'wisdom' and 'compasssion'.'Wisdom' is essentially the realisation of the illusory nature of the self, but such realisation is held to be indissolubly linked with the growth of compassion.Even in our ordinary unenlightened state we sometimes quite naturally lose our sense of having a separate identity.A door is slammed and someone catches their fingers in it: here we may quite naturally respond emotionally as if *we* had been hurt.From a Buddhist point of viewthere is no separate self that has the pain, hence there is no important difference between me having it and you having it.'Selves' drop out of the picture, so that for the enlightened person concern for 'others' arises as spontaneously as concern for 'self'. As Schopenhauer, that most Buddhist of Western philosophers put it, " ...the better person is the one who makes least difference between himself and others, and does not regard them as absolutely non– ego; whereas to the bad person this difference is great, in fact absolute."(Schopenhauer, 1844; translation in Payne, E.F.J., 1974, p. 507).It is no doubt right to acknowledge that the idea of the dissolution of the self in Buddhism goes well beyond the idea of the dissolution of the self– concept (or persona) in counselling practice.Allthough I cannot discuss the matter here, I believe that the difference is closely linked with the distinction between therapeutic and spiritual change.Therapy, I would say,aims to soften or dissolve the persona (the mask, the self– concept), so as to allow the real experiential self or ego to emerge.The traditional spiritual paths, as I understand them, aim to soften or dissolve the ego– – the self– centred self itself.

MEDITATION AND THERAPY

The parallels I have discussed so far have centred around the conceptual frameworks of Buddhism and client– centred therapy. But there also seem to be parallels between what Buddhists and client– centred therapists *do* in their respective quests for increasing enlightenment and congruence.

I can do little more than touch on this comparison in the space available, but it is interesting that in both approaches the basic procedurescan hardly be called techniques, or even means to an end: what we have, rather, are certain ways of embodying attitudes that are intrinsically valuable.In client– centred therapy the central procedure is that of reflection by the therapist of the client's expression of feelings and thoughts.One function of this reflection, according to Rogers, is to establish anempathic link with the client, but it also seems clear that close listening and reflection manifest a high degree of respect for the client. Thus reflection is a simple way of embodying the two aspects of acceptance which clients need if they are to become more congruent.That is, the necessary closeness to the client's world is manifested in the accuracy of the therapist's empathy, while the necessary distance is manifested in the way the therapist respects the *client's* view of things.What is so effective in close listening is the *combination* of respect and empathy.

In Buddhism there are various types of meditation, but the two central practices are those known as 'tranquillity' (shamatha) and 'insight' (vipashyana), or 'stopping' and 'seeing'. Tranquillity meditation involves simply focussing one's attention on a particular experience, such as the sensations involved in breathing.In this kind of meditation one does not make any judgements about one's experiences, although one may notice that judging is taking place.The point is simply to stay with the experience, allowing the mind to become still.In client– centred language tranquillity meditation involves respect for one's experience in its immediacy and uniqueness. (It is – in the traditional imagery – like the flickering flame of a lamp becoming steady).Insight meditation is usually introduced after some proficiency in tranquillity has been attained.When the meditator can 'stay with' an experience, the experience can then be reflected on, and understoodfor what itis. (The steadily burning flame now becomes brighter and clearer). In client– centred language this'insight meditation' could well be called self– empathy, a clear seeing into one's own being.It is said that it is the union of tranquility and insight which leads to, or constitutes, the enlightened state, a state of deep acceptance free of all craving (see e.g. Namgyal, 1986; Thrangu, 1993; Thich Nhat Hanh, 1991).

It seems then that Buddhism and the client– centred approach use similar methods as well as seeking essentially the same goal.The only really significant difference in method is that in client– centred therapy the client's increasing congruence is facilitated by the empathy and respect embodied in the therapist's presence, whereas in Buddhism the meditator is developing self–respect and self– empathy in a more direct way.(But I should add that it is a very common view in Buddhism that meditation is difficult to learn without some personalcontact with a teacher who has attained a measure of tranquility and insight themself).

THE THREEFOLD ROOT OF RELATIONSHIP

One of the advantages of theoretical understanding over simple empirical knowledge is that it enables us to see not just that things are the way they are but *why* they are so.I would like now to apply this principle to a question which may seem trivial at first, but which leads quickly into quite deep waters.It is the question of why there are just three core conditions.Why not four, six or more? It is true that fourth and further conditions have been suggested by several writers, including myself(Purton, 1989), but none of these have quite caught on, whereas the three original conditions have maintained themselves in therapeutic theory and practice far beyond the confines of the client– centred approach. It is curiously the same in Buddhism.The list of three troubles (attachment, aversion, ignorance) runs all through Buddhism.There is, it is true,an extended list which includes two extra troubles, and it would be interesting to link these with possible fourth and fifth conditions of therapy, and then there are 'secondary afflictions' such as laziness, spitefulness and so on, but the original list of three has remained at the core of Buddhist thought.The question arises of whether there really is something significant about there being just three?

I think there is, and that it has to do with the fact, as I maintain, that the three conditions (or the three troubles) are not *just* a listof facilitative conditions for therapy (or just a list of afflictive emotions). Rather they are aspects of what could be called the structure of the personal. I mean that to think about persons essentially involves thinking of relationships, and a relationship involves two people (or possibly two personal elements within a single person).Now where there are two people their relationship involves either closeness, distance, or neither– one– nor– the– other.Two people in a relationship are either together or apart, or they are in some in– between or muddled state.There really are no further possibilities at this most basic level of analysis.

Now we have seen that client– centred therapy, or the Buddhist path, involves moving from states of greed, aversion and illusion towards states of empathy, respect and congruence. But what this seems to amount to in terms of relationship is the following:

(1)A person moves from an unsatisfactory form of closeness (e.g. greed, possessiveness, attachment) to a more satisfactory form of closeness (i.e. empathic communion).What was unsatisfactory about the initial closeness was that it had no element of distance or respect in it. The person involved was not prepared to let the 'winds of heaven' dance through the relationship.

(2)A person moves from an unsatisfactory state of separation (e.g. aversion, fear, hate) to a more satisfactory form of separation (i.e. respect). What was unsatisfactory about the separation was that it had no element of togetherness or communion about it.The person involved was not prepared to acknowledge or experience his or her common humanity with the other person.

These two situations are clearly opposites, where an extreme of either separation or closeness is rectified by the therapeutic admixture of something of the opposite quality. What helps with suffocating closeness is the distancing of respect; what helps with cold separation is the togetherness of empathy.The basic idea here is very familiar in Buddhism;Gampopa,a twelfth– century Tibetan teacher put it succinctly : "...when we have found out which is our strongest emotion, we must seek its remedy. This is done in each case by meditating on the opposite quality" (sGam.po.pa: translation 1959, p. 191).

But what of third, and most central, therapeutic movement, the one from illusion to congruence? In terms of relationship I think it involves the movement from an unsatisfactory state of not knowing where one is in a relationship, a state of painful confusion, to a *satisfactory* state of not knowing where one is, i.e. a sparkling relationship where nothing is certain because nothing is fixed, where we don't quite know, perhaps, where our boundaries are, but where that is a delight, a dance, a depth of relationship which defies any classification into 'together' or 'separate'.

A glimpse of this might be seen in the remarks of a participant in one of Roger's workshops (Rogers, 1980, p. 197):

> – it was like a meditative experience when I feel myself as a center of consciousness, very much part of the broader universal consciousness.And yet with that extraordinarysense of oneness, the separateness of each person present has never been more clearlypreserved.

In Buddhist terms the path leads away from fixed categories to the unfixed.Where there is fixed closeness we need some separation; where there is fixed separation we need some togetherness.Paradoxically it is as if we *need* a degree of confusion, an alchemical mixing of the opposites, and it is only out of the confusion, muddle, illusion, *moha*that the lotus blossom of the enlightened mind emerges.In Nietzsche's words:"One must still have chaos in oneself to be able to give birth to a dancing star". (Nietzsche 1883, I, 5)

The structure of the personal, then, is the structure of relationship, and the basic form of relationship is threefold:Together, Apart and Uncertain.Each of these modes of relation can exist in a satisfactory or an unsatisfactory form.The unsatisfactory form of togetherness covers the area of collusion, smothering, overprotection, infatuation and so on.The satisfactory form of togetherness covers such things as sharing, communion and empathic understanding.

The unsatisfactory form of separation takes us into the region of hate, fear, rejection, isolation, loneliness and so on.The satisfactory form of separation is the sphere of respect, independence, valuing, prizing, etc.

The unsatisfactory form of uncertainty is confusion, muddle, ambivalence, self– deception, mixed messages, etc. The satisfactory form of uncertainty is flexibility, idiosyncracy, openness, freedom, and so on.

Looking at it like this, the movement along the therapeutic (or Buddhist) path consists in moving from the unsatisfactory to the satisfactory version of each of the three modes of relationship, i.e. from possessive closeness to empathic closeness, from aversive separation to respectful separation and from confusion to freedom.

SOME IMPLICATIONS FOR PRACTICE

I will end by returning from these rather ethereal heights to a question of therapeutic practice. As client– centred therapists we try to offer our clients the core attitudes of respect, empathy and genuineness, but we often have to make choices about which of these attitudes should have priority with particular clients at particular times.Getting a balance between the core attitudes, a balance which is appropriate to the individual client, seems a comparatively unexplored area in the client– centred approach.Rogers (1980, p. 160) does suggest ways in which the balance may helpfully be tipped in different kinds of personal relationship,but he does not ground these suggestions in his clien:– centred theory.

I want to suggest now some rough guidelines based on my previous discussion.It is that the core attitude which is especially likely to be therapeutic is that which tends to balance out the trouble which prevails in the client at the time.While all the troubles are to some extent with us all the time, it seems likely that in particular clients, or during particular sessions, one or other of the troubles may predominate.That is, the client's difficulties at the time may be especially rooted in either *lobha, dosa* or *moha* , so that the preferential emphasis would be respect for the *lobha* client, empathy for the *dosa* client, and genuineness for the *moha* client.

The *lobha* client is one whose difficulties are rooted in such things as over– involvement, possessiveness, demandingness, perfectionism, clinging to relationships, 'loving too much', and maybe compulsions and addictions.Also in this territory, I think, is depression, which arises when the demands of *lobha* are not met, when we lose what we feel we must have. *Lobha* is a disorder of 'closeness', and the 'antidote' is a degree of separation.Hence my suggestion is roughly that with depression, for example, or with clients who 'love too much' the preferred emphasis in therapy should be on respect, rather than empathy.What the client typically needs is to regain a sense of their own vitality and worth, so that the therapist's respect, valuing or prizing of the client seems crucial.

The *dosa* client will be one whose difficulties are rooted in such things as under– involvement, social isolation, suspiciousness, fear, coldness, 'loving too little'.*Dosa* is a disorder of separation, and the 'antidote' is a degree of closeness.Hence my suggestion is that with *dosa* the preferred emphasis in therapy should be on empathy rather than respect.I do not mean of course that *dosa* clients should not be prized and respected, but that the 'distance' that is involved in respect is something that these clients probably have enough of already.In *dosa* states there is often beneath the surface a tinge of arrogance, a sense of being 'special' and set apart from other people; in other words a *kind* of self– respect is already there.What is deeply missing is the sense of relatedness, of sharing, of being– with– others, and it is this sense of isolation which the therapist's empathy can can begin to dissolve.(It is tempting to see schizophrenia as involving an extreme form of *dosa* , and in this connection it is interesting that Rogers found in an extensive study of schizophrenia "that those patients receiving from their therapists a high degree of accurate empathy as rated by unbiassed judges, showed the sharpest reduction in schiozophrenic pathology".(Rogers, 1980, p. 151)

The *moha* client will be one whose difficulties are rooted in such things as confusion, aimlessness, uncertainty, lack of a sense of what one wants, lack of a sense of meaning or purpose in life, lack of a sense of identity, and so on.It is hard to empathise with confusion, and it is also hard to get a sufficient sense of who the person is in order to prize and respect *them.* So with *moha* , I think, the therapist is thrown back on his or her own genuineness or authenticity.With *moha* everything is uncertain, there are no tracks to follow, and the therapist can only trust in his or her ability to be at home in trackless country, to trust that it is out of chaos that the dancing star will be born.

These are of course only suggestions, and rather impressionistic groupings of types of counselling problems.Nevertheless it does seem to me that the suggestions are in principle open to empirical assessment. If it should turn out in practice that depression responds best to high levels of empathy, and schizoid states respond best to high levels of respect, well, then I would have to do some rethinking!

CONCLUSION

In comparing two paths as remote from each other in time and geography as Buddhism and client– centred therapy, there is clearly a danger of spinning a web of connections which is not very solidly grounded .However, I hope I have done enough to show that the connections between Buddhism and client– centred therapy are real and substantial.Both, after all, are concerned with the general aim of relieving the unsatisfactoriness of our lives; both see this unsatisfactoriness as rooted in our failure to be ourselves.Both take as axiomatic that our nature is inherently trustworthy, though it has in various ways become distorted or obscured.Both see a significant part of this distortion as arising from our adopting an external locus of evaluation, an external refuge in the views and attitudes of other people. Both see this unfortunate situation as remediable, since both conceive the human being in terms of process and flux, rather than in terms of a substantial unchanging essence.

So much is the backdrop; what I have tried to do in this paper is to explore the question of whether there are important parallels in the finer details of the path that leads away from *duhkha.*Such parallels do seem to exist, and I am begining to find them helpful in my counselling work.I am more aware now of the difference it may make when I lean more towards respect than towards empathy, or vice versa.But also I feel more sure about what I am doing as a client– centred counsellor. Given the lack of solid empirical support for the effectiveness of client– centered counselling (Levant & Shlien, 1984), I am glad to be able to ground my work in a tradition tried and tested over so many centuries.I do not for a minute doubt that other groundings are possible for client– centred practice; I suspect that such groundings can be found in any genuine spiritual tradition, though not necessarily in the mainstream expression of the tradition.Let me close with a quotation from Rabindranath Tagore:

The night has ended.

Put out the light of thine own narrow corner smudged with smoke.

The great morning which is for all appears in the East.

Let its light reveal us to each other who walk on the same path of pilgrimage.

REFERENCES

Ade, W.F.C. (tr.) (1972). *Nathan the Wise.*New York: Barron's Educational Series

Batchelor, S.*The Jewel in the Lotus.* London: Wisdom Publications.

Foy, W. (1978).*Man's Religious Quest: A Reader.* London: Croom Helm

sGam.po.pa (*translated* H. Guenther, 1959).*The Jewel Ornament of Liberation.*Boston and London: Shambhala

Gibran, K. (1964).*The Prophet.*London: Heinemann

Lessing, G.E. (1779, *translated* W.F.C. Ade, 1972). *Nathan the Wise.*New York: Barron's Educational Series

Levant, R.F. and Shlien, J.M. (eds.)(1984).*Client– centered Therapy and the Person– CenteredApproach.*New York: Praeger.

Namgyal, T.T. (1986).*Mahamudra: The Quintessence of Mind and Meditation.* Boston and London: Shambhala

Ñanamoli, B. (1972). *The Life of the Buddha.* Kandy, Sri Lanka: Buddhist Publication Society.

Nietzsche, F.(1883).*Thus Spake Zarathustra.* Translation in W.Kaufmann: *The Portable Nietzsche.*New York: Viking Press (1954), p.129.

Purton, A.C. (1989). *The person– centred Jungian.*Person– centred Review, *4* ,403– 418

Purton, A.C. (1993).*Philosophy and Counselling.*In Thorne, B. and Dryden, W.Counselling: Interdisciplinary Perspectives.Milton Keynes: Open University Press

Rogers, C.R. (1951).*Client– Centered Therapy.*London: Constable

Rogers, C.R.(1959).*A theory of therapy, personality, and interpersonal relationships, as developed in the client– centred framework.*In: S. Koch (ed.) *Psychology:*A study of a Science, Vol. 3. Formulations of the person and the social context (pp. 184– 256). New York: McGraw Hill.

Rogers, C.R. (1967).*On Becoming a Person.* London: Constable.

Rogers, C.R. (1980).*A Way of Being.* Boston: Houghton M ifflin.

Schopenhauer, A.(1813).Translation in Payne, E.F.J. *The Four– fold Root of the Principle of Sufficient Reason* (La Salle, Illinois: Open Court, 1974).

467

Schopenhauer, A.(1844). Translation in Payne, E.F.J. *The World as Will and as Representation*. Vol. II, (New York: Dover Publications, 1966).
Thrangu, K.(1993).*The Practice of Tranquillity and Insight.*Boston and London: Shambhala.
Thich Nhat Hanh (1991).*The Miracle of Mindfulness.*London: Rider.
Williams, P.(1989).*Mahayana Buddhism.* London: Routledge.

The Ending of a Story

REINHOLD STIPSITS

UNIVERSITY OF VIENNA

ABSTRACT

Unlike the initiation and first interviews, therapy endings are almost never considered a topic worthy of discussion, neither in general psychotherapy nor in its person– centred application. Carl Rogers in his earlier work (Rogers, 1942) paid some attention to this issue, and a few others (e.g. Mearns, Thorne, 1991; Swildens, 1992) do discuss the matter also.There is no proper training for these endings as such, but the end of a therapy is nevertheless of great importance. Unlike education, psychotherapy must have an end. This fact should also be taken into account in the training of therapists. In this paper I will discuss the idea that therapy, if regarded as a local narrative, has a tendency for quite individual endings. I will be drawing attention to some endings that do occur frequently. There are cold breaks, inconclusive departures and satisfactory endings. I intend to compare these endings with the aesthetic structure of elements encountered in other narratives, such as plays, novels, films etc. The ending implies a certain difficulty, which I would like here to discuss.[1]

The final stage of psychotherapy is a subject on which there is actually very little literature available. It differs in this from the many well–documented opening phases and initiations of encounters, not to mention first interviews – often with a didactic intention – which tend to have the character of a performance offering no real possibility for continuation. From my own point of view, the story of each psychotherapy is a local narrative, whereas interviews for illustration purposes might more justly be considered as microdramas, representing by themselves both the beginning and the end of a story.However, to begin with, I should like to make a few remarks on the way this problem was dealt with in the past, in order to give you a brief summary of the various opinions held by specialists in this subject. Rogers, particularly in his first book, "On Counseling and Psychotherapy" (Rogers, 1942), deals to some extent with the ending of psychotherapeutic sessions. He answers practical questions such as how to finish a session effectively, how to properly terminate a therapeutical relationship, what one should bear in mind as a counsellor or therapist and what one should avoid.

In this early phase of his work, Rogers refers both to ways of ending a single session within a longer relationship, and ways of terminating psychotherapy completely. One is undoubtedly justified in characterising the early Rogers as a very process– orientated therapist. He offers a number of remarks on how the client's development can be encouraged, what techniques are helpful to elicit relevant knowledge, and eventually, specific aspects concerning the final phases of therapy. The ultimate aim of "client– centred therapy" is not so much to enable the client to lead a satisfactory, problem– free life, but rather

> It is this unified purpose, this courage to meet life and the obstacles which it presents...The client takes from his counseling contact not necessarily a neat solution for each of his problems, but the ability to meet his problems in a constructive way. It follows that re– education is not, as has been sometimes supposed, the retraining of the individual in all aspects of life. It is rather a sufficient practice in the application of the new

insights to built up the client´s confidence and enable him to carry on in healthy fashion without the support of the counseling relationship. (Rogers, 1942, p. 218).

This is as much as Rogers imparts, as far as he is concerned with passing on his practical experience as a therapist. To Rogers, clients typically display ambiguous feelings towards their condition; on the one hand, they want to come to terms with their problems on their own, but at the same time they are somewhat frightened by the thought of having to survive without the help of the counsellor/therapist. It is up to them to make a decision between a responsible, independent and self– determined life, and the dependency on the safety and protection surrounding the relationship with the therapist. "It is entirely natural that there should be some regret at the dissolution of such a relationship and the counselor will do well to recognize this fact, and to admit his own as well as the client´s feeling about the matter." (Rogers, 1942, p. 222).

These lines may be taken as proof of the importance Rogers attributed to the congruence of the therapist. Being in a state of harmony with oneself may well be said to be the most fundamental guideline determining a therapist's behaviour, and therapists should take care to communicate this feeling of harmony to their clients. Towards the end of therapy, things begin to change for the clients, who have gradually gained insight into their feelings and behaviour. Not only has the clients' personal evaluation of their problems altered, even the interest they take in the therapist has undergone a modification. They will take to asking the therapist about his or her• personal concerns, the state of his health, and his opinions on topical issues. Some may even consider continuing the relationship on a social basis. With regard to this, Rogers clearly states his opinion in the form of advice: "The counselor should recognize these positve feelings toward himself, but in most instances will be wiser to close the contacts on a therapeutic, rather than a social, basis." (Rogers, 1942, p. 222). What Rogers very elegantly discusses here, without resorting to technical language, is in fact nothing other than the difference between congruence and abstinence. The act of taking leave is something personal which implies neither fusion nor renunciation of the counsellor's responsibility for his feelings towards the client.

In another passage, Rogers expresses his doubts concerning what has become common practice:

> Some therapists, notably Rank, have maintained that at times an arbitrary time limit should be set for the conclusion of treatment, this would seem to be unwised. The ending of the counseling interviews should be set primarely by the client, with the counselor serving again to clarify the isues that arise in connection with leaving. (Rogers, 1942, p. 228).

Rogers depicts the therapist's situation with insight and understanding:

> On the whole the end of counseling is likely to come sooner rather than later, than the counselor expects it. We are so prone to think in terms of unsolved problems that we may not be sufficiently aware of the client´s readiness again to "paddle his own canoe". (Rogers, 1942, p. 229).

As to the duration of counselling, Rogers suggests it will probably be something nearer three months than a year, thus emphasising the difference between psychotherapy and psychoanalysis. It must be admitted, however, that counselling periods have become a good deal longer in all forms of psychotherapy, and that therapies of several years' duration are no longer an exception. A comparable lengthening process in the duration of training periods and didactic analyses/therapies may be observed in the time between Freud and Rogers, but has been more apparent over the last fifty years. In his unmistakable tone, Rogers expresses the profound ambiguity inherent in any ending of a therapy. "Ordinarily the counseling ends with a sense of loss on both sides, but with a mutual reccgnition that independence is another healthy step toward growth." (Rogers, 1942, p. 238).

Unfortunately, Roger's earlier work has not been studied as attentively as his more famous publications and, therefore, is not quoted in a way corresponding to its merits. It must be noted that in his later days, Rogers was nc longer able to offer continuous psychotherapies, for the simple reason that various other obligations did not allow him to maintain regular client contacts (e. g. once a week). Another reason that perhaps made him withdraw from individual therapy, was probably his growing interest in other fields of person– centred study, such as group work or peace projects. Be that as it may, Rogers had a consistent and personal way of practising as a therapist over several decades, as was shown by Bozarth (1992). Although Rogers' earlier works do contain quite some practical knowledge, their constructivist aspects have only recently found critical appraisal (cf. Frenzel, 1991). If all things on earth necessarily come to an end, then Roger's person– centred therapy can certainly not escape this fate.

Swildens, Mearns and Thorne.

There are few other authors with anything relevant to say on the theme of ending psychotherapies. This is somewhat surprising perhaps, compared with the great number of studies on the "success" of psychotherapy (cf. e. g. Grawe, 1991).

The problem of terminating a therapy is dealt with by Swildens (1992) in his Process Oriented 'Gesprächs'– Psychotherapy, where the author clearly distinguishes between the individual phases of the process, which he classifies as follows: stagnation, pre– motivation phase, symptom/syndrome phase, problem/conflict phase, existential phase, and the leave– taking.

Swildens emphasises the phase of leave– taking and the specific feelings it arouses; of disappointment, anger, sadness, helplessness and fear of loneliness, which have to be properly "worked through". What Swildens refers to here are the cases of inconclusive departures, i. e. when clients seek to keep a door open for them to resume the relationship. He emphasises the necessity of a certain distance to be maintained in order to guarantee the psychotherapist's freedom and receptiveness to new challenges. Clients should learn to come to terms with leave– taking, not least as an expression of their increased independence.

The offer of a relationship going beyond that of client and therapist, will have to be unambiguously declined. I am not saying, though, that we ought not to understand the reasons that make the client propose such a relationship – just as we ought to admit the feelings (filtered carefully) which this impossibility causes in ourselves as therapists. (Swildens, 1992, p.68; my translation).

Swildens in particular describes the act of renouncing the alibi and of changing the myth as an essential processes which must occur before psychotherapy can be considered as successfully terminated. "A typical sign of the ending of a therapy is when the client renounces his alibi affirmation "I cannot go any further" and, with varying degrees of doubts and anxiety, decides to face the future." (Swildens, 1991, p.101; my translation).

After the leave– taking, which must be discussed, it is of course possible for the therapist to inquire after the client's condition. Swildens specifically mentions a case where he had contacts with a client during her epicrisis. Generally, however, the occasional exchange of letters following the actual end of the psychotherapy ought to be sufficient.

Mearns and Thorne (1988) also offer some precise remarks on the importance of an adequate therapy ending. To them, the ending should be marked by some specific act following upon the psychotherapy. This is of much practical use and can be positively checked at any time. If, for example, the aim of a psychotherapy was to change the client on an emotional and/or behavioural level, what is needed then, is an act expressive of such change. The authors share the conviction that a successful therapy is one which will eventually result in an increase of self-esteem. A new sense of self– worth, a "fondness of oneself", the reduction of strain, the recognition of new or hitherto unacknowledged opportunities; these are the usual signs characterising the final sessions with successful clients in psychotherapy.

"To regain the locus of evaluation". This seems to be a general expression of the client's newly– gained independence, and as such marks the beginning of the final phase of therapy (Mearns & Thorne, 1988, p. 138). The departure should be prepared with great care. If the authors suggest such tactful and tentative questions as: "Have you any thoughts on when we should stop?", they make it clear that they do not by any means expect the client's answer to be "Right now". Even if such were the clients response, the therapist would not be encouraged to actually stop at that very instant. The authors underline that as a general rule in person– centred counselling, it ought to be left to the client to determine the proper end of the therapy.

Mearns and Thorne give three further examples of questions recommended to be asked towards the end of a therapy. The first is the question of what the client still wants to "do" before the closure of the therapy. Here things remain entirely open; they may range from "beginning all over again" to "no problems left". The second possibility would be for the therapist to invite the client into a retrospective of the progress made so far. A final possibility of intervention suggested by Mearns and Thorne is to inquire about those things which have not yet been resolved. As this approach undoubtedly entails a greater directive intention, it requires the necessary circumspection on the part of the therapist so as not to stir any wounds in the healing process. Such is the advice from some significant examples taken from literature regarding helpful ways of closing a psychotherapy.

I have spent a long time in trying to formulate a useful, even original classification of the various forms of terminating psychotherapeutic relationships. I must admit that the result is all but satisfactory to me; roughly speaking, one can distinguish between three kinds of ending. Based on criteria as simplistic as they are questionable, the distinctions are these: cold breaks, inconclusive departures, and successful endings.

The term 'cold break' refers to cases in which the client stays away from therapy without having previously informed the therapist about his plans. The latter is reduced to conjectures concerning the reasons for the client's refusal to continue therapy. The break comes as a surprise, as a one– sidedness in a relationship, which by definition implies mutual respect but autonomous responsibility. Even if the therapist imagines plausible reasons for the client's evasion of the sessions, the invisible tie between the two persons will be impaired. In general, such a dramatic step is the last consequence of a crisis emanating from loss of confidence in the therapist. The cases in which reasons unrelated to the therapy prevent the client from mentioning an imminent break are in fact very rare. Sudden urgent changes in the client's professional life necessitating his abrupt relocation may be the reason for such a break. Still, if a good client–therapist relationship exists, the therapist will be informed in advance by the client of such an event. If it is true, as Shlien (1987) put it, that understanding in psychotherapy is a kind of lovemaking, then a sudden, unmotivated interruption of this relationship is unlikely. It rather suggests that the relationship had slipped into a state of crisis at an earlier stage.

Things are far more complex in the case of inconclusive endings. In these situations the therapist usually thinks of the relationship as largely unproblematic. The client seems to "respond" satisfactorily to the therapy, yet there is nevertheless something that prevents him from successfully taking leave. Either there are certain things which caused the client to seek a psychotherapist and which have not yet been discussed, or the client simply cannot acknowledge the impending separation. The ability to live alone is a prerequisite for a person to be able to live with others; those who are not comfortable living by themselves will often have difficulties in living with other people. Inconclusive endings often take place in connection with didactic therapies, under training conditions, i. e. in cases in which the client is likely to meet the therapist again in surroundings other than that of regular psychotherapy.

The term "inconclusive ending" as such, contains a rather negative connotation. On the other hand, the analysis of therapist behaviour is bound to yield a quality judgement. As psychotherapy is above all concerned with stories of relationships, an appropriate manner of inventing ways of successfully ending therapies seems to be by establishing a parallel with creative narratives. In and through language, we are in a position to invent the world, and to add to each story its own, particular ending.

Any spectator of a film assumes that it will have an ending. It may be surprising, boring, or may be a schmaltzy, happy ending, for which he has nevertheless secretly hoped – the one certainty is that it will have some ending. The charm of one of the most famous films in the history of cinema is said to be due to the fact that the actors did actually not know which ending the story was to take. Different versions were shot, and it was only after the shooting that they were told which of the various endings they had enacted was the "real" one. Although there existed a scenario for a stage version (entitled "Everybody Comes to Rick's", by Murray Burnett and Joan Alison), the ending of the film version was for a long time deliberately clouded in ambiguity. I am obviously not talking about Jens Jorgen Thorsen's "Stille dage i Clichy" ("Quiet Days in Clichy"), where many a bet might be lost too, as to the ending of the story, but of course about "Casablanca". Whatever we may think about the film, it undeniably owes its immense impact to a combination of pathos, serenity, irony, sense of justice, promotion of freedom, and humour. It was only in Woody Allen's superb parody, "Play it again, Sam", that the ending (a generous renunciation inspired by love) found a comparable artistic expression, heightened still by a subtle sense of tragicomedy. The relationship stories we are confronted with in our daily therapy sessions often have endings which are simply trivial; yet they are taken more seriously than certain film endings because they correspond to the feelings of the clients.

Inconclusive endings may be compared to TV serials. The hero of the story has all the qualities of the scriptwriter, lives his story and goes through it all under supervision, as it were. It does not matter how the story ends, there will always be a possibility to continue it under another title. It may be about a secret service agent who uses his licence on behalf of Her Majesty, or a caring mother who manages both to bring up her children and to make a career despite the difficulties of everyday life. We may even be transferred, in a genuine anticipation of the future, to the past from where it is possible to create the future, etc. Serials are fond of clichés, and the range of possibilities for continuation is almost unlimited. Both clients as well as trainee therapists, in their keenness for continuation, much resemble the heroes of serials. They stop without really stopping, so leaving it possible to continue later on. Unless the therapist doubts his own capacities – but which therapist would easily admit to that? – there will more often than not be a possibility to continue.

The successful ending of a therapy is much like the successful ending of a life. It can probably only be imagined the way one imagines the smile of the Mona Lisa: eloquent, profound, yet unfathomable. There is no relevance in the countless reinterpretations of its meaning; the meaning has to be totally reconstructed. It is this capturing of "real presence", as the cultural philosopher George Steiner put it in his opening address of this year's Salzburg Festival (1994), which psychotherapists ought to make their clients experience during their sessions.

The ending of a story equals the ending of a relationship. Taking inspiration from Bruner, Toukmanian and Rennie (1992) distinguish between two currents within psychotherapy process research: a "paradigmatic" and a "narrative" approach. In my opinion, this distinction does not only make perfect sense, it has also turned out to be extremely helpful in my reflection on the final stages of therapies.

The concept of "real presence" ought to make psychotherapists aware of a phenomenon worth discovering. In the course of the treatment, clients make experiences, they learn new things, they evolve. The story of the ending of a therapy would consequently have to be told in such a way that it never comes to an end or, in other words, that it represents the end, an end though which contains the germ of a new beginning.

I am looking for a way out. As I prefer the narrative model to the paradigmatic one, let me concentrate on the masters of narrativity, and take the writers as guides for my reflection on the ending of a story. How do they consider the ending of a story? The lesson the old masters of poetry teach us is no matter whether the aim is catharsis, chastening, enlightened understanding, integration into one's consciousness, homeostatic flux or a dramatic finale, there is only one inevitable truth: by the end, you must come to an end.

In more recent times we can find endings with similar intentions: the happy ending; the drama with the climactic moment of terror; the gentle fading away, undulating like waves; the interruption; and – for the generation that has come to appreciate this new æsthetic taught by Umberto Eco – the open work of art. Film, drama, and novels offer us a great diversity of the most amazing endings.

Apparently, the only thing we can know for sure is that there are no given rules on how to end a story. All in all, we cannot expect any further concrete or even technical guidelines on such specific situations as the various forms of ending a psychotherapy. After all, there is no straightforward rule for the teaching of psychotherapy, either. Generally speaking, we ought to be suspicious of any exercise promising to convey to trainees technical skills or concrete procedures for the ending of a therapy. This is why, in the following, I would like to make a few remarks on fundamental problems relating to the ending of therapies.

The close, confidential relationship between the client and the therapist is not only a prerequisite for a discussion embarking on the client's "problems", but is in itself the very element that supports the healing process. (Cf. Pawlowsky: Wie heilt der Personenzentrierte Ansatz? (What is the healing element in the person–centred approach?) 1992; Swildens 1992; Rogers 1973). Some authors (Truax– Carkhuff, 1951; Barrett– Lennard, 1958; Speierer, 1993; Tscheulin, 1994) have tried in various ways to describe the success of therapy in terms of measurable changes. In this paper, I am not so much interested in changes that can be proved empirically, nor in the client's prolonged good feeling towards his capacity thereafter to deal more successfully with his problems. My question aims right at the fundamental problem in connection with the ending of a psychotherapy: What must happen for the guiding and supervising presence of the therapist to lose its character of necessity for the client and become a simple presence? How can the therapist be discharged from his freely– contracted engagement to be at the client's disposal. In other words, how therapy can come to an end. The (temporarily limited) independence must be restored to the client. This will be painful. The client must recover the authorship of his story, then he will again be in a position to write his own history or, better still, to control his own destiny.

The narration of the ending of narratives. If Education is said to be a life– long process, which in the case of self– education is bound to be a continuous activity, this must be considered a distinctive feature separating Education and Psychotherapy.

It is in the nature of psychotherapy that the treatment will have an end. The psychotherapist's aim is not to be a companion and sympathetic listener to the client throughout his entire life. Psychotherapy needs to have an end. The end of a psychotherapy is the ending of this concrete relationship between client and therapist.

Let me postulate psychotherapy as being a narrative process, a therapeutic dialogue involving both, therapist and client, though each with a different degree of responsibility. I tell a story therefore I am. This is the credo of psychotherapy (Stipsits, 1994). By listening, I encourage your story to develop, says the psychotherapist to the client. As I tell the story, I become aware that I can talk about things in a way different from that I used to. In the process of telling, I can remould the story. Together with my companion, the therapist, I can deconstruct it, says the client. Psychotherapy uses the medium of language, and is quite basically dependent on language. If we think of psychotherapy as a local narrative, opposing the great narratives of truth and legitimation with their claim for unlimited, universal validity, it is essentially the psychotherapist's task to supervise and accompany these individual, finite stories. A successful psychotherapy is one which succeeds – together with the client – in coming to a proper end.

The era of great narratives has come to an end. I will make mine this postulation by Lyotard (1986) and claim it to be true of psychotherapy as well. Once again we are talking of endings. Although the philosophers of post–modernism (for example Derrida, with his "Apocalypse not now") give us an ironical warning not to indulge too readily in this feeling of the end of time, to confront the end has something of a morbid charm. The postulation says that there cannot be any reasons justifying a belief in a development that goes essentially towards creating a better world. This way of reasoning is in direct contradiction to the idea of growth, as formulated by Rogers. Personal growth is a central feature underlying the person–centred approach considered as a great narrative. Such views can no longer be maintained, neither in the history of the individual, nor in that of mankind as a whole. There are no rules of behaviour generally applicable to any given situation. Seen from a paradigmatic point of view, the idea of personal growth implies an image of the client as a plant which, by the help of the therapist, is brought to full development. If, on the other hand, person–centred psychotherapy is considered within a narrative context, it assumes the quality of an event narrated by a person embedded in a specific historical context, capable of making judgements relating to his or her own narrative. This is a fine problem we have inherited from Rogers and his inclination to flirt with the various scientific traditions of his time. If self– determination is to be possible – and for me and a number of others, such as Wijngarden and Pfeiffer, this is one of the central categories of person–centred psychotherapy – then there does exist a choice between Good and Evil. A prerequisite for this is freedom; at least in the sense of the freedom to choose from among a number of alternatives.

The implications of this for psychotherapy are that in our profession we cannot rely on general rules of conduct. For each specific situation within a unique therapist / client relationship, we must – before taking any steps – carefully consider our motives leading up to a certain action, and the consequences it may have. Respecting Roger's basic conditions, the therapist attempts to establish a unique, personal bond with the client. As it was the client who, by consulting the therapist, autonomously decided to embark upon a psychotherapy, it must also be left to the client to decide when it should end. To live alone again is one of the things the client has to learn during psychotherapy. The assistance of the therapist is designed to help him over the crisis. The client's long–term objective is to be once more free and independent of the therapist. Psychotherapy principally aims at unlimited independence and autonomy, which – if limited at all – ought to be so only by willingly engaged relationships to another person.

Narratively speaking , psychotherapy might even be considered as an initiation into the art of dying. Taken in so comprehensive a manner, the task of psychotherapy may no longer be distinguishable from the classical task of education, as described by Seneca. These questions do have some bearing on the definition of local narratives in psychotherapy. Over and over again we come across these existential situations of human life that in some way or other call for a specific, personal response, and which have become the great issues of psychotherapy.

A problem that arises sooner or later in psychotherapy is that of taking leave. In different degrees, this problem may be observed in every kind of psychotherapy. If person–centred psychotherapy is based to such an extent on the relationship between therapist and client, as Rogers suggests, the beginning and development of this relationship is of great importance. It's trial is then the degree of success in which two people who appreciate each other can leave one another. The Japanese tradition of the tea ceremony shows us what mastership in the art of leave–taking other cultures have developed. Condensed in a single gesture incorporating all the importance of a departure, the ceremony is acted out in a way implying the utmost degree of intensity and intimacy. It has nothing of a furtive encounter; it stands for an embrace, with style and dignity. Self–centredness vanishes; there is no place for a self, nor for any kind of self–assertion. It symbolises a service to a loved person. Therapy is such an intricate term, which here reveals a facet containing the notion of serving in its most simplistic meaning. Purely positivist research has no means of grasping this mutual relation between therapist and client. Something profound happens, which is partly beyond our comprehension. The therapeutic relation may be seen as a source of energy, encouraging us to try old things afresh, rather than search for a completely new beginning.

If a therapeutic relationship is based on confidence, acceptance of each other, and honesty, then love may be a healing force (cf. Pawlowsky, 1992; Tscheulin, 1994). In this case, psychotherapy is concerned with a matter which once, in a description of the work of the Austrian author Evelyn Schlag, was called "the initiation into the most difficult thing in life: to give love and to take leave".

Psychotherapy as a narrative process? Yes, if attention is paid to the narrative. This means that I would have to try to tell the ending in a new manner. I would have to start out anew with the problem. In this case, that which I have told so far would not have been in vain. It would rather be subject to a constant re–evaluation, and it might serve as a new beginning for the story of the end. What I know of a story would not have to be re–told, but adapted and provided with new meaning. I tell stories therefore I am. While telling, I change a few things, telling thus what things will have been like. Failure of course constantly endangers the project, but we live in the hope of success. It would perhaps not be too bad an ending for a person–centred psychotherapy if it succeeded in giving rise to a new beginning.

Finally, let there be no résumé; no summary about the ending of a story. Starting out with a few examples taken from the literature on psychotherapy, I have endeavoured to draw a parallel with narrative literature in general. The question we must ask ourselves is this: How are we to proceed so as to come to a harmonious ending? The end is when it is over. This sentence, worthy of Karl Valentin, one of the world's greatest comedians (or philosophers, if you like) ends my story of the ending of stories.

REFERENCES:

Bozarth, J. *The essence of client–centered therapy*. In: Lietaer, Rombauts, Van Balen. Leuven 1990, p. 59. Also in: Stipsits/Hutterer (Hsg.) Perspektiven Rogerianischer Psychotherapie. Wien: WUV.

Frenzel, P. (1991). *Selbsterfahrung als Selbsterfindung*. Stuttgart: Roederer.

Grawe, (1993). *Wirksamkeit von Psychotherapie*. Bern.

Mearns, D. & Thorne, B. (1988). *Person– centred Counselling in Action*. London: Sage Publ.

Pawlowsky, G. (1992). *Wie heilt der Personenzentrierte Ansatz?*

Rogers, C. R. (1942/1973). *Counseling and Psychotherapy*. Boston: Houghton Mifflin.

Schlag, E. (1992). *Der Schnabelberg*. Frankfurt.

Shlien, J. M. (1987). *A Countertheory of Transference*. In: Person Centered Review. London: Sage Publ.

Stipsits, R. (1994). Selbst-verständlich? In: Keil, W.W. et al. (Ed.): Selbst–Verständnis. Beiträge zur Theorie der Klientenzentrierten Psychotherapie Bergheim bei Salzburg: Mackinger.

Stipsits, Reinhold and Hutterer, R. (Eds.) (1992). Perspektiven Rogerianischer Psychotherapie. Kritik und Würdigung zu ihrem 50jährigen Bestehen, Wien:WUV Universitätsverlag.

Swildens, H. (1991). *Prozeßorientierte Gesprächspsychotherapie*. Cologne: GwG.

Toukmanian, S. G. & Rennie, D. L. (eds.), (1992). *Psychotherapy Process Research*. Paradigmatic and Narrative Approaches. London: Sage Publ.

Tscheulin, D. (1994). *Heilung aus Liebe?* Würzburg: (unpublished manuscript).

---

[1] The author's appreciation goes to Josef Dallinger for the translation of the manuscript.

Severe Disturbances

Dealing with Schizophrenia — A Person–Centered Approach Providing Care to Long–Term Patients in a Supported Residential Service in Vienna

GERLINDE BERGHOFER

VIENNA

ABSTRACT

After giving a brief overview of the model of supportive housing for psychiatric out–patients in Vienna, I will discuss the significance of diagnosis in treating schizophrenic people. Ideally this diagnosis involves a joint attempt of therapist and patient to understand and accept the patient better. Such a diagnosis leads *towards* the person and not away from him. I will summarize some core ideas of the person–centered approach to therapy with schizophrenic patients. In presenting my therapy with a residential patient, I will concentrate on selected aspects of the therapeutic relationship with schizophrenic patients. These aspects include the experiencing of closeness and distance, the establishing of boundaries, the handling of psychotic symptoms, the working at the patient's self–image, and the patient's "existential question". The most important element in psychotherapy with schizophrenic patients is the establishment and the maintenance of a reliable interpersonal relationship for an extended period of time.

INTRODUCTION

While attending to schizophrenic patients in a supportive group home, I encountered much pain and despair. There were also moments, however, when I could laugh wholeheartedly with these people whose reality often seems so very foreign to us. My article will begin with this joyful aspect of such a helping relationship. I thereby want to show that it is also possible to share light–hearted moments when working with schizophrenics, too, as the following two episodes illustrate.

One Wednesday afternoon, the usual resident group meeting in the group home took place. This time, we discussed one participant's specific fear of encountering the devil or of being pursued by the devil in the group home. All participants tried hard to alleviate the narrator's fear. Suddenly one of them had a brilliant idea: "In the group home, one could set up a galvanic, electronic device measuring the devil's vibrations thereby announcing the devil's approach!" This solution seemed so absurd even to the concerned that we all laughed heartily together.

Another patient approached with a troubled face to inform me in a concerned voice: "I once again hear voices." To my question, what these voices were saying, he replied seriously after a short pause, "They remain silent!"

I have begun with the amusing aspects of the therapeutic relationship since my humor and optimism repeatedly helped me to deal confidently with my patients' complaints and regressions. These attributes also aided me in accompanying my patients over a long time without expecting changes.

SUPPORTIVE HOUSING IN THE "PSYCHOSOZIALER DIENST WIEN" (PSYCHOSOCIAL SERVICES VIENNA)

In Vienna the psychiatric care of out–patients is provided by the "Kuratorium für Psychosoziale Dienste", the community mental health service of Vienna. At a total of eight regional *out-patient clinics* physicians take care of the patients' medical needs while social workers support their practical and legal needs. Each of these clinics is connected to a day clinic and a group home. The *day clinics* provide the patients with structured programs which usually intend to prepare the patients for an occupational re–entry. In the *group homes* the actual supportive housing takes place. The goal of the supportive housing is to allow the patient slowly to achieve greater self–reliance, which will then allow him to live alone.

Most of the group home's occupants are long–term schizophrenic patients. Therapeutic work with them centers around the facilitation of social interaction and the learning of practical skills necessary for daily life, which the occupants have forgotten due to their repeated hospitalization. The chronically schizophrenic patient tends strongly to social withdrawal and isolation. Here he directly takes part in the present and shared living situation – a very difficult task which is therapeutic in itself. The group home is a therapeutic community. Living together and dealing with each other is strongly therapeutic. As Uchtenhagen (1980, p. 237) summarizes his experience with psychiatric patients: "Living conditions have a major impact on the course of illness and treatment in psychiatric patients."

The group homes of the "Psychosozialer Dienst" allow for a possible transition from the institutional care in a psychiatric hospital to the independent life in one's own apartment. Supportive housing has proven successful in preparing patients' social re–integration (Eikelmann & Reker, 1991; Macmillan & Hornblow, 1992). For this reason Hogan and Carling (1992, p. 216) demand that "All people with long–term mental illness should be given the option to live in ... settings that maximize their integration into community activities and their ability to function independently."

What then is the actual supportive element of supportive housing? It consists of exposing the patient only to that with which he can cope, and of avoiding both overstraining and overprotecting him. It further includes a combination of exposing the patient to reality and allowing him the freedom to take small experimental steps. Sandal, Hawley and Gordon (1975, p. 617) emphasize that the support offered in such residential programs should be flexibly adapted to the changing needs of their occupants. The authors report that in such a setting many occupants were able to use their experiences as a "starting point to personal growth and autonomy".

SUPPORTIVE HOUSING AND PSYCHOTHERAPY: FRAMEWORK AND SETTING

Most patients entering the group home have a long history of treatment which usually includes repeated psychiatric hospitalization. Between their stays in psychiatric hospitals they are attended to in the above–mentioned social psychiatric out–patient clinics. About two thirds of the patients move directly from a psychiatric hospital to the group home. By the time the patient enters the group home, the team has usually known the patient for a long time already.

The framework for psychotherapy with schizophrenic patients in the group home is unusual. Rather than having the patients come to me, I went to see them in their apartments every day. Not all my patients appreciated my daily visits. It often took a long time before they were willing to accept my offer of a relationship and not to see me as an intruder checking up on them.

Let me give you an example for the often unusual ways of establishing a therapeutic relationship with patients in the group home. One of our occupants, a 32–year old man, had slept in trash–cans before he came to us. During that time he had survived on stolen or begged–for food. At the beginning, he completely refused my visits, felt supervised and wanted to be left alone. Only after I had understood and accepted that he considered his room very private and after I had suggested taking walks for our meetings, did he begin to trust me and to talk about himself.

One aspect of the framework of my therapy in the group home was my ability to adjust the frequency of my contact with the patient to his needs. Accordingly, my quick and intensive support during especially difficult times could sometimes prevent threatening re–hospitalization.

One problem which commonly occurs in the psychotherapeutic treatment of schizophrenic patients is neuroleptics. Today, drug therapy of schizophrenic patients is generally recognized as necessary. Also when patients live in the group home, they continue drug therapy at the associated out–patient clinic. In fact, regular appointments with an appointed psychiatrist at the out–patient clinic and the continued use of the prescribed neuroleptic medicineare formal conditions for the admission to the group home. In practice, however, the occupants of the group home often do not continue to meet these conditions. Schizophrenic patients often refuse to take drugs. In their psychotherapeutic treatment they often raise questions and complaints about their medication. There are very different reasons for their complaints. For psychotherapeutic intervention, it is important to respond to these different reasons.

If a patient refuses to take his drugs because of the unpleasant side–effects, I refer him to the responsible physician. I encourage him to discuss his questions and complaints with his physician directly. I consider it very important not to convey this referral as a rejection. Therapeutically, I assist the patient in clarifying his relationship and his attitudes toward his physician.

Besides rejecting their drugs because of side–effects, patients also have other reasons for refusing to take them. For example, one of the group home's patients associated his bi–weekly injections with the beatings which as a child he had gotten from his father. "My father used to cripple me – today I am still beaten with injections". Only the realization and acceptance of this connection allowed the patient and me to understand his refusal. The patient explaining his position to his physician lead to an unproblematic change to oral medication.

THE SIGNIFICANCE OFDIAGNOSIS IN TREATING SCHIZOPHRENIC PATIENTS

A diagnosis is considered a prerequisite for predicting the course of an illness. However, it is precisely this function that a diagnosis cannot fulfil in the case of a schizophrenic patient.

For if one considers the causes and course of schizophrenia,one reaches anything but clear conclusions. Concepts as broad as the aetiological Vulnerability–Stress–Model (Zubin, 1977; Nüchterlein & Dawson, 1984) and a careful terminology ("group of schizophrenias") are reactions to the contradictions and multiplemanifestations of "schizophrenia". As Pao states, "No two schizophrenics are alike."

Referring to the different course of the illness, Strauss states that no clear prognosis is permitted:

> At the two year follow–up, a woman who was still very delusional was functioning socially in a way better than many 'normal' people. She was working, looking after her child, and taking care of her house on a relatively limited income, all while frequently

being psychotic. Another patient I saw, a woman whose symptoms had essentially disappeared, was sitting in a darkened room in her house, and had not worked or had contact with friends for most of the time since I had seen her at the initial evaluation two years before. Thus, there did not seem to be one outcome, but many.

He concludes that "For schizophrenia therefore, it appeared that diagnosis did not equal prognosis..., and that many interacting processes were involved including normal and abnormal functioning" (Strauss, 1992, pp. 20 f.).

What position can the diagnosis then have in the therapy of schizophrenic patients? Is the diagnosis entirely superfluous?

Especially in his early works Roger criticises the diagnosing of clients. He regards doing so as not only superfluous to the therapy, but even detrimental (Rogers, 1951). For diagnosing leads to placing the responsibility for the comprehension and improvement entirely in the hands of the therapist. The relationship therapist–patient is transformed to a relationship between expert and observed object. Such a relationship, however, renders an encounter between two persons impossible.

My own experiencein my work with psychiatric patients confirms this danger. Patients then become *derived* persons, characterized by their symptoms, deviating behavior patterns, and deficient social relationships. The individual, the active and influencing person, is lost. The thinking about the patient more than with the patient (Reisel, 1992, p. 156) leads to the search for a confirmation of the diagnosis and away from the question with *whom* I am establishing a relationship. A diagnostic exploration of the schizophrenic patient hinders the establishment of an authentic relationship. Questions such as can he sleep well, does he take his medication regularly, does he feels pursued, does he experience a change in his environment, and so on, create much distance and do little to facilitate the relationship. Moreover the patient forms the impression that he is being cross–examined by an expert who knows much better than he what is wrong with him. The therapist rather than the patient is responsible for the situation.

Later Rogers expands his position about diagnosing. He now believes that the diagnostic information is not important for the client, but may be helpful to the therapist. Sometimes such information provides security for the therapist so that he can encounter the client with real empathy and acceptance (Rogers, 1957). Binder and Binder (1991, p. 34) also accentuate this aspect of the diagnosis. According to them, the therapist can accept some of his client's bizarre behavior better through the diagnosis. A diagnosis emerges as if by itself, especially when the therapist deals with schizophrenic patients.

Cain (1989, p. 176), too, does not necessarily consider a diagnosis a disadvantage. For him diagnosing does *not* mean simultaneously depriving the patient of his independence and rights. In his Collaborative Model of diagnosis he places a substantial and active responsibility for the diagnosis on the patient. In this model the therapist is only an assistant in the patient's process of self–diagnosis. Diagnosis and therapy are inseparable. Here diagnosis is a search for "Knowing the Self".

My knowledge about schizophrenic experiencing can help me adjust to the individual patient in the joint search for "Knowing the Self". My knowledge about schizophrenia then allows me a freer access to the other. I will then be less scared by his odd behavior and I will be able to understand his sporadic handling of closeness and distance better. I will also be able to accept the patient's regressions and therapeutic stagnation more easily. Schmid, too, states that a "differential classification of suffering" is justified and even necessary when it leads to a greater understanding for the patient and to higher empathy and congruence by the therapist (Schmid, 1992, p. 112). On the other hand, ignorance and a lack of experience may lead to therapeutic mistakes and breaks in the relationship.

Diagnosis, therefore, is neither final nor unalterable. In the best case, it is rather an attempt to understand and accept the patient's behavior better. Such a comprehension of the diagnosis never leads to one–sided therapeutic instructions. "Knowledge of specific deficits of schizo-phrenic patients serve ... not as an explanation of the illness or instruction, but rather as aid for comprehension and action" (Binder & Binder, 1991, p. 80).

FROM DIAGNOSIS TO PERSON: SCHIZOPHRENIA AND PERSON–CENTERED PSYCHOTHERAPY

Many of the schizophrenic patients I encountered in my work in the group home had lost their sense of being a person. Shaped by their long institutionalization, by the loss of their work as well as by the decline of their social contact and acceptance, they consider themselves more as an illness or a fragmented being than as a person (see Strauss, 1992, p. 22). Almost all schizo-phrenic patients have a deep tendency to devalue themselves, to feel unimportant and exposed. Rogers deals with the schizophrenic patients' self–devaluation. He describes how their self–awareness includes the possibility of becoming crazy again at any time. They perceive themsel-ves as maladjusted and dependent people in whom there are hidden energies beyond their con-trol. This self–image, however, cannot foster self–confidence (Rogers, 1959, p. 55).

For people with such a fragmented self, the person–centered approach is suitable as this ap-proach focuses on the healing of the self in the therapeutic process. Pawlowsky (1992, p. 128) states:

> The person–centered approach heals through the strengthening of the client's self, not through the solving of a concrete problem... The client's self becomes stronger, if it suc-ceeds in dissolving elements that have so far been integrated but distorted, and if it can integrate so far disintegrated organismic experiences into a now widened self–concept.

Empirical studies about the effectiveness of the person–centered approach with schizophrenic people are rare. The best known and most comprehensive has been done by Rogers, Gendlin, Kiesler and Truax (1967), the Wisconsin Research Study. Rogers' Team worked with chroni-cally hospitalized, extremely inaccessible patients. The study shows that schizophrenic people hardly perceive therapeutic conditions (empathy, congruence and positive regard), regardless of the extent to which these conditions are actually present. These therapeutic conditions also did not lead to *significant* therapeutic progress. Wherever there was however some progress, this progress was dependent on these relationship variables. The number of patients released from hospital and those having to be re–admitted was slightly lower in the therapy group than in the untreated control–group. "At the end of the period the therapy group were less vul-nerable, psychologically, and more capable of facing themselves and their environment than were the control group" (Rogers, 1967, p. 81).

More recent person–centered ideas about psychotherapeutic work with schizophrenic persons have been developed by Prouty, Binder and Binder, and Swildens.

Prouty's pre–therapy method describes an impressive way of establishing contact with chroni-cally hospitalized schizophrenic patients (Prouty, 1976 , 1988, 1990). With this method he establishes contact with severely fragmented people who are otherwise considered unable to establish contact and unsuited for psychotherapy. Prouty succeeded in building up contact with entirely autistic and severely hallucinating schizophrenic patients. Prouty's interventions direct themselves towards:

• the client's immediate environment (*situational reflections*): "You're looking out of the window right now",

• the client's facial expression and the feeling it expresses(*facial reflections*): "your eyes look discouraged",

• the repetition of the client's utterances (*word for word reflections*). In this case the therapist repeats, for example, the intelligible parts of a fragmented sentence full of neologisms,

• *body reflections*, "you're sitting there completely bent–over", and

• *reiterative reflections*. Here the therapist re–uses interventions which have previously facilitated the client's experiencing and expressing himself.

Binder and Binder (1991, p. 347) believe that person–centered psychotherapy with schizophrenic patients does not require modification of the therapist's basic attitudes. They however emphasize however that only a penetrating understanding of the impairment's structure allows for a sound therapeutic procedure. They point to four issues which constitute important starting points for the therapeutic understanding of schizophrenic patients. These are:

• The *closeness–distance issue*. This includes for example the desire for a symbiotic union, which is contrasted by a fear of fusion and loss of autonomy.

• The *lack of ego boundaries*. This becomes evident in the permeable border between the schizophrenic patient and other people or his own experiencing.

• The *power–impotence issue*. For schizophrenic people it is difficult to deal with their own and other people's power. They are noticeably sensitive toward power, dominance, and competition.

• *Hierarchization deficit and time experience*. The perceptions of schizophrenic patients often lack hierarchic order, according to subjective importance, for example. As a result, the patient is overwhelmed by internal and external impressions. Furthermore, schizophrenic patients often experience the present as isolated from the past and the future (Binder & Binder, 1991, pp. 160 ff.).

Swildens describes how the patient's longing for help changes during the course oftherapy. Swildens differentiates among four phases.

• During the *pre–motivating phase* it is important to develop the patient's necessary trust in the therapy and the therapist.

• During the *symptom phase* (also called *acting out phase*) it is necessary to pay attention to the also protective function of the patient's symptoms.

• Only during the *verbal phase* can the feelings previously represented by the symptoms begin to be discussed .

• During the *existential phase*, which is the most significant phase in the treatment of schizophrenic patients, the question of a meaningful life with the illness is addressed (Swildens, 1991, pp. 188 ff.).

One should certainly not expect psychotherapy to lead to a complete healing and recovery of the self in chronic schizophrenic patients. My own therapeutic goal in the group home was to enable the schizophrenic patient to remain in the community and to lead a relatively independent and satisfying life.

ESTABLISHING THE RELATIONSHIP:
CENTRAL POINT OF PSYCHOTHERAPY WITH SCHIZOPHRENIC PERSONS

Therapy with schizophrenic persons focuses less on the self–exploration of the patient than on the establishment of a reliable and trusting relationship. For the therapist, however, initiating the relationship with the schizophrenic patient is often rendered difficult because of the patient's recurrent long silences or floods of bizarre words (Rogers, 1983, pp. 198 ff.). On the other hand, for the schizophrenic patient the therapists' offer of a relationship is hard to accept because this offer frequently contrasts the patient's existing experience. "The more the therapeutic relationship offered is in contrast to the former experience of the client, the more difficult it is for the client to realize this relationship emotionally...", Binder and Binder (1979, p. 202) state.

The therapist's offer of a relationship in his therapeutic work with schizophrenic patients, as anywhere, is based on the therapist's empathic understanding, positive regard, and genuineness. However, it is essential to know that merely offering these conditions does not imply that they are at all perceived by the patient. "... Schizophrenic patients tended to perceive a relatively low level of these conditions as existing in the relationship, and only slowly over therapy did they perceive somewhat more of these therapist attitudes" (Rogers, 1967, p. 75). In addition, in the work with schizophrenic patients, the prerequisite for the therapeutic relationship, psychological contact, often has to be established first. Frank and Gunderson (1989) report how long it can take to establish such contact.

The weight assigned to the therapist's attitudes in the relationship with the schizophrenic patient is special. Among the "classical" therapist attitudes (empathy, positive regard, genuineness), Rogers (1983, p. 199) directs his main attention to the genuineness of the therapist. Schizophrenics are particularly sensitive in regard to the discrepancies between the words, gestures, and feelings of others. In order to be able to trust, they must perceive clearly that the therapist is present in a real way and that he is openly genuine.

In the group home, too, I often felt that my transparency about my own feelings and expectations helped reduce the distance between my patients and me which had been there at the beginning. My openness about myself seemed to help the patients move from their initial distrust to more security in our relationship. I have experienced that – next to this warm openness – my perceptibly showing interest and my actively approaching the others were the most efficient ways of making contact. "Summarizing the perceptions and results of different schools leads one to the conclusion that these schools concur that the most important quality of the therapist may be seen in his strong and persisting interest, which aims at and maintains the therapeutic relationship with the patient", writes Krull (1987, p. 61).

THERAPY IN THE GROUP HOME: MR. P.

My therapy with Mr. P., a 28–year old resident of the group home, was terminated by his referral back to the psychiatric hospital. During the two and a half years of our contact, I learned much about the therapeutic relationship with schizophrenic people. One of its constant characteristics moved me time and again: Mr. P.'s struggle between his strong desire for contact and his equally strong fear of it.

Mr. P.'s biography, full of losses of relationships, helps to understand his caution and fear of new persons in his life. He is one year old when his parents get divorced. After the divorce, he lives with his grandmother since his mother rejects him and does not look after him. His mother, in psychiatric treatment herself, commits suicide when he is six years old. One year later, his grandmother dies, too. Mr. P. now moves in with his father, who has become a stranger to him since they have had no common contact in the meantime.

Mr. P. loses his first job as a technical designer after one and a half years. As a result of the loss of his job, he withdraws completely and often stays in bed for days. Briefly thereafter, his father kicks him out of the apartment because of Mr. P.'s "laziness". From now on Mr. P. commutes between the psychiatric hospital and various group homes.

At the age of 23, Mr. P. gets to know a female fellow patient. Their relationship stabilizes his life for a brief period. They move into a shared apartment, and Mr. P. finds a protected workplace in a joiner's workshop. When their son is two years old, Mr. P. and his partner increasingly have conflicts. He becomes burdened too much by the situation, loses his position at work, and again has to be hospitalized several times. His girlfriend does not want to live with him any more and kicks him out of the apartment. After one hospitalization Mr. P. moves into our group home. In the meantime he has turned 28.

When I first met Mr. P., he was very restless despite the strong neuroleptic medication he had to take at that time. It was difficult for him to sit still on his chair. During our first meetings, I could hardly follow his erratic thoughts. Since a longer contact seemed to strain him, all our meetings were initially only very brief.

It was important to Mr. P. that our meetings always took place at the same time and in the same room. It seemed that this firm structure made him experience our contacts as reliable and predictable.This reliability laid an important foundation for the development of a trusting relationship.Knowing that I would come again tomorrow and the day after tomorrow, too, provided Mr. P. with a feeling of security. Binder and Binder (1991, p. 69) emphasize the importance of continuity in the relationship with schizophrenic patients. They call for a setting which "... allows for the experience of continuity through reliable rituals and thus can become familiar."

It took almost three months until Mr. P.'s trust in me had grown noticeably and until he seemed more relaxed during our encounters. The contents of our discussions now focused more on Mr. P.'s present life situation. More and more segments of his past also came up. In the account of his experiences of ostracism, uprooting, and the loss of close people, the insult of his father's rejection became especially pronounced.

During the first year of his life in the group home, Mr. P. met his ex–girlfriend and his son only on weekends. In the beginning he was very afraid to become gradually estranged from his son. The separation from his girlfriend had triggered a strong inner strife in Mr. P. On the one hand, he felt relieved because they had never really understood each other, on the other he was worried by the resulting distance. He felt that his only "outside" contact was at stake.

After his girlfriend had entered a relationship with another man, Mr. P.'s hopes for the future collapsed. He now felt completely rejected, did not see any meaning in his life, and did not have any hope any more ever to get better. He now was only allowed to visit his son very rarely. News that his girlfriend's new partner wanted to adopt his son triggered new despair. Mr. P. felt that his contacts with his son would now break off entirely.

The final break with his girlfriend led to his complete withdrawal from his other social contacts. Mr. P. distanced himself from his fellow patients in the group home. In the day clinic, he felt excluded by the others. They would reject him and not take him seriously. Finally, he broke off his visits to the day clinic. Mr. P. now only rarely kept his appointments with his physician and hardly took his medicine. His home situation deteriorated visibly. He needed more and more support to keep his apartment clean and to groom himself. At that time I had known Mr. P for two and a half years. After my summer holidays I found him completely confused and dishevelled in his apartment. He was just about to seal his ears with glue in order to escape the voices that pursued him. A little later Mr. P. was referred back to the psychiatric hospital because a more intensive and continuous care had become necessary.

My therapy goal with Mr. P., his independent life outside psychiatric institutions, had not been achieved. During the time of our common work, his development was characterized by the constant change between the achievement of new abilities, stagnation, and the loss of recently won competencies and possibilites. The conception of my therapeutic mission changed during this time. I no longer tried to change him but rather to accompany him and to be there as a reliable support.

In my subsequent discussion about my therapy with Mr. P., I want to take up some aspects of the work with schizophrenic people that seem essential to me: dealing with closeness and distance, establishing boundaries, responding to psychotic symptoms, working on the patient's self–image, and Swildens' "existential question".

Dealing with Closeness and Distance

Especially in our early meetings, I felt that our encounters were simultaneously important and burdening to Mr. P. To me, it was important to find a balance between expressing my interest and considering his need for distance. This consideration was not alwayseasy. I vividly remember my frustration when, after a number of very intensive encounters, Mr. P. closed himself markedly. It was almost as if there had been no previous closeness at all. In order not to feel hurt or rejected it was important for me to learn to understand and accept better his changing need for closeness and distance (see Binder & Binder, 1991, p. 169). The therapist should enable the patient to experience the latter's frequent change between a need for closeness and distance without consequences to the relationship (Binder & Binder, 1991, p. 175).

Swildens describes another important aspect of the handling of closeness and distance. He writes that the establishment of a trusting relationship succeeds, "if the therapist succeeds in clarifying that there is nothing to be afraid of; that he will neither pull nor confront; that there will also be no magic involved, that he merely has to offer safe and accepting contact..." (Swildens, 1991, p. 197).

Defining Boundaries

The difficulties of schizophrenic patients to distance themselves from their environment and their own experience is often described as a consequence of identity diffusion or a lack of ego boundaries (see, for example, Binder & Binder, 1991, p. 197).Mr. P., too, often experienced the establishing of boundaries towards external events and other people as a problem.

Mr. P., for example, became friends with a fellow patient who repeatedly visited him in the group home. In our sessions Mr. P. described the extent to which he felt this contact to be a burden. He found it extremely difficult to establish boundaries in his relationship with this acquaintance. At the end, Mr. P. was so overburdened by these visits that he could only escape them by referring himself to a psychiatric hospital.

Mr. P.'s problems in establishing boundaries did not only appear outwardly, i.e. in his dealing with other people or specific events, but also internally his experience and his feelings could literally overwhelm him. For instance, Mr. P. once wanted to visit his girlfriend and his son without appointment but was not permitted into their apartment. During our next session he was still outraged: "I hate myself! I feel empty! Like a puppet which floats and can't do anything!" In this situation his self-hatred and feeling of emptiness seemed to overwhelm him entirely, and he seemed at the mercy of these feelings.

In Mr. P.'s therapy it was important to work out concrete possibilities of establishing boundaries for these overwhelming situations, such as a timely withdrawal to another room. Many authors (see, for example, Swildens, 1991, p. 213) see in the joint recognition and discussion of the circumstances which lead to psychotic experiencing an important part of therapy with schizophrenic patients.

Psychotic Symptoms

In Mr. P.'s case, psychotic symptoms often manifested themselves in an altered perception of his body. "I feel my nerves flow"; he agitatedly pointed to parts of his arm. "My backbone is getting stiff; here, I can't feel it any more!" While making these statements, Mr. P. continually checked whether I took his descriptions seriously and whether I believed them. Only after he had convinced himself that I took his experience and his fears seriously was he able to calm himself down. As a result, he could usually continue our conversation in a more intelligible manner.

The serious acceptance of the schizophrenic patient's psychotic experience is an important prerequisite for authentic contact in therapy. This acceptance does not mean that my reality corresponds to that of the patient. Rather it means that I can accept the reality of the other in the way it exists for him and that I can leave it unchanged with him.

For the therapist, the psychotic experience of the patient can however be very upsetting. Often the psychotic contents are completely foreign to the therapist's perception and experience. Their description can lead to great fear and insecurity in the relationship. What would it be like if voices suddenly commanded *me* to throw myself in front of the subway or to poison my family? What do *I* have to fear of a person who has such experiences?

Primarily the following two considerations have helped me deal with my own insecurities and initial fears when dealing with the patient's psychotic experience:

• Rather than empathically understanding the unrealistic content ("my brain is turning around"), it is important to stay with the associated, usually intelligible feeling(for example, despair or confusion) (see Binder & Binder, 1991, p. 107).

• The psychotic symptom is not only a derailment from reality. It can also be regarded as the simultaneous effort to prevent an even greater derailment from reality and from contact with the other (see Swildens, 1991, p. 200). Such a view of the psychotic symptom's meaning leads to respecting it as something meaningful. It then no longer needs to be attacked as meaningless or unnecessary. Thus Binder and Binder (1991, p. 297) conceive of paranoid delusions as efforts to control the environment in which "... no matter how distortedly ... the effort shows the patient's attempt to act towards the world and others."

Realistic Self-Image

In therapy with Mr. P., the development of responsibility for his own situation and of a self-image beyond over- and underestimation of his own capacities were important themes. Most of the time he did not see himself responsible for the problems in his life. He primarily held his father responsible for his desperate situation, and he considered the psychiatric system responsible for his ongoing suffering. In the discussion of his conflicts with his girl-friend, Mr. P. sometimes did recognize his own contributions, only to return soon to his belief that she was the cause of all his difficulties. Rogers describes the schizophrenic patient's tendency to externalize responsibility. He writes that even if a relationship is established and if the client comprehends something new about himself, it is still not likely that he will continue in this direction. It is more likely that the client will continue to externalize his responsibility by projecting it onto the environment (Rogers, 1983, p. 197).

In our conversations we also often dealt with a realistic perception of Mr. P.'s abilities. One day, for example, he talked about his intention to look for work in the free labor market although even his trip to the day clinic had become too threatening to him. Mr. P. seemed to have to defend himself against accepting a depressing reality through his unrealistic plans. More often, however, Mr. P. devalued his true actual abilities. After having successfully finished tasks, he discarded all recognition by others and pointed out the deficiencies in his work instead.

My very careful confrontations with my own perceptions prove helpful while working at responsibility and at a more realistic self–image with Mr. P. Doing this work, I confronted Mr. P. only after I had sensed that he would not experience my questioning of his protection as a threat and as a questioning of his self.

The "Existential Question"

The existential question (Swildens, 1991, pp. 205 ff.) – "what is the meaning of life with this illness? How can I continue life in these circumstances?" accompanied Mr. P., too,in our conversations. For long periods he did not see any hope for the future any more. Our therapeutic work then primarily consisted of our jointly carrying and tolerating his rage and aggression about his situation.

At these points of therapy it was crucial for Mr. P. to sense that our relationship would not get lost despite his overwhelming and negative feelings. I then perceived my task primarily as my being there for him perceptibly and constantly by listening and by thereby reassuring him that he was not left alone completely in his despair.

When Mr. P.'s anger was pointed directly at me or when he devalued our relationship as well, I sometimes found it difficult not to feel insulted. Rogers' consideration "If I had had the same background, the same circumstances, the same experiences, it would be inevitable in me, as it is in this client, that I would act in this fashion" (Rogers et al., 1967, p. 103) helped me stand Mr. P.'s aggressive rage and made it nevertheless possible for me to accept him warmly. Of course I did not always succeed in doing so. Whenever this happened, I preferred showing my insult and anger rather than putting up a professional facade and making true encounter impossible.

CONCLUSION

When dealing with schizophrenic people the therapist should not limit himself by his diagnostic reflections. The interpersonal relationship is and will remain the core of therapy, also in the case of the schizophrenic person. In the best case, diagnosis is a joint attempt to understand and accept the patient better. Such a diagnosis leads *towards* the person and not away from him.

For the therapist, a sound understanding of core aspects of the relationship with the schizophrenic person is important. These aspects include the patient's changing need for closeness and distance. The therapist also needs to truly accept the patient's psychotic experience. Psychotic symptoms can best be seen as the patient's distorted efforts to establish contact. Focusing on the feelings associated with the patient's psychotic experience often helps to understand these symptoms. Another important part of the therapy with the schizophrenic patient is the joint effort to establish boundaries for threatening external and internal events. The article also describes the cautious working at the patient's realistic self–image, and the supportive dealing with the patient's "existential question" about the meaning of life with the illness.

Providing care to schizophrenic patients in a supportive group home helps to adapt the therapeutic support offered to the individual patient's needs. In the helping relationship with the schizophrenic person, the therapist has to be willing and able to support the other's fragile self reliably and for a long period of time. The discussion of my therapy with Mr. P. shows that some circumstances (as the therapist's leaving for her holidays) make it difficult for one person alone to provide the necessary constancy of support. Only the joint offers of many supporting others can ensure the required continuity of support, thereby integrating the patient in a social network. The most important element in psychotherapy with schizophrenic patients is the active establishment and maintenance of a reliable interpersonal relationship for an extended period of time.

REFERENCES

Binder, U. & Binder, J. (1979). *Klientenzentrierte Psychotherapie bei schweren psychischen Störungen*. Frankfurt am Main: Fachbuchhandlung für Psychologie.

Binder, U. & Binder, J. (1991). *Studien zu einer störungsspezifischen klientenzentrierten Psychotherapie*. Eschborn: Dietmar Klotz.

Cain, D.J. (1989). *The client's role in diagnosis*. Three approaches. Person Centered Review, 4 (2), 171–182.

Eikelmann, B. & Reker, T. (1991). *A modern therapeutic approach for chronically mentally ill patients – results of a four year prospective study*. Acta Psychiatr Scand, 84, 357–363.

Frank, A.F. & Gunderson, J.G. (1990). *The role of the therapeutic alliance in the treatment of schizophrenia*. Arch Gen Psychiatry, 47, 228–236.

Hogan, M.F. & Carling, P.J. (1992). *Normal housing: a key element of a supported housing approach for people with psychiatric disabilities*. Community Mental Health Journal, 28, 215–226.

Krull, F. (1987). *Psychotherapie bei Schizophrenie – Theorie und Praxis der Einzelbehandlung. Eine Übersicht*. Fortschr. Neurol. Psychiat., 55, 54–67.

Macmillan, M. & Hornblow, A. (1992). *From hospital to community: a follow up of community placement of the long term mentally ill*. New Zealand Medical Journal, Sept., 348–350.

Nüchterlein, K. & Dawson, M.E. (1984). *A heuristic vulnerability/stress model of schizophrenic episodes*. Schizophrenia Bulletin, 10, 300–312.

Pao, P.N. (1979). *Schizophrenic disorders*. New York: International University Press.

Pawlowsky, G. (1992). *Die Heilung*. In Frenzel, P., Schmid, P.F. & Winkler, M. (Eds.), Handbuch der Personzentrierten Psychotherapie (pp. 127–136). Köln: Edition Humanistische Psychologie.

Prouty, G.F. (1976). *Pre–therapy, a method of treating pre–expressive psychotic and retarded patients*. Psychotherapy, Theory, Research and Practice, 13, 290–294.

Prouty, G.F. & Pietrzak, S. (1988). *The Pre–therapy method applied to persons experiencing hallucinatory images*. Person Centered Review, 3 (4), 426–441.

Prouty, G.F. (1990). *Pre–therapy: A theoretical evolution in the person–centered/experiential psychotherapy of schizophrenia and retardation*. In Lietaer, G. et al. (Eds.), Client–

centered and experiential therapy in the nineties (pp. 645–658). Löwen: Leuven University Press.

Reisel, B. (1992). *Die Diagnose.* In Frenzel, P., Schmid, P.F. & Winkler, M. (Eds.), Handbuch der Personzentrierten Psychotherapie (pp. 153–163). Köln: Edition der Humanistischen Psychologie.

Rogers, C.R. (1951). *Client–centered therapy. Its current practices, implications and theory.* New York: Houghton Mifflin. Quotation taken from: Rogers, C.R. (1983). Die klientenzentrierte Gesprächspsychotherapie. Frankfurt am Main: Fischer.

Rogers, C.R. (1957). *The necessary and sufficient conditions of therapeutic personality change.* Journal of Consulting Psychology, 21, 2, 95–103.

Rogers, C.R. (1959). *A theory of therapy, personality, and interpersonal relationships, as developed in the client–centered framework.* In Koch, S. (Ed.),Psychology. A study of science. Vol. III: Formulations of the person and the social contexts (pp.158–256). New York: McGraw–Hill. Quotation taken from: Rogers, C.R. (1991). Eine Theorie der Psychotherapie, der Persönlichkeit und der zwischenmenschlichen Beziehungen. Köln: GwG.

Rogers, C.R., Gendlin, E.T., Kiesler, D. & Truax, C.B. (1967), *The therapeutic relationship and its impact: A study of psychotherapy with schizophrenics.* Madison: University of Wisconsin Press.

Rogers, C.R. (1967). *The findings in brief.* In Rogers, C.R., Gendlin, E.T., Kiesler, D. & Truax, C.B. (Eds.), The therapeutic relationship and its impact: A study of psychotherapy with schizophrenics (pp. 73–93). Madison: University of Wisconsin Press.

Rogers, C.R. (1983). *Therapeut und Klient.* Frankfurt am Main: Fischer.

Sandall, H., Hawley, T.T. & Gordon, G.C. (1975). *The St. Louis community homes program: graduated support for long–term care.* Am J Psychiatry, 132:6, 617–622.

Schmid, P.F. (1992). Das Leiden. In Frenzel, P., Schmid, P.F. & Winkler, M. (Eds.), *Handbuch der Personzentrierten Psychotherapie* (pp. 83–125). Köln: Edition Humanistische Psychologie.

Strauss, J.S. (1992). *The person – key to understanding mental illness: towards a new dynamic psychiatry, III.* British Journal of Psychiatry, 161 (suppl.18), 19–26.

Swildens, H. (1991). *Prozeßorientierte Gesprächspsychotherapie.* Einführung in eine differentielle Anwendung des klientenzentrierten Ansatzes bei der Behandlung psychischer Erkrankungen. Köln: GwG.

Uchtenhagen, A. (1980). *Geschützte Wohn– und Arbeitsmöglichkeiten für psychisch Kranke in der Region Zürich – Angebot, Erfahrungen, Entwicklungen.* Psychiat. Prax., 7, 237–246.

Zubin, J. & Spring, B. (1977). *Vulnerability – a new view of schizophrenia.* J. Abnorm. Psychol., 86, 103–126.

Reflections and Reactions to
Carl R. Rogers with Mr. Vac: Implications for
Futrue Therapeutic Interactions with
Severely Disturbed Clients

JEROLD D. BOZARTH
UNIVERSITY OF GEORGIA

ABSTRACT

Carl R. Rogers' therapy with a diagnosed schizophrenic hospitalized client, Mr. Vac (also identified as Mr. Brown) is reviewed from the perspective of future implications for working with severely disturbed clients. My understanding and reactions to Rogers' work with this client are presented in context of client–centered theory and Rogers' comments. It is concluded that the implications for work with such clients *continues* to be: (1) the connection of one's self with the other's self and (2) the therapist's intention of creating an atmosphere by embodying the core conditions in order to promote the natural constructive process of the individual. The only intention of the dialogue is to try to connect one's self with the person's frame of reference, and to trust "..the remarkable resiliency of human beings when they are given adequate opportunity to grow."

Carl Rogers sent me a paper five months before his death titled, *The essence of psychotherapy: Moments of movement* He wrote on it: "I just discovered this 1956 paper and I like it—I hope you do too." The paper suggests that there are moments in therapy sessions when clients' experience irreversible moments of change. Rogers perceived a change in Mr. Vac (also referred to as Mr. Brown) after such a moment. Rogers believed that his expression of genuine caring to Mr. Vac stimulated such a process. One interchange was determined by Rogers to be a "crucial turning point" in the therapy.

In an interview published the year of his death, Rogers (Baldwin, 1987) referred to his work with Mr. Vac in the following way:

> Over time, I think I have become more aware of the fact that in therapy I do use myself, I recognize that when I am intensely focused on a client, Just my presence seems to be healing and I think this is probably true of any good therapist. I recall once I was working with a schizophrenic man in Wisconsin whom I had dealt with over a period of a year or two and there were many long pauses. The crucial turning point was when he had given up, did not care whether he lived or died, and was going to run away from the institution. And I said; "I realize that you don't care about yourself, but I want you to know that I care about you, and I care about what happens to you." He broke into tears for ten or fifteen minutes. That was the turning point of the therapy. I had responded to his feelings and accepted them but it was when I came to him as a person and expressed my feelings for him, that it really got to him. That interested me, because I am inclined to think that in my writing perhaps I have stressed too much the three basic conditions (congruence, unconditional positive regard and empathic understanding). Perhaps it is something around the edges of those conditions that is really the most important element of therapy—when my self is very clearly, obviously present. (p. 45)

Although I believe moments of irreversible change may periodically occur, I have never been convinced of the universality of that phenomenon as depicted by Rogers. His more recent statement referring to the presence of himself is more consonate with my own thinking. I found the enduring qualities of equal humanness of Rogers with Vac to be the most impressive. That is, Rogers willingness to set in silence, his efforts to find cigarettes for Vac, and to loan him money. Much of which, I suppose, might be considered an ethical violation through a dual relationship. My reaction (Bozarth, in press) to Rogers' sessions with Mr. Vac is summarized in an upcoming book in which I concluded:

> Finally, what Rogers (1967) did in these two "crucial sessions" can be summarized in his own words: "I felt a warm and spontaneous caring for him as a person, which found expression in several ways—but most deeply at the moment when he was despairing" and "..we were relating as two real and genuine persons" (p. 411).

Before responding to the questions posed for consideration, my personal reaction to Rogers' work with Mr. Vac is summarized in the above noted book. I stated the following:

> I was pleased to have the opportunity to review and comment upon Carl R. Rogers' sessions with Mr. Brown because of my early experience working with chronic long term hospitalized clients. I learned client–centered therapy working with such clients during the late 1950's and early 1960's. I was a Psychiatric Rehabilitation Counselor who began one of the first "vocational/therapeutic" programs for incarcerated mentally ill in Illinois. I did individual and group therapy with the "patients" and also provided resources and opportunities for them to leave the hospital. Patients I worked with were considered "impossible" patients. They, however, achieved an incredibly high discharge and "improvement" rate and low recidivism record. Most of these individuals had been in the hospital for twenty or thirty years. I don't remember any "moments of movement" or "crucial turning points" but do remember over

> 100 patients who changed their behaviors and attitudes in ways that enabled them to get out of the hospital or, at least, to get out of locked wards. Their major therapeutic contact was with me and that sometimes consisted of primarily talking about jobs or training possibilities.

> Rogers' review of Mr. Brown's sessions reminded me of sessions that I had with one young man. I had over fifty sessions that were predominantly silent. I experienced him as exuding anger to the point that I was often uneasy being with him and would occasionally express my feelings towards him without ever getting a response. Yet, I learned many years later that he had married, graduated with a professional graduate degree and was a successful professional.

> I was struck with the fact that Rogers had 166 hours of therapy with this client without intervening or judging or interfering with the client's way of being. The client could choose! He did not need to be threatened by conditions of worth put on him. I wonder if it is what one does not do as a therapist that is just as important as what one does. I was also struck with Rogers' dedication to the client; he searched for cigarettes, was obsessed about his next appointments, looked for magazines to give to Brown, and loaned him money. All of these actions seem to me to be very human acts of caring and interest towards a person. In addition, there was the tenacious, dogged determination of Rogers to understand the experiences of the individual; the determination to understand the experiential world of the other person. I viewed this intent as the primary reason for his almost insistent "pushing" for the intense feelings of Mr. Brown. I thought that it might have

been difficult for Rogers to allow the client to redirect the focus. Nevertheless, Rogers seemed able to return to the client's world even when it was more murky in meaning to Rogers than the intensity of the sobs. I wonder if it would have made a difference in the direction of the therapy if Rogers had responded to Mr. Brown's statements of defiance rather than to the sobs and self discounting. Could Mr. Brown have perceived the caring and understanding from a defiant stance as well as from experiencing his "defensive shell" as one which was to "..crack wide open, and..never be quite the same" (P. 411).

I feel somewhat that Rogers' willingness to search for cigarettes for Brown may have been as significant a factor in Brown's progress as the one moment that Rogers' believed was crucial. I fantasize Mr. Brown saying, "Doc always found me a cigarette and that's what I needed to help me get through all those bad times." Is there a crucial moment of movement in therapy? This was true to Rogers in this case. But was it even necessarily so in this case?

Overall, I found these two sessions to be meaningful representations of Rogers' theoretical and therapeutic intent. They represented Rogers' consistent intent to experience and communicate accurate empathy and unconditional positive regard while being a congruent therapist. They were of special interest because they were not typical of other demonstrations by Rogers. I believe the sessions revealed the reality of long term sessions with labeled psychotics and the personhood of the individuals with whom we work. I am mostly reminded, however, of the remarkable resiliency of human beings when they are given adequate opportunity to grow.

So, was therapy a moment of movement for Mr. Brown, as such, dependent upon one of a series of recognizable experiential changes? Although Rogers saw this occurrence with Mr. Brown, he was also dedicated to the more holistic influence of "..relating as two real and genuine persons" (Rogers, 1967, p. 411). John Shlien's (1971) comment on therapy when writing about a client–centered approach to schizophrenia seems apropos to this discussion as well. "Therapy" , said Shlien, "is bigger (a whole atmosphere) and smaller (moments of internal experience) than can be conveyed by the synopses we can offer" (p. 156). I believe Shlien (1971) provides us with a memorable description of this definition in his interaction with a client who was diagnosed as schizophrenic. The description:

> He blew his nose, dropped his handkerchief, and as he picked it up, glanced at me. He saw tears in my eyes. He offered me the handkerchief, then drew back because he knew he had just wiped his nose on it and could feel the wetness on his hand. We both knew this, each knew the other knew it; we both understood the feel and the meaning of the handkerchief (the stickiness and texture, the sympathy of the offering and the embarrassment of the withdrawal) and we acknowledged each other and the interplay of each one's significance to the other. It is not the tears, but the exquisite awareness of dual experience that restores consciousness of self. A self *being*, the self–concept can change. (p. 164)

MY RESPONSES TO THE QUESTIONS POSED FOR DISCUSSION ARE THE FOLLOWING:
Question 1. In what aspects would you personally act differently in the interview from your point of view today?

Although I would act out of the same theoretical base as Rogers, it is unlikely that I would have had the same responses then or now. It is likely, for example, that I would respond more to Mr. Vac's defiance of "to hell with them." This is not because I believe anything particular about the content of this defiance; rather, it is because it seems a more integral part of the being of Mr. Vac.

Generally, I would enter therapy sessions with "psychotics" the same way now that I did forty years ago, hopefully, with more patience and sagacity but with just as much naiveté and absence of particular preconceptions. I would enter sessions with the hope and the intention of connecting and blending with the individual as a human being and, hence, promoting the natural growth process of the individual. What I would particularly do would be dependent upon the client at the moment, myself at the moment and the interaction at the moment. My dedication would be to the client's perception of the world.

Question 2. And, if so, why?

I would NOT act from a theoretical stance different from Rogers' fundamental theoretical view because the theoretical base is the same as nearly forty years ago. The interchange of, as Rogers said, "..relating as two real and genuine persons." and, as Shlien said, "..the exquisite awareness of dual experience that restores consciousness of self" have not changed over the years.

Question 3. Consequently, what is the status quo of the Client–Centered or Experiential Therapy or Person–Centered Approach, where do you see a possible development?

I see the possible development as being in a renewal and clarification of understanding of Rogers' fundamental theoretical position of Client–Centered Therapy. That is: (1) the clarification of the connection of one's self with the other's self and (2) the understanding that the only therapist intention is to create an atmosphere by embodying the core conditions in order to promote the natural constructive process of the individual. The only intention of the dialogue is to try to connect oneself with the person's frame of reference, and to trust, as I previously stated, "..the remarkable resiliency of human beings when they are given adequate opportunity to grow."

REFERENCES

Baldwin, M. (1987). *Interview with Carl Rogers on the use of the self in therapy.* In Baldwin, M. & Satir, V. (Eds.), The use of self in therapy (pp. 45–52). New York: The Haworth Press, Inc.

Bozarth, J. D. (in press). *A silent young man: The case of Mr. Brown.* In B. Farber, A. D. Brink, & P. Raskin (Eds.), Carl Rogers: Casebook and critical perspectives. New York: Guilford.

Rogers, C. R. (1967). *A silent young man.* In C. R. Rogers, E. T. Gendlin, D, J. Kiesler, & C. B. Truax (Eds.), The therapeutic relationship with schizophrenics. (pp. 401–416), Madison: The University of Wisconsin Press.

Shlien, J. M. (1971). *A client–centered approach to schizophrenia: First approximation.* In C. R. Rogers & B. Stevens (Eds.), Person to Person: The problem of being human. (pp. 149–165), Layfaette, CA.: Real People Press.

The delicate approach to early trauma

TON COFFENG
THE NETHERLANDS

ABSTRACT

A client–centered approach is described for survivors of child sexual abuse. The complexity and multi–layering of childhood trauma is explained. The therapy starts with Rogers by considering the client as the expert, and with Prouty by respecting symptoms. Basis is found in Gendlin's 'experiencing' and in Prouty's 'pre–experiencing' and 'pre–symbolic processing'. The center of attention is the body: a source for memory and for healing. The Inner Child–concept serves as a vehicle to re–contact and re–formulate old experience. An overlap is described between grief and trauma. To assist the client's recovery various techniques are offered, as Prouty's contact–reflections, Olsen's boundary issue and imagery, Pesso's holding, possibility sphere etc., Gendlin's blue print, the re–establishment of moral rules and the use of extrapolation. Finally necessary preconditions are discussed.

INTRODUCTION

More survivors of severe childhood trauma (a.o. incest) present themselves for therapy, since society is becoming aware slowly of what seemed not to exist before (Boon & Draijer, 1993). It goes with a stream of articles by experts discussing diagnosis and treatment. Till now the discussion is dominated by medical/psychiatric thinking and by analytical, behavioristic, directive and hypnotic orientations (Conference Reader, 1992; van der Hart, 1991; Herman, 1992; Kluft, 1982, 1991a; Kluft & Fine, 1993; Ochberg, 1988; Putnam, 1989; Willis & Ochberg, 19-91). A client–centered view is lacking an approach traumatized clients need, one would expect (1).

Another point is the distinction between trauma / dissociation and disorders of the 'self' (Kernberg, 1984; Kohut, 1977; Masterson, 1981). It seems as if trauma and dissociation is a clinical syndrome to be treated in a certain way, and personality disorders problems of another planet. I consider this distinction as artificial: the impact of trauma on the individual is multi–dimensional and could be approached by integrating both schools, as illustrated by Brown & Fromm (1986) and Haaken & Schlaps (1991).

The model introduced here is based on Rogers' (1951) view to restore the client as the one in charge of her therapeutic process: as the expert, who knows which trauma occured and which approach fits. The theory of *'experiencing'* (Gendlin, 1964) helps to understand the small 'experiential' steps of healing. Prouty's (1976, 1977, 1994) *'pre–experiencing'*, describig the slow, primitive and repetitive process of confused clients, applies also to clients, who were traumatized in childhood. The trauma has been inflicted upon the *body* of the client: therefore the body is the source of information, of symptoms, of memory ('body memory'), and the source of recovery. Focusing/experiential language (Gendlin, 1968, 1981,) serves to contact the body. The *'Inner Child'*–concept is used as a metaphor to reconstruct what happened, to re–contact early experience („Re–contacting the Child", Coffeng, 1992b), and to concretize the therapist's empathy. Attention will be given to *grief* because of the overlap between grieving and the working through of trauma.

To assist the re–contacting of trauma and the process of healing various therapeutic models are incorporated, as Prouty's *contact reflections*, Olsen's *boundary issue*, Pesso's *true scene*, *possibility sphere*, *holding*, Gendlin's *blue print*, the introduction of *moral rules*, the use of *extra–polation* and Olsen's *imagery*. Finally several conditions are discussed, which should provide a safe environment for an intensive and long lasting therapy as this one.

CHILDHOOD SEXUAL ABUSE

Childhood sexual abuse is not a single incident but a set of repeated traumatic violations of the child's physical and emotional ego–boundaries. It is associated with many other factors and consequences which are traumatic as well. First there is the use of violence, eliciting pain and anxiety; the breaking of ego–boundary, leading to feelings of powerlessness and loss of respect as a human being: to be treated as a thing. The perpetrator's threat to surrender, not to cry, not to make any sound, not to tell anybody (e.g. by the showing of a knife) leads to extreme death–anxiety of the child, together with feelings of abandonement and isolation. Again, this is not a single nightmare like with adult victims of rape, but a repeated sequence of daily experiences, happening for years from childhood.

In addition there is the shocking experience of loosing one's parent. The perpetrator is usually the father: the person who was trusted before behaves as a criminal suddenly. The abuse happens in secrecy without any witness, and the child is forced to keep it secret. So the child is isolated from the other parent and family members, she looses the other parent as well as the pre–existing safety of the family.

The secrecy of the abuse can happen either by the way in which the perpetrator succeeds to keep the other family members ignorant of what happens, or because of defenses of the family members who deny signals of the abuse.

The child is faced with isolation, not understanding why nobody notices what happens and why nobody is there for rescue or comfort. Faced with this ignorance and lack of logic, the child invents her own logic: saying to herself that she deserved this bad treatment because she was bad. In addition to the dissociation due to the severe abuse, the child has to handle two opposite strong feelings: on one hand she wishes badly that the abuse is discovered, that the truth comes out and that she will be rescued; but on the other hand she is frightened that it will come out and that the abuser will kill her or that she will be punished or sent away.

Next to this is the schizophrenic situation, that the abuse takes place daily and that 'normal family life' goes on as if nothing happened! As a consequence the child has to split herself too. Because of fear that the abuse comes out the child isolates herself at school, hiding physical marks of the abuse, hiding her feelings of sadness and anxiety. The dissociation, the early grief, the denial, the splitting and the isolation may lead to various symptoms as e.g. bed–wetting, stammering. These symptoms give way to despite and labeling in these families, mis–diagnosis and stigmatization by family–doctors, and to further isolation from siblings and peers. Adolescent and adult victims with symptoms are often mis–diagnosed, mis–labeled and sometimes mis–treated in psychiatry. So the traumatization is multiple and complex and multi–layered in time, and gradually the victim herself does not see any connection any more between her symptoms and the original trauma.

As described in the case of childhood grief (Coffeng, 1992b) the trauma and all its consequences are mixed up with the emotional development of the child, leading to personality disorders as well. The child learns to trust nobody and not to trust her own experience as a source of truth. She experiences herself as fragmented and of no worth and of no power. Adult survivors live in a continuous state of anxiety, suffer from flashbacks, nightmares and 'day–mares' (Prouty & Pietrzak, 1988); at the same time they suffer from gaps in their memory, which is also fragmented and distorted. So they are very unsure about the reliability of their memory, doubting if all these nightmares have elements of truth, and wishing deeply it all did not have happened! Dissociation, auto–mutilation, substance abuse, suicide attempts serve to escape from the terror.

Notwithstanding negative experiences in psychiatry some have the courage to find a therapist who takes them seriously, and is willing to engage into the investigation of what really did happen.

THE EXPERIENTIAL APPROACH TO EARLY TRAUMA

General.

The client is the expert; respect of symptoms.
As the client had to survive in the middle of horrible experiences she is the only one who can tell of what happened, is an expert in surviving techniques and in assessing danger. She is the only one to know whether the helping profession helps. Symptoms are respected as defenses which might avoid worse, and which might lead to the disclosure of true traumatic events (Prouty, 1977, 1983, 1986). The client is the translator of these symptoms into historic events.

It applies also to the therapeutic techniques used and to the speed of the process: the client is the monitor who gives feed–back (Coffeng, 1991). This rogerian pre–condition is important especially in the case of detection of what happened: the therapist should not hurry to discover, neither conclude too early to know. Because of the multi–layered traumatic experience, memory fragments can be hidden under other memory fragments, and the client may feel betrayed when the therapist took half of the truth in stead of the whole (Brown & Fromm, 1986).

The issue, – the client is the expert –, is crucial in case of crisis. The respect of symptoms, even auto–mutilation or suicide attempts, is the understanding that this behaviour prevents worse. It's like with 'borderline' clients, who show all kinds of symptoms to prevent terror, pan anxiety or desintegration (de Blecourt, 1991). And symptoms can imply cues, which are on the way to reveal traumatic details of the past, (Prouty, 1983, 1986, 1991). This does not mean approval of risky behaviour, which should be limited in case of real danger. But the symptoms and coping mechanisms of the client, how crippled they might be, are seen as fragments of real historic life events which are distorted by succeeding life events, and which may reveal themselves in due course.

Experiencing: the process of healing.
Experiencing was conceived by Gendlin (1964) as the core process of therapeutic change: the mere attending to preconceptual body felt sense – about a certain life issue – and the subsequent symbolizing in words or images produces an experiential felt shift. The issue is felt differently, which is followed by integrating and understanding emotionally and mentally. The therapeutic process consists of small experiential steps (Gendlin, 1990). The individual feels change in these micro–steps: she feels that she is on the right track of feeling better and understanding herself better. Another important fact Gendlin (1964) discovered was an ease and relaxation which occured during the felt shift. Even when one is faced with a highly anxiety provoking situation, but assisted in attending to the felt sense or crux of that anxiety, anxiety

subsides. Contrary to catharsis or forced discharge of emotions, feeling the complexity and typical flavour of that issue, enables the emotionally heavy topic to be understood bodily and carried forward, followed by a real relief, and *then* followed by the discharge of emotions. This mechanism was visible in experiential grief–therapy, where subjects could face emotional topics without being overwhelmed, which enabled them to digest it slowly, experientially and specifically (Coffeng, 1992a).

As with grief, it is not only the severity of the trauma, but also the typical contextual flavour of the trauma in each individual case, which is essential in the working through: to which experiential therapy fits so well.

However, for many survivors of childhood trauma even the gentle approach of experiencing is hardly reachable, as if this process is too fast.

Pre–experiencing
Prouty (1976, 1977) introduced a new type of process, when he studied the lack of succes of client–centered therapy for confused and psychotic patients. Rogers and Gendlin (Rogers, 1967) concluded that there was no therapeutic process, and no experiencing, but Prouty discovered a process on a different level, which he called 'pre–experiential' and 'pre–expressive' (Prouty, 1994). He pointed at the slow, primitive, repetitive and cyclical processing in these clients. He designed therapeutic procedures to restore the 'psychological contact' and to process hallucinatory material to enable usual experiencing to follow. Eventually clients started to tell about early traumatic events!

Central in Prouty's approach is the respect of symptoms, which, – when attended to experientially –, will unfold into true life experiences in due time. This respect is realized by literal reflecting the expressions of the client at the level of the client. There is also the attendance to the slow processing, by slowly reflecting what the client expresses and by slowly repeating of what one reflected before. In this way one trusts that a pre–experiential process is necessary before the client reaches the point where usual conversation and interaction can take place.

This involves a most literal reflecting, very basic, realistic and simple. Without adding any semantic understanding, as this process is almost a physical one, and of a different order than usual therapy. It requires a different and specific language (Prouty, 1990; Prouty & Kubiac, 1988).

Prouty pointed also to the cyclical and repetitive character of this process: repetition of symptoms or utterings of the client should not be seen as a standstill, but as a cyclical recurring of something which seeks to be expressed. In this sense he considers hallucinations as pro-active and creative, which are finding ways to be expressed, though not yet understandable. Hallucinations are called 'pre–symbols': not pointing semantically or symbolically to real life experiences, but as distorted and fragmented parts of the self, refering to, indicating and implying other experience or hallucination and evolve from there slowly into a real life experience. It has to be followed and reflected literally before it can express itself semantically and understandably.

I found this concept applicable to multi–traumatized clients: contrary to techniques to reveal forcibly what is yet unconscious or to fill amnestic gaps, I prefer to attend to symptoms, as flashbacks, dissociation or sudden somatic com- plaints, in a pre–experiential way, until the symptoms reveal themselves. The speed of the client is followed as well as her indication of being able to face the traumatic memory.

The body

The body is the place where the trauma occured, where the pain, anxiety and sadness is felt; the body is also considered to be the place where the amnesia and flashback are originating. As described with early grief (Coffeng, 1992b+c), there is a *body memory*: many clients have strong physical feelings without any mental image or memory of the event. Pesso (1990) stated that the body is the center of truth: although the client has been brainwashed by the perpetrator and others, it is trusted that the body will translate the physical memory into a real story of the abuse with all details. It is also the body where the healing of trauma takes place and from where the energy of recovery and integration originates.

Focusing (Gendlin, 1980, 1981) assists the client to contact body memory and to process traumatic physical memory into experience and symbolization. It is the intermedium between the therapist and the client's actual feeling. Suggestions of the therapist are translated by the client into questions to her body; reactions of the body are again translated by the client into language understandable by the therapist, (,,The client's client", Gendlin, 1984).

Traumatized clients suffer frequently from severe anxiety and pain: it is hard for them to feel. They have all reasons not to feel and try to avoid it. In the teaching of focusing (Coffeng, 1984, 1985) clients learn to differentiate between experiential feelings (felt sense) and strong emotions. Especially the first step of focusing, 'clearing a space' (McGuire, 1982/83), helps to create a distance between oneself and overwhelming traumatic emotions.

Focusing should be handled with caution: as stated above most clients are not yet able to focus/experience and are in a stage of pre–experiencing, to which Prouty's approach applies. But now and then bits of focusing are possible, provided the therapist is aware of the phasing and timing and feed–back of the client (Coffeng, 1991). In a later phase many clients come back to focusing and practice it spontaneously and fluently.

The Inner Child

In the experiential practice the 'Inner Child'–concept is used as a metaphor for what the felt sense of a person is trying to express, and as a metaphor to restore the contact between the client and her inner self in the way she experienced events when a child. It is supposed that the child, who suffered when young, is still present and suppressed by the client (Gendlin, 1991, 1992). It is a metaphor for experiences of the past which could not be integrated or 'experientially carried forward' and hence still exist as 'frozen wholes' (Gendlin, 1964). It is a metaphor to discover the original potency of the child, and to restore communication between the client and her inner self.

In the case of early trauma, the child is invited to come out and to tell what happened and to experience it afresh. The simple act of telling what really happened, experiencing it and being believed and being supported by the therapist as a reliable parent has a healing effect. This is contrary to what happened before: the client was abused, not believed, not helped and hence mistrusted her own experience and denied the inner child.

For many clients this is a helpful metaphor, to go back to early experiences, to feel like a child and to restore the contact with themselves. When memory fragments come to the surface, by images or mere physical feelings, the therapist translates it into something like: ,,I think the child has to tell us something about what happened."..etc.

Early grief

In various ways early grief is connected with early trauma. First, the child looses a parent she trusted before, and because of the imposed secrecy she avoids and looses the other parent as well. She looses her childhood, her innocence and sponaneity as a child, the safety of the family, her schoolmates, etc. In addition to the trauma there is a big loss. But there is also an overlap between the process of grieving and the working through of trauma: books and papers about trauma discuss grief, and vice versa (Ochberg, 1988; Stern, 1985). The enormous strain and heavy emotions connected with the grieving process and the phases are very similar.

But one aspect has to be added in the case of *early* grief: in young children grief is often disrupted and mixed up with the emotional development of the child: it is connected with it and it interferes with the emotional development. This complicates the therapy of adults who suffered a loss when a child. One has to understand the cyclical character of the process: elements of grief are alternating with development issues, and are coming back in cycles (Coffeng, 1992b). A similar pattern can be seen in the therapy of early trauma. Issues are coming back again and again, and this should not be considered as a repetition or standstill.

Specifics

Till now several concepts were discussed to understand the process of healing from early traumatization. The client as an expert, respect of symptoms, the experiential approach, and more specific: the pre–experiential process; the body as the place to attend, the typical language to contact the body; the inner child–concept and the aspects of early grief. The healing process can be assisted by various concepts and techniques, of which some are mentioned below.

Contact reflections

Prouty understood the difficulty of pre–expressive and pre–experiential clients to engage in therapeutic interaction as a lack of *contact functions*: the absence of *reality contact* (contact with the world,people,places,events), *affective contact* (contact with self, with own feelings), and *communicative contact* (ability to express experience to others). Realizing that his clients were extremely isolated in their confused state because of lack of contact, Prouty invented a client—centered and experiential way to restore these contact functions, by reflecting techniques, very basic, realistic and simple. He called this 'contact reflections' or 'pre–therapy'. *Situational* reflections assist the contact with reality; *facial* reflections assist the contact with self; *body* reflections assist the contact with self and reality; *word–for–word* reflections support the communicative capability of the client by literal reflecting; and *reiterative* reflections repeat reflections which had an experiential effect in the client and reinforce the process (Prouty, 1976, 1990, 1994; Prouty & Kubiac, 1988).

These contact reflections, basic and not intrusive, support both confused clients and the clients we deal with: traumatized clients who are overwhelmed by flasbacks and looze contact with their environment, themselves and the therapist.

Boundary issue

Olsen (1982/83) pointed to this important issue. It was reformulated by Gray (1990). The ego–boundaries of victims of sexual abuse were violated. This should be restored. Before any therapy starts, the client is assisted to define where her ego–boundary should be. It can be done in an exercise in which she establishes the right distance between herself and the therapist. The therapist acknowledges this boundary and promises never to cross it without the explicit permission of the client. As soon as the client is able to focus she can define this boundary in more detail. Often the therapist mentions where the boundary is, and that this was violated in the client's history.

505

However, when the client engages in the process of therapy and contacts childhood experience, she might need the therapist's near presence. But even then the therapist expresses explicitly how near he will come, asks the client's permission to come nearer, and asks the client to check whether this fits. The more clients have the experience that their definition of the boundary is respected, the more a dynamic change in distance can occur. The more they rely on the therapist, the more they allow him to come nearer.

Holding, containment
True scene, possibility sphere. Pesso (1972, 1988a, 1990), a psychomotor therapist, designed the group setting as a place to experience childhood events afresh. He considers the body, body feelings and experiential process as the core of therapeutic change. Clients are assisted to enter a 'true scene': something which happenend in the past. Groupmembers are asked to take the role of the real historic parents and act as they did. But he introduced also the 'possibility sphere': other groupmembers act as ideal parent figures and give symbolically what the child should have received. Other members act as supporting figures by holding the client when anxious, or comforting the client when sad, or protecting the client against automutilation or toxic parent interactions. So next to the re–experiencing of real historic events there is the healing facility of supporting figures and the presence of symbolic ideal parent–figures. The figure of the 'witness' was invented too: a person who should have been there when the child was abused.

For victims of childhood sexual abuse Pesso (1988b) added 'holding' and 'containment': the client is held by supporting figures when emotions are so overwhelming that the client fears to fall apart. By being held the client is able to bear these emotions, to feel and to process them.

With some imagination and creativity these techniques can be applied in an individual setting. The 'possibility sphere' can be created with an image in which reliable persons can assist and hold the client, or protect her from intrusion. Provided the boundary (3.2.2.) is defined clearly, gradually the therapist can take the role of an assisting figure, and propose to hold the client literally the way the client wishes, verbalizing exactly what he is doing, and what an assisting person should say. It can both ways: the therapist holds the client and he creates imaginary policemen who put the perpetrator in prison. As soon as the client is used to this procedure she will ask herself to be held or come over to sit near the therapist to seek protection, and order the therapist what he should say or do (Coffeng, 1994).

Blue print, morality
Recently Gendlin (1991, 1992, 1993, 1994) mentioned the 'blue print': the child has an original physical preverbal sense of what is naturally required, of what should happen, and of what should *not* have happened. The child has a sense of *morality* : preverbally it knows that it should be held when frightened; that it should not be raped; that it should be protected ; that lies should not be believed. But because of the abuse and threatenings it is afraid to listen to this blue print. It has been forced to mistrust her own sense and to betray herself. Gendlin suppports the inner knowing of the child about truth by expressing his indignancy loudly when the client tells about bad events: „It should not have happened!", thereby reflecting the inner oppressed indignancy of the child. At which Gendlin adds: „What should have happened?" He points to the inner felt sense of the client which knows what should have happened or what should happen.

Therapists dealing with trauma underline the importance of re–establishment of morality and truth. Victims suffer from false and distorted moral rules, wrong assumptions, false explanations and distorted truth/memory because of the enforced brainwashing by the perpetrators in a noxious atmosphere. Clients have guilt–feelings, that they were wrong, that it was their own fault. Again and again these misconceptions have to be corrected by refering to the client's inner blue print, which can confirm that the therapists remarks are more reliable than those of the criminal parent. Pesso confirms the blue print with the witness–figure who testifies of what happened, expresses that it was bad, and confirms which harm it did to the child.

As the false truth and misconceptions were imprinted in the vulnerable mind of the child so frequently, insidiously, verbally, by acts and by indirect ways of manipulation, the restoration of the real truth and moral rules has to be expressed explictly, repeatedly and clearly by the therapist.

Extrapolation
The process of healing from severe dissociation and trauma happens in very small experiential, even pre–experiential steps. Traumatic memories come to the surface, can be felt and experientially worked through when the client can handle it. The client can experience them fully as a small child when she feels safe with the therapist. So first there has to be built a reliable bond between therapist and client, like in early grief (Coffeng, 1992b). However, clients who suffer from nightmares and mis–diagnosis for years tend to burst and to tell all, when they find a therapist finally. They have a strong wish to get rid of it all quickly, quite understandably. It requires some skill to explain that the traumatic events can only be told really, and experientially worked through, when there is a reliable bond, and in small steps. But then the therapist risks to give the impression that he is not interested to hear the truth, like many other persons in the client's life.

By 'extrapolation' the therapist makes clear that he is going to listen to all, that he is wanting to know all *in due time*. That emotions connected with the recurrent traumatic memories are too heavy for one person in one day, lest for the moment the client feels herself as a small child. That the therapist will help to feel it step by step. Prouty's literal and slow reflection has a similar effect: one does not enter the topic by enquiring what it is about, but one attends to it slowly.

Extrapolation refers also to the therapeutic tools which will be used, as focusing, Pesso's structures, etc. One mentions these techniques, saying that it can be applied in due time, when the client feels ready for it.

Imagery, symbols
Gendlin and Olsen (1970) demonstrated the powerful effect of imagery in experiential focusing. Images and symbols have the potency to capture the implicit felt meaning of the client more exactly and in a broader sense than words. This appeared to be helpful in focusing and grief: the expression of grief feelings became easy and more differentiated with the help of images (Coffeng, 1992a). In the therapy of early trauma clients show a lot of creativity in finding ways to express and support their process: they bring with them dolls, drawings, letters, poems, etc.. They hardly have to be encouraged.

But more than imagery has to be used in the case of recapturing traumatic memories. Often there are mere physical memories, e.g. a tight feeling around the wrists, a knowing that the wrists were tied once with a rope, without any clear picture of the scene involved; or a feeling of strangulation without images. In those instances the therapist assists the client by imagining what could have happened possibly, and to offer this image to the client. As with the therapy of early grief, he assists the client in the reconstruction of all memory fragments (physical feeling, a smell, fragments of dreams/nightmares) into a possible historic event. The client checks the accuracy of this reconstruction with her felt sense (focusing).

Imagery is used also with Pesso's techniques, when imaginary supportive figures and ideal parent figures are created. And of course with Gendlin's blue print: to imagine what should have happened.

Pre–symbols

In the beginning of therapy the process is usually still pre–experiential, and the memory fragments and the content of flash backs and nightmares bizarre and yet not understandable. These should be processed in a pre–symbolic way by literally reflecting (Prouty, 1977, 1986). They will refer and evolve to other experiences and explain themselves later on. Pre–symbolic processing (Prouty, 1994) should be applied as long as the client is in this pre–experiential stage, as long as traumatic fragments are split–off or dissociated. As soon as the client experiences all, – when the memory of the trauma is complete and the client is able to feel the complexity of it all –, then one can reflect in the usual experiential way and assist the client to focus. A similar processing of pre–symbols was practiced before by the swiss psychiatrist Sechehaye (1947, 1971, 1972), in: „la réalisation symbolique". Drawings of her client had a pre–symbolic character. Similar drawings were reported by Brown & Fromm (1986) and Santen (1993).

Relationship

Obviously therapists dealing with severely traumatized clients face transference issues. The client cannot believe that somebody will trust and believe her and will be reliable. How could someone not be annoyed by her symptoms, but interested really to know what these symptoms refer to? Clients don't feel at ease with a person who takes them serious. Clients themselves don't take their complaints serious. They are used to be left alone, and hence frightened that all traumatic memories come to the surface and that they will be left alone then. So first the reliability of the therapist is tested, and trust and confidence has to be built.

Sooner or later the therapist will be identified with the perpetrator or with the neglecting parent. With the concept of 'the interactional space'(Gendlin, 1991, 1992) the therapist can express his understanding of mistrust and fear, because the client had no positive experience. But this item is coming back repeatedly, often triggered by a single word, or something the therapist wears (a belt) which reminds the client to the perpetrator.

Slowly the client starts to test and to trust the therapist's reliability, and the therapist becomes a substitute parent (van de Veire, 1993) who assists the client to recover traumatic memories, to work them through, and to resume her natural emotional development. However, there is a strong ambivalence in the client. Her ties of loyalty to her parents are strong. She starts to realize that her real parents did not behave like parents should have done, that she lost in fact her parents. The therapist should not compete with these loyal ties, but respect the client's hardship to believe that she was betrayed by her real parents.

SETTING ETC.

Most authors agree, that the therapy of severe and early trauma should be and can be performed on an individual and out–patient basis. Trauma–clients are sensitive to imposed rules and procedures, as in clinical settings; and few clinical settings consider the client as her own expert (Kluft, 1991b; Sackheim & Hess, 1988). Most clients prefer individual therapy, rather than sharing their experience with other victims in a group. Medication is hardly indicated, which is in line with the contradicting reports about its effect (Loewenstein, 1991).

Crises are frequent, which require only the availability of the therapist by telephone: short therapeutic interventions, as the restoration of contact or contact–reflections, are usually sufficient (de Blécourt, 1991; Fine, 1991). Crises are often a parameter of the speed of the process, or refer to interventions of the therapist or misunderstandings.

Both client and therapist need a supportive net–work (van der Hart, 1991). The therapist needs a co–therapist, preferably of the other sex, who can replace him in case of holidays etc., to whom the client can go when she feels like, and who can assist in other ways. But she is also a support to the therapist. A supportive team is desirable too. For the client friends/collegues etc. are needed to whom she can go just for a cup of coffee, or whom she can call at unusual times. These friends should set limits, because support has to be offered for a long time. In the same sense support is needed from the general practioner, by the offering of contact, leaving the client as an expert to tell what she needs. The G.P. explains to his medical collegues the required carefulness, when medical interventions are unavoidable. The same applies to the dentist, who should know that the setting may trigger old sexual trauma.

DISCUSSION

Clients with severe and early childhood trauma, who suffer from dissociation, MPD, flashbacks, amnesia and anxiety can be met by client–centered/experiential therapy. Attention has to be given to the typical pre–experiential character of the healing process, which is slow and repetitive. The body is the place where the trauma occured and the source of restauration. Pre–symbolic process will be followed by experiencing and symbolic process. It should be noted that pre–experiencing can alternate and sometimes go together with experiencing: like with borderline clients symbols can be pre–symbols and symbols at the same time and hence have to be reflected both ways. This may complicate reflecting.

Various therapeutic tools assist the recovery, as Prouty's contact reflections, Olsen's boundary issue, Pesso's techniques etc..

This heavy and long lasting therapy can be carried out on an indivual out–patient basis, if supported by a network of both client and therapist. Provided one respects the slow speed of the process, severe crises, medication or admission are rather exceptions than the rule.

REFERENCES

Blécourt, A. de (1991) *Het borderline syndroom*. In, Blécourt, A. de (ed), Voelen, denken en handelen in de psychoanalyse, 195–306. Assen: van Gorcum.

Boon, S. & Draijer, N. (1993) *Multiple personality disorder in the Netherlands*. Amsterdam: Swets & Zeitlinger.

Brown, D.P. & Fromm, E. (1986) *Hypnotherapy and hypnoanalysis*. Hillsdale NJ: L. Erlbaum Associates.

Coffeng, T. (1984) *Teaching focusing to clients: a way of pre–therapy*. The Focusing Folio, 3 4), 130–138.

Coffeng, T. (1988) The use of focusing in experiential therapy. Videotape (engl.titles) Int. Conf. Leuven.

Coffeng, T. (1991) *The phasing and timing of focusing in therapy*. The Folio, a Journal for Focusing and Experiential Therapy, *10* (3), 40–50.

Idem, In, Keil, W.F., Hick, P., Korbei, L. & Poch, V., (1994, eds), *Selbstverständnis*. Bergheim: Mackinger verlag.

Coffeng, T. (1992a) *Focusing and grief. The Folio,* J. for Focusing and Experiential Therapy, 11 (2), 41–48. (German, 1994: Focusing und Trauer, *Personzentriert, 1*, 80–94.)

Coffeng, T. (1992b) *Re–contacting the child. The Folio,* J. for Focusing and Experiential Therapy, 11 (3), 11–21. (Idem 1994:, GWG–Zeitschrift 25 (93), 5–12. German: 1993: GWG–Zeitschrift, 24 (89), 19–24. 1994: Personzentriert, 1, 95–115.

Coffeng, T. (1992c) *Re–contacting the Child.* Videotape (engl.titles) Int. Conf. Focusing, Chicago.

Coffeng, T. (1994) *The delicate approach to early trauma.* Videotape (engl.titles) Int. Conf. Client–c. and Experiential Therapy, Gmunden.

Conference Reader (1992) *International Conference on Multiple Personality Disorder & Dissociative States.* Amsterdam: Post Academisch Onderwijs Geneeskunde.

Fine, C.G. (1991) *Treatment stabilisation and crisis prevention: pacing the therapy of multiple personality disorder.* Psychiatric clinics of North America, 14, 661–675.

Fisher, M. (1991) *On making parents disappear: regression in the therapeutic process with reference to the re–experiencing of childhood trauma. 2nd Internat.* Conf. on Client–centered and Experiential Psychotherapy, Stirling. Book of Abstracts.

Gendlin, E.T. (1964) *A theory of personality change.* In, Worchel, P. & Byrne, D. (eds), Personality Change, 4. New York: Wiley.

Gendlin, E.T. (1968) *The experiential response.* In, Hammer, E.F., Use of interpretation in treatment, 208–227. New York: Grune & Stratton.

Gendlin, E.T. (1980) *Client–centered therapy as a frame of reference for training.* In, de Moor, W. & Wijngaarden, H. (eds), Psychotherapy and research. Amsterdam: Elzevier Biom. Press.

Gendlin, E.T. (1981) *Focusing.* New York: Bantam.

Gendlin, E.T. (1984) *The client's client. In, Levant,* R.F. & Shlien, J.M. (eds), Client–centered therapy and the person–centered aproach, 76–107. New York: Praeger.

Gendlin, E.T. (1990) *The small steps of the therapy process: how they come and how to help them come.* In, Lietaer, G., Rombauts, J. & van Balen, R. (eds), Client–centered and experiential psychotherapy in the nineties, 205–224. Leuven: University Press.

Gendlin, E.T. (1991, 1992, 1994) *Focusing in the interactional space.* Therapists workshops, Chicago.

Gendlin, E.T. (1993) *Focusing ist eine kleine Tür.* Würzburg, D.A.F.

Gendlin, E.T. & Olsen, L. (1970) *The use of imagery in experiential focusing Psychotherapy: Theory,* Research & Practice, 7, 221–223.

Gray, L. (1990) *The function of the boundary in facilitating experiential focusing.* The Focusing Folio, 9, 112–127.

Haaken, J. & Schlaps, A. (1991) *Incest evolution therapy and the objectivation of sexual abuse.* Psychotherapy, 28, (1), 35–47.

Hart, O. van der (1991) (ed) *Trauma, dissociatie en hypnose.* Amsterdam: Swets & Zeitlinger.

Herman, J.L. (1992) *Trauma and recovery.* New York: Basic Books.

Kernberg, O. (1984) *Severe personality disorders.* Nes Haven/London: Yale University Press.

Kluft, R.P. (1982) *Variety of hypnotic interventions in the treatment of multiple personality.* American Journal of clinical Hypnosis, 24, 232–240.

Kluft, R.P. (1991a) *Multiple personality disorder.* In, Tasman, A. & Goldfinger, S.M. (eds), American Psychiatric press Review of Psychiatry, 10, 161–188. Washington DC: American Psychiatric Press.

Kluft, R.P. (1991b) *Hospital treatment of multiple personality disorder: an overview.* Psychiatric Clinics of North America, 14, 695–719.

Kluft, R.P. & Fine, C.G. (eds, 1993) *Clinical perspectives on multiple personality disorder.* Washington DC: American Psychiatric Press.

Kohut, H. (1977) *The restoration of the self.* Madison CT: Internat. University Press.

510

Loewenstein, R.J. (1991) *Rational psychopharmacology in the treatment of M.P.D.* Psychiatric Clinics of North America, 14, 721–740.

Masterson, J.F. (1981) *The narcissistic and borderline disorders.* New York: Brunner/Mazel.

McGuire, M. (1982/83) *Clearing a space with two suicidal clients.* The Focusing Folio, 2, (1), 1–4.

Ochberg, F.M. (ed, 1988) *Posttraumatic therapy and the victims of violence.* New York: Brunner/Mazel.

Olsen, L. (1982/83) *How, I do body work.* The Focusing Folio, 2 (3), 1–8.

Pesso, A. (1972) *Experience in action.* New York: New York University Press.

Pesso, A. (1988a) *Ego development and the body.* Bewegen en hulpverlening, 5, 239–248.

Pesso, A. (1988b) *Sexual abuse, the integrity of the body.* Bewegen en hulpverlening, 5, 270–281.

Pesso, A. (1990) *Center of truth, true scene and pilot in Pesso system/psychomotor therapy.* Bulletin Netherl. Assoc. Pessotherapy. Eelde, The Netherlands.

Prouty, G.F. (1976) *Pre–therapy, a method of treating pre–expressive psychotic and retarded patients.* Psychotherapy: Theory, Research & Practice, 13 (3), 290–294.

Prouty, G.F. (1977) *Proto–symbolic method: A phenomenological treatment of schizophrenic hallucinations.* Journal of Mental Imagery, 1 (2) 339–342.

Prouty, G.F. (1983) *Hallucinatory contact: a phenomenological treatment of schizophrenics.* Journal of Communication Therapy, 2 (1), 99–103.

Prouty, G.F. (1986) *The Pre–symbolic structure and therapeutic transformation of hallucinations.* In, Shorr, J.E. & Krueger, L. (eds), *Imagery*, 99–106. London: Plenum Publishing Corporation.

Prouty, G.R. (1990) *A theoretical evolution in the personcentered/esperiential psychotherapy of schizophrenia and retardation.* In, Lietaer, G., Rombauts, J. & van Balen, R. (eds), Client–centered and experiential psychotherapy in the nineties, 645–685. Leuven: University Press.

Prouty, G.F. (1991) *The pre–symbolic structure and processing of schizophrenic hallucinations: the problematic of a non–process structure.* In, New directions in client–centered therapy. Practice with difficult client populations. Chicago: The Chicago Counseling Center.

Prouty, G.F. (1994) *Theoretical evolutions in person–centered/experiential therapy applications to schizophrenic and retarded psychoses.* New York: Praeger.

Prouty, G.F. & Kubiac, M.A. (1988) *The development of communicative contact with a catatonic schizophrenic.* Journal of Communication Therapy, 4 (1), 13–20.

Prouty, G.F. & Pietrzak, S. (1988) *The pre–therapy method applied to persons experiencing hallucinatory images.* Person–centered Review, 3 (4), 426–441.

Putnam, F.W. (1989) *Diagnosis and treatment of multiple personality disorder.* New York: The Guilford Press.

Rogers, C.R. (1951) *Client–centered therapy.* London: Constable.

Rogers, C.R. (ed, 1967) *The therapeutic relationchip and its impact.*Westport CT: Greenwood Press.

Roy, B. (1991) *A client–centered approach to multiple personality and dissociative process.* In, *New directions in client–centered therapy: practice with difficult client populations.* Chicago: The Chicago Counseling Center.

Sakheim, D.K.; Hess, E.P. & Chivas, A. (1988) *General principles for short–term inpatient work with multiple personality–disorder patients.* Psychotherapy, 25, 117–124.

Santen, B. (1993) *Focusing with a dissociated adolescent.* The Folio, Journal for Focusing and Experiential Therapy, 12 (2), 45–58.

Sechehaye, M.A. (1947) *La réalisation symbolique.* Revue suisse de psyhologie et de psychologie appliquée, 12. Bern: Hans Huber, Editions médicales. (dutch transl. 1971, 1972; Rotterdam: Lemnisc aat).

Stern, E.M. (1985) (ed) *Psychotherapy and the grieving patient.* New York: Harrington Park Press.

van de Veire, Chr. (1993) *Steunende/structurerende client–centered therapie bij een borderline cliënt.* VRT–periodiek, 31 (2), 4–20.

Warner, M.S. (1994) *Dissociation.* Paper third international conference client–centered and experiential psychotherapy. Book of abstracts.

Willis, D.J. & Ochberg, F M. (1991, eds) *Psychotherapy with victims.* Psychotherapy, special issues, 28 (1+2).

Youngson, S.C. (1991) *Ritual child abuse. A challenge to the person–centered approach?* 2nd Int. Conference Client–centered and Experiential Psychotherapy, Stirling, Book of abstracts.

Working with the Mentally Handicapped in a Person–Centered Way:
Is it possible, is it appropriate and what does it mean in practice?

MARLIS PÖRTNER

SWITZERLAND

ABSTRACT

Subject is the daily work in institutions for people with special needs. Given the fundamentals it is based upon, the person–centered approach is capable to
– extend the handicapped persons' frame of action and improve their quality of life
– make easier the staff's work
– minimise the negative effects of frequently changing staff
In working with mentally handicapped or – to use the Britsh term – people with special needs, the emphasis mostly is on training or caretaking aspects. Though probably everyone in this field would agree that it is extremely important to foster the independence of each person, it is sometimes not very clear what this really means. Often the aiming for this goal is guided more by the staff's concepts than by the impulses and capacities of the handicapped persons themselves.
Based on the principles of person–centered approach, completed with Prouty's concept of pre–therapy, we can develop practicable guidelines for working in a person–centerd way with mentally handicapped adults. These should give a basic orientation as well as leave enough space for various ways of being adapted to the practice of each specific individual and institutional situation. I am not talking here of psychotherapy, although I do client–centered psychotherapy with mentally handicapped clients. My issue here is how to work in a person–centered way with mentally handicapped people in the daily life of communities and institutions where they live. The idea to develop a person–centered concept for this field emerged from doing supervision with staff members of such institutions for many years. I realized how much the person–centered approach actually has to offer here. Also I discovered that social workers who do not know the person–centered approach, sometimes intuitively develop ways of working which do quite conform with its principles.

TWO EXAMPLES

Example 1

Gertrud is constantly hurting herself by picking bits of skin off her hands. For years the staff of the institution where she lives, tries in vain to stop her doing that. She rubs her bleeding hands on the walls, which are blood stained wherever she comes by. This absorbes her so much, that she is hardly able to participate in the activities of the group. One day the staff decides to give up trying to stop her. Gertrud is now allowed to pick the skin off her hands, but on certain conditions: she has to decide if she wants to stay with the others and participate in their activities or if she wants to pick her skin. If she decides to do that, she can do it in the area of the room reserved for the handicapped to retire for a rest . If she wants to join the group activities, she has to stop it. The effect is amazing: Gertrud still picks the skin off her hands, but considerably less now. The walls are not blood–stained anymore. Her hands are less sore. In the morning, before the goup activities start, she now mumbles: "I have to decide, I have to decide," and she always keeps the agreement, not to pick the skin off her hands as long as she participates in the activities of the group.

Example 2

Eva does not like to do housework. She scolds violently, when she has to do it. Everybody knows that and tries to calm her down. She continues to scream about the vacuum–cleaner. One day one of the staff members examines it more carefully and discovers that indeed there is a loose switch which has to be hold down with one finger in a very uncomfortable way. It is easy to get this switch fixed.

What do we learn from these examples? At first Gertrud and Eva were met with a – so to speak – "diagnostic" and "pedagogic" attitude. The staff members knew their deficiencies and, out of experience and knowledge, considered themselves, able to interpret the behaviours of the two women. In vain they tried to change the "undesirable behaviours" which, on the contrary, increased and escalated into power fights with the staff. In the solutions which finally were succesful, appears a different attitude. This attitude corresponds to person–centered principles, even if those were not explicitly known to the staff.

WHAT DO WE UNDERSTAND BY PERSON–CENTERED ATTITUDE?

It is a basic assumption of the person–centered approach that the individual has within him or herself ressources for growing, for changing and for resolving problems. For various reasons – like retardation, traumatic experiences, lack of encouragement, illness – these ressources may be blocked or inhibited. To meet individuals with an attitude based on this assumption, helps them to discover, develop and use this hidden potential.

Is this also valid for people with special needs? Both examples showed that it was this attitude which led to changes. The staff, instead of assuming that they knew better what would be right for the handicapped women, took them seriously and let them participate in the process of searching for better ways to handle the situation. This had the effect that instead of destructive power fights, constructive solutions became possible.

Instead of trying to stop Gertrud's inadequate behaviour, she was given space to take her own decisions, as well as a structure which helped her change her behaviour.

Eva's scolding was no longer dismissed as her usual well known reaction to something she did not like, but was taken seriously. And it turned out that Eva's perception was quite realistic and that there was a concrete reason for her scolding.

The very essential is to meet a handicapped person with the conviction that for her this strange and unintelligible behaviour makes sense and to aim for understanding instead of stopping her behaviour.

The two examples are situated on different levels, and two very different personalities were involved. Gertrud showed a severely disturbed behaviour which did not only affect herself strongly, but also her surroundings. With Eva, it was a banal everyday situation which nevertheless caused tension and bad feelings. Gertrud is a severly retarded woman who does not talk much. She lives for years in this institution, where she participates in a special program for those who are not able to work in a sheltered workshop.. Eva is much less handicapped, she lives in a small flat–sharing community together with other mentally handicapped people and works in a sheltered workshop.

A "side effect" which perhaps was even more important than to resolve the problem itself, was that the women's self–confidence had been reinforced, that they experienced themselves as being able to move and change things. And the staff learned that they could trust the handicapped people much more than they had imagined.

In both cases, as different as they might be, the staff's acting in a person–centered way provided some positive changes. These are just two out of many examples, where social workers discovered a person–centered way without having a specific knowledge of this approach. It seems as if the experience of getting stuck with what has been tried before, sometimes would lead quite naturally to ways which offer the handicapped person more space for own responsibility and intitiative.

But a consistent person–centered attitude and a solid knowledge of it's foundations seems to be nowhere the very base of working with people with spevial needs. Yet the person–centered approach is highly suitable to provide guidelines for working in this field. I am persuaded that working on its principles could

– *extend the handicapped persons' frame of action*

– *improve their quality of life*

– *facilitate the staff's work*

– *diminish the negative effects of frequently changing staff*

I shall describe in short the foundations of the person–centered approach and demonstrate how they can be transfered into practical work with mentally handicapped people.

FOUNDATIONS

The person–centered approach has developed from client–centered psychotherapy. It proved that the attitude of EMPATHY, ACCEPTANCE AND CONGRUENCE which facilitates the therapeutic process, is also helpful in other fields. Yet it is crucial to be clearly aware of and to *acknowledge the structure* of a situation. Neglecting this aspect has been the cause of many misunderstandings and disappointments. A therapeutic situation is different from an everyday situation in an institution. The structure of psychotherapy is the therapy hour, where the client's experience and the therapist's trying to understand her as accurately as possible, is central. In the structure of an institution, the staff has not only to be empathic with the client, but also to acknowledge the conditions of the institution. A simple example may illustrate this:

Example 3
Eva lives in a small flat–sharing community for people with special needs. She does not like the cleaning. Yet the inmates live in this community on condition that the housework is mainly done by the themselves. Eva does it reluctantly and grumbling. How can the staff, in this situation, be empathic and accepting? Not, of course, by doing the cleaning themselves, nor by telling somebody else to do it. But by accepting Eva's bad feelings and communicating that to her (for example: "you don't like the cleaning", "you are angry right now because you have to help with the cleaning", and the like).

This is a crucial distinction: on one hand to take seriously and accept the woman's reactions and feelings and on the other to respect and represent the structure of the community. It is not always easy to carry something through and at the same time accept the feelings of the other person. Sometimes we have a hard time to cope with "negative" reactions like anger, hurt, disappointment. We wish that our demands would be met with pleasure and – consciously or unconsciously – do communicate this. Thus human beings are trained to not acknowledge their feelings, to not express and perhaps to not even perceive them, unless with bad conscience, and to deny, rationalise and repress them. To have no or only poor acces to one's own feelings is, as we know, one of the main causes for psychological disorders and life problems. This becomes quite obvious in Carl Rogers' theory of the self–concept, to which I will come back later.

People with special needs in particular, are frequently cut off from their emotions. Growing up they are rarely encouraged to trust their feelings which often show in bizarre and unintelligible ways. Most people around them make no effort to understand this strange behaviour, but spend a lot of energy to stop it. This way the mentally handicapped learn, even more than other people, to repress their feelings or to not even perceive them. As this is only possible to a certain extent, the blocked feelings, from time to time, break out the more violently and inadequately. The handicapped person is overwhelmed and frightened by this outbreak and does not know how to cope with it. People around then again react rigorously, the handicapped person feels guilty – and the vicious circle is turning.

In my experience the moderate handicapped particularly have difficulties to acknowledge their feelings. Their wish to appear "normal" has a fatal effect as it promotes over–adjustment. Out of fear to appear "handicapped", the person only dares to show "positive" and "adequate" feelings. Because she is afraid such feelings would be labeled inadequate and "not normal", on no account she would admit that she feels depressed, angry or irritate. And very often, this attitude is – consciously or unconsciously – reinforced by the surroundings. Handicaped people who appear well adjusted and "normal" cause less trouble and are easier to live with, than those who rebel and express their feelings – often by queer and striking ways of behaviour. We tend to forget that this well adjusted behaviour of the handicapped person often is caused by her not being in touch with her feelings and that this further diminishes her already weak self–confidence.

Example 4

Irene, a woman of 62, who is in therapy with me, expresses her feelings mostly in indirect ways by accusing others. Only after several years could she express how irritated and angry she feels, because her sister–in–law talks to her as if she were a child. Up to then, she had only dared to critisize her for speaking a specific dialect. This dialect was the language of Irene's childhood, she hated it and had refused to speak it ever since her mother died and she was moved to another town.)

So the feelings of the person must be accepted at the same time as the structure has to be respected. The structure is not only determined by the conditions of the institution and its everyday demands, but also by the possibilities and limitations of the staff. And of course the different personalities of the handicapped people have to be taken into consideration, their strong sides, as well as their weak sides and their limitations.

Both is needed: **structure and free play**. They are interdependent, complementary and *have to be maintained in an appropriate balance*. In its early years – an this has still some influence today – special education emphasized in offering mentally handicapped people a solid structure. It is true that such a structure is necessary. Yet, if this structure does not at the same time offer the mentally handicapped a free space for own decisions and initiatives, it will more inhibit than promote their growth. On the other hand, if the free play is too wide and open for the handicapped person to survey it, she will get stressed and unable to use it. The structure is necessary to make the free play visible. The free play is necessary to make sure that the structure does not just restrict people with special needs, but offer a safe space where they are encouraged to try out own impulses and take their own decicions.

Example 5

Herman is collecting everything. He stuffs his room with hundreds of toy cars, old papers, empty boxes, etc. He is not able to throw anything away, but keeps everything. His room gets so stuffed that it is hardly possible to keep it clean. The responsible social worker, on one hand, feels that Herman should be allowed to decide himself about his room, but on the other hand, that the dimensions of the mess get somehow out of control. She is asking herself how much she can tolerate without neglecting her professional duties. During supervision the idea arises, that she could mark with colored scotch tape those areas in Herman's room which absolutely have to stay free, so that the cleaning can be done. Everything else is left to his own responsibility. It works. Hermann keeps this agreement.

To find and to maintain *an adequate balance between structure and free play* is a demanding and crucial task for professionals working with the mentally handicapped. There is no rigid balance which can be found by diagnostics and then be fixed. It is a subtle balance, which continuously has to be watched and if necessary altered *together with* the handicapped people, *not for them.*

Example 6

Herman cannot deal with his money. Every time he gets his salary at the workshop, he immediately spends it to the last penny at the shopping center across the street. He already has accumulated hundreds of toy cars and he continues to buy new ones. He then has no money left for other things. If for instance the group goes out to have a coffee together, sombeody else has to pay for Herman. All attempts to persuade Herman that he should spare money for other things and not spend it all on toy cars, failed. The very day Herman gets his salary, compulsively, he spends it all on toy cars. The social worker agrees with Herman to split up the money in different envelopes, one for each week, and to take just one at a time, on the day indicated on the envelope. It works. Herman even seems to appreciate this support and keeps the agreement. Yet it is important for Herman to know that on the day of payment, the social worker will be there when he gets home and, together with him, prepare the envelopes.

Sensitivity to recognize individual possibilities and limitations, openness for changes and flexibilty to react to them are necessary. But equally important is clarity about what is given and cannot be discussed. There is nothing worse than to arise the illusion that there are choices if there are none. Staff members, wishing to be democratic, often tend to blur such facts, even for themselves, and only after discussing with the handicapped, do they realize that the decision has been made before.

Example 7

A small communtiy will admit a new inhabitant. Two people have applied. Both are invited for a visit. Afterwards the staff discusses with the group whom they would choose. They express a clear preference. Only later staff and management realize that for resaons the handicapped could neither know nor judge, this young man can not be accepted They decide for the other one. It is quite justified that the inhabitants are irritated and complain that their choice hat not been acknowledged and that the staff would ask them but then anyway decide by themselves.

Management and staff definitely should have verified if there was a real choice, before discussing with the group. This would have spared the handicapped people another experience of being disappointed and not taken seriously. Such experiences do not reinforce trust, but discourage the person. A little more reflection in time could help to avoid that.

More principles are essential for the person–centered work. I have described them in detail in my book "Praxis der Gesprächspsychotherapie". In this context I just want to point to some aspects which seem particularly relevant for working with people with special needs.

The road is as important as the destination: The crux with defining educational or behavioural goals for the handicapped person, is that only achieving this goal is considered a success. The eyes are so fixed on the goal, that what happens on the way, is not seen. Impulses pointing in another direction are not paid attention to, though they might open up quite new perspectives. For a person with special needs, the experience to be on the road is often more important, than to arrive at the destination. She experiences herself not as blocked anymore, but as moving. This movement should be perceived and encouraged by the staff.

Example 8
In an adult education program, mentally handicapped people learn how to express their concerns. Paul had always wished to have a single room. But he never dared to say it. In a role play, he is given the opportunity to try out how he could expresss his concern to the responsibles in his institution. The next evening at the program, he happily tells the other participants: "I said it" and "lottery". As there are only few single rooms in that institution and several applicants, the staff had decided to do a lottery next time a single room will be available. And Paul is lucky: he wins the single room ticket. This happens just before the summer vacation. After the summer a new program starts in which Paul again participates. The facilitator asks him, how he is feeling in his single room. Paul says: "No single room anymore. Much too boring."

This PROCESS–ORIENTED VIEW which acknowledges changes, rather than to stick to what was known before, is characteristic for the person–centerd approach in which *experience* has an important place. In the example above whe could see how Paul's concern has been taken seriously, how he was allowed to make his own experiences, how he then changed his mind and how this too was accepted. Though the staff felt, they could have told in advance that Paul would not like the single room, they let him experience this process, step by step, himself. It is obvious that this is much more rewarding for a handicapped person than decisions made by others "for her best".

The SMALL STEPS have to be paid particular attention to. Steps of growth will only be integrated if a person is allowed to do them *in her own rhythm*. This is not only, but particularly true for the mentally handicapped. They usually are much slower, survey smaller segments than we do. In a life determined by the rhythm of the "normals", they experience permanently to be overrun and to stay behind. Some of them develop considerable skills to hide this, so that people around them do not even notice it and stress them further. The experience of not being able to follow is so omnipresent and overwhelming for most mentally handicapped, that they hardly become aware of the small steps they manage to achieve here and then.

The staff therefore should look very carefully for these small steps and welcome them. Each step, as small as it may be, proves that the person is able to take a step, and bears the potential for further steps. Much too often the small steps go down, because we look too much at what is not functioning. Yet it is very important to point to and reinforce them, in order to arise and strengthen the handicapped people's trust in their own ressources.

Not the deficiencies are crucial but the ressources is another principle of the person–centered approach which is particularly valid for working with the mentally handicapped. Only out of their own ressources they may change and grow. Therefore it is necessary to discover and foster these ressources. The "diagnostic eye" which constantly looks at the deficiencies, tends to fix people with special needs on what they cannot do and blurs the view on what they can do.

Why it is so important, for mentally handicapped people *to experience their strong sides and their ressources* and why the staff should rather emphasize on facilitating and fostering them, than on trying to "fill up holes" (which mostly does not work anyway), becomes very clear when we look at

Carl roger's theory of the self–concept: The notion self–concept embraces the image a person has of herself and how she values this image. The self–concept is developing on one hand out of the immediate experience of the child (for example hunger–satisfaction) and on the other hand out of the values which are communicated to the child by his surroundings (for example: "if I get dirty, I am bad"). The self–concept is not fixed, but permanently developing and changing through life experience. Obstructions and emotional difficulties arise when experiences, feelings, sensations cannot be accepted because they do not conform with the self–concept. In other words, if the self–concept has become rigid, due to rigid external values or taboos (like "getting angry is bad", for example).

Congruence means: the self–concept conforms with experience. The self–concept is flexible and can allow the integration of new experience.

Incongruence means: a rigid self–concept which cannot allow new experiences, feelings or perceptions, unless they conform with the existing narrow limits.

Unfortunately, though not intentionally, the education of mentally handicapped children often tends more to foster incongruence than congruence. I have mentioned before, how people learn not to trust their feelings. But in daily life too, they again and again experience: "I cannot do that", "I do it the wrong way ". As there are indeed many things they cannot do or do the wrong way, they constantly are corrected. Sometimes much more than neccessary, because their surroundings wish them to appear as "normal" as possible. And they forget, how important it is for the handicapped to try out their own ways, wherever it is possible, even if their behaviour then may not quite conform to the norms. They anyway have to be corrected more than enough in situations where it is indeed impossible to follow their impulses. Yet we should not define each little queerness by the fact of retardation, but consider, that it could be just a somewhat strange personal behaviour which we would easily tolerate with a "normal" person.

Example 9
Eva is not able to fix a salad dressing. The social worker again and again has tried to demonstrate and explain her how to do it. She cannot get it and takes the bottle with the ready–made dressing. The social worker is disappointed that she is not able to learn such a simple thing and that she is handicapped to that point.

The retardation may well be the reason, why Eva is not able to understand how to prepare a salad dressing. On the other hand many "normal" people think they cannot make a good dressing and prefer the ready–made. By this I do not mean that the retardation should be denied. It is a reality, which the handicapped are expected to accept. This is not a small demand on people who are mentally handicapped. The more, as they are confronted with discrimination wherever they go – at the store, at the bus, at the swimming pool, on the street. No wonder do they tend to deny their handicap as much as possible and to keep distance from the other handicapped people. It is easier for the more severely handicapped, because they are less conscious of their being handicapped. But they too are very sensitive to the reactions of other people and do realize, that they are not how they should be.

To accept being handicapped is only possible, if the handicapped person can also experience *positive aspects* of how she is. For this she needs the support and encouragement of people around her, and this requires that these *can see* the positive aspects. Mentally handicapped, like other people, have to live with their weak points . But also with their strong points. The emphasis should not be on the label "handicapped", but on *the strong sides and the weak sides* of each individual. The handicapped should get to know these – their own as well as those of the others including the staff – and learn how to cope with them. To discover that other people too have weak points, as well as strong points, to experience that different people are different, and to accept these differences, is an indispensable condition for finding an acceptable way to live together in a community.

In Great Britain the term "mentally handicapped" has been replaced by *"people with special needs"*. Although this is an important step in order to overcome a discriminating labeling, the term does not cover all aspects I want to discuss here. Therefore I still use the traditional language too. But it is true that we need to find alternatives, especially for the valuations the handicapped are continuously confronted with: mildly, moderately, severely, profoundly retarded, more handicapped than others, less handicapped than others. The handicapped people fully adopt this rating among each other and establish a hierarchy of retardation, in which everybody tends to place him– or herself in higher ranges than the others. This does not exactly foster good relations among people with special needs..

Example 10
For Irene it is very important to what degree the other women in her community are handicapped. She is very happy to tell of one of her mates: "she belongs to the more severely retarded", or of another: "she gets attacks and has to take medication, I don't". It was terrible for her when a few years ago, after an accident, she had to move to a group of more severly retarded women. It is not relevant for her if she feels better or worse there, what counts is the blemish: "I now belong to the more severely retarded."

It would be much more constructive, instead of communicating this kind of rating, to try to stimulate sensibility for the differences of different people, to promote – and to practise – tolerance. The handicapped people should be encouraged to benefit from each other's strong sides, to help each other with the weak sides and to recognize: what can I better than others, what can others better than I, where do I need help, where can I help others?

Is it possible at all, to change the rigid patterns which have been marked in the handicapped person's childhood? It seems realistic not to have too large expectances, yet at the same time *to be open to surprises*. It is amazing to see, how sometimes a handicapped person, all at once, takes an unexpected step which nobody thought her capable of. And even if nothing of the like happens: for the staff, *to not reinforce further the stereotype behaviour* is a considerable success which is not always fully recognized.

As a support for the staff in meeting their various demanding tasks, we can deduce from the person–centered concept some useful

GUIDELINES FOR EVERY–DAY WORK

Listening

is one of the basic foundations of the person–centered approach. To listen patiently to the handicapped person, who may have difficulties to express herself, to listen carefully for nuances, hints for change, impulses, needs, feelings and moods, is an indispensable condition for any step towards better understanding what the person needs and how she feels and how the staff could respond to her in a helpful way.

Not letting us guide by what we already know

We should not rely on our knowing how a person will react, even if we have experienced it a hundred times. It is possible, at any time, that a handicapped person will act completely different from what we are used to. We should be open to that and not let us guide by what we already know. Of course, in many situations, our knowledge may be very helpful, yet we should not use it to pin ourselves – and the handicapped person – down to it. We have to *stay open to new and unknown aspects of her personality.*

Taking the handicapped person seriously

– even if she expresses herself in an unintelligible way and her behaviour appears bizarre – is another basic condition. We have to acknowledge that the handicapped person is trying to convey something which she cannot express properly. We should not dimiss that with the label "handicapped" or "regressed", but try to *"feel into" and understand her perception, her experience and her frame of reference.*

Staying with the obvious

We should avoid intepretations and explanations based on retardation, but stay with the obvious, exactly with what the handicapped person tries to express. The example with Eva and the vacuum–cleaner showed that clearly. With a "normal" person we would first check if something is wrong with the vacuum–cleaner, before we assume that something is wrong with the person. It should be the same with the mentally handicapped: first stay with the obvious and only if this does reveal any sense, try to find out what is behind. Yet the only chance to approach a hidden meaning, is to stay accuratley and concretely, with what the handicapped is expressing and to go with it, step by step.

Facilitating the person's own experience

As much as possible, whe should allow the handicapped to make their own experiences, not only in major issues like in the example of Paul's wish for a single room. Very small every–day things, which frequently, without much thinking, are done for the handicapped, would offer an opportunitiy for them to make their own experiences and to learn from. It is much more helpful, for example, to take somebody outside for a minute and let him try out, if he would be too warm with the coat or too cold without it, than to just say: "today you need your warm coat".

Of course there are limits. There are situations where people with special needs have to be protected from bad experiences. But this is done rather too much than not enough. To protect the handicapped from any bad experience also means to prevent them from learning to confront their reality and to make them miss chances for a good experience. It is very important though, not to leave them alone with a bad experience, but to talk about it and to consider together what could be learned from it.

522

Fostering Independency

The life of people with special needs is to a high degree determined by others. Therefore most of them feel a strong need for independency, even those who seem well, even too well, adapted. Very frequently this wish for autonomy is diffuse and hidden behind rebellious and strange behaviour, or it manifests by sticking stubbornly to something the staff considers a minor detail.

Example 11

Every morning it is a dreadful struggle for the staff to wake up Anna. She complains, refuses to leave her bed, does not come down for breakfast and has finally to be forced to get up. Particularly with new staff members, of whom she senses that they feel insecure, she goes to extremes with this fight. In supervision I suggest to try it with an alarm-clock – it works. Anna gets up without any problem and is at breakfast on time. Obviously the alarm–clock makes her feel that she is getting up by herself, not by being urged to by the staff.

Daily life offers countless opportunities to foster independency. Clothing, for example, is a large field. It is alarming how sometimes, from the way the handicapped people are dressed, the taste of the staff can be detected.

Example 12

Eva is very concerned to dress in a way to please people around her. On weekends she dresses after her mother's taste (which is considered awful by the staff), on weekdays she wears the clothes she thinks would please the staff. Looking at her wardrobe, it is easy to make out which piece of clothes has been bought with which staff member.

The staff can avoid that by helping the handicapped person to *find out what she* likes. For example, instead of saying: "this sweater does not go with the pants", to let her look at the mirror and try out: "how do you like yourself better, this way or that way?". It is necessary to emphasize, again and again, that not everybody has to have the same taste. For instance by saying: "I like this one, John likes the other one, which one do you like?"

Example 13:

In an adult education program, the mentally handicapped do a role–play: "how to buy clothes". A week later, Paul's mother tells the facilitator that she had to buy Paul a dark sweater for a funeral. They went from shop to shop, finally Paul had to decide between two sweaters. Both, the mother and the shopkeeper suggested the darker one, which would better suit the occasion and in which they thought Paul looked better. But Paul insisted on the other, a flushy, bright blue sweater. When he was asked why, he said: "because it feels so soft when I touch it".

Such experiences could be provided in the institution as social activities. Entertaining and yet instructive plays with clothes and cloths could be arranged for the handicapped people – offering them an opportunity to try out, to look at the mirror, to look at each other and to share their different tastes.

Helping the handicapped to perceive what they eperience

Most mentally handicapped have learned not to trust their experience. They feel that others do not understand it or consider it inadequate. Sometimes the handicapped do not even know what they experience and when they are asked, refer to what others are saying or to common-places.

Example 14

When I ask Irene, if she likes the new job at the workshop, she answers: "I always work hard." Or when the question is discussed if, because of her age, she would like to stop working or prefer to continue, she says: "At the workshop they are still grateful for my help."

Whe have to try, again and again, to draw the person's attention to what she feels and experiences in herself: "you were pleased", "you don't like that so much", "now it is getting too much for you". This way, at least we will not reinforce her being cut off from her experiencing process and, hopefully, help her to become, little by little, more aware of what is going on in herself.

Encouraging

People with special needs, very often in their life, are discouraged. So many things, they would like to do, are impossible. So they cannot build up a solid self–confidence. Some feel completely worthless, others compensate by overestimating themselves and then again get discouraged. Therefore it is extremely important that the small steps are paid attention to and encouraged. They should not go down in daily routine.

Example 15

Eva has to prepare a carrot salad. She bought two pounds of carrots and asks the social worker: "Do I have to prepare them all?" The social worker shows her the tomato salad and lettuce, already prepared, and asks her to guess how much carrot salad they would need in addition. "I can't ', is her clear statement. In supervision the social worker expresses his disappointment about her not being able to make any progress. I point out to him, that it *is* a progress for Eva to recognize her limits realisticly and to ask for help.

Even if achievements are tiny and hard to perceive, we have to point them out to the handicapped again and again, in order to encourage them to take another step.

Providing supports which enable the handicapped person to act independently

We can provide simple supports which help a handicapped person with something she cannot do and yet leave a space where she can act independently. Herman's envelopes for the money are an example for such a support. And with Eva, we could try, for instance, to have her fill the carrots in a bowl and see if this would help her to get an approximative idea of how much of them she would need for the salad.

Transparence

It is very important for the mentally handicapped that the actual situation, even if it is unpleasant, always is clear and transparent, . People with special needs should never be outwitted or taken by surprise, even if it seems easier at the moment. But the mistrust arising from that, would, in the long run, create new difficulties. Sometimes quite simple situations which only slightly differ from what they are used to, may be very mysterious and confusing the mentally handicapped. Then, a clear statement which describes the situation can be very helpful.

Reflecting the situation

is a method which can be appropriate and very helpful on various occasions and in different ways. Many critical situations might be eased and put on another level,

from where it is easier to find a solution. For instance if

– discussions turn in circles

– powerfights are going on

– agressions escalate

to reflect the situation helps to interrupt the circle, for example by saying: "we both are speaking very loud right now", "I tell you to wash your hair and you say no", "you don't like what I say", "you would like to hit me", "you are angry and I am impatient", etc. By reflecting the situation, we take a step back, look at it and, for the time being, accept it at it is. This may open up a way to change it. At least it provides a break for breathing and interrupts the vicious circle. This method is highly developed and refined in

Garry prouty's concept of pre–therapy

where reflections are used for the purpose to establish contact with profoundly retarded, very withdrawn and autistic people and to help them getting in contact with reality, with themselves and with others. Prouty's clinical experience proves that working in a person–centered way is not restricted to the moderately handicapped. Pre–therapy is a way to establish psychological contact, which is the first necessary condition for psychotherapy, and it also offers various helpful opportunities to be used in everyday–life with the people .

These are some of the guidelines we can deduce from the person–centered approach. It is up to the staff, to use their experience as well as their creativity to transfer them into the practice of their specific work situation.

HOW CAN A PERSON–CENTERED WAY OF WORKING BE TRAINED?

The attitude based on empathy, acceptance and congruence is the main foundation

of the person–centered concept. But it cannot just be put on like working clothes. As we have seen, this attitude implies some guidelines and methodic approaches which have to be known and transposed into practice. To listen accurately, to be empathic with another person's world, to discern between what is going on in ourselves and what we perceive from the other person, requires a discipline which, to some extent, can be practised. Yet learning, in this field, first of all means: working on ourselves to become conscious of our inclinations, our fears and our blind spots.

And those who work in institutions also have to be well grounded in it's structures. They must know it's possibilities, it's limitations and it's patterns, in order to have a clear view of the conditions on which they work.

Trainers should develop, together with the staff, a person–centered way which takes into account their specific work situation. The trainers contribute their profound knowledge of the person–centered approach and it's applications, the trainees contribute their experience with the mentally handicapped and with the institution. This is how, for example, a training program could be designed:

1. An inaugurative workshop for the whole staff where they are introduced to the basic foundations of the person–centered approach.

2. Regular supervision, based on person–centered principles, for those who work directly with the handicapped people.

3. Follow–up workshops where, what has been learned and transfered into practice, can be reviewed, deepened, further developed and, if neccessary, modificated.

We have dealt with professionals and institutions, so far. Now we may ask ourselves:

IS THE PERSON–CENTERED CONCEPT USEFUL ALSO IN FAMILIES?

Basically, in a family, a person–cantered attitude can help to deal with tensions and conflicts and with the daily routine. Yet it has to be acknowledged that the structure of a family is different from that of an institution. Then the described guidelines can be very useful for the family of a mentally handicapped person. An example may ilustrate this:

Example 16

Jonas is an autistic young man. He has no ears (due to a prenatal damage), does not speak, but is able, to a certain degree, to grasp what is told him very loudly, slowly and with distinct lip mouvements. He lives in an institution and comes home two or three times a year for holidays. There he loves to watch television (as he has no opportunity to do that at his institution), and it is difficult to prevent him from doing that too extensively. One evening his mother has to go cut for two hours. She is in a hurry and does not want to upset Jonas. So she does not tell him, knowing that he is upstairs watching television. Also, his younger sister Nadine is at home. Nadine goes down to her room in the basement, too without telling Jonas, knowing that he will not move away from the television set until somebody goes and gets him.

But this time, unexpectedly, Jonas comes down and finds the living room empty. He goes wild and sreams. Nadine gets panicked, not knowing how to calm her brother. She remembers that he likes to take a bath and that this usually has a soothing effect. So she prepares him a bath. He puts up a fierce struggle and splahes water everywhere. Desperately, Nadine phones her older sister for help. Together, with great difficulty, they manage to calm Jonas down.

Which of the described guidelines could help to avoid such a critical situation, or at least it's escalation?

Not letting us guide by what we already know: Jonas' mother knows that Jonas, once he is watching television, does not move until somebody goes and gets him. She acts according to this knowledge and without considering that he could behave differently for once.

Transparence: In order to avoid long explications and the possibility of his protest, she does not tell him, that she is going out. The sister too does not tell him where she ist. For Jonas, the situation is not transparent at all and he gets panicked.

Staying with the obvious: Nadine, who does not often see her brother, is terrfied by his going. She does not think of the obvious: Jonas is upset because he discovers that mother is not there. Instead of being empathic, Nadine only thinks of how to stop him getting wild. She remembers that a bath sometimes used to soothe hiim. But he does not want to take a bath, what he wants is *to be taken seriously*, so he gets even more wild. The situation escalates. If she would have explained to him: "Mom went out, she will be back soon, I am downstairs in my room", he very probably would have calmed down soon and gone back to watch television.

This example shows us that in families too, there are situtations which the person–centered approach could help to cope with in a better way. Yet the family situation is different from that of ian institution which is designed specificly for mentally handicapped people. In a there must be room for the needs, concerns, sorrows and pleasures of its other members as well as for those of the mentally retarded, as it is the living space for all of them.

Family relationships are not the same as relationsships in an institution. Parents, sisters and brothers are much more involved emotionally with each other. It is harder for them, in difficult situations, to take some distance. The fact of mental retardation has a much stronger impact on the family of the handicapped person than on those who have to deal with her professionally.

For professionals, living with mentally handicapped people, is their job. After work they go home to their privacy, where they can take a breath and live their own lives. Their relationship with the handicapped is different.

THE RELATIONSHIP BETWEEN STAFF AND PEOPLE WITH SPECIAL NEEDS

There is common agreement that relationship is central in this work. But the characteristics of this relationship often are not seen very clearly..

In person–centered view, the relationship between staff and people with special needs is based (just as the therapeutic relation in client–centered therapy) on empathy, acceptance and congruence. Congruence implies that the specific character, as well as the limitations of this relationonship, have to be clear and transparent for the people involved. It is, to some degree, a one–sided relationship, in which the well–being of the handicapped persons and the fostering of their independence take priority. It is *their life* which takes place in the institution, not that of the staff who live their private life somewhere else. As warm and affectionate the relationship may be, it still remains *a professional relationship.* Social workers sometimes tend to blur this fact. They try to establish a very close personal relationship, get very involved, cannot keep it up, are soon burnt out and have to look for another job. For the handicapped this means, once more, to feel abandoned and disappointed, an experience they know only too well. It is interesting to observe how the handicapped people, according to their different personalities,in different ways, try to protect themselves from new disappointments. Some cling persistently to the staff members, hoping to hold them this way, wherea others, on the contrary, refuse the closeness the social workers try to offer them.

A **reliable professional relationship which keeps some distance, but offers continuity,** is more honest and finally more helpful for people with special needs, than a closenesss the social worker is not able to keep up. "Professional" does in no ways mean cold or unconcerned. Professional means, that the staff maintains the necessary distance to be able to put aside their own wishes, ambitions and ideas and emphasize on the needs and development of the handicapped. If those can rely upon all staff members to work on this same base, it will be much easier for them to cope with the fact, that people around them change frequently, be it due to the work–schedule or to the fluctuation of the staff.

Even if everybody works on the same base, each relationship will still remain unique and have its own idiosyncratic feature. Different staff members have different access to different people with special needs. All the mentally handicapped will have staff members they like better than others. But they can be sure, that all staff members will try to foster their growth as much as possible, to accept them in their individuality and to offer them a structure which meets their individual needs and abilities. This is a grant for

CONTINUTITY

If an institution's work is based consistently on the person–centered approach, if the priority is on being empathic to the world of the mentally handicapped, on trying to realize and understand how they feel and what they experience, then many useless and disappointing experiments could be avoided. Often new staff members start their work full of ideas, deriving from their diagnostic knowledge and pedagogic concepts. With best intentions, they eagerly want to try them on the people with special needs. But very rarely this leads to the results they aim for. Frequently handicapped people, confronted with ideas brought from outside and not developed out of empathy with their specific world, fall back instead of progressing. If an institution would employ people who are willing to work in a person–centered way and have them trained carefully in this approach, this kind of disappointment could be avoided and new staff members could use their energy and their creativity in a more useful and rewarding way.

To provide this continuity might not only improve the quality of life for the mentally handicapped, but also, for the staff, make work more interesting, more pleasant and less frustrating as well as create a better climate for the institution.

REFERENCES

Pörtner, M. (1990): *Client–Centered Therapy with Mentally Retarded Persons: Catherine and Ruth.* In: Client–Centered and Experiential Psychotherapy in the Nineties, hrsg. von Lietaer, G., Rombauts, J. & Van Balen, R. Leuven (University Press).

Rogers, C. (1951): *Client–Centered Therapy.* Boston (Houghton Mifflin). Deutsch: Die klientenzentrierte Gesprächspsychotherapie. München 1972 (Kindler).

Pörtner, M. (1994): *Praxis der Gesprächspsychotherapie – Interviews mit Therapeuten.* Stuttgart (Klett–Cotta). english version edited by Allan Turner: *The practice of Client–Centered Psychotherapy – Dialogues with Therapists.* Unpublished script, Zürich 1993.

Prouty, G. (1994): *Theoretical Evolutions in Person–Centred/Experiential Therapy: Applications to Schizophrenic and Retarded Psychoses.* New York (Praeger).

Pörtner, M. (1990): *Klientenzentrierte Psychotherapie mit schizophrenen Patienten.* In: Die Kerbe, Nr. 3 + 4. Stuttgart, (1993) Klientenzentrierte Therapie mit geistig Behinderten un d Schizophrenen. Garry Prouty's Konzept der Prae–Therapie. In: Brennpunkt, Nr. 54. Zürich. english: Client–Centered Therapy with Mentally Retarded and Schizophrenic Clients – Garry Prouty's concept of Pre–Therapy. Unpublished script, Zürich 1992.

Client–Centered Therapy with Very Disturbed Clients

NATHANIEL J. RASKIN

NORTHWESTERN UNIVERSITY

ROGERS' INTERVIEW WITH "LORETTA."

In discussing the use of client–centered therapy with very disturbed clients, I have employed two sources. One is a tape–recorded interview conducted by Carl Rogers in 1958 with a woman in a psychiatric hospital diagnosed as schizophrenic. My second source for exploring the topic is the experience that comes from my own practice. Rogers' interview, with"Loretta," is a rich reservoir of verbatim material; my own work is more impressionistic.

I have written a detailed analysis of Rogers' interview with the woman known as "Loretta" which the Guilford Press will soon publish as a chapter, "The Case of Loretta," in "Carl Rogers: Casebook and Critical Perspectives," Barry Farber, Debora Brink, & Patricia Raskin (Eds.). The book includes a verbatim typescript of the interview.

In brief, Loretta was a patient in a state psychiatric hospital. Rogers' was the last of three demonstration interviews conducted during the 1958 Annual Workshop of the American Academy of Psychotherapists. Albert Ellis had demonstrated Rational–Emotive Therapy and Richard Felder had given an example of the experiential approach used by his Atlanta, Georgia psychiatric group. Rogers' interview has become a classic audiotaped demonstration of his hypothesis that client–centered therapy can be used effectively with all kinds of people, including some sufficiently disturbed to be diagnosed as psychotic and hospitalized.

The interview is also classic in the consistency with which Rogers provides empathy, congruence, and unconditional positive regard. His opening statement conveys these attributes in a seminal fashion: "I'm Carl Rogers...This must seem confusing and odd, and so on, but I, I felt when you left, I felt really sorry that the interview had been kind of...cut short 'cause I sort of felt maybe there were other things you wanted to say."

Even though the session is less than thirty minutes long, Loretta uses it constructively in at least five different ways:

(1) She resolves the problem of whether she will cooperate with an impending transfer to another ward, about which she had a great deal of conflict.

(2) She deals with the question of whether she is able to trust people in general, and the hospital staff in particular.

(3) She expresses upset and confusion about the treatment of a patient heard screaming in the background throughout the interview, and talks about the fears aroused by this experience.

(4) She gains insight into peculiar sensations of a tickling in her knees, and of a feeling of electricity in the air when she had worked in the hospital laundry.

(5) As the interview progresses, she manifests attitudes of positive self–regard, in a number of concrete ways.

Loretta's reaction to Rogers is so positive that the listener may question, "Does this woman belong in a psychiatric hospital? Is her diagnosis correct?" Loretta's history and symptoms do lend credence to her classification, but her responsiveness to Rogers also supports the belief she articulates in the interview that talking as she has to these three therapists is more helpful than the medications and the shock therapy she has been given.

MY OWN WORK WITH VERY DISTURBED PERSONS

Aside from five years as Chief Psychologist at a major children's hospital in Chicago, my clinical work, since 1950, has been in the context of a part–time private practice , averaging ten to twelve hours a week. My clientele has been quite diverse, in terms of age, socio–economic status, kind of problem, and degree of disturbance. I remain committed to seeing any kind of person, but there have been changes in the kind of people I see, and in my beliefs.

For some reason, many of the people I see have turned out to be quite disturbed. I mean by this that they have had breakdowns, have been hospitalized psychiatrically, have difficulty holding jobs, come from non–nurturant families, can't establish families, and often feel dependent on medication. In addition, they may be depressed, thought–disturbed, or paranoid. In my practice, they happen to be mostly women.

When I began seeing people in therapy, I had a totally positive outlook. This was partly a function of having a therapeutic orientation based on a profound belief in the capacities of the client and may also have been a function of my youth. I was only 19 years of age when I began my graduate study with Carl Rogers, who was himself only 38. I felt very good about the training I was getting to be of help to people. My expectation was that I would be able to help all kinds of people to help themselves.

It was not till decades later that I was dismayed to observe that a couple of the clients I had seen years earlier and had apparently profited were having the same problems or worse. They were more rigid or felt more persecuted. I had always rejected a disease model but found myself thinking these people were in the grip of a disease. While I was sobered by this experience, I stuck with the people I was seeing who had serious problems. Sometimes one of these individuals will say I must be bored with hearing the same complaints and problems. I seem to have a great capacity to keep working with people who are stuck and not become bored or discouraged.

I believe that continuing to be there for such people is probably the most powerful factor in being of help and in eventually seeing change and growth.

I think the second most important thing is to remain as empathic as possible with the world of the very disturbed person. I do not always succeed in doing this. Sometimes I feel that I have to tell my client that I do not understand her train of thought. This is in the interest of my being congruent but I find that, usually, rather than succeeding in bridging the gap between myself and my client, I drive her further away. In terms of our relationship, I am better off trying to be empathic.

Another situation where it is difficult for me to remain empathic is with a client who keeps complaining, complaining, complaining how people mistreat her. I find myself wanting this person who is acting weak and helpless, to act in a way which expresses some independence and strength. Since my confidence in her is greater than her own, this usually results in her feeling, not only that I do not understand her, but that I am taking sides against her.

An example is a client who lives in a residence for people who have at some time required psychiatric hospitalization. She is intelligent, pretty, and artistically talented, but finds it difficult to believe in herself and is emotionally fragile. She is supported by the state and has no income of her own. She has siblings who give her small sums of money from time to time. They have medical and interpersonal problems of their own. My client feels entitled to their help and gets angry when they do not give it. Recently, as a result of her artistic ability, she earned a little money on her own, but became angry when she got the impression that her sister was expecting her to pay her own train fare to visit the sister over the weekend. As it turned out, the sister picked her up and drove her to her home, but my client spent a substantial amount of emotional energy feeling angry and resentful that her sister was expecting her to pay for her own train fare. My own feeling was that this was a reasonable expectation, and an expression of respect, but I knew that if I expressed this, my client would feel misunderstood and be angry at me. I believe that I learn over and over again that it works better to be empathic and respect my client's own way of viewing herself and the problems she experiences.

I believe that I have been of help to the client I described and many others with severe emotional disturbance. There are others with whom I have not been successful. On the whole, I believe with some conviction that a person–centered approach without any special modifications is effective in helping many individuals who have had breakdowns, been hospitalized, have thought disturbances, and find it difficult to work and to establish families.

Accomodating Psychotherapy
to Information–Processing Constraints.
A Person–Centered Psychiatric Case Description.

LUC ROELENS
BELGIUM

ABSTRACT

An individually tailored residential psychiatric treatment is reported. The patient was admitted in a state of severe alcohol toxicomania, complicated by paranoid psychotic episodes. He was diagnosed as a borderline personality. His cumbersome clinical evolution during the first three years of treatment demonstrated that the suffocation of fundamental positive tendencies by destructive patterns had to be handled successfully before real progress could be made.

Improvement of self–disclosure by the patient inspired the author to develop a suited method of process directivity based on recent neurobiological knowledge of the human cerebral infor-mation–processing mechanisms. This process–directive method accelerated the process of ge-neralization of experiential shifts, recently obtained in therapeutically sheltered interactions. Relevant information–processing aspects are analyzed.

This case history elucidates the relevance of combining client–centered attitudes with accep-tance of the complexity of the psychopathological problems and with correct understanding of the basic psychophysiological processes at issue.

INTRODUCTION

According to Rogers (1951), "therapy is basically the experiencing of the inadequacies in old ways of perceiving, the experiencing of new and more accurate and adequate perceptions, and the recognition of significant relationships between perceptions" (p. 222).The knowledge about the neurobiological mechanisms underlying the replacement of patterns of "significant relati-onships between perceptions" by "new and more accurate and adequate" patterns is gro-wing.The human neural information processing system as described by Edelman (1989) dis-plays the organizational features needed to "separate out, and to bring into figure, any signifi-cant perceptual element which has heretofore been unrecognized" (Rogers 1951, p. 145).

This case history documents a person–centered application of a recent human information–processing model (Koukkou, 1987, 1988).Knowledge of information processing constraints proved decisive in helping the patient to automatize recently developed and more adequate interpersonal schemes and strategies.In doing so, he bootstrapped the process of generalization of experiential shifts obtained in therapeutically sheltered interactions.

CASE DESCRIPTION :GUIDED 'FUNCTIONAL STATE SHIFT' AS A RELEVANT FRAGMENT OF LONG–TERM RESIDENTIAL TREATMENT
Clinical picture on admission

After divorce, at the age of twenty–seven, John found himself living alone for the first time in his life.He slipped into a massive abuse of alcohol.At the age of thirty–three, he was sent to our mental hospital.Upon admission he was in a state of severe alcohol toxicomania.His usual level of functioning had to be characterized as : a chronic state of personal and social neglect; alcohol toxicomania; depression; anxiety and loss of personal security.

Once we enjoyed his confidence, other elements were added to this picture : he had for his lifetime experienced himself as a very anxious person, very dependent on a supporting person but shying away from getting too close to that person.The death of his father had been a heavy blow for him.He perceived himself as having totally broken down after the separation from his wife.

Psychopathology

John was diagnosed as a borderline personality with good intelligence.In the course of the hospitalisation he displayed a broad spectrum of psychopathological symptoms.

– He had to be protected from his tendency to abuse alcohol which lasted for more than three years after admission.

– He behaved for a long time as a person who was capable to adapt to his environment in a formal way and who was at the same time unable to accept more closeness in contact.

– For several years, he displayed a need of preoccupation with vague but rigid convictions about physics, astrophysics, the macrocosmos and the "All".He claimed to discern hidden relations between the facts involved in his belief system and said that these relations made a clear and deep sense to him.

– Several times, in situations of stress or following alcohol abuse, these abstract beliefs evolved into overrunning paranoid micropsychoses.

– Huge interpersonal anxiety emerged as the elading symptom in the course of the hospitalisation.

Evolution

After acute treatment and general observation, the psychiatric revalidation proved cumbersome.Nor the building of a sufficiently strong psychotherapeutic alliance nor a good solution of the anxiety problems were within reach.During the first three years of hospitalisation John's level of functioning was highly situation–dependent.In periods of severe anxiety he was unable to accomplish very simple tasks in the occupational therapy.In such times he reacted in an hypochondrical way, suffering mostly from pain in many joints.This pain disappeared each time he progressively recuperated from those periods of anxiety.John continued to need a sheltered life as he persisted to be a recluse person with problems of anxiety and of episodic alcohol abuse.These problems made short trials of living outside the hospital fail.Nevertheless, John partly recovered.He manufactured in a very motivated way the furniture he lacked.During two years while living at the hospital, he attended an evening course on the restauration of antique furniture and he obtained the certificate.Without displaying whole–hearted attachment, he had built to a limited extent therapeutic alliances with several team members.Although I estimated the progress made as insufficient, John was discharged upon his request on day 1093.Again, he slipped into alcohol abuse and invalidating anxiety.He was unable to attend the provided day hospitalization.In two months, he got three readmissions to and two discharges from full hospitalization.

Alcohol abuse and suicidal thoughts urged him to ask for a new long–term readmission on day 1152.He was completely demoralized.His mood turned to a depressive state, colored by fear and submissiveness.From day 1176 onwards, he gradually but incompletely relaxed.The nurses observed an uncommon element in his behaviour : he clearly needed the opportunity to talk with them, sharing all his preoccupations.This was the first sign of an important shift in his interpersonal attitudes : from avoiding to approaching nurses.This shift was expanded systematically.From that time onwards the personalized therapeutic prescriptions included :

– "Your own judgment and wishes are to be distrusted as guidelines for a successful evolution; instead, your concrete way of behaving is reliable."

– "Your pattern of escaping has to change : don't flee into loneliness, fly towards trustworthy persons (as soon as possible after a short period of withdrawal)".

– "Rely on the guidance of dependable persons when your mood is dominated by anxiety. At such moments you are not able to be your own guide."

This interpersonal approach was concretely implemented.Simultaneous pharmacological treatment consisted of a high daily dosis of benzodiazepines and of antidepressive medication.

John's huge interpersonal anxiety continued to dominate the clinical picture for several months.But progressively John learned to switch from being the victim, paralyzed by anxiety and paranoid ideation, to sharing those terrifying thoughts and feelings.After a sheltered period of 137 days on the closed ward, he was able to join his former open ward on day 1375.There he was confronted with some brazen fellow patients and he slipped into a new episode of sensitivity, paranoid ideation and behavioural inhibition.He was able to talk about it spontaneously with his coaches.

On day 1421, John explicated to me very concretely that every morning he experienced an irreconcilable contrast between his own mood (anxious awakening at night, unpleasant dreams, feelings of shame about his past and the vitality he perceived in other people.Talking about it, he suddenly became anxious and frozen, relaxing again after having confessed that towards me he got ashamed by being honest about the feelings mentioned. I accepted this happening as a concrete advance in the development of a trusting relationship.Clearing the space and careful reframing of the ad–hoc experience together provided him a sense of relief : "It feels good to have someone backing me".

Instigated by this level of self–disclosure, I wrote that evening a procedure to process those morning difficulties which I offered him the next day.The following days, John made a single adjustment : he changed the order of the different substeps of step 5.One week later, on day 1429, the nurse noted : "The written proposal gives him much support. He is able to adjust himself and to join the therapeutic activities."On day 1431, John reported that he got up from bed earlier in order to seek a quiet place to proceed trough the different steps without being disturbed.During the following weeks, John improved dramatically.On day 1469, I noted richer facial expressions while he commented on his positive evolution.That day, we started the reduction of the benzodiazepine doses (to abolition) and we anticipated changing the treatment regime into day hospitalisation.He succeeded in living in his home town from day 1480 onwards.

John needed some ten months to adapt to the exigences of living at home.He went trough some subjectively harsh episodes without recurring to alcohol or to tranquillizing medication.Progressively, he laboriously adjusted his self–perceptions to a more flexible interaction with other people.Management of his behaviour now could totally rely on his personal efforts and control.From about day 1790 onwards he took personal initiative in order to resume work.One month of half time working was enough to give him the self–confidence necessary to engage successfully in fulltime work (day 1861) after five years of psychiatric treatment.He regularly kept contact.It was a pleasure to observe John growing into self–confidence as he coped successfully with daily life.At that level of change he could rely on what he had internalized.During his follow–up appointments most of the time we focused on his reports of autonomous progress without hampering difficulties.After a few months already the psychologist expressed his appreciation of John's behavioural change by saying : "It is remarkable how John has got sucked up by normal behaviour patterns now."Successful evolution after discharge is documented for more than three years now.Up to now, the only psycho~patho~logically recognizable sequelae of the illness consist of three upsurges of preoccupations about the "All", marking three episodes of stressful fear without endangering the level of daily functioning.

The guided functional state shift manual

("Morning processing manual", John's rearrangement of step 5).

Step 1 – *Awakening*

Step 2 – *Accepting the automatism*: 'Everything comes down on me and I would prefer to wal off.'

Step 3 – *Getting a correct understanding*: 'Looking at life from an anxious attitude, while lacking self–confidence, my automatic way of appreciation remains unshakable.If I succeed in finding another perspective, everything can change.'

Step 4 – *A sound foundation for reframing*: 'The moments that I really feel backed up by someone, I feel much stronger.For a little while I evoke memories of such moments ... .If this does not succeed very well today, I keep on knowing rationally that the behaviour of dr. Roelens, Robert, Paul, Steve, Anny and John proves that each of them goes on backing me up, each in their own way. I consider this thought for a moment ... .'

Step 5 – *A correct framing*: 'I accept that I still have to learn many things.'

5.1. Looking from my present perspective is only a starting point. I accept that the unpleasant subjective outlook gets installed automatically and that this outlook is far to restricted. I have to learn to put this outlook in a larger context : the total situation, the position of other people with their particularities and needs... .

5.2. My capacities do exist.I have demonstrated them regularly.Starting the day as open–minded as possible will give my vitality the opportunity to be elicited by situations that call for it.

5.3. Other people offer me opportunities for cooperation.Seeing their offer can require a lot of deduction.This quest makes better sense than sticking to my view of people as opposed to me (threatening me or being unapproachably superior).

5.4. In order to escape more easily the situation of being trapped as a plaything of unpleasant emotions I will have to search everytime for a practical and realistic approach of those emotions (I gather concrete examples).

5.5. The development of trust has to go on acquiring subtle distinctions indefinitely. It starts from an affective "all or nothing" basis, which gradually takes up many distinctions by inter-action with reality if the circumstances are favourable to this development.Everyone has the inevitable duty to find each time the right distinctions. This asks for many steps in the deve-lopment of nuances.

Clinical comments

Before the admission John had committed himself to strategies and attitudes of self–protection with self–destructive consequences.These were automatized in a way that precluded direct personal exploration.Without external interference, these strategies could to go on dominating the automatized stages of individual information processing and behaviour for ever.Such a po-werlessness of the patient implies a large responsibility for the psychiatrist who has to develop, select and evaluate the most promising ways of "selective attunement" (Stern, 1985, p. 207–211).

During three years John was unable to engage into concrete constructive self–disclosure.Confronted with the treatment failure after those three years, "not knowing what else to do", he got very depressed.He "tumbled into a bottomless pit".Only then his basic inter-personal behaviour changed, indicating that his breakdown opened the way for more basic forms of relatedness (Stern, 1985).This gave him a starting point for learning to accomodate to the dependency of his further development on a favourable surrounding interpersonal athmosphere.

Retrospectively, it seems that the basic anxiety had to acknowledged in a direct way before it became possible to process it in a suited interpersonal climate.Even then, it was a hard job for John to get out of his old ways of coping and to elaborate more efficient new ones.After ha-ving accepted the necessity of relying on trustworthy people, he needed several more months, filled with intense suffering, to elaborate new ways of coping with his anxieties and to develop progressively new ways of perceiving and experiencing.

This development was greatly accelerated by the use of the "morning processing ma-nual".Linking up with recently developed and spontaneously occurring mood, the manual gave enough instrumental help to produce a decisive 'functional state shift' (Koukkou, 1988, p. 88–90) every morning.From then on, the new ways of perceiving and experiencing progressively got automatized by daily practice, by the guided functional state shift and by application to new situations.

ANALYSIS OF RELEVANT INFORMATION–PROCESSING ASPECTS

Introduction

The psychotherapeutic interaction on day 1421 will be familiar to many psychotherapists.From an information–processing perspective this interaction shares several aspects with John's per-sonal effort when using the guided functional state shift manual.Drawing on the information–processing model developed by Koukkou (1987, 1988), this section clarifies those similarities.

Day 1421 : the psychotherapeutic interaction displays spontaneous shifts in the functional brain state

While talking about feelings of weakness, John realized that he had engaged into unusual self–disclosure.This obviously induced a feeling of relative unsafety.As a result, his behaviour chan-ged automatically from fluent talking into an inhibiting anxiety.Only after some time he was able to relax again, after further self–disclosure and after perceiving my unconditional acceptance of his way of being of that moment.Thus, in this segment of therapeutic interaction we can discern three different phases separated by two observable shifts, the first from spontaneity to inhibition and the second from the inhibited to a more relaxed state.

From a neurobiological point of view, these both shifts in emotional state and overt behaviour reflect transitions between different functional brain states.Koukkou's information–processing model helps us to understand these transitions.

John's instinctive impression of unusual self–disclosure induced an instantaneous reappreciation of the situation.This was executed by pre–attentive processes (which are not under conscious control).They identified the situation as relatively unsafe according to the standards of interpretation that were automatically and unconsciously available to him at that moment.

What were the standards that John had used in constructing his interpersonal world ?He had never been intimate with his parents.When growing up, he had been a weak shy boy for years.His attachment behaviour was restricted : he always had shyed away from getting too close to the persons on whom he felt dependent; after the loss of his father and his wife, he never had accepted new persons to support him.During the first three years of residential treatment he did not overlearn this core of reticence and fearful awe.Different attitudes with a restricted degree of generalization only appeared from day 1176 onwards.On day 1421 the older attitudes continued to be the dominant ones.For John the most salient feature of other people still was their negative influence on his feelings of well–being, as it had been for years.Concomitantly, the 'suited' behaviour was automatically activated by those salient features : John got struck into an anxious inhibition.

Information about unsafety is information to which an "attention" response gets attached.As a result, the controlled or cognitive mode of information–processing gets activated as a next step in the processing (Koukkou, 1988, p. 86). So, John was consciously confronted with his incongruency : while confiding personal feelings to his psychiatrist his spontaneous behaviour had walled off this trusting.From this moment onwards, he was able to analyze the event more completely : what were the advantages and the disadvantages of each of both behaviours ?Now John could check the adequacy of the two conflicting behaviours in an experiential way.He felt that trusting me had priority.At that moment his brain was able to engage into a corrective shift as his experiential feeling instigated the here and now strongest motive to override the older, well–established motive.John thus engaged in further self–disclosure.This shift matched his needs as was proven by the result, his sense of relief.It was accompanied by a conscious reframing, "it feels good to have someone backing me".This statement confirmed that his standards of security had been met in a new way by the ongoing interaction.

Of course, this shift to a more extensive form of trust was also dependent on my lasting ability to offer John the client–centered core conditions.In fact, at that time I felt very committed to the fate of John.It had been hard to be for many months the witness of his invalidating anxieties and paranoid ideas.I felt responsible as I was the rigorous psychiatrist who had kicked him out of his usual ways of cripple coping with anxiety.I could imagine how he suffered each morning from the confrontation of his own feelings of worthlessness with the vividness of other people.At this point my knowledge of the information–processing perspective made me sensitive for an additional opportunity of therapeutic progress.I felt that all prerequisites were met for John to learn to influence these automatic shifts of information processing.So, that evening at home, I wrote the morning processing manual.

Biological constraints on voluntary change

John's automatic inhibition was grounded in very old appreciative patterns.These patterns had not been updated during childhood, adolescence and adulthood.On the contrary, John had for his lifetime experienced himself as a very anxious person. Patterns leading to interpersonal inhibition had been reinforced during childhood, as he had shyed away from the rougher boys in school to whom he had been an easy victim.The development of interpersonal trust had been arrested on an early level : as an adult John felt himself very dependent on a supporting person while at the same time avoiding closeness.This dependency need had been satisfied by the presence of his father and his wife.After the death of his father and the separation from his wife, John had broken down totally.

John had acquired his current basic appreciative patterns at an age by which his brain had not yet reached maturity.He had retained them although his brain since then had acquired many possibilities of differentiation and representation that were unavailable to it in the first years of life.This developmental distance installed a large gap between the functional state of his brain upon acquisition of the basic appreciative patterns and the functional state of his brain later in adult life.Whatever the reasons might have been, as a child John had been deprived from the circumstances favorable to a continuously developing concrete sense of interpersonal security.A corrective education would have provided him with many small steps of transformation from the archaic appreciation towards better suited, more efficient ways.In a healthy development coping strategies (or programs for responses and actions) would have been regularly actualized and differentiated.But this actualization is a vulnerable process.Motivationally strong affective states with adverse effects on candid openness (such as fear, intense shame, pain, experiencing lack of respect or devaluation of personal worth, ...) can take over priorities and install disruptive loops of automatized appreciation, unsuited for fruitful interpersonal behaviour.

As John's basic appreciative patterns never got updated, they continued to be recalled by the pre–attentive processes.In their archaic condition they continued to serve as a standard of comparison used for the first evaluation of incoming information.The automatic attribution of the meaning "it is unsafe to disclose myself" proved to be dysfunctional in the situation of trusting and closeness, occurring on day 1421.

Perpetuated restriction to old ways of appreciation is a common problem.The victim has the difficult task of changing old automatisms to more appropriate strategies while automatically functioning in the dysfunctional pattern and without being able to gain direct and conscious access to the long–term memory storages in which the automatized strategies were originally developed.The more primitive the point of stagnation, the more difficult the job.

For clients with this kind of problem, one biologically suited way out is the formation of new patterns of appreciation.The client–centered therapeutic attitudes offer a suited interpersonal climate to which the client may respond sooner or later by perceiving it unconsciously ("subception", Rogers, 1951, p. 506–507) as satisfying his basic needs of security.The second shift during the interaction on day 1421 demonstrated that John had successfully formed a new appreciative pattern.But he still had to automatize and generalize this new pattern.

Guided functional state shift as a way of automatizing new basic appreciative patterns

The goal of the intervention was to deflect John's early waking information processing mechanisms in such a way that they could evade from the functional brain states associated with and characterized by the habitual negative mood.By using the manual John got the opportunity to add a deliberate attention response, founded on motives originating from personal experience, to this automatically appearing mood.In doing so, he fostered shifts to other brain states selected from the new repertoire, acquired during the nine preceding months.He had to succeed these shifts at moments on which therapeutic help was not available.However, he had already indicated that he had acquired new 'RIGs' (representations of interactions that have been generalized – Stern, 1985, p. 97–99) : on day 1400 he had commented that discussing problems with a nurse had brought him partial relief, but that he would have enjoyed total relief if I had been available to him at that moment.Somehow I trusted the combined effect of this 'RIG' with the evoking qualities of the manual (the manual could function as an object leading to "subception" of qualities of the person who had given it). Indeed, the effect was strong enough to back John with a sufficient amount of proper symbolized interpersonal components (Kiesler, 1982, p. 12) in that specific situation.

The five steps were phrased in a process–centered way.This prevented the intrusion of subjective values foreign to John.

Step 1 (awakening) and step 2 (accepting the unagreable automatic mood shift) were formulated to remind and convince John that automatic shifts in functional brain state are inevitable.Like many other people he still continued to stick to his preconceptions on how his behaviour should be, putting irrealistic demands on himself.In doing so he failed to make any differentiation between biologically sensible and biologically absurd ways of coping.By rehearsing steps 1 and 2 each morning John acquainted himself with the idea that the totality of his personality was much larger than his conscious self–image or his ideal self.This encouraged him to accept himself as an holistic organism which encompasses his conscious intentions and feelings.

John himself had uttered several times the ideas written down in steps 3 and 4.Repeatedly, he had lived trough these experiences.So, technically his problem of disruptive morning mood could be conceptualized as an incapacity of keeping the new experiences prominent by slipping back into the older and better automatized affective routine, as had happened in the interaction on day 1421.

The genesis of these instructions defines this guided functional state shift procedure as a truly person–centered 'self–actualization'–technique.First, in a therapeutic athmosphere the acquisition of new interpersonal experiences developed at a personal pace.Next, their existence was communicated to the therapist in a self–disclosure that progressively tapped deeper layers of authenticity.In this way the patient elicited the commitment of the psychiatrist who had assimilated strategies suited for preparing change which were out of reach of the patient.Finally, the psychiatrist succeeded in implementing his technical knowledge with the concrete life experiences of the patient.This order distinguishes this procedure radically from so–called cognitive approaches.

The different substeps of step 5 were intended to embed the shift in a larger context of confidence in his growing capacities to acquire new interpersonal attitudes.Again, in the course of the residential treatment John had already gathered personal experience with the substeps 5.1 to 5.4.Substep 5.5 invited him to accept and trust the stratified nature of development.It presented him a better paradigm than the borderline 'all or none'–dichotomy.It added a suitable cognitive component to the corrective interpersonal experiences he enjoyed.

Effect of the procedure

For some time, every morning John took serious the task of rehearsing meditatively his newly acquired interpersonal experiences (steps 3 and 4).He concentrated on them in a relaxed way, while putting them in a more global context of acceptance of what already existed (step 1 automatically brings along step 2) and of confidence in the possibilities of acquiring more advanced interpersonal attitudes (step 5).This method helped him to reach a functional brain state, characterized by a better mood, which was better suited for efficiently engaging into the daily interpersonal interactions.

Daily rehearsal partly automatized the fluidity of the morning shift.This guided shift in information processing and experiencing tipped the balance between old and new ways of perception, attribution of meaning and behaviour sufficiently to produce relevant shifts in interpersonal behaviour and in self–esteem (a far more natural "drug" against anxiety than benzodiazepines).Already the ease with which his tranquillizers were lifted was remarkable.But far more important was the fact that the capacities of self–reliance, needed for living in the home town, at least became available in a sufficient degree.

DISCUSSION

In the course of John's treatment, the suffocation of fundamental positive tendencies by destructive patterns had to be handled successfully before real progress could be made.John gives the impression to have taken this necessary turning point only after fully acknowledging his invalidation by asking readmission on day 1152.In Rogers' words one could say that John then entered the necessary state of incongruence (Rogers' second condition, 1957).From that moment onwards, the therapeutic management helped him, first to develop new ways of coping and later to gain more flexibility and more autonomy.

Rogers (1957, 1959) did not explore the many ways that human organisms have at their disposition to escape the necessary confrontation with "a state of incongruence".Some are wired into our cerebral information processing technology.Others are actively pursued by persons to sooth their distress.Mental illnesses can interfere with the capacities needed to find constructive ways of coping with incongruency.So, Rogers' second of six conditions "necessary and sufficient for therapeutic personality change" is inaccessible to many patients.A biologically correct pacing of therapeutic expectations will facilitate the process of personality change for some of them.

This blending of attention for opportunities of constructive personality change with a realistic approach to impeding factors is not new in the history of client–centered and experiential psychotherapy.Rogers (1957, 1959) was familiar with the findings of Kirtner (Kirtner and Cartwright, 1970).Gendlin (1969, 1981) started a successful trend by teaching focusing to clients who fail to discover spontaneously the fruitful interaction between felt sense and conscious symbolization.Prouty (1994) developed a way to help autistic, delusional and retarded people meet the first of Rogers' (1957) conditions ("Two persons are in psychological contact").On the clinical level, Prouty's paradigm assigns to the therapist the task of understanding the powerlessness of the client with its unique experiential aspects.

This stance is also fruitful for people with more subtle interpersonal and experiential difficulties, such as John, the borderline patient presented.The helplessness or coping inefficiency of the client has to be taken serious.Moreover, in order to be really congruent the therapist has to be arti~culatedly transparant about the way the client has to be respectful to the conditions he needs.

CONCLUSION

This clinical report demonstrates that information processing concepts add new opportunities to treat maladaptive patterns at the intersection of biological specificity, personality and interpersonal interaction.It corroborates the perspective that differential contributions of the clients ask for differentiation of the therapeutic approach (a.o. : Kirtner and Cartwright, 1970; Rice, 1984; Tscheulin, 1990).

Ostensibly, client–centered process directivity can take several forms.Here, at a suited point of evolution, the patient was trained to seek a more fruitful personal appreciation of his situation, starting from a disadvantageous state of mood and in the absence of the therapist.Similarities and differences between different forms of client–centered process directivity point to the fact that appreciative–cognitive reorganisation and reorientation are much more global processes than our theories suggest.They are grounded in fundamental neurobiological mechanisms.

In order to unfold their guiding power for people such as the patient presented, client–centered core ideas and principles have to be put in a larger frame of reference, which also includes the neurobiological aspects of psychological functioning.Many descriptions in "Client–Centered Therapy", a.o. those emphasizing the concepts of 'perceptual field' and 'phenomenal field', show us that Rogers (1951) clearly was in touch with the flavor of human information processing.At this point, his pioneering efforts deserve a thorough update.

REFERENCES

Edelman, G.M. (1989). *Neural Darwinism.*The theory of neural group selection.Oxford: Oxford University Press.

Gendlin, E.T. (1969). *Focusing.* Psychotherapy : Theory, Research and Practice, 6, 4–15.

Gendlin, E.T. (1981). *Focusing (revised edition).* New York: Bantam Books.

Kiesler, D.J. (1982). *Interpersonal theory for personality and psychotherapy.*In : Anchin, J.C. and D.J. Kiesler (eds.), Handbook of interpersonal psychotherapy (pp. 3–24). New York: Pergamon.

Kirtner, W. and D. Cartwright (1970). *Success and failure in client–centered therapy as a function of client personality variables.*In : J. Hart and T. Tomlinson (eds.), New Directions in Client–Centered Therapy (pp. 179–189). Boston: Houghton Mifflin Company.

Koukkou–Lehmann, M. (1987). *Hirnmechanismen normalen und schizophrenen Denkens.* Berlin: Springer.

Koukkou, M. (1988). *A psychophysiological information–processing model of cognitive dysfunction and cognitive treatment in depression.* In : C. Perris, I.M. Blackburn and H. Perris (eds.), Cognitive Psychotherapy (pp. 80–97). Berlin: Springer.

Prouty, G.F. (1994). *Theoretical evolutions in person–centered/experiential therapy. Applications to schizophrenic and retarded psychoses.* Westport: Praeger.

Rice, L.N. (1984). *Client tasks in client–centered therapy.*In : R.F. Levant and J.M. Shlien (eds.), Client–centered therapy and the person–centered approach : New directions in theory, research and practice (pp. 182–202). New York: Praeger.

Rogers, C. (1951). *Client–centered therapy.*Boston: Houghton Mifflin Company.

Rogers, C.R. (1957). *The necessary and sufficient conditions of therapeutic personality change.* Journal of consulting Psychology, 21, 95–103.

Rogers, C.R. (1959). *A theory of therapy, personality, and interpersonal relationships, as developed in the client–centered framework.* In S. Koch (ed.), Psychology : a study of a science. Vol. III. Formulations of the person and the social context (pp. 184–256).New York: MacGraw–Hill.

Stern, D.A. (1985). *The interpersonal world of the infant. A view from psychoanalysis and developmental psychology.* Basic Books: New York.

Tscheulin, D. (1990). *Confrontation and non–confrontation as differential techniques in differential client–centered therapy.* In : G. Lietaer, J. Rombauts and R. Van Balen (eds.), Client–centered and experiential psychotherapy in the nineties (pp. 327–336).Leuven: Leuven University Press.

Group Psychotherapy and Facilitating

Facilitator Training in South Africa

FRANS CILLIERS
SOUTH AFRICA

ABSTRACT

Since the last visit by Carl Rogers and Ruth Sanford in 1986, many businesses in South Africa showed enthusiasm to train Person–Centered facilitators as change agents for the post–apartheid South Africa. Unfortunately, this training never really got momentum because of (amongst other reasons) the misconception about facilitation, its process and skills. This research can be seen as a continuation of Rogers and Sanford's work in an effort to explain facilitation to management, train facilitators working in cross–cultural communication situations in South African industries and evaluate this training. Facilitation is conceptualised from the PCA and operationalised by making use of different training models form the human potential movement. A training model and an experiential learning workshop were constructed. As representative and random sample, 50 personnel and training officers attended the workshops. The evaluation battery included the Carkhuff scales and the Personal Orientation Inventory. The pre and post measurement showed statistical significant improvement in performance on all four core dimensions of respect, empathy, realness and concreteness; intrapersonal awareness, emotional maturity and internal locus of control. Suggestions towards accelerated training of PCA facilitators in South Africa are formulated.

Workshops in cross–cultural communication by means of the Person–Centered approach, are presented in many countries around the world (Devonshire, 1991; McIlduff & Coghlan, 1993), especially in troubled countries, where constitutional and social change manifest in uncertainty and violence. This description fits South Africa where probably the most challenging time in history in terms of political and social change is now taking place. In the business sector the main issue is to integrate previously separated working groups, communities and races. In this process, the underlying feelings of threat and uncertainty manifest itself in aggression and violence.

Since the last visit of Carl Rogers and Ruth Sanford to South Africa in 1986 (Rogers & Sanford, 1991; Sanford, 1991), many efforts were made to implement the Person–Centered approach in this change process. In industry this resulted in enthusiasm to train personnel and training officers in facilitation skills, to act as change agents in trans–cultural communication situations, informally, as well as formally as it applies to affirmative action, social responsibility and community development.

MISCONCEPTIONS IN INDUSTRY ABOUT FACILITATION

Unfortunately, this training never got momentum in industry. Although the term facilitation is used extensively, it has been made superficial to refer to autocratic and pedagogic ways and mean something close to training, instructing, chairing or leading. Furthermore, it is used in practice to empower the manager (as first person in the interaction, instead of the second person). By pretending to care, he can actually manipulate. An appointed „facilitator" could be any person in the organisation without insight or training in human behavior. He is expected to „make it right" according to the set rules, by taking responsibility, structuring and directing on a content level. This input is supposed to relieve the working group from having to do it themselves or to contribute something. Typical verbal expressions heard in this regard, are: „The facilitator really got them" / „Go and facilitate them – and be sure to tell them exactly what I want". Thus, the misconception about facilitation inhibits and harms individual, group and organisational independence and growth towards fully functioning and a democratic organisation and community.

The above could be a manifestation of the controlling and telling style of the „old regime" in the country, resisting democracy, Person–Centeredness with its emphasis on congruence and respect towards processes and the individual's frame of reference.

PROBLEM STATEMENT AND AIM

This research addresses the relevance of facilitation and its personality profile as conceptualised in the Person–Centered approach, in the present South African need for open cross–communication in a post–apartheid work situation. The following research question can be stated: is it possible to stimulate the characteristics of this profile in change agents working in cross–cultural situations in industry, in order to contribute to a more harmonious and fully functioning work environment? As a first step to an answer, the aim of this research is to psychometrically evaluate a facilitating skills workshop for change agents in South African industries.

FACILITATION DESCRIBED

Facilitation is conceptualised from the Person–Centered approach (Rogers & Stevens, 1967, Rogers, 1973; 1975a; 1975b; 1982; 1985; Hirschenbaum & Henderson, 1993), as a process of providing an open and trusting climate and opportunity for learning how to learn. This implies an interpersonal relationship between the facilitator and a second person(s). The facilitator functions on high levels of specific core behavioral dimensions or interpersonal skills, and personality characteristics or intrapersonal characteristics. These conditions facilitate personal growth and learning about ways of changing behavior (such as stereotypes and preconceived ideas) towards more fully–functioning or self–actualisation in the second person(s).

Fully–functioning or self–actualisation refers to the necessary personality characteristics and skills of the facilitator as well as the resulting process of growth in the personality of the second person(s) in facilitation. It is defined as a natural, dynamic and creative growth process, in which the person, while fully acknowledging own responsibility, gradually develop a unique sense of wholeness through self–definition and the optimisation of mental and psychological potentials, and in whom the expression of the actualising tendency leads to enhancement and enrichment of life, intrapersonally as well as interpersonally, including cross–cultural communication.

THE PERSONALITY PROFILE OF THE FACILITATOR

The profile refers to knowledge, interpersonal skills and intrapersonal characteristics (Maslow, 1954; 1971; Collingwood et al.. 1970; Rogers, 1973; 1975a; 1975b; 1982; 1985; Hekmat, 1975; Brazier, 1993; Hirschenbaum & Henderson, 1993; Segrara & Araiza, 1993:83).

Knowledge

This includes knowledge about and insight into individual and group behavior and dynamics form the Person–Centered approach, as a result of substantial personal experiences in encounter groups (Rogers, 1975a).

Interpersonal skills

Interpersonally the facilitator shows an optimistic and unconditional acceptance of and respect towards all other people, a preference for qualitative, intimate, deep, rich and rewarding interpersonal relationships, and sensitivity, consideration and love towards others. This will allow him/her to make nonverbal and verbal contact with another person and to do so effectively, genuinely, spontaneously, non–exploitatively and responsibly, in terms of the unique demands of each situation. This ability to form relationships sensitively involves the initiation of facilitative interpersonal processes or the creation of a relational climate that can stimulate constructive processes between one person (say, the supervisor) and another (a colleague or subordinate including one form a different race group).

Operationally, these skills are referred to as the core facilitative dimensions, respect, empathy, realness and concreteness.

* Respect may be defined as a profound recognition and appreciation of and regard for the value of the other person as a unique creature and for his or her rights as a free individual. Respect is manifested in warmth, unconditional positive regard and in the quality of the attention given to that person.

* Empathy refers to a person's ability to transcend his or her own self–consciousness in order to arrive at a conscious and accurate understanding of the other person's deepest feelings and intentions, in terms of the latter's own frame of reference, and to explicitly communicate this understanding to the second person.

* Realness involves the degree of correspondence, congruence and transparency between what a person says or does and what he or she truly feels and means. This the facilitator does in a honest and sincere way without affectations.

* Concreteness refers to the extent to which the personal or task–related information that is conveyed to the second person is specific and factual rather than vague or over–generalised. Concreteness aids accurate and clear communication.

Intrapersonal characteristics

The above mentioned interpersonal skills depend upon the level of sensitivity as a pre–requisite. This is the extent to which the facilitator is able to become aware of his/her own feelings and perceptions and to deal with this information respectfully, honestly and responsibly. This is supported by the following cognitive, affective and conative behavior.

On the cognitive level, the facilitator thinks in an objective and flexible way and does not allow inappropriate feelings such as guilt, shame, inferiority or superiority to influence the thinking process.

Affectively the facilitator is sensitive to and aware of own feelings and emotions (yet neither hypersensitive nor insensitive). These are recognised, taken responsibility for and expressed in a natural, independent and autonomous way. This stimulates the person's self–knowledge, insight and a realistic selfconcept, characterised by self–respect, acceptance, confidence and a sense of own worth. Consequently the facilitator purposefully seeks involvement in meaningful life situations to enhance own self–actualisation.

Conatively the facilitator acts in a self–directed way, experiencing freedom of choice and not feeling victimised by external forces.

550

Method

To satisfy industry's demand for exact proof in human resource matters, quantitative research is undertaken.

Model for facilitator training

The above profile is operationalised in a training model.

* For the gaining of knowledge about behavior and group dynamics, an instructional self study and examination method was used.

* For the interpersonal skills, an Integrated Facilitation Process Model was compiled, based on different training models within the humanistic paradigm and the Person–Centered approach. These are the Human Potential Development Model by Carkhuff (1972; 1978; 1983), the Skilled Helper Model by Egan (1973a; 1973b; 1975) and the Micro Skill Training Model by Ivey (1971). These models provide operationalisations of the core dimensions as interpersonal skills.

* For the intrapersonal characteristics, encounter group experiences were used (Rogers, 1975a).

The workshop format

The workshop lasts 24 hours (three working days). It is presented experientially in a small group of ten participants and one facilitator. It contains five modules.

Module 1 – Theory. The aim is to study theory on behavior and group dynamics from the Person–Centered approach and encounter group movement, as well as the application of facilitation in the work situation. The format used is a handout given four weeks prior to the workshop for self study and examination.

Module 2 – Encounter group 1. The aim is to enhance intra– and interpersonal sensitivity. The format is an encounter group with one facilitator.

Module 3 – Interpersonal skills training. The aim is to master the interpersonal skills of facilitation. The format is role–play as facilitator in one–to–one and group situations with feedback form a trainer / facilitator according to the mentioned Integrated Facilitation Process Model.

Module 4 – Encounter group 2. The aim and format are as in Module 2.

Module 5 – Application group. The aim is to process the training experience and give support for the transfer of learning to the work situation. The format is the same as in Module 2.

The sample

With 320 registered personnel and training officers from 35 companies in the Johannesburg–Pretoria area, with at least a Bachelors degree in Psychology or Industrial Psychology, 10 years work experience and a mean age of 31 years, as the population, a random sample of 140 was drawn. Of these 100 indicated their willingness to take part in the study. Of these a randomly divided 50 formed the experimental and 50 the control group.

The measuring battery

According to the personality profile of the facilitator, a psychometric battery was complied. (Knowledge was not measured.)

* For the interpersonal skills, the Carkhuff scales (1969b) were chosen.

* For the intrapersonal characteristics, the Personal Orientation Inventory (POI) (Shostrom, 1963; 1974; Knapp, 1975), and the Inventory of Self–actualising Characteristics (ISAC) (Banet, in Pfeifer & Jones, 1976), were chosen.

All three instruments correspond conceptually with the operational definitions in the profile above. Cilliers (1984) reports high reliability and validity for the POI and Carkhuff scales in the measurement of these characteristics and skills. Little information is available on the ISAC, except for Butler (1980) who reports on its reliability in sensitivity training.

Procedure

The sample of 100 was randomly divided into an experimental (N=50) and control group (N=50). To fit in with the workshop format and to optimise the learning opportunity, both groups were paired into five subgroups. Thus the workshop was presented five times.

At the start of every workshop, the measuring battery was administered as a pre–measurement to both groups (N=20). Then the control group (N=10) went on with their daily activities and the workshop was presented to the experimental group (N=10). At the end, the measuring battery was administered as a post–measurement to both groups again (N=20).

The Carkhuff scales were administered in two situations. The first was a written communication situation administered in the group. This contains typical verbal racial discrimination expressions in the work situation on which the respondent has to react and record his own spontaneous verbal reaction. The second is an individual role–play recorded on video, with the respondent as acting facilitator in a five minute interaction with a second person who threatens to resign because of racial tension.

The psychometric data was processed collectively for all the experimental and all the control groups. The significance of differences between pre and post measurement (t–test) were calculated by means of the SAS Computer package (SAS Institute, 1985).

RESULTS

The results of the interpersonal skills are presented in table 1. The results of the Carkhuff scales show that the workshop lead to the significant improvement in performance on all four core dimensions respect, empathy, realness and concreteness.

The results of the intrapersonal characteristics are presented in table 2. The POI results show that the workshop stimulated the following characteristics significantly: time competence focussing on the here and now, behavior motivated form a sense of inner–directedness, living according to the values of self–actualisation, flexibility in the application of values, sensitivity towards own feelings and needs and the spontaneous expression there–of, selfregard and acceptance in spite of weaknesses, the acceptance of opposites (eg. good/bad, masculine/feminine social roles) as non antagonistic, acceptance of own aggression and anger in an interpersonal situation, and the capacity to form warm and intimate interpersonal relationships.

The ISAC results show that the workshop stimulated the following characteristics significantly: acceptance of self, others and the nature of man, spontaneous, uncomplicated and natural behavior, problem centeredness, independent and autonomous behavior with a preference to privacy, independence from culture and environment, freshness in perception, capacity for peak experiences, a positive feeling towards the community, intimacy and closeness in interpersonal relationships, living according to democratic values and ethical standards, creativity and a decline of violence in humor.

TABLE 1 :

SIGNIFICANCE OF DIFFERENCES BETWEEN PRE AND POST SCORES FOR THE INTERPERSONAL SKILLS OF FACILITATION AS MEASURED BY THE CARKHUFF SCALES IN THE WRITTEN COMMUNICATION AND ROLE–PLAY SITUATIONS

ITEMNO	ITEM NAME	EXPER GROUP		CONTR GROUP		t–VALUE
		X	S	X	S	
1	Respect	01,60	00,50	00,06	00,25	0,0007 *
2	Empathy	01,46	00,51	00,20	00,41	0,0009 *
3	Realness	01,72	00,45	00,01	00,01	0,0011 *
4	Concreteness	01,79	00,41	00,06	00,25	0,0004 *

- $P < 0,01$

TABLE 2:

SIGNIFICANCE OF DIFFERENCES BETWEEN PRE AND POST SCORES FOR THE INTRAPERSONAL CHARACTERISTICS OF FACILITATION

ITEM NO	ITEM NAME	EXPER. GROUP		CONTR. GROUP		t–VALUE
		X	S	X	S	
POI 1	Time competence	18,76	02,51	15,06	02,72	0,0100 *
POI 2	Inner–directedness	95,06	09,74	80,35	10,05	0,0041 *
POI 3	Self–actualisation values	23,66	03,45	20,74	02,74	0,0027 *
POI 4	Existentialism	22,06	04,08	14,98	03,95	0,0025 *
POI 5	Feeling reactivity	17,57	02,85	15,08	02,39	0,0002 *
POI 6	Spontaneity	14,43	03,05	11,58	02,83	0,0046 *
POI 7	Self–regard	14,05	02,59	12,32	03,21	0,0004 *
POI 8	Self–acceptance	19,28	04,93	14,03	04,16	0,0005 *
POI 9	Nature of Man	12,75	02,45	10,34	01,98	0,0713
POI 10	Synergy	06,54	01,22	07.25	01,68	0,0156 **
POI 11	Acceptance of aggression	20,73	04,21	18,35	03,57	0,0032 *
POI 12	Intimate contact	22,05	06,40	18,29	02,18	0,0056 *
ISAC 1	Perception of reality	03,57	00,48	03,46	0042	0,0642

ISAC 2	Self–acceptance	03,90	00,49	02,80	00,25	0,0010 *
ISAC 3	Spontaneity	04,37	00,47	02,73	00,33	0,0002 *
ISAC 4	Problem–centeredness	04,01	00,39	03,10	00,26	0,0096 *
ISAC 5	Self–sufficiency	03,90	00,46	03,08	00,32	0,0182 **
ISAC 6	Autonomy	04,42	00,46	02,43	00,29	0,0001 *
ISAC 7	Fresh perception	04,36	00,48	02,96	00,34	0,0008 *
ISAC 8	Peak experiences	03,66	00,38	02,85	00,31	0,0038 *
ISAC 9	Gemeinschafts feeling	04,32	00,50	02,60	00,41	0,0001 *
ISAC 10	Intimacy	03,97	00,47	03,06	00,36	0,0442 **
ISAC 11	Democratic behavior	04,20	00,37	03,21	00,34	0,0028 *
ISAC 12	Ethical standards	03,86	00,43	03,12	00,32	0,0447 **
ISAC 13	Non–violent humor	03,70	00,38	02,91	00,29	0,0069 *
ISAC 14	Perception of reality	03,89	00,38	02,87	00,25	0,0011 *
ISAC 15	Resistance / encultur.	04,18	00,45	03,19	00,41	0,0027 *

• $P < 0,01$ ** $P < 0,05$

DISCUSSION

The research shows that facilitative behavior can be enhanced significantly by means of this workshop. Interpersonally the skills of the trainees changed to respect and accept the second person as a human being (which implies the awareness of the own frame of reference, ideas, stereotypes, prejudices and the skill to temporarily put this aside). Secondly, the skills to move into the second person's frame of reference in a honest and genuine way, to reach more awareness, sensitivity, understanding and acceptance of the second's ideas, needs and feelings, and to communicate this understanding and acceptance in a concrete way by means of micro skills to such an extent that the second person experiences the facilitator's presence and communication as emphatic, improved. In other words, the tendency at the beginning of the workshop (in the pre–measurement) to play games, manipulate and prescribe their own solution, diminished significantly. This will possibly lead in future to more respectful, real and emphatic interactions in the work situation.

Intrapersonally the behavior changes can be integrated to mean personality integration, contact with reality, emotional maturity and internal locus of control.

* Personality integration include a growing awareness of behavior dynamics and processes and a life style according to ethical, moral and self–actualisation values, congruent to the demands of the situation.

* Reality contact includes objectivity, a focus on the task and a more rational problem centeredness, decision–making without emotional over–involvement and heightened concentration.

* Emotional maturity is characterised by ego–strength, emotional insight, calmness, stability, discipline, autonomy and independence. This leads to greater sensitivity and awareness of own needs and feelings, self image based upon self knowledge, insight, respect, confidence and acceptance in spite of weaknesses, the acceptance of own feelings (especially aggression) and the spontaneous and natural expression of all feelings, a moving away from rule boundness, self

defiet, moralising, rigidity, inhibiticn and self laid restrictions. These changes may in future lead to more acceptance of responsibility for own behavior, heightened sensitivity in the handling of own and other's affective behavior in a facilitating situation and the modelling of flexibility.

* Internal locus of control includes self motivation, inner–directedness with own integrated values, needs and feelings, in stead of a focus on the needs of others, the making of conscious choices in an independent and autonomous way, flexibility according to the demands of the situation in stead of rigid, compulsive and dogmatic behavior. These changes may in future lead to stronger self motivation in decision making and the modelling there–of in a facilitation situation.

CONCLUSIONS AND SUGGESTIONS

This research shows that facilitative behavior as defined in the Person–Centered approach, can be stimulated amongst personnel and training officers in the work place. Accelerated training of facilitators by means of this model and workshop, is suggested to cope with the demand for effective cross–cultural communication in South Africa.

It can only be assumed that the change agent will also be able to facilitate learning in a real cross–cultural work situation. To ascertain this, it is suggested that the research model be extended to include a follow–up phase by means of a phenomenological approach in terms of interviewing and measuring trainee's in vivo performance. This extended research model will evaluate the effectiveness of the training over a time period as well as its contribution towards more effective communication amongst and between all race groups.

REFERENCES

Brazier, D. (1993). *Beyond Carl Rogers*. London: Constable.

Butler, R.R. (1980). *Actualizing counselors in training – three small group approaches*. Small group behaviour, 11(1), 13–21, Feb.

Carkhuff, R.R. (1969a). *Helper communication as a function of helpee effect and content*, Journal of counseling psychology, 14(2), 126–131.

Carkhuff, R.R. (1969b). *Helping and human relations Vol. 2. Practice and research*. London: Holt, Rineholt & Winston.

Carkhuff, R.R. (1972). *New directions in training for the helping professions: toward a technology for human and community resource development*. Counseling Psychologist, 3, 12–30.

Carkhuff, R.R. (1978). *The art of helping. Trainers manual*. Amherst: Human Resource Development Press.

Carkhuff, R.R. (1983). *The art of helping V*. Amherst: Human Resource Development Press.

Cilliers, F. (1984). *A developmental programme in sensitive relationship forming as managerial dimension*. Potchefstroom (Doctorate thesis (PhD) – Potchefstroom University).

Collingwood, T., Hefele, T., Muehlberg, N. & Drasgow, J. (1970). *Toward identification of the therapeutically facilitative factor*. Journal of clinical psychology, 26, 119–120.

Devonshire, C.M. (1991*). The Person–Centered Approach and Cross–Cultural Communication*. The Person–Centered Approach and Cross–Cultural Communication – An International Review, 1, 15–42.

Egan, G. (1973a). *A two–phase approach to human relations training*. The 1973 annual handbook for group facilitators. La Jolla: University Associates.

Egan, G. (1973b). *Face to face. The small–group experience and interpersonal growth*. Monterey: Brooks/Cole.

Egan, G. (1975).*The skilled helper*. Monterey: Brooks/Cole.

Hekmat, H. (1975). *Some personality correlates of empathy*. Journal of consulting and clinical psychology, 43(1), 89.

Hirschenbaum, H. & Henderson, V.L. (1993). *The Carl Rogers Reader*. London: Constable.

Ivey, A.E. (1971). Microcounseling: Innovations in interviewing training. Springfield: Charles C. Thomas.

Knapp, R.R. (1976). *Handbook for the Personal Orientation Inventory*. San Diego: Edits.

Maslow, A.H. (1954). *Motivation and Personality*. New York: Harper.

Maslow, A.H. (1971). *The Farther reaches of Human Nature*. Harmodsworth: Penquin.

McIlduff, E. & Coghlan, D. (1993). *The Cross–Cultural Communication Workshops in Europe – Reflections and Review*. The Person–Centered Approach and Cross–Cultural Communication – An International Review, 2, 21–34.

Pfeiffer, J.W. & Jones, J.E. (1976). *The 1976 annual handbook for group facilitators*. La Jolla: University Associates.

Rogers, C.R. (1973). *Client–centered therapy*. London: Constable.

Rogers, C.R. (1975a). *Encounter groups*. London: Penguin.

Rogers, C.R. (1975b). *On becoming a person: A therapist's view of psychotherapy*. London: Constable.

Rogers, C.R. (1982). *Freedom to learn for the 80's*. Columbus: Charles E. Merrill.

Rogers, C.R. (1985). *Carl Rogers on Personal Power*. London: Constable.

Rogers, C.R. & Sanford, R. (1991). *Reflections on our South African Experience (January/February, 1986)*. The Person–Centered approach and Cross–Cultural Communication – An International Review, 1, 87–90.

Rogers, C.R. & Stevens, B. (1967). *Person to Person: The Problem of being human*. Moab: Real People Press.

Sanford, R. (1991). *The Beginning of a Dialogue in South Africa*. The Person–Centered Approach and Cross–Cultural Communication – An International Review, 1, 69–86.

SAS Institute. (1985). *SAS user's guide: statistics, version 5 edition*. Cary: SAS Institute Inc.

Segrera, A.S. & Araiza, M. (1993). *Proposals for a Person–Centered model of Social conflict resolution*. The Person–Centered Approach and Cross–Cultural Communication – An International Review, 2, 77–86.

Shostrom, E.L. (1963). *Personal Orientation Inventory*. San Diego: Edits.

Shostrom, E.L. (1974). *Manual of the Personal Orientation Inventory*. San Diego: Edits.

Family Therapy – a Client–Centered Approach

HIPÓLITO, J. AND MENDES COELHO, F.

LISBON– PORTUGAL

ABSTRACT

The authors develop one approach of family therapy. The Person Centered Approach being their main frame of reference they refer to the concept of socio–anthropological system, developed by C. Caldeira. After an initial time of client (the family) centered intervention they reflect on a second moment on their experiences which have been through during the intervention. The authors propose the construction of amodel: the socio–anthropological system with at least six dimensions of relational dimension and understanding. This model pretends to pick up in a non–reducing way, oneobjective "image" of the family, contrasting with the one the family gives. The conceptualization is then enriched by the utilization of an open and interacting systemic model with a lecture grid of one reality – the family having such a complexity degree that can never be perceived in his totality, but only under some of his aspects. At the hinge of the clinical work, of the psychology and social sciences, the family has been the object of clinical practice andresearch from the authors, who emphasize some aspects of the setting and the methodology they use.

INTRODUCTION

All along his evolution – from the non–directive approach to the person–centered approach, passing by the client–centered therapy – C. Rogers has manifested a profound interest in the groups, including the family group (Rogers, 1970, 1972) and their development as well. An important number of papers demonstrate the interest of his disciples in this field of investigation. However, as far as we know, the family group hasn't benefited the same effort and even the same development since then (Levant, 1978; Raskin & van der Veen, 1970; Barret–Lennard, 1984; Levant 1984; Guerney Jr., 1984; Gaylin, 1993). Apparently only late in his life C. Rogers (Rogers, 1977, 1980) has shown any relevant importance to the social–cultural, economical and political aspects. Within the Portuguese cultural and scientific framework, these dimensions are seen altogether as very important and therefore the centered approach to the groups in general and the family approach in particular have received a great attention.

The socio–anthropological system concept occupies a central position in the model developed by C. Caldeira (Caldeira, 1981). In it, the approach to the person is built in two moments: one, the intervention, the encounter, and two, the understanding, the analysis. In the socio–anthropological system, which goes from the physical body to the social relationships, one might describe the following dimensions:

the personal dimension (a certain concrete person)

the groupal dimension (the group, the family, the community)

the inter–personal dimension (the serial, the encounter)

the organizational dimension (place for the world and life bureaucratization).

the societary–institutional dimension (within which the production and reproduction of dominant social relationships is analyzed).

the dimension related to the Absolute (concerning the Transcendence and the Absolute)

Therefore, we face a multidimensional universe or, by another words, a multidimensional system of interdependent social relationships where the different relation dimensions (social-personal or production/salary/consumption) are present in a variable degree and in correlation one to the others.

The person is the center of this open system, one of the poles of all relationships, described within a perspective at same time diachronic and synchronic. We then can define the analysis of the socio–anthropological system as the analysis of the concrete man, in situation, inserted in his family and socio–cultural context: synchronic and diachronic analysis of the socio–anthropological system through a dialogical practice centered in six dimensions of listening: - personal, dyadic, groupal, organizational, societary–institutional and Absolute related (Campiche, Hippolyte & Hipólito, 1992).

The person–centered intervention (Rogers, 1951) shows through the empathic understanding how the person lives his relationship within these different dimensions; that is the face of the system which we call "per Se". On the other hand, according to the sciences applied to each concrete case, the analysis which arises from what is lived by allows us to build up the other face of the socio–anthropological system which we might call "in se".

The *per se* and the *in se* systems (Sartre, 1943) are then two different ways of regarding the same object – the person – the insight that goes from the inside to the outside and the reverse insight going from the outside to the inside, that is, two points of view which are not possible to be wholly coincident but that otherwise complete themselves one to another towards the building of a system which does not intend to reproduce the real person but to approach it the most possible in every moment. (To be understood like quantic pairs, complementary but irreducible, obeying to the Heisenberg principle of uncertainty, within the spirit of the "Copenhagen interpretation": uncertainty, complementation and perturbation of the system by an act of observation) (Stapp, 1972; Gribbin, 1984).

The aim of the analysis of the socio–anthropological system, science of the individual (Granger, 1975) is to reach the socio–anthropological system by the dialectical construction/knowledge movement; by counter–induction (Feyerabend, 1979) and by the generalization of the generic socio–anthropological systems, it reveals to have a foreseeing scientific value notwithstanding keeping itself open to the unexpected and to the surprise.

FAMILY GROUP AND THERAPEUTIC GROUP

After what has been said, we consider the family as an open system, a "holon" (Koestler, 1968), making above all reference to the groupal dimension, which is composed by people, a socio–anthropological system in relation, but being much more than their total sum. Within this system, the dimension permeating the milieu is the one of the family transactions.

The interventions within a family are based upon investigation researches concerning, among others, the structure of families without an identified mental patient or without social transgressions, compared to other families that include a schizophrenic patient (Caldeira, Mendes Coelho, Dias, Almeida & Rebelo, 1981). This intervention is based upon a general theoretical elaboration (Dias, 1979; Dias, Mendes Coelho, Almeida & Rebelo, 1983; Caldeira, 1981) enriched by the experience acquired in these last years with the family intervention either for diagnostic purposes or as a socio–communitary animation or even of therapeutic facilitation.

In relationship to the therapeutic group, the family has some specific characteristics: while the therapeutic group has a memory, a semantics (verbal and non verbal language) and a way of functioning which are common to their members and to those in which the facilitator has participated since the beginning, the family has, on the other hand, a memory, a semantics (which has included in it a very important non verbal language), ways of functioning and a patrimony pre–existent to its own elements and even more to the facilitator who is then confronted with a universe unknown to him.

In the family dimension, there is a predominance of circular causality upon linear causality without the total suppression of this last one, these two terms behaving like quantic pairs subjected to the Heisenberg principle of uncertainty. The family must be seen as a system within which an element might be the expression of the family suffering but also within which the suffering of the family might be the expression of the trouble of one of its elements.

When a suffering family demands help, the given answer respects to the explicit demand: if this one is made on behalf of the family, the help is proposed to the family as a whole – family therapy –; if the demand is made by the couple or by a member of the family, the response will be in function to the acceptance of the demand – couple therapy or designed member therapy.

Sometimes, however, during the treatment there is a change in the demand; for instance, as soon as this is formulated by a member of the family, the therapy leads the family to the discovery that the therapeutic process has all to gain if is extended to the whole family group. Then the family becomes the therapeutic subject. When the designed patient is a child, it's frequently possible, if not desired, to suggest, a preliminary family interview. Teenagers accompanied by their parents during one of the initial consultation are frequently received with them, at least the first time.

Asking for help, the family attributes to the facilitator a phantasmic hierarchic power, in which the restitution to the family itself, the real source, constitutes one of the aspects of the therapeutic process in itself. The therapist has a know how and a technical competence which he uses on behalf of the family but, more than an expert, he is the participant and the facilitator of the therapeutic process. While the therapist is the facilitator of this change, the center of the decisions and evaluations remains within the family.

THE FAMILY CENTERED APPROACH:

We think that the basic postulate of the person centered approach (Rogers, 1959) where our family therapy approach comes from, remains valid in the case of the families, while at the same time we are aware that researches should and must be undertaken in order to demonstrate it in the most explicit possible way. We could say conversely: every person, group or family placed in a situation of adequate facilitation is going to change itself in the sense of its potentialities actualization (are they indeed possibilities?). We are then aware of the theoretical difficulties posed by the enlargement of the actualizing tendency concept or the utilization of the formative tendency concept in the specific case of a family and a group. Both in Portuguese and in French, the word organism is applied not only to a vegetal or animal organism but to a social organism as well. Within the family, the facilitation which is the catalytic element of this type of change supposes from the therapist an attitude of congruence, of positive unconditional acceptance an of empathic understanding as described by C. Rogers (Rogers, 1961).

This facilitation is concretized in the therapist activity who sends the communication of each person to the family group and from this one to each of its members, in a constant integration of the individual discourses within a family group discourse which does not annihilate or deny their differences, but on contrary is based upon their acceptance.

It develops the person to person relation inside the family, it respects the family competence in the decision making which best suits themselves, including those decisions related to all the aspects of the therapy (who will participate and how much will be involved, which are the significant sectors the interview will focus upon, which sense to give to their experience and which actions or decisions shall be accepted or rejected).

By his warm presence and by his support to the family, the facilitator is implicated in a non possessive manner in his leading role. Also, he constantly tries to understand the framework of the internal references of the family, communicating its understanding of the his experiences, maintaining himself sensitive to the way their livers have been lived, to the changes already occurred and to the meaning of all that.

The attitude of congruency, positive unconditional acceptance and empathic understanding might become the object of learning and training (e.g. one can learn how to intervene upon his own feeling in relationship to the silence, much more than directly upon the silence itself).

THE THERAPEUTIC SETTING:

The technical aspect must be adequate to the situation of the group and to the situation of this specific group that is the family. The reflecting technic (in which we include the reflection through action as well as the utilization of closed video circuit) (Caldeira & Dias, 1982) take place in a person to person relation that is beneficial to the person himself, excluding all manipulation.

As an example, we might say that if the setting is always structured by the therapist(s) in an implicit or explicit way, its explicit structureness might be used as a reflection through action: there is then always a seat for each member of the family either present or not in the séance as far as the family is presenting itself as a client. The members of the family choose their place, showing this way to the therapist his own.

Our practice with family therapy has lead us to organize its setting in such a way that it becomes not much different from other therapeutic groups whatever type they might assume: verbal (Paulino, Sequeira, & Pinto 1985; Paulino, Pires, Tavares & Vicente,1985), psychodrama (Hipólito, Mendes Coelho & Garcia, 1988) or relaxation (Hipólito, Laroche & Lazega, 1987). Like what happens with other groups, we video register the whole seance and have present one or two therapists, by preference a heterosexual couple and (in meta" position), and one or two observers using a closed video circuit.

This setting, that is explicit to the family, allows us to increase our intervention capacity, our disposability near the family and our understanding and analysis. In case of non–acceptance by the family, insufficient personal or technical means, we admit a possible reduction of the setting, though increasing that way the difficulties of the intervention

Normally seances last between an hour and half and two hours. Some minutes before the end of each seance, the seance is interrupted and the therapist(s) leaves the room in order to make a synthesis of the seance with the observers, to structure a reflection of the synthesis which after that is given back to the family. If the therapist is alone he formulates a synthesis in the end of the seance just like we do with the other therapeutic groups. The aim of the synthesis formulation is neither a judgment of value nor a diagnosis and it does not foresee either a prescription or a home work. It addresses itself to the family as a group to which is recognized an existence in time and space. Placing itself at the conscious level of the seance, it permits to establish a connection as well, a continuity of the seances aiming an integration of each seance ill the totality of the therapeutic process along the course of time.

The synthesis reflection in the family therapy is jointly elaborated by the therapist(s) and by the observer(s) who take into consideration the need to avoid partialization and involuntary manipulation by the therapists, acknowledging the multiple digital and analogical aspects to take into consideration within the family system and the difficulty during the seance in order to be simultaneously successful, to accompany the family and being present in the now and here of the intervention. The synthesis reflection and the way it is prepared are usually lived by the family as a concern, as an expression of a responsibility sense by the therapists towards the family itself. After each seance and during thirty to ninety minutes, the therapist(s) and the observer(s) discuss the seance and its integration in the therapeutic process, taking into consideration their own personal experience, their empathic understanding of the personal experience of the members of the family and what they had watched in the video. If the therapist is alone, ill this job is mainly based upon the video recording which becomes a most important work ool contrarily to other therapeutic groups.

One discusses now the attitudes and the utilization of technics by the therapists (empathy, congruency, positive unconditional acceptance, partiality, manipulation, etc.) Particularly important are the most significant relational moments concerning each member of the family, the family system and the therapists who try to avoid reductionism; what leads the therapist to taking into consideration, every time it is pertinent, the different dimensions of each socio–anthropological system, of the family system (in its quality of group and specific group which the family is), considered also in its different dimensions and finally the therapeutic system (family, therapists, setting), considered in its multiple dimensions as well.

CONCLUSIONS:

The intervention within the family, in its multiple aspects of investigation, theorization, socio–communitary animation, diagnosis and therapeutic facilitation is one of the domains where in one hand the critical reflection about the experience is the most needed because of the importance of the family dimension in the illness and in the mental health and in another hand because of the need to overcome the resistance and the individualistic and ideological individual prejudices towards the family

REFERENCES

Barret–Lennard, G. T. (1984). *The World of Family Relationship: A Person Centered Systems View.* In Levant, R. F. & Shlien, J . M. (Eds.). Client Centered Therapy and Person Centered Approach: New Directions in Theory, Research, and Practice. New York: Praeger.

Caldeira, C. (1981), *Análise sociopsiquiátrica de uma comunidade terapeutica. Aplicação do modelo antropoanalitico em psiquiatria social.* Dissertação de Doutoramento. Lisboa.

Caldeira, C., Mendes Coelho, F., Dias, G.F., Almeida, M.J., Rebelo, T. (1981), *Estruturas familiares: aproximação antropoanalitica.* Lisboa: Centro de Informática da Universidade Nova de Lisboa.

Caldeira, C. & Dias, G.F. (1982), *Psicoterapia da esquizofrenia. Abordagem dialógica centrada no cliente como prática da antropoanálise.* in: Progressos em terapeutica psiquiátrica. Coord. GUIMARÃES LOPES. Porto: Hospital Conde Ferreira.

Campiche, C., Hippolyte, J & Hipólito. (1992). *A Comunidade como Centro.* Lisboa: Fundação Gulbenkian.

562

Dias, G.F. (1979), *Teoria dos grafos e métodos das grelhas de Kelly aplicado ao estudo da estrutura familiar*. Lisboa: Centro de Informática da Universidade Nova de Lisboa.

Dias, G.F., Mendes Coelho, F., Almeida, M.J. & Rebelo, T. (1983). *Aplicação da teoria dos grafos à determinação da liderança. Estruturas familiares.* Lisboa: Centro de Informática da Universidade Nova de Lisboa.

Feyerabend, P. (1979), *Contre la methode. Esquisse d'une théorie anarchiste de la connaissance*. Paris: Seuil.

Gaylin, N. L. (1993). *Person Centered Family Therapy*. In Brazier, D. (Ed.). Beyond Carl Rogers. London: Constable.

Granger, G.G. (1975), *Pensamento formal e ciências do homem*. Lisboa: Presença.

Gribbin, J. (1984), *Search of Schrodinger's cat*. London: Corgy.

Guerney Jr., B. G. (1984). *Contributions of Client Centered Therapy to Filial, Marital, and Family Relationship Enhancement Therapies*. In Levant, R. F. & Shlien, J. M. (Eds.). Client Centered Therapy and Person Centered Approach: New Directions in Theory, Research, and Practice. New York: Praeger.

Hipólito, J., Laroche, R. & Lazega, M. (1987*). Relaxation: An Anthropoanalytical and Person Centered Approach.* Acta Psiquiátrica Portuguesa. 33. (2). 65–69.

Hipólito, J., Mendes Coelho, F. & Garcia, R., (1988) , *Expérience de deux groupes de psychodrame – Perspective anthropoanalytique –*.Psiquiatria Clínica. 9 (1).

Koestler, A. (1968), *Le cheval dans la locomotive*. Paris: Calmann–Lévy.

Levant, R.F. (1978). *Family therapy: a client–centered perspective.* Journal of marriage and family counseling. Vol. 4 (2). 35–42.

Levant, R. F. (1984). *From Person to System: Two Perspectives*. In Levant, R. F. & Shlien, J. M. (Eds.). Client Centered Therapy and Person Centered Approach: New Directions in Theory, Research, and Practice. New York: Praeger.

Paulino, M., Sequeira, M., Pinto, M.J., (1985*), Therapeutic group in a psychiatric consultation in a general hospital: results. Communication.* XIII International Congress of Psychotherapy. Opatija.

Paulino, M., Pires, R., Tavares, J., Vicente, E., (1985*). Therapeutic groups: problems. Communication.* XIII international Congress of Psychotherapy. Opatija.

Raskin, N. & van der Veen, F., (1970). *Client Centered family therapy: some clinical and research perspectives.* In J. T. Hart & T. M. Tomlinsom (Eds.), *New directions in client–centered therapy.* Boston: Houghton Mifflin.

Rogers, C. (1951), *Client–centered therapy.* Boston: Hougthon–Mifflin.

Rogers, C. (1959), *A theory of therapy, personality and interpersonal relationships.* in: S. Koch (org.) Psychology: a study of a science. (vol.3). New York: McOraw–Hill.

Rogers, C.(1961), *On becoming a person.* Boston: Houghton–Mifflin..

Rogers, C. (1970), *On encounter groups.* New York: Harper and Row.

Rogers, C. (1972). *Becoming partners: marriage and its alternatives.* New York: Delacort.

Rogers, C. (1977), *A way of being.* Boston.: Houghton–Mifflin.

Rogers, C. (1980), *On personal power.* New York: Delacort Press.

Sartre, J.P. (1943), *L'être et le néant.* Paris: Gallimard.

Stapp, H. (1972), "The Copenhagen interpretation and the nature of Space–Time".American Journal of Physics, 40 .

Client–Centered Group Psychotherapy in Dialogue with other Orientations: Commonality and Specificity

GERMAIN LIETAER AND PAUL DIERICK

CATHOLIC UNIVERSITY LEUVEN, BELGIUM

ABSTRACT

Following a brief historical overview of client–centered group therapy and group work, we focus on the client–centered therapist's working–method and more specifically on the question of whether or not client–centered group therapy is more than a form of 'individual therapy in a group'.Our chapter is largely based on research findings and makes a dual comparison: on the one hand, that of client–centered group therapy in relation to other therapeutic orientations and on the other, individual versus group therapy within our own therapeutic orientation.

This analysis leads to the conclusion that client–centered therapists do indeed pay attention to typical group therapeutic processes in their everyday practice.Hence we appeal for development of theoretical concepts with increased emphasis on group dynamics and the interactional aspects of the process.

We conclude with a discussion of a number of characteristics of client–centered group therapy which we believe to be largely unique to our approach: trust in the group process, a consistent experiential focus and personal presence of the therapist.

THE GROUP AS INSTRUMENT IN THE CLIENT–CENTERED APPROACH
BRIEF HISTORICAL OVERVIEW

Although the client–centered approach came into being as a form of individual therapy, work with groups has taken a prominent place from the start (Raskin, 1986a).We can roughly distinguish three periods in the development of group work, with ramifications and overlaps: The Chicago period (1945–1960), the Human Potential Movement period (1960–1980) and the present period, from 1980 on.

Group–centered therapy had already started by the late 1940s (Hobbs, 1951) and Rogers' students remained active in the ambulatory and residential group psychotherapy after his departure from Chicago (Truax, 1961. Beck, 1974).Rogers had, also right from the start, shown a keen interest in the group as a tool in fields other than that of psychotherapy proper.Thus he experimented with student–centered teaching and– in the framework of care for the war veterans – organized crash courses for counselors in which the group approach to training and supervision was paramount (Bloksma & Porter, 1947).Rogers also applied his client–centered principles to the organization and management of the University of Chicago Counseling Center itself: a group–centered leadership in which responsibility and power were largely delegated to staff members (Gordon, 1951).

During the sixties and seventies – the hey–day of humanistic psychology and the Human Potential Movement – the use of groups assumed enormous proportions (Lieberman, Yalom, & Miles, 1973).Rogers and many of his co–workers played a key role in this: it was the time of encounter groups (Gendlin & Beebe, 1968; Rogers, 1970; Solomon and Berzon, 1972; Barrett–Lennard, 1974; Bebout, 1974, 1976; Meador, 1975).Typical of these groups was their pursuit of personal growth, self–actualization and the development of interpersonal skills.But these goals were quickly broadened: the intensive face–to–face group was soon pressed into the service of organizational development and social change (W.R. Rogers, 1979, 1984; Seewald, 1988; Terjung, 1990).Famous in this context is the 'Immaculate Heart Project: an experiment for self–directed change in an educational system' (C.R. Rogers, 1974, 1983; Coulson, 1972): a large–scale action–experiment in which members of all branches of a school system participated in encounter groups.Workshops for multicultural and conflicting groups were also held (Devonshire & Kremer, 1980; McIlduff & Coghlan, 1993).Out of these grew Rogers' Peace Project in which he worked with black and white South Africans and with political leaders and people in charge of Central American issues (see complete issue nr. 3 and pages 275–384 of Journal of Humanistic Psychology 1987).Within this social–political framework, leaders of client–oriented groups also directed their attention to the use of non–professionals as group facilitators (Bebout & Gordon, 1972), to work with large groups and to the founding of person–centered communities (Coulson, Land & Meador, 1977; C.R. Rogers, 1980; McGuire–Boukydis, 1982; Wood, 1984, 1988; Thorne, 1988; Barrett–Lennard, 1994).

Towards the end of the seventies, the 'group movement' subsided, perhaps partly because of the economic recession.But group therapy had in the meantime established itself more firmly in ambulatory and residential clinical practice.Within this altered framework, group therapy remained an important working method within the client–centered orientation (in Europe at any rate), and for some even a preferred method.Attention had thus shifted to group therapy with clinical populations and this was accompanied by closer investigation of the theoretical basis of client–centered group therapy (Franke, 1978; Swildens, 1979; Berk, 1984; Spittler, 1986).For an overview of the publications of the last 15 years, see: Mente and Spittler, 1980; Coulson, 1981; Lietaer, 1981; Tausch & Tausch, 1981; Ködel & Froburg, 1988; Esser & Sander, 1988; Sander and Esser, 1988; Gundrum, 1989; Beck, 1991; Thomas, 1991; Snijder–van den Eerembeemt, 1993; Schmid, 1994; Finke, 1994.

When examining the totality of the literature on client–centered group therapy, we are struck by the following.

*The process is usually described in fairly concrete terms and close to the facts.Texts are rich in verbatim excerpts and testimonies of group members.Exceptions to this trend that do advance general or abstract theory (Barrett–Lennard, 1975; Braaten, 1991) have not attracted great attention.

*A fair amount of empirical research has been done (see Truax & Carkhuff, 1967; Barrett–Lennard, 1974–75; Raskin, 1986b; Eckert & Biermann–Ratjen, 1985; Beck, Dugo, Eng & Lewis, 1986; Pomrehn, Tausch & Tönnies, 1986; Frohburg, Di Pol, Thomas & Weise, 1986; Speierer & Hochkirchen, 1986; Murayama, Nojima & Abe, 1988; Braaten, 1989; Dierick & Lietaer, 1990; Nakata, 1992).

*No clear–cut distinction is made between group psychotherapy proper and growth groups: Rogers and numerous others with him (Speierer & Hochkirchen, 1986; Johnson, 1988) believe the process to be fairly similar.

*There is little emphasis on the specificity of group therapy.The principles of individual client–centered psychotherapy are applied 'with little revision' to working with groups.There is however some theorizing about the phases in the group process (C.R. Rogers, 1970, pp. 14–

42; Beck, 1974; Braaten, 1975) and about structural aspects of the group (Barrett–Lennard, 1979), but little is said about specific tasks and interventions of the group therapist.

Rogers substitutes 'the group' for 'the organism' and lends it an actualizing tendency:

> To me the group seems like an organism, having a sense of its own direction even though it could not define that direction intellectually. ... A group recognizes unhealthy elements in its process, focuses on them, clears them up or eliminates them, and moves on toward becoming a healthier group (1970, p. 44).

Furthermore, the group therapist has to communicate the basic attitudes of acceptance, empathy and authenticity to the group members, exactly as in individual therapy. It is expected that group members will gradually take over these attitudes and experience them towards each other. Thus Hobbs in 1951 already wrote:

> It is one thing to be understood and accepted by a therapist, it is a considerably more potent experience to be understood and accepted by several people who are also honestly sharing their feelings in a joint search for a more satisfying way of life. More than anything else, this is the something added that makes group therapy a qualitatively different experience from individual therapy (p. 286).

Is client–centered group therapy then a kind of individual therapy in a group? Our theories seem to point in that direction. But there is often a large gap between theory and practice. Hence, we would like to examine 'the facts'.

INTERVENTIONS BY CLIENT–CENTERED GROUP THERAPISTS. A COMPARATIVE STUDY

As part of the Leuven study of group therapeutic processes (Dierick & Lietaer, in preparation) some 80 therapists were asked to describe their interventions within a given episode (12–18 hours) in a group process under their direction. Several of them completed the 'Intervention–style questionnaire' at least twice (in reference to different groups), yielding 102 therapist protocols, 65% of which belong to group therapy proper (clinical and outpatient), 35% to growth and experiential learning groups (mainly within a training setting). In this sample, 5 orientations with a 'sufficiently large' sample are represented: client–centered (n = 37); classical psychoanalytic (n = 13); Gestalt (n = 9); behavioural (n = 20); psychodrama and body work (psychomotor therapy of Pesso, bonding, bio–energetics; n = 19). These five orientations will be discussed, focusing on the position of client–centered therapists. Therapeutic and growth groups within the client–centered orientation will also be compared. Discussion of methodological aspects will be limited; for this we refer to a more extensive article (Lietaer and Dierick, in preparation).

The Intervention–style questionnaire consists of 45 items, worded in concrete behavioural terms which are to be judged in terms of frequency of occurence. For example 'Explaining how to work in a productive way in a group': Never (0); seldom (1); every now and then (2); often (3). It should be kept in mind however that the frequency ratings may reflect a complex interaction between what therapists want to do and believe in doing (on the one hand) and what they notice or observe themselves doing (on the other hand). A cluster and factor analysis yielded 9 scales, and in addition 5 individual items which were retained because of their potential clinical significance. Here follows a content description of the different dimensions which we subsequently classified into four umbrella sections (For the dutch version of the questionnaire, see Lietaer & Dierick, 1994).

A. Facilitating the experiential processs

Scale 1. Deepening individual exploration: reflect implicit feelings; stimulate expression of feelings; invite further exploration, e.g. in the context of the here–and–now.

Scale 2. Stimulating interpersonal communication: ask feedback or feelings about feedback; clarify, concretize, or pithily restate the communication.

B. Personal presence

Scale 3. Personal commitment and support: communicate commitment, care, respect and positive regard; encourage, confirm; relate own life experiences.

Scale 4. Give personal here–and–now feedback about a group member or about own feelings in relation to what happens in the group.

Item 10. 'Bring explicitly one's own values or what one finds personally important, to the group'

Item 11.'Have informal contact with group members outside of the sessions'.

C. Meaning attribution

*Scale 5.Providing individual insight.*Point out: perpetuating factors, behaviour or experiential patterns, discrepancies, underlying anxieties or wishes about the group as a whole, consequences of behaviour.

*Scale 6.Clarification of interactions and group processes.*Focus on: implicit messages among group members, relationship patterns, processes of the group as a whole, differences between group members.

Scale 7.Psychodynamic interpretation of underlying conflicts and defensive patterns; genetic interpretations.

D. Executive function

*Scale 8.Direction, advice and procedures.*Determine the direction or theme of the conversation; explicitly reinforce or disagree; give information and suggestions; ask actual information; introduce procedures, exercices, homework.

*Scale 9.Process rules and evaluation.*Draw attention to 'contractual' agreements, to constructive communication rules and work methods; insert moments of evaluation.

Item 12. 'Work explicitly *with one member* separately'.

Item 13.'React in a challenging or provoking manner to one or several group members'.

Item 14.Make room for interaction and communication among group members by not intervening as group leader at particular times'.

We believe this questionnaire to cover the array of possible group therapist interventions fairly completely.Indeed, we recognize in our material – but then in a more differentiated manner – the main factors found by Lieberman, Yalom and Miles (1973): *emotional stimulation, caring, meaning attribution* and *executive function.*

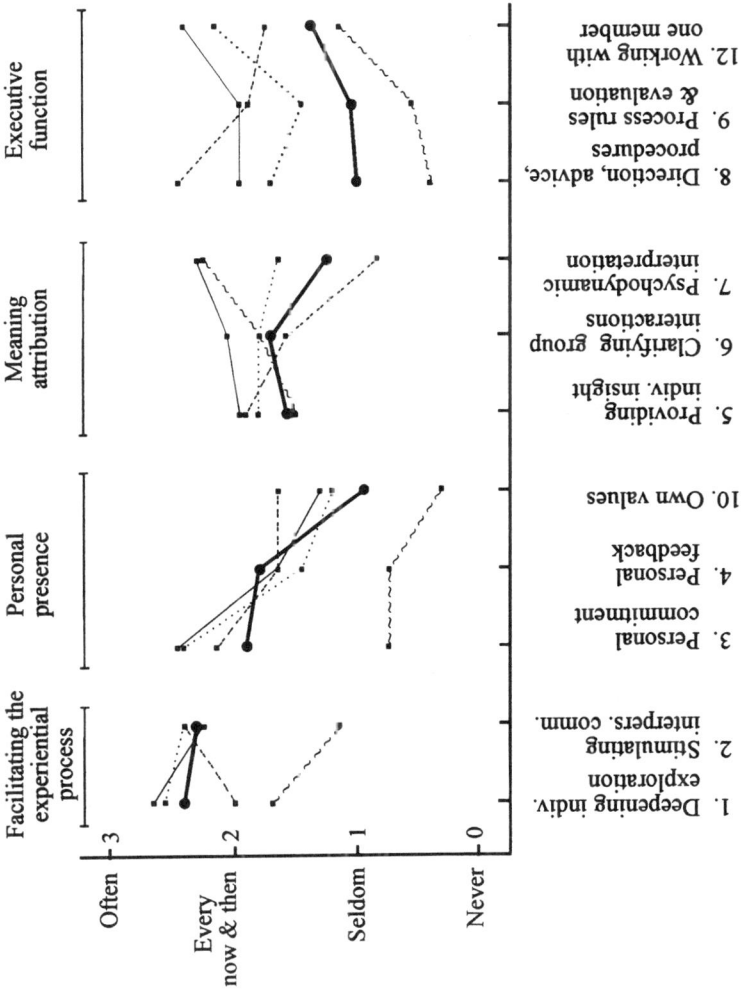

Figure 1. Intervention style of group therapists: *mean therapist perception in five orientations*
(——— CC: n = 37; ~ ~ ~ AN: n = 13; ···· GEST: n = 9; - - - BEHAV: n = 20; ——— DRAMA/BODY: n = 19)

Figure 1 shows the results of our investigation (items 11, 13 and 14 being omitted for clarity's sake).What do these findings tell us about the similarities and differences between orientations and about the client–centered group therapist's position in relation to colleagues from other orientations?We discuss a few salient findings.

*Within sections 'Facilitating the experiential process' and 'Personal presence', the psychoanalytic orientation contrasts sharply with the four other orientations: psychoanalysts intervene much less often at these levels.

*Within section 'Meaning attribution', all five orientations are approximately at the same level except for scale 'Psychodynamic interpretation' where client–centeredand behaviour therapists score much lower than psychoanalysts and practitioners of psychodrama.

*The largest differences between the five orientations are to be found in section 'Executive function'.Here the client–centered orientation finds itself closest to the psychoanalytic one, both showing a low level of structuring.In spite of the marked differences in structuring between the five orientations, no differences are found in explicitly giving room to the group by not intervening as a therapist (item 14): all averages are high, in between 'every now and then' and 'often'.Neither are there marked differences in provoking (item 13): all averages are low, around or under 'seldom'.

Considering the results in their totality, the client–centered group therapist appears to be minimally structuring but often stimulating the experiential process, both on the individual and the interactive level.In meaning–providing work as well, attention goes as much to group and interactive processes as to individual structures.Furthermore, he comes across as a 'visible' person in the group by communicating explicitly his concern and support, every now and then, and by giving regularly here–and–now feedback.Yet he believes putting forward only occasionally his own values.

This profile of the modal client–centered group therapist should however not obscure the large spread in the data.In almost all sections – especially the meaning–providing one – as many as three out of the four response categories are used (from 'never' to 'every now and then' or from 'seldom' to 'often'): every therapist provides thus his own accent.The obvious exception is the scale 'Deepening individual exploration' where responses are almost unanimously situated between the two highest scale values.In the context of group therapy facilitating individual exploration thus remains a dominant way of intervening for client–centered therapists.

Besides this, we notice a few marked differences between growth and therapy groups; client–centered therapists in therapeutic work score significantly higher on the two scales referring to 'Structure and procedures' and on scales 'Providing individual insight' and 'Psychodynamic interpretation'.In therapy groups client–centered therapists apparently direct more than in growth groups and interpret more in a cognitive way.A more 'steering' approach is thus adopted for clients with more serious problems.Besides, client–centered therapists in growth and training groups have markedly more informal contact with their groups than in therapy groups.This is no doubt partly due to situational factors: often such a training context includes common meals.However, it also reflects an option about visibility, with psychoanalytic group leaders withdrawing in such a context; in the 13 questionnaires filled out by psychoanalysts for our study, the item was unanimously answered 'Never'.

This investigation yields an empirically based profile of client–centered group therapists' own perception of their interventions: minimal structuring (be it markedly more so in psychotherapy than in growth groups); actively facilitating the experiential process and the reflection on it;

personal presence; balanced attention to both the interactive and the intrapsychic aspects of the process.This last characteristic arouses the suspicion that client–centered theory of group therapy has not kept up with actual practice.In the next paragraph we will try to highlight what is characteristic of the group therapeutic approach and to integrate it more explicitly in client–centered theory.

FROM INDIVIDUAL TO GROUP: SHIFTS AND NECESSARY ADDITIONS

The foremost task of a group therapist: to create a well–functioning group

In group therapy, a therapist finds himself in a position which is essentially different from that of the individual therapist.While the individual client's therapeutic process proceeds in and through the relationship with the therapist, the group therapist's relationship to the group members is mainly that of a context in which the proceeding mutual interactions between group members are the nuclear event.As Gendlin and Beebe put it: "The group leader is not a switchboard or funnel through whom everything must go".What happens between group members themselves is the most important part of the event – as is shown in many studies (see e.g. Berzon, Pious & Farson, 1963; Dierick & Lietaer, 1990) – and it is there that the main therapeutic processes are to be found.This implies a specific task for the group therapist which we believe has not been sufficiently highlighted in client–centered literature: that of creating, getting started and keeping going a well–functioning group (Yalom, 1985, pp. 112–134).

Rogers also sees it as his task to guard the group climate – especially in the beginning stages of the group – but he describes this task in a rather limited way and in highly individual terms (1970, pp. 46–48); he wants to create a climate of security by making it clear that he does not want to steer the group process in any particular direction and by listening as sensitively as possible to each group member who wants to express something of his own.In this way he wants to convey that each group member is worth being understood.This is no doubt very important but, we believe, not sufficient.We suggest that this task should be given more weight and content in client–centered therapy.In fact, the focus on group functioning has to start even before the first meeting: clients are to be selected and prepared carefully.During the sessions the therapist has to maintain a group–dynamic orientation which means, among other things: facilitating group cohesion (for example by stimulating mutual communication and involvement); the timely recognition and curtailing of processes which could endanger the cohesion; paying attention to and promoting therapeutic group norms; uncovering and investigating antitherapeutic norms; paying attention to typical group phenomena such as informal leadership, formation of coalitions, scapegoating, group flight, phase–specific processes etcetera.

The group as interpersonal laboratory: preference for the here–and–now

A second principle of client–centered theory of group therapy should be given a more prominent place alongside the group–dynamic focus: the group as interpersonal laboratory.In the interpersonal approach to group therapy (Yalom, 1985; Leszcz, 1992; Dies, 1992) the group is viewed as a social microcosm in which each member interacts sooner or later – and especially when structural limitations of the group are minimal – with group members in the same way as with others in his social environment.Each group member repeats thus in the here–and–now of the group his interpersonal patterns, and the 'working through' of these interactions in the here–and–now is seen as the nucleus of the process of change.This is justified by the idea that an *in vivo exposure* with possiblity of feedback from other group members offers more chance of breaking through rigid interpersonal schemes than the exploration of experiences from one's personal life or from the past.This gives the therapist a double task: to bring the group into the here–and–now and to stimulate reflection on this interpersonal process (Yalom, 1985, pp. 135–172).This means that the therapist has to think in the here–and–now and has to try to bring the material brought by the group members to life in the here–and–now through selectively directed interventions.

As a matter of fact, the motive for an interpersonal focus is experiential in nature: here–and–now interactions are experienced vividly and there is reality confrontation with the reactions of others.This is an important element in favour of this, but it does not exclude the possibility of exploring and working through personal life and past experiences in a felt manner.Hence we appeal for a flexible approach on the part of the therapist: a clear preference for the here–and–now (by which the therapist exerts a non–negligible influence on the direction which the group process will take by his selective attention) and simultaneously sufficient attention to the link between the here–and–now and what members are experiencing or have experienced in their personal lives.It is exactly this spiral movement between 'here, elsewhere and past' which makes the group therapeutic process so deep.Although Rogers has a preference for the here–and–now as well, he emphasizes strongly having no intention of imposing this on the group.Perhaps he felt that steering a group towards the here–and–now was too firm a way of controlling the content: "I respond *more* to present feelings than to statements about past experiences but am willing for both to be present in the communication.I do not like the rule: "We will only talk about the here and now"(Rogers 1970, p 50).

Clarifying the here–and–now interactions requires comments on the process.Here Yalom sees a specific task of the therapist: as a slightly more distant 'historian' of the group, he is best placed to play a central role in uncovering patterns, discussing gains and losses, guiding towards change.We believe that Rogers incorrectly considers process comments as something objectifying and detached, and that he sees too little value in providing meaning (1970, p. 57).On the other hand, he mentions feedback and confrontation, two important vehicles of process comment, as belonging to his repertoire.

We want to emphasize that viewing a group as an interpersonal laboratory follows an evolution which is to be found in individual client–centered therapy as well.Both Rogers and Gendlin gradually came to view the therapist as a separate pole in the interaction and not only as an alter ego (Lietaer, 1993, Van Balen, 1990).This interactional view has been elaborated by Kiesler (1988) and by Van Kessel and Van der Linden (1993).They make the client–therapist interaction a preferred process–enhancing medium.Besides the fact is that Yalom's handbook of group psychotherapy constitutes an important source of inspiration for numerous client–centered group therapists.The emphasis and method proposed by Yalom can easily be integrated in a client–centered approach.This is perhaps due to the fact that Yalom does not stress the gaining of (genetic) insight but rather the corrective interpersonal experience.Client–centered therapists too, want to orient themselves towards the breaking down and transcending of repetitive rigid patterns and view relationships between group members (as well as the relationship with the therapist) as a preferential arena for doing this.With Yalom they are convinced that this is the major and specific force behind group therapy.Indeed, where else can metacommunication about how people interact with one another occur in such a thorough, varied and (generally) constructive way?

The client–centered group therapist's intervention pattern

The previous two points were intended as a plea for increased attention to the specificity of group therapy, since this aspect is not sharply outlined in our literature.Our study (Fig. 1) shows however that client–centered group therapists, when asked about their own concrete practice, do pay sufficient attention to specific group–therapeutic aspects.If their perception is a reflection of reality, then the question arises how this is reflected, at a microscopic level, in their concrete intervention patterns. We will now explore this by means of an objective analysis of a client–centered group therapist's interventions in a growth group (a training group for clinical psychology students running over three weekends with eigth one and a half hour sessions each; De Bruycker, 1993). We will compare these findings with two cases of individual client–centered therapy (the first four or five sessions; Plessers, 1992). This material is of course not sufficiently representative, but the clearly emerging trends do allow us to formulate tentatively a number of typical characteristics of the client–centered group therapist's intervention pattern.

Table 1. Frequently used response categories by client–centered therapists: percentages in two cases of individual therapy first 4 or 5 sessions) and in a growth group (3 weekends of 8 sessions each)

| Response categories | Individual therapy | | Growth group | | | | |
| | Casus 1 | Casus 2 | All sessions | WE 1 | WE 3 | Individual | Group |
				Fase		Focus	
1. Open exploratory questions	7	13	20	18	19	18	28
2. Restatement of narrative aspects	12	12	3	4	3	2	3
3. Reflection of expressed feelings	23	28	11	16	8	12	7
4. Reflection of underlying feelings	22	19	21	31	12	23	8
5. Feedback and confrontation	8	5	18	13	27	17	21
6. Here–and–now disclosure of T.	2	0	6	2	9	4	11
N response segments	500	538	846	291	342	672	134
N therapy hours	4	5	36	12	12		

The analysis was carried out using a revised form of the Hill Counselor Verbal Respons Category System (Hill 1986) in which each intervention (or part thereof) is assigned to one single category. The results show that the following six categories occur rarely (less than 5% of all interventions) in client–centered therapy and that there is no difference between individual and group therapy. They are: affirmation or reassurance; providing information (especially about the therapeutic process); instructions (about in–session procedures or 'homework'); closed questions; interpretation; disclosure of personal life experiences by the therapist. Alongside these, there are six more frequently used categories where we do notice a difference between individual and group therapy. Only these categories are shown in Table 2. The main findings are as follows.

*Comparing the number of intervention segments per therapy hour, we notice four times as many in individual therapy as in group therapy. This illustrates the less central position of the group therapist.

*The three reflection categories together (2, 3 and 4) represent 60% of all interventions in individual therapy compared to only 35% in group therapy. Remarkable is that this low percentage concerns the reflections on the *manifest* content (cat. 2and 3) whereas reflections on *underlying* experiences yield a similar percentage in both types of therapy. Perhaps the group therapist does not consider it as his primary task to give 'maintenance reflections', but tends to reveal rather what has not been heard, has been said in a veiled way or what has fallen between the cracks.

*On the other hand, group therapy shows a higher percentage of exploratory questions and especially a higher percentage of interventions which start from the personal frame of reference of the therapist: feedback and confrontation, and self–disclosure in the here–and–now.The fact that a group therapist asks more exploratory questions may reveal his desire to remain in contact with what *all* group members experience and to stimulate the active participation and mutual communication between all members.

*Looking at the evolution of the group therapist's interventions from the first to the third weekend, we notice a number of marked shifts.Whereas the intervention pattern during the first weekend resembles closely that of individual therapy, by the third weekend the difference has become striking: reflection of feelings (cat. 3 and 4) decreases from 47 to 20% whereas feedback, confrontation with discrepancies and introduction of here–and–now feelings rise from 15 to 36%.This increasing proportion of process comments demonstrates clearly the increasingly interactional character of the process as the group progresses.

*In this group 95% of the interventions took place in the context of a discussion of mutual relations within the group.We looked at the focus of these interventions: does the therapist address one group member, or several, or the group as a whole?Analysis shows thet 16% of these interventions were addressed to the group and 79% to one person.However, group–directed interventions increased clearly as the weekends went by: from 7% in the first to 21% in the third.Next we looked at the relative weight of the six response categories in the interventions directed at an individual and those directed at the group.This weight is clearly different in three categories: exploratory questions and the therapist's here–and–now feelings play a larger part in the group–directed interventions; on the other hand, reflections of underlying feelings occupy a larger place within the individual–directed interventions.

With regard to the intervention focus, we want to point out that even interventions addressed to one person often have a relational goal, which is to promote communication *between* group members.A number of intervention categories found in a previous study by one of the authors (Lietaer, 1981) illustrate this clearly: a request for feedback from a group member, a request to relate the given feedback more clearly to the here–and–now interactions, clarification of the feedback given by a group member, explicitation of the experiential impact of the feedback etc.This sort of intervention enhances the self–exploration of the person addressed by the therapist but aims also at facilitating communication with the interacting partner.

These findings, as well as our clinical experience allows us to draw – tentatively – the following picture of what is typical in the intervention pattern of the client–centered group therapist: more exploratory questions than in individual therapy, fewer reflections of manifest content and proportionally more reflections of underlying feelings; more interactional process comments through feedback and self–expression of here–and–now experiences.Moreover, the 'volume of interventions' is markedly less than in individual therapy and a significant number of interventions is addressed to the group or to several group members.Even individual–directed interventions often aim indirectly at enhancing communication *between* group members.Finally, group therapy presents a larger problem in selecting which theme to pursue: often a lot is happening at the same time.Preference for the here–and–now is always an important criterion.

PERSONAL ACCENTS

From the above and especially from our comparative study, it has become clear that similarities between group therapists of different orientations exceed their differences.But this is not to say that client–centered group therapy does not have its own specificity.In our literature we find accents which can be traced back individually in other orientations, but which as a Gestalt, we believe, put a very personal stamp on our work method.At any rate, they are aspects which touch the nuclear identity of client–centered therapy.By way of conclusion to this chapter, we would therefore like to present them to the reader, enhanced by a few side–notes.

Trusting the group process

As mentioned in the introductory part of our chapter, client–centered literature stresses belief in the wisdom and self–corrective capacities of the group as an all–important basic attitude on the part of the therapist.Thus, Rogers emphasizes strongly the capacity of group members to help each other.Even in acute situations in the group process, when someone shows psychotic symptoms or bizarre behaviour, he has learned to trust the therapeutic capacities of the group members (1970, p. 58).He believes the professional helper to be more likely to put the person in question into a category and to treat him more readily as an object.It has been his experience that untrained group members keep reacting more as a person and thus in a more therapeutic way.

This trust in the wisdom of the group process includes that the role of the therapist is, first and foremost, that of a facilitator who 'follows while deepening' and does not act as a guru who 'directs' the group process by means of his know–how of techniques along well–defined roads and towards a well–defined goal.He respects the group's own direction and the pace of members.He does not structure a lot and joins largely what develops from within the group.Rogers likes to quote in this respect what Lao–Tse wrote twenty five centuries ago about a good leader:

> But of a good leader, who talks little,
>
> When his work is done, his aim fulfilled,
>
> They will all say, "We did this ourselves" (1980, p. 42).

This trust in the constructive forces of the group is however not shared by everybody in the client–centered orientation.Swildens (1979) for example writes: "Who can expect eight to ten neurotically disturbed people to provide each other in mutual interaction those favourable conditions which, according to the humanistic–experiential theory, only a fully functioning person can provide?" (p. 4); and further on: "There is no basis for extending the growth potential of the individual to that of social structures such as groups" (p. 7).Although we would not put it as strongly as Swildens, we do agree with him: he points at a weak spot in our theory.Our literature does indeed sometimes make it look as if a constructive group process arises 'by itself' and underlines too little the necessity of the therapist's process directivity.A group can be subject to constructive as well as destructive processes.In this last case, but more generally as well, steering interventions may be necessary.Perhaps our directivity–phobia has played tricks on us in the past and has not allowed us to write about it without a certain embarrassment.But in the meantime, change has taken place.It has now been realized, more clearly, how influential a therapist – even a non–directive one – really is.Thus, the 'minimal–structure' set–up forces the group members into a greater self–reliance.The therapist's (sometimes unconscious) selective attention to personal connotations in the group members' statements and to what is happening here–and–now exerts a strong steering influence in a direction soon picked up and focused on by group members.Even accepting the group 'exactly where it is' (Rogers, 1970, p. 48) may paradoxically lead to a point where change becomes possible.Thus, we do influence in any event.But we try to avoid control and manipulation by which group members are pushed in a certain direction against their will and under external pressure.The point is not whether our interventions are following or steering (the difference is sometimes hard to tell anyway), but whether or not they are imposed on the client, and whether or not the client remains free to pursue them (Coghlan & McIlduff, 1990).

By means of such non–manipulative process directiveness we try to get a process going which largely takes its origin in what happens in the group and is sufficiently carried and approved by the group members; a process in which we give the group members as much credit as possible and whose nucleus is mainly situated in what happens among the group members themselves.This may lead to episodes in the group process in which we as therapists disappear temporarily into the background and where the group almost forgets about us.'To learn to be unimportant' is thus part of our task as a group therapist.

Experiencing as a continuous touchstone

Client–centered therapy has a marked phenomenological character: entering the client's experiential world and continuously testing the interventions against the client's *felt sense* are basic principles of our approach (Vanaerschot, 1990, 1993; Leijssen, 1990).This experiential listening continues to feed our interventions in group therapy.Although group therapy is often concerned with the exploration of what happens *between* people, this analysis never limits itself to a behavioural analysis of the interaction as such.We always try to follow a back and forth motion between obtaining a clearer picture of what happens at the interactional level, on the one hand, and the experiential basis in which this way of interacting is embedded, on the other.Just as we focus on the experiential source of the client's words in individual therapy, so we focus on the experiential source of the interaction in group work.This means that we always try to evoke the experience behind the relational problem: how do the group members experience – at a deeper level – their way of interacting?Which anxieties and desires are taking part?Which life experiences have 'marked' them in this respect?Our experience tells us that reaching this underlying experiential layer and communicating it to one another often provides a turning point in defrosting relationship patterns which have become stuck.That the therapist has hereby an important role to play shows in our study of therapeutic processes: the category 'clarifying and deepening empathic interventions' is the only one in which group members refer clearly more often to the therapist than to other group members (Dierick & Lietaer, 1990, p. 762).

Our focus on experiencing also means that the goal of client–centered therapy is more than mere symptom removal.Group members are continuously invited to turn to their experience and take this 'inner compass' seriously as primary source of their choices and decisions.We are thus stimulating a broader capacity which can not only be of use for the problem at hand but also for problems which may arise in the future.This focus on *'inner–directedness'*, on growth and self–determination, is eminently enhanced by what Greenberg, Rice & Elliott call 'empathic selection':

> The therapist reflects aspects of client experience that involve emerging experience, or ownership; strengths, progress or active coping; desire for change, mastery, or contact with others; personal rights, mature interdependence and mutuality; positive aspects of self; and plans or projects for the future (1993, p. 114).

This broader orientation towards experience–based growth leaves also room for existential moments during the group process, moments in which *being* is more important than *coping* (Bugental & Bracke, 1992; Mullan, 1992): A journey into self (Rogers, McGaw & Farson, 1968), a common search for a meaningful and authentic existence, for what leads to deeper life–fulfillment.

Personal presence of the therapist

The comparative study discussed above (see Figure 1) shows that client–centered group therapists – together with therapists from three other orientations – allow themselves more visibility than psychoanalysts.Rogers has always rejected the idea of the therapist as a blank screen and has gradually – partly through his work with groups – promoted therapist authenticity as the most important basic attitude.But how does this attitude show concretely in the way of being and the interventions of the client–centered group therapist?A number of aspects will be mentioned here briefly (for extensive discussion, see Lietaer, 1993).

*Authenticity has an inner and an outer component.The inner component (congruence) refers to the degree to which the therapist has access to, and is receptive to, *all* aspects of his experience.The outer component (transparency) refers to the therapist's explicit communication of personal impressions and experiences.In fact, congruence, with its accent on self–knowledge and ego–strength, has always been given the most weight in client–centered therapy.This attitude allows the therapist to fulfill properly his holding–function in the group; he can be quietly receptive and respond to everything that occurs in the process, and receive as a 'rock of Gibraltar' the violent emotions and conflicts without being flooded himself.

*A congruent therapist has *presence*.He is personally involved in the process.His working method rests on an underlying attitude and is shaped by his personality; he is 'himself'.Even though his attention is largely centered on the group members' experiential world, his understanding remains nevertheless a personal event in the sense that his interventions take root in his own experience of what group members say, and are thus never a rigid–scolarly application of a technique: the therapist does not only summarize what a patient says but puts into words 'what strikes him', 'what the client's discourse evokes in him'.Even empathic guessing and listening 'with the third ear' is fed by the therapist's roots in his own experience.Rogers describes as follows how he gradually came to trust his own deeper intuitive layer:

> I *trust* the feelings, words, impulses, fantasies, that emerge in me.In this way I am using more than my conscious self, drawing on some of the capacities of my whole organism.For example, "I suddenly had the fantasy that you are a princess, and that you would love it if we were all your subjects."Or, "I sense that you are the judge as well as the accused, and that you are saying sternly to yourself, 'You are *guilty* on every count'" (1970, p. 53).

*In his interactional work, a client–centered group therapist regularly provides here–and–now feedback: impressions about how group members deal with each other and with him as well as the feelings elicited in him by certain group members or the group as a whole.Here too, his congruence plays a vital role: that of an interactional barometer.But can a therapist in his here–and–now feelings make a distinction between what is largely elicited by others and what has to do with his personal sensitivities and problems?Can he word his relational feedback clearly as an 'I–statement' and remain open to how it is received?Can he face his own contribution to the interactional process without being unduly on the defensive?All this requires a sufficiently congruent therapist who can use his own here–and–now experience to discuss and break through certain relationship patterns without interference by personal needs.

*Moreover, therapist transparency can refer to communication of personal life experiences.This occurs however rarely.It may be used as an expression of empathy, in order to show the client that one knows from experience what he goes through and 'what it means'.Furthermore, in case an event in the therapist's private life weighs heavily on his therapeutic work (such as the death of a close relative) it may be advisable to mention it.Finally, a therapist may bring in a personal life experience as 'point of comparison' against which the client may explore further and clarify his own experience, position or choice.This will usually only occur in the last phases of the group process, in which the therapist is no longer automatically seen as an authority figure but can also be viewed as 'only a fellow pilgrim'.

Our emphasis on a real and visible therapist (Boy, 1990) certainly does not mean that we feel he should continually be in the spotlight, as a kind of charismatic leader.His self–revelations remain in the service of the group process and remain sober.But a client–centered therapist does not primarily aim at becoming a symbolic figure or a projection screen.He chooses a natural spontaneous attitude whereby he shows his concern in an open an direct manner.This is considered to be an important factor in the building of trust and gives the therapist the possibility to serve as a model for the group members.Perhaps it is this very difference in attitude which is at the basis of Eckert and Biermann–Ratjens's findings in their comparative study of client–centered versus psychoanalytical clinical group psychotherapy (1990, p. 463).The *degree* of improvement was similar in both cases but the *nature* of the change was different: in the psychoanalytic groups, patients localized their improvement more on an intrapsychic level; in the client–centered groups, on the other hand, more at the level of capacity for interpersonal relationships.

The client–centered group therapist's transparent attitude, however, does not do away with his special, separate position as a process facilitator; he never becomes *one of the guys*, something which has occasionally been overlooked in the days of encounter groups.It also does not mean that he cannot be emotionally charged or distorted by group members: although we do not provoke regression and transference, paratactic distortions can occur and it is our task to deal with them in an expert way.

CONCLUSION

We are convinced that the training of client–centered therapists makes them eminently suited for group therapy: the basic attitudes of acceptance, empathy and authenticity – and the ensuing responses and interventions – provide them with a number of interpersonal skills which are all important for facilitating relational processes.Besides, they are mostly specially trained and sensitized to these issues by participating in a long–term psychotherapeutically–oriented training group.Numerous client–centered therapists are indeed group therapists.Typical of our orientation is also our interest in using groups in the broader field of personal growth, prevention, societal problems, revalidation and health psychology.We find publications about group counseling for teachers (Groddeck, 1988), the jobless (Grimm, Dircks & Langer, 1992), single parents (Brendemühl, 1988), the elderly (Sherman, 1990), cancer patients (A.–M. Tausch, 1981; Dircks, Grimm & Tausch, 1982) and infarct patients (Esser, 1988).Client–centered therapists are furthermore active in the field of self–help groups, in which non–professional helpers are often involved as aids (Goodman & Esterly, 1988).

In summary: both on the preventive and on the curative level, client–centered therapists frequently use groups as a tool for change, support and growth.Publications about the client–centered approach to outpatient and clinical group psychotherapy in the narrow sense are, however, still scarce although a change can be noticed since 1980.We find for instance publications about outpatient group therapy as a supplement to individual therapy (Snijder–Van den Eerenbeemt, 1990), about group therapy in psychiatry (Thomas, 1988; Marchiori et al., 1990; Marques–Teixeira et al., 1990), with borderlines (Eckert & Biermann–Ratjen, 1986), schizophrenics (Teusch, 1990), anorexia nervosa patients (Schmitt, 1980), problem couples (Tausch, Langer & Bergeest, 1984), alcoholics (Pattyn, 1982) and delinquents (Melk, 1980).

In the further elaboration of client–centered group therapy we will be confronted with a certain tension between 'orthodoxy' and openness to integration.It is typical of client–centered group therapists, we believe, to cast themselves as relatively non–dogmatic, both in terms of theoretical insights into the group process and in terms of concrete interventions and procedures.According to one's personal affinities, one's 'training history' and the setting in which one is active, different features are stressed and elements from other orientations are added (as in: Van Dantzig–van Amstel & Lehmann, 1977; Tausch, 1988, 1990; Martens, 1990; Berk, 1991; Leijssen, 1992).We wholeheartedly encourage such a non–dogmatic attitude and openness.Indeed, not everybody has to re–invent the wheel.Numerous insights into group processes are useful to all group therapists, whatever their orientation, and a certain assimilation of work methods should be possible as well.Nevertheless, we believe it remains important to give sufficient attention to our 'own model' and study its specific potential.After all, there is richness in diversity.

REFERENCES

Barrett–Lennard, G. T. (1974) *Experiential learning groups.* Psychotherapy: Theory, Research and Practice, 11, 71–75.

Barrett–Lennard, G. T. (1974–75).*Outcomes of residential encounter group workshops: Descriptive analysis of follow–up structured questionnaire data.*Interpersonal Development, 5, 86–93.

Barrett–Lennard, G. T. (1975). *Process, effects and structure in intensive groups: A theoretical–descriptive analysis.*In C. L Cooper (Ed.), Theories of Group Processes (pp. 59–86).London: Wiley.(Published 1975; corrected paper–cover reprinting, 1976).

Barrett–Lennard, G. T. (1979). *A new model of communicational–relational systems in intensive groups.*Human Relations, 32, 841–849.

Barrett–Lennard, G. T. (1994).*Toward a person–centered theory of community.*Journal of Humanistic Psychology, 32(1), 90–105.

Bebout, J. (1974), *It takes one to know one: Existential–Rogerian concepts in encounter groups.*In D.A. Wexler & L. N. Rice (Eds.), Innovations in client–centered therapy (pp. 367–420).New York: J. Wiley & Sons.

Bebout, J. (1976), *Basic encounter groups: Their nature, method, and brief history.*In H. Mullen & M. Rosenbaum (Eds.), Group psychotherapy: Theory and practice.New York: MacMillan.

Bebout, J., & Gordon, B. (1972).*The value of encounter.*In L. Solomon & B. Berzon (Eds.), New perspectives on encounter groups (pp. 83–118).San Francisco: Jossey–Bass.

Beck, A. P. (1974), *Phases in the development of structure in therapy and encounter groups.*In D. A. Wexler & L. N. Rice (Eds.), Innovations in client–centered therapy (pp. 421–463).New York: Wiley.

Beck, A. P., Dugo, J. M., Eng, A. M., & Lewis, C. M. (1986).*The search for phases in group development: Designing process analysis measures of group interaction.*In L. S. Greenberg & W. M. Pinsof (Eds.), The psychotherapeutic process: A research handbook (pp. 615–705).New York: Guilford Press.

Berk, T. (1984).*Groepsdynamische experiëntiële groepstherapie.*In G. Lietaer, Ph. H. van Praag, & J. C. A. G. Swildens (Eds.), Client–centered therapie in beweging (pp. 521–534).Leuven: Acco.

Berk, T. J. C. (1991). *Cliëntgerichte groepspsychotherapie.*In H. Swildens, O. de Haas, G. Lietaer, & R. Van Balen (Eds.), Leerboek gesprekstherapie.De cliëntgerichte benadering (pp. 433–478).Amersfoort/Leuven: Acco.

Berzon, B., Pious, C., & Farson, R. E. (1963).*The therapeutic event in group psychotherapy.A study of subjective reports by group members.*Journal of Individual Psychology, 19, 204–212.

Blocksma, D. D., & Porter, H. F. Jr. (1947).*A short–term training program in client–centered counseling.*Journal of Consulting Psychology, 11, 55–60.

Boy, A. V. (1990).*The therapist in person–centered groups.*Person–centered Review, 5, 308–315.

Braaten, L. (1975). *Developmental phases of encounter groups and related intensive groups.*A critical review of models and a new proposal.Interpersonal Development, 75(5), 112–129.

Braaten, L. (1989). *The effects of person–centered group therapy.*Person–centered Review, 4, 183–209.

Braaten, L. (1991).*Group cohesion: A new miltidimensional model.*Group, 15(1), 39–55.

Brendemühl, U. (1988).*Prophylaktische Angebote in der Erziehungsberatung am Beispiel der Arbeit mit Alleinerziehenden.*In K. Sander & U. Esser (Eds.), Personenzentrierte Gruppenarbeit (pp. 125–132).Heidelberg: Asanger.

Bugental, J. F. T., & Bracke, P. E. (1992).*The future of existential–humanistic psychotherapy.*Psychotherapy, 29, 28–33.

Coghlan, D., & McIlduff, E. (1990).*Structuring and nondirectiveness in group facilitation.*Person–centered Review, 5, 13–29.

Coulson, W. R. (1972). Groups, gimmicks and instant gurus.New York: Harper & Row.

Coulson, W. R. (1981).*Client–centered group therapy.*In R. Malnati, J. Donigion, & D. Kendall (Eds.), Critical situations in group counseling.Monterey, CA.: Brooks/Cole.

Coulson, W., Land, D., & Meador, B. (Eds.). (1977).*The La Jolla experiment: Eight personal views.*La Jolla: Landmark.

Dantzig–van Amstel, B., & Lehmann, B. (1977). *Synthese van psychodynamisch en interactioneel georiënteerde groepstherapie.*Een praktijkervaring.Tijdschrift voor Psychotherapie, 3, 23–32.

De Bruycker, D. (1993).*Therapeutinterventies in groepstherapie.Een aanpassing van het Hill Counselor Verbal Response Category System.*De studie van één case. Unpublished master's thesis, Katholieke Universiteit Leuven, Belgium.

Devonshire, C. M., & Kremer, J. W. (1980). *Toward a person–centered resolution of intercultural conflicts.*Dortmund: Pädagogische Arbeits–stelle.

Dierick, P., & Lietaer, G. (1990). *Member and therapist perceptions of therapeutic factors in therapy and growth groups: Comments on a category system.*In G. Lietaer, J. Rombauts, & R. Van Balen (Eds.), Client–centered and experiential psychotherapy in the nineties (pp. 741–770).Leuven: Leuven University Press.

Dierick, P., & Lietaer, G. (doctoral dissertation in preparation).*Cliënt–, therapeut– en groepsprocessen in groepstherapie en groeigroepen.Een belevingsonderzoek bij 600 cliënten en 80 therapeuten.*Centrum voor client–centered therapie en counseling, Katholieke Universiteit Leuven, Belgium.

Dies, R. R. (1992).*Models of group psychotherapy: Sifting through confusion.*International Journal of Group Psychotherapy, 42(1), 1–17.

579

Dircks, P., Grimm, F., Tausch, A.–M., & Wittern, J. O. (1982).*Förderung der seelischen Gesundheit von Krebspatienten durch personenzentrierte Gruppengespräche.*Zeitschrift für Klinische Psychologie, 11, 241–252.

Eckert, J., & Biermann–Ratjen, E.–M. (1985).*Stationäre Gruppenpsychotherapie: Prozesse, Effekte, Vergleiche.*Berlin: Springer.

Eckert, J., & Biermann–Ratjen, E.–M. (1986).*Ueberlegungen und Erfahrungen bei der gesprächspsychotherapeutischen Behandlung in Gruppen von Patienten mit einer Borderline–Persönlichkeitsstörung* Zeitschrift für personenzentrierte Psychologie und Psychotherapie, 5, 47–54.

Eckert, J., & Biermann–Ratjen, E.–M. (1990).*Client–centered therapy versus psychoanalytic psychotherapy.Reflections following a comparative study.*In G. Lietaer, J. Rombauts, & R. Van Balen (Eds.), Client–centered and experiential psychotherapy in the nineties (pp. 457–468).Leuven: Leuven University Press.

Esser, P. (1988).*Aspekte stationärer Gruppenarbeit mit Herzinfarktpatienten.*In K. Sander & U. Esser (Eds.), Personenzentrierte Gruppenarbeit (pp. 162–180).Heidelberg: Asanger.

Esser, U., & Sander, K. (Eds.). (1988).*Personenzentrierte Gruppenpsychotherapie. Therapeutischer Umgang mit der Person und der Gruppe.*Heidelberg: Asanger Verlag.

Finke, J. (1994).*Gruppen–Gesprächspsychotherapie.*In Empathie und Interaktion (pp. 150–159).Stuttgart: Thieme.

Franke, A. (1978).*Klientenzentrierte Gruppenpsychotherapie.*Stuttgart: Kohlhammer.

Frohburg, I., Di Pol, G., Thomas, B., & Weise, K. (Eds.). (1986).*Forschung und Praxis in der Gruppengesprächspsychotherapie.*Berlin: Gesellschaft für psychologie.

Gendlin, E. T. & Beebe, J. (1968). *Experiential groups.*In G. M. Gazda (Ed.), Innovations to group psychotherapy (pp. 190–206).Springfield: Thomas.

Goodman, G., & Esterly, G. (1988).*The talk book.The intimate science of communicating in close relationships.*New York: Ballantine Books.

Gordon, T. (1951), *Group–centered leadership and administration.*In C. R. Rogers, Client–centered therapy (pp. 320–383).Boston: Houghhton Mifflin.

Greenberg, L., Rice, L. N., & Elliot, R., *Facilitating emotional change.The moment–by–moment process.*New York: Guilford.

Grimm, F., Dircks, P., & Langer, I. (1992).*Prozesse und Auswirkungen personenzentrierter Gesprächsgruppen bei Arbeitslosen.*In M. Behr, U. Esser, F. Petermann, W. M. Pfeiffer, & R. Tausch (Eds.), Personzentrierte Psychologie & Psychotherapie.Band 3.Jahrbuch 1992 (pp. 116–131).Köln: GwG Verlag.

Groddeck, N. (1988).*Lehren und Lehren als Person.Ein Erfahrungsbericht aus einem Hochschul–Praxisprojekt für Lehrer und Lehrerstudenten der Sekundarstufe.*In K. Sander & U. Esser (Eds.), Personenzentrierte Gruppenarbeit (pp. 13–42).Heidelberg: Asanger.

Gundrum, M. (1989).*Client–centered therapie en systemen.Een overzicht van de duitstalige literatuur.*Unpublished master's thesis, Katholieke Universiteit Leuven, Belgium.

Hill, C. (1986).*An overview of the Hill counselor and client verbal response modes category systems.*In L. S. Greenberg & W. M. Pinsof (Eds.), The psychotherapeutic process: A research handbook (pp. 131–158).London: Guilford Press.

Hobbs, N. (1951), *Group–centered psychotherapy.*In C. R. Rogers, Client–centered therapy (pp. 278–319).Boston: Houghton Mifflin.

Johnson, F. (1988).*Encounter group therapy.*In S. Long (Ed.), Six group therapies (pp. 115–158).New York: Plenum.

Kessel, W. J. H. van, & van der Linden, P. (1993).*Die aktuelle Beziehung in der Klientenzentrierten Psychotherapie; der interaktionelle Aspekt.*GwG Zeitschrift, 24, No. 90, 19–32.

580

Kiesler, D. J. (1988).*Therapeutic metacommunication: Therapist impact disclosure as feedback in psychotherapy.*Palo Alto: Consulting Psychologists Press.

Ködel, R., & Froburg, I. (Eds.). (1988).*Grundbegriffe der Gruppen–Gesprächspsychotherapie.* Berlin: Ges. für Psychologie.

Leijssen, M. (1990).*On focusing and the necessary conditons of therapeutic personality change.*In G. Lietaer, J. Rombauts, & R. Van Balen (Eds.), Client–centered and experiential therapy in the nineties (pp. 225–250).Leuven: University Press.

Leijssen, M. (1992).*Experiential focusing through drawing.*Focusing Folio, 11(4), 35–40.

Leszcz, M. (1992).*The interpersonal approach to group psychotherapy.* International Journal of Group Psychotherapy, 42, 37–62.

Lieberman, M. A., Yalom, I. D., & Miles, M. B. (1973).*Encounter groups first facts.*New York: Basic Books.

Lietaer, G. (1981), *Client–centered groepstherapie: grondhoudingen en interventies van de therapeut.*Leren en leven met groepen, 13, 2200/1–36.

Lietaer, G. (1993).*Authenticity, congruence and transparency.*In D. Brazier (Ed.), Beyond Carl Rogers: Towards a psychotherapy for the twenty–first century (pp. 17–47).London: Constable.

Lietaer, G., & Dierick, P. (1994).*Een onderzoekslijst voor de werkwijze van de therapeut: de 'GIS–V'.*In T. J. C. Berk et al. (Eds.), Handboek groepspsychotherapie (W8: pp. 1–19).Houten: Bohn Stafleu Van Loghum.

Lietaer, G., & Dierick, P. (in preparation).*Interventiestijl van groepspsychotherapeuten: vergelijkende studie van vijf oriëntaties.*Centrum voor client–centered therapie en counseling, Katholieke Universiteit Leuven, Belgium.

Marchiori, L. et al. (1990).*Il "piccolo gruppo": modalità d'incontro con lo psicotico nell'istituzione.*Psichiatria Generale e dell'Eta Evolutiva, 28, 53–64.

Marques–Teixeira, J. et al. (1990).*Evolução de um grupo de psicodrama num hosptial psiquiátrico.*[Evolution of a client–centered psychodramatic group in a psychiatric hospital.]O Médico, 123, 536–550.

Martens, J. (1990).*Ontdekkende klinische psychotherapie in de therapeutische gemeenschap.*Tijdschrift Klinische Psychologie, 20(2), 126–134.

McGuire–Boukydis, K. (1982), *Building supportive community: Mutual self–help through peer counseling* (Available from ISCCEP, 186 Hampshire Street, Cambridge, MA 02139).

McIlduff, E., & Coghlan, D. (1993).*The cross–cultural communication workshops in Europe.Reflections and review.*In E. McIlduff & D. Coghlan, The person–centered approach and cross–cultural communication: An international Review.Vol. 2 (pp. 21–34).Linz: Sandkorn.

Meador, B. D. (1975).*Client–centered group therapy.*In G. M. Gazda (Ed.), Basic approaches to group counseling and group psychotherapy (pp. 175–195).Springfield, Il.: Thomas.

Melk, G. (1980).*Groepspsychotherapie in een huis van bewaring.*Tijdschrift voor Psychotherapie, 6, 45–57.

Mente, A. (1990).*Improving Rogers' theory: Toward a more completely client–centered psychotherapy.*In G. Lietaer, J. Rombauts, & R. Van Balen (Eds.), Client–centered and experiential psychotherapy in the nineties (pp. 771–778).Leuven: Leuven University Press.

Mente, A., & Spittler, H. D. (1980).*Erlebnisorientierte Gruppenpsychotherapie* (Vol. 1–2).Paderborn: Junfermann.

Mullan, H. (1992).*Existential therapists and their group therapy practices.*International Journal of Group Psychotherapy, 42, 453–468.

Murayama, S., Nojima, K., & Abe, T. (1988).*Person–centered groups in Japan: A selective review of the literature.*Person–centered Review, 3, 479–492.

Nakata, Y. (1992).*On research and practice of encounter groups.*The Japanese Journal of Humanistic Psychology, 10(1), 25–29.

Pattyn, M. R. (1982).*Bedenkingen in verband met groepstherapie met alcoholisten.*Tijdschrift Klinische Psychologie, 12(2), 14–36.

Plessers, S. (1992).*Onderzoek naar plaats en betekenis van het empathisch antwoord binnen het interventierepertorium van de psychotherapeut.*Unpublished master's thesis, Katholieke Universiteit Leuven, Belgium.

Pomrehn, G., Tausch, R., & Tönnies, S. (1986). *Personenzentrierte Gruppen–psychotherapie: Prozesse und Auswirkungen nach 1 Jahr bei 87 Klienten.*Zeitschrift für personenzentrierte Psychologie und Psychotherapie, 5, 19–361.

Raskin, N. J. (1986a).*Client–centered group psychotherapy, Part I. Development of client–centered groups.*Person–centered Review, 1, 272–290.

Raskin, N. J. (1986b).*Client–centered group psychotherapy, Part II. Research on client–centered groups.*Person–centered Review, 1, 389–408.

Rogers, C. R. (1970), *Carl Rogers on encounter groups.*New York: Harper & Row.

Rogers, C. R. (1974).*The project at Immaculate Heart: an experiment in self–directed change.*Education, 95, 172–196.

Rogers, C. R. (1980).*Building person–centered communities: The implications for the future.*In A Way of being (pp. 131–206).Boston: Houghton Mifflin.

Rogers, C. R. (1983), *Freedom to learn for the 80's.* (Rev. ed.). Columbus, Ohio: Charles Merrill.

Rogers, C. R., McGaw, W. H., & Farson, R. E. (1968).*Journey into self.*A 45 min. film of a 16 hr. encounter group.La Jolla, CA: Western Behavioral Sciences Institute.

Rogers, W. R. (1974).*Client–centered and symbolic perspectives on social change.*A schematic model.In D. A. Wexler & L. N. Rice (Eds.), Innovations in client–centered therapy (pp. 465–496).New York: J. Wiley & Sons.

Rogers, W. R. (1984).*Person–centered administration in higher education.*In R. F. Levant & J. M. Shlien (Eds.),Client–centered therapy and the person–centered approach: New directions in theory, research and practice (pp. 317–336).New York: Praeger.

Sander, K., & Esser, U. (Eds.). (1988).*Personenzentrierte Gruppenarbeit.*Förderung und Entwicklung der Person und der Gruppe in Ausbildung und Beratung.Heidelberg: Asanger.

Schmid, P. F. (1994).*Personzentrierte Gruppenpsychotherapie.Ein Handbuch, Band I: Solidarität und Autonomie.*Köln: Edition Humanistische Psychologie.

Schmitt, G. M. (1980).*Klientenzentrierte Gruppenpsychotherapie in der Behandlung der Pubertätsmagersucht.*Praxis der Kinderpsychologie und Kinderpsychiatrie, 29, 247–251.

Seewald, C. (1988).*Der personenzentrierte Ansatz in der Management–Entwicklung.*In GwG (Ed.), Orientierung an der Person.Band 2 (pp. 235–243).Köln: GwG Verlag.

Sherman, E. (1990).*Experiential reminiscence and life–review therapy with the elderly.*In G. Lietaer, J. Rombauts, & R. Van Balen (Eds.), Client–centered and experiential psychotherapy in the nineties (pp. 709–732).Leuven: Leuven University Press.

Snijder–van den Eerenbeemt, A.–M. (1990).*Systeemtheorie en client–centered groepstherapie: naar een gedifferentieerde psychotherapie–praktijkvoering*VRT–Periodiek, 28(3), 3–13.

Snijder–van den Eerenbeemt, A.–M. (1993).*De experiëntiële groepen.*In T. J. C. Berk et al. (Eds.), Handboek groepspsychotherapie (A4: 1–16).Houten: Bohn Stafleu Van Loghum.

Solomon, L. N., & B. Berzon (1972), *New perspectives on encounter groups.*San Francisco: Jossey–Bass.

Speierer, G. W., & Hochkirchen, B. (1986).*Erlebensentwicklung und der Prozesz der individuellen Problembearbeitung in der klientenzentrierten Selbsterfahrungsgruppe* .Zeitschrift für personenzentrierte Psychologie und Psychotherapie, 5, 32–46.

Spittler, H. D. (1986).*Das Konzept der Gruppe in der Gesprächspsychotherapie.*In H. Petzold & R. Frühmann (Eds.), Modelle der Gruppe in der psychotherapie und psycho–sozialer Arbeit.Bd. 1. (pp. 373–388).

Swildens, H. (1979).*Is er een Rogeriaanse groepstherapie?*Tijdschrift voor Psychotherapie, 5, 1–7.

Tausch, A.–M. (1981).*Gespräche gegen die Angst.Krankheit: ein Weg zum Leben.*Reinbek: Rowohlt.

Tausch, C., Langer, I., & Bergeest, H. (1984).*Personenzentrierte Gruppengespräche bei Paare mit Partnerschwierigkeiten.*Zeitschrift für personenzentrierte Psychologie und Psychotherapie, 3, 489–497.

Tausch, R. (1988).*Reappraisal of death and dying after a person–centered behavioral workshop.*Person–centered Review, 3, 213–228.

Tausch, R. (1990). *The supplementation of client–centered communication therapy with other valid therapeutic methods: A client–centered necessity.*In G. Lietaer, J. Rombauts, & R. Van Balen (Eds.), Client–centered and experiential psychotherapy in the nineties (pp. 447–455).Leuven: Leuven University Press.

Tausch, R., & Tausch, A.–M. (1981).*Gesprächspsychotherapie.*Göttingen: Hogrefe.

Teusch, L. (1990).*Klientenzentrierte Gruppenpsychotherapie schizophrener Patienten.Ein Erfahrungsbericht.*InM. Behr, U. Esser, F. Petermann, & W. M. Pfeiffer (Eds.), Jahrbuch für personenzentrierte Psychologie und Psychotherapie.Band 2 (pp. 144–158).Salzburg: Müller.

Terjung, B. (1990).*Person–centered approach und Organisationsentwicklung.*In M. Behr, U. Esser, F. Petermann, & W. M. Pfeiffer (Eds.), Jahrbuch für personenzentrierte Psychologie und Psychotherapie. Band 2 (pp. 122–143).Salzburg: Müller.

Thomas, B. A. (1988).*Zur Verwirklichung von Gruppen–Gesprächspsychotherapie in der Psychiatrie – Standortbestimmung und eigene Erfahrungen.*In GwG (Ed.), Orientierung an der Person.Band 2 (pp. 308–313).Köln: GwG Verlag.

Thomas, B. A. (1991).*Gruppen–Gesprächspsychotherapie in der Versorgung psychisch Kranker.*In J. Finke & L. Teusch (Eds.), Gesprächspsychotherapie bei Neurosen und psychosmatischen Erkrankungen.Neue Entwicklungen in Theorie und Praxis (pp. 163–177).Heidelberg: Asanger Verlag.

Thorne, B. (1988).*The person–centered approach to large groups.*In M. Aveline & W Dryden (Eds.), Group therapy in Britain.Open University Press.

Truax, C. B. (1961).*The process of group psychotherapy: Relationship between hypothesized therapeutic conditions and intrapersonal exploration.*Psychological Monographs, 75(7), 1–35.

Truax, C. B., & Carkhuff, R. R. (1967), *Toward effective counseling and psychotherapy: Training and practice.*Chicago: Aldine.

Vanaerschot, G. (1990).*The process of empathy: Holding and letting go.*In G. Lietaer, J. Rombauts, & R. Van Balen (Eds.),Client–centered and experiential psychotherapy in the nineties (pp. 269–293).Leuven: Leuven University.

Vanaerschot, G. (1993).*Empathy as releasing several micro–processes in the client.*In D. Brazier (Ed.), Beyond Carl Rogers: Towards a psychotherapy for the twenty–first century (pp. 47–72).London: Constable.

Van Balen, R. (1990).*The therapeutic relationship according to Carl Rogers: Only a climate?A dialogue?Or both?*In G. Lietaer, J. Rombauts, & R. Van Balen (Eds.), Client–centered and experiential psychotherapy in the nineties (pp. 65–85).Leuven: Leuven University Press.

Westermann, B., Schwab, R., & Tausch, R. (1983).*Auswirkungen und Prozesse personenzentrierter Gruppenpsychotherapie bei 164 Klienten einer Psychotherapeutischen Beratungsstelle.*Zeitschrift für Klinische Psychologie, 12, 273–292.

Wood, J. K. (1984).*Community for learning: A person–centered approach.*In R. F. Levant & J. M. Shlien (Eds.),Client–centered therapy and the person–centered approach: New Directions in Theory, Research and Practice (pp. 297–316).New York: Praeger.

Wood, J. K. (1988). *Menschliches Dasein als Miteinandersein.Gruppenarbeit nach personenzentrierten Ansätzen.*Köln: Edition Humanistische Psychologie.

Yalom, I. D. (1985).*Theory and practice of group psychotherapy.* (Rev. ed.).New York: Basic Books.

"Group effect"?
Implementation of the Portuguese Translation
of the Barrett–Lennard Inventory on 5 Individual group types.

João Marques–Teixeira, M. Manuela Pires de Carvalho, Ana Maria Moreira
and Clara Pinho

Portugal

ABSTRACT

This research is about group members' facilitative qualities perceptions and attempts to answer the question: is there any group effect that works by itself and accounts for the development of the group members? Five individual group types were used to test the hypothesis that in different types of groups there are some characteristics of the communication patterns that are similar between groups and other that are different. Those similarities and differences characterise group effect.

Subjects were recruited from a person–centered psychotherapy training group, a religious group, a close friends group, a psychiatric outpatients psychodramatic group and from a workers group of an enterprise. Trainees and religious groups had designated facilitators and the remain groups had not.

Barrett–Lennard's Relationship Inventory was used to assess subjects perceptions and feelings about the relationship with the other members of the group they belong.

Results suggest on one hand, that group effect is not universal (meaning that is not present in all groups) but rather dependent on the characteristics of each group (mainly on the presence or absence of a designated facilitator), and on the other hand that the way it operates is, itself, universal: group effects operates through empathic communication, being in a direct proportion to it.

1. INTRODUCTION

The question of groups and the way they work requires a kind of recursive relationship between its constituent elements and the group itself as an individual unit. Interactions between subjects create groups and these ones, in turn, retro–act upon subjects.

The theoretical reference frame that has better expressed this group question is the General Systems Theory (Bertalanffy, 1968). According to this theory, a group is a system which, by definition, is an organised set made of the interactions between its constituents. Those interactions presume the existence of attractions, of affinities, of possibilities of linkage, but also, in order to obtain some balance, the maintenance of differences. This means that the maintenance of forces should, at least, safeguard something essential in the originality of its constituent elements.

The self–organisation concept is intrinsic to this systemic principle, and involves (1) the variety organisation (by hierarchy, differentiation, specialisation, communication), (2) self–regulation (by negative feedback and by homeostasis), (3) multistasis (the ability to accept as satisfactory a great number of several different states), (4) equifinality (the ability to attain a goal through different ways according to the difficulties found) and finally (5) aptness to development and evolution (from the capacity of potentialities actualisation).

This sort of conceptualisation can be summarised in Agazarian's (1992) happy expression "systems–centred thinking", which essentially involves the conception of a group as a system that exists in a systems hierarchy, and the system itself is a systems hierarchy too. In other words, and using Agazarian's very same words, "systems are self–reflexively isomorphic in structure and function" (Azagarian, 1992).

A group, like any other living organism, obeys to a general development principle, enunciated by Rogers as the "formative principle", which can be formulated, in the light of the systems–centred thinking, as a function of discrimination and of information integration. In this sense, a group, as long as it is a system of systems, progresses and develops through the facilitation of the process of discriminating, communicating and integrating perceptions of differences in the apparently similar and similarities in the apparently different. We designate this process as *group effect*, this being a common characteristic to the individuals sets that may be considered groups (obeying, as such, to the already defined characteristics). The communication process and the attitudes perception emerge, in this way, as the main operators of the *group effect*. Communication takes place in the boundaries between sub–systems at all levels of the hierarchy: the group as a whole, the different subgroups and, particularly, the subjects.

So, in order to characterise *group effect*, and according to the paradigm frame we are following, we'll have to describe the communications net that is established between the different boundaries that make up group hierarchy. From this, it follows that the information flow carried through the different levels in the group, is one of the key–elements for group description and development. However, the main element is not quite the communication content but rather the nature of the communication conveyed by that content. Carl Rogers, with regard to the meaning of communication, kept an interest in the organism impulses of the individual, rather than in psyche (Arnett, 1989). That means that Rogers focused his attention on the more immediate and less elaborated aspects of communication. Besides, this nature is directly dependent on the way each group member perceives the other group members and, as a result, this perception depends on the fundamental attitudes that impregnate the group atmosphere. Thus, and by the application of Rogers' postulates (1957), the perception that each group member has about the other members is the result of the degree to which that member perceives the qualities of the unconditional positive regard, the empathic understanding, and the genuineness or congruence.

In spite of evidence of the growing importance of these aspects in groups development and characterisation (e.g. Marques–Teixeira, 1993), a comparatively little effort has been made in order to determine which relationship pattern and which communication aspects constitute and are related to what was called *group effect*. According to the principles of the Person–Centred Approach (PCA), *group effect* will come as a result of the qualities of the relationships the different group members establish with each other, and of the perception those very same members get from those qualities. As we have already seen, Rogers (1957) enunciated the three related qualities needed for personal development, and he postulated that this development depends on the extension to which a person experienced, at present and in the past, those very same qualities, when exhibited by significant people. Subsequently, Barrett–Lennard (1962) proposed four variables which facilitate personal development, subdividing the unconditional positive regard in level of regard and uncontionality of regard.

We can, thus, summarise, as a thesis for this research, that *group effect* expresses the extension to which each group member experiences, and the degree to which he or she perceives, from the other group members, the four facilitating qualities: (1) level of regard, (2) unconditionality of regard, (3) empathic understanding and (4) genuineness or congruence.

Adding to this, PCA assumes that personal development is not restricted to the therapeutic setting, but that it may also extend to significant relationships outside that setting. Besides, the presence in a group constitutes, very often, an happening which could evolve to the development of significant relationships and, in this way, to conform to the postulates formulated by Rogers.

Thus, and keeping in mind what has just been said, the group self–construction produces an effect upon its members (*group effect*) that it is necessary to test, as most works have centred their topics on therapeutists' or counsellors' qualities, and don't say much about the perception group members have of each other (cf. Mclennam, 1988). According to this author, any study that attempts to lean over these aspects should be grounded on a phenomenologically based research methodology, which gives importance to the participants' experience.

One of the difficulties of this sort of studies is to be able to decide beforehand which groups and which relationships are relevant, so as to provide the communicational atmosphere with the facilitative qualities. Rogers (1970) enunciated some of the group characteristics in order to be able to consider the existence of some learning from group experience. Of those characteristics we give special importance to (1) the "group's intensive experience", (2) to the shortness of the groups (from 8 to 18 elements) and (3) to their fairly small structure. In addition to the proposal of these characteristics, Rogers (1970) considered also that group learning tends to extend to relationships between workfellows and between cultists of the same religious cult. In turn, Crammer (1987, 1988 and 1989) considers that close friends may have an important role in personal development, and Dryden and Thorne (1991) give special emphasis, in psychotherapy training, to the aspects attached to personal development in group. Finally, therapeutic groups make up the preferential setting for group personal development, which has been the subject of the attention from researchers (Marques–Teixeira, Moreira, Almeida, Viegas, Silva, Torres and Carvalho, 1990; Mente, 1990, among others). These considerations guided us in our choice of groups for this research.

Thus, the main goal of this investigation is to test the *group effect*, starting from the communication patterns conveyed through the group members' perceptions of facilitative qualities, which in turn are assessed from the present relationships with other group members. To attain this goal, we used 5 groups, in which we presumed beforehand to exist, according to the considerations formerly made, the facilitative conditions that enable us to consider them an adequate means for their members' personal development: (1) a group of psychotherapy trainees, according to the PCA model; (2) a religious group; (3) a group of close friends; (4) a psychiatric outpatients psychodramatic group and (5) a group of workers from the same enterprise.

From the theoretical developments made before, one of this research predictions is that, at the more structural level, there will be communication patterns that will be common to the different groups and, for that same reason, they will help in the characterisation of the *group effect*, making it possible. That means that, in order to be able to talk about a *group effect*, we'll have to get some invariance in the different groups, so as to give sense to that effect. On the other hand, *group effect* depends itself on the sort of communication its members establish with each other and, for that reason, the other prediction is that it should exist some variation in certain communicational elements, which make the distinction between the different types of groups possible.

Thus, the working hypothesis to be tested sustains that there are communication patterns, expressed by the main attitudes perception mentioned above, which constitute elements at the same time invariant and variant ones, between groups, and that they make *group effect* characterisation possible.

Two important details must be considered when our working hypothesis is being tested. The first one deals with the rogerian postulate according to which a minimal degree of all facilitative qualities must be present for a certain psychological development or adjustment to occur. This detail implies that none of those single qualities can, alone, distinguish groups. For that reason, this aspect has to be taken into account in the statistical analysis of results.

The second detail deals with the unconditionality of regard. From the moment Barrett–Lennard (1962) made the distinction between unconditionality of regard and level of regard, this variable has been dealt with separately. It becomes, thus, necessary to understand what its affective value is, if we want to clarify its meaning. As far as the level of regard is concerned, Barrett–Lennard considers it to be the "composite 'loading' of the distinguishable feeling reactions of one person toward another, positive and negative, on a single abstract dimension" (Barrett–Lennard, 1986). When it is positive, "it is concerned in various ways with warmth, liking/caring, and 'being drawn toward'"; on the other hand, when it is negative, "feelings of extreme aversion (except for contempt), or of anger to the point of rage, are not encompassed" (Barrett–Lennard, 1986). This is, thus, a variable that positions itself in an "axis of experienced response in a particular relationship" rather than in the immediate moment of a relational episode.

As far as unconditionality of regard is concerned, it refers to the "degree of regard constancy felt by one person for another who communicates self–experiences to the first" (Barrett–Lennard, 1986). It varies in the conditional/unconditional axis, being the unconditional side stable, "in the sense that it is not experienced as varying with or otherwise dependently linked to particular attributes of the person being regarded" (Barrett–Lennard, 1986).

In order to proceed to the testing of the hypothesis above enunciated, we designed a research which aims at defining the communication characteristics of 5 different individual group types, when assessed by an appropriate instrument for the characterisation of interpersonal relationships main attitudes: Barrett–Lennard's (1978) Relationship Inventory (BLRI). We used its simplified form (BLRI 40) to be more usable in field settings, measuring the same constructs and retaining acceptable reliability.

The use of this instrument comes from its confirmed ability to elicit from clients their perceptions of the communicational behaviours of the members with whom they establish a relationship, which make a positive contribution to the quality of the experienced relationship (Ganley, 1989). Further evidence for its validity comes from nonclinical studies where subjects described a current close relationship (Cramer, 1986a, 1986b).

2. METHODS

2.1. Subjects

Recruitment procedures were designed to obtain subjects from a set of groups who would be representative of groups where there is intensive group experience, and minimal degree of external structure provided, leaving the development of the group's structure to emerge in an informal manner as a result of group member interaction. This was achieved by recruiting subjects from a person–centred psychotherapy training group, from a religious group, from a close friends group, from a psychiatric outpatients psychodramatic group and from a workers group of an enterprise.

The total sample consisted of 5 groups, which included 50 subjects. Table 1 represents the main characteristics of these groups.

GROUPS	Females	Males	Total of Subjects	Ages
Group 1 (trainees g.)	7	8	15	32–45
Group 2 (religious g.)	4	5	9	23–45
Group 3 (close friends g.)	3	4	7	26–37
Group 4 (patients g.)	8	0	8	18–44
Group 5 (workers g.)	3	8	11	22–37

Table 1
Main characteristics of the total sample

Groups 1 and 4 had a facilitator, oriented according to the PCA principles, and group 2 was animated by a Jesuit priest who supervised the spiritual reflexion sessions, Groups 3 and 4 didn't have designated facilitators, but the hypothesis of the existence of natural leaders in these groups was not excluded.

2.2. Instruments

After the translation, into the Portuguese language, the Barrett–Lennard's Relationship Inventory (Form OS–M–40), and also after the assessment of that very same version by a group of 3 judges[1], data from the 5 groups were used to analyse the 40 items of the BLRI, namely, the Empathy (E), Regard (R), Unconditionality (U) and Congruence (C) Subscales (Form OS–M–40), with the subjects rating their perceptions and feelings about the relationship with the other members of the group. The six–choice–response format (Barrett–Lennard, 1978) was used, with response choices ranging from $+3$ (Yes, I strongly feel that it is true) to -3 (No, I strongly feel that it is not true). Half of the items on BLRI are worded positively and half are worded negatively. The instructions were as follow: "Below are listed a variety of ways that one person may feel or behave in relation to another. Please consider each statement with reference to your *present relationship with (mentally adding his or her name on space provided)*". They were told to complete the Inventory toward the group they were supposed to be linked. Specific items for each subscale were collected following Barrett–Lennard's (1986) indications. Forms were filled, all at the same time, coinciding with different moments of relationship for the different groups. Thus, for the trainees group, the filling up of the forms coincided with 2 years of group work; for close friends group, the filling up of the forms coincided with the 8th. day of holidays together; for the patients group, it coincided with the 30th. psychotherapy session (of a 40 sessions set), and for the workers group, it coincided with about 2 years of companionship.

2.3. Procedures

Groups were contacted for one of us, and 5 to 10 minutes of their time was request to explain our research project. Subjects were given the forms to complete at home and return. Nonresponders were contacted by phone at 3 week–intervals to encourage participation. Forms were returned by 86% of those recruited.

The standard scoring method was used (Barrett–Lennard, 1969) by a computer scoring program. The data set was then composed of four subscale scores (arithmetic total of positive items and negative ones for each of the four subscales), and the raw data was made up of subscale scores for each person for each in–group relationship that they answered.

2.4. Statistical analyses

Four statistical analyses were performed:

1. Multivariate analysis of variance to examine if there was differences between the groups through the four subscales. In this case a MANOVA 5 x 4 (groups by subscales) was performed using all subscales and all subjects in the groups.

2. Univariate tests of variance was performed to examine which subscales accounted to the difference between groups.

3. A discriminant function analysis (DFA) was done to determine the degree of separateness of the four subscales.

4. A cluster analysis was used to determine how the subjects in each group cluster around each subscale.

3. RESULTS

3.1. Multivariate Analysis of Variance

To check whether the groups did or did not have different types of communication patterns, a 5 x 4 (groups x RI subscales) multivariate analysis of variance (MANOVA) was computed on subjects' responses to the RI. The effects of type of groups were clearly significative (F apr. $(16,177)$= 7.352, p=0.0000), showing that there were significative differences between groups. Hence, some subscales were more representative than the others and, of direct interest for this manipulation check, the subscales reflected differentiated patterns of subjective feelings. To check whether all subscales were indeed subjectively differentiated, separate 5 x 1 (groups x subscale) ANOVAs were computed. In all instances, all groups had clearly differentiated patterns of subjective feelings, as indicated by significant Groups x Subscales interactions (Table 2).

Subscales	F	p
Regard	10.616	0.0000
Empathy	12.165	0.0000
Unconditionality	6.172	0.0000
Congruence	4.13	0.003

Table 2
ANOVA 5 x 1 (groups by subscale). F value and significance

3.2. Discriminant function analysis

Since there is no single question or subscale that clearly differentiates any particular group from all the other groups (see pp. 5), a method was sough that would make use of several subscales in combination. We expected that a profile would emerge for each group on two or more subscales, and that the profile would successfully differentiate the group with a particular pattern of communication, from all other groups.

The statistical procedure selected was the DFA. The DFA takes the five groups and asks the question: are these five groups statistically separate from each other? For the purpose of this study, the five groups were considered to be the independent variable, and the score of the subscales were the dependent variable. The analysis was done using all the four subscales and the 367 responses from the 5 groups. The results of this analysis define the four subscales as empirically differentiated from each other, at a statistically significant level.

Table 3 shows the four canonical discriminant functions (there are $n - 1$ independent functions describing the five groups, where $n =$ the number of groups).

Function	Eigen Value	% of Variance	Wilks' Lambda	Chi square	Degrees of Freedom	Significance
1	0.2147	63.4	0.7314	112.44	16	0.0000
2	0.1089	32.16	0.8884	42.52	9	0.0000
3	0.0124	3.66	0.9852	5.37	4	0.251
4	0.0026	0.78	0.997	0.946	1	0.33

Table 3
Canonical Discriminant Functions

The first function accounts for 63.4 % of the variance, and the second function accounts for 32.16 %. It is clear that these two functions provide the greatest degree of discrimination (95.56 % of the total variance).

Table 4 shows the canonical discriminant functions evaluated at the group centroids for each group, across all the subscales. The centroid is the point which has co-ordinates that are the group's mean on each of the variables. The first two functions have been plotted for each of the 5 groups (Figure 1).

Groups	Function 1	Function 2
1	0.174	–0.336
2	0.427	–0.277
3	0.353	0.262
4	–0.836	–0.137
5	0.0349	0.465

Table 4

Canonical discriminant functions evaluated at group means

This plot shows two pairs of the five groups in different quadrants and one group distinctly separated from the other pairs.

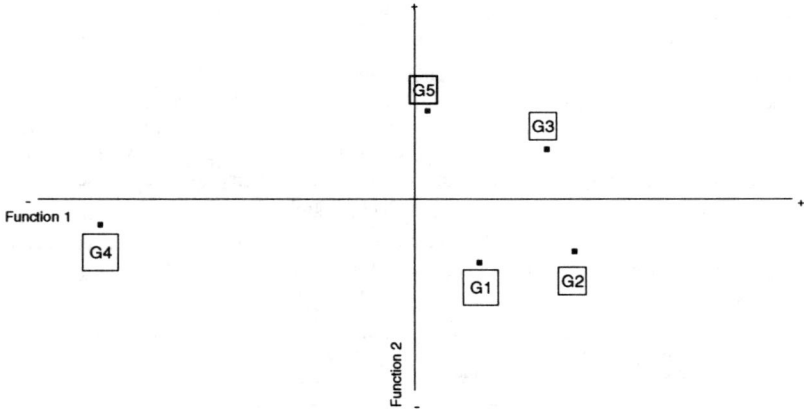

Figure 1
Plot of groups on function 1 by function 2

G1 = Trainees group G4 = Patients group
G2 = Religious group   G5 = Workers group
G3 = Friends group

The DFA test maximises differences between the categories of a single sample. When applied to a second sample, differentiation may not be as great. Apparently, in terms of perceived facilitative attitudes seen through dimensions of relationship, trainees and religious groups show similar patterns, which in turn differ from close friends and patients groups. The workers group falls close to the centre. It should be pointed out that this group is not a remainder group, but it rather indicates that there are not enough communication patterns to consider this group as having a closer relationship between its members.

3.3. Cluster analysis

In order to estimate how the members of each group cluster themselves around the subscales, a cluster analysis on each group and across the four subscales was performed.

This analysis aims at exploring the differences found through the DFA, now in terms of respondents clustering around the four facilitative variables being studied.

The algorithm used for determining cluster membership is based on nearest centroid sorting (Anderberg, 1973). That is, a case is assigned to the cluster for which the distance between the case and the centre of the cluster (centroid) is smallest. Table 5 contains the values of two centres selected for each group. They are labelled "Final Cluster Centres", and each centre corresponds to a type of score (on the positive side of zero and on the negative side of zero).

		Regard	Empathy	Unconditionality	Congruence	N° Responses
G1	1	0	0.6136	2.7955	1.9773	44
	2	−2.444	−5.8333	−4.0556	−3.8333	18
G2	1	0.434	0.1321	5.6981	7.5283	53
	2	−2.5429	−3.7429	−3.6	−4.0857	35
G3	1	6.25	3	9.875	11.5	8
	2	0.4	−3.9	3.1	3.2	30
G4	1	2.9032	5.4032	3.6129	4.3065	62
	2	1.0625	1.4375	−8.75	−5.5	16
G5	1	−1.5472	−4	−0.2642	−2.9245	56
	2	9.1975	8.2826	10.8478	14.4565	46

Table 5
Cluster Analysis of scores of RI subscales.

G1= Trainees group; G2= Religious group; G3= Friends group; G4= Patients group;
G5= Workers group.

The examination of the table shows, for the trainees group (1), that the most representative cluster (N=44) is the positive one with its highest value in U subscale; for the religion group (2), the most representative cluster (N=53) is also the positive one, with its highest value in the C subscale; for the close friends group (3), the most representative cluster (N=30) has it's highest value in E subscale and it is the negative one; for the patients group (4), the most representative cluster (N=62) is the positive one with its highest value in E subscale; finally, for the workers group (5), the most representative cluster (N=56) is the negative one with its highest value in E subscale, but another cluster, the positive one, has a great number of responses (N=46) with its highest value in C subscale.

Figure 2 is a plot of the scores of RI subscales on the highest positive and negative clusters, for each group.

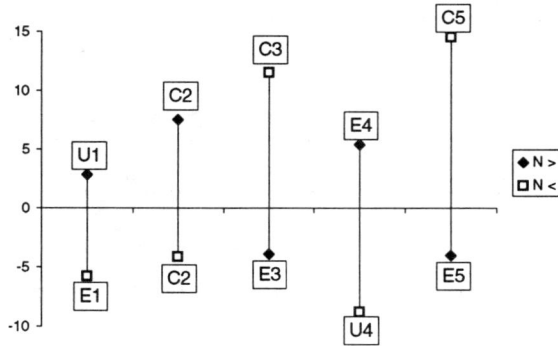

U1 = Trainees Group (Unconditionality)   E1 = Trainees Group (Empathy)
C2 = Religious Group (Congruence)   C2 = Religious Group (Congruence)
C3 = Friends Group (Congruence)   E3 = Friends Group (Empathy)
E4 = Patients Group (Empathy)   U4 = Patients Group (Unconditionality)
C5 = Workers Group (Congruence)   E5 = Workers Group (Empathy)

Figure 2
Plot of groups and clusters of scores of RI subscales on positive and negative clusters

Figure 2 shows that trainees group, religious group and patients group have positive centroid clusters with the highest number of responses, but with different subscales referred to that clustering: the trainees group centred on the unconditionality subscale, the religious group centred on the congruence subscale and the patients group centred on the empathy subscale. The close friends and workers group, on the contrary, have more negative centroid clusters with the highest number of responses, and both of them on the empathy subscale.

4. DISCUSSION

Having noticed that groups differ from each other through the average scores of the RI subscales (Table 2), we tried to sort out what shape those differences took. As none of the subscales in particular can define or distinguish groups from each other, we carried out a DFA in order to determine the profile in two or more subscales so that the distinction of groups could be made. The results from that analysis (Table 4) show the existence of a similar profile for the trainees and the religious groups, enabling us to separate them from the patients and the close friends groups (Figure 1). In addition to this, these two groups are also different from each other, as they have a position in opposed quadrants in the DFA. Finally, as far as the workers group is concerned, the same analysis suggests that this is a group with a weak relationship between its members and, for that reason, it stands clearly out of the other four groups.

Having noticed the existence of the clustering of two groups, and also the clear differentiation in relation to the other three, we needed to know which were the intrinsic characteristics of each group, that would enable us to characterise either the differences or the resemblances made conspicuous by the DFA.

For that purpose, we made a cluster analysis on each members' responses in all groups and in the four subscales, aiming at determining the responses clustering pattern in each subscale and in each group.

The results from that analysis (Table 5 and Figure 2) suggest that the responses from 3 out of the 5 groups being analysed cluster themselves around positive clusters (the trainees group, the religious group and the patients group), and that the remaining two groups cluster themselves around negative clusters.

Comparing these results to those from DFA, we notice that groups located on the same side of Function 1 show similar clusters (cf. Figure 1). That means that the trainees group, the religious group and the patients group show a greater number of responses clustered around the positive scores of the RI subscales, while the close friends group and the workers group show a greater number of responses clustered around the negative scores of those very same scales.

The conjugation of these two analyses allows us, in the first place, to suggest that, in terms of facilitative attitudes perceived by the groups members, there are similarities between the trainees group, the religious group and the patients group, on the one hand, and between the close friends group and the workers group, on the other hand.

It remain for us to know which differences those very same groups show between themselves. The same clusters analysis reveals those differences (cf. Figure 2): for the trainees group, the greater number of responses occurs around the positive scores of unconditionality and the negative scores of empathy; the religious group clusters, in terms of responses, around congruence (with a great cluster of negative scores); in the patients group, empathy emerges as the subscale which congregates the greater number of responses with positive scores, and unconditionality as the one with greater negative scores. As far as the close friends and the workers groups are concerned, they show a greater number of responses with negative scores around empathy, and positive scores around congruence.

These results suggest that the three groups clustered around the positive scores can be differentiated through the more representative subscales (U1; C2 and E4) and the two groups with negative scores cannot be separated as far as the subscales are concerned.

As these results organise themselves in terms of negative scores and positive scores, and because they suggest there are differences between the groups with positive scores, but not between the groups with negative scores, we carried out separate multivariate analyses of variance for the means of the subscales scores, for those responses that show positive scores in all subscales and negative scores in all subscales as well.

As it was expected, the results from these analyses confirm those from the previous ones. For responses with only positive scores, all subscales showed significative differences between groups (Table 6); for responses with only negative scores, only the subscales related to empathy and unconditionality showed significative differences between groups.

3POSITIVE SCORES	F	p
REGARD	8.813	0.000
EMPATHY	6.192	0.000
UNCONDITIONALITY	9.609	0.000
CONGRUENCE	10.598	0.000
NEGATIVE SCORES	F	p
REGARD	1.89	0.156
EMPATHY	4.65	0.01
UNCONDITIONALITY	3.94	0.02
CONGRUENCE	1.378	0.271

D.F (4,91)

Table 6

Separate multivariate analyses of variance on mean scores of RI subscales,
for responses with all positive and all negative scores in all subscales. F value and significance.

In order to ascertain how the four subscales correlated with the different types of groups, a
Pearson product–moment correlation was made between the four subscales and the five types
of groups, for each one of the positive and the negative scores. This analysis revealed, for the
positive scores, positive and significative correlations in all scales for the different groups, whereas, for the negative scores, only empathy shows a negative and significative correlation for
the different types of groups (Table 7).

	POSITIVE SCORES	NEGATIVE SCORES
REGARD	0.48 **	–0.0085
EMPATHY	0.41 **	–0.47 *
UNCONDITIONALITY	0.49 **	–0.077
CONGRUENCE	0.49 **	–0.155

* – p<0.05; ** – p<0.01

Table 7

Pearson's R correlation and significance for positive and negative scores with RI subscales.

This suggests that the only subscale that significatively and simultaneously varies in these ranks
of groups is empathy, which establishes a positive correlation with the positive scores rank, and
a negative correlation with the negative scores rank.

5. CONCLUSIONS

The main goal of this research was to determine the main characteristics of the communication
patterns in different groups, when assessed through the facilitative qualities perception made by
the members of those groups.

Keeping in mind the theoretical developments made in the introduction, it was predicted that
group effect was represented by invariances and differences between groups, as far as the
communication patterns were concerned. This prediction was confirmed. The multivariate
analysis of variance made for the five groups and for the four subscales was highly significative, which indicated the existence of differences in the five groups members' perceived attitudes. Furthermore, it was expected that the different subsacles produced different group pat-

terns, as they measured exactly different qualities. This prediction was also confirmed, with a high significance for all subscales, except for the congruence one, which showed an F value of less magnitude. These results enable us to conclude that all subscales differentiate the 5 groups, with a greater incidence for the level of regard, empathy and unconditionality.

Having confirmed the existence of differences in the communication patterns of the 5 groups being studied, the next question was to know whether the groups showed a specific profile, in terms of communication, which could justify this differentiation. Discriminant Function Analysis enabled us to group the trainees and religious groups in terms of communication patterns, and clearly separate them from the close friends group and from the patients group. This one, in turn, could be clearly distinguished from all the others. Workers group wasn't much characteristic, as far as communication patterns were concerned.

These results enables us to suggest that, in those groups where a facilitator is present (in the trainees group and in the patients group designated as such, and in the religious group present in an implicit way), similar patterns (in terms of their members' perceived attitudes, shown through the way the group works) cluster around the empathy, the unconditionality and the congruence attitudes; in those groups where a facilitator is not present (there will eventually be a natural leader), the group atmosphere is characterised by a lack of empathic understanding.

Thus, empathy, emerges as the more differentiating attitude in groups, as it is the only attitude that simultaneously correlates to those two ranks of groups, in a positive way for groups with a facilitator, and in a negative way for those without one.

At last, what can these results suggest as far as group effect is concerned?

Given the differences between the 5 individual group types, and the similarities between the two ranks of groups (rank of groups with a facilitator, and rank of groups without facilitator), the results from our research suggest that the group effect isn't universal but rather dependent on the characteristics of each group. The facilitator's presence emerges as one of the characteristics that may be similar to group effect, but the similarities and the differences in those groups still coexist. In this sense, the group effect is a resulting effect from facilitative qualities developed levels, through the "group's intensive experience". Those qualities, in turn, depend on the group's own structure, as it was plainly demonstrated.

Finally, in the introduction to this research, we defined group effect as a process characterised by the integration of differences in the apparently similar, and of the similarities in the apparently different. After our results analysis, we came to the conclusion that empathy is the only attitude that enables us to make groups alike in spite of their difference, and at the same time to tell them apart in spite of their similarities. Having formerly concluded that group effect is not an universal effect (that is, it is not present in all groups), we come now to the conclusion that the way it operates is, itself, universal: group effect operates through empathic communication, being in a direct proportion to it.

REFERENCES

Agazarian, Y. (1992). *Contemporary theories of group psychotherapy: a systems approach to the group–as–a–whole*. International Journal of Group Psychotherapy, 42 (2), 177–203.

Anderberg, M. (1973). *Cluster analysis for applications*. New York: Academic Press.

Arnett, R. (1989). *What is dialogic communication? Friedman's contribution and clarification*. Person Centered Review, 4, 42–60.

Barrett–Lennard, G. (1962). *Dimensions of therapist response as causal factors in therapeutic change*. Psychological Monographs: General and Applied, 76 (43, whole n° 562).

Barrett–Lennard, G. (1969). *Technical note on the 64–item revision of the Relationship Inventory.* University of Waterloo.

Barrett–Lennard, G. (1978). *The Relationship Inventory: Development and adaptation.* Catalogue of Selected Documents in Psychology, 8, 68 (MS # 1732).

Barrett–Lennard, G. (1986). *The Relationship Inventory now: Issues and advances in theory, method, and use.* In L. S. Greenberg and W. M. Pinsof (Eds.), The Psychotherapy Process: A research handbook. New York: Guilford.

Bertalanffy, L. (1968). *General System Theory. Foundations, Development, Applications.* New York: George Braziller.

Cramer, D. (1986a): *An item factor analysis of the original Relationship Inventory.* Journal of Personal and Social Relationships, 3, 121–127.

Cramer, D. (1986b). *An item factor analysis of the revised Barret–Lennard Relationship Inventory.* British Journal of Guidance and Counseling, 14, 314–325.

Cramer, D. (1987). *Self–esteem, advice–giving and the facilitative nature of close personal relationships.* Person Centered Review, 2, 99–110.

Cramer, D. (1988). *Self–esteem and facilitative close relationships: a cross–lagged panel correlation analysis.* British Journal of Social Psychology, 27, 115–126.

Cramer, D. (1989): *Self–esteem and the facilitativeness of parents and close friends.* Person Centered Review, 4, 61–76.

Dryden, W. and Thorne, B. (1991). *Training and supervision for counseling in action.* London: Sage Pub.

Ganley, R. (1989). *The Barrett–Lennard Relationship Inventory (BLRI): current and potential uses with family systems.* Family Process, 28, 107–115.

Marques–Teixeira, J. (1993). *Client–Centred Psychodrama.* In D. Brazier (Ed.), Beyond Carl Rogers. Towards a Psychotherapy for the 21st Century. London: Constable.

Marques–Teixeira, J., Moreira, A., Almeida, A., Viegas, E., Silva, I., Torres, L. and Carvalho, M. (1990). *Evolução de um grupo de psicodrama num hospital psiquiátrico.* O Médico, 123 (2004), 536–550.

McLennan, J. (1988). *Conceptualizing and measuring client–centered relationships.* Person Centered Review, 3 (3), 292–303.

Mente, A. (1990). *Improving Rogers' theory: toward a more completely client–centered psychotherapy.* In G. Lietaer, J. Rombants and R. van Balen (Eds.), Client Centered and Experiential Psychotherapy in the Nineties. Leuven: Leuven University Press.

Rogers, C. (1957). *The necessary and suficient conditions of therapeutic personality change.* Journal of Counsulting Psychology, 21, 95–103.

Rogers, C. (1979). *Carl Rogers on Encounter Groups.* New York: Harp and Row.

---

[1]This process consisted in retranslating into English the translated version (by one of the judges) which, in turn, was standardised to the version in the original language by the second judge, and the needed corrections were made. The third judge took the task of standardising this final correction to the original version.

The Facilitation of Large Groups: Participants Experiences of Facilitative Moments

MHAIRI MACMILLAN AND COLIN LAGO
SCOTLAND, ENGLAND

ABSTRACT

The authors describe the basis of their interest in large group process and facilitation. They outline some of the literature on the relationship of client–centred therapy and the person–centred approach to groups – small, encounter groups through large groups and communities. A small–scale research project on participants' experiences of "facilitative moments" in large groups is described briefly, some findings sketched in and some speculative conclusions drawn on the alterations to a "person–centred psychology" that might be made in the light of large group experience.

INTRODUCTION

Our interest in Large Groups stems from participation in and facilitation of many large person–centred approach workshops. In a paper presented at the Fifth Forum on the Person–centred Approach, Terschelling, Netherlands (Lago and MacMillan, 1993), we concentrated on themes such as the negotiation of meaning in large groups and the complex relationship between the dynamics of staff teams and their impact upon the large group.

Analysis of western society today would reveal, we argue, a breakdown in the sense of community and the emergence of atomised individuals (Hofstede, 1980; Kingdom, 1992; Orbach, 1994; Lago, 1994). Large groups, we contend, offer one possibility whereby individuals may experience the relationships and phenomena of being in community. They offer a vehicle for experiential learning and might even become one of the therapeutic forms for the future, especially for impoverished communities. Indeed, a hypothesis from analytical writings is that, for the purposes of theoretical understanding, large groups may be likened to society itself (de Marre, 1985).

The theoretical basis for conducting and understanding large groups has been extrapolated from the theory underpinning individual therapy. In Rogerian terms (client–centred and person–centred), this is fundamentally an application, to groups, small and large, of the core conditions, which are summed up as empathic understanding, congruent relating and unconditional positive regard, along with the trust in the tendency of the organism to actualize itself (Rogers, 1961, Mearns and Thorne 1988). Other approaches to group work have also taken this line (de Marre, 1994; Samuels, 1993), but the further one moves from the original situation of individual therapy, the less likely it is that applying these principles will as accurately determine quality of relationship and eventual outcome. Although it is helpful in guiding and informing group interactions, over–reliance on the theory of individual therapy may have acted as a deterrent to further research.

'Trawling' the literature

This section covers some of the literature on groupworking, from small, encounter groups through large groups to group communities, especially as it concerns facilitation or facilitative behaviours.

Small 'encounter' groups

1. Carl Rogers (1970) "Can I be a facilitative person in a group?"
This is the classic statement of the application of client–centred principles into a small group setting. Rogers re–states his trust in the wisdom of the group and in its sense of its own direction. He hopes to set the environment right from the start with (a) a considered opening statement, (b) listening attentively, (c) responding to individuals, (d) accepting the group and the individuals in it, (e) being fully present himself ("operating in terms of my own feelings"), and (f) confronting on specific behaviour and so on.

This is a descriptive and personal statement which acknowledges that other people will have their own styles of facilitation, which may be different from and complementary to Rogers' own. However, he lists what he believes to be –facilitative behaviour; and here he makes a clear distinction between the "perceived facilitator" and a participant. Non–facilitative behaviour in the facilitator "tends to set a norm for the group" when it occurs early on before group members have found their own power. He ends with the hope that others will be encouraged "to speak for their own styles of group facilitation".

2. Bebout (1974), applying "Existential–Rogerian" concepts to encounter groups, teased out the concept of empathy into several forms: vicarious empathy (as it is usually understood in therapy), physiognomic empathy (connecting with the bodily 'felt sense' of the other) and cognitive empathy (assimilation of others' values, meanings, symbols, intentions and ideation). Bebout's view is that these empathic processes must come into being as essential pre–cursors to a sense of "experiential communality".

Experiential communality is multi–dimensional. It occurs when, for example, someone "feels a real physical pain from the hurt of another" (Rogers 1970). That is, a "direct intimacy" between persons is established which affects the others present as well, not merely as witnesses but at an intrapsychic level. Another sense of experiential communality is a feeling like "we're in this together". He gives the example of the closeness between the few workers who have struggled through a snowstorm to make it into the office – a closeness which fades when conditions are back to normal. And he tells of the Ik, a starving tribe in Uganda who would expend considerable energy just to come and sit in "the communal sharing of the pangs of hunger".

Bebout suggests that a quality of experiential communality is that it "can by itself evoke an expanded sense of self" and reminds us of the tendency of a group towards actualization. But when the group is unable to overcome a significant "group incongruence or deceit" the actualization process is impeded. It is most significant when the incongruence or self deceit is perpetuated by the group facilitator or leader (or facilitator team), but may arise during the process of the group and, if not addressed and cleared, prevents the group achieving significant communality of experiencing. Group , therefore, which entails honesty, candour and risk–taking, is the bedrock upon which acceptance and empathic understanding, pre–requisites for experiential communality, can be built.

3. Ariadne Beck (1974) suggests a category of "emotional leader": one who is "responsive to the feeling aspect of any issue that is raised and [who] usually can be quite articulate about such content". Beck questions whether a leader whose previous training has been in intensive individual therapy may be able to hold a group–wide perspective (including a perception of the stage of development the group may have reached). Such a leader may, rather, feel "overwhelmed by his concern for attending to several clients simultaneously".

Large Groups

4. Rogers (1977) re–presented his view on facilitation with respect to large groups, and in the light of his appreciation of the work of Paulo Freire. This takes into account the more overtly political dimensions of "a situation involving minority groups, the oppressed or anyone who feels powerless" (which covers most large groups). He makes a series of "if" conclusions, starting with "if a person with facilitative attitudes can gain entry into the group", and continuing:

– if this facilitator is genuinely free of a desire to impose ready–made truths or to control the outcome

– if the facilitator respects the capacity of the group to discover the nature of their own problems and has skills in helping people express that capacity

– if a respectful hearing is given to all attitudes and feelings, no matter how "extreme" or "unrealistic"

– if the members of a group are permitted to choose, collectively and individually, their own goals

... and goes on to predict certain outcomes.

5. Thorne (1988) believes, in contrast to Beck, that the skills required of the large group facilitator are "unlikely to be attained by someone who is not deeply involved in therapeutic work in the course of his or her professional life". At the heart of Thorne's writing, there lies an essential self–acceptance; his recounting of his "collapse" in the group, for example, and that he "did not feel a less effective facilitator as a result". And he refers to the humility of the facilitators, which prevents them feeling expert, or know–it–all.

6. J.K. Wood (1984) relays a sense of the freedom that can be part of the experience of a large group – terrifying freedom. When the large group convenors, who were well–known, experienced people to whom others would be likely to look for leadership, refused to function as leaders because they believed that "they were no better equipped than other participants" to deal with the complex human issues that would inevitably arise in the group, participants became free to deal with the issues themselves.

To reach this point the convenors have to shed themselves of their "institutionalized authority". This is even harder to do as a group culture builds up (especially when a series of annual workshops such as the FDI summer workshops or the cross–cultural communication workshops continues over a 20– year period).

Community

Community is a concept often associated with large groups. Just when and how does a large group become a "community"? or does it? – calling meetings of the whole group "community meetings" does not result in all participants feeling part of a community.

7. G.T. Barrett–Lennard. (1994) reports on research carried out in a large group workshop. Barrett–Lennard concluded that the large group moved in the direction of becoming a community, the foundations were laid, but that the group did not "reach this destination". The three top selected "indications of community" were: climate of respect/caring/trust; attentive listening to others; tolerance for ambiguity and conflict.

Large Groups and Society

8. P. Homans (1974) suggests that the effect of imposed and introjected conditions of worth is to "split the actualizing tendency from the self–actualizing tendency". He contrasts this with the "organismic valuing process" which, when allowed to operate, not only restores that connection, but also " " (our emphasis). It is "unconditional positive regard" which mediates this return.

Homans suggests that Rogerian psychology thus points to a way in which persons can free themselves from the "manipulative public sphere" and overcome a sense of alienation. But, he warns, this "mode or structure of experiencing" (which is now known as the person–centred approach) could itself become institutionalized.

9. M.M. O'Hara (1989) compares the work of Carl Rogers with that of Paulo Freire. She notes that each has a different focus of attention in the context of a large group; Rogers to the individual person's experience (often emotional experience) and Freire to human societies and their oppressive aspects. She considers the contradictions between the "individualistic core" of Rogers' theory of developing human awareness (or "critical consciousness") and his later emphasis on large group contexts in which to tackle some of the difficulties of society.

The contradiction can be resolved, she believes, in the context of a large group if the conditions are right for what has been called (above) experiential communality. O'Hara's example is of two group participants, who, when they spoke about their own, very different, personal experiences of apartheid, increased not only their own "critical consciousness" of this political issue but also the consciousness of the rest of the group. (This passage was pointed out to us by Alan Coulson). But for this kind of "resolution" to remain part of the gain from work in the large group, there must already exist a willingness to consider political issues, to let them be voiced.

10. In his keynote address to the second conference of the Australian Centre for Archetypal Studies **(February 1994), Andrew Samuels** – a post–Jungian and author of "The political psyche" (1993) suggested that a whole set of "collective psychologies" has been virtually suppressed by the "individualistic tradition", out of distrust of "unscientific" transpersonal notions. Individualistic psychology is about separateness, whereas what Samuels calls "the psychology of community" is about how we (human beings) share things in common and implies that "we are already in relationship with one another".

Samuels also questions whether too much has been extrapolated from a psychology based on clinical work with individuals and small groups into our view of large groups and of society itself. "Let's trawl the textbooks', says Samuels, "for the suppressed psychology of what is shared. There is such a thing as shared psychological dynamics that show up in groups, particularly groups larger and more complex than small therapy groups". (Samuels, 1993, 1994).

THE RESEARCH

Purpose and Method

The purpose of our research was to enquire into what participants in large groups have experienced as . We investigated four broad areas: an experience of being facilitated or enabled; general facilitative qualities and characteristics; a sense of personal involvement or engagement; being facilitative. The complete questionnaire is reproduced as an appendix to this paper.

A total of 139 questionnaires, in three languages, were distributed during the spring of 1994 to past participants of cross–cultural workshops. Eleven completed questionnaires and two other written responses were returned. Several more people commented that they had found the questionnaire very difficult to complete. They had difficulty in remembering one discrete event and in describing an event which had many aspects and linked phenomena around it. Their awareness and memory was tuned to the workshop as a whole and not an isolated moment within it.

Responses to the questionnaire

An experience of being facilitated / enabled

"Facilitated" was broadly defined as "contributed to your personal learning or added meaning to your experience in the large group". Respondents described situations in which they were directly involved as well as situations in which they "assisted" (from the French "assister") or witnessed. The numbers of people involved in the events ranged from 2 to 320 (a whole group). Only four out of the 11 events described involved a designated facilitator. The facilitative behaviours described came in 4 broad categories: making integrative comments; directly responding to an individual's emotive state; standing out (perhaps against the prevailing mood) as "fearless" and "powerful"; conveying a sense of effectiveness.

General facilitative qualities / characteristics

Individuals described as having been facilitative covered a wide range (as would be expected) – female, male, silent, speakers, different nationalities and cultural backgrounds, speaking the same or a different language, translated or not, designated facilitators and participants. Characteristics cited included warmth, inviting, interest in understanding, verbally responsive, safe, strong, confident, flexible, competent, perceptive, courageous, intelligent, motherly, "persons by whom I felt loved". In terms of the broadly defined core conditions of the person–centred approach to therapy, there were 10 references to understanding / empathy, 16 references to warmth / acceptance and 47 references to allowing oneself to be seen (congruence / transparency).

A sense of personal involvement / engagement

For several respondents this was when personal emotions were being described or expressed by others e.g. "when culture and race were overcome by simple emotional identification". Others felt deeply engaged when they themselves or people they knew were speaking or otherwise in the centre of attention of the group. For some, it was the sense that only they could make the necessary or appropriate response to a person or a situation: "I felt that the outcome of things depended upon me".

In contrast to these rather uplifting occasions, one respondent was most engaged at a time of conflict and when she sensed injustice: "When a black USA woman was misunderstood, undervalued and attacked by white Europeans". One person described how she could not stand her sense of over–involvement; "I am buffeted by the contrary winds of the group process ... at times my very identity is threatened ... I prefer to walk out."

Times of greatest engagement tended to be accompanied by intense emotional arousal, some "positive" – joy, release, enormous bliss, discovery – others "negative" – grief, rage, frustration, powerless to help, despairing.

On being facilitative

Describing a time when they, themselves, were facilitative for another person, 3 respondents referred back to their response to Q1 ('an experience of being facilitated or enabled') and one connected being facilitative with the time of greatest engagement in the group. One gave a general description of her facilitative comportment in groups – looking at or touching a person, letting her own feelings show, making contact. Three other distinctive events were described. One person had supportively moved to be beside someone who was under pressure from the group; a second had "facilitated someone through an argument" with a third party and a third had made a personal statement which brought resolution to the group. Three respondents could not give an instance of being facilitative for others.

When asked "why did you believe your behaviour was facilitative?" some responses described the feedback received or the effect on the group or person. For example: person(s) stated that it was helpful; the facilitative person felt warmth and openness or "tremendous unforeseen approval" towards themselves, the course of the group changed or the climate changed (greater clarity, harmony, resolution, relief). The intervention/behaviour was "against the main stream", met unspoken needs, created a break allowing people to reconnect with themselves. One person commented: "the timing was right".

Another set of responses described the internal experiencing of the facilitative person. One said: (it is) when I am in touch with myself; something deep inside rises to consciousness or feeling in the body; a sense of wholeness in the behaviour; calmness and impartiality; or, in contrast, very risky feeling, trembling, courageous.

DISCUSSION AND CONCLUSION

Our discussion falls into three parts:

(a) on the usefulness of this research and the feasibility of attempting to identify concrete skills, attitudes and behaviours through examining "moments of facilitation".

(b) some findings

(c) implications for a "more adequate" person–centred psychology.

Usefulness of the Research

The number of respondents was low, but so were the numbers of respondents in studies conducted by Jeanne Stubbs (1994) and Kristen Sturdevant (1994) (both below 10). Some respondents said they found the questions "repetitive and confusing". Some of this will be due to faulty design (there was no time for a trial) We did not try to define facilitation in the questionnaire so as not to tighten the linguistic frame within which people might respond. Generally, we have not used facilitate in a transitive sense (i.e. facilitate the group, facilitate the process).

It is likely that the confusion, repetition and difficulty in separating events reflect the nature of large groups themselves. Alan Coulson (1994) expressed a reservation that the questionnaire fragmented the learnings from large groups by emphasising incidents or events. He agrees with those who assert that most significant learning occurs when there is a degree of alignment among members, the group has settled down to real listening and a fairly high degree of mutuality has been achieved.

We would not dispute this assertion, but our interest remains in a large group reaches this state. Is it enough for 200 people to spend an extended time together in close physical proximity (especially in a pleasant setting?) Or, to put it another way, can we not unpack some of the standard person–centred language and describe some specific happenings and their effects on people in the group?

Difficulties remain even if we are able to identify concrete skills, behaviours and attitudes. The problem is the tendency for writings to be read and absorbed as if they were . As we have stated previously (MacMillan and Lago, 1993) "even someone who acts a facilitator role perfectly cannot be as facilitative as someone who is present, totally and genuinely themselves in the group".

Findings

It is immensely complex to identify and locate discrete facilitative skills, behaviours and attitudes. Partly this is because "we can never know who is going to say or do something which is facilitative for someone else" (Coulson, 1994). Nevertheless, a range of incidents have revealed a very wide set of responses. At the most basic, a look, a touch or even another's attentive silence were experienced as facilitative and it was confirmed that being directly responded to can prove a powerful experience.

Our results are in general accord with Stubbs's (1994) research. For example, although acknowledging the core PCA conditions (which have by now largely become part of the culture), facilitator characteristics appear to be non–specific alongside the perceived pivotal presence of the facilitators. In other words, the presence of facilitators is perceived as important yet what they do seems less important, or harder to define. The large group workshop at Zinal, 1981, where there were no designated facilitators seems to confirm this. Then the participants looked to the organisers as if they were facilitators, which they were not.

We have speculated that the most important feature of one who is a designated facilitator as well as those persons whose behaviour is facilitative relates to their willingness to be seen, not to hide either by withdrawing from the arena or behaving falsely within it. Here is a concrete example: a correspondent wrote that a significant episode in his first ever large group workshop (and for many persons both in our study and that of Jeanne Stubbs the first large group was of special significance) was when a facilitator responded to his first ever remark in the large group arena by saying he thought it was "nonsense". This is not part of the ideology of how facilitators should be. But for the participant the significance of the incident was that he did not feel hurt or rejected or put down by an "authority figure". He wrote: "My views, right or wrong, were heard and I felt accepted, received. And I felt that my perspective was just as likely to be correct as D's (the facilitator's)." He had felt he had taken a risk in speaking, having been brought up not to "stick his neck out". He goes on:

> "...even such a minor risk taken within a context of acceptance or trust is quite a significant advance. It seems to me these are straws in the wind or blips which lead us to say 'Wait a minute what's going on here?' ...it felt as though I could allow my mouth to open and things to pop out and it would not be necessary or, perhaps by that stage, possible, to edit, filter or censor what was said on the grounds of some 'ought' or 'should' .... It is a very liberating experience!" (Coulson, 1994)

Translation

We now consider the notion that has sometimes been expressed in workshops where there has been extensive professional translation that the translators are the real facilitators. Whilst translators often do a difficult job well (and sometimes not) it seems astonishing that translation is considered to be synonymous with facilitation. The use of translators makes it more likely that some languages are squeezed out of translation altogether. Moreover, the provision of official translation could be argued to be depriving the group of an opportunity for resolving its own communication problems.

In the Zinal workshop referred to above, the whole group (about 150 persons) had to take responsibility for translating from one language to another. Thus, individuals had to ask for translation at times and speakers with knowledge of more than one language would translate – often paraphrase – themselves. Sometimes, the whole group would be involved in searching for the exact meaning of a person's utterance. One respondent became so "tuned in" that he could understand most of what was going on in the large group without translation and even found himself (a person who hardly speaks his native English in large groups) speaking in French in the community meeting. In contrast, when official translators have been used, participants have been asked not to translate themselves (far less given the chance to try out latent language skills) because it is confusing for the translators.

Altered state

Several respondents referred to some kind of "altered state of consciousness", a "different frame of mind" from their normal experience. This can be manifested in the example just cited (which has been reported by others, including the authors) of understanding a speaker even though one has no conscious knowledge of their language. We do not believe that there is anything magical or mysterious in this phenomenon; it is more a demonstration of the latent potential in each one of us for realising our ability to understand each other when we put our minds to it.

A more adequate psychology?

It is not part of our purpose here to stir up any further the debate between "client–centred" and "person–centred" therapy. But there may be, in continuing and reflective research into large groups, some clues to "an adequate psychology to deal with the present realities" which Wood (1994) suggests needs to be developed if a "new entity" called person–centred therapy should be introduced. (It seems to us that such a new entity has indeed developed; see Mearns and Thorne, 1988). Very tentatively, we suggest that the following features would be included in this new psychology.

1. An expanded sense of self, implying a change in the self–concept to allow for experiencing the connectedness between persons. In this we follow the work of writers like Samuels (1993) and Holdstock (1992).

2. A shift in the view of the core conditions of client–centred therapy when translated into a large group context, and extrapolated to wider social contexts. There is less importance on reflection as a manifestation of empathic understanding and much more in the way of idiosyncratic empathy expression (Bozarth 1984). Empathic expression, in its various forms, sets the scene for emergence of experiential communality. Acceptance (of self, others and the group) and its manifestation in unconditional positive regard has to it a deeply social, mutually interconnecting dynamic. The large group is where this can be directly experienced.

3. Visibility, authenticity, congruence or "wholeness of expression" are of great importance in enabling the realisation of connectedness or interdependence. This is not licence to do or say whatever one wishes; but it is difficult to concur with Holdstock's view that "intense experiences of ego–focused emotions are to be avoided". Our belief is rather that the large group arena is a forum or learning community (MacMillan and Lago 1993) where, having learned what wholeness is like, "ego–focused emotions" are less urgent and need not be expressed abusively. Clearly, those of us from western–northern cultures can learn much from persons from eastern–southern cultures.

Future directions

When can we have a large group organised and facilitated in Japan or India or Zimbabwe, please? For people of western cultural backgrounds there would be a great challenge and much to learn from participating. A "La Jolla Program International" was conducted in Istanbul in 1988; but most of the Turkish participants lived locally and the effect was to leave only the few foreign participants as residents at the programme location. The design of the programme included only two large group meetings in the week. Nevertheless, western persons could experience some very different cultural elements – the food, a non–European language, the regular call of the muezzin – as a backdrop to the process of the group. If participants could reside together in the same non–western living space, the backdrop would become part of the process.

Large group workshops are difficult, time–consuming and expensive to organise. It may be that further research may have to take place more frequently in 'median' groups of about 30 – 40 participants: about the size of a 'small group' at a large group workshop. Much might still be learned about the collective psychology which a person–centred approach to individual therapy ought also to take into account.

APPENDIX

Questionnaire on Facilitative Behaviour in Large Groups
Introduction

We would like you to provide examples of facilitative behaviour in the following pages only from experience in large groups.

We would prefer responses in English but we hope also to be able to translate from French and German should you find these languages easier to respond in.

We ask that you . For example, personal encounters happening during the social time of such workshops are not valid. Also, incidents and experiences in small group workshops are not valid for this research.

Thank you.

An experience of Being Facilitated/Enabled

1. Please describe one significant incident or event, that is, an episode with a distinct beginning and end, that contributed to your personal learning or that added meaning to your experience in a large group.

2. (a) How many people were involved in this event?

(b) Please describe the persons involved in this event/interaction including whether they were:

(i) male/female

(ii) participants, facilitators or translators

(iii) nationality.

3. If possible, can you remember if the persons in the interaction were speaking different languages being translated through the interpreter, or not?

4. Please describe the specific behaviour that was facilitative and enabling.

5. If possible, can you explain why you think that behaviour was effective?

General Facilitative Qualities/Characteristics.

6. In general, what person or persons were significantly facilitative for you during workshops?

608

(Please indicate if they were male/female, participant / facilitator / translator, nationality).

e.g. Person One – Female, participant, Spanish

Person Two – Male, translator, French.

7. How would you describe the personal characteristics and/or the behaviour of these persons?

E.g. Person One – she ....

Person Two – he ....

A sense of Personal Involvement / Engagement

8. On what occasion did you feel most involved / engaged with what was going on in the group?

9. Can you remember your feelings at this time?

10. Please describe why you think your sense of involvement was high at this point.

On being facilitative

11. Can you describe an episode or personal encounter in which you believe that you, yourself were facilitative for another person or for the group?

12. Can you describe why you think your behaviour was facilitative?

REFERENCES

Barrett–Lennard, G.T. (1994) *Towards a Person–Centred Theory of Community.* J. of Humanistic Psychology, vol. 34, No. 3.

Bebout, J. (1974) *It takes one to know one: Existential–Rogerian concepts in encounter groups;* in Wexler, D.A. and Rice, L.N. (eds.) Innovations in Client–Centred Therapy, Wiley.

Beck, A.P.,(1974) *Phases in the Development of Structure in Therapy and Encounter Groups*; in Wexter and Rice (op.cit.)

Bozarth, J.D. (1984) *Beyond Reflection: Emergent Modes of Empathy*; in Levant, R.F. and Shlien, J.M. (eds.) Client–centred Therapy and the Person–centred Approach, New York, Praeger.

Coulson, A. (1994) *Personal Communication.* De Marre', P.: Large Group Perspectives. Group Analysis, 18 (2). 1985

Hofstede, G. *Cultures Consequences: Sage*, Beverley Hills, 1980.

Holdstock, T.L. (1992) *Incongruence between the Person–Centred Theories of Self and of Therapy;* paper presented at the Fifth Forum for the Person–Centred Approach, Terschelling, Netherlands.

Kingdom, J. (1992). *Buckingham.* Open University

Lago, C.O., (1994) *Therapy for a Masturbatory Society : The need for Connectedness* Counselling (Journal of the British Association for Counselling) Vol 5, No. 2.

Orbach, S. *Behind the Political Psyche,* London Weekend Guardian, November 1993.

MacMillan, M.I. and Lago, C.O. (1993) *Large Groups: Critical Reflections and some Concerns;* in The Person–Centred Approach and Cross–cultural Communication: An International Review, vol 11.

Mearns, D and Thorne, B. (1988) *Person–Centred Counselling in Action, London, Sage.* O'Hara, M.M. (1989) Person–centred approach as conscientizacao: the Works of Carl Rogers and Paulo Freire; Journal of Humanistic Psychology, vol. 29, No. 1.

Rogers, C.R. (1970) *Encounter Groups*, Penguin

Rogers, C.R. (1979) *On Personal Power*, London, Constable.

Samuels, A. (1993) *The Political Psyche*, London, Routledge.

Samuels, A. (1994) *The Political Psyche*; keynote address to the second Conference on the Australian Centre for Archetypal Studies. (audio–tape)

Stubbs, J. (Forthcoming) *Individual Experiencing in Person Centred Community Workshops: A Cross–cultural Study* (A forthcoming article from Jeanne Stubbs doctoral research 1993).

Sturdevant, K. (1994) *A Pilot Study: Intentions and Expectations of Members of a Large Person Centred Community Group*. Renaissance – Newsletter for the Development of the Person–Centred Approach, Vol. 11, No. 1.

Thorne, B. (1988) *The Person–centred Approach to Large Groups*; in Aveline, M. and Dryden, W. Group Therapy in Britain, Open University Press.

Wood, J.K. (1984) *Communities for Learning: a Person–centred Approach*; in Levant & Shlien (op.cit.)

Wood, J.K. (1994) *Approaching the Approach*; unpublished.

"Probably the Most Potent *Social* Invention of the Century" Person–Centered Therapy is Fundamentally Group Therapy

PETER F. SCHMID

HOCHSCHULE ST. GABRIEL / VIENNA

ABSTRACT

The Person–Centered Approach is traditionally seen as a method for individual therapy, which in the course of time has been applied to many other areas, including group therapy. Consequently it has often been criticized for being individualistic in its thinking and acting.

In contrast to this the thesis is presented and justified — supported by historic and conceptual arguments — that the Person–Centered Approach is by its very nature already a social approach and thus fundamentally also a group approach. In this way a new idea of encounter is being generated — in the sense of the French encounter philosopher Emmanuel Lévinas: from the enclosed "I and Thou" to the open "We". Such a view has important theoretical and practical consequences for the understanding of the approach, for the question of indication and for individual (dyadic) therapy as a "special form" of group by offering a specific protective climate.

"In the beginning was the group" — it is the interface between the person and the community and the original locus of therapy and of the person–centered relationship.[1]

For many people, the question of what takes precedence, the group or the individual, may seem a bit like the chicken and the egg debate. Anthropologically, both aspects are equally important to personhood: Being a person means being substantial, independent, individual and created from within, *but it also means* being relational, in relationships, created by others (Schmid, 1991; 1994). From a psychological and therapeutic point of view, the question is far from insignificant. An aspect that comes immediately to mind is the status of individual therapy versus group therapy and how this status relates to the concept of personality development. The basic question arises: How should we view the relationship between a pair and a group? Is the group an extension of the "one–to–one relationship" or something independent of it, a "primary social factor"?

Mentioning before: What happens between persons can be viewed from either perspective, the individual as well as the social. Neither should the one be played off against the other nor should one aspect be put absolutely — both perspectives form a creative tension. This article, however, stresses the so far widely neglected aspect of the group as a phenomenon as such and thus underlines the necessity of the mentioned tension between the individual and the relational dimension for an appropriate understanding of the approach.

Without a doubt, the Person–Centered Approach has quite consciously turned an increasing amount of attention to the group relationship and its significance in the course of its development. But I would like to go one step further and assert something which flies in the face of a generally accepted view: *Person–Centered Therapy, as an approach, has, from the very outset, already been a social approach, thus also a group approach.* Historically, it may have been *described and developed*, at least *theoretically, for* use largely, almost exclusively, in individual therapy, but, in actual practice and from the very beginning, it incorporated ideas that originated in group experiences, ideas which, in turn, influenced theory. To put it even more pointedly: *Person–Centered Therapy is by its very nature not merely a process of individual therapy which just happens to be applicable to groups. Rather, it is, in its essence, also a social approach, an approach relating to groups, and thus a "group approach". In its application to relationships between two people, the dyad (pair) can be seen as special type of a group by offering a specific protective climate.[2]*

THE ONE–TO–ONE RELATIONSHIP AS A SPECIAL TYPE OF GROUP WORK

Person–Centered Therapy involving two people, also known as "individual therapy", can be defined as a special type of group event, a "group of two". (This definition is not meant either to deny its importance in certain cases nor its uniqueness: As a pair relationship, it certainly has a character all its own and is not simply *just* a mini group; I'll return to this point later.) However, the focus of attention now shifts: Human beings generally live in groups, the "natural" and, in this sense, original living arrangement of human beings is the group. This fact appears to me to have enormous implications for the Person–Centered Approach.

Others have expressed thoughts along these same lines and called for Person–Centered Group Therapy to be revised accordingly — especially, John Keith Wood (1988, pp. 23, 39, 80), but also Anne–Marie and Reinhold Tausch (1990, p. 7), late in their careers, for example. They underscore the importance of the group, without maybe going to the full implications of doing so, namely, *to view the Person–Centered Approach, as such, as a group approach.*

Like the French psychologist Max Pagès or Jacob Moreno, founder of psychodrama, I think this means to conceive of the smaller unit in terms of the larger, not vice versa. From this point of view, the group is a primary phenomenon, because it is where relationships of an equally primary nature occur. Pagès (1968, pp. 288, 322), for instance, views individual psychotherapy as a special form of family therapy or of treating organizations to which the individual belongs. He sees them as two different aspects of a uniform methodology for change. For him, group training is psychotherapy for the individual. *Individual therapy is thus a special form of group training.* Moreno's (1959, p. 9) thoughts on the matter: "In the beginning was the group; in the end, the individual." Since the individual is a more recent phenomenon in the development of mankind than the group, it is only logical that, initially, the individual methods of psychotherapy were consciously developed before forms of group psychotherapy had matured, Moreno states.[3]

THE PERSON–CENTERED APPROACH AS A GROUP APPROACH: THE HISTORICAL ARGUMENT AND ARGUMENTS RELATING TO THE SUBSTANCE OF THE APPROACH

To legitimate the assertion made above, it is necessary for us to look back on the history of how the Person–Centered Approach developed. A review of the publications would seem to contradict the assertion, almost without exception. According to them, the Person–Centered Approach — including all the other labels it took throughout the years — was developed as a procedure for counselling individuals.

This was how Rogers himself described it in his main theoretical work "A theory of therapy, personality, and interpersonal relationships, as developed in the client–centered framework" (1959a), where he had this to say about his theory on interpersonal relationships (ibid. 61): "This formulation springs [...] primarily from the theory of the therapy, viewing the therapeutic relationship as simply one instance of interpersonal relationship." But he went on to say: "This is still a theory in the making. It does not grow out of consideration of research data and grows only partly out of experience." (ibid. 65).

Rogers' description is echoed by many other authors in the person–centered tradition: Beyond its roots and

> its principal form of practice, there is another sense in which its main emphasis lies with the individual person. As a system of ideas, client–centered therapy is also a psychology of the individual. It is a psychology that has focused on the uniqueness of each person. (Wexler & Rice, 1974, p. 313)

However, they conceded the aspect of application, as well:

> Since its beginnings, client–centered therapy has also sought wider spheres of influence, beyond the individual, both in attempting to explore the relevance of its ideas in contexts broader than traditional dyadic therapy and in seeking to apply its approach to wider social milieus (ibid.).[4]

This is a general consensus as well as a point brought up by critics. For example, by Hans Swildens (1988, p. 34) when he stresses:

> It is characteristic of Rogers' way of thinking that contact is only a secondary phenomenon. In the beginning was the individual: the individual establishes contact with another individual. Rogers pays scant attention to the individual's inevitable connections with others, connections that begin from the moment of conception.

According to Swildens, Rogers' main concern even in the 70's was with

> unconnected individuals who happen to meet each other [...] Even at this point there is no mention of self–evident with–ness [...] In other words, Rogers' central idea is still that the individual is the primary factor. Others are simply other individuals the individual meets and gets along with or not, as the case may be. (ibid.)

These words also reflect the views commonly held about the different psychotherapeutic schools: Freud and Rogers are seen as having developed an individual therapy approach. It gave rise to group approaches, which, in turn, are applications of the individual procedure. By contrast, Moreno and Iljine are said to have created a group therapy, on the basis of which individual therapeutic procedures were developed (for example the monodrama) that are thought of as special forms based on group therapy.

The role of the group in the person–centered theory

I will concede that Client–Centered Therapy, when viewed in isolation, might actually originally have been a psychology of the individual, at a certain point in its historical development; however, as soon as Client–Centered Therapy came to be understood as a subtype of person–centered interaction, the foundation was laid for a shift in the entire view — and I believe this shift has theoretical implications much more far–reaching than it has yet been paid attention to.

Work with "intensive groups", as Rogers (e. g. 1980b, p. 2165) himself often called them, contributed significantly to the development of the Person–Centered Approach as such. This view is traditionally accepted. The reciprocity of help Rogers often experienced in these types of groups exceeded such experiences in individual therapy. The conception the group "leader" had of himself as a facilitator affected the conception the person–centered therapist had of himself in the therapist–client relationship. The work with and within groups were not only important in helping to develop Client–Centered Psychotherapy to the broader Person–Centered Approach, it was instrumental in helping to understand human beings within relationships and interpersonal relationships as such. After all, therapeutic and person–centered relationships are simply special types of interpersonal relationships. The definition of the "fully functioning person" not only as an individualistic self, but as a self within society, and the social and, by extension, political dimension of the Person–Centered Approach also originate largely in experiences from small and large groups. Last but by no means least: the fundamentally equal participation in groups with "anyone", highly democratic in itself, has been and remains important for overcoming elitist thinking, even within the Person–Centered Approach. These points justify Nat Raskin's (1986, p. 281) comment that: "The encounter group was and remains one of the most outstanding forms of expression for the person–centered approach." (cf. also Carkhuff, 1969, p. 130)

But a closer look brings even more revelations to light.

Rogers worked and lived in groups: A historical argument

1. On a closer examination of the history of Person–Centered Therapy, a history inseparable from Carl Rogers' personal stages of learning, it is Rogers' *own learning experiences in his relational groups — family, church and university* — and his references to his own experiences in these groups which are of initial significance. It becomes apparent that while Rogers may at times have been "solitary" (Rogers, 1961a, p. 6) and outstanding, he was anything but a loner: He lived and worked in groups. Applying Rogers' own argument that experience was the final authority, this learning in and from groups is anything but insignificant.

Even in what is — as far as known — his first publication, an article on an international student conference (World Student Christian Federation Conference) in Peking, which Rogers attended as a 20–year–old student (Rogers, 1922: "An Experiment in Christian Internationalism" in the YMCA publication "The Intercollegian"), he voices his fascination with the group experience (and with intercultural understanding by the way) involving 800 students:

> Men and women from 34 countries, living together, meeting in the same room, frankly discussing their common problems, differing strongly on many points, yet with a spirit of agreement that went deeper than their differences — doesn't that sound a little like a description of the millenium. Yet it was an accomplished fact at the Peking Conference [...] Students [from around the world and from many different races] came together at Tsing Hua College, for the purpose of understanding one another, of comparing and discussing their problems and their opportunities, and in the hope of binding together in a real and vital fellowship the Christian students of the world. (ibid. 1).

After praising the speeches at the conference, he continued:

> Perhaps the most valuable part of the Conference, however, was found in the forums, where the students from all over the world discussed frankly and openly the questions involved in making Christ's principles rule in international relations, in social and industrial relations, and in campus life. [...] The forums were a challenge to every delegate to go back to his own Movement and bring them face to face with the fact that together the students of the world must think through these questions in the light of Jesus' teachings. (ibid.)

In the remainder of the article, he continues to express his enthusiasm about the friendly spirit which prevailed despite the differences in race and nationality, despite the tensions among the nations of the representatives in attendance, despite the differences in opinion on various issues.

> When it is possible for Indians and British, and Japanese and Chinese, to get together in small groups and discuss openly and frankly the difficult international relations existing between their respective countries as they did here at Peking, then we can begin to hope for a solution for those problems. (ibid.)

Another aspect he emphasized: "It was far from being a conference *for* the students. It was a conference *of* the students" (ibid.) who unanimously criticized the things that did not meet their expectations. And finally: There was widespread consensus that the major challenge of the times was not to preach Christianity, but to actually live Christianity. If Americans would implement Christian principles in their social and economic life, he wrote, there would be no need for missionaries. A society re-established on the basis of Jesus' precept of love would unleash a greater revolutionary change than Bolshevism. However, Rogers continued, all this enthusiasm did not give rise to false optimism, it wasn't a "hip–hip–hooray spirit" (ibid., p. 2) destined to dissipate quickly. "The students of the world have been brought face to face within that challenge" (ibid.) In many of the passages, it is almost as if one is listening to Rogers reporting 60 years later on an international large–group workshop and its political implications ...

In his first book, "The Clinical Treatment of the Problem Child" (1939a), Rogers emphasizes the importance of the group for therapy and dedicates a chapter, "The intelligent use of clubs, groups and camps" (ibid., p. 249–275), to the group.[5]

2. Along with Rogers' (1940b) Minnesota speech in 1940, 1945 can be considered the year of birth for Person–Centered Group Therapy. Something usually overlooked is that Rogers himself became interested in group work rather early on. By his own account, he had already begun in 1945 to work with students in groups as a professor at the University of Chicago. The actual work conditions that Rogers created are a central fact of his professional life. And his *staff groups* played an increasingly important role. It was in these staff groups that the theoretical ideas were discussed and further developed based on actual experiences (cf. already Rogers, 1939a, pp. 367–371).

3. The *teaching and learning situations* in which Rogers presented his ideas were also almost exclusively group settings: Rogers taught about the approach within a group — very unlike Freud, for example, and his practice of engaging in one–to–one conversations, often during long strolls through the Vienna Woods. (These conversations are considered the precursors of didactic psychoanalysis.) Even the fundamentals in Rogers' publications originated in groups (which occasionally gave rise to disputes about the authorship of many an idea that Rogers published under his own name).

4. By the same token, the approaches to person–centered *training* were set from the very beginning in groups — to such an extent, in fact, that many training courses for individual psychotherapists did not even include individual psychotherapy. In 1947 Rogers had already developed a model to train counsellors for war veterans — the same year, by the way, that the first T–groups of the NTL were set up in Bethel, building on the ideas of Kurt Lewin. The success of Rogers' model made it a prototype for summer workshops, where it was further tested. Unlike Bethel, however, the focus tended to be more on therapeutic and empirical aspects and personality development rather than on training people to acquire specific capabilities, such as leadership skills. Much later, Carl Rogers (1973b, p 39) had these comments about this period: "They have all been encounter groups, long before the term was coined."

(Historically speaking, these observations about Carl Rogers are also applicable, in many respects, to person–centered associations: The theory was and remains primarily a theory on the individual with a focus on the pair relationship. The number of publications, conferences, symposiums, seminars devoted primarily to groups is very low in comparison to other subjects. Nevertheless, the group was almost always the setting for practicing, training and developing the theory.)

5. The first *publications* which included the subject of group work appeared fairly early on, as well. In 1947(e), Rogers published his first article dedicated, even in its title, to the group: "Effective Principles for Dealing with Individual and Group Tensions and Dissatisfactions". In a 1948(d) article entitled "Some Implications of Client–Centered Counseling for College Personnel Work", Rogers also wrote extensively about group work and group therapy, touching on many of what later become his key principles, such as trust in the group, which he sees as an organism in its own right.

6. The fact that Rogers puts the individual at the center of his description of the Person–Centered Approach as a group approach (e.g. Rogers, 1970a) and describes the individual as virtually the only relevant variable — with few exceptions — in his theory (not just with regard to the Person–Centered Approach) is an indication more than anything of the lasting effects of the *US American "pathology" about individual happiness*. Rogers appears to have put more things in motion than he explicitly incorporated into his theoretical writings. In this case, we have to pit "Rogers against Rogers" and be consistent, as he himself would have intended.

Any encounter transcends those encountering each other: The philosophical and psychological argument

The posited assertion is supported not only by historical events but by arguments relating to substance, as well. Let us turn first to a number of substantive reasons from outside the Person–Centered Approach:

1. In *personal development*, the group is the "natural" setting in which human beings experience life, whether in a family, at school, at work, in recreational and interest associations, etc. In all those contexts, one–to–one situations are the exception, groups are the rule. Every pair relationship is usually based on a group or at least imbedded within a group, from the mother–infant relationship to marriage to a partnership between a man and a woman. From the very outset, human beings are born into a group — at least as a rule.

One might object that the first relationship — that between mother and child, intrauterine and postnatal — is a pair relationship. However, even disregarding the significance of the third person involved, the father, whose role is being given increasing recognition even in these early phases, and the fact that the mother–child relationship is normally imbedded within a group, one central truth must not be forgotten; namely: human beings are, *phylogenetically,* group creatures. It is within groups that we discover our identity. Groups give rise to identification: Through them, we know who we are and where we belong.

2. The primary factor, then, is not the individual, but the human being together with other human beings: The human being is a *social being*, a ζωόν πολιτικόν [zoón politikón] (Aristotle) and, from the very beginning, is predisposed by his or her very *corporeity* to communicate with the world and with human beings (cf. Plessner, 1928; Goldstein, 1939; Marcel, 1978).[6] On a purely biological level, the human being originates in a human relationship and dies when at least a minimum thereof no longer exists, as hospitalism research has shown. *Human existence is coexistence.*

3. Besides the anthropological argument, the epistemological one is also important. *Human knowledge is not possible without human society*: Body, awareness, sociality, values — none of these would exist without community. Language, communication, and the search for values and meaning all point to previous social contexts without which they would not exist.[7]

4. Intersubjectivity is another powerful argument from the realm of personality theory. The understanding of the individual as a person is rooted essentially also in the relational aspect of being a person: The human being is and becomes a person within his interpersonal relationships (Schmid, 1991). *It is within groups that a human being becomes a person.*

The thoughts of the French encounter philosopher Emmanuel Lévinas (1961; 1974) on the "third person" are of special relevance in this context. He argued that the physical presence of a third person is not even necessary, because this person is already present in the "visage" of one's fellow human being, whereby Lévinas actually speaks in terms of fellow *human beings*, not fellow *human being*. *An encounter always transcends the persons encountering each other, for its ultimate goal is to rise from isolated duality to open plurality, from the I–Thou dyad to a "We"* (of those who keep "on track", in Lévinas' terminology).[8]

5. Community has a central place in major value systems like *Christianity* or *Marxism* as well as in many of the Far Eastern religions and philosophies. In Judeo–Christian tradition, the human being is defined in terms of his relationship with God as the creator and source of life. God, in turn, is viewed as a trinity, as triune, a community of three persons in one God. In Marxism, human beings are seen first and foremost as social beings, as Feuerbach emphasized in his theses: "Human nature is not an abstract quality inherent in the individual. In its essence, it is the ensemble of the social relationships." (Marx, 1958)

6. Such a view is shared by a large number of *psychotherapists and schools of therapy*: For instance, like the psychoanalyst Harry Stuck Sullivan (1953), Erich Fromm (1941), too, believes that man is primarily a social being, not just in his needs but in his very essence. That is why psychology is also a "psychology of human relations". Hilarion Petzold refers to the "prior nature of sociality" (Petzold & Schneewind, 1986, p. 128). And the client–centered psychiatrist Hans Swildens (1988, p. 46) emphasizes that a "human world is always a world of interactions, not simply or primarily the malleable interactions within encounter groups, but above all the interactions, contexts and ties from our personal history which determine our lives today and shape our attitude toward the future." The increased interest in many schools of therapy in systemic interconnections is also important to note in this context (cf. Schmid, 1995; 1996).

"Human beings are incurably social": The person–centered argument

The most cogent substantive argument in support of our thesis comes from the Person–Centered Approach itself.

1. Firstly: Rogers' way of thinking is remarkably non–individualistic, especially for a US–American of his time. From the very beginning, it is social, relational and relationship–oriented. As his life progressed, he steadily expanded on these tendencies, which were there from the very outset.

Rogers' writings contain no explicit musings about what a person is or about what a group is. Rogers was as little interested in "the group" as such as he was in "the individual" or "the person". He derived his personality theories from theories based on his therapeutic experience. It was there — in a theory about growth conditions and personality development — that his main interest lay. However, these theories are all, at the very least implicitly and usually explicitly, theories about relationships: The actualization tendency turns out to be, not least, a socially constructive force and is attributed not only to the individual but also to the group as a political entity (Rogers, 1977a), and as a formative tendency even to the structural aspects of the entire universe (Rogers, 1979a). The conditions for constructive personality development are eo ipso conditions for relationships. That is why they were described as conditions for a relationship — for "two persons" — already at the time of their first presentation (Rogers, 1957a): from the contact of the participants to the description of authenticity as "congruence in a relationship". The process of the clients in therapy, too, is described essentially as an account of how individuals experience themselves within social relationships (e. g. Rogers, 1980b).

Thus, the starting point, in both, practical and systematic terms, is the theory of therapy and personality change. It is only after this that the personality theory comes, then the theory of the fully functioning person, and the theory of interpersonal relationship (in general) and the theories of application — and that is the structure of his theoretical opus (1959a). *The very fact that Rogers starts with the (therapeutic) relationship and personal development influenced (facilitated) by relationships in developing his theory and not with the individual as such shows that this theory is rooted in social psychology, not individual psychology.* From the very outset, Rogers is interested in the human being within relationships (i.e. in the person), not in the individual as such, the suffering human being whom another human being sets about to help, then the human being as a person growing within relationships, the human being as a person learning within relationships that foster this learning, the human being as a member of a group (not the group as such), the human being as part of society and as a political animal (not society or politics as such).

In fact, the human being's dependence on relationships is such a given for Rogers that he doesn't even bother to discuss this axiom, for him a human being is simply "incurably social". (Rogers, 1965b; Rogers & Tillich, 1966), has "a deep need for relationships" (ibid.), is a "social animal" (Rogers, 1961a, p. 103) for whom "the need for love and affection is innate" (Rogers, 1971f).

Conflicts, incongruence, personal problems, emotional suffering have their origins (though not exclusively) in social relationships. In terms of developmental psychology, the setting of values which prevent a constructive and flexible self from emerging also rests on values that a human being received from others. His happiness as well as his suffering arise largely from social relationships.

It is therefore categorically incorrect to accuse Rogers of one-sided, individualistic ideas and to view the Person–Centered Approach as anything but one rooted in relationships.

2. Rogers sees a parallel and a profound *connection between individual development and social relationships, and therefore with the groups,* in which a person grows up and lives. It is thus to follow the view of Foulkes (Foulkes & Anthony, 1957) — for whom the group is a more fundamental entity than the individual — that group psychotherapy simply brings the problems back around to the point where they belong: The group is the arena in which conflicts which arose likewise in a social context "belong". It is only logical then that it is within and through relationships that problems arising from relationships can be worked out. Since, however, most relationships are relationships within groups (or at least oriented toward groups), as mentioned above, it follows that the group must again be seen as the therapeutic medium.

We can either criticize Rogers, justifiably, for never actually developing his own theory on groups or we can look at it from another perspective: If it is true that Rogers' starting point was always group experiences — although he did not at first conceptualize them theoretically — that would mean that the group is the obvious "arena" for pair relationships, a place where relationships (can) occur between one person and another. The group, then, is the arena for encounters. The arena takes on a definite shape as soon as the relationships are described. *Thus the group is the arena in which the game of encounter is actualized, from which it draws sustenance, and it, in turn, is actualized and draws sustenance from the personal encounters that occur within it.*

3. A logical step, as mentioned earlier, would be to *"take Rogers more seriously" on this point than he perhaps took himself* and to incorporate his experiences into a more consistent theoretical framework. For many years he obviously drew on only a part of his therapeutic and other learning experiences to cast his theoretical concepts, not paying due attention to the relational aspect until much later. It was not least the influence of Buber which prompted Rogers to focus increasingly on the phenomenon of the encounter, a phenomenon which, from the very outset, had obviously influenced his views, indeed shaped them. A similar observation was made by John K. Wood (1988, p. 65), who noted this contradiction between theory and practice and concluded: "We have to find out much more about the profound role played by therapist and client in a complete relationship" so that we may "better understand the social factors involved in successful therapy" (ibid., p. 66; cf. Wood, 1994, pp. 9, 16).

Rogers' actions were certainly guided by the principle that the primary social fact was that of the human being with his fellow human being. His increasingly frequent use of the term "encounter", his closer attention to the immediacy of the relationship and the presence in the relationship, his view of the group as having its own identity to which a special "collective knowledge" can be attributed (Rogers, 1987n), all these developments can be verified in his texts. If Rogers had seen the need 20 years later to present his theory in a comprehensive and systematic manner, he undoubtedly would have gone about it much differently than he had in 1959.

4. *Thus, the most powerful argument supporting the thesis of the "therapeutic primacy of the group" in the Person-Centered Approach is the image of man* on which it is based: The human being as a person, characterized by sovereignty and commitment (Schmid, 1991), is inconceivable without the relational settings in which he is able to actualize his personhood in a relational sense, that is without the relationships in which he is not only born into as a person, but in which he also grows to become more of a person: *The human being as a person is inconceivable without the other persons, his fellow human beings, with whom he lives in groups and with whom he actualizes his personhood.* This is further underscored by ideas about encounter and presence, play and action, interaction and effectiveness, the "anthropology of relationality", ideas which cannot be described in greater detail here (v. Schmid, 1994; 1996).

It is also but a short step to extend the concept of encounter beyond Buber's I–Thou relationship to a concept of encountering the Other in whom we always encounter yet a "third person", as Lévinas believes; not to stop at the therapeutic I–Thou relationship but to go beyond it to a "We" and thus to the group as the "arena for encounters", *to view the triad and not the dyad as the basic element of interpersonality.*

THE GROUP AS THE INTERFACE BETWEEN PERSON AND SOCIETY

All of these ideas suggest the following concept of the group: *The group — a social psychological fact — is a totality of persons which as an interface between individual on the one hand and society on the other hand is an excellent setting for personal encounters.* Just as independence and autonomy, i.e. substantiality, are equally important to a person as his dependence on relationships, i.e. relationality, so too are both of these aspects constitutive elements of the group: By its very nature, a group constitutes both the persons belonging to it as well as its own autonomy as a social entity and its connection to other groups in a broader social context, the all-encompassing totality of society, of which it forms a section. This tension is inherent in the group. That means, on the one hand, that without persons, without members, groups cannot exist, and on the other hand, that in the absence of certain social factors, even several persons might not constitute a group. The persons bring their life and experiential history with them into a group, which includes their earlier relationships and group experiences as well as their evaluations of them. Society is the social and cultural framework. Within this framework, the persons constitute, under certain conditions, a group with its own specific processes as an autonomous organized totality.

As was already stressed earlier, *this means that the group is neither a mere collective nor is it the sum total of the persons making it up. It is a complex system existing in a state of tension between person and society, a process in which individual and collective problems become clear and subsequently influence each other in many different ways. Its essence is in the relationship it has to its members, whose relationships in turn are shaped by the group.*

The group is where a human being experiences himself in his social and his individual qualities. Where he experiences his self as a self–in–relationship; where he can learn through action to appreciate others to an increasing extent and to actualize his own potential more and more fully. The group is where the human being lives in solidarity and autonomy, where he learns to be solidary and autonomous, to offer solidarity and to receive it, to respect autonomy and to achieve it (cf. Schmid, 1994).

SOME OF THE IMPLICATIONS FOR THE PERSON–CENTERED THERAPY

What significance does the posited assertion of the originality of the group have? In a certain respect, the implications arising from the image of man underlying personal encounter reverse the whole premise on which person–centered thought and action are based:

1. The primary setting for the person–centered relationship is the group: The group is thus the "first", the initial point of approach to therapy. In other words, unless other reasons make another decision obviously preferable, the group is the place of choice for the human being to come to terms with himself, just as it is the natural setting in which he lives his life. It is in the group that one learns best — and most consistently — to treat oneself and others in a person–centered manner, with the goal of allowing space in one's life for personal encounter. Thus one could speak of a "therapeutic primacy" of the group if one likes.

2. The group is taken seriously as a therapeutic or helpful medium. The ultimate goal of person–centered relationships is the fully personal encounter. The reciprocity which this requires and which Rogers always strove for is much easier to achieve in group therapy than in individual therapy. Under this approach it is the task of the entire group to act as therapist, counsellor, facilitator. It is not focused or not limited to a single person or several persons: The understanding is that the entire group, all its members, are facilitators for each other. In this way, the approach is even "more democratic", even less likely to become elitist, because the fundamental equality of everyone is taken seriously. The moment each individual is seen as someone who can facilitate, give support to another and is called on to do so, an enormous potential is unleashed which would otherwise lie dormant.

3. The diversity of life "lives" in the group. In individual therapy, the diversity of life is often merely discussed, relived, or reflected; in the group, it can, to a great extent, be directly experienced "live", because it can occur there directly. The group has much to teach us about achieving lively and effective individual therapy.

4. The status of the pair relationship as a special relationship is based primarily on its protective function. In my opinion, the two–person relationship is made more valuable in this view, not less. The pair is neither "two individuals" nor a "reduced group", but a special form of relationship which Rogers called "person to person" (e. g. Rogers & Stevens, 1967). The special character of the pair is that each of the two people has a relationship to the other and, within the pair, only to each other. Every dyadic relationship is thus a potentially intimate situation, which, as such, offers protection against every situation and person outside the pair.

5. The pair also offers special protection within therapy. The therapeutic pair relationship, indeed any helping pair relationship in general, is not a matter of individuals but of persons subject to demands relating to their relational qualities. One could call them a "mini encounter group". Their real value stems from the fact that this type of pair is a special relationship, in a special framework which offers an unusually high degree of protection. A therapeutic dyad is also an intimate relational constellation. Here, too, the special quality of the pair is its (relative) exclusivity, which offers a special protective function. It is clearly a type of facilitative relationship which is appropriate under certain circumstances. In all cases in which the pair relationship is more facilitative for the affected person, it should be used as a therapeutic framework — nevertheless, in this perspective, the therapeutic pair is more the exception than the rule.

To touch on the key indications briefly: Firstly, if the client desires a therapeutic pair relationship, because he believes it is more appropriate for him, he should be offered the possibility of it. For example, persons who can't imagine working within a group as such, because they are too afraid of it or have had bad experiences in groups and thus lack the trust required. There are also reasons relating to the nature of the problems or task at hand which make individual work more preferable: For instance, if the client requires undivided attention, the group is definitely inadvisable. If the client has a difficult time building a stable and sustainable relationship, the pair relationship with its concentration on a *single* relationship is also appropriate. This is the case with persons whose social behaviour creates major problems for them in this regard or who find themselves in an acute crisis requiring intensive caring. In short: The pair relationship is the preferable framework whenever it is able to provide better growth conditions. (A completely different type of reason for a pair relationship is when a person wishes to work through his own personality, as is the case in training therapy. Initial hours or orientation counselling also can often be more fruitful and expedient in the one–on–one setting.)

6. The pair relationship, when defined in this way, cannot lead to isolation — the others are virtually present. From the above description, it is equally clear that all pair relationships are imbedded in a larger entity. There is not only I and Thou and Thou and Thou ...; there is I and We; there is We and Thou. Whenever pairs isolate themselves and withdraw from society around them, there is a danger of blind self complacency and sterile isolation. Pfeiffer (1993, p. 21) writes about the danger of a "dyadic autism":

> As important as dyads are for the development of relationships with our fellow human beings, they are nevertheless insufficient unto themselves. They must be supplemented by other persons or they become sterile [...] For this reason, the larger family, the play group, etc. takes on great significance even in early childhood. And through dyads and especially through groups, the diversity of others, society, the world, becomes accessible.

Hence follows not to overlook the virtual presence of the others in dyadic Person–Centered Therapy.

7. Group egoism is also a danger. Just as there is egoism in individuals, so too can it arise in a pair or a group. It seems to be appropriate to coin the term "group autism" to describe this phenomenon. Groups, too, can shut themselves off from the larger community and from the society at large. Many sects demonstrate this tendency to an alarming degree. Many of the procedures in psycho–groups can inspire the same type of fears. (It remains an open question whether the danger of a group "becoming stuck" in isolation is much less than it is for pairs.)

8. No "systemic supplement" is required. A significant trend in psychotherapy in general seems, to a certain respect, to be headed in the same direction: namely, systemic thinking in psychotherapy. According to many traditions, psychotherapy is a course of treatment which begins with the individual; most classic psychotherapies are conducted as individual therapies. Many group therapy procedures change the setting but not the major thrust, i.e. that the therapy is ultimately there to serve the individual. With the development of systemic approaches — that is: the therapist's understanding of the situation and his treatment are rooted in the system in which the individual lives, for example in the family, and no longer in the individual himself — a change has taken place not only in the therapeutic method but also in the point at which therapy is to be applied. In our view, the Person–Centered Approach, with its fundamental social dimension, does not require a "supplemental" systemic aspect of this kind nor does it require a supplemental political aspect. It already is a political approach and an approach which from the very outset takes into account an aspect which is of such importance to systemic therapists: The setting in which a person lives his life, his social environment, has an especially strong presence in the group, too. In cases when others are not present physically, the relationship to them is part of the person's understanding of himself. What the Person–Centered Approach needs to do, however, is to take this fact seriously and to implement these consequences in practice.

9. It creates a starting point for developmental psychology. It is in groups that human beings learn how to have relationships. What we become is primarily what we become in groups. In particular, we learn the essential process of setting values in groups and for a person, the process of valuing never takes place without his referring back to the groups that are relevant to him. This has to have a number of implications for developmental psychology and not least, for educational practices in particular.

10. The political significance of the group is in its "anticipatory function". Pagès (1968, p.136) states:

> Another consequence of this concept of the group is that it can be seen as the place where societal processes can be examined and understood, where political action can be tested. Groups can be seen, in general, as a place for trial political action. Groups play a crucial role not only for the person, for example as a therapeutic medium, they also have an anticipatory function in that they offer creativity to the larger groups to which they belong.

Just as the small groups at a workshop make essential contributions to the work of the large group, person–centered work is always an activity with social political relevance, as well.

11. The approach still is "person–centered", not "group–centered". Although the Person–Centered Approach is from the outset a group approach, it does not allow the individual to disappear in the collective. It maintains the delicate balance or tension between the individualistic and the relational. The term "person" ensures that due attention is paid to both the individual and the social dimension, preventing an individualistic as well as a collectivist misunderstanding. The concept thus remains "person–centered". (After all, calling the approach "group–centered" in this context would be just as incorrect as referring to it as "subject–oriented" or "individual–oriented".)

12.Taking into consideration the group phenomena, the Person–Centered Approach as such can be developed further. If we develop the social psychological perspective and view the Person–Centered Approach accordingly new aspects for understanding the approach and its

623

philosophy and psychology will evolve. Furthermore this will lead to the "retroactive" effect of new theoretical and practical consequences for individual therapy. In refining our thinking in the context of social relationships, we later can project back our knowledge on the individual case which will also give individual therapy more effectiveness.

REFERENCES

Carkhuff, R. R. (1969). *Helping and human relations: Vol. II. Practice and research.* New York: Holt, Rinehart and Winston.

Cain, D. J. (1989). *From the individual to the family.* Person–Centered Review 4 (3), 248–255.

Foulkes, S. H. & Anthony, E. J. (1957). *Group psychotherapy.* London: Penguin.

Fromm, E. (1941). *Escape from freedom.* New York: Rinehardt & Co.

Goldstein, K. (1939). *The organism.* New York: American Book.

Lévinas, E. (1961). *Totalité et infini: Essai sur l'extériorité.* Den Haag: Nijhoff; [7]1980.

Lévinas, E. (1974). *Autrement qu'être ou au delà de l'essence.* Den Haag: Nijhoff; [2]1978.

Lynch, J. J. (1985). *The language of the heart.* New York: Basic.

Marcel, G. (1978). *Leibliche Begegnung.* In Kraus, A. (Ed.). Leib, Geist, Geschichte (pp. 47–73). Heidelberg: Hütig.

Marx, K. (1958). *Thesen über Feuerbach.* In Marx Engels Werke 3. Berlin: Dietz.

Moreno, J. L. (1959). *Gruppenpsychotherapie und Psychodrama: Einleitung in die Theorie und Praxis.* Stuttgart: Thieme; [3]1988.

Pagès, M. (1968). *La vie affective des groupes.* Paris: Dunod [quotations from German edition: *Das affektive Leben der Gruppen: Eine Theorie der menschlichen Beziehung.* Stuttgart: Klett 1974].

Petzold, H. G. & Schneewind, U.–J. (1986). *Konzepte zur Gruppe und Formen der Gruppenarbeit in der Integrativen Therapie und Gestalttherapie.* In Petzold, H. G. & Frühmann, R. (Eds.). Modelle der Gruppe in Psychotherapie und psycho–sozialer Arbeit, vol. I (pp. 109–254). Paderborn: Junfermann.

Pfeiffer, W. M. (1993). *Die Bedeutung der Beziehung bei der Entstehung und der Therapie psychischer Störungen.* In Teusch, L. & Finke, J. (Eds.). Krankheitslehre der Gesprächspsychotherapie: Neue Beiträge zur theoretischen Fundierung (pp. 19–39). Heidelberg: Asanger.

Plessner, H. (1928). *Die Stufen des Organischen und der Mensch: Einleitung in die philosophische Anthropologie.* Berlin/Leipzig.

Raskin, N. J. (1986). *Client–centered group psychotherapy, I: Development of client–centered groups.* Person–Centered Review 1 (3), 272–290.

Rogers, C. R. (1922). *An experiment in Christian internationalism.* The Intercollegian (YMCA) 39 (9), 1f.

Rogers, C. R. (1933). *A good foster home: Its achievements and limitations.* Mental Hygiene 17, 2–40.

Rogers, C. R. (1939a). *The clinical treatment of the problem child.* Boston: Houghton Mifflin.

Rogers, C. R. (1940b). *Some newer concepts of psychotherapy.* Manuscript.

Rogers, C. R. (1947e). *Effective principles for dealing with individuals and group tensions and dissatisfactions.* Executive Seminar Series in Industrial Relations, Session 10. Chicago: University of Chicago Press.

Rogers, C. R. (1948d). *Some implications of client–centered counseling for college personnel work.* Educational and Psychological Measurement 8 (3), part 2, 540–549.

Rogers, C. R. (1957a). *The necessary and sufficient conditions of therapeutic personality change.* Journal of Consulting Psychology, 21(2), 95–103.

Rogers, C. R. (1959a). *A theory of therapy, personality, and interpersonal relationships, as developed in the client–centered framework.* In Koch, S. (Ed.). Psychology. A study of a science. Vol. III. Formulations of the person and the social context (pp. 184–216). New York: McGraw Hill.

Rogers, C. R. (1961a). *On becoming a person. A therapist's view of psychotherapy.* Boston: Houghton Mifflin.

Rogers, C. R. (1965b). *A humanistic conception of man.* In Farson, R. (Ed.). Science and human affairs (pp. 18–31). Palo Alto: Science and Behavior Books.

Rogers, C. R. (1970a). *On encounter groups,* New York (Harper and Row) 1970.

Rogers, C. R. (1971f). *Interview with Dr. Carl Rogers.* In Frick, W. B. (Ed.). Humanistic psychology: Interviews with Maslow, Murphy and Rogers (pp. 86–115). Columbus: Charles E. Merrill.

Rogers, C. R. (1973b). *My philosophy of interpersonal relationships and how it grew.* In Rogers, C. R., A way of being (pp. 27–45). Boston: Houghton Mifflin, 1980.

Rogers, C. R. (1977a). *On personal power: Inner strength and its revolutionary impact.* New York: Delacorte.

Rogers, C. R. (1979a). *The foundations of the person–centered approach.* education 100 (2), 98–107.

Rogers, C. R. (1980b). *Client–centered psychotherapy.* In Kaplan, H. I. & Sadock, B. J. & Freedman, A. M. (Eds.). Comprehensive textbook of psychiatry, III (pp. 2153–2168). Baltimore, MD: Williams and Wilkins.

Rogers, C. R. (1987n). *Questions and answers.* In Zeig, J. K. (Ed.). The evolution of psychotherapy. New York: Brunner/Mazel.

Rogers, C. R. & Carson, C. W. (1930). *Intelligence as a factor in camping activities.* Camping Magazine 3 (3), 8–11.

Rogers, C. R. & Schmid, P. F. (1991). *Person–zentriert: Grundlagen von Theorie und Praxis.* Mainz: Grünewald; ²1995.

Rogers, C. R. & Stevens, B. (1967). *Person to person. The problem of being human.* Moab: Real People Press.

Rogers, C. R. & Tillich, P. (1966). *Dialogue between Paul Tillich and Carl Rogers. Parts I & II.* San Diego: San Diego State College.

Schmid, P. F. (1991). *Souveränität und Engagement: Zu einem personzentrierten Verständnis von "Person".* In Rogers & Schmid, 1991, 15–164, 297–305. 19

Schmid, P. F. (1994). *Personzentrierte Gruppenpsychotherapie: Ein Handbuch. Band 1. Autonomie und Solidarität.* Köln: Edition Humanistische Psychologie.

Schmid, P. F. (1995). *Die Person im System: Systemische Therapie und Personzentrierter Ansatz, I & II.* apg–kontakte 2 & 3.

Schmid, P. F. (1996). *Personzentrierte Gruppenpsychotherapie in der Praxis. Ein Handbuch. Band 2. Die Kunst der Begegnung.* Paderborn: Junfermann.

Sullivan, Harry S. (1953). *The interpersonal theory of psychiatry,* ed. Perry, H. S. & Gawel, M. L. New York: Norton.

Swildens, H. (1988). *Procesgerichte Gesprekstherapie: Inleiding tot een gedifferentieerde toepassing van de cliëntgerichte beginselen bij de behandeling van psychische stoornissen.* Löwen/Amersfoort: Acco/de Horstink [quotations from German edition: *Prozeßorientierte Gesprächspsychotherapie: Einführung in eine differentielle Anwendung des klien-*

tenzentrierten Ansatzes bei der Behandlung psychischer Erkrankungen. Köln: GwG; 1991].

Tausch, R. & Tausch, A.-M. (1990). *Gesprächspsychotherapie: Hilfreiche Gruppen- und Einzelgespräche in Psychotherapie und alltäglichem Leben.* Göttingen: Hogrefe; [1]1960, [9]1990.

Wexler, D. A. & Rice, L. N. (1974) (Eds.). *Innovations in client-centered therapy.* New York: Wiley.

Wood, J. K. (1988). *Menschliches Dasein als Miteinandersein: Gruppenarbeit nach personenzentrierten Ansätzen.* Köln: Edition Humanistische Psychologie.

Wood, J. K. (1994). *From the person-centered approach to client-centered therapy: Towards a psychology.* Keynote address IIIrd ICCCEP, revised version. Jaguariúna: Manuscript; v. this volume, pp. 163–181.

---

[1] "'Die vermutlich größte *soziale* Erfindung des 20. Jahrhunderts' [Rogers, 1970a, p. 9]. Personzentrierte Therapie ist vom Ansatz her Gruppentherapie"; translation by Mark Wilch. — I would like to thank Nat Raskin, Leif Braaten, Doug Land and especially John K. Wood for helpful remarks and critical comments on the paper.

[2] I would like to state that the use of "he / him / himself" as a pronoun for human being / person is stylistically motivated and not a reflection of ignorance, misogyny, anti-feminism, etc.

[3] By the way, in "Group Psychology and the Analysis of the Ego" even Freud (1921) admitted that, "in the individual's mental life, someone else is invariably involved, as a model, as an object, as helper, as an opponent; and so from the very first, individual psychology [...] is at the same time social psychology as well". Wood's comment (personal communication, 1994): "And practically everyone has forgotten."

[4] Cf. also Cain, 1989, p. 249.

[5] "As to the treatment methods used, the most vital and important was of course the camp regime itself. Away from home, in an interesting and stimulationg environment, the challenge of group activity was in itself enough in many instances to bring about normal behavior." (Rogers, 1939a, p. 268) Cf. also Rogers & Carson, 1930, about camping groups and Rogers, 1933, about the family.

[6] Wood (1994, p. 12) points out that human existence as coexistence is very well demonstrated by James Lynch's (1985) work dealing with the cardiovascular system.

[7] Cf. "con-scientia, co-gnoscere, con-sensus, com-municatio" (Petzold & Schneewind, 1986, pp. 128f).

[8] Concerning the importance of Lévinas' philosophy for person-centered anthropology and ethics v. Schmid, 1994, pp. 136–154, 292, and Schmid, 1996.

Pamela Rosengard

A Comparative Analysis of Four Psychotherapy Manuals and a Proposed Model for Psychotherapy Manuals

Frankfurt/M., Bern, New York, Paris, 1991. 386 pp.
European University Studies: Series 6, Psychology. Vol. 347
ISBN 3-631-44180-0   pb. DM 99.--*

The development of psychotherapy manuals may be critical to modern comparative psychotherapy research and the training of therapists. Based on this assumption, four manuals were comparatively analysed according to structural design and content. Furthermore, an empirical study compared how a sample of inexperienced versus experienced therapists (American and German), evaluated the four manuals. Finally, based on these analyses, a generic model for psychotherapy manuals is presented. Since the four manuals studied cover supportive-expressive psychoanalytic therapy, time-limited psychodynamic therapy, interpersonal therapy for depression, and cognitive therapy for depression, this work also provides an overview of how varying approaches can be presented in manual form.

Contents: Purposes of psychotherapy manuals · Manual background · Essential features · Therapeutic change · Strategies/techniques · Contextual factors · Therapist-patient relationship · Termination · Readers' evaluations of manuals · A model for psychotherapy manuals

Peter Lang ⚜ **Europäischer Verlag der Wissenschaften**
Frankfurt a.M. · Berlin · Bern · New York · Paris · Wien
Auslieferung: Verlag Peter Lang AG, Jupiterstr. 15, CH-3000 Bern 15
Telefon (004131) 9402121, Telefax (004131) 9402131
- Preisänderungen vorbehalten - *inklusive Mehrwertsteuer